DATE DUE

THE PSYCHOLOGY
OF
LEARNING
AND
INSTRUCTION

PRENTICE-HALL, INC.
Englewood Cliffs, New Jersey

JOHN P. De CECCO
San Francisco State University

WILLIAM R. CRAWFORD
University of California, Los Angeles

THE PSYCHOLOGY OF LEARNING AND INSTRUCTION
EDUCATIONAL PSYCHOLOGY

Second Edition

Library of Congress Cataloging in Publication Data

DE CECCO, JOHN P.
The psychology of learning and instruction.

Includes bibliographies.
1. Educational psychology. I. Crawford,
William R., joint author. II. Title.
[DNLM: 1. Psychology, Educational. LB1051 D292p 1972]
LB1051.D352.1974]   370.15   73–13995
ISBN 0-13-732917-2

THE PSYCHOLOGY
OF
LEARNING
AND
INSTRUCTION
EDUCATIONAL PSYCHOLOGY
John P. De Cecco and William R. Crawford

© 1974, 1968 by Prentice-Hall, Inc., Englewood Cliffs, New Jersey

Printed in the United States of America

10 9 8 7 6 5 4 3 2

Prentice-Hall International, Inc., London
Prentice-Hall of Australia, Pty. Ltd., Sydney
Prentice-Hall of Canada, Ltd., Toronto
Prentice-Hall of India Private Limited, New Delhi
Prentice-Hall of Japan, Inc., Tokyo

To the students and colleagues
who have trusted us

CONTENTS

PART TWO
ENTERING BEHAVIOR AND DEVELOPMENT

PART THREE
INSTRUCTIONAL PROCEDURES AND LEARNING

PART FOUR
PERFORMANCE ASSESSMENT AND RESEARCH

A SPECIAL NOTE
TO THE STUDENT

There is a time for speculation and a time for teaching, but equally important for you as a prospective teacher there must be a time for acquiring basic knowledge about the conditions of learning which can improve teaching. The purpose of this book is to introduce you to the present state of knowledge about learning and teaching. If the book fulfills this purpose you should be a better teacher after you read it than you were before.

This general purpose suggests four ways in which this book can be useful to you. (1) It provides you with a general conception, or model, of teaching which is useful in describing and analyzing the instruction you read about and observe and in organizing and executing your own teaching. (2) It provides you with a body of knowledge which can be useful to you throughout your teaching career as you engage in the description of instructional objectives, in the accommodation of the entering capacity and behavior of individual students, in the selection of instructional materials and procedures, and in the assessment of student performances. (3) It provides you with a theoretical and factual basis for making teaching decisions which are apart from but not necessarily inconsistent with or opposed to your own preferences, intuitions, and impressions about teaching. (4) It provides you with some fairly specific guidelines for important teaching functions, such as stating your objectives, analyzing student behavior, providing the necessary conditions for various types of learning, programing instructional materials, constructing tests and interpreting test scores, and evaluating research reports. If you learn or only begin to learn to perform the teaching functions described in this book, you may indeed become a very skilled teacher.

There are three ways in which this book is *not* useful. First, you will find that it does not always concur with many of your present opinions about teaching. Instead it gives you knowledge you may not have and, in this way, may change and develop your behavior.

Second, you will find that the book is *not* a list of do's and don't's. Although suggestions for performing some teaching functions (e.g., programing and constructing tests) are more specific than are those for other teaching functions (e.g., teaching concepts and problem solving), the level of discourse is somewhat more general than you may expect. The book provides a basic core of knowledge which should have general applicability throughout your teaching career. Lists of do's and don't's are usually very specific and pertain to particular instructional objectives, students, procedures, and tests. You should acquire most of this specific knowledge in other professional courses and in your teaching experience in the classroom.

Third, you will find that the book is *not* based on a conception of teaching which places the personalities of the teacher and of the student at the center of the stage. In a refrain we hope you do not find tedious we reiterate that the important focus of all classroom effort, the teacher's and the student's, is the student's achievement of the instructional objectives. The teacher should provide those conditions of learning which will lead to the student's full achievement of the instructional objectives.

ON GETTING THE MOST FROM THIS BOOK

We have designed both the textbook and the *Student Guide* to help you achieve the objectives more easily. Consider the textbook first. A perusal of the Contents (which you can do after reading this paragraph) shows that the book has four parts. The Contents also lists the major headings in each chapter.

The following suggestions should be helpful to you in achieving the instructional objectives of each chapter:

1 Read the introduction to the chapter. It briefly describes the general purpose and the contents of the three or four sections of the chapter.

2 Read the list of instructional objectives which precedes each section. These statements tell you in advance what you should be able to do upon completing the section. By checking your own performances you can determine what you have learned well and what requires further study. You should make generous use of these lists.

3   Read the headings within the chapter. These are distinguished by type size and location on the page. Some students find it useful to turn headings into questions and to return to the questions upon completing the material to which the headings refer.

4   Read the contents of the chapter. Very often the definition of a technical term occurs at the beginning of the paragraph. The subject index will tell you where to find an explanation of technical terms. Make full use of the tables, charts, and figures. They have been chosen carefully to help increase your understanding of the text.

5   Read the summaries. Written in paragraph form, they list the major points of each section.

6   Read and answer the embedded questions. At the conclusion of chapter sections a question, usually in multiple-choice form, assesses your achievement of the major objectives of the section. In selecting your answer, explain to yourself the basis for your choice and for your rejection of the alternatives. *After* this self-explanation, turn to the answer section at the back of the book and read the correct answer and its defense. If you miss a question, return to the pertinent portion of the chapter and review it.

7   Read the summary which concludes the chapter. It draws together the major points and enables you to review important conceptual relationships.

8   Use the sources of suggested readings. The annotated list of suggested readings following the chapter summary usually contains references to both elementary and advanced treatments of the chapter topics.

The purpose of the *Student Guide* is to facilitate the learning of the instructional objectives. The *Guide* contains:

1   A discussion of how to study with instructional objectives and how to anticipate the various ways in which test items could measure a given objective.

2   A detailed outline of each textbook chapter.

3   Sample multiple choice questions for each chapter in the text indicating the various ways in which an objective can be measured. Correct and incorrect alternatives are explained.

4   Controversial issues from each chapter in the text.

The bibliography at the end of the book describes all the references mentioned in the text. It is an excellent source for suggested readings, especially for research articles in educational psychology.

A NOTE TO
THE INSTRUCTOR
ON THE SECOND EDITION

The first edition, published in 1968, was extremely successful as a synthesis of new areas of educational psychology in the sixties. The book synthesized the knowledge we had for basing teaching and learning on empirically-based theory and practice. It included the teaching and learning innovations of the sixties—particularly the use of performance objectives, behavior modification, programed instruction, computer-assisted instruction, the new science and mathematics, and recent developments in research technology.

The second edition retains much behavioral theory and data but includes more cognitive and linguistic theory to reflect the growing research and interest in those areas. The outstanding features of the second edition are as follows:

1 The basic teaching model is retained. Instructors using the book reported that they found its use a convenient way for them to organize their courses and for their students to synthesize and retain what they had learned. In the first chapter the basic teaching model has been contrasted with historical and contemporary models of current interest.

2 The use of instructional objectives has been expanded to include cur-

ricular, teacher, and student objectives so that the choice of objectives does not exclude any important group of educators and learners.

3   The lists of instructional objectives for each chapter have been broken into shorter lists and these shorter lists have been inserted in the chapters at the points that new topics are introduced.

4   One whole chapter is devoted to the development of intelligence. It is based on the most sophisticated theory of intellectual development—that of Jean Piaget and his coworkers. This chapter is considerably more detailed than the material presented in other educational psychology textbooks. The richness of Piagetian theory for all branches of educational psychology is only now being fully appreciated. Current research is linking his theory to the psychology of learning, to emotional development (particularly moral development), and to the measuring of intellectual performance. The standard material on intelligence testing has been moved to the measurement and research section of the book (Part Four).

5   One whole chapter is devoted to the development of language. It is based on learning, linguistic, and psycholinguistic theory. It reflects the growing concern of parents, teachers, and students to develop more fully the ability to speak, read, and write. This chapter replaces the one in the first edition on the education of the disadvantaged child. It reflects the growing belief of many educators that so-called "disadvantaged" children need to read, write, and speak clearly just as other children do and that their past linguistic experience can be an asset as well as a disadvantage. This chapter includes a section on Black English.

6   The research references have been updated where it seemed that some genuinely new research themes were being developed.

7   The measurement and research sections reflect new trends in those areas. For example, the idea of criterion-referenced measures has been introduced to reflect the current interest in competency-based instruction and curriculum.

This textbook is the major part of an instructional package which also includes the *Instructor's Manual* and the *Student Guide*. This package provides the student with the essential materials for independent study and the instructor with the materials for periodically assessing what the student has learned. The careful organization of the textbook, with its systematic interrelationship of topics, lists of instructional objectives for each chapter, and embedded questions with accompanying answers and explanations, makes this book a maximally effective teaching instrument in its own right. Although there is ample opportunity to amplify, omit, and add topics, the careful presentation of material here relieves the instructor of much of the burden of explaining the text as well.

The book allows considerable flexibility in the assignment of material because each chapter divides clearly into three or four sections and thus it is possible to assign particular sections only. The Contents indicates these section divisions and facilitates the choice of assignments.

The textbook provides several sources of supplementary reading. The list of suggested readings at the end of each chapter contains references which treat the related subject matter at different levels of complexity and allow the student to pursue a topic in a way consonant with his objectives, interests, and abilities. The extensive Bibliography at the end of the book lists innumerable research reports.

The *Instructor's Manual* contains 400 multiple choice items keyed to the chapter objectives in the text. The manual discusses the use of these items for exemption purposes as well as for formative and summative evaluation in a competency-based course. Classroom discussion topics and projects designed to actively involve the class are presented.

The instructional package suggests several classroom uses, some of which are listed here:

1 For any given class session the instructor may select particular instructional objectives from the lists for each chapter and require the student to demonstrate his achievement of that objective. The instructor, of course, must provide the student with the necessary conditions and materials for performance.

2 The instructor may select discussion issues from the *Student Guide* and direct discussion in a way which elucidates concepts and principles the student has learned in reading the text and which enables the student to achieve the chapter objectives.

3 The instructor may use the projects described in the Instructor's Manual. Most projects can be completed within one classroom period.

4 The instructor may require the student to teach a concept or principle explained in the text and to demonstrate in his teaching the knowledge he has gained in reading the text. The instructor may also administer a test to determine the effectiveness of his teaching.

5 The instructor may ask the student to make reports on those chapters which are not required reading for all the class and to apply these materials to teaching situations with which he is familiar.

6 The instructor may administer quizzes based on questions in the *Instructor's Manual* and use the scoring of the tests as a basis for classroom discussion.

7 The instructor may assign particular projects for which the text offers considerable guidance. Among these are the following: (a) the explicit description of instructional objectives; (b) the analysis of student entering behavior; (c) the arrangement of teaching conditions for a particular type of learning; (d) the programing of instructional materials; (e) the construction of a classroom test; (f) the administration of a standardized test and the interpretation of the test scores using particular statistical concepts; and (g) the evaluation of research reports.

ACKNOWLEDGMENTS

It is impossible to name all the individuals who have contributed to the writing and revision of this book and whose help we deeply appreciate.

Among the educational psychologists whose research and articles we have found exceedingly fruitful are the following: Professor Robert M. Gagné of Florida State University, whose *Conditions of Learning* provided a firm bridge between experimental learning psychology and the psychology of school learning, and Professor Robert Glaser of the University of Pittsburgh, whose teaching model enabled us to organize and present the vast amount of information this book contains.

For reviews and critiques of the manuscript at various times in its development we express our deep appreciation to Professor Donald Ross Green of the California Test Bureau, to Professor John R. Feldhusen of Purdue University, to Professor Anne Terrill of the University of Pittsburgh, and to Mr. James Monahan of the University of Illinois.

We also want to thank our many current and former colleagues in education and psychology at Florida State University; Michigan State University; San Francisco State University; and the University of California, Los Angeles. We especially wish to thank Professor Bernard R. Corman of the University of Alberta, Professors Russell Kropp, Howard Stoker, and Hazen Curtis of the Florida State University, Professor John Krumboltz of Stanford University, Dean Rheba de Tornyay of the University of California, Los Angeles, Professor Morton Keston of San Francisco State University and Dr. Harold Ladas of Hunter College. For their help with the chapter on educational technology we thank Professors A. Daniel Peck and Francis X. Moakley of San Francisco State University.

For their invaluable help in shepherding the manuscript through its various stages we are indebted to Joy Thornbury, Jill Soula, and Betty Gardiner.

San Francisco and Los Angeles
1973

John P. De Cecco
William R. Crawford

THE PSYCHOLOGY
OF
LEARNING
AND
INSTRUCTION

PART ONE

INSTRUCTIONAL MODELS AND OBJECTIVES

CHAPTER ONE

A
BASIC TEACHING
MODEL

The general purposes of this chapter are reflected in three main sections. The first section explains the contents of a theory of teaching and how such a theory differs from theories of learning and development, educational philosophies, and the institutionalized practices of the school. The second section describes a basic teaching model which is general enough to cover a wide range of teaching, concrete enough to have practical utility, and simple enough to be remembered and used throughout this book. The last section compares the basic teaching model with two psychological views and three historical views of teaching.

After reading the first section, you should be able to meet the following objectives:

1-1 Write three questions about teaching behavior that a theory of teaching should be able to answer.

1-2 Write three questions about learning behavior that a theory of learning should be able to answer.

1-3 Write three questions about development that a theory of development should be able to answer.

1-4 Write three questions about teaching and learning that a philosophy of education should be able to answer.

A THEORY OF TEACHING

Although we are all students for many years, we develop no systematic conception of teaching because we are inclined to believe that teaching is something one does, not something one studies. Yet we need a general conception of teaching for organizing our present knowledge about teaching, proposing research which will advance our knowledge, and guiding our teaching practice. In asserting the need for a theory of teaching, however, we should sound two precautionary notes. First, with proper veneration of the past, we should remind ourselves that teaching has been with us a long time; to the extent that human beings (and teachers) learn from experience, teaching has not been carried on in total ignorance of its conditions and effects. Thus, experience and tradition have been sources of knowledge. Second, we should appreciate that there is no single conception of teaching. Perhaps every teacher has at least a primitive notion of teaching which may very well fail to stand the test of research and time. At this early point in the development of our knowledge about teaching, one should be willing to consider alternative conceptions of teaching for whatever light they may shed on its nature and practice. The time is hardly ripe for doctrine and dogma.

A theory of teaching should answer three questions (Gage, 1963, p. 133): How do teachers behave; why do they behave as they do; and what are the effects? It should be a general concept which applies to all teachers, to all students, to all subject matter, and to all situations, both in and out of school, in which teaching may occur. It should consider the behavior of teachers, the cause, and the learning of students, the effect (Gage, 1964) p. 272). Further, it should explain, predict, and control the ways in which the behavior of the teacher affects the learning of the students. You must remember that we do not presently have theories of teaching which embody these characteristics. We can indicate which questions theories of teaching must answer—that is, we can describe the form or shape theories must take—but we cannot describe the theories themselves. The fact that our knowledge is in such a primitive state may increase your skepticism about educational psychology and teacher training and confirm your fears that these are rather prosaic rituals based more on myth than on fact. If you will bear with us, however, you will discover that, even though we have no well-developed theories of teaching, we do have a firm base of knowledge upon which to build them.

We will probably never have a single theory of teaching. Nathaniel Gage (1964, p. 274) points out that teaching embraces "far too many kinds of process, of behavior, of activity, to be the proper subject of a single theory. We must not be misled by one word, 'teaching,' into searching for one theory to explain it." Gage uses the analogy of getting rich. We can get rich by inheriting, gambling, stealing, making profits, or earning wages—no single theory covers all the possible ways.

Theories of Learning

Theories of learning describe and explain the conditions under which learning does and does not occur. A theory of learning is a general concept which applies to all organisms, to all learning tasks, and to all situations where learning occurs. It considers the conditions which give rise to learning as the cause, and the learning itself as the effect. It explains, predicts, and controls the way in which environmental conditions affect the learning of the organism. For example, Edward Thorndike (1913) developed a theory of learning to explain how animals and human beings learn to make particular responses to particular stimuli in their environments. According to this theory, two conditions provide for the gradual "stamping in" of stimulus-response connections: The stimulus and the response must occur together, and the response must be followed by a satisfier, or reward. In a typical experiment, Thorndike placed a hungry cat in a cage and an irresistible piece of fish outside. To obtain the fish, the cat had to learn to pull a string which opened the cage door. Through trial and error, the cat gradually learned to pull the string, escape from the cage, and devour the fish. In this simple experiment, the key stimulus was the string which opened the cage, the key response was pulling the string, and the satisfier was the fish. An annoyer (punishment) could substitute for the satisfier. For example, a mild electric shock given to the cat each time it pulled the string would prevent it from learning a particular mode of escape. Thorndike's theory (described more fully in Chapter 7) fulfills the requirements of our original definition of a theory of learning: It describes and explains the conditions under which learning does and does not occur.

This brief explanation and illustration of learning theory show that a theory of learning is much broader and more basic than a theory of teaching. In fact, theories of teaching must be based on theories of learning. You will recall that a theory of teaching considers the behavior of teachers to be the cause, and the learning of students to be the effect. But, the behavior of teachers is only one special category of environmental conditions under which learning occurs. Similarly, the learning of students is only one special category of effects produced by these conditions. For example, learning occurs in animal as well as in human organisms. It also occurs without teachers. Children learn before they enter school, and adults who do not entirely surrender their intellectual prerogatives upon graduation, continue to learn all their lives. Learning then is a more ubiquitous experience than teaching.

Theories of learning are much more highly developed than theories of teaching. Yet learning theory is itself a young and growing field in much need of further development (Hill, 1963). We have no single theory of learning, and the prospects for one are dim. Considerable controversy takes place even over the form learning theory should take. Winfred Hill (1963, p. 204) distinguishes between narrow theories, which are developed in the laboratory and which are more precise than the broad ones, and the broad theories, which deal with everyday situations and which are less precise than the narrow ones. The narrow theories have greater rigor, the broad theories have greater relevance. Hill uses this illustration:

> For a person who deals with a great variety of people in different situations, it may be both useful and more satisfying to have such a broad generalization as, "Learning is most effective when the learner is 'motivated' but not 'threatened.'" As a scientific law, this generalization is not very meaningful since it leaves unspecified what we mean by "motivated" and by "threatened." It does, however, have a valuable use in telling us what to look for in a learning situation. Another person, dealing with one particular learning situation, might find it both more useful and more satisfying to know that "Infantrymen learn to use this weapon most effectively if they are trained three hours after breakfast, given knowledge of results after every shot, and told their scores will go on their service record." This generalization permits more precise predictions than the previous one and hence can be more easily and accurately used, but its range of application is too narrow to give it any general significance. Ideally we would like to be able to combine the precision of the second generalization with the breadth of the first. This goal keeps many theorists working.

David Ausubel (1971) has urged that further development of the psychology of education and learning should result from research in classrooms and schools. Such field research, if it were to rely heavily upon open-ended discussions with children, teachers, parents, and school officials about the changes and effects they want to bring about, would greatly increase the scope, richness, and relevance of contemporary learning theory. In the meantime, we shall see that teaching theory and alternative views of teaching derive from many sources. Some of these are (1) the developmental psychology of Jean Piaget, (2) different social and political views of the organization and role of the school, (3) alternative systems of values and social priorities, (4) aspirations for various types of utopias, and (5) favored choices of new life styles.

Theories of Development

Theories of development describe the biological and psychological changes that occur in people during various stages of their lives. Theories of development apply to all people with similar biological capabilities and similar physical and social backgrounds. These theories assume that people experience about the same stages or steps of development approximately in the same sequence and at the same time in their lives. Theories of learning derive from studies which show how changes in environment produce changes in behavior. Theories of development, however, are broader than theories of learning because they derive from studies which show how our biological capabilities grow and develop with our various encounters with environment. Theories of learning, consistent with the tradition of research in the physics and chemistry, link behavioral change to environmental change. Theories of development, by contrast, link behavioral change both to biological inheritance and growth and to environmental change.

Theories of development are also much broader than theories of teaching. In fact, theories of teaching must be based on theories of development as well as on theories of learning. The behavior of teachers is only one category of environmental conditions. The child is also learning to utilize biological and physical abilities in ways which promote further expression and growth. The teacher cannot change these abilities but can facilitate their development.

Philosophies of Education

We should also distinguish theories of teaching from philosophies of education. Philosophies of education deal with the goals and values that educational systems embrace and propagate. They include not only Western philosophy and political theory from that of Socrates to the latest brand of existentialism but also the ideas of those schools of psychology like psychoanalysis and phenomenology which are broad value orientations to modern life. Their primary concern is with ends rather than with means, and their importance lies in keeping us aware of the alternative goals of all our educational efforts. When educators caution parents and teachers about the tender psyches of children and the need to foster Athenian democracy in the classroom, their primary attention is not on teaching or on educational method but on the ultimate welfare of the child and the survival of the community. In a democratic society the electorate determines the values of the schools and the goals toward which they work.

Philosophies of education influence theories of teaching. Philosophers of science have made scientists aware of how subjectivity enters their work. And even though the psychologists may cherish the belief that theories of learning and teaching can develop in a climate of philosophical and ethical neutrality, we know now that such absolute neutrality is not possible, especially since we have the dual and overlapping roles of educators and citizens. As teachers we can aspire only to relative neutrality. Our teaching expertise must consist of the knowledge of means—of how we should behave to produce effective learning in our students. There may be considerable folly in professional educators' fiercely pursuing goals and values that are seriously at odds with those of the lay public, which provides both the children and the money we need to run the schools.

School Practices

Theories of teaching often contrast sharply with actual school practices. The gap between theory and practice has been the bane of most training pro-

8 grams for teachers. School practices are much more diverse than those prescribed by theories of learning and development. The practices are responses to many social and political factors as well as to the demands of classroom teaching and learning.

QUESTION 1-1   The speaker raised his arms, fixed his eyes, and, with deep conviction, uttered these words: "What we need are teaching methods which free the mind of the child. Teachers who make all the classroom decisions, materials which are remote from the child's interest, and procedures which make the child an automaton reduce the child to slavery and increase his feelings of frustration and guilt."

Is the above quotation chiefly (a) a theory of teaching, (b) a theory of learning, (c) a philosophy of education, or (d) a theory of development?

After you have selected your answer, list the characteristics which are absent in the quotation and by which you justified your rejection of the remaining choices.

After reading the sections which follow, you should be able to meet these objectives:

1-5   Name the four components of the basic teaching model and illustrate how a feedback loop from performance assessment results in adjustments in the three remaining components.
1-6   Describe the psychological teaching models of Stolurow and Flanders in terms of the components of the basic teaching model.
1-7   Describe the historical teaching models of lecture-recitation, Montessori, and human relations in terms of the components of the basic teaching model.

PSYCHOLOGICAL TEACHING MODELS

The best substitute for a theory of teaching is a model of teaching. Teaching models merely suggest how various teaching and learning conditions are interrelated. In many fields, models are prototypes of theories because they make possible our early conceptualization and study of phenomena. Unlike theories, in their early state of development models lack factual support. Eventually useful models give way to empirically supported theories. In this section of the chapter we shall examine and relate several models of teaching.

A Basic Teaching Model

Robert Glaser (1962) has developed a stripped-down teaching model which, with modifications, is the basic teaching model of this book. The basic teach-

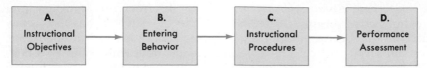

FIG. 1-1 A basic teaching model (after Glaser, 1962, p. 6).

ing model divides the teaching process into four components or parts. You will find it useful in several ways. It provides an uncomplicated, yet fairly adequate, conceptualization of the teaching process. It helps you organize the great body of facts, concepts, and principles which makes up the field of educational psychology. And it helps you understand other, more complicated, teaching models. In this book, we use the basic teaching model for all three purposes.

Figure 1-1 is a diagram of the basic teaching model. The four parts of the model correspond to the basic divisions of this book. Box A, instructional objectives, includes the material in Part 1 (Chapter 2). Box B, entering behavior, includes the material in Part 2 (Chapters 3–6). Box C, instructional procedures, makes up the material in Part 3 on the teaching of skills, concepts, principles, problem solving, creativity, and educational technology. Finally, box D, performance assessment, covers the material in Part 4 on the construction and use of tests. A final chapter on research in educational psychology, applies to the four components of the basic teaching model. Figure 1-1, with its connecting arrows, shows only the major sequence of events in the instructional process; you could add many more connecting lines. Lines which connect components later in the sequence with earlier ones are called *feedback loops*. The three feedback loops in Figure 1-2, for example, connect performance assessment with each of the earlier components of the model. In the ensuing chapters, discussions of the model components will refer to several feedback loops.

We will briefly define here the components of the basic teaching model. Later chapters will give detailed consideration to each component. *Instructional objectives* (box A) are those the student should attain upon completion of a segment of instruction. In theory, objectives can vary in scope and character from the mastery of a spelling list to the acquisition of Greek virtue. Chapter 2 tells you how to make useful statements of your instruc-

FIG. 1-2 Feedback loops for performance assessments.

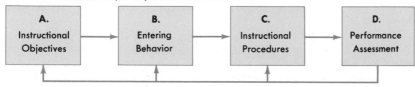

tional objectives. *Entering behavior* (box B) describes the student's level before instruction begins. It refers to what the student has previously learned, his intellectual ability and development, his motivational state, and certain social and cultural determinants of his learning ability. Entering behavior is a more precise term than its usual alternatives—human ability, individual differences, and readiness. This precision may come at the price of seeing the student as less complex, less able, and less experienced than he may in fact be. Schools tend to define entering behavior in terms of the traditional curriculum rather than in terms of student ability, experience, and interest. A student with the more abstractive ability and interest of the mathematician, therefore, may be viewed as having a higher level entering behavior than that of a student whose major interest and ability are in creating the visual, geometric forms of modern painting and sculpture. Although the model gives priority to the selection of instructional objectives over the assessment of entering behavior, in practice these two components must interact.

Instructional procedures (box C) describe the teaching process; most decisions a teacher makes are on these procedures. Proper management of this component results in those changes in student behavior which we call learning or achievement. Procedures must vary with the instructional objectives. Later chapters describe procedures for teaching skills, language, concepts, principles, and problem solving. Finally, *performance assessment* (box D) consists of the tests and observations used to determine how well the student has achieved the instructional objectives. If performance assessment indicates that the student has fallen short of mastery or some lesser standard of achievement, one or all of the preceding components of the basic teaching model may require adjustment. The feedback loops in Fig. 1-2 show how the information provided by performance assessment feeds back to each component.

You should note that the personality of the teacher is not the central element in the present conception of the teaching process. The model indicates that teaching includes a broad range of decision and practice—much of which requires little or no personal contact between teacher and student. The widespread use of technological devices, team teaching, and nongraded instruction (see Chapter 12) will undoubtedly modify the traditional nature of the personal contact between teacher and student. Depending on the requirements of the instructional situation, particularly on the entering behavior of the student, the classroom of the future will provide for more or less personal contact than the conventional classroom does now. Accordingly, the model implies a greater emphasis on teacher competence than on personal charisma without, of course, objecting to a useful combination of the two.

To illustrate the possible interrelationships among the four components of the basic teaching model and the varying emphasis we can give each component, we will describe two additional psychological models of teaching. These models are more complex than the basic teaching model, but they include each of its components.

By far the most complex teaching model you will study is one developed by Lawrence Stolurow and Daniel Davis (1965). In this model the computer replaces the teacher in making decisions and providing the actual instruction. Stolurow and Davis divide the teaching process into two phases. The *pretutorial phase* has a single purpose: to select for a particular student a teaching program that will achieve particular instructional objectives. The *tutorial phase* has two purposes: to put the program which has been selected into use, and to monitor the student's performance to discover whether a new program may be more suitable than the original one.

Figure 1-3 diagrams the pretutorial phase; it indicates the decisions the computer must make before instruction actually begins. This phase includes decisions on instructional objectives and entering behavior. (See boxes under Input in Figure 1-3.) For instructional objectives, three factors must be considered: (1) the final level of performance, P_f, (2) to be achieved in a given topic or subject matter, T, (3) within a given time, t. For entering behavior, the decisions are somewhat more difficult. Figure 1-3 shows the two aspects considered: the student's achievement level P_e, or what he has already learned that is relevant to the instructional objectives and his aptitude level Ap, or set of skills, which is not necessarily tied to a particular subject.

Given particular instructional objectives and entering behavior, the

FIG. 1-3   The pretutorial decision process (after Stolurow and Davis, 1965, p. 176)

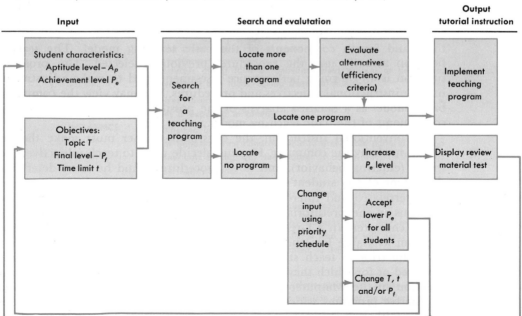

authority" or he can put them into one of the six other categories. He can classify the statements of the students as response or initiation. In one study (Flanders, 1964), the observer also kept a record of the six different types of classroom activity. During one hour he collected data separately for all periods of routine administration (settling down to work, passing out materials, collecting materials, cleaning up); for all periods of evaluation, in which homework and tests were being corrected; for all periods in which new material was being introduced; for all periods in which the students and the teacher planned activities together; for all class discussions; and for all periods in which the students worked individually at their desks or in groups. At the end of the hour, the observer added up all the different kinds of statements for each of these six classroom activities and combined them into a grand total for the entire hour.

Flanders (1964, p. 202) states the three principles of teacher influence to which the interaction model applies.

> Restricting student freedom of participation early in the cycle of classroom learning activities increases dependence and decreases achievement.
> Restricting student freedom of participation later in the cycle of classroom learning activities does not increase dependence but does increase achievement.
> Expanding student freedom of participation early in the cycle of classroom learning activities decreases dependence and increases achievement.

The teacher restricts student freedom of participation when he exercises direct influence (categories 5, 6, and 7 in Table 1-1) through lecturing, giving directions, and criticizing or justifying authority. In these behavior categories the teacher talks more and therefore plays a dominant role in the classroom. Expansion of student participation occurs when the teacher employs categories 1 through 4: The teacher accepts feeling, praises or encourages, accepts or uses student ideas, and asks questions. The phrase *early and late in the cycle* refers to Flanders' particular conception of the order in which events recur in the classroom. Flanders (p. 203) describes this cycle as follows:

> First, an intellectual difference or problem is created; second, the major dimensions of the problem are identified; and third, relationships within the problem are isolated. Fourth, work occurs—such as the gathering of information, the application of a formula, or the trial solution of a problem. Fifth, progress is evaluated and tested. Sixth, the new knowledge is applied to additional problems and interpreted in some meaningful way.

Steps 1 and 2 represent the early part, and steps 5 and 6 represent the late part of the cycle.

The directness or indirectness of the teacher's influence in each part of the cycle affects two aspects of learning: the student's dependence and his achievement. Flanders defines dependence in terms of the degree of concern the student has for pleasing the teacher. A dependent student is more concerned about which method the teacher wants him to use than about which method will solve the problem. According to Flanders, sustained direct influence by the teacher results in increased dependency. Achievement is the difference in pretest and posttest scores. Again, the directness or indirectness of the teacher's influence, in the interaction model, increases or decreases this variable.

We can now compare the interaction model with the basic teaching model. First, the interaction model does not explicitly provide for the statement of instructional objectives or for the adjustment of entering behavior and instructional procedures to different objectives. In his description of the classroom cycle, Flanders refers to the creation "of an intellectual difference or problem." But, since his principles indicate that the teacher should avoid direct influence early in the cycle, when the problem is created and identified and its relationships isolated, we may conclude that the model does not recommend the prior establishment of clear instructional objectives. Second, although the model makes no explicit provision for accommodating differences in entering behavior, the student may be able to adjust the instruction to his own entering behavior since he can control so much of the direction of the learning activity. Also the flexibility of teacher influence, in theory, allows for adjusting the instruction to meet the needs of the students. Third, the model makes no explicit provision for instructional procedures. Rather, it strongly suggests that the most suitable procedures will emerge from the sensitive interaction of students and teacher. Finally, performance assessment, where it is mentioned at all, seems to depend on posttest scores and possible differences in student attitudes. Also, the model does not explicitly provide for using the results of the performance assessment to make changes in objectives, entering behavior, and instructional procedures.

Table 1-2 shows the common elements of the three psychological teaching

COMMON ELEMENTS OF THREE PSYCHOLOGICAL TEACHING MODELS   **TABLE 1-2**

BASIC TEACHING MODEL	STOLUROW	FLANDERS
Instructional objectives	a. Subject matter b. Minimum level of final achievement c. Maximum amount of time	Determined by interaction of teacher and student.
Entering behavior	a. Aptitude level b. Previous relevant knowledge	Student's feelings, ideas, and present information.
Instructional procedures	a. Teacher function b. Professor function	Interactions between teacher and student ranging from direct to indirect teacher influence
Performance assessment	Included in teacher and professor functions	Achievement tests and attitude questionnaires used at conclusion of instruction

models. Inspection of the table reveals that the model of Stolurow easily fits the basic teaching model. Stolurow's is the most explicit for all four components. Flanders' is the least explicit but perhaps the most easily applied to the conventional classroom.

In a teaching method developed by Friedrich Herbart (1883), the first step was called *preparation*. In it, the teacher was to inventory the student's *apperceptive mass,* which was composed of clusters of ideas, roughly equivalent to knowledge the student had acquired. The teacher roughly outlined what he might find, questioned the class, and encouraged the student to mention everything that related to the topic. In this way the teacher tried to call into consciousness those ideas which were most crucial for learning (Herbart says *apperceiving*) the new material.

Which of the following teaching models (and which part of the model) does this first step of Herbart's method fit: (a) the computer-based model, or (b) Flanders' interaction model?

After you have selected your answer, explain your basis for rejecting the alternative.

HISTORICAL TEACHING MODELS

To show the relationship between traditional concepts of teaching and the basic teaching model, we shall now describe three historical models: the lecture-recitation model, the Montessori model, and the human relations model.

Lecture-Recitation Model

The lecture-recitation model is the traditional style of teaching still found in many schools and colleges. Historically, it is best illustrated by the Jesuit schools which flourished from the fifteenth to the nineteenth centuries and which were models of classical, humanist education. Broudy (1963, p. 22) describes the Jesuits as "masters of method," with a genius for organizing materials, methods, and teachers into uniformly effective instructional systems. The *Ratio Studiorum,* first published in 1586, is the most detailed description of their method.

Jesuit education was largely a product of the Renaissance, a period of intense revival of interest in the literature of the Greeks and Romans and in their ideals and styles of life. The educated man of the Renaissance was the cultured gentleman at home in many worlds—the royal courts of Europe, the world of wily diplomacy, the new world of trade, and the world of music, painting, sculpture, and literature. Even today many members of liberal arts faculties wistfully dream of their students attaining this breadth of culture. More specifically, the instructional goals were the acquisition of a high degree of skill in speaking, writing, reasoning, and criticizing. Students gained these skills in the process of mastering Latin and Greek, logic, natural and moral philosophy, metaphysics, theology, and sacred scripture (Fitzpatrick, 1933). Broudy (1963, pp. 22–25) observes that these materials had built-in sets of values, even though the focus was not directly on inculcating them. Critics who see only the avid formalism and intellectualism of the classical schools ignore this value orientation.

The curriculum was fairly standard, and the student had to accommodate himself to the instruction rather than the other way around. We might say that the method selected the student. Those who succeeded under this classical program of studies went on to the universities. Although in the main these students were the children of the old landed aristocracy and the new merchant class, the Jesuits always had an eye for talent, no matter what its socioeconomic trappings. Therefore, children from the lower classes who manifested brightness often found themselves the beneficiaries of the Jesuit schools. The talented aside, the provision for repetition and review in Jesuit education enabled a docile student of even moderate ability to succeed.

The Jesuits had highly developed instructional procedures. The *Ratio Studiorum* contained very specific directions for the teacher. The chief method of presentation was the *prelection*. The teacher studied the assignment in front of the class, and the student was expected to repeat this model performance as precisely as possible. Broudy (1963, pp. 22–23, following Fitzpatrick, 1933, pp. 212–13) quotes the following passage from the *Ratio*, which contains directions for the prelection of an oration or poem:

> If an oration or poem is being explained, first its meaning must be explained, if it is obscure, and the various interpretations considered. Second, the whole method of the workmanship, whether invention, disposition, or delivery is to be considered, also how aptly the author ingratiates himself, how appropriately he speaks, or from what topics he takes his material for persuading, for ornament, or for moving his audience; how many precepts he unites in one and the same place, by what method he includes with the figures of thought the means of instilling belief, and again the figures of thought which he weaves into the figures of words. Third, some passages similar in subject matter and expression are to be adduced and other orators or poets who have used the same precept for the sake of proving or narrating something similar are to be cited. Fourth, let the facts be confirmed by statements of authorities, if opportunity offers. Fifth, let statements from history, from mythology, and from erudition be sought which illustrate the passage. At last, let the words be considered carefully, and their fitness, their elegance, their number, and their rhythm noted. However, let these things be considered, not that the master may always discuss everything, but that from them he may select those which are most fitting.

The Jesuits also retained the medieval disputation for some teaching purposes. The disputation was a formal debate, a kind of formal Socratic dialogue, usually between two students, the defender and the assailant. A master teacher presided over the student debaters, his chief task being to keep the debaters and their audience from muddling their chief points and confusing one another. The rules and the arguments of debating were explicit and had to be learned. Perhaps the only survival of the disputation is the oral examination of doctoral candidates in our graduate schools.

According to Broudy (1963, p. 24), the most important aspect of Jesuit teaching was the method for securing overlapping review. Review of the prelection and other tasks followed immediately upon completion of the work. Students reviewed the work of the week on Saturday; and, for promotion, they reviewed thoroughly the work of the entire year. Students submitted homework assignments at least once a week; grammar students, every day.

The Jesuits made important use of rivalry as a teaching device. They charged each student with catching and correcting every mistake of his opposite number. They also grouped the students into teams, with the success of the team depending on such individual performance. Teachers consistently praised every correct response and blamed every incorrect one, a practice designed both for motivation of the students and for feedback.

The Jesuits built performance assessment intimately into their system. The standard of achievement was mastery of the material and its retention for a year and longer. The teacher or fellow students under the direction of the teacher regularly checked assignments and returned them to the student. The frequent reviews in themselves uncovered what was learned and how well.

Comparing the Jesuit method of instruction with the basic teaching model, you can see that it was explicit for each component of the model. The instructional objectives consisted of good performance in speaking, writing, reasoning, and criticizing. Other objectives, considerably less explicit, were the acquisition of certain attitudes and values. It appears, however, that the Jesuit teachers consciously tried to develop specific performances and hoped that the desirable attitudes and values would evolve from the Greco-Roman materials studied. No conscious variation in objectives and procedures accommodated differences in entering behavior. The Jesuits expected all students to achieve the same objectives and in about the same way. This standardization of objectives and procedures is still characteristic of the classical-human curriculum of today. The Jesuit method was most explicit about instructional procedures. Although their methods smack a little of what today we deprecatingly call *rote learning,* the thoroughness of Jesuit teaching often resulted in the students' long-term mastery of a wide range of subjects.

Today there is considerable debate over use of the lecture-recitation method as the major instructional procedure. One important reason for this is that American society has become information-rich and action-poor (Coleman, 1971). Information is no longer a monopoly of schools and teachers. We have many new and easily available sources of information: our own experience and travel, computer data banks, institutional reports, paperback books, magazines and journals, movies, radio, television, and so on. At the same time, the school has become action-poor because it provides students few opportunities to use information to make changes in schools and communities.

The Montessori Model

There has been a sharp increase in interest in the work of Maria Montessori, an Italian physician who, in 1909, published her *Scientific Pedagogy as*

Applied to Child Education in the Children's Houses. (See the McV. Hunt edition, 1964.) Her work, in addition to that of John Dewey, has influenced the development of the British primary schools (Featherstone, 1971). Montessori's method emphasized the importance of *liberty,* the freedom of both child and teacher to observe and experiment. Montessori believed that the collective or lecture-recitation method failed because the teacher, like the inept concertmaster, tries to teach the same monotonous and discordant rhythms at the same time and in the same way to the most diverse instruments and voices. Better, she writes, for the concertmaster to teach each scholar one by one and for each artist to perfect himself as an individual and, in this way, to produce great collective works of harmony and beauty.

Montessori describes two major options teachers have in deciding how to teach (McV. Hunt, ed., 1964, p. 114):

> Let us suppose . . . that an architect shows you a dome, the form of which interests you. He can follow one of two methods: (1) He can call attention to the beauty of line, the harmony of the proportions, and may then take you inside the building and up into the cupola itself, in order that you may appreciate the relative proportion of the parts in such a way that your impression of the cupola as a whole shall be founded on general knowledge of its parts. (2) Or he can have you count the windows, the wide or narrow cornices, and can, in fact, make you a design showing the construction; he can illustrate for you the static laws and write out the algebraic formulae necessary in the calculation of such laws.
>
> In the first place, you will be able to retain in your mind the form of the cupola; in the second, you will have understood nothing, and will come away with the impression that the architect fancied himself speaking to a fellow engineer, instead of to a traveller whose object was to become familiar with the beautiful things about him. Very much the same thing happens if we, instead of saying to the child, "This is a square," and by simply having him touch the contour establish materially the idea of the form, proceed rather to a geometrical analysis of the contour.

Montessori's method stresses simplicity. If, for example, you want to teach a child the colors red and blue, you attract his attention by saying, "Look at this." You hold up the red object and say, "This is red," pronouncing the word slowly and clearly. You do the same with the blue object. To be certain that the child understands, you ask him to give you the red and then the blue object. If the child makes a mistake, do not repeat and insist. Smile at the child, give him a friendly caress, and remove the colors.

Montessori claimed that her method stresses objectivity and observation. By objectivity she meant that the focus of the child's attention should be on the objects he seeks to understand and not on the personality of the teacher. By observation she meant that the focus of the teacher's attention should be on the changing level of the child's interest rather than on pressing the child beyond the limits of spontaneous interest.

How does the Montessori method compare with the basic teaching model? It appears that the objectives are fairly clear—engaging the child in performances which will show how well he has learned such things as geometric and color concepts. The objectives seem to be chosen by both child and teacher in that the Montessori schools allow children sufficient freedom of choice and movement; the child can select objects and materials to play with and to learn about. The method provides great sensitivity to entering behavior. Montessori's objection to the lecture-recitation method was that not all children are predisposed to give their attention to the particular lesson at hand. Even after the instruction has begun, the method urges discontinuation of instruction when the child's interest wanders and he begins to make mistakes. Brief, successful learning experiences are emphasized. The teacher is merely calling attention to forms and experience that the child sees and has in his daily life. As for materials, the child is provided with a rich environment of objects which appeal to wide ranges of individual preference and ability. Montessori's materials include solid insets, objects of varying thickness and thinness, rods of varying length, large and small objects, trays of geometric insets, color tablets, series of little whistles, and so on. Both the method of instruction and the assessment of performance is individual—the teacher adjusts the method to the child on the basis of the results that have been observed in the child. There is no formal testing, since individual performance and observation make this unnecessary. Observation provides the feedback necessary for lesson adjustment, discontinuation, and the introduction of new lessons.

How does the Montessori method differ from the basic teaching model? The method resembles the model in that it includes the notion of individualized instruction which uses carefully designed instructional materials. Montessori, however, emphasized that the child learn how to control his own learning and performance through the selection of his own learning tasks.

The Human Relations Model

The origin of teaching models which concentrate on improved human relationships among teachers and students can be traced to the *life-adjustment movement* (Cremin, 1964, p. 133). This was the last phase of the progressive education movement; the name stemmed from the Commission on Life Adjustment Education for Youth which was established in 1948. The Commission first believed that training in occupational skills was the chief means of helping the youth of the nation adjust to the occupational and social order. Later, the psychological dimensions of life-adjustment became the predominant concern as was seen in the mental hygiene movement, sensitivity group therapy, and humanistic education (Alschuler, 1969).

Soon after the birth of the Commission, Donald Snygg and Arthur Combs wrote a book which has served as an authoritative reference for those whose major professional concern is the personal adjustment and development of their students. In the first edition (1949), the authors discussed individual behavior; and in the revised edition (Combs and Snygg, 1959), they included two chapters—one on goals and purposes, the other on teaching relationships—which related individual behavior to education.

Alfred Alschuler (1959, p. 2) described the following six steps as a guideline for courses in humanistic education:

1 Focus attention on what is happening here and now, and create moderate novelty that is slightly different from what is expected.
2 Provide an intense, integrated experience of the desired new thoughts, actions, and feelings.
3 Help the person make sense out of his experience by attempting to conceptualize what happened.
4 Relate the experience to the person's values, goals, behavior, and relationships with others.
5 Stabilize the new thoughts, actions, and feelings through practice.
6 Internalize the changes.

Alschuler states that these courses depart from traditional classroom formats in that they have large blocks of time, they are organized as workshops, and they are often removed to locations where activities occur without interruption.

A comparison of the human relations model and basic teaching model reveals several important points. The goals of the human relations model deal primarily with individual styles of communication, including physical gesture, facial expression, bodily posture, and use of words. The goals emphasize seeing yourself as others see you. These goals are usually not translated into instructional objectives that can be assessed readily.

The goals are implemented through various exercises selected by the training leader. Exercises occur in groups of two or more people and seem to be drawn from a pool of exercises rather than devised for particular problems and individuals. Feedback is continuously invited within the exercises themselves or as an aftermath in reaction sessions. The feedback centers on the impact of one individual's behavior on another individual or on the whole group, rather than on situations in the past that stimulated this behavior. In some ways the exercises of this model seem as highly structured and preordained as those of the lecture-recitation model. The Montessori method, however, seems to present a more sensitive response to changes in students' feelings and interests than does the human relations model.

SUMMARY

This chapter described what a theory of teaching must include. It distinguished a theory of teaching from and related it to a theory of learning and a philosophy of education. The chapter also described the four components of the basic teaching model: instructional objectives, entering behavior, instructional procedures, and performance assessment. It then described psychological teaching models—a computer-based model (Stolurow) and an interaction model (Flanders)—and compared them with the basic teaching model. Finally, it described three historical teaching models—the lecture-recitation, Montessori, and human-relations models—and compared them with the basic teaching model.

QUESTION 1-3   Othanel Smith (1960) has developed a teaching model which describes what he calls the *ebb and flow* of teaching or the *cycle of giving and taking instruction*. A cycle consists of a teacher phase and a student phase, which mirror each other. In the teacher phase the teacher perceives the student's behavior, diagnoses the student's state of interest, readiness, knowledge, and so on, and, finally, acts. In the student phase the student perceives and diagnoses the teacher's behavior and, finally, acts. Which of the following models is least like Smith's: (a) the Montessori model, (b) the lecture-recitation model, or (c) the human-relations model? After you have selected your answer, list the characteristics of the model you chose and point out the differences between it and Smith's model.

SUGGESTED READINGS

The following articles are useful and comprehensive discussions of teaching theory (with its relation to learning theory):

COLEMAN, JAMES S., "Education in the Age of Computers and Mass Communication," in *Computers, Communication and the Public Interest*, ed. M. Greenberger. Baltimore: The Johns Hopkins Press, 1971.

FEATHERSTONE, JOSEPH, "Schools for Children: "What's Happening in British Classrooms," *The New Republic*, Aug. 19, 1967.

GAGE, NATHANIEL S., "Paradigms for Research on Teaching," in *Handbook of Research on Teaching*, ed. N. L. Gage, pp. 94–141. Chicago: Rand McNally & Co., 1963.

———, "Theories of Teaching," in *Theories of Learning and Instruction*, ed. E. R. Hilgard, pp. 268–85, part 1 of the 63rd Yrbk. of the National Society for the Study of Education. Chicago: University of Chicago Press, 1964.

The following works give fuller descriptions of the psychological models we have used:

ALSCHULER, ALFRED, *Human Relations Education: A Guidebook to Learning Activities*. Albany, New York: Curriculum Development Center, State Education Department.

CARROLL, JOHN B., "A Model of School Learning," *Teachers College Record*, 64 (1963), 723–33.

COMBS, ARTHUR, *The Professional Education of Teachers: A Perceptual View of Teacher Preparation*. Boston: Allyn and Bacon, Inc., 1965.

FLANDERS, NED A., "Interaction Analysis and In-service Training," *California Journal for Instructional Improvement*, 9 (1966), 14–31.

MONTESSORI, MARIA, *The Montessori Method*, ed. McV. Hunt. New York: Schocken Books, 1964. (paperback)

STOLUROW, LAWRENCE M., and DANIEL DAVIS, "Teaching Machines and Computer-Based Systems," *Teaching Machines and Programed Learning, II: Data and*

Directions, ed. R. Glaser, pp. 162–212. Washington, D.C.: Department of Audio-visual Instruction, National Education Association, 1965.

The following works give fuller descriptions of the historical models:

BROUDY, HARRY S., "Historic Exemplars of Teaching Method," *Handbook of Research on Teaching,* ed. N. S. Gage, pp. 1–43. Chicago: Rand McNally & Co., 1963.

BROUDY, HARRY S., and JOHN R. PALMER, *Exemplars of Teaching Method.* Chicago: Rand McNally & Co., 1965.

CHAPTER TWO

INSTRUCTIONAL OBJECTIVES

This chapter has the following general purposes. First, it distinguishes between three types of objectives—those of schools, teachers, and students. The objectives of teachers and students are called *instructional objectives*. Second, it shows how each type of objective can guide development, learning, and instruction. Third, it shows you how to write behavioral statements of instructional objectives—a process also called *task description*. Fourth, it describes the various ways of classifying instructional objectives—a process called *task analysis*.

Upon reading the first section of this chapter you should be able to meet this objective:

2-1 Distinguish between school, teacher, and student objectives by giving examples of each type.

In this section, three types of objectives are discussed. School objectives are distinguished from *instructional objectives,* a term used in reference to both teacher and student objectives. All three types of objectives—school, teacher, and student—will be considered.

School Objectives

We shall use the term *school objectives* to refer to the broad goals which nations and communities pursue through their educational systems and the administration of their schools. School objectives are broad statements of goals and reflect economic, political, and social philosophies. They serve as general frameworks for stating the narrower, more specific teacher and student objectives. Because these frameworks are so broad, different teachers and students derive different objectives from them.

There is often general agreement in American communities about the goals of the school. Educational controversy mostly centers around the practices we use or should use to attain those goals. In 1955, *The Committee for the White House Conference on Education, A Report to the President* had little difficulty in stating fifteen goals pertaining to general education, citizenship, values, vocations, leisure time, physical development, mental health, and family life. A more recent effort by a research team at Teachers College, Columbia University developed a manual of goals for civic education (De Cecco and Richards, 1974, Appendix B) the following goals were included:

1 The citizen participates in the decision-making processes of his society.
2 The citizen makes use of alternative courses of action. If he finds no viable options open, he creates new alternatives for democratic action.
3 The citizen analyzes courses of action for their democratic bases, feasibility, and anticipated and actual consequences.
4 The citizen employs negotiation, mediation, and arbitration in resolving conflicts.
5 The citizen understands and analyzes issues from viewpoints other than his own.
6 The citizen distinguishes personal issues and conflicts from institutional issues and conflicts and attacks the two accordingly.

These six goals are examples of school goals which high school students believe are appropriate for democratic society.

In an earlier report, the Educational Policies Commission (1961, pp. 11–12) expressed this general purpose of American education:

The purpose which runs through and strengthens all other educational purposes—the common thread of education—is the development of the ability to think. This is the central purpose to which the school must be oriented if it is to accomplish its traditional tasks or those newly accentuated by recent changes in the world. To say that it is central is not to say that it is the sole purpose or in all circumstances the most important purpose, but that it must be a pervasive concern in the work of the school.

Other groups have put considerable effort into developing outlines of school objectives which reduce these broad objectives to narrower categories more useful to the teacher. The Russell Sage Foundation (Kearney, 1953, and French, 1957) sponsored the development of two such outlines, one for the elementary school and another for the high school. The outline for the elementary school stressed four broad categories of behavior: knowledge and understanding—the memorizing or understanding of content so well that it can be easily recalled; motor and intellectual skill and competence; attitude and interest, including basic human needs and drives, the exercise of the will, and the play of the emotions; and action patterns—broad, generalized ways of behaving. The outline divides further into nine broad curriculum areas; three age-grade levels (ages 6 to 15, grades 1 to 9); and "determining conditions," which are "the biological and social context in which the children and the school work together" (Kearney, 1953, p. 91). The outline for the secondary school curriculum contains these educational goals: growing toward self-realization; growing in the ability to maintain desirable small (face-to-face) group relationships; and growing in the ability to maintain the relationships imposed by membership in large organizations. Each of these major categories reduces to several levels of sub-categories, with the statements becoming slightly more explicit. For example, "can learn independently and shows desire to do so" finally reduces to (among other statements) "tries to improve his own written work by revising it so that it will convey his attention as clearly as possible." Both these outlines attempt to bridge the gap between broad school objectives and specific instructional objectives.

Teacher Objectives

Teacher objectives are narrower in scope than school objectives. Their chief purpose is to guide the teacher in the selection, emphasis, and omission of subject matter, materials, and activities when preparing lesson plans, classroom instruction, or field studies. Some examples of teacher objectives are:

1 Understanding of the political dilemmas facing the Tudor monarchs in the sixteenth century.
2 Appreciating the religious themes expressed in seventeenth-century poetry, painting, and architecture.
3 Learning the major religious leaders of the Protestant and Catholic Reformations.

As these examples show, teacher objectives are traditionally expressed in terms of knowledge (or understanding), attitudes (or appreciation), and skills (spelling, reading, listing, and the like). In the traditional lesson plan, teacher objectives introduce a more specific description of the subject matter and activities the teacher will cover.

You can now see that teacher objectives can be subcategories of school objectives. By helping students "understand the political dilemmas of Tudor monarchs" (a teacher objective), the teacher may also help them "understand and analyze issues from viewpoints other than their own" (a school objective). Similarly, when a teacher enables students to "appreciate the religious themes in seventeenth-century poetry" (a teacher objective), he may also help students "grasp and act on principles involved in concrete problems in democracy" (a school objective). The relationship between school and teacher objectives cannot be left to chance. Their coordination must be the result of discussion and planning by school officials, teachers, and students.

Student Objectives

The student protest movement of the 1960s in high schools and colleges and the growing prominence of the British primary schools strongly suggested that students should play a larger role in deciding *what* to learn as well as how to learn it. The traditional practice was to determine the content of the curriculum at the state level by leaving decisions in the hands of state boards of education and state superintendents of schools. Local boards and administrative staffs merely implemented the state educational mandates. The responsibility for making curriculum decisions was almost entirely separated from the responsibility for teaching and learning. This growing discrepancy between what the schools traditionally teach and what the students need in contemporary society has led to increased student demands for responsibility in formulating objectives.

Student objectives refer to the options and plans expressed and pursued by students (DeCecco and Richards, 1974). For example, students may have certain reasons for taking a given course. The objective may be to get an easy grade or to get knowledge necessary for later employment. In specific courses, student and teacher objectives may be at odds. Thus, student input is useful at the curriculum planning stage as well as in particular courses.

After reading the subsequent sections of this chapter, you should be able to meet these objectives:

2-2 Distinguish between behavioral and nonbehavioral statements of instructional objectives and identify terminal performance.
2-3 Describe the arguments for and against the use of behavioral statements of instructional objectives.
2-4 Write behavioral statements of instructional objectives, using Mager's three requirements for task description.
2-5 Identify the missing requirements in faulty task descriptions.
2-6 List the behavior categories used in two systems of task analysis (Gagné's and Bloom's) and identify and provide examples of instructional objectives for each category.

One way to define instructional objectives is to identify the end product of instruction in terms of observable performance. The way to determine whether or not a student has learned something is to observe the outcome of his behavior. These outcomes have been conventionally referred to as *behavioral objectives*. It is more precise to refer to these end products of instruction as *terminal performances*. In most school situations these are verbal performances or motor skills. The following three statements are instructional objectives which describe observable terminal performances:

1   Student names the planets of our solar system.
2   Student distinguishes between the Renaissance and the Reformation.
3   Student lists the major systems of the body.

By contrast, the following statements do not refer to observable terminal performances:

1   Student really understands the poetry of John Donne.
2   Student appreciates the beauty of Gothic architecture.
3   Student grasps the significance of the impact of the French Revolution on later political developments in Europe.

We may refer to the second set of objectives as *nonbehavioral statements* of instructional objectives because the terminal performances are not specified —how the student will visibly demonstrate his understanding or appreciation of Donne, Gothic architecture, or the French Revolution is not indicated—and because the performances implied are interior states, responses, and processes not open to observation.

    The distinction between behavioral and nonbehavioral statements lies chiefly in the choice of verb. The verbs in the behavioral statements were *to name, to distinguish,* and *to list.* These are publicly observable acts. In the nonbehavioral statements the verbs were *to understand, to appreciate,* and *to grasp the significance of.* These do not indicate how the student will visibly show his understanding and appreciation. Also, much of his understanding and appreciation is neural and cerebral activity which is hardly open to observation by the teacher. Without denying the importance of nonbehavioral objectives for the educational enterprise, this chapter will stress the practical importance of behavioral statements of instructional objectives.

    The following example will further clarify this behavioral distinction. Compare these two statements:

1   Joe and Lucille are hopelessly in love.
2   One rarely sees Joe without Lucille, or Lucille without Joe.

The first statement describes a joyful (sometimes painful) internal state of two individuals, which can be exemplified in a number of observable acts. Conceivably, Joe and Lucille may be hopelessly in love because their families, teachers, or community do not approve of their relationship. They may be hopelessly in love because they have no time except for each other—which at least is a hopeless situation for other interested candidates. Or the description may refer to the inevitable quarrels when they are together and the inevitable statements of nostalgia when they are apart—a kind of hopeless compatibility. Or Lucille may be about to die of leukemia or Joe about to enlist in the Navy—both very hopeless situations.

The second statement, however, refers to behavior—the physical and therefore observable presence of two individuals. Even the word *rarely* implies that we could count the number of times Joe and Lucille are not seen together. Now we can scarcely deny that Joe and Lucille may be together for reasons other than love or that they may demonstrate their love in more ways than by a symbiotic existence. Perhaps no one else will have anything to do with them—they may be social outcasts thrown into each other's company. They may be brother and sister or Siamese twins. Or they may be very private in their love, with few or no public appearances. In any case, whether it be love or hate, biological or social necessity, we can at least agree on when and how often we see them together. The performance is explicit.

Now let us analyze two partial statements of instructional objectives for this distinction between behavioral and nonbehavioral performance.

1   The student should know what the Renaissance embraced and how it arose, and appreciate its great cultural significance.
2   Given the complete unit of the Italian Renaissance, the student should be able to list and discuss its classical origins and its chief literary and artistic products, and to illustrate its survival in the literary and artistic products of our century.

The important verbs in the first statement are *to know* and *to appreciate*. In the second statement they are *to list, to discuss,* and *to illustrate.* The implicit nature of the first statement opens it to considerably more ambiguity than does the explicit nature of the second statement, although, as instructional objectives, both statements leave much to be desired. We know, for example, that the Renaissance included important religious, commercial, political, and social developments which have their legacy in our century. In the first statement, the requirement that the student appreciate the great significance of the period could refer to something as parsimonious as making a general statement that "the Renaissance surely changed the course of events in Europe." Or, the same sentence could refer to something as elaborate as making a detailed analysis of social, political, religious, economic, and cultural events of the centuries after the Renaissance in order to identify specific instances of surviving influence. The second statement, however, indicates that what the student should know best is only the cultural part of the historical period. And even this knowledge is limited to cultural products and does not necessarily include the producers—the artists and the writers. In this instance, to name particular artistic and literary works and to show how they have been influenced by the Renaissance describes performance which involves a very limited appreciation or perhaps no appreciation at all. In any case, in the second statement, as against the first, it is easier to agree on the occurrence or nonoccurrence of the performance in question.

Usefulness of Behavioral Objectives

Ralph Tyler (1949, 1950, 1964) and Robert Gagné (1965b) provide three persuasive reasons for the careful definition of instructional objectives. First, such a definition provides guidance in the planning of instruction. If you are not certain where you are going, you may very well end up someplace else. Thus, the teacher must determine at the start what the student will be able to do at the finish. A careful statement of this terminal performance enables the teacher to plan the steps the student must take to achieve it. The teacher can provide for all the responses the student must make in order to accomplish the major final responses only after he has adequately described the characteristics of these final responses. You may recall that in the pretutorial phase of the computer-based teaching model the search for the appropriate program is based on the instructional objectives and the entering behavior of the student. One of the possible outcomes of this search is the modification of objectives—by changing the amount of time, the expected level of mastery, or the topics covered. These changes can occur only if the objectives first appear in behavioral form. In the same way, instructional procedures cannot accommodate differences in entering behavior unless the teacher determines in some precise form what the student is able to do before instruction and what he is expected to do after instruction. By far the most important reason for using explicit statements of instructional objectives is the guidance they provide the teacher in planning his instructional procedures. Later in the chapter, when we describe task analysis, we will carefully consider the relationship between instructional objectives and procedures.

A second reason for making explicit statements of instructional objectives is that they are useful in performance assessment. In education, the original concern for adequate statements of instructional objectives came from men chiefly interested in test construction and curriculum evaluation. They discovered that using ambiguous statements of objectives made it difficult or impossible to construct tests and test items. One has much more difficulty constructing test items for objectives which contain the verbs *to know* and *to understand* than for those which contain the verbs *to solve* and *to differentiate*. In a programed textbook on descriptive statistics (Gotkin and Goldstein, 1964, p. 1), for example, one of the first objectives is: Identify whether a set of data represents a sample or a population. Later (p. 243) the authors present this test item:

List some possible populations that each of the following samples might represent:

a   A bushel of McIntoch apples.
b   Sixty fourth-grade boys.
c   A quart of milk.
d   All members of the New York City chapter of Alcoholics Anonymous.

By correctly identifying possible populations for each of these samples, a student demonstrates his achievement of the instructional objective. The statement of the objective specifically suggests the test item. In this way, the proper statement of objectives and the construction of test items interweave.

A third reason for using explicit statements of objectives pertains more to the student than to the teacher. If the student knows beforehand what he must learn in any given unit of instruction, he can better direct his own attention and efforts. When you contemplate how frequently students are unable to make even an approximate statement of what the teacher is trying to explain, the importance of this practice becomes convincing. Take, for example, the list of objectives for Chapter 1. Although the student cannot define every term in the list the first time he reads it, he does obtain some preliminary idea of what he should look for and be able to do upon completion of the chapter. He knows in summary form and at the outset that, after reading the chapter, he should be able to (1) distinguish between a theory of teaching and theories of learning and philosophies of education; (2) describe the four components of the basic teaching model; and (3) describe the relationship of the model to various psychological and historical teaching models. While reading the chapter, the student can match the responses he makes to the responses given in the list. In programed instruction, the requirement that the student make overt responses throughout the program greatly facilitates this matching process.

A study by Mager and McCann (1961) provides empirical support for the benefits students derive from knowing at the start the specific objectives they should attain. The researchers investigated three groups of engineers being trained on particular engineering tasks. In the first group the instructor selected and ordered all the content. In the second group the students selected and ordered all the content which they studied. In the third group the investigators presented the students with a detailed list of the instructional objectives, each one illustrated by the kinds of questions they were expected to answer. Mager and McCann then allowed these students to instruct themselves in any order and by whatever procedures they desired; the students reported to the instructor when they were ready to demonstrate their achievement of the objectives. The investigators found that the training time for the third group was 65 percent less than that for the other groups without any loss in achievement. Thus much learning can occur when the teacher does nothing beyond presenting the student with the list of instructional objectives.

In the late sixties there was growing criticism of the use of behavioral objectives as the *sine qua non* of effective teaching. Much of the criticism came from teachers who had tried behavioral objectives and discovered how constraining they could be. Much criticism also came from students who felt that the objectives were efforts to program their learning in the way we program computers.

The movement for the adoption of behavioral objectives was led by those who were interested in developing curriculum packages, such as Robert Mager (1962) and W. J. Popham and Eva Baker (1970). In fact they developed packages that taught people how to make and use behavioral objectives. Mager provided his instruction in programed book form. Popham and his associates developed a series of filmstrip/tape recorder programs with tests and answer sheets. Neither set of materials requires a live teacher except, perhaps, as a materials administrator and legitimator of the activity. Popham and Baker (1970) believed that teachers resisted the use of behavioral objectives because they were threatened by precision: They preferred to rely on intuitive and capricious judgment rather than face their teaching failures. Behavioral objectives insist upon accountability, and the resisting teachers wanted the protection of unaccountability. Since 1967 Popham has modified his position. His slogan now appears to be: Help Stamp Out *Some* Nonbehavioral Objectives!

One of the first critics of behavioral objectives was Robert Ebel (1963). He argued that instructional objectives pertain to processes as well as products. To limit instructional objectives to products results in an overemphasis on conformity. Ebel (1963, p. 34) writes:

> For, if the goals of education are defined in terms of narrowly specific behavior desired by curriculum makers and teachers, what need is there for critical judgment by the student; what freedom is there for creative innovation; what provision is there for adaptive behavior as the cultural world changes?

Ebel also argued that there was practical difficulty in the use of behavioral objectives. To try to list all the behavioral objectives for a unit or course requires books rather than statements or paragraphs. Even books of behavioral objectives would not be able to fully describe all the particular behaviors desired. What is gained in concreteness is lost in complexity.

Elliot Eisner (1967) added to the basic criticism of behavioral objectives. In complex subject matters and skills behavioral objectives may be neither possible nor desirable. Eisner (1967, pp. 253–54) believes that in the "arts and subject matters where novel or creative responses are desired, the particular behaviors to be developed cannot easily be identified. Here curriculum and instruction should yield behaviors and products which are unpredictable. The end achieved ought to be something of a surprise to both teacher and pupil."

Eisner further argues that there is a vast difference between making a qualitative judgment and applying an objective standard. We can make a behavioral judgment of a piece of writing in terms of grammar, syntax, and even logic. But what shapes our preferences for the writing of Truman Capote or Gore Vidal over that of Ernest Hemingway is the result of the esthetic impact of content and style—a qualitative judgment that varies with individuals and times. It is often the uniqueness of what these writers say and do rather than their conformity to a standard that gives their writing literary and artistic value.

Eisner also distinguishes between the logical and psychological development of a course of study. Although it seems logical that a person should know where he is going when he embarks on a trip, it is often not the most psychologically satisfying way to travel. It is often more exciting to leave some of the itinerary unplanned or to change it when more interesting alternatives are discovered. James MacDonald (1967) believes that our objectives are known to us only after the completion of instruction. Teachers first ask the question "What am I going to do?" and out of the doing comes the final accomplishment.

Reasonable Use of Behavioral Objectives

It now appears that not all instructional objectives can or need be defined in behavioral terms. Those that are defined in behavioral terms need not be atomistic and trivial. Tyler (1964) believes that at the most useful level of specificity the teacher describes the concrete behavior he wants the student to acquire. These instructional objectives should express a purpose which is meaningful in the larger context of the life goals of the student, and this purpose should be distinguishable from others. Following Tyler's criteria, Gagné (1965a) suggests that teachers seek statements of objectives such as these:

> "Reads a French newspaper," rather than "reads French"; "solves problems requiring the use of sine, cosine, and tangent," rather than "understands trigonometry"; "makes a quantitative description of dispersion errors in observations," rather than "knows statistics."

Not all topics or courses are equally adaptable to behavioral objectives. Moreover, age and grade level differences must also be adapted to the substantive behavioral objectives. For example, the behavioral objectives for history courses at the graduate level and at the elementary school level cannot be identical because of the differences in course content and ages of the students. Both substance and age considerations are important in setting the objectives.

TASK DESCRIPTION

A task description is a full description of terminal performance. Although it involves more than reference to explicit terminal performance, such references are one of its major elements.

QUESTION 2-1   The student teacher was preparing a list of instructional objectives for his history lesson. At this point he was interested in identifying terminal performances. The following three items were part of his list:

1   The student should demonstrate his genuine understanding of the French Revolution.
2   The student should be able to name the political leader of the Revolution.
3   The student should be able to explain in concrete terms the causes of the Revolution.

Which of the following is the best evaluation of the list? (a) The list meets all the major requirements of explicit statements of instructional objectives. (b) The list satisfies only one requirement—each statement designates a terminal performance. (c) The list contains only one statement that adequately describes a terminal performance.

After you have made your choice, indicate your basis for rejecting the two alternatives.

Mager's Procedure

Robert Mager, an experimental psychologist, has developed a method of task description. In the light of our previous distinction between explicit and implicit behavior, Mager's method is the easier to explain. According to him, a statement of instructional objectives (what we are calling task description) requires each of the following:

1   Identification of the terminal performance which the instruction attempts to produce.
2   Description of the important condition under which the behavior is expected to occur.
3   Description of how good a student's performance must be to be acceptable.

Now examine two of Mager's (1962) examples of task description:

A   Given a linear algebraic equation with one unknown, the learner must be able to solve for the unknown without the aid of references, tables, or calculating devices [p. 26].
B   Given a list of factors leading to significant historical events, the learner must be able to select *at least five factors contributing to the depression of 1929* [p. 27].

Let us apply Mager's three requirements of task description to these two examples. The first requirement, the identification of the terminal performance, should be the easiest of the three for you to apply because it rests on the distinction between explicit behavior considered earlier. The two examples identify terminal performance as follows:

A   The learner must be able to solve for the unknown. . . .
B   The learner must be able to select . . . factors contributing to the depression of 1929. [Note: Mention of how many factors has been omitted.]

You will agree that these are explicit, publicly observable performances.

We have not previously discussed the second and third requirements of task description. Their inclusion, however, further reduces ambiguity about what we are attempting to teach and gives the teacher much more guidance. The second requirement is to describe the important conditions under which the behavior is to occur. The two examples identify these condition as follows:

A   Given a linear algebraic equation with one unknown . . . without the aid of references, tables, or calculating devices.
B   Given a list of factors leading to significant historical events. . . .

The third requirement is to describe the level of acceptable performance. This may be a somewhat arbitrary standard ranging from 100 percent mastery (spelling correctly all fifty words in a spelling list) to only minimal mastery (spelling correctly only one of the fifty words in the list). The two examples describe these levels of performance (or standards) as follows:

A   To solve for the unknown. . . . [The implication is 100 percent mastery.]
B   To select at least five factors. . . . [Five, of course, is a minimum standard.]

We will fully discuss the implications of Mager's third requirement in the chapter on test construction.

QUESTION 2-2

Select the statement below which fills all the requirements of Mager's method of task description:
  (a) Given a list of human muscles, the student selects all those which are striated.
  (b) The student is able to distinguish between similes and metaphors in poetic passages presented to him.
  (c) The student lists 75 percent of the common characteristics of two biological species.
  After you have selected the best task description, indicate what is missing in the two faulty descriptions.

TASK ANALYSIS

It is possible not only to describe but also to analyze the tasks we expect the student to perform. In this task analysis we identify classes of behavior which differ in respect to the conditions necessary for learning (Gagné, 1965b). In somewhat less technical language, once we have made adequate statements of the instructional objectives (or task descriptions), we can analyze these objectives by fitting them into various classes of behavior. The chief purpose of task analysis is to help the teacher determine the specific tasks the student has failed to perform.

Consider, for example, the following task descriptions:

1 When given examples of various types of geometric figures, the student selects only (and all) those which are triangles.
2 When given a list of French words, the student gives all the correct English equivalents.

These two objectives involve different classes of behavior. The first involves *concept learning;* the second, *verbal learning.* The conditions for learning these two tasks (as you will see in Part 3 of this book) are quite different. In a proper task analysis the teacher would correctly classify the behavior involved in each objective and establish the best learning conditions for each.

A task analysis may also identify the subtasks which must be learned in the process of learning the task proper. This procedure is important because the subtasks may fall into different classes of behavior and require, therefore, different learning conditions. Robert Glaser and James Reynolds (1964) provide an example of how a disingenuously simple instructional objective requires further task description and task analysis. They developed an instructional program for time telling appropriate for six- and seven-year-olds. Ignoring what we have said about task description, they could have settled for this statement of their objective: to teach children to tell time. Such a statement is very ambiguous: It does not define the terminal behavior, the conditions, or the standard of judgment. In it, *time* could have any of the following meanings: (1) the concept of time; (2) the passage of time from midnight, the zero hour, to midnight, the last hour; (3) the units of time, such as seconds, minutes, weeks, months; or (4) the judgment of time units, such as observing that ten hours is longer than ten minutes. Glaser and Reynolds adopted a much more explicit statement of their instructional objective: The child is able to write and to say aloud the time indicated by the clock to an accuracy of one minute. With an adequate task description they proceeded to list the subtasks or subbehaviors the children had to learn in working toward the terminal performance. These are some of the subtasks Glaser and Reynolds identified (C and D are omitted):

SUBTASK A   FOR WRITING THE HOUR AND MINUTE IN SEQUENCE, e.g., 7:35
1 Reading the number on the clock face to which the little hand is pointing.
2 Reading the number on the clock face which the little hand has just passed.
3 Determining the number indicated by the little hand.
4 Writing the number of hours the little hand indicates.

SUBTASK B   SAME PURPOSE AS A BUT FOCUSING ON THE BIG HAND
1 Writing "00" when the big hand points to top center of clock.
2 Associating the word *o'clock* with 00 and top center of clock (this ties in with subclass D—saying "o'clock").

3 Counting clockwise by one's every single mark from the zero point to determine number indicated by big hand.

4 Counting clockwise by five's every fifth mark from the zero point to determine the number indicated by the big hand.

5 Counting clockwise by five's from zero point and then by one's to determine the number indicated by the big hand.

6 Determining the number indicated by the big hand.

7 Then, writing the number of minutes the big hand indicates.

FOR SAYING THE MINUTE AND HOURS IN SEQUENCE, e.g., 35 MINUTES AFTER 7 SUBTASK E

1 Associating *minutes after* with number indicated by the big hand.

2 Associating *hours* with number indicated by little hand.

3 Associating *minutes after* with numbers the big hand indicates when it is off top center.

4 First saying the number the minute hand indicates when it is off top center.

5 Then saying "minutes after" when minute hand is off top center.

6 Then saying number hour hand indicates when minute hand is off top center.

These are only some of the subtasks the children had to learn to reach their instructional objective.

Task analysis is only practical for the teacher as a way of diagnosing learning failure. For example, the teacher can determine the particular subtasks (behaviors) the child has not mastered in telling time. We shall now consider two systems for the classification of behaviors which have particular educational relevance.

Gagné's Classes of Behavior

The most complete description of Gagné's classes of behavior appears in his *The Conditions of Learning* (1970). Here he distinguishes eight types of learning, beginning with the simple forms and ending with the complex. Although Gagné refers to these classes as learning types, he is primarily interested in the observable behavior and performance which are the products of each such class. In Part 3, we will treat these learning types together with the conditions necessary for producing them in detail. Here we shall give only a brief description and example of each.

Signal learning In this type of learning (often also called *classical conditioning*) the animal or individual acquires a conditioned response to a given signal. Pavlov studied such learning in great detail. In it the responses are diffuse and emotional and the learning is involuntary. Examples are the withdrawal of the hand upon sight of a hot object, the salivation of a dog upon hearing food poured into his metal feeding dish, and the tearing of the eyes upon sight of an onion. The signals are the sight of the hot object, the sound of food being poured in the dish, and the sight of the onion. The conditioned responses are withdrawal of the hand, salivation, and tearing of the eyes.

Stimulus-response learning   In this kind of learning, exemplified by animal training, the animal makes precise responses to specific stimuli. At first this training usually requires the use of a leash and a choke chain. As the dog learns particular responses for particular jerks of the leash and chain, his master rewards him with pats and praise. Later the master does not have to use the leash and chain; the animal sits, stays, or lies down upon hearing the simple verbal command. Whereas the responses in signal learning are diffuse and emotional, the responses in stimulus-response learning (often called *operant conditioning*) are fairly precise. Stimulus-response ($S \rightarrow R$) learning may be used in acquiring verbal skills as well as physical movements. For example, the child may learn to say "Mama" on request, or an adult may learn the appropriate response to the stimulus of a word in a foreign language.

Chaining   In this type of learning the person links together previously learned $S \rightarrow R$'s. The links may involve physical reactions such as an animal learning a series of tricks, each of which gives the cue to perform the next trick. For example, in one 45-minute show involving dolphins, the dolphins are able to perform an unbroken series of tricks; each trick is the stimulus for performing the next trick. Gagné uses the example of a child who learns to say "doll" at the sight of a doll, then learns to lie down, hug the doll, and say "doll." This type of learning often seems to occur so naturally that we do not notice the specific series of events which led to it. The case of trained dolphins is an exception since the trainer takes special care to chain each event to the next one.

Verbal association   This learning is a type of chaining, but the links are verbal units. The simplest verbal association is the activity of naming an object, which involves a chain of two links: An observing response enables the child to identify properly the object he sees; and an internal stimulus enables the child to say the proper name. When the child can name an object "ball" and also say "the red ball," he has learned a verbal association of three links. Gagné calls another common verbal association *translation responses;* in these, for example, the individual gives the German or French equivalent of an English word, or one nonsense syllable or English word in response to another syllable or word. The learner frequently acquires verbal associations by verbal mediation—an internal link which helps him associate, for example, the French word and its English equivalent. If the student were learning *hand* in response to the French word *main,* the English word *manual* would provide verbal mediation.

Discrimination learning   In this type of learning the student must learn different responses for stimuli which might be confused. The student learns to distinguish between motor and verbal chains he has already acquired. In studying French, for example, the student must associate *faim* with *hunger* and *femme* with *woman*. When American boys undertake to identify all the new models of automobiles produced in this country in a particular year, they are engaging in discrimination learning. They must associate each individual model, with its distinctive appearance, with the correct model name, and with no other name. When there is only one model to consider, linking the correct name with the right model illustrates verbal association. When there are several models and names, linking that name with the same model and no other model illustrates discrimination learning. Teachers, Gagné suggests, engage in discrimination learning when they devise means for calling each student by his correct name.

Concept learning In learning a concept we respond to stimuli in terms of abstract characteristics like color, shape, position, and number as opposed to concrete physical properties like specific wavelengths or particular intensities. Gagné uses this example. A child may learn to call a small cube a "block," and also to call similar objects which vary in size and shape "blocks." Later he may learn the concept *cube* and discover that cubes can be made of wood, glass, wire, and other materials; can vary in color; and can be of any size. Or, if a student is given a series of numbers, he is able to select those which belong to the class *odd* as opposed to those in the class *even*. In concept learning, the student's behavior is not under the control of particular physical stimuli but of the abstract properties of each stimulus. Concepts have concrete references even though they are learned with the use of language.

Rule learning In learning a rule we relate two or more concepts. According to Gagné, the simplest rule may be depicted in the form: "If X, then Y," as in the example, "If a feminine noun, then the article *la*." Or, "If the temperature of the water is above 212° F, then the water boils." Rules are, in effect, chains of concepts. We may represent knowledge as a hierarchy of rules, in which we must learn two or more rules before learning a higher-order rule which embraces them. If the student has learned the component concepts and rules, the teacher can use verbal instruction alone in leading the student to put the rules together.

Problem solving In the set of events called problem solving, individuals use rules to achieve some goal. When the goal is reached, however, the student has learned something more and is then capable of new performances using his new knowledge. What is learned, according to Gagné, is a higher-order rule, the combined product of two or more lower-order rules. Thus problem solving requires those internal events usually called *thinking*. Gagné suggests these examples. A driver who maps his route through traffic rather than being swept along by it is solving a problem. In replanning his luncheon schedule to accommodate a new appointment, the individual is solving a problem. When the housewife shops selectively for particular items on the basis of price variations, she is solving a problem. Without knowledge of the prerequisite rules, the problems cannot be solved.

We have now completed our description of Gagne's learning types. In Part 3 we shall describe each type further and carefully consider its application to instructional procedures. We can now turn to another system for classifying behavior which also is relevant to education.

Bloom's Classes of Behavior

For instructional and testing purposes Benjamin Bloom and his associates developed a method of classifying educational objectives, a process we have called *task analysis*. As in Gagné's system, the different classes of behavior are arranged in hierarchical order from the simple to the complex: Behaviors in one class are likely to make use of and build on behaviors in the preceding classes. Bloom and his associates explain their system in the *Taxonomy of Education Objectives* (1956). The system includes two broad categories—(a) knowledge and (b) intellectual abilities and skills—which produce six classes of behavior. We shall describe each class and provide examples of educational objectives for each.

Knowledge　This class involves the recall of specifics and generalizations; of methods and processes; and of pattern, structure, or setting. Recall simply means bringing the appropriate material to mind, usually without alteration. The *Taxonomy* uses this analogy: If you think of the mind as a file, in a test of knowledge you must find in each problem the signals, cues, and clues which best bring out whatever knowledge you have filed. This class of behavior covers several educational objectives. Here are some examples:

> To define technical terms by giving their attributes, properties, or relations.
> To make pupils conscious of correct form and usage in speech and writing.
> The recall of major theories about particular cultures.

Bloom categorizes the remaining five classes of behavior as intellectual abilities and skills.

Comprehension　This class is the lowest level of understanding. The student knows what is being communicated and can use the material or idea without necessarily relating it to other material or seeing its full implications. The following examples of educational objectives fit this class:

> Skill in translating mathematical verbal material into symbolic statements.
> The ability to grasp the thought of the work as a whole at any desired level of generality.
> Skill in predicting continuation of trends.

Application   This class of behavior requires the student to use abstractions in particular and concrete situations. The abstractions may be general ideas or they may be procedures, technical principles, and theories which must be remembered and applied. These two examples of educational objectives involve application:

Application to the phenomena discussed in one paper of the scientific terms or concepts used in other papers.

The ability to predict the probable effect of a change in a factor on a biological situation previously at equilibrium.

Analysis   This behavior class requires the student to make clear the relative hierarchy of ideas in a body of material or to make explicit the relations among the ideas or both. Analysis clarifies the materials and indicates how they are organized and how they can vary their effects. These examples of educational objectives involve analysis:

The ability to recognize unstated assumptions.

Ability to check the consistency of hypotheses with given information and assumptions.

The ability to recognize form and pattern in literary and artistic works as a means of understanding their meaning.

Synthesis   This behavior class requires the student to assemble parts into a whole. It involves the process of arranging and combining pieces, parts, and so on to constitute a pattern or structure not clearly there before. These examples of educational objectives involve synthesis:

Skill in writing, using an excellent organization of ideas and statements.

Ability to propose ways of testing hypotheses.

Ability to make mathematical discoveries and generalizations.

Evaluation   This class consists of judgments about the value of material and methods used for particular purposes. The judgments may be quantitative or qualitative, and they may involve the application of standards of acceptability determined by the student or given to him by the teacher. The following examples of educational objectives involve evaluation:

The ability to indicate logical fallacies in arguments.

The ability to compare a work with others of recognized excellence.

The *Taxonomy* includes test questions which apply to each of the six classes of behavior and which ingeniously illustrate both the behavior each class embraces and the type of item which can measure achievement of the objective of each class.

How do the two schemes for classifying behavior compare? The test of any system for classifying behavior is its usefulness for task analysis, which, in turn, should enable the teacher to distinguish various performances and to establish the necessary learning conditions for achieving these performances. If we use this test, we find that Gagné's classes of behavior are more useful than those of Bloom and his associates. Although the *Taxonomy* has greater breadth and variety in the number and type of instructional objectives it embraces, it presents two difficulties for task analysis. First, the educational objectives lists do not meet Mager's requirements for task descriptions, usually because they lack a careful description of the conditions under which the desired performance must occur. For example, the *Taxonomy* lists as an objective the "ability to propose ways of testing hypotheses." Does this mean that when the student is given various experimental procedures and materials he can select and combine those which will be valid and reliable tests of hypotheses? Or does it mean that when presented with a theoretical problem and the available data the student can deduce appropriate hypotheses and procedures for testing them? The general objective may indicate either or both of these more specific objectives, even though each requires significantly different performance. A student could be capable of performing one objective but not the other. Second, each of the formal characteristics listed in the *Taxonomy* does not clearly fall into one distinct class. Gagné (1965b, p. 40), for example, asks how "knowledge of generalization" is distinguished from "interpretation" (which falls under the class *comprehension*) and how both are distinguished from "comprehending the interrelationships of ideas" (which comes under *analysis*). Of course, when the classes of behavior are not distinct, it becomes difficult to classify instructional objectives and to determine their appropriate learning conditions—the major purpose of task analysis.

On the other hand, Gagné's classes of behavior provide for both explicit statements of instructional objectives and for relatively distinct behavior categories. Because his behavior classes are themselves products for research on conditions of learning, they have particular usefulness for task analysis. What we may lose in richness and breadth in Gagné's classification, we gain in greater precision in the design of instruction.

QUESTION 2-3   Miss Pegg tried to decide which class of behavior (or type of learning) her instructional objective involved. This was the objective: Given ten rock specimens, the students will identify the five which are fossils. Which of the following classes of behavior includes this objective: (a) verbal association; (b) concept learning; (c) problem solving?

After you have made your choice, explain your rejection of the two remaining choices.

SUMMARY

This chapter distinguished between school, teacher, and student and pointed out their relationships. The chapter also described how to state instructional objectives in behavioral terms. Task analysis was defined and described, and two systems for classifying instructional objectives were compared. In general, the chapter considered the relationship between behavioral statements of instructional objectives and important decisions the teacher must make.

SUGGESTED READINGS

Four very readable articles and books discuss the relationship between educational and instructional objectives:

DeCecco, John P., and Arlene K. Richards, *Growing Pains: Uses of School Conflict*. New York: Holt, Rinehart, and Winston, 1974.

Gagné, Robert M., "Educational Objectives and Human Performance," in *Learning and the Educational Process*, ed. P. D. Krumboltz, pp. 1–24. Chicago: Rand McNally & Co., 1965.

Popham, W. J., and E. L. Baker, *Systematic Instruction*. Englewood Cliffs, N.J.: Prentice-Hall, Inc., 1970.

Tyler, Ralph W., "Some Persistent Questions on the Defining of Objectives," in *Defining Educational Objectives*, ed. C. M. Lindvall. Pittsburgh: University of Pittsburgh Press, 1964.

A very delightful programed book teaches you how to make adequate task descriptions:

Mager, Robert F., *Preparing Objectives for Programed Instruction*. Palo Alto, Calif.: Fearon Publishers, Inc., 1962.

Task analysis is a much more complicated topic. Substantial discussions appear in the three following articles:

Gagné, Robert M., "The Analysis of Instructional Objectives for the Design of Instruction," in *Teaching Machines and Programed Learning, II: Data and Directions*, ed. R. Glaser, pp. 21–65. Washington, D.C.: Department of Audiovisual Instruction, National Education Association, 1965.

Miller, Robert B., "Analysis and Specification of Behavior for Training," in *Training Research and Education*, ed. R. Glaser, pp. 31–62. Pittsburgh: University of Pittsburgh Press, 1962.

———, "Task Description and Analysis," in *Psychological Principles in System Development*, ed. R. M. Gagné, pp. 187–230. New York: Holt, Rinehart & Winston, Inc., 1962.

PART TWO

ENTERING BEHAVIOR AND DEVELOPMENT

CHAPTER THREE

ENTERING BEHAVIOR

This chapter concerns what the student has already learned, or should have learned, when he presents himself for further instruction. The primary purpose here is to describe what entering behavior includes and how it relates to instructional objectives. The primary emphasis is on a description of entering behavior which is useful for the planning and execution of instruction. The first section of the chapter defines entering behavior and distinguishes it from and relates it to terminal performance. It then compares the concept of entering behavior with similar concepts—development (readiness and maturation), individual differences, and personality. The second section of the chapter describes categories or classes of entering behavior—learning sets, learning abilities, and learning styles. The final section deals with the assessment of entering behavior and the use of this information in planning instruction.

After reading the first section of this chapter (on the definition of entering behavior), you should be able to meet these objectives:

3-1 List the major characteristics of entering behavior.

3-2 Distinguish entering behavior from and relate it to terminal performance by pointing out similar and dissimilar characteristics.

3-3 Distinguish entering behavior from and relate it to development, individual differences, and personality by pointing out similar and dissimilar characteristics.

3-4 Illustrate relevant entering behavior for an instructional objective of your own choice.

A DEFINITION OF ENTERING BEHAVIOR

The folly of requiring the student to perform in ways for which he is inadequately prepared is so often repeated we forget that it is entirely avoidable. No matter what feats of will, self-denial, and enthusiasm the student may perform and no matter how much dedication, love, and imagination the teacher may supply, the student cannot acquire new performances based on other performances which he has not acquired. Learning builds on learning in the way success builds on success. When the foundation blocks are missing, future construction, if possible at all, is a very precarious affair. To make your teaching less precarious, you should understand what entering behavior means and how to use it.

Characteristics and Illustrations

Entering behavior describes the behaviors the student must have acquired before he can acquire particular new terminal behaviors. More simply, entering behavior describes the present status of the student's knowledge and skill in reference to a future status the teacher wants him to attain. Entering behavior, therefore, is where the instruction must always begin. Terminal behavior is where the instruction concludes. We can describe teaching as getting the student from where he is to where we would like him to be—as moving from entering to terminal behavior. Together, descriptions of entering and terminal behavior define the limits of instructional responsibility for each discrete act of teaching.

Now you already know that teachers do not usually observe and test behaviors; they observe and test performances, which are the results of behaviors. We could as easily (and perhaps with great precision) refer to entering behavior as *entering performances* because the teacher is interested in these end products of previous instruction in planning future instruction. We use *entering behavior,* however, because this is the term used in the research literature and in journal discussions. Nevertheless, you should remember that, although we say entering *behavior,* we mean entering *performances.*

A list of entering behavior reveals two characteristics: The statements are explicit and refer to specific, observable performances; and the list as a whole is generally more comprehensive than the corresponding list of terminal performances. Consider the two subsequent lists of entering behavior. The first list (Glaser and Reynolds, 1964) is for the program on time telling, referred to in the previous chapter. The authors gave this description of the terminal performance for that program: "The abilities of writing and saying aloud the time indicated by the clock to an accuracy of one-minute intervals." Here is the list of entering behavior:

1 Select the smaller of two objects, e.g., the short hand or the long hand of the clock.
2 Follow pointer directions, e.g., "What does the little hand point to?"
3 Follow verbal directions, e.g., "Write the number in the little box," or "Turn the page."
4 Recognize, write, and say numbers from one to sixty.
5 Count by ones up to sixty and by fives up to sixty.

Consider now a second list of entering behavior with the corresponding list of terminal performances (Johnston et al, 1966). These objectives are for students in a physiology laboratory devoted to the study of the stimulation of muscles and reflexes.

Terminal performance no. 1: To be able to operate the grass model polygraph.
Entering behavior for terminal performance no. 1:
   1 Can state purpose of the polygraph.
     a Can state, define, and describe by example the three basic components of the polygraph.
     b Can identify the three basic components of the polygraph.
     c Can identify all the controls on the polygraph.
Terminal performance no. 2: To be able to operate the grass model S5 stimulator.
Entering behavior for terminal performance no. 2:
   2 Can state the purpose of the S5 stimulator.
     a Can state why this type (electrical) of stimulation is used.
     b Can identify all controls of the S5 stimulator.
Terminal performance no. 3: To demonstrate the various features of skeletal muscle contraction by experimental means and to explain these results and correlate them with what actually occurs in the living animal.
Entering behavior for terminal performance no. 3:
     a Stimulus (1) subliminal, (2) minimal or threshold, (3) maximal, and (4) supermaximal.
     b Latent period.
     c Muscle contraction (1) isometric and (2) isotonic.
     d Refractory period (1) absolute and (2) relative.
     e Can recognize experimental isometric muscle recording setup.
     f Can differentiate from graphs (1) simple muscle twitch, (2) wave summation, and (3) tetanization.

We can now review the first characteristic of a statement of entering behavior: It refers to specific, observable performances. In this respect entering performances are not distinguishable from terminal performances. Note, however, that descriptions of entering behavior (as illustrated in these lists) lack two characteristics of task descriptions: They do not describe the conditions under which the performance must occur, and they do not specify a standard of acceptability. Of course, a list of entering behavior could include all the characteristics of a list of task descriptions; the two lists here, which are typical of many, simply do not do so. In any case you should remember that, once the student can perform the tasks in the task description of today, that task description becomes the entering behavior statement of tomorrow.

The second characteristic of a statement of entering behavior is its generally comprehensive nature. In the list of entering behavior for the physiology laboratory, you can see that the student is expected to have acquired more entering behavior than he will acquire terminal performances. Even the list of entering behavior for the time-telling program is much more comprehensive than we would expect a list of terminal performances to be. We could not conceive a single program or lesson from which the student would learn all the performances included in this list—from performances as simple as understanding pointer directions to those as complicated as counting by fives and writing the correct time. The nature of teaching itself requires the teacher always to expect that the students have already learned more than what he plans to teach them.

Now that we have defined and illustrated entering behavior, we can consider four concepts—readiness, maturation, individual differences, and personality—which relate to it. We shall point out how these concepts are similar and dissimilar to the concept of entering behavior.

Development: Readiness and Maturation

Development is a product of inheritance and environment. What is inherited are biologically determined ways of interacting with the environment. The child develops by using his environment in biologically determined ways. (This will be explained in Chapter 4.) In educational terminology, development is often described as readiness and maturation.

Readiness is the adequacy of the student's existing capacity in relation to some instructional objective (Ausubel, 1959). For example, reading readiness refers to performances the student must have acquired before he begins to read: the identification of different marks on the printed page as particular letters, the association of these letters with sounds previously heard, the combination of letters into syllables and words, and so on. When readiness refers to particular performances it is identical to entering behavior. Note that the definition of readiness does not indicate how the student acquired his existing capacity; it merely refers to the adequacy of his capacity.

If teachers always used the term *readiness* in reference to entering behavior, we could have avoided introducing the new term, *entering behavior,* and the risk of sounding jargonish. Readiness, however, is frequently confused with a related but different concept—maturation (Ausubel, 1959). Maturation refers to biological growth which occurs largely under the influence of heredity. When, for example, we observe Steve's growth in height and weight, his increasing muscle size, and the deepening of his voice, we are observing his maturation. Note that the definition of maturation specifically indicates how it occurs—it is largely the result of hereditary influences. In maturation, certain structural changes must occur before a certain behavior can appear. When the psychologist observes certain capabilities occurring without the benefit of training and observes these same behaviors emerging in all children, he infers that maturation is at work (Martin and Stendler, 1959, p. 99).

What is the relationship between maturation and readiness? Readiness is a product of both training (or learning) and maturation. Several studies show that training is largely wasted if the child has not reached the prerequisite level of maturation. There is, for example, the classical study of Myrtle McGraw (1940) on toilet training. She used two sets of identical male twins to see whether she could speed up their toilet training. One member of each pair was given training from the second month of life. They were placed on the chamber daily at intervals of one hour, for seven hours a day. Their partners were started on toilet training at fourteen and twenty-four months, respectively. At the end of twenty-eight months, McGraw found that the boys whose training had been delayed had achieved as much control as their twins. She concluded that the maturation of certain muscles must precede effective toilet training. Readiness for toilet training, therefore, is based partly on maturation. The study also makes clear, however, that the training must be introduced sometime and that maturation alone will not provide the necessary control. This study and others like it merely indicate when training should be introduced—not whether it should be introduced. Readiness, then, is a product of both training and maturation.

What is true in physical development and training appears to hold true for cognitive development and school learning, as described in Parts Two and Three of this book. When the concepts of maturation and readiness are confused, the schools find themselves in the position described by David Ausubel (1959, p. 246):

> To equate the principles of readiness and maturation not only muddies the conceptual waters but also makes it difficult for the school to appreciate that insufficient readiness may reflect inadequate prior learning on the part of pupils because of inappropriate or ineffective instructional methods. Lack of maturation can thus become a convenient scapegoat whenever children manifest insufficient readiness to learn, and the school, which is thereby automatically absolved of all responsibility in the matter, consequently fails to subject its instructional practices to the degree of self-critical scrutiny necessary for continued educational progress. In short, while it is important to appreciate that the current readiness of pupils determines the school's current choice of instructional methods and materials, it is equally important to bear in mind that this readiness is partly determined by the appropriateness and efficiency of the previous instructional practices to which they have been subjected.

Ausubel implies that where lack of readiness is a product of lack of training, the teacher must increase readiness. Maturation alone will not manifest in the child the readiness to speak grammatically, read skillfully, and compose limericks with consummate poetical skill. Piaget's position (see Chapter 4) is that "learning failures" are often the result of teachers attempting to push the child beyond the level of his cognitive development.

Unlike the term *readiness,* the term *entering behavior* avoids conceptual confusion since it derives its meaning from the instructional design in which it is embedded. From the child's point of view, the behavior is an expression of his level of cognitive development. Since descriptions of entering behavior and terminal performances explicitly state the teacher's expectations and responsibilities, the use of descriptions avoids the vagueness of the term *readiness* and the consequent irresponsibility.

Individual Differences

The psychology of individual differences is largely the study of group differences. This study classifies individuals by age, trait, sex, race, social class, and so on, and observes the differences within and between these groups. For within-group differences—or differences within sex, race, and social class, for example—boys are compared with girls, whites with blacks, and those in the lower class with those in the middle class. Between-group differences may involve comparing middle-class blacks with lower-class blacks or ten-year-old boys with ten-year-old girls. The single individual enters this study only to the extent that his particular attributes fit those of the group being studied. That is, the study of how his various attributes are internally related is not the concern of the psychology of individual differences. The study of the individual in the totality of his attributes is the study of personality, a different branch of psychological inquiry.

Entering behavior, as you now know, refers to behavior the student must have acquired before he can achieve a new terminal performance; it refers to the present status of knowledge of a particular student in relation to some future status his teacher wants him to attain. Whereas the study of individual differences may yield information on, for example, the average intelligence of middle-class whites and middle-class blacks, the description and assessment of entering behavior will tell you exactly what the particular student must and does know in relation to the attainment of a particular instructional objective. In the former case we are dealing with group averages and in the latter with the specific capabilities of a single individual. For our purposes, information on group averages, despite its general interest and importance, is not so useful as a description of what a student must be able to do in order to learn something else.

The measurement of intelligence is an important segment of the study of individual differences. On the basis of individual and group IQs (as you will see in a later chapter), teachers can make fairly reliable predictions of the general level of academic success students will achieve. These predictions are a direct application of the knowledge of individual differences to educational practice. Now IQ is a very general description of a student's entering behavior; it measures his previous learning of a wide variety of tasks. The questions arise: How accurate a predictor is IQ when we radically improve the quality of instruction, and how does its accuracy compare with that of more specific measures of previous learning?

To answer these questions, consider the following two studies. To determine the relationship of intelligence to instructional method, Lawrence Stolurow (1964) in typical studies set up two different program sequences. For example, he developed two programs to teach fractions. In the first program (the easier one), he ordered the fractions consecutively so that the students could anticipate what fractions would come next. In the second program (the harder one), he presented the fractions in mixed or scrambled sequences. Stolurow then compared the achievement of high- and low-ability groups on both programs. Findings in several such studies have been consistent. With the easier program achievement between high- and low-ability groups differed little. With the harder program, however, the high-ability group obtained scores much higher than those of the low-ability group. Stolurow suggests that the easier program did for the poor-ability group what the high-ability group could do for themselves. He hastens to add, however, that such findings do not imply that intelligence is uncorrelated to learning. They merely indicate that the most efficient instruction for students of low mental ability will produce achievement which has zero correlation with intelligence.

Lewis Eigen and John Feldhusen (1964) conducted a study with students in the ninth, tenth, and eleventh grades using a programed text and machine instruction on sets, relations, and functions. They found that what the student already knew about a particular subject indicated how much he would learn better than did IQ. This study suggests that a direct assessment of entering behavior under optimal instructional conditions is more useful than a general assessment of intelligence. Similarly, the ability to transfer what has been learned by programed instruction is also determined more by how much the student has learned than by IQ.

Two chapters which follow, one on development of intelligence and the other on the development of language, make extensive use of the study of individual differences as an approach to the description of entering behavior. The assumption of those chapters is that knowledge about individual differences helps the teacher locate areas of entering behavior in which students may be deficient. In reading those chapters, however, you must remember that the description of individual differences is not equivalent to the description of entering behavior.

Personality

The psychology of personality is largely the study of the hypothetical structures and processes within a person that dispose him to act in certain ways (Lazarus, 1963). A wide range of personality structures and processes have been proposed and, to some extent, investigated. If you are a Freudian, you explain your own and your friends' behavior in terms of conscious and unconscious processes and of the almost interminable, always exciting, and occasionally resolved conflicts among id (libido), superego, and ego. If you are a Rogerian (a follower of Carl Rogers), you believe that the self-concept determines behavior—the individual does not respond to the objective environment but to his perception of that environment no matter how personalized or distorted his perception may be. He sees himself as reformer, realist, and so on, and organizes his behavior to preserve and enhance this self-concept. You can also conceive of personality as the organization of a number of traits of the individual. In this case you describe the behavior of your friends as manifesting various degrees of dominance (or submission), capacity (or incapacity) for status, sociability (or unsociability), self-acceptance (or rejection), and so on. You assume these traits are consistent patterns of behavior in the individual. You emphasize not so much why the individual behaves as he does as how he behaves. You can also explain behavior in terms of the individual's secondary needs, such as the need for acquisition, achievement, dominance, or autonomy. Or you may prefer a different set, such as the need for self-actualization, esteem, love, or safety. The needs theoretically refer to psychological forces which organize our thinking and acting. To distinguish them from physical needs we often call them psychogenic needs. Finally (and our list is far from exhaustive), you can explain the personal behavior of your friends in terms of the psychology of learning by applying such concepts as drive, reinforcement, stimulus (or cue), and response. In Chapter 6, on motivation, we attempt to apply learning concepts to the explanation and management of student motivation.

What is the relationship between entering behavior and the study of personality? Undoubtedly entering behavior is a product of the many personality structures (or something like them) which the study of personality hypothesizes. Since entering behavior refers to present performances which reflect previous learning and since this previous learning both influences and is influenced by various personality structures and processes, we must conclude that a relationship between entering behavior and personality exists. The existence of this relationship does not mean, however, that we can use the terminology of personality theory to describe the entering behavior for particular instructional objectives or of particular students who try to achieve those objectives. As intriguing as your search for your students' self-concepts, ids, traits, and psychogenic needs may be, none of these concepts yields the precise descriptions of student performance which entering behavior requires. In fact, too great a preoccupation with the internal structures and processes of the student, whatever these may be, has often led the teacher away from an objective description of instructional objectives and entering behavior and, consequently, from any precise description of the limits of his instructional responsibilities. Although personality theory and research have considerable clinical importance and popular appeal, at this stage in their development, they are too general and too little tied to observable behavior to be applied in the design of instruction.

Chapter 6 uses the study of personality as an approach to the description of entering behavior to the extent that this type of study relates to maintaining and increasing student motivation. The assumption of that chapter is that knowledge of personality structures and processes, when tied to observable behavior, may help the teacher define certain of his continuing instructional responsibilities. These instructional responsibilities are described as *functions,* to distinguish them from the instructional *procedures,* which are capable of more specific description and application.

Miss Pegg wants to teach her pupils to select correctly the vowel in all trigrams with the consonants, b, f, d, t, s, and w. (Examples are bat, den, fun, won, sit.) She makes certain each pupil can recite the alphabet without error and that he can name all printed letters.

Which of the following alternatives is your best prediction of the outcome of Miss Pegg's efforts?

(a) She is likely to succeed because her task is well described, and she has made adequate provision for entering behavior.

(b) She has adequately defined neither entering nor terminal performance.

(c) She is likely to fail because she has not adequately defined entering behavior.

After making your choice, point out any inadequacies which you think exist in Miss Pegg's description of either entering or terminal performance.

CLASSES OF ENTERING BEHAVIOR

If you had to describe the entering behavior of your students as minute responses to minute stimuli, the description would be monumental and impractical. If you could classify these stimuli and responses and avoid both the generality of descriptions based on the study of individual differences and personality and the multiplicity of highly detailed descriptions, you would have a practical means for describing entering behavior. Although research on learning sets, abilities, and styles as entering behavior has only recently begun, it promises to distinguish classes of entering behavior which have relevance to and practical application in the design of instruction. This section describes learning sets, learning abilities, and learning styles, and relates each of them to the concept of entering behavior.

After reading this section of the chapter, you should be able to meet these objectives:

3-5 List the major characteristics of these concepts: learning to learn, learning sets, learning structures, learning abilities, conceptual tempos, and selection strategies.

3-6 Provide an illustration of each of the concepts listed in the previous objective.

3-7 Describe and illustrate the usefulness of each concept as a description of entering behavior for particular instructional objectives.

3-8 Describe the similarities and differences among these concepts by referring to their characteristics.

Learning Sets

We shall now describe two types of learning sets. The first is properly called *learning to learn*. The second is called *learning set* and *learning structure*.

Learning to learn We commonly observe that our capacity to learn new tasks increases when we have practiced similar tasks. Henry Ellis (1965, p. 32) uses this illustration: After a person practices solving linear equations for several days, he improves his speed and accuracy in solving new linear equations. This progressive improvement in performance is known as learning to learn.

A series of experiments by Harry Harlow and his associates (1949), using both monkeys and children as subjects, provided some of the most convincing evidence for the usefulness of this concept. Figure 3-1 illustrates the apparatus Harlow used in his experiments with monkeys. The stimulus tray contained food wells which could be covered with various objects (similar to the game of concealing a coin under one of three shells). The forward opaque screen prevented the monkey from seeing which well the food (usually a raisin) was placed in. The one-way vision screen separated the monkey and the experimenter during trials. The objects placed over the wells were two blocks. For each test the two blocks were different in some dimension which could be easily seen—one black, the other white; one cylindrical, the other conical; one striped, the other plain; and so on. In each trial, the monkey was allowed to look under only one block. The

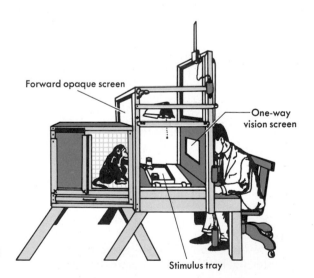

FIG. 3-1 Apparatus used in experiment on learning to learn (after Harlow, 1949, p. 52).

best strategy for the monkey would be, for example, to look under the black block if he had failed to find the raisin under the white block in the preceding trial. In one experiment, eight monkeys learned to solve a series of 344 such problems. Figure 3-2 shows the results for the first six trials on different sets of these problems. If you carefully examine the legend for this figure, you will see that the bottom curve shows the performance of the monkeys on the first eight problems. This curve represents their worst performance. Their best performance is represented by the top curve, which shows that they made almost 100 percent correct choices by the second trial for the last fifty-six problems. The other curves (with one exception) show that the speed and accuracy of the monkeys increased as the number of problems they learned to solve increased. By the end they attained almost total accuracy on the second and third trials. The monkeys had learned to learn.

What did the monkeys learn? You could say that they acquired insight. But we can be more precise. When we (monkeys and people) meet new situations, we must attend and respond to a great many things. Eventually we begin to see similarities between our previous learning and the new situation. The monkeys learned what to attend to and what to ignore in the problems. They learned, for example, not to respond to the position of the block (whether it was right or left), but rather, to the color of the block (whether it was black or white). They also learned to switch. If the raisin was not under the first pattern they selected, they would try the second pattern the next time.

FIG. 3-2 Learning curves for the same subjects for the first six trials in a series of more than 300 problems (after Harlow, 1949).

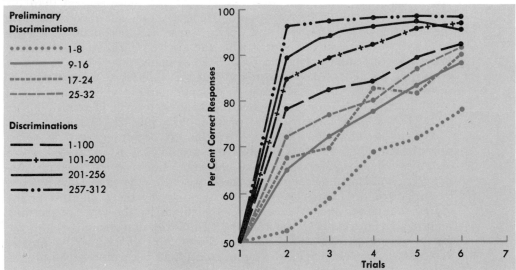

Additional evidence supports these findings on learning to learn. Harlow (1949) found about the same learning curves for children solving series of similar discrimination problems. An earlier study (Ward, 1937) required subjects to learn several lists of nonsense syllables. In this study, Lewis Ward found that subjects learned every succeeding list in fewer trials than they needed for learning those which preceded a given list. A more recent study (Keppel and Postman, 1966), using paired-associate materials, found that subjects gained skill in learning one pattern of associations by practicing on another pattern—evidence that the subjects were acquiring general paired-associate learning skill.

On the basis of this evidence we may conclude that entering behavior can sometimes be conceived as the general modes of attack available to the student for learning various tasks. If these general modes are to be useful, however, the tasks or instructional objectives must be similar to them—that is, the student must be expected to show about the same terminal performance under about the same conditions. When we introduce wide variation in the conditions or the performances, the advantages of learning to learn dissipate.

Learning set and structures Robert Gagné and his associates (1961, 1962) developed a more specific idea of learning sets. Gagné defines learning sets as the capabilities the student possesses at any given stage in the learning of a given task. Although these capabilities are internal to the student, they are directly measurable as performances.

You can discover the sets necessary for learning a particular task by working backward from the task to the prerequisite capabilities. Beginning with the final task (the instructional objective), you ask: What capability does the student need if he is to perform this task successfully? The answer identifies a new task which is simpler and more general than the final task from which it was derived. However, the new task is basic to the learning of the final task and, in this sense, is subordinate to it. You continue this process of inquiry with the derived task. Again you ask: What must the student know to be capable of doing this task? The answer gives you the second level of subordinate capabilities. The process continues until you have discovered increasingly simple and more general capabilities, which, with the higher capabilities, form a hierarchy. These hierarchies are *learning structures* (Gagné, 1970, pp. 328–29).

Figure 3-3 shows the learning hierarchy for beginning reading—sometimes called decoding. This involves the pronunciation of printed words by following particular rules. What the child learns is the rule for pronouncing words like *democracy, personality,* and *exuberance.* Gagné (1970) has indicated the highest point in the hierarchy by the single box at the top of the figure. As you move down the hierarchy the types of learning required are increasingly simple. The two boxes immediately below the top box require rule learning but at a lower level of complexity. As you move down the left side of the figure, the type of learning capability required is in the nature of concepts involving the pronunciation of single

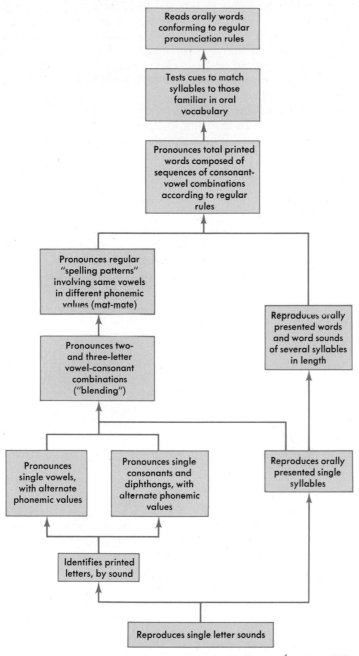

FIG. 3-3 A learning hierarchy for a basic reading skill (Gagné, 1970. p. 271)

letters such as hard *a,* soft *c,* and so on. Since the pronunciation of words requires more learning than the pronunciation of letters, Gagné classes word pronunciation as rule learning and letter pronunciation as concept learning. Proceeding further down the hierarchy, we see that there are simpler concepts to learn—the identification of single letters by their sounds. The right side of the diagram shows still simpler forms of learning—chaining or the oral repetition of strings of syllables. Simple imitative speaking is lower in the hierarchy than symbol identification, although both are necessary for learning to read.

A comparison of learning to learn and learning sets suggests the following conclusions. The capabilities in learning to learn are often those at the base of Gagné's learning structures. These are the most basic and general capabilities that the student requires. Learning sets differ from these capabilities in two ways: They are more specific and are defined in relation to particular instructional objectives; and they are hierarchically related. The idea that some learning sets are more basic than, or are subordinate to, other sets is an important expansion of the concept of learning to learn. Both concepts enable us to describe entering behavior as *classes of performances:* printing numerals and symbols, distinguishing between any object or symbol that is alike or different, and adding to and taking away from any set. By describing classes of performances the teacher is often spared the necessity of describing every required detail of performance as entering behavior.

The concept of learning sets and structures applies to the curriculum in English and social sciences as well as to that in mathematics and science. Fred Tyler (1964) suggests that an analysis of the former curriculum in terms of learning structures would answer questions like these: When should the student study restrictive and nonrestrictive clauses? When is the student ready for the *Ode to Immortality* and *Macbeth?* Tyler provides two examples from William James in which the student (James) lacked the necessary learning sets. First, James (1892) misinterpreted what the boatman in *Lord Ullin's Daughter* expected to receive for his services:

> I'll row you o'er the ferry.
> It is not for your silver bright,
> But for your winsome lady.

James, at eight years, concluded that the boatman was to receive the lady as payment, whereas the boatman intended to win merely the lady's favor. Second, misinterpretation is even more likely when the student lacks the learning sets for the figurative use of language, as in this example from *Troilus and Cressida.* Here, the lovesick Troilus answers Pandarus, who has just been praising Cressida, Troilus' sweetheart:

> . . . thou answers't, she is fair;
> *Pour'st in the open ulcer of my heart*
> *Her eyes, her hair, her cheek, her gait, her voice.*

One hesitates to conjecture what interpretation of the italicized lines a student who lacks the learning sets for figurative language would provide. Would such a student compassionately suggest medical treatment for an ulcerated heart when psychological help was what poor Troilus needed?

Learning Abilities

Learning abilities are the various processes by which the individual acquires new performances. Arthur Jensen (1960) hypothesizes that individuals differ in learning abilities in a limited number of ways. He gives two examples of such differences: Some students learn better when they pace their own work, while other students learn better when the machine sets the pace; and, although two students may do equally well under spaced-practice conditions, one student may do considerably better than the other under massed-practice conditions. Jensen (1965) found that individuals also differ in their susceptibility to the factors which cause forgetting: retroactive inhibition, proactive inhibition, and response competition (see Chapter 8). According to Jensen (1965), a student's performance on any given task will be a product of the levels of his learning abilities and the degree to which the task involves these abilities. As of now, the basic learning abilities have not been identified or measured—a job for the educational psychologist of the present and future.

Jensen (1963) provides one study which suggests that there are several learning abilities rather than a single, unitary ability and that these abilities sometimes bear little relationship to IQ. Jensen argued that the usual intelligence tests are achievement tests: They tell us more about what the child has learned outside the test situation than about his capacity to learn in a novel environment. He contrived a learning situation which was equally novel for mentally retarded, average, and gifted children of varied socioeconomic backgrounds. The experimental apparatus required the children to push buttons in response to various stimuli—geometric forms such as triangles and squares displayed on a small screen. The children had to learn which of the twelve push buttons would turn on a green light for each of the twelve stimuli. The findings were what one would generally expect. The gifted children performed better than the average children, the average children better than the retarded. Figure 3-4, however, shows some very interesting exceptions within the retarded group. The two top curves show the performances of four of the retarded children on the first and last tests. These four children, whom Jensen calls *fast learners,* scored above average on all the tests. The bottom two curves show the performances of the six slowest learners in the retarded group. Clearly the performance of the retarded group as a whole varied widely. One of the two fastest learners in the entire group of subjects was a retarded child whose IQ was 65! The other was a gifted child whose IQ was 145. The retarded child was below average in scholastic achievement; the gifted child, far above average.

This study lends support to Jensen's notion of learning abilities. For

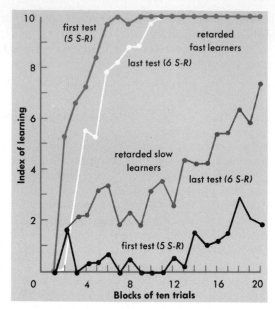

FIG. 3-4 Learning curves on the first and last tests of four retarded subjects who had learning scores above the mean of the gifted group and curves on the same tests of the six slowest learners in the retarded group (after Jensen, 1963, p. 133).

this particular task, some retarded children had the special ability required. On some other learning task the four successful retarded children might have been slow learners. Jensen suggests that retarded children may turn in poor school performances because they lack verbal learning ability. For example, we know that attaching names to objects allows us to refer to those objects in their absence and to use their verbal symbolic form in many abstract contexts. Jensen refers to this as *labeling behavior*. A child who does not have the ability to use labels is severely handicapped in many scholastic functions.

Learning abilities, as conceived by Jensen, are related to learning to learn, learning sets, and entering behavior. As basic processes which the individual employs in learning a wide assortment of tasks, learning abilities are similar to the concept of learning to learn. Because learning abilities are involved to varying degrees in different tasks, they are similar to the concept of learning sets. Because they are prerequisite capabilities for achieving instructional objectives, learning abilities relate to entering behavior. Since learning abilities occupy an intermediate position between overspecified and overgeneralized descriptions of entering behavior, their identification will quite possibly prove useful in designing instruction.

Learning Styles

Learning styles are personal ways in which individuals process information in the course of learning new concepts and principles. Here we discuss two types of learning styles—conceptual tempos and selection strategies. In Chapter 10 you will discover how learning styles are related to the learning of concepts. Here they are discussed as aspects of entering behavior.

Conceptual tempos   These are basic dispositions of the individual either to reflect upon his solution of a problem or to make impulsive and un-considered responses. Jerome Kagan and his associates (1964, 1965, and 1966) have identified children with two different conceptual tempos: The child with the impulsive, or fast, tempo solves a problem with little or no delay. The child with the reflective, or slow, tempo considers alterna-tive problem solutions and, therefore, delays his responses. To determine tempo Kagan used a Matching Familiar Figures (MFF) test and a Haptic Visual Matching (HVM) test. Figures 3-5 and 3-6 illustrate sample items from these tests. In the MFF test the researcher shows the child the draw-ing at the top and six strikingly similar ones. The child must select the drawing which is identical to the one at the top. The researcher records the amount of time the child uses to make his response. In the HVM test the child explores with his fingers a wooden figure which he cannot see. The researcher then presents the child with five wooden figures he can see. His task is to select the figure that corresponds to the form he explored with his fingers. Again, the researcher records the decision time.

   This study of the reflection-impulsivity dimension yielded these results (Kagan, 1965): (1) Reflection tends to increase with age, as does accuracy; (2) the tendency to display fast or slow decision times was relatively stable over periods as long as twenty months; (3) the tendency toward reflection or impulsivity shows in the performance of many tasks—such as selecting the correct response from a list of alternatives, providing the correct re-sponse in the absence of an alternative, and answering questions in an

FIG. 3-5   Two sample items from Matching Familiar Figures (MFF) test (after Kagan, 1965).

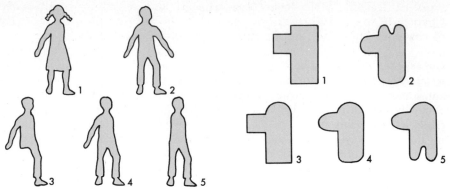

FIG. 3-6 Two sample items from Haptic Visual Matching (HVM) test (after Kagan, 1965, p. 137).

interview situation; and (4) the dispositions seem to be linked to some basic aspects of the child's personality. Kagan (1965, pp. 154–55) writes:

At present it is believed that a major determinant of a child's position involves the differential value placed upon two standards espoused by the child's social milieu that are inconsistent. One standard demands, "Get the answer quickly," while the second exhorts, "Do not make a mistake." When problems are difficult, as in MFF or HVM, these standards are mutually exclusive. It is suggested that the impulsive child places a greater value on "quick success" than he does on "avoiding failure". . . . This argument suggests that the reflective child is a low-risk child who avoids situations that are potentially dangerous and productive of failure, humiliation, or harm. The impulsive child prefers a high-risk orientation.

One study (Kagan, Pearson, and Welch, 1966) showed that impulsive children can be trained to be reflective under two specially designed tutoring conditions: a normal nurturant condition, in which the tutor merely comments positively on the child's choices on the two tests; and an adult-identification condition, in which the tutor persuades the child that if he becomes more reflective he will be more like the tutor. In a one-hour training period all children delayed each response for a period of ten or fifteen seconds, answering only when the experimenter told them they were allowed to. The one-hour training in delay did cause the impulsive children to take more time to answer items on tests taken up to a few weeks after the training period. Unfortunately, however, the additional time did not increase their accuracy; and the attempt to get impulsive children to identify with an adult did not produce significantly better results, either.

Kagan believes that the study of reflective and impulsive children has three educational implications. First, the teacher should adjust his procedures and the tempo of his teaching to accommodate the two different modes of learning. He should avoid the tendency to view the reflective child as slower and less bright than the impulsive child. This tendency shows up in bright, impulsive children themselves, who tend to think that they are brighter than bright, reflective children. Second, the teacher should not punish the impulsive child for incorrect answers with sarcasm, laughter, or rejection, especially when he rewards children who offer correct answers quickly. The teacher who behaves in this way handicaps the impulsive child with only average ability. Finally, teachers vary in their teaching tempos, some speaking fast and offering a rapid flow of ideas and others encouraging the child to consider alternatives and placing no premium on speed. The tempo of the teacher should be tailored to the tempo of the child.

Selection strategies   Jerome Bruner and his associates (1956) describe various ways in which individuals can learn concepts. These methods, called *selection strategies,* control the order in which examples and nonexamples of a concept appear. Selection strategies have three purposes: They maximize the opportunity to obtain useful information about the concept; they reduce the strain of assimilating and keeping track of information; and they regulate the amount of risk we take in reaching a solution—we may take either the risky or the safe course.

Four selection strategies have been identified. In the first of these, *conservative focusing,* the individual uses an example of the concept as a focus and changes one attribute of the example at a time to find those attributes which are essential. Robert Travers (1963, pp. 129–30) uses this example. The student visits a large furniture store and finds a piece of French Provincial furniture, a chair. Wishing to acquire the concept *French Provincial furniture,* he uses the first example as his focus and finds another chair similar in every respect but one, its finish. He discovers that this chair is also French Provincial. He then finds a chair in which only the upholstery is different and discovers that this chair is also French Provincial. By selecting different chairs and varying one attribute at a time, the student will eventually discover the essential and nonessential attributes of French Provincial chairs. This strategy almost guarantees success: It maximizes the opportunity to obtain useful information; it reduces the strain of remembering information through the use of the focus example; and every choice is safe, in the sense that every choice will yield some useful information. *Focus gambling* is a similar selection strategy in that the individual uses a focus example, but it is dissimilar in that he changes more than one attribute at a time. In Travers' example, the student using this strategy chooses as his next example of a French Provincial chair one that has a higher back, straighter legs, and a different finish (three attributes). If the clerk tells him that he has not chosen a French Provincial chair, he does not know which attributes should be excluded. He has gambled and lost. This strategy holds out the possibility of acquiring the concept with the use of fewer examples than those required in conservative focusing. When the student, however, uses as an example a chair which is not

French Provincial, he loses the possible gain in time. In Kagan's terms, impulsive children use focus gambling while reflective children use conservative focusing.

In the two other selection strategies, *simultaneous scanning* and *successive scanning,* the student formulates one or more hypotheses of what the concept may be and then looks for examples. In *simultaneous scanning* the student formulates several hypotheses about the attributes a French Provincial chair must have. Each time he encounters a different French Provincial chair, he decides which hypotheses to keep and which to eliminate. Simultaneous scanning is, as you can see, very exacting for the individuals must deal with several independent hypotheses and carry them all in his mind. In *successive scanning* the student tests a single hypothesis at a time. He forms his idea (hypothesis) of the characteristics of a French Provincial chair, and he tests his hypothesis against each chair he encounters. Successive scanning reduces the amount of information which must be remembered, but it also reduces the amount of relevant information each encounter may provide. If he tests one hypothesis at a time, the student must return to chairs he has previously encountered in testing other hypotheses.

Individuals may vary their strategy with the concept or they may retain a particular strategy regardless of the concept they seek to acquire. In the light of Kagan's findings, one is tempted to believe the latter. Travers suggests that the teacher should adjust the selection strategy to the ability of the child. A simultaneous scanning strategy requires more ability than a conservative focusing strategy. In the former, one must carry and discard hypotheses, while in the latter one accepts and rejects examples one by one. Also, in line with Kagan's findings on reflective and impulsive children, the strategies which involve higher risk (simultaneous scanning and focus gambling) may be attractive to impulsive students with fast tempos, while the low-risk strategies may attract reflective students with slow tempos. In any case, selection strategies are one means of classifying entering behavior for instructional objectives which involve the learning of concepts and rules and problem solving.

QUESTION 3-2   Mr. Chips selected this statement as his instructional objective: When presented with examples of the figurative use of language in poetry, the student always correctly indicates the figure of speech employed. In determining the entering behavior for this objective, Mr. Chips did two things: Working backward from the objective, he asked what the student must be able to do before he could achieve the objective, and, in this way, Mr. Chips identified several levels of prerequisite performance; and in choosing examples of the various figures of speech during instruction, he decided which word order he would allow students to use. Which two different classes of entering behavior was Mr. Chips considering: (a) conceptual tempos and selection strategies; (b) learning sets and learning abilities; (c) learning sets and selection strategies; (d) learning to learn and learning abilities?

Make your choice and defend it by pointing out your reasons.

After reading the last section of this chapter (on the use of entering behavior), you should be able to meet these objectives:

3-9   Describe the basis for determining what entering behavior is required and provide an illustration of this basis.
3-10   Describe how entering behavior can be assessed and provide an illustration of this assessment.
3-11   Describe all the alternative decisions the teacher can make in the case of too much or too little entering behavior.

THE INSTRUCTIONAL USE OF ENTERING BEHAVIOR

In this section we briefly consider the problems of incorporating entering behavior in the actual planning of instruction. To do this we must determine what entering behavior is required, assess the entering behavior of the student, and make decisions based on the results of the assessment.

What Entering Behavior Is Required?

After you have made explicit statements of your instructional objectives, you can determine what entering behavior you will require. Essentially instruction should begin with what the student presently knows and should continue to where he is capable of the terminal performance under specified conditions and to a specified standard. Once objectives have been stated, decisions on instructional procedures can be made. As you may see later, an instructional objective can be changed, if it proves to be impractical. You will also see that instruction for new objectives does not begin strictly with new material but rather with the recall of previously learned responses appropriate to the learning of the new material. Finally, different entering behavior is required for different learning. Concept learning, for example, requires as entering behavior the previous learning of verbal associations and discriminations, while rule learning requires as entering behavior the previous learning of concepts. We treat the kinds of entering behavior required for skill, concept, and rule learning in detail in Part 3.

Assessing Entering Behavior

After you have determined what entering behavior is necessary for your instructional objective, you must find out whether or not the student has acquired this behavior. This knowledge is best obtained through an interview with the student or a test of entering behavior, especially if the list of entering behaviors is extensive. Each prerequisite behavior is the basis for writing three or four test items. You should distinguish a test of entering behavior from a pretest, which measures terminal performance before instruction begins. The pretest is frequently the same as, or an alternate form of, the posttest. A test of entering behavior, however, measures previous rather than present learning. On many occasions the teacher may wish to administer both a test of entering behavior and a pretest. Or occasionally the test of entering behavior may include items which measure how well the student can perform the component tasks of the terminal performance. It is often wise to include such items to find out whether the student has more entering behavior than you require.

Decisions on Entering Behavior

Once the objective has been stated various decisions can be made. If the student has more than enough entering behavior, you may decide either to carry out your instructional plans or alter your plans and begin instruction at a more advanced point. The teacher also has the option of adding more depth, breadth, or applications of the material than originally planned. If the student lacks the necessary entering behavior, several al-

---

QUESTION 3-3   Mr. B. Wright prepared a test of entering behavior on the topic of kinetic energy. He carefully included three or four items to measure each terminal performance in his list of instructional objectives. He then administered the test to his physics students, and all obtained scores of zero. Which of the following decisions should Mr. Wright make?

(a) He should prepare a new test of entering behavior.

(b) He should adopt a new list of instructional objectives.

(c) He should move ahead with his instructional plans because he has now ascertained that none of the students has knowledge about kinetic energy.

After selecting your answer, explain the basis for your selection and for your rejection of the two alternatives.

---

ternatives are available. First, his entering behavior can be increased by review exercises, which will recall material learned earlier but now forgotten. Second, more instruction can be provided than originally intended by beginning at an earlier point. Finally, your instructional objective can be changed either by choosing a different terminal performance or by lowering the standard. All these decisions are made in the pretutorial phase of the computer-based teaching model (Chapter 1). In any case the results of the determination and the assessment of entering behavior must become an integral part of the instructional plans.

SUMMARY

This chapter has developed the concept of entering behavior, the second component of the basic teaching model. We can describe entering behavior only in the context of particular instructional objectives and particular students. By doing this, we avoid much of the ambiguity of related concepts—readiness, maturation, individual differences, and personality. The chapter also described three ways of classifying entering behavior: as learning sets, as learning abilities, and as learning styles. The most practical classification at this stage of our knowledge is learning sets, which, by using Gagné's procedure, we can translate into learning structures. Finally this chapter considered the practical use of entering behavior and the decisions we can make once entering behavior has been determined and assessed.

SUGGESTED READINGS

These articles will help you develop a proper conception of readiness and its relation to teaching:

AUSUBEL, DAVID P., "Viewpoints from Related Disciplines: Human Growth and Development," *Teachers College Record,* 60 (1959), 245–54.

TYLER, FRED T., "Issues Related to Readiness to Learn," in *Theories of Learning and Instruction,* ed. E. R. Hilgard, Part I of the 63rd Yrbk. of the National Society for the Study of Education, pp. 210–39. Chicago: University of Chicago Press, 1964.

These articles deal with the different classes of entering behavior:

GAGNÉ, ROBERT M., "The Acquisition of Knowledge," *Psychological Review,* 69 (1962), 355–65. Here Gagné explains learning sets.

JENSEN, ARTHUR R., "Individual Differences in Concept Learning," in *Analyses of Concept Learning,* eds. H. J. Klausmeier and C. W. Harris, pp. 139–54. New York: Academic Press Inc., 1966. Here Jensen describes learning abilities.

KAGAN, JEROME, "Impulsive and Reflective Children: Significance of Conceptual Tempo," in *Learning and the Educational Process,* ed. J. D. Krumboltz, pp. 133–61. Chicago: Rand McNally & Co., 1965.

CHAPTER FOUR

INTELLECTUAL DEVELOPMENT

The three main sections of this chapter reflect the following general purposes. The first section describes some of the basic concepts in Jean Piaget's theory of intellectual development. The second section describes the four periods of intellectual development: sensorimotor, preoperational, concrete operational, and formal operational. The third section describes some applications of Piaget's theory to teaching and learning.

After reading the first section, you should be able to meet the following objectives:

4-1 Distinguish *schemes* from responses and particular acts.

4-2 Give examples of schemes, using physical actions common to infants.

4-3 Distinguish between *assimilation* and *accommodation* by describing the different effects each has on schemes.

4-4 Using a particular scheme, illustrate the different influences of assimilation and accommodation.

BASIC THEORETICAL CONCEPTS

Piaget and his coworkers at the Rousseau Institute and the Centre International d'Epistémologie Génétique, both in Geneva, Switzerland, have given us our most elaborate theory of intellectual development supported by extensive research. This section is devoted to an explanation of some basic theoretical concepts in Piaget's system, a description of the major periods of intellectual development, and an examination of the possible applications of Piaget's work to the assessment of entering behavior. Piaget's system is introduced here to indicate to the interested student where he may find more detailed treatment of Piaget's monumental work.

Schemes

In Piaget's theory, to know an object one must act upon it, either physically or mentally. These physical or mental actions can displace objects or connect, combine, take apart and reassemble them (Piaget, 1970, p. 704). The activities that people perform on objects are known as *schemes*. Schemes are *not* particular actions or responses; they are what can be repeated and generalized in particular acts. Particular acts of sucking, for example, share commonalities. The sucking scheme, once the child develops it, enables him to suck a variety of objects in a variety of positions. Similarly, the pushing scheme enables the child to push a variety of objects with or without the use of various implements. As soon as the child learns to coordinate the various actions involved in sucking and pushing, Piaget describes the child as having *constructed* the respective schemes. For Piaget, the development of intelligence is not the passive unfolding of experience and heredity. It is the result of the increasing ability of the child to coordinate his actions, both physical and mental. These abilities or capabilities are the child's schemes (Piaget and Inhelder, 1969).

In the early development of the child, the schemes are physical actions on the objects in his immediate environment. As the child moves toward adolescence these actions become internal mental operations. Like mental arithmetic, older children and adults do not have to move objects physically in order to add and subtract them. We can perform the physical movements by converting the objects to numbers, and we can even do the operations on the numbers without setting them on paper. Although Piaget believes that learning (more properly development) is doing, much of the doing is mental as well as physical.

Assimilation

The child needs the environment in order to develop his intelligence. Intellectual assimilation is similar to biological assimilation. Using the example of food, Piaget (1970, p. 707) wrote:

From a biological point of view, assimilation is the integration of external elements into evolving or completed structures of an organism. In its usual connotation, the assimilation of food consists of a chemical transformation that incorporates it into the organism.

The "evolving or completed structures" are the schemes. Assimilation is the process of extracting from the environment what is needed for developing and maintaining schemes. If the schemes are stable or completed, assimilation operates as a simple digestive process in which the organs of digestion undergo relatively little change. Assimilation is not exclusively dependent upon what is available in the environment. It also depends upon the schemes already available even in the process of changing them. The child's response to the environment, therefore, is not unlimited—that is, it is not controlled only by the environment. For example, if the child lacks the scheme for object permanence (as do most children under the age of eight months), he makes no response to vanished objects and very little effort to search for them. As soon as the child develops the scheme for objective permanence (from 12 to 24 months), he makes active search for objects in places where he has seen them disappear. Similarly, the child may lack the scheme for understanding that substances can be present although invisible (for example, salt dissolved in water). After witnessing a demonstration of salt dissolving in water, the child will say that the salt is no longer present, if asked about what happened.

Assimilation accounts for the child's ability to act on and understand something new in terms of what is already familiar (his available schemes). If the child were limited to assimilation, he would not develop new schemes—new capacities for assimilating new objects and events. To explain how new schemes develop out of the old ones, Piaget has described a second process, known as accommodation.

Accommodation

Piaget (1970, p. 708) defines accommodation as any change of a scheme by the elements it assimilates. To return to the metaphor of food assimilated through digestion, we know that American children grow taller than their immigrant parents. If the "digestion schemes" remained the same for immigrant parents and children, as adults the offspring be the same height. But the bodies of the children are able to assimilate new substances in improved diets and thereby grow taller. The accommodation of the new food substances changes the existing digestive schemes. The progressive modification of schemes through accommodation allows the child to develop his capabilities beyond the point of dealing only with the immediate physical environment. The child can reach a stage where he can solve problems through mental calculation alone.

Equilibration

Equilibration is the process of seeking mental balance. The balance, or equilibrium, that is sought lies between assimilation and accommodation.

Equilibration functions as the thermostat that maintains a balance between cold and hot. In the body it functions to keep a balance between such states as activity and rest.

According to Piaget, equilibration is a dynamic, not a static, function. It moves development from simple to more complex schemes through the dual action of assimilation and accommodation. Although the simpler schemes and early stages form resting points in the child's intellectual development, these resting points are only temporary states of equilibrium. The child's actions on his environment and his rudimentary understanding of it leave him unsatisfied. He seeks better control and better answers to his questions. Recurrent frustration and curiosity in the development of children are states of disequilibrium prodding them on to develop more complex schemes and more stable states of equilibrium. Only when children reach the final stage of intellectual development (in their adolescent years) does intelligence take the stable (equilibrated) form we recognize as adult intelligence. Before adult intelligence is achieved, children experience imbalances of too much assimilation or too much accommodation. Too much assimilation produces fantasy as when the child uses play objects to represent only what he imagines. He may make a meal with pebbles standing for bread, grass for lettuce, and so on. Too much accommodation produces mere imitation that simply reproduces the forms and movements of the persons or objects it models.

Equilibration is the process that produces progressive equilibrium between assimilation and accommodation. It is a process of decentration whereby the child moves from stages in which he is centered on his own actions and viewpoints to stages in which he can take the points of view of objects and other people. The decentering is complete when the adult achieves this objectivity. Until the decentering reaches levels of objectivity, the child experiences successive stages of perplexity, confusion, and curiosity. Adult curiosity and confusion are often useful regressions to lower developmental stages when the adult is making an effort to change old points of view. The decentered stability of adult intelligence gives it more mobility—the ability to apply mental operations quickly and efficiently to the solution of new problems.

Miss Rose notices that Maria sometimes separates the red, white, and blue blocks by color and ignores shape. Othertimes Maria separates the blocks both by color and shape. The sorting by shape is done by separately grouping the cubes and pyramids. Which of the following statements best describes the present state of Maria's intellectual development?

QUESTION 4-1

    (a) Maria has a scheme for color but not for shape.

    (b) Maria's development shows disequilibrium.

    (c) Assimilation outweighs accommodation.

    (d) Accommodation outweighs assimilation.

    (e) Maria's development shows stabilization.

Upon reading the second section of this chapter, you should be able to meet the following objectives:

4-7   Using the example of the disappearance of objects, describe the six stages of the *sensorimotor period.*

4-8   Describe development in the sensorimotor period in terms of the developing relationship of child with physical objects and space.

4-9   Describe the two stages of the *preoperational period* in terms of the child's ability to form concepts (for example, beads, dogs, and so forth.)

4-10   Describe the developing ability of the child to assemble objects that are alike.

4-11   Describe the developing ability of the child to use the concepts "all" or "some."

4-12   Describe the child's ability in play and imitation in terms of accommodation and assimilation.

4-13   Describe the period of *concrete operations* in terms of reversibility and interiorization.

4-14   Illustrate the period of concrete operations by using the child's knowledge of conservation.

4-15   List the characteristics of groupings in the period of concrete operations and illustrate each grouping.

4-16   Using the terms *possible* and *real,* distinguish between the periods of concrete and *formal operations.*

4-17   Referring to the three derived characteristics of the period of formal operations, distinguish between concrete and formal operations.

Sensorimotor Period

The first period of intellectual development is the sensorimotor period that lasts to about 1½ years of age. In the first half of this period, the child's activity is centered on his own body. In the second half, the child develops schemes of practical intelligence that enable him to deal with objects in space.

Mary Ann Spencer Pulaski (1971, pp. 207–8) described the six stages of the sensorimotor period as follows:

Stage I (0–1 month)   Characterized by neonatal reflexes and gross, uncoordinated body movements. Stage of complete egocentricism with no distinction between self and outer reality; no awareness of self as such.

Stage II (1–4 months)   New response patterns are formed by chance from combinations of primitive reflexes. The baby's fist accidentally finds its way into his mouth through a coordination of arm moving and sucking.

Stage III (4–8 months)   New response patterns are coordinated and repeated intentionally in order to maintain interesting changes in the environment.

Stage IV (8–12 months)   More complex coordinations of previous behavior patterns, both motor and perceptual. Baby pushes aside obstacles or uses parent's hand as a means to a desired end. Emergence of anticipatory and intentional behavior; beginning of search for vanished articles.

Stage V (12–18 months) Familiar behavior patterns varied in different ways as if to observe different results. Emergence of directed groping toward a goal, and of new means-end manipulations for reaching desired objects.

Stage VI (1½–2 years) Internalization of sensorimotor behavior patterns and beginnings of symbolic representation. Invention of new means through internal experimentation rather than external trial and error.

To illustrate these sensorimotor stages, consider the infant's reactions to the presence and disappearance of objects. In the first stage (0–1 month), the infant is passive to the world of objects. The newborn infant will close his hand on anything that lightly touches it. He grasps passively, but he does not search actively for any objects. In a random effort to assimilate the object environment the newborn makes impulsive movements of his limbs, but there is no attempt to direct these movements toward the grasping of particular objects. This passive release by stimulation gives way to active groping, as we see in the infant's sucking behavior. Very early in the infant's life he learns to grope with his mouth for the nipple of the breast. He "assimilates" the nipple to the innate sucking scheme.

At the second sensorimotor stage (1–4 months), the world of objects is still only an extension of the infant's needs and movements. As an object the nipple has no permanence or constancy. When it disappears, he makes no active effort to find it. Out of sight, out of mind! By the second stage, however, the infant knows when he is in the vicinity of the nipple. He is sensitive to the smooth breast skin surrounding the nipple and moves his mouth around until he makes contact with the nipple. He is, therefore, more actively engaged in the nipple search than when he merely awaited its insertion.

At the third sensorimotor stage (4–8 months), there is still more progress from passive responding to active search. The infant's behavior becomes intentional—centered on producing some result in the environment. For example, Piaget (1963, p. 158) describes how Lucienne (one of his daughters), at the age of 5 months, learned to move her foot to shake the doll hanging from the hood of her bassinet. She began by shaking the bassinet (a scheme already developed) and added the movements of her foot. She even looked at her foot after shaking the doll—an awakening understanding of the connection between the movements of foot and doll. During this stage objects begin to acquire permanence. If the doll dropped from the hood, the infant's eyes followed it and searched the bassinet in which she was lying. At about 8 months of age, Laurent (Piaget's son) would search the floor for everything Piaget dropped above him. According to Piaget, Laurent was developing a scheme for the movement of falling. In this stage the child begins to develop primitive notions of space, causality, and time and shows the beginnings of imitation. The child, in short, begins to construct a basic reality (McV. Hunt, 1961, p. 133).

At the fourth sensorimotor stage (8–12 months), the infant's behavior becomes even more intentional and active. This is illustrated most graphically in the child's search for vanished objects. In his experiments for this period, Piaget would hide an object (often his watch) under a cushion. He would then allow the infant to search for the watch and find it. After the child found the watch under the cushion, Piaget would then hide it under a second cushion in another location. The infant would be allowed to watch while the watch was transferred from one location to the other. At this fourth stage the child immediately began the search for the watch. But alas! Even with several repetitions of the transfer of the watch, the child looked only under the first cushion, failing to find the vanished object. Still, the search under the first cushion shows the development of more purposive behavior. The infant no longer behaves as if an object ceases to exist when it disappears from sight.

At the fifth sensorimotor stage (12–18 months), there is more active experimentation by the infant. The child discovers new means for attaining various goals. Laurent, for example, developed an interest in dropping objects, experimented with various ways of dropping them, and finally converted dropping into throwing. The infant had achieved object constancy. When the watch, hidden under one pillow, was transferred to a place under a second pillow, Laurent lifted the second pillow to find it. If, however, the infant did not see the transfer, he may continue to search for the watch under the first pillow. When the infant does not witness an event, it lacks reality for him. Aside from attaining a somewhat better scheme for object permanence, in this stage the child develops a greater interest in novelty and in the imitation of new models and gains better understanding of space, time, and cause-effect relationships.

In the sixth (last) sensorimotor stage (1½–2 years), the infant develops schemes that allow him to represent mentally objects and events. He can imagine actions as well as execute them. Like the Kohler (1925) chimpanzees, the infant can invent means for using an instrument to achieve some goal. Piaget (1963) described how his daughter Jacqueline could find a disappearing coin. Piaget placed the coin in his hand and then placed his hand under the cushion. Next he brought the hand forward while keeping it closed. Piaget then immediately hid his hand under a coverlet; he withdrew his hand and held it out. Jacqueline pushed the hand aside because she had experience in opening her father's hand and not finding the coin. Instead of looking in his hand, she looked under the cushion and then under the coverlet where sho found the coin. Several repetitions with various objects and disappearances were solved easily by Jacqueline. Even though she did not witness the actual concealment of the object under the coverlet, she finally searched there and found the coin.

The process of making new schemes out of old schemes involves both assimilation and accommodation. When the infant's old schemes of objects as simple extensions of his motions prove to be inadequate for his growing physical potential, assimilation of new aspects of the environment results in the accommodation of the old schemes and the development of new ones. The new schemes are more inclusive and absorb the old schemes in a kind of intellectual hierarchy. We can say, therefore, that the infant's schemes for sucking and object permanence contain all of the schemes of earlier stages but become subordinate to the new, more general schemes that enable the child to manipulate his environment more fully.

Because of this hierarchical ordering of primitive schemes into more developed schemes, the sensorimotor period foreshadows the structure of adult thought. Inhelder and Piaget (1958, p. 15) wrote:

> Thus, the scheme of pulling a support to obtain a coveted object will tend to the eventual differentiation of a sub-scheme where the support is rigid like a plank: It can be pivoted on its axis. The subject will then have a general scheme of using a support to gain an object, subdivided into two schemes, one of which consists in simply pulling the support while the other involved pivoting and sliding it.

By emphasizing the hierarchical organization of sensorimotor schemes, Piaget has shown how infant intelligence is continuous with the development of child and adult intelligence.

In summary, the sensorimotor period begins with the infant centering its attention on its own body, a period lasting from seven to nine months. It is followed by a period of approximately equal length in which the child becomes aware of the independence of objects and space outside his own body.

Preoperational Period

The second period of intellectual development begins around 1½ to 2 years of age and extends to the age of 7 or 8 years. Piaget calls this a period of representational intelligence because the child is able to represent reality as language and mental imagery. For the child, it is the period of magic during which words, pictures, emotions, fantasies, and dreams all seem part of an external reality. The child is not decentered in this thinking. He sees everything from a single point of view, his own. During this period, assimilation appears to outweigh accommodation. There is pleasure in activities themselves (swinging a yoyo, for example); real objects become symbolic (using playing cards to build a house); and in rule games symbols are defined by social convention (playing marbles).

This period can be divided into two stages. Pulaski (p. 208) described these stages as follows:

> *Preconceptual Stage* (2–4 years) Development of perceptual constancy and representation through drawings, language, dreams, and symbolic play. Beginnings of first overgeneralized attempts at conceptualization, in which representatives of a class are not distinguished from the class itself (e.g., all dogs are called by the name of the child's own dog).
> *Perceptual or Intuitive Stage* (4–7 years) Prelogical reasoning appears, based on perceptual appearances untempered by reversibility (e.g., Grandma in a new hat is not recognized as Grandma). Trial and error may lead to an intuitive discovery of correct relationships, but the child is unable to take more than one

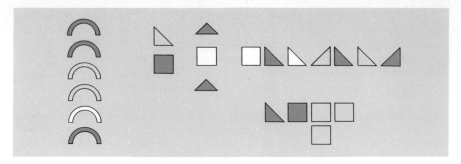

FIG. 4-1   From Inhelder and Piaget, 1969. (New York: Humanities Press, Inc.)

attribute into account at one time (e.g., brown beads cannot at the same time be wooden beads).

To illustrate preoperational thinking, we shall borrow from Piaget's studies of children's behavior in collecting objects (Inhelder and Piaget, 1969). Children are presented with materials similar to those in Figure 4-1; these objects consist of triangular, rectangular, and half-ring shapes. The children are then given directions such as these (Inhelder and Piaget, 1969, p. 21):

Put together things that are alike.
Put them so that they are all the same.
Put them so that they're just like one another.
Put them here if they are the same, and then over there if they're another lot (group) different from this one but the same as each other.

What responses do the children make to the materials and directions? In Figure 4-2, the child has made a number of separated arrangements. One child called the arrangement at the lower right-hand side of the figure a house. Some children make alignments using fluctuating criteria. With a different set of materials, one child began by arranging in a row five rec-

FIG. 4-2   From Inhelder and Piaget, 1969, p. 21. (New York: Humanities Press, Inc.)

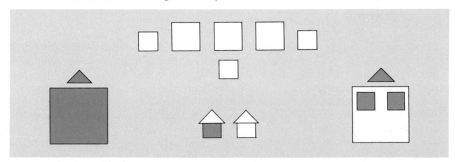

FIG. 4-3 From Inhelder and Piaget, 1969, p. 22. (New York: Humanities Press, Inc.)

tangles, the fifth of which was yellow. The child then arranged four yellow triangles and followed this with two yellow semicircles. This led to five more semicircles of various colors as shown in Figure 4-3. Some children made both alignments and complex figures. As shown in Figure 4-4, one child began with an alignment of five rectangles and six squares and finally ended with a two-dimensional figure in the arrangement of the five circles.

Other children make what are called collective objects. Inhelder and Piaget (1969, p. 27) define a collective object as a two- or three-dimensional collection of similar elements which together form a unified figure. The arrangement in Figure 4-4 is a collective object. Also the squares in the upper part of Figure 4-2 form a collective object with two dimensions—the three large squares forming a rectangle with the three smaller squares lying against three of its sides. Figure 4-2 also contains complex objects made with arrangements of squares and triangles.

The various ways in which children collected the objects seemed to arise spontaneously; the children moved back and forth between the ways in successive attempts to make graphic collections. These graphic collections show the transition in development of intelligence from the sensorimotor period to the period when a child can truly classify objects. According to Inhelder and Piaget, graphic collections are not true classifications. The actual spatial arrangement determines how the child groups the objects.

> Thus he [the child] may place a triangle over a square, because he thinks that these two forms must be related. The triangle reminds him of the roof of a house while the square can be the main part of the building. To him, this means that the triangle must be placed over the roof of the building and nowhere else (Inhelder and Piaget, 1969, p. 18).

FIG. 4-4 From Inhelder and Piaget, 1969, p. 25. (New York: Humanities Press, Inc.)

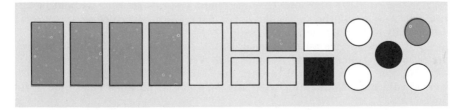

FIG. 4-5 From Inhelder and Piaget, 1969, p. 60. (New York: Humanities Press, Inc.)

In this summary we cannot consider all the aspects of preoperational thinking that have been studied by Piaget and his coworkers. We shall, however, consider how the child develops the concepts of "all" or "some"—what Piaget calls *class-inclusion*. The form of the experiments is ingeniously simple. The child is required to answer the question whether all the X are *y*. For example, are all the squares in Figure 4-5 red? Are all the circles blue? To be sure that the children do not learn the composition of a row by heart, they are given three kinds of tests: (1) They are asked to reproduce the row by picking out circles and squares of different colors from four boxes; (2) they are asked to reproduce the row by memory; and (3) they are asked a set of standardized questions. Apparently, there are three stages of preoperational thinking that children experience before they master this task. In the following illustration taken from Inhelder and Piaget (1969, pp. 66–61), the numbers in parentheses indicate the child's age. For example, Pie is 5 years and 0 months old.

Pie (5; 0) is shown five blue circles with three red squares. The red squares are scattered in the row: "What boxes do you need to remake this?—*Red circles and blue circles.*—Are you sure?—*Yes.*—What is this?—*One of those* (red squares).—And this?—*Blue circles.*—Well, look, are all the circles here blue?—*Yes . . . no.*—Why?—*There are red ones.*—Where?—*There are red squares and blue circles.*—Are all the squares red?—*Yes.*"

Series II (three red squares, two blue squares, two blue circles): "Are all the circles blue?—*No, there are only two.*—Are all the squares blue?—*No.*—And all the circles are blue?—*No, there are blue and red ones.*—What are the red ones like?—*Square.*"

Tin (5; 1). Series I: "Which boxes do you need?—*Red squares and blue squares.*—(The two collections are partially separated by moving the blue circles slightly upwards.) And like this?—*Red circles and blue circles.*—(The two collections are now completely separated by putting the five blue circles on the right of the row and the three red squares on the left.) And like this?—*Red squares and blue circles.*—And now (alternated irregularly as before)?—*No.*—Why?—*I don't know. Because there are also blue ones* (= other counters which are blue without being squares!)—And are all the circles blue?—*Yes.* (There is no difficulty, for they form the majority.)—And all the squares are red?—*No!* (confidently)."

Ire (5; 5). Series I: "Are all these squares red?—*I don't know.*—Why?—*There are circles as well.*—But the squares are all red?—*Yes.*—And all the circles are blue?—*Yes.*—(a blue square is added to form the beginning of series II). And are all these squares red?—*No, because there is a blue one.*—And are all the blue ones circles?—*Yes.*"

Bar (5; 0). (The experimenter starts with a row (I) of 6 blue circles and 2 red squares (inserted after the 2nd and 5th circles). After looking at the row, Bar declares that she needs only the boxes containing red squares and blue circles to remake it. She puts aside the other two boxes and reproduces the row correctly. The experimenter goes on to series II, rows made up of 7 blue circles, together with a varying number of red and blue squares, 1 or 2 red, 1 to 5 blue.) Bar remembers the rows exactly every time; she puts aside the box of red squares, keeps the three others, and reproduces the rows correctly. She is asked the following questions about the last two:

(IIA). "Are all the squares red?—*No.*—Why?—*There are red ones and blue ones* (Right)—Are all the blue ones circles?—*No.*—Why?—*There are circles and squares* [which are blue] (right).—Are all the red ones squares?—*Yes, because there were blue squares and red squares* (right).—Are all the circles blue?—*No* (wrong).— Why?—*Because there were* [blue] *squares and circles.*—Are all the squares blue?— *No* (right) *because there were* [blue] *circles and* [blue] *squares.*"

With the last row (IIB): "What did we have?—*Blue circles and red and blue squares* (right).—Are all the circles blue?—*No* (wrong), *because there are* [blue] *squares and circles.*—Are all the blue ones circles?—*No* (right), *because there were* [blue] *squares and circles.*—Are all the red ones squares?—*Yes, because there were only the squares.*—Are all the circles blue?—*No* (wrong), *there were circles and squares* [blue]."

Older children give completely correct answers:

Cor (6; 8) "Are all the red ones squares?—*Yes.*—You are sure?—*Yes.*—Are all the blue ones circles?—*No, not all. There are also* [blue] *squares.*—Are all the squares blue?—*No, there are also red ones.*—Are all the circles blue?—*Yes.*"

Oec (7; 9). "Are all the circles blue?—*Yes.*—Are all the squares red?—*No, not all.* —Are all the red ones circles?—*No.*—Are some of the blue ones circles?—*Yes.*— Are all the squares blue?—*No, not all.*—Are some of the squares blue?—*Yes.*"

Table 4-1 shows that the accuracy of response increases with age. The lack of consistency in the results is due to the disequilibrium of the classificatory schemes for this period. Because of this, a child may answer some of the questions correctly and other questions incorrectly. In general, however, the results show that accuracy increases with age. Only at stage 3, does the child attain equilibrium.

Piaget (1970, pp. 718–19) believes that the development of mental images is the necessary precursor of the development of mental operations in older children and adolescents. He distinguishes between two kinds of images: reproductive images in which the child mentally visualizes something he has observed in the past and (2) anticipatory images in which the child mentally visualizes something which could happen but which he has not yet witnessed. Children in the earlier stage of preoperational thinking experience only reproductive images. They could mentally visualize the vertical fall of a straight stick. But only older children could mentally visualize the intermediate rotating positions of the falling stick.

TABLE 4-1   PERCENTAGE OF CORRECT ANSWERS GIVEN TO THE FOUR QUESTIONS
BEARING ON THE USE OF "ALL"

AGE (AND NO. OF SUBJECTS)	CB	RS	BC	SR	AB	BA	+	MEAN CB + SR	MEAN BC + RS
5(12)	67	54	79	66	42	58	8	66	66
6(10)	90	55	80	80	45	70	20	85	67
7(10)	100	70	80	90	70	70	50	95	75
8(10)	100	80	100	90	80	88	70	95	90
9(10)	100	85	100	90	80	90	80	95	92

Legend: CB = Are all the circles blue?
RS = Are all the red ones squares?
BC = Are all the blue ones circles?
SR = Are all the squares red?
AB = Are all the As Bs? (if $A < B$) = CB and RS
BA = Are all the Bs As? (if $A < B$) = BC and SR
+ = correct answer to AB and BA
From Inhelder and Piaget, 1969, p. 64.

In the preconceptual stage of this period, the child's thinking is fuzzy. He distorts reality partly because of his dependence upon immediate perception. In the graphic collections, we saw how the young child shifts from one criterion to another in grouping objects; a new criterion is chosen because the child hits upon it accidentally. Collecting by color, for example, gives way to collecting by geometric shape. Similarly, when arranging materials in response to questions of "some" and "all," the child has difficulty keeping color and shape separated. He can think of red *circles* and blue *circles,* but it is difficult for him to deal with blue *circles* and red *squares.* Concepts are classifications of objects. When Piaget calls the child in the early preoperational period *preconceptual,* he means that the child cannot reliably classify objects that vary in more than one characteristic.

Later in this period the child has an intuitive grasp of reality. His groupings and classifications become more reliable, but the child still lacks the stable equilibrium of operational thought. Children in this period believe that evening has not come until they have had their dinner, or that they are not awake until the alarm clock has rung. They intuitively grasp the relationships between dinner and time of day and between alarm clocks and morning, but the relationships they construct are rigid and unidimensional. This resembles the failure to see that circles and squares can be either red or blue and that color and shape are independent.

The two stages of preoperational thinking can also be described in terms of assimilation and accommodation. In the earlier (preconceptual) stage, assimilation outweighs accommodation. In the later (intuitional) stage, accommodation outweights assimilation. The preconceptual stage, therefore, is dominated by symbolic play in which the child makes mud pies, sand castles, and stick guns—an assimilation of reality distorted to fit the schemes he has available. The intuitional period is dominated by imitation. The child reproduces the movements of the monkeys in the zoo, jet airplanes, and even the bent hollyhocks. He models the behavior of parents and siblings.

In one of his early studies, *Play, Dreams, and Imitation in Childhood* (originally published in 1951), Piaget carefully documents his observations of children passing through the stages of imitation and play. Imitation, for example, begins with using action to model objects and persons that are present; it then becomes deferred imitation when the objects and events are not present; and finally it is interiorized imitation when the child can imagine the action without performing it. When the child is able to imagine the action, accommodation is then subordinate to the child's intellectual schemes. Play is similar.

Play begins with exercise games which are movements made for the pleasure gained from the activity itself. Children often let out horrible screams just for the fun of screaming and for the effects it can cause in adults. Exercise games give way to symbolic games which transform commonplace objects of the environment into new, playful uses; large leaves become plates for serving the pebble food. Finally, symbolic games give way to rule games (checkers, and later, chess), in which the rules are fixed, arbitrary, and do not represent reality. In the development of play, therefore, assimilation becomes subordinate to the properties of the objects or to the situations entailed. With the gradual subordination of both assimilation and accommodation, the child's thinking begins to stabilize. He achieves the equilibrium necessary to move toward more advanced and realistic forms of thinking. Pulaski (p. 122) summarized the preoperational period as follows:

> We have seen, during the intuitive period, the use of symbolic play declines in favor of imitation of real-life activities. This is so because the child is reaching a better balance between assimilation and accommodation, and is more interested in the real world than in his private fantasies. . . . Adaptive thought reaches a state of permanent equilibrium, ushering in the period of concrete operations. This is possible because of the development of representation. The ludic (play) symbols of earlier childhood tend more and more toward the reality they symbolize; in other words they become more like the representational images developed through imitation. However, they do not become mere carbon copies of reality but are enriched and extended by the child's imaginative experiences in fantasy play. With the establishment of equilibrium between representations of imitation and representations of fantasy comes a speeding-up of the thought processes, an ability to range forward and backward in time and space. This, of course, entails reversibility, the ability to retrace one's steps mentally and to think inductively as well as deductively.

Let us now turn from the preoperational period to the period of concrete operations.

Concrete Operations Period

Beginning at the age of 7 or 8 children are able to engage in activities of the mind which Piaget calls *operations*. These operations are interiorized—

they are actions on objects that can be carried out mentally without being carried out physically. These operations are also *reversible* in the sense that they can be followed by another mental act which restores objects to their original states.

Conservation   To clarify the difference between preoperational thinking and concrete operational thought, we can note the differences in children's understanding of the conservation of liquids. Consider the use of three bottles—one narrow, one wide, and one still wider. If the preoperational child is asked to predict the height of a liquid as it is poured from the narrow into the wide and still wider bottles, he is able to predict correctly. He will say that the height of the water will change and that it will be lower as the bottles get wider. He does not understand, however, that the amount of water remains the same. In conection with this, Piaget (1968, p. 19) has stated:

> The essential characteristic of preoperational . . . identity . . . is that it deals with simple qualitative invariants, without quantitative composition. For example, the 4 or 5 year old, who maintains that the amount of water has changed, will admit that it is "the same," in the sense that the nature of the matter "water" has not changed. Similarly, if he draws his own body as he was when he was little and again as he is now, he will recognize that it is still the same individual, even if he is bigger in size ("It's still me").

How does the concrete operational child handle the matter of conserving liquids? This child understands the relationship of shape of bottles to quantity of liquid. We say that he is able to *coordinate* both factors—shape of bottles and quantity of liquid—at one time. He is able to think simultaneously about the two factors because of his capacity for interiorized thought (or operations) and for reversibility. This latter capacity enables him to think what would happen to the amount of water if it were poured back into the original container. Baldwin (1967, pp. 192–93) illustrated some concrete operations the child can perform during this period:

> He can, for example, arrange objects in order of size and fit new ones into the series. He can understand that equality of number of two sets of objects depends upon a one-to-one correspondence between the objects in the two groups. He understands that the number of objects in a group is not changed by purely spatial rearrangements. He can understand many of the simpler relationships between classes of objects; for example, he can realize that a class cannot have fewer members than any of its subclasses. He understands what will happen to the sequence of objects if they are rotated. He can distinguish between the distance between two objects and the length of the path between them. In short, he has acquired a rudimentary conception of time, space, number, and logic, those fundamental conceptions in terms of which our understanding of events and objects is ordered.

Grouping   According to Piaget, during this period the child understands the relationships among various concrete operational groups. *Grouping* is a term derived from logic and mathematics and, as such, is difficult to define briefly in nontechnical language. In general, it refers to logical operations. Piaget describes nine distinct groupings for the period of concrete operations. We can say that these nine groupings describe the cognitive structure (or schemes) of the child in this period. Groupings are, therefore, intellectual schemes which possess particular characteristics—closure, associativity, reversibility, and identity.

David Berlyne (1957b, pp. 7–8) has defined and illustrated each of these characteristics of groupings:

1 *Closure.* Any two operations can be combined to form a third operation (e.g., $2 + 3 = 5$; *all men and all women = all human adults;* A *is two miles north of* B *and* B *is one mile north of* C = A *is three miles north of* C).

2 *Reversibility.* For any operation there is an opposite operation which cancels it (e.g., $2 + 3 = 5$ but $5 - 3 = 2$; *all human adults* but *all human adults except women = all men;* A *is two miles north of* B *and* B *is one mile north of* C = A *is three miles north of* C; but, A *is three miles north of* C *and* C *is one mile south of* B = A *is two miles north of* B).

3 *Associativity.* When three operations are to be combined, it does not matter which two are combined first. This is equivalent to the possibility of arriving at the same point by different routes (e.g., $(2 + 3) + 4 = 2 + (3 + 4)$; *all vertebrates and all invertebrates = all human beings and all subhuman animals;* a *is the uncle of* b *and* b *is the father of* c = a *is the brother of* d *and* d *is the grandfather of* c).

4 *Identity.* There is a "null operation" formed when any operation is combined with its opposite (e.g., $2 - 2 = 0$; *all men except those who are men = nobody; I travel one hundred miles to the north and I travel one hundred miles to the south = I find myself back where I started*).

Berlyne also adds a fifth characteristic, which Flavell (1963, p. 175) has called *special identities.* This characteristic has two versions. First, *tautology* merely indicates that repetition of a classification or relation does not change it. Saying something repeatedly does not add information (for example, all men and all men = all men). Second, *interation* indicates that a number combined with itself produces a new number (for example, $3 + 3 = 6$; $3 \times 3 = 9$).

In the concrete operations period, children are able to construct *groupings.* These groupings are mental structures that enable children to deal with part-whole relationships, to join classes in order to form larger classes, and to multiply classes. These groupings also enable children to think in terms of relationships as in a serial ordering of objects based on size. We shall illustrate each of these groupings.

One kind of grouping involves combining classes to form larger classes. The larger classes can be divided into subclasses through a reverse operation. A typical example of this kind of grouping is shown in Figure 4-6. In the discussion of graphic collections and class-inclusion for the preoperational child, we saw the difficulties the children had in combining classes to form larger classes. As these children moved into the concrete operational period, these difficulties of classification were overcome.

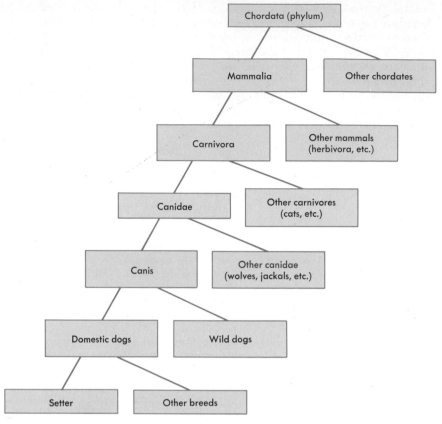

FIG. 4-6 From A. L. Baldwin, 1967, p. 185.

Arranging objects in proper serial order is another type of grouping Piaget has studied (Inhelder and Piaget, 1969, p. 250). In an early experiment, children were presented with ten small rods ranging in length from 9 to 16 centimeters. After the child tried to arrange these rods in order of length, he was given a set of rods of intermediate length to insert into the original series. In the preoperational period children were capable of only two types of manipulations: (1) The child could arrange the rods into subgroups containing two to four rods but then was unable to put the groups together. (2) The child could arrange the original set of rods in a correct series by trial and error, and he could also insert the additional rods by trial and error, sometimes starting over from the beginning. At the age of 7 or 8, when the child reaches the level of concrete operations, he proceeds systematically by first looking for the largest or smallest rod and then looking for the smallest or largest rods among those remaining. The correct ordering of the rods involves the coordination of two operations: (1) understanding that any given rod is both larger than the one preceding it and smaller than the one succeeding it, and (2) mastering reversibility, or the ability to insert the rods of the second set correctly without trial and error.

A third type of grouping deals with multiplicative classification. This is a mental operation in which objects can be classified in various ways. Figure 4-7 shows how objects are classified in at least two ways: (1) Objects in the left half of the figure have four wheels, while those in the right half have two wheels; and (2) objects in the upper half have motors, while those in the lower half do not have motors.

Here is an example taken from Inhelder and Piaget (1969, pp. 172–73) of how a preoperational child tried to sort the objects:

Grei (6; 6) starts with four lots: (1) wagon, shopping basket, (2) bicycle, motor-scooter, motor-bike, (3) car and lorry, (4) pram. Then he puts the pram with the

FIG. 4-7 After Inhelder and Piaget, 1969. (New York: Humanities Press, Inc.)

wagon *"because the pram has four wheels.—And (2)?—Because they have two wheels."*

Given two boxes, Grei puts everything in a single box. *"I'm going to put everything with wheels here* (he starts with the total class).—How would you put them in two boxes?—*Here* (wagon, pram and shopping basket) *they're all wagons.* —And here (2, in which all the others are placed)?—*Because there's nowhere else to put them."*

Given two boxes once again: (1) *"They're all the ones with two wheels"*; (2) *"They're all those with four wheels."*

With four boxes, "Do it differently from the way you did it the first time": (1) lorry, car, *"They have a motor and they have four wheels"*; (2) motor-bike, motor-scooter, *"They have a motor* (and two wheels)"; (3) shopping basket and wagon, *"They're wagons. They have two wheels and four wheels"*; (4) bicycle and pram.

Grei was finally able to sort objects into four versus two wheels and motorized versus nonmotorized, but he was unable to keep both of these characteristics in mind at the same time.

A child who is capable of this grouping easily sorts objects using both characteristics at the same time and can even think of additional subclasses.

Bon (8; 3). Given four empty boxes, Bon immediately divides the vehicles into the four simplest multiplicative classes: motorized and non-motorized, four-wheeled and two-wheeled. But when asked to place the objects in two boxes, he discovers eight possible criteria: two or four wheels, with or without a roof, with or without a handle-bar, with or without a door, with or without a saddle, with or without a bell, with or without brakes, and with or without tyres [sic]. Their associations would engender 256 multiplicative classes! When he is given four empty boxes again, Bon tries several different combinations, all of which are incomplete. But when the boxes are arranged to form a matrix, he returns to the four initial exhaustive classes (Inhelder and Piaget, 1969, pp. 175–76).

Flavell summarized three limitations of the period of concrete operations: (1) The operations are oriented toward concrete things and events in the immediate present, so movement toward the nonpresent, or potential, is limited. The child during this period acts as if his primary task were to organize and order what is immediately present; the real does not become a special case of the possible. (2) The child has to relinquish the various physical attributes (such as mass, weight, volume) of objects and events one by one. If, for example, he understands that there is as much clay in object A as in object B (mass), despite the difference in shape, the child will still need considerable time to understand that the weight and the volume of the clay also remain the same. (3) Each of the groupings which the child develops in this period remains an isolated organization and does not form an integrated system of thought. All three of these limitations are removed in the period of formal operations.

From Concrete to Formal Operations

We will illustrate how the child moves from the period of concrete operations to the period of formal operations by using experimental data provided by Inhelder and Piaget (1958, chap. 1). In the following example, we begin with the preoperational period to illustrate the transition to concrete operations.

First consider Figure 4-8, which shows a kind of billiard game. In order to understand why the balls propelled by the plunger succeed or fail in hitting the target, the child must construct the principle of the relationship between the angle of incidence and the angle of reflection. In other words, the angle (of incidence) formed by the plunger and the buffer wall must equal the angle (of reflection) formed by the path the ball travels from the wall to its target. The angle of incidence is increased as the plunger is aimed lower on the rebound wall and decreased as the plunger is aimed higher. To understand the law the child must combine the notions of reciprocity and equality. Understanding the relationship of movement of target and plunger requires an understanding of reciprocity. To understand why the ball proceeds toward its target, the child must understand equality—the ball will return to the starting point if the plunger is perpendicular to the rebound wall. The progression in understanding this principle is illustrated by the following interviews.

Preoperational period Inhelder and Piaget (1958, p. 4) described the reactions of Dan (about 5 years old) to the billiard game. Dan explained his first success as follows: "I think it works because it's in the same direction." He adjusted the plunger by trial and error. Then he asked, "Why do you have to turn the plunger sometimes? No, you have to put it there (he fails). If it could be pushed a little further." He did this and succeeded. Dan could control the rebounds successfully, but he had no idea that they were made up of angles. When asked to describe the ball's path with his finger, Dan traced a curve which accounted for the starting point and the goal but which did not touch the wall at the rebound points.

Dan (about 5½ years old) was surprised by the detour of the ball after it struck the wall. He said, "It always goes over there." But he did not vary his aim. "Oh, it always goes there . . . it will work later." Per, a third child about 6½ years old said, "It goes there and it turns the other way"—his gestures also traced a curve.

Inhelder and Piaget (1958, p. 6) analyzed the actions of the three children as follows. These children were not even at the level of concrete operations. They acted *only* with a view toward achieving the goal, and they did not ask themselves why they succeeded. They did not seem conscious of either rebounds or angles. In effect, they failed to internalize their actions as operations. Their behavior was mostly trial and error with little or no awareness of the effects of their own behavior with the plunger.

Concrete operations (period three) In the first years of this stage, children show a distinct awareness of straight lines and angles in their explanations of why the ball reaches its targets. For example, Vir (about 7½ years old) traced two lines at right angles to each other. He stated, "To aim more to the left, you have to turn (the plunger) to the left." Truf (about 3 months older) stated, "I know where it will go." His gestures showed that he knew

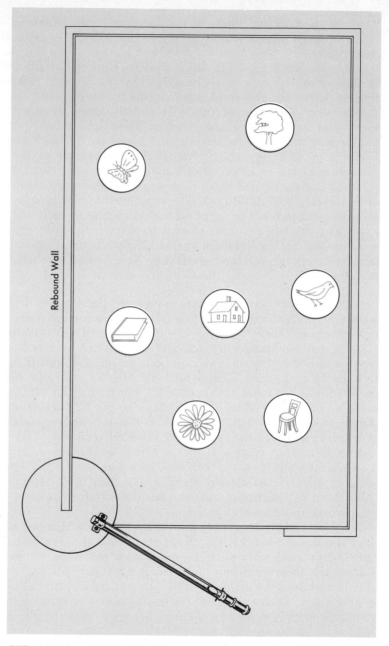

FIG. 4-8 The principle of the billiard game is used to demonstrate the angles of incidence and reflection. The tubular spring plunger can be pivoted and aimed. Balls are launched from this plunger against the projection wall and rebound to the interior of the apparatus. The circled drawings represent targets which are placed successively at different points. After Inhelder and Piaget, 1958, p. 5.

that the angle of rebound is acute when the plunger is raised and obtuse when it is lowered. But Truf did not divide the total angle shown by his gestures into two equal answers. Inhelder and Piaget (1958, p. 7) concluded that Truf had a global and implicit understanding of the principle.

In the later years of this period, the explanations of the relationship between inclination of the plunger and reflection of the rebound are more clearly explained. Nic (about 9½ years old) said: "You have to move the plunger according to the location of the target; the ball has to make a slanting line with the target." Kar (about the same age) said: "The more I move the plunger this way (to the left), the more the ball will go like that (extremely acute angle), and the more I put it like this (inclined to the right) the more the ball will go like that" (increasingly obtuse angle). He almost reached the point of discovering why the ball returns to the starting point when the plunger is "straight" or perpendicular to the rebound wall.

How do children in the period of concrete operations differ from the children in the preoperational period? The preoperational (period 2) children knew only how to attain their goal. They never looked for reason behind their reactions—for example, how the different positions of the plunger affected the direction of the ball. The concrete operational (period 3) children, however, had become aware of some very important facts. First, they were aware that the plunger can be fired at different angles to the rebound wall. Second, they knew that the ball's path is composed of two straight lines. Third, they knew that these two lines form an angle at the point of rebound. Fourth, they knew that the size of this angle varies with the position of the plunger. Fifth, they could order these relations into amounts such as "sharper," "more to the left," and "higher." They could also order the path of rebound: "The ball keeps going higher." And finally, they could establish correspondences between the direction of the plunger and the path of the ball from the point of rebound. "The more the plunger is to the left, the more the ball will go downwards."

What characteristic distinguishes the explanations of period 3 children from those of period 4 children? The period 3 children never look for reasons why the concrete rank orders and correspondences they find are true. According to Inhelder and Piaget (1958, p. 9), they "stick to dealing with facts whose accuracy is due to serial ordering and correspondence operations, but they do not explain these facts. . . ." They remain at the level of rough, global observation—certainly a great advance over that of period 2, but still too global to lead to an analytic breakdown of the observed angles. Period 3 children are content to point out slopes of directions and to deal with the total angle composed of the two segments of the trajectory; they do not divide this total angle into two equal parts that would give us the angle of incidence and the angle of reflection.

Formal operations (period 4) Children in the early development of this stage slowly discover the law of the equality of angles. They try several hypotheses, until they find one they can verify. Bon (about 14½) first hypothesized that the launching force is the determining factor; he then realized that the paths are the same whether the balls are shot hard or soft (Inhelder and Piaget, 1958, p. 10). Next he hypothesized about the effect of distances ("how you have to place the rod"). He proceeded to set up correspondences as do period 3 children: "It's the position of the lever: the more you raise the target, the more you raise it here." Bon then used a ruler to mark the path of the ball between the rebound point and the target in such a way as to verify its correspondence with the position of the plunger. Bon hypothesized that the angle is always a right angle. "It has to make a right angle with the lever." But after several trials he concluded: "No, above (when the plunger is straightened) it won't work." He agreed that it could be at a right angle for one position. "But other than that position?" he was asked. He responded: "When you turn, one should be smaller, the other larger. Ah! They are equal!" He pointed out the angles of incidence and reflection.

Arriving at the understanding of the law of equality of angles is rapid and complete in children who have fully attained the stage of formal operations. There is less need to try and discard several hypotheses (as in the case of Bon). The search for the law tends to be systematic as in the case of Mul (about 14 and 3 months). After beginning with a series of trials, Mul stated: "I was here and it went in this direction. You change the angle to see how it goes." He systematically reduced the angle until he discovered, "If I shoot it straight, at a right angle, it (the ball) will come right back." Then he discovered that "the smaller you make the angle here, the larger the angle there." Next Mul discovered the need for equal angles: "This angle is the same as that one; you have to make it parallel to that one. I am going to see." He checked for several different angles. Finally: "Yes, I think that's it. You have to carry over exactly that angle" (Inhelder and Piaget, 1958, p. 13).

Lam (about 15) was even more direct: "The rebound depends on the inclination (of the plunger). . . . Yes, it depends on the angle. I traced an imaginary line perpendicular (to the buffer): the angle formed by the target and the angle formed by the plunger with the imaginary line will be the same."

Finally, Fort (16) had this to say after several trials: "You have to move the lever according to the target position and vice versa (reciprocity). You must have an angle there, but it isn't always the same. It's obvious that everything changes." Then: "You have to think in straight lines. To the extent that the lever is displaced, you will find the same distance to the other direction: you have to displace it according to the mean. The two distances, the two sides, always indicate the angles (of incidence and reflection)" (Inhelder and Piaget, 1958, p. 14).

What is the central feature that distinguishes thinking in the stage of formal operations from thinking in the earlier stage? The distinguishing feature would seem to be connecting the idea of reciprocity to the idea of equality. Most of the formal operations subjects first established the idea of reciprocity. That is, they discovered the similarities in the relationship of the angle of the plunger to the path the ball took after it struck the rebound wall. The idea of equal angles became clear only after the subjects realized that the ball returned to the starting point when the plunger is perpendicular to the rebound wall. After this discovery, it becomes clear that the incline of the plunger must be equal to the incline of ball's rebound.

At this point the subject can arrive at the law in two ways. He can imagine a perpendicular line extending from the rebound wall at the point the ball strikes the wall and in this way discover the equality of the angles of incidence and reflection. Or he can look for complementary angles between the plunger and the rebound wall or the rebound wall and the path of the ball to its target. In either case the discovery of the law of equal angles is the result of the quest for an explanation of the observed inclinations. The discovery results from calculating possibilities and not merely from describing the facts.

Formal Operations Period

During the period from 11 to 15, the adolescent acquires the adult capacity for abstract thought. In the previous period the child is only beginning to extend his thought from the actual to the potential (Inhelder and Piaget, 1958). Flavell (1963) uses this analogy: The cognitive structure of the previous period is like a parking lot in which the parking spaces are alternately empty and occupied. The spaces themselves endure, and their owners can and do look beyond the cars which are present toward the future (potential) when other spaces will be occupied and empty.

We shall now summarize the major characteristics of the period of formal operations. These characteristics explain what Berlyne (1957b, p. 9) has described as the "adolescent's taste for theorizing and criticizing." The major characteristic of this period, according to Bärbel Inhelder and Piaget (1958), concerns the possible versus the real. In describing this new quality of thought, Flavell (1963, p. 205) wrote:

> No longer exclusively preoccupied with the sober business of trying to stabilize and organize just what comes directly to the senses, the adolescent has, through this new orientation, the potentiality of imagining all that might be there—both the very obvious and the very subtle—and thereby of much better insuring the finding of all that is there.

The adolescent, therefore, theorizes about and criticizes the present operation of the world because he conceives of many possible ways in which it could operate and many alternative ways in which it could be better.

From this major characteristic we derive three other characteristics of the period of formal operations. First, the adolescent's thinking is basically *hypothetico-deductive*. To discover the real among the possible requires that the possible be cast as hypotheses, which may be confirmed or rejected. The reasoning of the adolescent, in the words of Flavell (1963, p. 205), may take this form:

Well, it is clear from the data that *A* might be the necessary and sufficient condition for *X,* or that *B* might be, or that both might be needed; my job is to test these possibilities in turn to see which one or ones really hold true in this problem.

Second, thinking in this period is *propositional thinking.* The adolescent does not consider only raw data but also sentences which contain these data. In the period of concrete operations the child deals with concrete objects and events, which he learns to classify, set in correspondence, and so on. In the period of formal operations he takes the results of these concrete operations, puts them in sentence form, and begins to find relationships among the sentences (or propositions). Berlyne (1957, pp. 7–8) uses these examples of propositional thought: *"Either sentence* p *is true or sentence* q *is true;"* or *"If sentence* r *is true, then sentence* s *must be true."* Third, thinking in this period involves *combinatorial analysis.* In considering all the possible solutions to a problem, the adolescent isolates all individual factors and all possible combinations of factors that may figure in the solution. The factors are propositions or statements and the combinations of statements are hypotheses.

Flavell (1963, p. 207) has selected two examples from Inhelder and Piaget (1958, pp. 108–9, 111, and 117) to illustrate the differences in the thinking of children in the periods of concrete and formal operations.

In experiment I, the child is given four similar flasks containing colorless, odorless liquids which are perceptually identical. We number them: (1) diluted sulphuric acid; (2) water; (3) oxygenated water; (4) thiosulphate; we add a bottle (with a dropper) which we will call *g;* it contains potassium iodide. It is known that oxygenated water oxidizes potassium iodide in an acid medium. Thus mixture $(1 + 3 + g)$ will yield a yellow color. The water (2) is neutral, so that adding it will not change the color, whereas the thiosulphate (4) will bleach the mixture $(1 + 3 + g)$. The experimenter presents to the subject two glasses, one containing $1 + 3$, the other containing 2. In front of the subject, he pours several drops of *g* in each of the two glasses and notes the different reactions. Then the subject is asked simply to reproduce the color yellow, using flasks 1, 2, 3, 4, and *g* as he wishes.

The report on Ren illustrates thinking at the level of concrete operations; that on Cha illustrates the level of formal operations:

Ren (7;1) tries $4 \times g$, then $2 \times g$, and $3 \times g$: *"I think I did everything. . . . I tried them all."*—"What else could you have done?"—*"I don't know."* We give him the glasses again: he repeats $1 \times g$, etc.—"You took each bottle separately. What else could you have done?"—*"Take two bottles at the same time"* [he tries $1 \times 4 \times g$, then $2 \times 3 \times g$, thus failing to cross over between the two sets (of bottles), for example 1×2, 1×3, 2×4, and 3×4].—When we suggest that he add others, he puts $1 \times g$ in the glass already containing 2×3 which results in the appearance of the color: "Try to make the color again."—*"Do I put in two or three?* [he tries with $2 \times 4 \times g$, then adds 3, then tries it with $1 \times 4 \times 2 \times g$]. *No, I don't remember any more,"* etc.

Cha (13;0): *"You have to try with all the bottles. I'll begin with the one at the end [from 1 to 4 with g]. It doesn't work any more. Maybe you have to mix them [he tries 1 × 2 × g, then 1 × 3 × g.] It turned yellow. But are there other solutions? I'll try [1 × 4 × g; 2 × 3 × g; 2 × 4 × g; 3 × 4 × g; with the two preceding combinations this gives the six two-by-two combinations systematically]. It doesn't work. It only works with"* [1 × 3 × g].—"Yes, and what about 2 and 4?"—*"2 and 4 don't make any color together. They are negative. Perhaps you could add 4 in 1 × 3 × g to see if it would cancel out the color [he does this]. Liquid 4 cancels it all. You'd have to see if 2 has the same influence [he tries it]. No, so 2 and 4 are not alike, for 4 acts on 1 × 3 and 2 does not."*—"What is there in 2 and 4?"—*"In 4 certainly water. No, the opposite, in 2 certainly water since it doesn't act on the liquids; that makes things clearer."*—"And if I were to tell you that 4 is water?"—*"If this liquid 4 is water, when you put it with 1 × 3 it wouldn't completely prevent the yellow from forming. It isn't water; it's something harmful."*

The protocol of the younger child (Ren) shows that he is able to make some of the possible combinations and that he makes the few he thinks of (some with considerable help from the experimenter) in nonsystematic ways. On the other hand, the older child (Cha) in the very beginning thinks of all possible (and feasible) combinations, and he does this in an orderly and systematic way: $(1 \times g) \times (2 \times g)$, and so on, and then $(1 \times 2 \times g) + (1 \times 3 \times g)$, and so on. The number of if-then statements shows the hypothetico-deductive characteristic of his thinking.

It should be clear by now that during the period of formal operations the adolescent engages in his first scientific reasoning. He is capable of planning truly scientific investigations, and he can vary the factors in all possible combinations and in an orderly fashion. In fact, he appears to be capable of discovering the basic laws of physics with the help of simple apparatus. By observing whether the student attempts to explain a given state of affairs in terms of various combinations of factors and to verify his hypotheses by observing their consequences, the teacher can determine whether the student is operating at the level of formal operations.

Inhelder and Piaget (1958) believe that the development of adolescent reasoning may account for changes in adolescent behavior. Unlike the younger child, who lives in the present, the adolescent lives in the world of the possible and the hypothetical—the world of the future. Since he is capable of reflective thought, he can consider his own future and the future of the society in which he lives. According to Piaget, he develops a special egocentricism, in which he combines an extravagant belief in thought with sweeping disregard for the practicality of the designs and the reforms he proposes. Flavell (1963, p. 224) quotes Inhelder and Piaget (1958, pp. 345–46):

The adolescent goes through a phase in which he attributes unlimited power to his own thoughts so that the dream of a glorious future or of transforming the world through ideas (even if his idealism takes a materialistic form) seems to be not only fantasy but also an effective action which in itself modifies the empirical world. This is obviously a form of cognitive egocentricism.

This brief description concludes our consideration of the periods of intellectual development as identified by Piaget and his associates. In the next section we consider the educational applications of Piaget's psychology, especially as it pertains to entering behavior.

Jacqueline is given several dolls of varying heights and color and several canes of varying lengths and color. She is asked to put the correct cane with the correct doll. She proceeds to arrange the canes in a row, beginning with the shortest, then moving to the next longest, and so on to the longest cane. She arranges the dolls in the same order, placing the shortest doll above the shortest cane, the next longer doll above the next longer cane, and so on. When asked to make a new arrangement, she reverses the rows, placing the longest cane and tallest doll on the left. Although the colors of the canes and dolls correspond, Jacqueline never matches canes and dolls by color. At what level of intellectual development does Jacqueline appear to be: (a) sensorimotor period, (b) preoperational period, (c) concrete operational period, (d) formal operational period?

After reading the final section of the chapter you should be able to meet the following objectives:

4-18   List three instructional applications of Piaget's study, referring to intelligence tests, curriculum development, and instructional procedures.
4-19   Using the characteristics of the periods of concrete and formal operations, illustrate how the teacher may utilize these characteristics for instructional purposes. Also indicate how the application of these schemes is limited.

ENTERING BEHAVIOR AND INTELLECTUAL DEVELOPMENT

In Piaget's terms, the educational problem is to discover ways to govern the encounters children have with their environments in order to foster rapid rates of intellectual development and satisfying lives (McV. Hunt, 1961, p. 363). In achieving this solution, however, we must avoid both a fruitless pushing of the child beyond his intellectual resources and a fruitless delay in the introduction of intellectual tasks he is ready to pursue. Instruction must accommodate the intellectual level of the student, and, since we can ascertain this level only by studying his behavior, we can say that it must accommodate his intellectual entering behavior. Flavell (1963, pp. 365–69) has suggested three ways in which Piaget's system can be applied to entering behavior.

First, we may be able to develop intelligence tests based on the intellectual tasks Piaget has used in his extensive research. Presently, at the Universities of Geneva and Montreal, developmental scales of reasoning are being evolved in the following content areas: number, quantity, space, geometry, movement, velocity, time, change, causality, logical deduction, logic of relations, and the child's beliefs about the world (realism, animism, and artificialism). Preliminary evidence indicates that the various responses children give to Piaget's tasks in a given content area do show the age and stage differences his theory describes. Further development of these intelligence tests will make possible the assessment of the entering behavior of the child for the learning of particular cognitive tasks as, for example, the learning of certain mathematical and scientific concepts, principles, and problem solutions. In other words, it may be possible to develop a scale of instructional objectives which has a one-to-one correspondence with a scale of reasoning.

Second, we may be able to plan the curriculum on the basis of Piaget's discoveries. This planning should include both the proper grade placement of particular instructional objectives and provisions for guarding against the student's misacquisitions, which are likely to occur when he attempts to master a new area. Flavell gives these examples of questions which could arise and decisions which could be made: Do Piaget's discoveries suggest that teaching the scientific method should be deferred to early adolescence, when the child is capable of formal thought? Is it possible to teach geometry earlier than usual because the child of 8 or 9 has adequate concepts of spatial representation and measurement? Regarding misacquisitions, the teacher may have to steer the child away from the concept of volume, which pertains only to the interior contents of an object, until the student is able to relate the concept to the surrounding space. British educational psychologists are particularly active in linking curriculum development to Piaget's studies (Lovell, 1959, and Peel, 1959).

The third possible application of Piaget's system is in the proper matching of entering behavior and instructional procedures. Indeed, this may be the most important application. It would require the teacher to perform a task analysis based on the operations described by Piaget. The content of instruction implies the operation the student must perform to learn it. And, since these operations possess certain properties, these properties should be incorporated in the instruction. For example, Piaget believes that both reversibility and associativity are essential aspects of thought. If the teacher wanted to incorporate the property of *reversibility*, he would teach multiplication and division, as well as addition and subtraction in alternation. He would follow a problem like ($5 \times 5 = ?$) with the problem ($25 \div 5 = ?$). If he were considering the economic effects of the War Between the States, he would also consider the economic causes of the War (effect to cause). As for the property of *associativity*, in this system the teacher would show the student different routes to the same problem solution. Flavell suggests the example of deriving the equation for the perimeter of a rectangle. The teacher would lead the student to see the equality of the following expressions: $2(b + h) = 2b + 2h = h + b + h + b = h + h + b + b$, and so on.

The recommendation that the teacher analyze the instructional content in terms of intellectual operations rests on two implicit assumptions. First, as Piaget expresses many times, the student must engage directly with the content he is learning. He must perform real actions on these materials, as concrete and direct as possible. These external actions, according to Piaget, become the internal concrete and formal operations of student thought. In Chapter 11, in which we consider discovery learning, we examine the need for student participation in the learning process. Second, Piaget stresses the great importance of having the student interact with his fellow students to liberate him from his egocentricism. Rationality and objectivity are acquired by pitting one's ideas against those of others and observing the distinctions and similarities. Instruction, therefore, must be conducted on a group as well as on an individual basis.

None of these applications of Piaget's system to education gives specific directions for formulating instructional objectives, assessing entering behavior, and selecting instructional procedures. More specific guidance for the teacher must come from research directed toward finding procedures that are consistent with Piaget's theories and that result in the desired level of thought. Although this research is now underway (see, for example, Smedslund, 1961a and b), some basic theoretical issues must be settled before more direct classroom application of Piaget's findings is possible. In the meantime, since Piaget has given us our only well-developed theory of intellectual development, we should use the general guidelines it provides for dealing with the entering behavior of our students.

QUESTION 4-3   A science teacher designed an ingenious apparatus which consisted of a game resembling billiards. The balls were launched from a tubular spring-plunger (as in pinball games), or lever, which could be pivoted in various directions to aim the ball at various points along a projection wall or buffer. The object was to pocket the ball by deflecting it from the wall. The teacher used this game to help students learn the law that the angle of incidence equals the angle of reflection. In presenting this game to children in the third grade, which of the following statements would be most useful in explaining how to make successful shots?

    (a) "You have to move the lever according to the target, and vice versa."

    (b) "If the lever is straight the ball returns exactly."

    (c) "The ball hits the middle of the wall when you hold the lever like this."

After selecting your answer, explain the reasons for your choice and for your rejection of the alternatives.

SUGGESTED READINGS

BALDWIN, ALFRED L., *Theories of Child Development*. New York: John Wiley & Sons, 1970.

HUNT, J. McV., *Intelligence and Experience*. New York: Ronald Press, 1961.

INHELDER, BARBEL, and PIAGET, JEAN, *The Early Growth of Logic in the Child: Classification and Seriation*. New York: The Norton Library, 1969. Selections reprinted by permission of Humanities Press, Inc., New York.

INHELDER, BARBEL, and PIAGET, JEAN, *The Growth of Logical Thinking from Child-*

hood to Adolescence: An Essay on the Construction of Formal Operational Structures. New York: Basic Books, 1958.

PIAGET, JEAN, On the Development of Memory and Identity. Worcester, Mass.: Clark University Press, 1968.

PIAGET, JEAN, The Origins of Intelligence in Children. New York: W. W. Norton & Co., 1963.

PIAGET, JEAN, "Piaget's Theory," in Carmichael's Manual of Child Psychology, ed. Paul H. Mussen, pt. I, pp. 703–32. New York: John Wiley & Sons, 1970.

PIAGET, JEAN, Play, Dreams, and Imitation in Childhood. New York: W. W. Norton & Co., 1962.

PIAGET, JEAN, Psychology and Epistemology. New York: The Viking Press, 1970.

PIAGET, JEAN, Science of Education and the Psychology of the Child. New York: The Viking Press, 1971.

PIAGET, JEAN, and INHELDER, BARBEL, The Psychology of the Child. New York: Basic Books, 1969. One of the clearest and shortest descriptions of their work.

PULASKI, MARY ANN SPENCER, Understanding Piaget: An Introduction to Children's Cognitive Development. New York: Harper & Row, Publishers, 1971.

CHAPTER FIVE

LANGUAGE DEVELOPMENT

The five major sections of this chapter reflect the following general purposes. The first section deals with the nature of language as described by structural linguistics and transformational grammar. The second section describes three theories of language development—those of Piaget, Chomsky, and Jensen. The third section describes four stages of language development: prelinguistic, one-word sentences, two-word sentences, and morphosyntactic. The fourth section deals with sociolinguistics—the influence of social environment on the child's cognitive-linguistic development. The fifth section deals with the implications for teaching modern studies of language and language development.

After reading the first section you should be able to meet the following objectives:

5-1   Describe the major characteristics of human language and relate them to expandable and flexible form and meaning.

5-2 Define phoneme in terms of sound units.

5-3 Define morpheme in terms of phoneme.

5-4 Distinguish between the purposes of structural linguistics and transformational grammar.

5-5 Distinguish between surface and deep structure.

5-6 Define transformational grammar in terms of surface and deep structure.

5-7 Define kernel sentences in relation to other sentences.

THE NATURE OF LANGUAGE

Dolphins and bees have language or communication, but, as far as we know, their languages lack the unique combination of features of human language. Susan Ervin-Tripp (1964) lists three particular features which combine to produce human language: the combination and the recombination of a limited number of elements; the creation of arbitrary meanings for combinations which are conventional in a social group; and the reference to distant objects and events and to intangible concepts. These three characteristics make human language expandable and flexible in form and in meaning. The first characteristic, combination and recombination, makes language expandable in form, so that we can always create sounds, words, and grammatical parts and rules. We continually engage in the rather marvelous act of composing sentences which have never been uttered before, a feat unmatched even by computers with the largest capabilities. The second and third characteristics make language expandable and flexible in meaning. We can invent new terms or give old terms new meanings which are quickly accepted and used by various social groups. The whole nation is frequently delighted by the expansion of vocabulary which accompanies our exploration of space and our attempts to make a safe landing on the moon. The Russians are able to describe their space program in their language. Even the Chinese and French have nuclear and missile programs which their languages if not their foreign policies accommodate very well. All nations, with all their languages, are engaged in a universal discourse on international government and law, which demonstrates the flexibility of all languages. Also, many of the things we talk about—world government, world peace, and an era of human equality—are distant and not always tangible concepts. Unlike animal communication, human communication is not limited to discussion of the present. We can talk about the past and the future and the highly abstract. In education, language accommodates scientific subjects and the physical and creative arts as easily as it accommodates literature and history.

Structural Linguistics

Structural linguistics is the study of language based on actual samples of speech (Bloomfield, 1933). This analysis reveals the basic structures to be found in language itself. Consciousness of language (consciousness, for example, that one has spoken or heard a sentence that makes sense) is *not* the concern of the structural linguists. It ignores both performance and competence and looks to the language itself for its own structure. Their work has been important because of their discovery of what is now called the "surface structure" of language, particularly its sound patterns. To the structural linguists we owe the early study of the phoneme and morpheme.

Phonemes   These are the basic sound units of a language. More particularly, they are bundles of mutually exclusive sounds (Eric Hamp, 1967). In English, for example, *p* has four sounds: A breathed *p* appears at the beginning of words like *peace;* an unbreathed *p* occurs in words such as *spit* and *span;* an exploded *p* occurs in a word like *cup;* and a glottalized *p* is heard when we say the word *peace* immediately after we have taken a drink of water. Each of these is a distinct sound, but in English we have bundled these sounds together into one phoneme, for *p*. That is, we will recognize the phoneme within the range and limits of these four sounds. Similarly, in English we recognize distinctive sounds not heard in other languages. The Spaniard, for example, does not hear the *d* sound in the middle or the end of the word as a distinctive phoneme. For this sound most Spaniards use a voiceless *th*. The characterization which we give foreign languages is the result of hearing those languages through our own patterns of phonemes. When we say that German sounds "guttural," we have only observed a phonemic pattern different from our own, such as *shl* and *tzt* in *shlange* and *jetzt* and the liberal use of the phoneme *ch*. When we call Italian the "lilting" language, among others things we have noticed the double consonant clusters in words like *fratello* and *madonna*. Both the German and the Italian consonant clusters are usually lacking in English. All known languages now employ between twelve and eighty phonemes, and in English (depending on your dialect) we employ between forty and forty-five. Hamp (1967, p. 12) describes phonemes as follows:

> The sounds have no intrinsic meaning of their own; they are merely the smallest contrasted units that can be isolated in a stream of speech. They may be likened to bricks which, though each has its own color, consistency, and character, may be put together to build a wall, a sewer, a well, and even a statue.

Henry Gleason (1965) observes that if you listen carefully when you ask an English-speaking child to utter nonsense, you will notice that it is English nonsense. It is interesting to note that the phonemes do not occur with equal frequency. Nine English phonemes account for 50 percent of the spoken language. The *i* in *hit* is used one hundred more times than the *z* in azure.

Morphemes   These language units consist of phonemes and convey meaning. A morpheme is any form which cannot be divided into two or more forms (Carroll, 1964). Carroll uses these examples: In the words *lighthouse, redbook,* and *unreconstructed,* the morphemes are *light, house, red, book, un-, re-, construct,* and *-ed.* Of the two types of morphemes, *free forms* are those which can stand alone, such as *fish, gold, boy,* and *goldfish. Bound forms* cannot stand alone and occur in ordinary speech with some accompanying form. Examples are *un, -struct,* and *con-.* Hamp points out that many but not all words are free forms. And all free forms are not single words. *The,* for example, is a word, but it is not a free form because it cannot stand alone. Also, *the house* is not a single word, but it is a free form. For the linguist the spaces between words are simply an accident of history. The word *the* could conveniently be attached to the words it precedes.

Originally the linguist saw these units as combining in various ways to produce the grammar or syntax of the language. For example, if he found out how frequently free forms and bound forms occurred and discovered that the bound forms occurred with much higher frequency, he would then state the rules which governed their combination. In this way, he would assemble the forms into a grammar, or a description of the basic structure of the language. Current linguistic theory, however, sees a very different relationship between basic language structure and grammar.

Transformational Grammar

Modern linguists object to the analysis of language in its constituent parts because this analysis obscures aspects of the language about which the native speaker is fully aware. The native speaker, for example, realizes the relationship between sentences which may be quite different in structure. Gleason (1965) states that the native speaker of English would match these sentences without difficulty and in the same way as any other native speaker:

Where are you going?	That is a book.
What is that?	I like that one.
Which one do you like?	I am going tomorrow.
Are you going tomorrow?	I am going home.

The relationship of these sentences does not depend on meaning but on grammar. These sentences are related by rules called *transformations.* All the rules (or transformations) for the English language link together large sets of sentences.

The idea of a transformational grammar was set forth by Noam Chomsky (1957), who tried to explain why the native speaker is able to produce and understand sentences that have never before been written or spoken. Transformational grammar assumes that language is a system of rules and that the application of these rules makes possible the formation and comprehension of new sentences. Knowledge of the language is based on the intuitive mastery of the rules. The rules, in a sense, generate sentences: Applying the rules in a carefully prescribed manner creates only grammatical sentences.

TABLE 5-1   DIFFERENCES IN DEEP AND SURFACE SENTENCE STRUCTURE (after McNeill, 1970, p. 1146)

SENTENCES WITH SAME SURFACE STRUCTURE	PARAPHRASES DIFFERENCES IN DEEP STRUCTURE	NONPARAPHRASES
a. They are buying glasses.	—	—
b. They are drinking glasses.	They are glasses to use for drinking.	They are glasses that drink.
c. They are drinking companions.	They are companions that drink.	They are companions to use for drinking.

Deep and Surface Structure   Examine the three sentences in Table 5-1. We will compare the outer (surface) and inner (deep) aspects of these sentences. All three sentences have the same outer appearance: they begin with *they* (a pronoun), which is followed by *are* (a verb form), followed by a word ending in *-ing* (a progressive form), followed, finally, by words ending in *s* (to indicate a plural noun). A closer look shows that the sentences have different surface structures because the pauses and the articles occur in different locations. Even the stress and intonation of the uttered sentences varies. The difference in surface structure, as you can see, pertains to sound or phonology.

Now look at sentences (*b*) and (*c*). McNeill (1970, p. 1147) points out that these two sentences have the same surface structure but different deep structures. They differ in meaning because of the difference in deep structure. McNeill explains this difference in deep structure as follows:

> Sentence (*b*) means "they are glasses to use for drinking," and sentence (*c*) means "they are companions that drink." Exchanging the form of the paraphrase between (*b*) and (*c*) leads to a nonparaphrase. Sentence (*b*) does not mean "they are glasses that drink" any more than sentence (*c*) means "they are the companions to use for drinking." Despite the identity of surface form, (*b*) and (*c*) differ in underlying form.

McNeill described the distinguishing characteristics of (*b*) and (*c*) as differences in *deep structure*. Although the surface and deep structures are identical in most sentences, every sentence has some kind of surface structure related to some kind of deep structure.

Transformational or generational grammar   Transformational grammar is the name given to the rules that state the relations between surface and deep structures. It is sometimes called *generational* grammar since the use of the rules can theoretically "generate" all the sentences of a language. *Grammar* in this sense does *not* refer to performance (the grammar of performance that we learned in English classes); here, grammar refers to a set of logical relations among sentence parts. The deep structure of sentences is abstract. Deep structure gives the sentence meaning but it is not present in the overt form of the sentence.

All languages require rules of transformation because sound and meaning are independent parts of languages. The transformational rules are the descriptions of the ways sound and meaning are related. The rules themselves do not contribute meaning as much as reveal meaning. According to most scientists of language development, what the child must learn as he acquires language is transformational grammar. To repeat, this is *not* the grammar of how phrases are put together, or the grammar of exercise books used in English class.

Kernel sentences Basic to this conception of transformational grammar is the idea of kernel sentences—those underlying sentences of the language from which all other sentences derive. Here are two examples:

> The puppy came in.
> Alfredo played hooky.

Kernel sentences have two main structures, a *noun phrase* and a *verb phrase*. In the preceding sentences the noun phrases are *The puppy* and *Alfredo*. You will note that Alfredo is a single word, but it is still a noun phrase. The verb phrases are *came in* and *played hooky*. You may believe that the linguist has been guilty of term swapping. After all, is not noun phrase a fancy name for subject, and verb phrase another name for predicate? The distinction is that noun and verb phrases refer to structure, while subject and predicate refer to functions of structures. You recall that the subject is usually defined as the performer of an action, and the predicate as the action. Many sentences, however, contain no performer-action relationship. Some of these may even be kernel sentences, like the following:

> Harriet appeared ecstatic.
> Archibald was funny.

Single transformations Using an example of Gleason (1955), let us consider single transformations. Below are two columns of sentences. The sentences in the first column have been changed into the sentences of the second by the application of a rule.

1	John is writing a letter.	John isn't writing a letter.
2	Jim has been trying to do it.	Jim hasn't been trying to do it.
3	James will come tomorrow.	James won't come tomorrow.
4	Ruth was a beautiful girl.	Ruth wasn't a beautiful girl.
5	Mary could have been there.	Mary couldn't have been there.

This rule covers these transformations: Add *n't* as a suffix to the first word in the verb phrase. Sentence 3 contains a minor complication, since *will* and *n't* do not yield *won't*. But this can be shown to be quite regular. Here, then, is a single rule for negative transformations.

Transformations operate on particular sentence structures and not on others. For example, in these sentences the rule which governs changing a noun phrase to an object position applies:

> We saw Juan on Tuesday.
> Juan we saw on Tuesday.

It does not apply to a noun phrase in these positions:

> We wanted the name of the boy with Michael.
> Michael we wanted the name of the boy with.

In the negative transformation above, the rule about adding *n't* to the first word does not always apply:

> His father walked home.
> His father walkedn't home.

Words like *walked* must be changed to *did walk,* and the *n't* added to the *did.*

Chomsky's transformational grammar is of major importance in studying the relation of language and thought. The transformational rules are a product of the structure of the language and of the psychological processes within the speaker. Jacques Mehler (1963) has found that the recall of English sentences is related to the applications of these rules. George Miller (1962) has explored the relationship of memory to syntactic categories (roughly, parts of speech) and the relation of these categories to the understanding of sentences.

You should now determine how well you have achieved the objectives for section one.

QUESTION 5-1 Which of the following statements best describes the major use of transformational grammar?
   (a) It relates phonemes to language meaning.
   (b) It provides the best analysis of language into its visible constituent parts.
   (c) It is the only analysis available of deep linguistic structure.
   (d) It explains how language competence becomes language performance.

After completing the second section of the chapter, you should be able to meet the following objectives:

5-8 Describe Piaget's theory of language development in terms of sensorimotor and preoperational thinking.

5-9 Describe Chomsky's theory of language development in terms of language competence.

5-10 Describe Jensen's theory of language development in terms of verbal mediation.

5-11 Critique each theory on the basis of how well it relates intellectual and language development.

THEORIES OF LANGUAGE DEVELOPMENT

We shall review three theories of language development. The first theory has been developed by Piaget who believes that language is a construct of intelligence (Piaget, 1970, p. 706). The second theory belongs to Noam Chomsky (1965, 1968) who wrote that language development is the result of maturation—the unfolding of the child's genetic capability for language. The third theory held by learning theorists such as Skinner, Jensen, Palermo, and Lipsit states that language is the result of adults reinforcing the child's attempts to imitate adult speech.

Piaget's Theory: Language as Intelligence

According to Piaget, language emerges only at the end of the sensorimotor period of intellectual development. By the end of that period the child has mastered the notion of objects that are independent of his body and existing in space and time. The child is also sufficiently decentered to know that movements of these objects in space and time are independent of his own body movements. According to Piaget, objects exist only as "indexes and signals" at the end of the sensorimotor period. Indexes are signifiers that stand for objects but are not differentiated from them. For example, the mother's voice is an index of the mother (for the child) but not distinct from the mother. Signals are also not distinct from the object whose presence they signal; the ring of the bell is not differentiated from the bell, for example. In the course of his second year of development, the child acquires a symbolic (or semiotic) function—the ability to use signs and symbols to represent an object that is not present. In games, blocks become symbols of bricks or people. Through the process of imitation, the child begins to make the transition from indexes to symbols. As he develops interiorized imitation (he can imagine an object or event or act), it becomes a source of symbols and language. Piaget (1970, p. 711) states his language theory as follows:

> Why do language and the semiotic function emerge only at the end of a long sensorimotor period where the only significance are indexes and signals, where there are no symbols or signs? (If the acquisition of language were only dependent on an accumulation of associations, as is sometimes claimed, then it could occur much earlier.) It has been shown that the acquisition of language requires at least two conditions be satisfied. First, there must exist a general context of imitation allowing for interpersonal exchange, and second, the diverse structural characters which constitute the basic unit of Chomsky's transforma-

tional grammar must be present. For the first of these conditions to be met means that in addition to the motor techniques of imitation (and this is by no means an easy task) the object, spatiotemporal, and causal decentrations of the second sensorimotor subperiod must have been mastered. For the second requirement, our collaborator H. Sinclair, who specializes in psycholinguistics, has shown (in her recent work which will shortly be published) that Chomsky's transformational structures are facilitated by the previous operation of the sensorimotor schemes, and thus that their origin is neither an innate physiological program (as Chomsky himself would have it) nor an operant or other conditioning "learning" process (as Chomsky, 1959) has shown conclusively.

The following sample of Sinclair's research, illustrating the dependence of language development upon prior intellectual development, is described by Piaget and Inhelder (1969).

> Two groups of children were chosen. The first was clearly preoperatory, that is, these children did not possess the least notion of conservation. The children in the second group accepted one of these notions and justified it by arguments of reversibility and compensation. Both groups were shown several pairs of objects (a large object and a small one; a group of four or five marbles and a group of two; an object that is both shorter and wider than another, etc.) and were asked to describe the pairs when one element of the pair is offered to one person and the other to a second person. This description is thus not related to a problem of conservation. The language of the two groups differs systematically. The first group uses "scalars" almost exclusively (in the linguistic sense): "this man has a big one, that man a small one; this one has a lot, that one little." The second group uses "vectors": "this man has a bigger one than the other man": "he has more," etc. Whereas the first group describes ony one dimension at a time, the second group says: "This pencil is longer and thinner," etc. In short, there is a surprising degree of correlation between the language employed and the mode of reasoning.

In the preoperational period, the child develops the capacity to manipulate signs and symbols—things that stand for objects. At the end of the sensorimotor period, the child's world is still one of concrete objects. His only "thought" about these objects represents his actions upon them. In the preoperational period he can follow signs that point to objects and understand symbols that stand for objects. By using images, perception, and memory, the child is able to represent objects without attempting to move or transform them. Piaget calls these mental images of reality *schema* to distinguish them from schemes which are physical or mental operational activities (Piaget, 1970, p. 704).

Chomsky's Theory: Language as Innate Capacity

Chomsky (1968) believes that the child is programmed at birth with the capacity to master transformational grammar. Chomsky describes this mastery of grammar in the three-year-old as *intuitive*, obviously because three-year-olds could hardly formulate or state transformational rules as described in the previous section. Chomsky (1965) calls this innate language capacity *Language Acquisition Device* (LAD). This device enables the child to produce transformational rules by his analysis of the language he hears and speaks. Thus far there is little empirical evidence to support the existence of LAD.

Chomsky (1965) was one of the first linguists to distinguish between linguistic performance and linguistic competence. McNeill (1970, pp. 1139–40) defines language performance as the "actual acts of speaking and hearing, taking place in time, subject to various distractions, limited by memory and by the general weakness of human flesh." He defines language competence as "knowledge of syntax, meaning, and sound that makes performance possible." Performance refers to observable language behavior, while competence refers to mental phenomena.

Chomsky (1968) believes that children are born with full linguistic competence. Individual differences in performance, even adult as compared with child performance, are *not* due to differences in competence. Performance may lag behind competence because of incidental factors like fatigue and variation in size of memory capacity.

The characteristics of language that help the child utilize his innate language competence are *language universals*. These are general characteristics of all human languages. For example, all languages require that complete sentences have both subjects and predicates. The form of the predicate may vary greatly, but a predicate is always required. The child's innate language competence gives him foreknowledge of these language universals. According to McNeill (1970, p. 1064), these universals are attributable to factors existing outside of language, as in the case of cognition and perception.

Learning Theory: Language as Reinforcement

Two basic components of learning theory apply to language development. The first is reinforcement. In effect, the theory holds that the child acquires adult language as he is reinforced for correct responses and ignored or punished for incorrect responses. Adults reinforce those infant sounds that are closest to adult language performance. Essentially the child produces sounds that he has heard adults utter so that the accurate imitated responses are those for which he is reinforced. The second basic component is pairing. The theory holds that words become associated with other words until elaborate verbal hierarchies are developed.

Arthur Jensen (1966) proposed the following theory for the learning of verbal behavior. (Table 5-2 lists the various types of verbal learning which Jensen describes and the approximate ages at which these learning types develop.)

S_v-*R learning* Verbal learning begins when the child hears words in connection with other stimuli in his environment. Before the age of one the child's environment presents a confusion of noise. The child makes little or no distinction between human speech and other sounds he hears.

TABLE 5-2   TYPES OF VERBAL LEARNING (after Jensen, 1966, 1968)

	LEARNING TYPE	AGE DEVELOPMENT BEGINS
1	S_v-R	One year
2	S-R_v	Two years
3	R_v-R or V-R	Three years
4	S-V-R	Three years
	or S-r-s-R	Three years
5	S-V-R-V_c	Three years
6	S-V-V-R	Three years
7	V-V-V	
	(Verbal hierarchies)	
	V	

Note: R_v refers to an overt verbal utterance, and V refers to a covert verbal utterance.

In S_v-R learning, the child begins to distinguish human speech from other sounds in his environment. In Jensen's notation, S_v refers to a *verbal stimulus*—a syllable, a word, a phrase, and so on. R refers to the physical movement the child makes in response to the verbal stimulus (or S_v). The movement may involve touching, grasping, or otherwise manipulating some object. For example, mother may tell Percival (age 1) to get the ball, and Percival, distinguishing the sound "ball" from the clatter of other household noises, responds by fetching the ball and bringing it to his mother. Ball is the S_v (verbal stimulus), and Percival's action is the response (R). At Percival's age, children respond to words about four times faster than they respond to other sounds in their environment. It is not clear why this is so, but it is possible that the reinforcing effects of making proper responses to verbal stimuli are sufficiently strong to cause a rapid development of this behavior. S_v-R learning represents, then, the simplest form of verbal behavior.

S-R_v learning   In the second and third years of Percival's (or any child's) life, he progresses to more sophisticated verbal behavior. (After all, even the puppy is capable of S_v-R learning.) In S-R_v learning, Percival acquires the ability not only to fetch the ball at his mother's command but also to utter the word "ball" when he sees the ball or has the ball presented to him. In this example, the ball (as object) is the stimulus *(S)* and Percival's utterance of the word "ball" is the response *(R_v)*. To distinguish verbal responses (that is, speech or utterance) from physical movements, Jensen uses the notation R_v instead of R. Between two and three years of age the child is obsessed with pointing to objects, hearing the parent label the object, and then imitating what the parent has spoken. It would almost appear that the child is attempting to catalog everything in his environment. Presumably, at this stage in his development, the child has learned to discriminate between various objects. His verbal learning now consists of discriminating certain sounds and associating these sounds with particular objects. The child's responses constitute labeling behavior which may be seriously lacking in the development of disadvantaged children.

R_v-R and V-R learning   In the third or fourth year the child's movements come under the control of his own verbal behavior. At earlier stages the child's movements are mostly involuntary actions. He responds rather indiscriminately to many stimuli in his environment, and these stimuli control his behavior. At this later stage, however, the child can think the word "run" and start propelling his body through space. Or he can audibly say "run" (really saying it to himself) and start running. Similarly he can control his walking, crawling, grasping, and other manipulatory behavior. At this stage he is no longer tied solely to the physical environment. With his ability to say and think various words he has the capacity to direct his behavior. His movements, however, are not entirely divorced from his environment. R_v-R learning consists of making an overt response to his own spoken response. Percival says "bite" (R_v), and indeed he does bite (R) you. V-R learning consists of making an overt response to his own thoughts. Percival thinks "bite" (V), and he then proceeds to sink his teeth into your flesh.

S-V-R learning   To show the proper relationship among environment, verbal response, and movement, Jensen describes the V-R level as S-V-R learning. S is the environmental stimuli, V is the verbal response (which the child speaks to himself), and R is the physical movements which finally result. For example, Percival sees his big, red ball; he thinks or states to himself that he will run after it (V); and he does run after it (R). He could just as well have thought "crawl," "roll," "throw," "pinch," or "eat"—all covert verbal responses (V) which may be esthetically less appealing but within the possibilities of Percival's verbal behavior. At the level of R_v-R and V-R or, more fully, S-V-R learning, we can begin to distinguish between animal and human behavior. For the most part animal learning does not progress beyond S_v-R learning. The puppy, you may remember, is a slave to the physical stimuli of his environment. He cannot think or say "paw," and, on his own volition, raise his paw. He must wait for the signal (S_v) from Chuck; without this verbal stimulus the puppy is helpless. Human beings, however, can and do respond not only to environmental stimuli but also to words and symbols which these stimuli evoke.

    The addition of the V_c in S-V-R-V_c learning does not indicate another learning type but simply another aspect of S-V-R (or V-R) learning. V_c refers to a verbal confirming response or feedback. Percival sees his big, red, soft ball (S). He thinks that he would like to bite it (V), and he does (R). He then says, "Yum, yum!" (V_c). Percival's approval of his own response, biting the ball, is simply a form of self-reinforcement. His words evoke various responses, and these responses bring certain consequences. If the ball were hard and Percival cracked a tooth in the process of biting it, the V_c would be negative, and Percival might in time give up biting hard balls (or any ball) and limit his consumption to food. The addition of V_c to the S-V-R notation indicates the relationship of reinforcement, particularly self-reinforcement, to the development of verbal behavior.

S-V-V-R learning. Words may also become linked to words in ways which facilitate the association of stimulus and response. Later in the chapter, you will read about the teacher's mediation function in making these associations, and you will see how mediation operates. (At that time we shall also explain the notation, *S-r-s-R,* which also appears in Table 5-2.) In the laboratory study of verbal learning, the subject is sometimes given a particular word and asked to respond with the first word which comes to mind. For example, if we give the subject the word *table,* he will most likely respond *chair.* If we give him the word *man,* he will respond *woman.* Among individuals with the same cultural background, the first responses are very similar. The notation *S-V-V-R* indicates such connections between verbal responses as well as connections between environmental stimuli and verbal responses. To take a crude example, Percival sees the ball *(S),* decides to touch the ball *(V),* which in turn suggests that he bite the ball (the second *V),* and he bites it *(R).* Touch is highly associated with bite in Percival's tender experience.

Verbal hierarchies The last notation in Table 5-2 shows that two words not directly associated with each other may be directly associated with a third word. For example, take the words *table, chair,* and *bed.* Table and chair are strongly associated with each other, but neither is strongly associated with bed. All three words, however, are associated with the word *furniture. Furniture,* in this example, is a higher-order, or more general, word. The relationship of all four words is a verbal hierarchy, with *furniture* at the apex and the words *table, chair,* and *bed* below.

Critiques of Language Theories

Piaget's theory of intellectual development is not a theory of language development. Yet his theory explains better than the others the rapid development of language from $1\frac{1}{2}$ years to 3 years, the end of the sensorimotor period and the beginning of the preoperational period. It is the only theory that links language development to the prelinguistic biological development of the child. Unfortunately Piaget's studies have concentrated on the child's growing ability to manipulate and mentally operate on his object world. He has not given special study to the linguistic world, although some of his co-workers are now turning to the study of the child's construction of language. Study of the child's language development as a product of his developing preoperational schemes is a most promising research area.

Chomsky's theory of innate capacity is not properly a theory of *development* because the child has full language capacity from the start. The chief value of his theory stems from his conception of transformational grammar. Chomsky describes the child's language competence in terms of grammatical rules that relate sound to meaning. As we shall see below, what the child learns (how to form plurals from singular forms, for example) appears to be more complex than the simple association of words. Chomsky's description of *what* the child learns during the process of achieving linguistic competence appears to be much closer to what is revealed by observations of linguistic development (Brown and Bellugi, 1964).

Jensen's theory of language development is really a description of increasingly complex levels of verbal associations. The difficulty with this theory is that verbal associations do not describe the basic language *structure* which the child must master to obtain language competence. The theory is a theory of performance with no underlying theory of the nature of language. Also, the evidence indicates that the child acquires language competence much faster than he could if he were tied to the laborious work of building verbal hierarchies. Finally, the conditions of reinforcement and generalization required by Jensen's theory are not consistently present in the linguistic environment of the child. There is even evidence that mothers typically reinforce their children's speech not on the basis of correct verbal associations but on the basis of the general truthfulness of what the child tried to say (Brown, Cazden, and Bellugi, 1969).

In summary, we can conclude that there is presently no theory of language *development*. However, the work of those psycholinguists and linguists who are studying the relationships between language competence (as defined by Chomsky) and intellectual development (as described by Piaget) holds the greatest promise for the construction of such a theory.

QUESTION 5-2

Percival sees his dog wagging his tail. Percival thinks "touch dog" and he proceeds to touch the dog. What level of verbal development has Percival reached? (a) S_v-R learning; (b) S-R_v learning; (c) S-V-R learning; (d) S-V-V-R learning.

After selecting your answer, give the reasons for your choice and for your rejection of the alternatives.

Upon reading the third section of this chapter you should be able to meet the following objectives:

5-12   Describe the prelinguistic stage in terms of crying, babbling, lallation, and echolalia.

5-13   Describe the one-word-sentence stage in terms of labeling and language structure.

5-14   Describe the two-word-sentence stage in terms of pivot and open classes.

5-15   Describe the morphosyntactic stage in terms of analogic formulations, generalization, telegraphic speech, sentence length, and syntax rules.

5-16   Describe some developmental examples (from the research reported) of language development as related to preschool learning.

STAGES OF LANGUAGE DEVELOPMENT

Harold Vetter and Richard Howell (1971) describe four stages of language development: (1) a prelinguistic stage; (2) a stage of one-word utterances; (3) a two-word stage; and (4) the stage of morphosyntactic developments. In this section, we shall describe each of these stages in turn.

Prelinguistic Stage

In one study (Eisenson, Auer, and Irwin, 1963), the vocal sounds made by the infants were divided into five substages: undifferentiated crying, differentiated crying, babbling, lallation, and echolalia. In the first month of life the infant cries in response to any (nondifferentiated) source of discomfort. In the second month the infant cries in order to get persons to attend to his needs for food, movement, warmth, sleep, and so on. During the third month he begins the cooing that gives way to babbling in the fourth and fifth months. About the sixth month lallation begins—the child appears to be reproducing his own speech sounds. About the seventh or eighth month the child engages in echolalia in which he imitates the sounds produced by others.

Vetter and Howell (1971, p. 4) believe that the child's prelinguistic behaviors are his first attempts to develop the phonemic system of his native tongue. They described the child's phonemic system as "collapsed" because it fails to make the sound-intonation distinctions made by the adult native speaker. They summarize this stage as follows:

> Babbling may result in a measure of cortical control over the quality of vocalizations, but there is no direct correspondence between the number, quality, or sequencing of sounds during babbling and the development of the child's phonemic system. Even if the child of ten months more or less randomly produces virtually any sound which is significant in any language in the world, he can take an additional several years to master the intricacies of his phonemic system without being considered to have a serious articulatory problem. This is well beyond the stage at which he will have mastered the basic grammatical patterns of his language. During the early stages of linguistic behavior phonemic systems are likely to be collapsed, in that a limited range of sounds in the child's repertoire may represent a broad range of sounds in the model. Yet so far as competence is concerned, it can be demonstrated that the child can hear and differentially respond to the greater variation of phonemes in the model. Finally, the child has a strong tendency to apply the findings from one contrast set across the board. That is, the distinctive features, such as voicing, are applied by analogy to contrast sets other than the one for which the discovery was originally made, or demonstrated.

During the last part of the sensorimotor period (from 1 to 1½ years), the child speaks in single words. According to Vetter and Howell (1971, p. 7), the child is learning patterns and structure rather than particular words. Adults seem to replay this experience in learning foreign languages—mastering pronunciation before they take up vocabulary and grammar. These authors also believe that single-word utterances could be studied for both their surface and deep structures to reveal the child's earliest construction of transformational rules. By linking the use of single words to the child's early construction of grammar, these authors follow Piaget in his linking of the use of indexes to the later use of signs and symbols. Vetter and Howell state that the single words can be simply labels rather than sentences, and, in this case, the single words would function only as indexes.

Two-Word Sentences

This period begins at the end of the sensorimotor period and affords evidence the child has reached the level of preoperational thinking that allows him to represent objects with signs and symbols. Vetter and Howell (1971, p. 10) describe this period as follows:

> A two-word sentence is more than a mere joining of two independent entities. As mentioned above, single words such as *push* and *car* carry primary stress and have a terminal intonation contour. But when placed into a single construction, the primary stress and higher pitch fall on *car,* while *push* carries a lesser stress and a lower pitch. . . . The terminal contour remains for car but disappears from *push;* the two-word sequence thus involves a higher level of complexity and implies mastery of two new rules, one having to do with the placing of terminal contours and the other having to do with different stress patterns. A study of the speech of children in the early part of this period revealed that their grammars had two word classes . . . . There were words that belonged to the *pivot* class such as *more, dirty, little, and two.* There were also words that belonged to the open class and made up the rest of the child's vocabulary. Using pivot and open class words the child was capable of such two-word sentences as *more melon* or *my mommy.* He made mistakes such as *a Mary,* or *two melon,* so that his grammar lacked elements of the adult model.

Words belonging to the pivot class are modifiers that indicate quantity (for example, *more*) and quality (for example, *dirty*). Words belonging to the open class are nouns indicating categories of objects (for example, *car, melon*). Vetter and Howell (1971, p. 22) believe that two-word, like one-word, utterances can function as labels (*a Mary* is an expanded name for Mary) as well as sentences such as *push car.*

Morphosyntactic Stage

Vetter and Howell (1971, p. 23) describe this period as containing a number of interrelated processes: analogic formations, overgeneralization, expansion

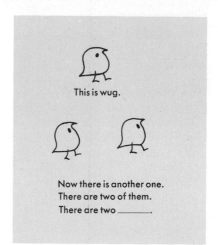

This is wug.

Now there is another one.
There are two of them.
There are two _____.

FIG. 5-1 Child to give the plural of wug after seeing this card (after Berko, 1958, p. 154).

of telegraphic speech, increase in sentence length, and increase in mastery of syntactic rules. Their example of the first two processes (analogic formations and overgeneralizations) are as follows:

> . . . *cat/cats* to *coat/coats*. Analogic formation but overgeneralization can yield forms which are not found in the model, as *foot/foots,* or of the sort *hit/hitted* by analogy with *pit/pitted*. Actually, such "incorrect" forms as *foots* and *hitted* show that the child has a rule for generating the plural and past tense, respectively.

Expansion of telegraphic speech, the next process, involves the omission of function words such as articles and auxiliary verbs.

Some of the earliest studies of the child's acquisition of grammar were done by Jean Berko (1958), Roger Brown (1961), and Brown and Bellugi (1964). Some evidence indicates that the child masters language structure and the transformational rules before he enters school. His mastery, of course, is intuitive in that he can seldom state the rules he is using to create and understand new sentences. Jean Berko (1958), for example, designed a study to find out how much mastery children had of these rules: forming plurals of nouns, forming two possessives of nouns (singular and plural), using the third person singular of verbs, and using the progressive and past tense. All are sophisticated rules, particularly for the children studied, who were in either preschool or the first grade. To be certain that the child had not memorized the correct linguistic form, Berko used nonsense words. She could not, for example, ask the child the plural of *witch* because he might have memorized *witches*. Instead she asked the plural of *wug,* a nonsense word. Figure 5-1 shows one of the cards presented to the child as a test of his knowledge of the rule for forming plurals. Here is one of the questions for testing the rule for past tense:

The card showed a man with a streaming pitcher in his hand and bore this question:
This is a man who knows how to spow. He is spowing. He did the same thing yesterday. What did he do yesterday? Yesterday he _____.

And one for testing the rule for the third person singular:

The card showed a man shaking an object and bore these words:
This is a man who knows how to naz. He is nazzing. He does it every day. Every day he _____.

For five of the nonsense words, well over half the children made the correct responses, which indicated their knowledge of the rule. Berko concluded that if a child's knowledge of English consisted of no more than storing up many memorized words, the child would refuse to answer because he had never, for example, heard of a *wug*. The children's consistent and orderly answers for the grammatical structures, however, indicated their knowledge of the rules.

Children of three to four years appear to be aware of parts of speech. Brown (1957) presented pictures which depicted action for verbs, mass for "count" nouns, and containers for particular nouns. In the case of the verb, for example, the child would be shown a picture and told that he could see *sibbing* (a nonsense verb). He would then be asked to choose one of three pictures which also showed *sibbing*. The child was expected to point to the one picture of the three which depicted motion. This study showed that very young children have knowledge of parts of speech and that they use this knowledge as a clue to the meaning of words.

Also, response terms of adults presented with a list of words for free association belong to the same part of speech as the stimulus terms, while those of young children do not. Adults, for example, respond the word *table* to the word *chair* (two nouns). Children respond *eat* to the word *chair* (a verb and noun). Ervin-Tripp (1961) found that with increasing age (starting from 7 to 12), children respond with the same part of speech.

Little Larry says "little truck" whenever he sees his yellow toy truck. On the basis of this evidence, which of the following sentences best describes the level of Little Larry's language development? **QUESTION 5-3**
  (a) He seems to be arrested at the stage of echolalia.
  (b) His morphosyntactic development has reached the level of verb phrases.
  (c) He has reached the level of two-word sentences if he uses *little* as a pivot word.
  (d) He has reached the level of one-word sentences if he uses *little* as a pivot word and *truck* as a label.

After reading the fourth section of this chapter, you should be able to meet the following objectives:

5-17   Distinguish psycholinguistics from sociolinguistics in terms of language structure and social variables.

5-18   Describe the effects of home environment in terms of Bloom's analysis of the effects of modified home and school environments.

5-19   Describe the effects of home environment on perceptual learning by referring to habits of attending and listening.

5-20   Describe the effects of home environment in terms of the differential between language comprehension and language expression.

5-21   Distinguish between restricted and elaborated codes and their relationship to roles and family context.

5-22   Describe the effects of home environment on types of verbal mediation: labeling, syntactical mediation, word-object stability, feedback, and learning styles.

5-23   Distinguish between Black English and Standard English in terms of vocabulary and language structure.

SOCIOLINGUISTICS

Psycholinguistics is the study of how the child learns the structure of the language that enables him to link sound and meaning. A related study is called *sociolinguistics*. This is the investigation of how the social environment of the child influences his learning of the language structure. According to Hymes (1967), some of these sociolinguistic variables refer to the person the child should speak to, when the child should speak, when the child should remain silent, whose point of view the child takes, and so on. The following section describes the effects of social variables on both cognitive and language development.

Effects of Early Environment

In an impressive analysis of several studies of stability and change in human characteristics, Benjamin Bloom (1964) marshals evidence which indicates that deprivation in the early years of childhood can have far greater consequences than deprivation in later years. Bloom based his conclusions on several types of studies: identical twins reared apart in enriched and impoverished environments; children originally reared in isolated environments and then educated in enriched environments (as in Wheeler's study); black children and the length of their residence in the North; and institutionalized retarded children presented with preschool stimulation. In Table 5-3 we see what Bloom calls the "hypothesized effects of different environments for three age periods." You can see that one-half of the development of intelligence occurs in the first four years. Early deprivation, therefore, can be much more serious than deprivation in the ten years from 8 to 17. You can also see that Bloom is hypothesizing that a change from a deprived

HYPOTHETICAL EFFECTS OF DIFFERENT ENVIRONMENTS ON THE DEVELOPMENT
OF INTELLIGENCE IN THREE SELECTED AGE PERIODS (Bloom, 1964, p. 72).

TABLE 5-3

AGE PERIOD	PERCENT OF MATURE INTELLIGENCE	VARIATION FROM NORMAL GROWTH IN IQ UNITS			
		DEPRIVED	NORMAL	ABUNDANT	ABUNDANT-DEPRIVED
Birth–4	50	—5	0	+5	10
4–8	30	—3	0	+3	6
8–17	20	—2	0	+2	4
Total	100	—10	0	+10	20

to an abundant environment can mean the gain of 20 IQ points. Such a
change, in the realities of our occupational world, can mean the difference
between a profession and a semiskilled laboring job. In Table 5–4 you can
see that the effects of the early environment on school achievement follow
the same pattern. One-third of school achievement is determined before
the child enters school.

Bloom's analysis shows the great importance of the early home environment, the nursery school, and the kindergarten. Much of the child's intellectual development occurs before he enters the first grade. We also see that
another 17 percent of the growth takes place between 6 and 13, which indicates that the elementary school years are the most crucial period of
achievement.

We shall need studies of much greater detail and more precise measures
of environment before we can establish exact relationships between environmental conditions and intellectual and educational development.
Bloom believes that measures of SES (socioeconomic status), social class,
and occupational and educational levels of parents will not give us the
information we need. Bloom refers to an unpublished study by Rich Dave
(1963) of six variables in the home environment: "achievement press," language models, academic guidance, stimulation to explore various aspects
of the larger environment, intellectual interests and activities, and emphasis
on work habits. Dave obtained a correlation of 0.80 between ratings of home
environment on these variables and achievement test battery scores of the

ESTIMATED PERCENTAGES FOR THE DEVELOPMENT OF LEARNING AS BASED
ON VARIOUS MEASURES OF ACHIEVEMENT (Bloom, 1964, p. 110).

TABLE 5-4

AGE	PERCENT OF AGE 18 DEVELOPMENT	
	EACH PERIOD	CUMULATIVE
Birth– 6	33	33
6–13	42	75
13–18	25	100

children. The usual correlations between SES and achievement are less than 0.50. From these results, we can see how studies are becoming more precise in identifying the environmental factors which enhance or block the growth of intelligence.

Perceptual Learning

The earliest form of learning must take place without the benefit of previous learning. Information feeds to the brain through our visual and auditory senses, and, in this way, the environment gains control over areas of the brain (Hebb, 1949). Jensen (1968) has reviewed some of the evidence we have for perceptual learning. Individuals who were blinded by cataracts at birth and who later had these cataracts removed were unable to use their eyes to judge distance, depth, size, shape, perspective, and so on. Although some of the patients were intelligent and successful students, they were unable to recognize a square without carefully counting the corners. They were unable to recognize the familiar forms of doctors and nurses. The patients lacked what is called *perceptual constancy,* or the ability to recognize an object as the same object under a variety of viewing conditions. Perceptual constancy, for example, enables us to recognize a person we know whether we approach him from the rear, the side, or the front. This recognition is probably the result of hundreds of exposures to the same object. Although most of these exposures occur in the earliest years of lives, adults are also capable of perceptual learning. Jensen refers to the experience of laboratory assistants who work with monkeys. At first they cannot distinguish the monkeys. After they have gained experience, however, the monkeys look as different to them as human beings do. Perceptual learning has enabled them to learn those "monkey" characteristics which distinguish individual monkeys.

The development of attention is also involved in perceptual learning. Attention is the central process of the brain which screens, selects, and steers the information we receive through our senses. When J. M. G. Itard (1932) tried to educate Victor, the Wild Boy of Aveyron, he had to teach Victor to pay attention. Victor had so much trouble distinguishing speech sounds from background noises that it was easier for him to understand printed than spoken words.

Cynthia Deutsch (1964) suggests that children living in the ghetto may have more trouble hearing than seeing. We know that repetitious or excessive stimulation causes the organism to become inattentive (see the discussion of optimal stimulation, p. 136). In hearing we often call this inattention *tuning out.* Deutsch suggests that the child raised in a noisy environment with little organized and sustained conversation may fail to distinguish and recognize speech sounds. This child fails to learn to pay attention to others' talking and he also fails to learn any skill, such as reading, which is dependent on auditory learning. Auditory learning should occur before the first grade, before bad listening habits develop. This learning requires a quiet environment, which concentrates auditory stimuli, reduces visual stimuli, and avoids too much repetition and variety. The ordinary nursery school, she suggests, may provide too many distractions and too much noise for these children to acquire auditory learning.

Verbal Mediation

One aspect of language which appears to have crucial importance is the use of verbal mediators. Jensen (1966b, p. 101) defines verbal mediation as "talking to oneself in relevant ways when confronted with something to be learned, a problem to be solved, or a concept to be attained." We think out loud only when problems become difficult. Most mediation is subvocal and unconscious. We shall describe two forms of mediation: labeling and syntactical mediation.

Labeling   An experiment of Vera John and Leo Goldstein (1964) illustrates the use of labels as mediators. They studied the test performance of high and low SES black students in the first and fifth grades. The test consisted of sixteen sample drawings which could be grouped into functional pairs, such as *sailor* and *boat,* or into logically consistent piles, such as *means of transportation* or *animals.* After sorting the cards, the child was asked for the basis of his sorting. One concept was represented by pictures of four men at work: a policeman, a doctor, a farmer, and a sailor. Here are some of the children's explanations for their piles (John and Goldstein, p. 272).

LOW SES CHILDREN	HIGH SES CHILDREN
1 Because the doctor nurses these other people	1 Because they are all men
2 Because the man and big Bill (the policeman) like each other	2 All the same
3 Because they look the same	3 They are both [sic] people

Inspection of these sample responses shows that the high SES black children produced the appropriate name or label, while the low SES black children attended to nonessential details.

Syntactical mediation   This type of mediation is called *syntactical* because it depends on the grammatical structure of the language. Jensen (1966b) illustrates that when normal subjects are asked to learn a list of paired words, they use additional words to link the pairs. For example, if you were asked to learn this list of pairs

HAT—TABLE
TREE—HOUSE
CAT—BED
etc.,

you would use additional words to link together hat and table, tree and house, and so on. Young children and mentally retarded children do not use mediators and, therefore, take longer to learn the list. If, however, the words are imbedded in sentences, then learning is almost immediate for all subjects. The following sentences give examples of imbedded words (Jensen, 1966b, p. 108):

The HAT fell off the TABLE.
The TREE stands beside the HOUSE.
The CAT ran under the BED.

When incomplete sentences are employed the mediators are less effective. For example, "The dirty HAT on the sleeping COW" is not so effective a mediator as "The dirty HAT rested quietly on the sleeping COW."

Word-object stability and feedback   Why do children often fail to develop verbal mediation? The average child learns words and labels by the repeated association of touching and seeing the object and of hearing the name of the object. They hear the name spoken by their mothers, fathers, brothers and sisters, relatives, and by other children. They experience the association of the name and the object as they view television. In low SES homes, John and Goldstein (1964) suggest that the label and the object fail to become associated for two reasons: Low SES homes do not provide the stable conditions which keep object and name properly tied together; and the low SES child is given little or no correction when he misapplies a label to an object.

In pursuing the study of word-object association, through the use of a picture vocabulary test which required the child to point to the correct picture when he heard a particular label, John and Goldstein found that low SES black children have more trouble with action words than with rural and other unfamiliar words. Examples of action words are: *digging, typing, pouring,* and *building.* Rural words are: *leaf, bee, bush,* and *nest.* Unfamiliar words (for these children) are: *kangaroo, caboose,* and *accident.* Why did the children have the most trouble with the action words? The reason may be that the low SES child has not had adequate experience in fitting a label to the various forms of action he has observed. He may have experienced digging or building in many different situations with many different individuals, but the connection between the action and its label was never made clear to him. Also, if the child were to misapply the label and if he were not corrected, or if he were not rewarded for the correct application of the label, the essential conditions for learning the proper use of action words would be lacking. Figure 5-2 indicates the postulated relationship between corrective feedback, stability of the word-referent relationship, and the type of label the child learns. He will find *Coca Cola* and *ball* easiest to learn, *key* and *teacher* more difficult, and the action words the most difficult to learn.

Bruner (1961) believes that some children lack both the richness of environment for developing models and strategies of thought and the cor-

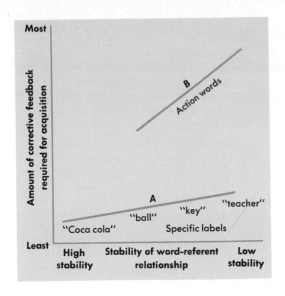

rective feedback necessary for their maintenance. Through models we con serve information in the form of concepts, and through strategies we learn to make inferences or to go beyond the information given.

In summary, evidence indicates that the cognitive development of the child is hampered by a lack of verbal mediators, as indicated by his difficulty in attaching labels to objects and people and by his difficulty with syntactical mediation. We can attribute many of these deficiencies to the lack of word-object stability and feedback in his early experience. Evidence also shows that some children fail to develop learning sets, learning abilities, and learning styles—categories of entering behavior which play a major part in school learning.

Language Codes

Frank Riessman (1962) describes the preference of ghetto children for motoric and physical activity. Even their primary religious expression involves handclapping and singing. Their preference for physical forms is reflected in their participation in and enjoyment of sports and in their physical forms of discipline. Riessman notes several characteristics of the language of these children. They use adjectives better than verbs; they understand more language than they use; they have the verbal ability to fantasize; and they express themselves best in spontaneous and unstructured situations, which precipitate a freer flow of language, because they are not required to make particular responses.

Evidence also indicates that some children comprehend more than they communicate. Arnold Carson and A. I. Rabin (1960) measured comprehension with a picture vocabulary test which required the children merely to point to a specific picture each time a word was read from the vocabulary list. To measure communication these children were required to give definitions for the vocabulary words of an intelligence test and also for the vocabulary words of a picture test. The children were fourth, fifth, and sixth grade black and white children. Some of the black children were born and reared in the North, and some were born in the South but reared in the North. Interestingly enough, the results showed that the children could understand more than they could communicate. On all tests, the whites did better than the northern-born blacks, who did better than the southern-born blacks. Whereas the whites were able to give the critical feature and function of the word they defined, the northern-born blacks often gave vague responses, and southern-born blacks gave many "don't know" responses.

Basil Bernstein (1961) distinguished between the *restricted code* (or language) of the lower SES group and the *elaborated code* of the higher SES group. These are the characteristics of the restricted code:

1 Short, grammatically simple, often unfinished sentences with a poor syntactical form stressing the active voice.
2 Simple and repetitive use of conjunctions (so, then, because).
3 Little use of subordinate clauses to break down the initial categories of the dominant subject.
4 Inability to hold a formal subject through a speech sequence; thus a dislocated informational content is facilitated.
5 Rigid and limited use of adjectives and adverbs.
6 Infrequent use of impersonal pronouns as subjects of conditional classes.
7 Frequent use of statements where the reason and conclusion are confounded to produce a categoric statement.
8 A large number of statements and phrases which signal a requirement for the previous speech sequence to be reinforced: "Wouldn't it? You see? You know?" etc. This process is termed "sympathetic circularity."
9 Individual selection from a group of idiomatic phrases or sequences will frequently occur.
10 *The individual qualification is in the sentence organization: It is a language of implicit meaning.* (Bernstein, 1961, p. 169)

The restricted code seriously limits the scope of expression and thought. Thoughts are strung together somewhat like beads on a frame and do not follow a planned sequence. Much information is repeated, as in the following illustration of the speech of a sixteen-year-old English boy of normal intelligence (Bernstein, 1961, p. 171):

It's all according like these youths and that if they get into these gangs and that they most have a bit of nark around and say it goes wrong and that and they probably knock someone off I mean think they just do it to be big getting publicity here and there.

The elaborated code has the following characteristics:

1 Accurate grammatical order and syntax regulate what is said.
2 Logistic modifications and stress are mediated through a grammatically com-

plex sentence construction, especially through the use of a range of conjunctions and subordinate clauses.

3 Frequent use of prepositions which indicate logical relationships as well as prepositions which indicate temporal and spatial contiguity.

4 Frequent use of the personal pronoun "I."

5 A discriminative selection from a range of adjectives and adverbs.

6 Individual qualification is verbally mediated through the structure and relationships within and between sentences.

7 Expressive symbolism discriminates between meanings within speech sequences rather than reinforcing dominant words or phrases, or accompanying the sequence in a diffuse, generalized manner.

8 It is a language use which points to the possibilities inherent in a complex conceptual hierarchy for the organizing of experience. (Bernstein, 1961, p. 172)

The elaborated code, according to Bernstein, makes the intended meaning of the speaker explicit. It also supplies him with many more alternatives for elaborating and expressing his thoughts. Middle-class children have access to both codes, working-class children, only to the restricted code. The problem with the restricted code is not the lack of vocabulary since the evidence indicates that the number of adjectives and adverbs does not vary in either code when speakers are matched for age and very high nonverbal IQ. Bernstein also notes that, despite the warmth and vitality of the restricted code, it tends to be impersonal because the personal meaning of the speakers is never explicit. Bernstein wrote that the use of the restricted code has far-reaching consequences for the child (1961, p. 174):

In the learning of this linguistic form, the child is progressively oriented to a relatively low level of conceptualization. It induces a lack of interest in processes, a preference to be aroused by, and to respond to, that which is given immediately, rather than responding to the implications of a matrix of relationships. In turn, this will affect what is to be learned and how it is learned and so influence future learning. There will be a tendency to accept and respond to authority which inheres in the form of the social relationship which maximizes the identifications with aims and principles of the local group rather than with the complex differentiated aims of the wider society. Finally, and of greatest importance, it is the language of implicit meaning in which it becomes progressively more difficult to make explicit, and to elaborate verbally, subjective intent.

The child experiences in school the consequences of knowing only the restricted code since the teacher uses the elaborated code. What is an opportunity for linguistic development for one child is a situation of linguistic change for the disadvantaged child. The teacher's job, according to Bernstein, is to preserve for the child the appeal and dignity of his accustomed code while making available to him the possibilities of expression in the elaborated code.

In later formulations of his theory of linguistic codes, Bernstein (1969) describes four family contexts in which the two codes can be used. (1) In the regulative context, the authority figures make the child aware of the "rules of moral order." (2) In the instructional context, the child learns about objects and persons and acquires skills. (3) In the innovative context, the authority figures encourage the child to experiment and invent his world in his own terms. (4) In the interpersonal context, the authority figures make the child aware of his own and other's emotional states. Elaborated and restricted codes interact with these four family contexts and produce particular language styles. The implication of this later formulation is that the socialization of the young within the family (as well as within the family's social class) affects the linguistic styles of the children.

There seem to be four major classes of effects deriving from the interaction of family context and linguistic code: (1) The style may be universalistic in the sense that it is independent of context. (2) The style may be particularistic or context dependent. (3) The style may be specific in the sense that the speaker shapes his meanings to the specific attributes of the problem or situation he is dealing with. (4) The style may be nonspecific when meanings are not shaped to context.

Black English

William Labov (1970) has presented evidence that there is a logic in nonstandard English, specifically the English spoken by black children in Harlem. Labov believes that this evidence weakens the "verbal deprivation" hypothesis and genetic theory of Jensen (1968).

The deprivation hypothesis asserts that, because black children receive so little verbal stimulation in their early years (especially as well-formed language), their means of verbal expression is seriously impoverished. This was the hypothesis which Jensen believed the Head Start programs had tried, but failed, to prove. Before Jensen published his article in the *Harvard Educational Review* (1968), he was impressed with the deprivation hypothesis.

Labov used the same theory and evidence to reject both the deprivation and genetic hypotheses, believing that the second hypothesis is the inevitable result of the first. The evidence came from interviews with black children in Harlem. Labov's analysis of the interview with a black adolescent named Larry, for example, showed the richness of Larry's logic, the speed and precision of his argument, the avoidance of unnecessary verbiage, and, indeed, the color of his speech. Linguistic analysis of the speech of black children showed a high-level logic which avoided the convolutions of middle-class speech. Labov believes that we are dealing with stylistic rather than grammatical differences.

Labov (p. 72) gives the following example of the logic of NNE—nonstandard Negro English:

> Let us consider for a moment the possibility that Negro children do not operate with the same logic that middle-class adults display. This would inevitably mean that sentences of a certain grammatical form would have different truth values for the two types of speakers. One of the most obvious places to look for such a difference is in the handling of the negative, since we encounter here one of the non-standard items which has been stigmatized as illogical by school teachers: the double negative, or as we term it, negative concord. A child who

says "He don't know nothing" is often said to be making an illogical statement without knowing it. According to the teacher, the child wants to say "He knows nothing" but puts in an extra negative without realizing it, and so conveys the opposite meaning, "he does not know nothing" which reduces to "he knows something." I need not emphasize that this is an absurd interpretation: if a non-standard speaker wishes to say that "he does *not* know *nothing*," he does so by simply placing contrastive stress on both negatives, as I have done here. He *don't* know *nothing*, indicating that they are derived from two underlying negatives in the deep structure. But note that the middle-class speaker does exactly the same thing when he wants to signal the existence of two underlying negatives: *He doesn't know nothing.* In the standard form *He doesn't know anything*, the indefinite *anything* contains the same superficial reference to a single preceding negative in the surface structure that the non-standard *nothing* does. In the corresponding positive sentences, the indefinite *something* is used. The dialect difference, like most of the differences between the standard and non-standard forms, is one of surface form, and has nothing to do with the underlying logic of the sentence.

We can summarize the ways in which the two dialects differ as follows:

SE
Positive: He knows something.
Negative: He doesn't know anything.
Double Negative: He *doesn't* know *nothing*.

NNE
Positive: He know something.
Negative: He don't know nothing.
Double Negative: He *don't* know *nothing*.

This array makes it plain that the only difference between the two dialects is in superficial form. When a single negative is found in the deep structure, SE converts *something* to the indefinite *anything*, NNE converts it to *nothing*. When speakers want to signal the presence of two negatives, they do it in the same way. No one would have any difficulty constructing the same comparison of truth values for both dialects.

Joan Baratz (1969) found evidence that Black English was a highly developed language, different than but not logically inferior to Standard English. In her study, sentences were constructed that used the language structure of Black English. Here are some of the sentences she used (Baratz, 1969, p. 12):

1 That girl, she ain' go ta school 'cause she ain' got no clothes to wear.
2 John gave me two books for me to take back the liberry 'cause dey overdue.
3 I's some toys out chere and the chil'run they don' wanna play wid dem no more.
4 Does Deborah like to play with the girl that sits next to her in school?
5 The teacher give him a note 'bout de school meetin' an he 'posed to give it ta his mother to read.
6 John he always be late for school 'cause he don't like ta go music class.
7 My aunt who lives in Baltimore used to come to visit us on Sunday afternoons.
8 Do Deborah like to play wid da girl that sit next to her at school?

The sentences were given to both black and white students who were asked to repeat them exactly as they heard them. She found that black children performed significantly better than white children in repeating these sentences. When the standard English versions of these sentences were given to both groups of children, the white children performed significantly better. Baratz believes her results indicate that black children are not bidialectical (equally skilled in standard and nonstandard English) and that Black English may actually interfere with their learning of Standard English. She believes that the schools should teach black children to read in their black vernacular before they are taught to read Standard English.

J. L. Dillard's *Black English: Its History and Usage in the United States* (1972) is the best treatment we now have of Black English. Dillard (pp. 43–45) points out the basic differences in Standard and Black English. He states that verbs in the aspect category

> . . . are marked for the ongoing, continuous, or intermittent quality of an action rather than for the time of its occurrence. This is the only obligatory category in the Black English verb system. This is perhaps the most basic difference from Standard English, since a speaker of Standard English must mark tense but can choose to indicate or to ignore the ongoing or static quality of an action. Black English gives the speaker an option with regard to tense, but its rules demand that he commit himself as to whether the action was continuous or momentary.
>
> The sequence *don' be* (or, in the affirmative *be*) has a special function which is not marked in the Standard English verb. It indicates that the time of the action is "stretched out"—that it is reportably long for the kind of action involved in the verb being used. [*He be waitin' for me every night when I come home.*]

Dillard provides convincing evidence that Black English differs in both structure and vocabulary from Standard English. He also believes that Standard English should be taught to blacks as a second language.

QUESTION 5-4   Mr. Peabody has a class of disadvantaged children. To teach them the concept *sailor*, he shows them various pictures of men at work. Several show men in white hats and bell-bottomed trousers, working on or about sailing vessels. Other pictures show policemen, firemen, carpenters, and farmers at work. Which of the following procedures should Mr. Peabody adopt to teach this concept?

(a) Have the children repeat "sailor" each time they see a picture of a sailor.

(b) As each picture is presented, ask the children, "Is this a sailor?" and have them reply "yes" or "no."

(c) Have the children identify the other workers by name, but have them say only "yes" when they see a picture of a sailor.

(d) Supply each child with a set of pictures and have him sort them into sailor and nonsailor piles.

After selecting your answer, give the reasons for your choice and for your rejection of the alternatives.

After completing the last section of this chapter, you should be able to meet the following objectives:

5-24 Describe the major reason why linguistics now has limited applications to teaching by referring to teaching methodology.

5-25 Distinguish between Fries's method and Pitman's method of teaching grapheme-phoneme relationships.

5-26 Illustrate the child's knowledge of grapheme-phoneme relationships through the use of pseudowords.

5-27 Describe the three characteristics of the audiolingual method of teaching foreign languages and distinguish it from the direct method.

5-28 Describe the major functions of the language laboratory and illustrate how it could be modified to provide for reinforcement of student responses.

LINGUISTICS AND TEACHING

It has been "embarrassingly fashionable" to discuss the contributions of linguistics to the teaching of the language arts. John Carroll (1964, p. 179) has written:

> One's embarrassment comes from the fact that despite certain very definite and positive contributions that linguistics can make to these endeavors, these contributions are of relatively small extent. Once we accept such fundamental tenets of linguistics as the primacy of speech over writing, the structure of the language code as a patterning of distinctive communicative elements, and the arbitrariness of standards of usage, and work out their implications in detail, we find that we are still faced with enormous problems of methodology in the teaching of such subjects as English, reading, and foreign languages.

With this caveat, we shall now consider the contribution of linguistics to the teaching of reading and foreign languages.

Instruction in Reading

Structural reading   The basic tenet of Charles Fries (1963) is that we should shift from a word-centered to a structure-centered view of language. Fries describes three stages of learning to read: (1) In the transfer stage, the child must learn to respond rapidly and accurately to the visual patterns of the printed page. This stage should be accomplished by presenting the child with two letters or two simple words at a time and asking him to respond by saying that they are alike or different. (2) The child should overlearn the printed shape of letters and words until he can respond to meanings implicit in the letters and shapes. The child should not be taught the connections between phonemes and graphemes (the printed forms) but should be allowed to discover the connections himself. Fries (unlike Sir James Pitman, whose method is discussed subsequently) uses only capital letters to accomplish this end. (3) Finally, the child should learn "vivid imaginative realization" of the values involved in the action or experience he reads about. For this the child should read poetry. Fries's method shows the linguistic emphasis on learning language structure and on deriving meaning from knowledge of structure.

Convincing evidence indicates that a child who learns to read well is forming useful spelling-to-sound habits which relate English phonemes to graphemes. In fact, linguists can predict pronunciation from spelling. The child masters the phonemes of his language before he begins to read. In learning to read he must discover how phonemes, or sounds, correspond to graphemes, or the written sound. Possibly the child learns grapheme-phoneme rules in the way he learns transformation rules. In any case, he is able to use both rules long before he is able to state them. Eleanor Gibson and her associates (1962) constructed pseudowords on the basis of spelling-to-sound rules. The pseudowords are of two types: (1) those which are pronounceable and follow the rules and (2) those which are unpronounceable and ignore the rules, but which consist of the same letters as the pronounceable words. Among the pronounceable words are *dink, vuns, glox, slub,* and *lods.* Some of the derived unpronounceable words are *nkid, nsuv, xogl, lbus,* and *dsol.* Gibson found that the curve for the pronounceable words was consistently higher than the curve for the unpronounceable words. Figure 5-3 shows the results of the study. The percentage of correct response rises sharply between the first and second exposure and increases very little thereafter. These findings strongly suggest that the proper unit for use in analyzing the processes of reading and writing is not the alphabetical letter but the spelling pattern which has a stable relationship with the phonemic pattern. The reading of words becomes inseparable from the hearing of words.

The initial teaching alphabet With considerable ardor, Pitman and his associates encourage the use of a reformed alphabet for use in beginning reading (Harrison, 1964). Pitman has developed an alphabet in which one

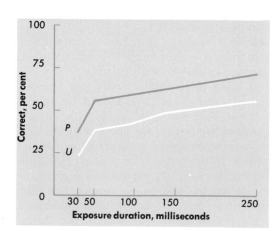

FIG. 5-3 Percentage of correct responses for pronounceable (*P*) and unpronounceable (*U*) words (Gibson et al., 1962, p. 562).

sign represents one sound and one sound only (see Tables 5-5 and 5-6). There is, for example, only one sign for the letter *g*. Pitman uses lower-case letters; if a capital is required, the lower-case letter is written large. He writes digraphs (two letters with a single speech sound) as one letter. For example, *mishap,* in which *s* and *h* have different sounds, can be distinguished from *bishop,* in which the *sh* has one sound. When the child is ready, the conventional alphabet replaces the new alphabet. Pitman and his followers have furnished some preliminary evidence that the use of the new alphabet with beginning readers enables them to learn to read conventional materials in less time than conventional reading programs require (Downing, 1964). Important is the fact that the forty-five characters of the new alphabet roughly reflect the English phonemes and try to preserve their sound value while the child is learning to make the transition from speaking to reading.

Instruction in Foreign Languages

Although there has been growing insistence that children learn foreign languages in our schools, very little research supports the feasibility of such a policy. Sometimes the available evidence has been ignored by those educators who are attempting to shape public school policy. One fact that has been ignored, for example, is the wide spread of individual differences in

THE INITIAL TEACHING ALPHABET (Harrison, 1964, pp. 110–11)   TABLE 5-5

b	bee	bat	bat	ϯh	ith	ϯhaut	thought
c	kee	cut	cut	ᵭh	thee	ᵭhis	this
d	dee	det	debt	wh	whay	whær	where
f	ef	fit	fit	ʒ	zhee	meʒuer	measure
g	gay	got	got	y	yay	yot, sity	yacht, city
h	hay	hunt	hunt	æ	aid	cæs	case
j	jay	jest	jest	a	at	caʃh	cash
k	kay	aks	axe	ɑ	ahd	cɑm	calm
l	ell	lip	lip	a	ask	casl	castle
m	em	mous	mouse	e	et	net	net
n	en	nævy	navy	ɛɛ	eed	nɛɛt	neat
p	pee	pens	pence	i	it	nit	knit
r	ray	rist	wrist	ie	ide	niet	night
ɼ	er	first	first	o	ot	not	knot
s	ess	sord	sword	œ	ode	nœt	note
t	tee	tiet	tight	u	ut	tuf	tough
v	vee	velvet	velvet	ue	ued	tuen	tune
w	way	wun	one	ω	oot	tωk	took
z	zed (or zee)	zɛɛbra	zebra	ω	ood	tωϯh	tooth
ᴢ	zess	horseᴢ	horses	au	aud	taut	taught
ᴄh	chay	ᴄhurᴄh	church	oi	oid	toi	toy
ŋ	ing	briŋiŋ	bringing	ou	owd	toun	town
ʃh	ish	ʃhaft	shaft				

a spesimen ov i.t.a. printiŋ

ie hav just cum from a scœl whær ðhe nue reediŋ is taut.
ie met ðhær a littl girl ov siks. ſhee is ðhe œldest ov a larj
family liviŋ on an œldham housiŋ estæt. tœ yeers agœ ſhee
wos a ſhie nervus chield, tœ frietend tœ tauk. ſhee has wun
priezd personal posseſhon—a dog-eerd antholojy ov vers,
given tœ her bie an œlder chield. ðhat littl girl ov siks has
just red tœ mee very buetifœlly wurdswurth's daffodils. ie
askt her whie ſhee chœs ðhat pœem. ſhee replied ðhat ſhee
luvd daffodils.

tœdæ ſhee speeks with charm and confidens. ðhe œnly
critisism ov her reediŋ ov ðhe pœem miet bee ðhat ſhee red
it raðher kwickly, tœ neerly at ðhe speed ov sielent reediŋ.
ſhee found ðhe pæj in ðhe bœk bie lœkiŋ up ðhe pœet's næm
in ðhe alfabetical indeks.

œnly ðhe sircumstanses ov ðhat story ar novel. ðhe
acheevment ov ðhat littl girl ov siks yeers is ov itself færly
commonplæs in œldham nouadæs.

octœber, 1963

language aptitude, even among students of average and superior intelligence. Here, however, we shall limit our attention to the contribution of
linguistics to the teaching of foreign languages.

The audiolingual method   George Scherer and Michael Wertheimer (1964)
describe this method in this way:

> The audiolingual method is characterized by intensive drills in speaking and
> listening through dialogues which are memorized and pattern drills which are
> thoroughly learned by the student. Instead of encouraging free conversation at
> first, the teacher uses directed dialogues which employ the learned patterns.
> While the foreign language is used as much as is practically possible in the class-
> room, English may be employed for the explanation of structure and, in varying
> degrees, for the teaching of meaning. Although grammar is not taught as an end
> in itself, the materials are constructed so that the students can arrive at its com-
> prehension by induction. After the examples have been drilled, the grammar is
> discussed and clarified.

The audiolingual method is distinct from the direct method of language instruction, which bans English entirely and excludes formal grammar.

Scherer and Wertheimer (1964) conducted an intensive evaluation of the comparative merits of audiolingual (AL) and traditional (T) language instruction using beginning students of German. At the end of two years of study, these were the results: (1) The groups were equal in listening ability; (2) the AL group was far superior in speaking; (3) the groups were equal in reading; (4) the T group was superior in writing; (5) the groups were equal in English-to-German translation; and 6) the T group was far superior in German-to-English translation. In brief, the new method did not result in equal or superior performance in reading, writing, listening, or translation. The AL students, however, did report a more positive attitude than did the T students toward German and themselves while speaking German. The results of the study hardly support a radical change in foreign language teaching.

The language laboratory In the past decade there have been several attempts to provide more opportunity for students to hear and speak the foreign language they are studying. The language laboratory has been the most popular technical innovation for providing this opportunity. The language laboratory, as Carroll (1960) remarks, is a misnomer since it is no more like a laboratory than a music practice room or a gymnasium is. It is essentially an opportunity for the students to hear the language spoken by a native and to practice speaking the language themselves. Traditional language teaching, unless the circumstances are ideal, does not usually allow as much time for oral and auditory experience as the student needs to develop speaking skill. Carroll remarks (p. 138), "Trying to teach a spoken foreign language without it [auditory stimulation] would be like trying to teach music appreciation solely from printed musical scores."

In the language laboratory, the student usually listens to a tape recording of a native speaker talking in a particular language. The tapes have spaces which allow the student to repeat what the speaker has said and then to listen once more to what the speaker said the first time. Lawrence Mace and Evan Keislar (1965) have found convincing evidence that the passive listening to tapes in the language laboratory is not enough. A more effective procedure requires the student to make overt responses which are evaluated for their accuracy. In their study, each student received discrimination training in the sounds of the language. The native voice spoke a pair of words, one of which was the correct pronunciation of a French phoneme. The student selected the word he thought correct and was then told the correct answer. He then heard the word again. Finally, the speaker said one word of each pair; the subject circled his choice of which word it was in the booklet and then was given the correct answer. This procedure provided for student participation and instructional feedback. In a later study, Mace (1966) found that training in speaking should precede training in listening to develop listening comprehension. This sequence reverses the ordinary procedure of the audiolingual method.

Many students in the past with traditional methods and many students in the present with a combination of traditional and audiolingual methods have learned and will continue to learn and even master foreign languages. The heralded technological changes for education have revolutionized foreign language instruction no more than they have any other part of the school curriculum.

Summary This section dealt with linguistics and teaching. Human language is unique because it is expandable and flexible in both form and meaning. It is composed of structural units such as the phoneme and the morpheme. Phonemes are the basic sound units of the language. Morphemes are phonemes which convey meaning. Transformational grammar explains why the native speaker is able to produce and understand sentences that have never been written or spoken before. It assumes that languages are systems of rules and that the application of these rules makes possible the formation and comprehension of new sentences. Kernel sentences are the underlying sentences of the language from which all other sentences derive. Some evidence indicates that the child intuitively masters language structure and transformational rules before his formal education. The application of linguistics to teaching appears at this time to be limited because of our lack of knowledge about teaching methodology and the language arts. Fries argues for discovery learning on the part of the child in linking phonemes and graphemes. According to him, beginning reading should emphasize visual patterns. The research of Gibson and her associates shows that the reading of words is inseparable from the hearing of words. The Initial Teaching Alphabet attempts to simplify beginning reading by making graphemes phonemic. As yet little or no evidence supports the use of the audiolingual over the direct method of foreign language instruction. The language laboratory provides the obvious advantage of allowing the student to hear the language spoken by a native speaker and to practice speaking the language himself.

SUGGESTED READINGS

These are published symposia and books of readings on many aspects of verbal learning and the psychological study of language (psycholinguistics):

BARATZ, JOAN C., "Teaching Black Children to Read," in *Teaching Black Children to Read,* eds. J. Baratz and R. Shuy, pp. 92–116. Washington, D.C.: Center for Applied Linguistics, 1969.

BERNSTEIN, BASIL, "Sociolinguistic Approach to Socialization," in *Direction in Sociolinguistics,* eds. H. Gumperz and D. Hymes. New York: Holt, Rinehart & Winston, 1969.

DE CECCO, JOHN P., ed., *The Psychology of Language, Thought, and Instruction.* New York: Holt, Rinehart & Winston, Inc., 1967.

DILLARD, J. L., *Black English: Its History and Usage in the United States.* New York: Random House, 1972.

KAUSLER, DONALD H., ed., *Readings in Verbal Learning.* New York: John Wiley & Sons, Inc., 1966.

LABOV, WILLIAM, *The Logic of Non-Standard English*. Georgetown University Monograph Series on Language and Linguistics, Monograph No. 22. Washington, D.C.: Georgetown University Press, 1970.

McNEILL, DAVID, "The Development of Language," in *Carmichael's Manual of Child Psychology*, ed. P. H. Mussen, vol. 1, pp. 1061–1161. New York: John Wiley & Sons, Inc., 1970.

OSSER, HARRY, "Language Development," in *Psychology and the Educational Process*, ed. G. S. Lesser. Chicago: Scott, Foresman & Co., 1971.

SAPORTA, SOL, ed., *Psycholinguistics*. New York: Holt, Rinehart & Winston, 1961.

VETTER, HAROLD J., and HOWELL, RICHARD W., "Theories of Language Acquisition," Florida State University, in mimeo.

CHAPTER SIX

MOTIVATION

This chapter chiefly helps you to develop a conceptualization of the motivational functions of the teacher. The first of the three sections, which is quite brief, defines motivation in a way which distinguishes it from learning and relates it to entering behavior. The second section introduces the basic theory of and research on motivation. The research reported forms the basis for the four motivational functions of the teacher described in the third section: the arousal, expectancy, incentive, and disciplinary functions. Motivational functions refer to rather broad categories of teacher behavior. Motivational functions, successfully enacted by the teacher, maintain and increase student effort without necessarily initiating or directing learning.

A chapter on motivation must deal with the student's attitudes, values, and, in general, his personality. Although these topics are often given more extensive treatment than they are in this book, everything about them in terms of instructional practice is contained in the description of the four motivational functions of the teacher.

Upon reading this first section, you should be able to meet these objectives:

6-1   List the characteristics of the concept of motivation and distinguish between behavior which is best explained in terms of motivation and behavior which is best explained in terms of habits, abilities, external stimuli, and so on.
6-2   Describe the relationship between motivation and entering behavior in terms of relative response strength.

A DEFINITION OF MOTIVATION

Motivation refers to those factors which increase and decrease the vigor of an individual's activity. Thus it determines the levels or degree of his activity. In the following treatment we will not use the concept of motivation to explain the initiation and direction of activity, which are more fully explained in terms of learning. Here we are concerned only with the factors which increase and decrease student activity. In educational parlance motivation is often called *effort*. In terms of effort, the study of student motivation searches for those factors which increase the student's effort to make desirable responses.

The modern teacher may motivate students by combining careful distribution of rewards with mild threats of punishment, somewhat forceful cajolery with benign tolerance of mistakes made in the line of duty, and concessions to immature interests and foibles with frequent reminders of what the student finally must learn. He may be warm and enthusiastic but may still insist on an orderly and businesslike classroom. If the modern teacher no longer slaps faces, thrashes bottoms, or rules the back of hands (at least in most suburban schools), he still furrows a mean brow and grimaces when displeased. He may no longer string gold stars after the names of successful students, but he has learned the advantage of a well-timed smile and a pat on the head or shoulder. To motivate his students, he may deliver short sermons on the ultimate salvation and glory of those who persevere and succeed and on the ultimate damnation of those who surrender the task of today to whim and fancy. He may consciously shape himself into the humane and intellectual model he wants his students to imitate. And at times he may share control of the classroom and of the lesson plan with the students, hoping that they will provide conditions which enhance their creative endeavors and satisfy their intellectual curiosity.

As students we have all been exposed to (and perhaps even victimized by) a magnificent array of motivational devices and procedures. For punishment teachers have used the verbal reprimand, either spoken or shouted; the check mark in the roll book; the birch rod; the ruler; and the dunce hat. Teachers have pulled ears and hair, made students stand in corners or corridors, detained them after school, banished them to the principal's office, expelled them from school, and made them return from exile in the company of their parents.

The list of rewards, although not so dramatic, is equally impressive and inexhaustible. Teachers have praised students, both publicly and privately, for work well done; have given the seat or seats of honor to those who distinguish themselves; have publicly displayed notebooks, paintings, and projects of superior merit; have awarded the perennial gold stars; and have devised graphs and charts to show how much the students are "growing in knowledge." They have arranged field trips, movies, special projects, and free periods. For some students reward takes the form of positions of privilege—teacher's chief helper, classroom president, aquarium caretaker, bird feeder, school president, and valedictorian. For others the reward is relief—relief that the class, semester, or school year is over; that the project is finished; or that, by law, their education is forever terminated.

Motivation As the Source of Vigor

Motivation is one of the most popular topics in educational, psychological, and business circles. Popular magazines frequently carry inspirational articles which suggest that by being sufficiently aroused or by finding the means of self-arousal an individual can solve all his problems of work, marriage, friendship, child raising, drinking, eating, and sexual relations. Vance Packard (1957, p. 5) reveals how psychology professors (in his opinion) have become merchandisers by using their knowledge to "sell you cake mixes, cigarettes, cars, soaps, and even ideas." These professors, he writes, use MR (motivation research) to find out how people make choices. In this research they employ techniques "designed to reach the unconscious or subconscious mind because preferences generally are determined by factors of which the individual is not conscious" (1957, p. 5). Packard continues (p. 4):

> What the probers are looking for, of course, are the *whys* of our behavior, so that they can more effectively manipulate our habits and choices in their favor. This has led them to probe why we are afraid of banks; why we love those big fat cars; why we really buy homes; why men smoke cigars; why the kind of car we drive reveals the brand of gasoline we will buy; why housewives typically fall into a hypnoidal trance when they get into a supermarket; why men are drawn into auto showrooms by convertibles but end up buying sedans; why Junior loves cereal that pops, snaps, and crackles.

Packard seems to conclude that the motivation researchers know the answers to all these and other questions and that we are now the passive victims of their artful manipulation. Lay and professional people seem to agree with Packard in assuming that motivation is the sole determinant of behavior.

In the above quotation Packard described the "probers" as looking for the "whys" of our behavior. He goes on to suggest that the whys are found in research on motivation. We now know that Packard's position would assign the entire study of human behavior to the area of motivation. His position represents a vast overcommitment to one among many areas of modern psychology. Why do we behave—at all, or as we do? The answer to this question embraces the whole field of psychology. We can distinguish many influences on our behavior other than motivation: (1) Innate structures (genes, for example) influence the direction and level of development; (2) our abilities (intelligence, for example) influence a wide range of behaviors; (3) we manipulate and adapt to the external stimuli, the environment; and (4) our habits—the acts we have learned—control us to some extent also. All these factors stimulate, control, and direct behavior.

Motivation and Entering Behavior

Entering behavior describes the present status of the student's behavior. It describes the responses he can now make to various stimulus situations. Any procedures a teacher may use to increase student motivation must account for the student's entering behavior. Later in this chapter we shall discuss discrepancies, expectancies, valences, anxiety, frustration, achievement motives, incentives, competition, and punishment. You will quickly discover that student performance varies considerably under each of these conditions. In motivation, as in no other aspect of human behavior, one man's sweat is another man's poison. For example, we shall review the evidence which indicates that some students actually achieve better under anxious, risky, competitive, and frustrating conditions than under the opposite ones. Other students' fears of failure make working under anxious and frustrating conditions an agony. Not all students react to verbal incentives in the same way. Some students feel that they must fail, and praise may only arouse their suspicions and their anxiety. They understand failure. What do they do with success (Van der Reit, 1963)? Students differ in their valences—what they consider to be desirable goals. They differ in their expectancies—what they believe to be realistic success for themselves.

Which of the following behavioral examples best illustrates the concept of motivation?   **QUESTION 6-1**

(a) Hortense has shown steady progress in her ability to relate past and present historical trends.

(b) Horatio has increased his practice time on the electric guitar from one to two hours per day.

(c) Havelock has always shown a keen interest and capacity in the breast stroke.

(d) Henrietta long ago developed the habit of looking up unfamiliar words in the dictionary.

After selecting your answer, explain the reasons for your choice and for your rejection of the alternatives.

The fact that there are no universal prescriptions and universal procedures for increasing student motivation greatly increases the difficulty of teaching. The teacher must make that analysis of the student's entering behavior which suggests the appropriate motivational procedures. The way the teacher makes this analysis and formulates procedures is the subject matter of this chapter.

After reading the second section of this chapter, you should be able to meet these objectives:

6-3   Define arousal in terms of the level of activity and provide illustrations of different arousal levels.

6-4   Define curiosity and exploratory behavior in terms of stimulus seeking and the conditions which give rise to it and provide examples of this behavior in animals and humans.

6-5   Define anxiety in terms of arousal and describe its relationship to student ability, learning tasks, and student performance.

6-6   Define frustration in terms of response competition and describe its relationship to anxiety and performance.

6-7   Define expectancy in terms of belief about outcomes and describe and illustrate its relationship to discrepancy, valance, and motive to achieve.

6-8   Distinguish between high- and low-achievement motivation and list the conditions which assist the development of the motive to achieve.

6-9   Define incentives and explain and illustrate how they increase response vigor.

BASIC THEORY AND RESEARCH

This section of the chapter introduces the theory and research on the motivational functions of the teacher. Three concepts—arousal, expectancy, and incentives—help us classify the factors which account for motivation. We may also use these concepts to designate the teacher's motivational functions: the arousal function, the expectancy function, and the incentive function.

Arousal

Arousal describes the general state of excitability of an organism—the general level of alertness, responsiveness, wakefulness, or vigilance. According to Donald Hebb (1955, p. 249), arousal is an "energizer but not a guide, an engine not a steering gear." The optimal level of arousal for our most efficient functioning is an intermediate level. We seek mild and avoid strong stimulation. The curve in Figure 6-1 shows that our most efficient performance in such activities as memorization, solving addition problems, and naming letters is at the intermediate level of arousal.

Humans have both internal and external sources of arousal. The external source is the stimulation provided by the environment. Although we cannot discuss here in detail the neural mechanisms which explain

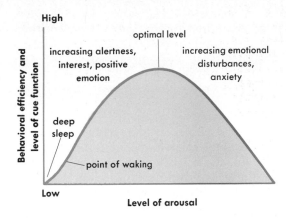

FIG. 6-1 Hypothetical, inverted U-shaped relationship between behavioral efficiency, or level of cue function, and level of arousal (after Hebb, 1955, Fig. 2).

arousal, Hebb (1966, p. 209) suggests that stimulation from the environment reaches the cortex through nonspecific pathways. These particular pathways tone up the cortex or, as we say, produce arousal. The internal source of arousal is a down-flow of thought, symbol, and fantasy from the cortex. Evidence for this internal source is the fact that humans do not necessarily go to sleep in a monotonous environment. Our students may day dream to keep themselves aroused when the classroom fails to provide adequate stimulation.

In his discussion of play, boredom, and the search for excitement, Hebb (1966, p. 248) stresses the fact that living things must be active. Ordinarily environmental stimulation and the satisfaction of biological needs keep the brain and the muscles active. He continues (p. 248), "There are times, however, when an animal has no threat to escape, no need of food, no young to care for, no sexual motivation, and no need of sleep. One need remains: to be active physically and mentally." In an economically prosperous society most of the physiological needs are routinely satisfied. "Life can become dull and the need to find excitement pressing—at least part of the time for the majority of citizens" (p. 253). At such times television is a necessity, not a luxury.

In summary we can state that activity is an intrinsic aspect of human nature—to be alive is to be active. The level of activity is called the *level of arousal,* and we ordinarily try to stay at an intermediate level between boredom and excitement. We shall now look at ways in which we escape boredom and seek stimulation through curiosity and exploratory behavior and then at ways in which we avoid stimulation through behavior which reduces anxiety and frustration.

Curiosity and Exploratory Behavior

In the 1950s investigators showed considerable interest in what appeared to be the spontaneous activity of animals. This behavior did not easily fit a drive-reduction model (explained below) of motivation since the behavior of the animal could not be attributed to any internal deprivation, such as the need for food, water, or sexual intercourse. For example, Harlow and his associates (1950) demonstrated that adult monkeys explore and handle mechanical puzzles and produce puzzle solutions in the absence of a hunger drive. They provided the first group of rhesus monkeys with an assembled mechanical puzzle for twelve days (a situation designed to stimulate curiosity and exploratory behavior—or to produce stimulus seeking). Disassembling the puzzle involved three or four sequential operations; there was no food or water reward. Harlow provided a second group of monkeys with the same puzzle for the same length of time. For this group, however, the puzzle was disassembled—no solution was necessary. Finally, examination day arrived, and both groups were presented new puzzles in their assembled states. The performance of the monkeys in the first group far surpassed that of the monkeys in the second. Harlow later repeated the experiment with hungry monkeys and gave food rewards for successful puzzle solutions. He found fewer solutions under this condition. The hungry monkeys attacked directly that part of the puzzle which obstructed their access to the food, and they ignored the necessary preliminary operations. In the first experiment it appeared that the monkeys attempted to increase stimulation. In the second experiment, they appeared to reduce the stimulation of the hunger drive.

Berlyne (1957) studied exploratory behavior in human subjects. Each subject sat alone in a dark room. By pressing a key, he could expose pictures on a slide projector for about one-quarter of a second. The subject could expose a single slide as frequently as he wanted; the next slide would be shown only when the subject indicated his readiness for it. The pictures varied in what Berlyne called *incongruity, complexity,* and *surprisingness.* An example of incongruity was a picture of an elephant's head attached to a dog's body. Subjects indicated a higher preference for incongruous than for normal pictures. The sequence of six complex pictures started with a simple circle. The following pictures showed the addition of circles until in the last picture a teddy bear was created. Subjects preferred the more complex to the simple pictures. The surprisingness slides were colored geometric figures. One series had twelve pictures. Figures 1 through 6 were red triangles. Figures 7 through 11 were green circles. Figure 12 was a violet square. Figures 7 (the first green circle) and 12 (the violet square) received more key responses than any other figures. Both figures provided new sources of stimulation. Again, as in the case of Harlow's experiment, the subjects appear to be seeking stimulation.

H. W. Nissen (1953) observed the behavior of sexually naive, or virginal, chimpanzees and noted that they tended not to copulate during the mating season. Instead they engaged in other activities, such as scratching, caressing, cleaning, or grooming one another. It would be difficult to claim that these animals were sexually deprived since they had never engaged in copulation before and were not doing so at the time. The grooming behaviors could not be called *secondary drives* since these behaviors occurred before the chimpanzees were sexually mature and between chimpanzees of the same sex. The grooming behaviors could satisfy only the search for new stimulation. Harry Fowler (1965, p. 18) wrote that a whole general class of behaviors cannot be explained by drive-reduction theorists—behaviors such as peering at a crack in the wall, looking around, twisting a paper clip out of shape, and cracking one's knuckles. These behaviors gradually were labeled *curiosity* and *exploration*.

Experiments were also conducted on *boredom*—also referred to as stimulus deprivation and isolation. Boredom arises from a monotonous environment or the performance of repetitive tasks. It often leads to inattention, and it can have disastrous consequences in automobile driving, military patrolling, and teaching. Experiments on boredom usually reduce the total amount of external stimulation. In an early study, William Bexton, Woodburn Heron, and T. H. Scott (1954) gave college students $20 a day to remain all day (except for eating and toilet needs) in a lighted, soundproof room. Lying on cots, the students wore translucent goggles, which prevented them from seeing objects in clear outline, and cardboard cuffs and gloves, which reduced touch sensitivity. They rested their heads on U-shape, foam-rubber pillows; the only noise was the air-conditioner. The students were free to terminate the experiment at any time. Most of the time they slept. After two or three days they grew increasingly restless. They became so desperate for stimulation they listened with relish to stock market quotations and to a talk for young children on the dangers of alcohol. Although they were required to take difficult tests, they looked forward to the testing periods. They tried to occupy themselves with fantasies of self-induced stimulation. One student terminated the experiment very early even though he took a job requiring heavy physical labor at considerably less pay. As in the studies on exploratory behavior we see the subjects seeking stimulation.

Fowler (1965, p. 33) believes that these studies indicate that organisms respond not only to a change in stimulation but also for a change. Fowler calls curiosity *incentive motivation* (p. 43). The animal learns that upon performing some response he will experience novel and unfamiliar stimuli. For example, monkeys will repeatedly press a button which opens shutters and gives them the opportunity to see other monkeys playing. The anticipated change in stimulation is the incentive for the monkeys' behavior. In terms of expectancy, we could say that the animal expects or anticipates a change by making certain responses. K. C. Montgomery (1954), for example, showed that female rats move to that arm of the Y maze which offers the opportunity to explore a checkerboard maze. They try the opposite arm when the checkerboard maze is attached there.

Boredom may often be the basis for curiosity. Boredom has the characteristics of drive motivation in that the animal is deprived of a change in stimulation by long exposure to familiar or relatively unchanging stimulus conditions. We say that familiarity breeds contempt (although more accurately it breeds indifference). It may also breed the necessity for change or new stimulation. According to Fowler (1965, p. 42), bored animals can become curious when they learn to anticipate the changes in stimulation which follow a particular response.

You will note that the common sense view of curiosity is not consistent with Fowler's theory. Fowler views curiosity as an acquired expectation—new stimulation is provided by the performance of a particular act. We do not become curious about the completely unfamiliar and novel. We can hardly be curious about sources of stimulation we are completely ignorant of.

Maria Montessori (1964 ed.) observed the spontaneous curiosity and exploratory behavior of children. In educating the senses, Montessori makes *observation* and *liberty* the hallmarks of her method (p. 169). The teacher supplies the child with graded materials and then allows the child a relatively unstructured exploration of the materials. Montessori (p. 169) notes the increased interest of children as they use one of her objects:

> Let us suppose we use our first object—a block in which solid geometric forms are set. Into corresponding holes in the block are set little wooden cylinders, the bases diminishing gradually in millimeters. The game consists of taking the cylinders out of their places, putting them on the table, mixing them, and then putting each one back in its own place. The aim is to educate the eye to the differential perception of dimensions.

According to Montessori (p. 170) the normal child develops "spontaneously a lively interest in this game. He pushes away all who would interfere or offer to help him, and wishes to be alone before his problem." By allowing only one correct solution, the material controls error and permits autoeducation. The student perfects himself through his own efforts. The teacher in no way interferes; she must only observe and "leave her little scholars in liberty" (p. 173). Montessori reports that children will repeat the exercise between five and twenty times before they tire.

The Montessori method utilizes curiosity and exploratory behavior. The child's disassembling of the blocks (his response) presents novel and unfamiliar stimuli which engage his attention and his effort. The very novelty of the problem and the fact that the child can anticipate this novelty each time he disassembles the puzzle strongly motivate him. The liberty to which Montessori refers is simply the opportunity the child has to assemble and reassemble the puzzle. To maintain optimum levels of arousal, to escape boredom, to experience slight discrepancies, we are all motivated to seek novelty and adventure.

Anxiety and arousal Anxiety describes the individual's level of emotionality. (Table 6-1 will illustrate this definition.) We can sometimes distinguish among our friends those who are mainly tense and worried (highly anxious) and those who are "cool" (hardly anxious). We know that anxiety and arousal are related because at the higher levels of arousal we find considerably more emotionality than at the lower levels. Since anxiety is an inferred emotional state of the organism and cannot be directly observed, investigations of anxiety rely heavily on having the individual report his own emo-

FACILITATING ANXIETY SCALE

1 I work most effectively under pressure, as when the task is very important. Always—never. (2)

2 While I may (or may not) be nervous before taking an exam, once I start, I seem to forget to be nervous. I always forget—I am always nervous during an exam. (9)

3 Nervousness while taking a test helps me do better. It never helps—It often helps. (11)

4 When I start a test, nothing is able to distract me. This is always true of me—This is not true of me. (12)

5 In courses in which the total grade is based mainly on one exam, I seem to do better than other people. Never—Almost always. (14)

6 I look forward to exams. Never—Always. (16)

7 Although "cramming" under pre-examination tension is not effective for most people, I find that if the need arises, I can learn material immediately before an exam, even under considerable pressure, and successfully retain it to use on the exam. I am always able to use the "crammed" material successfully—I am never able to use the "crammed" material successfully. (19)

8 I enjoy taking a difficult exam more than an easy one. Always—Never. (21)

9 The more important the exam, or test, the better I seem to do. This is true of me—This is not true of me. (24)

DEBILITATING ANXIETY SCALE

1 Nervousness while taking an exam or test hinders me from doing well. Always—Never. (1)

2 In a course in which I have been doing poorly, my fear of a bad grade cuts down my efficiency. Never—Always. (3)

3 When I am poorly prepared for an exam or test, I get upset, and do less well than even my restricted knowledge should allow. This never happens to me—This practically always happens to me. (5)

4 The more important the examination, the less well I seem to do. Always—Never. (6)

5 During exams or tests, I block on questions to which I know the answers, even though I might remember them as soon as the exam is over. This always happens to me —I never block on questions to which I know the answers. (10)

6 I find that my mind goes blank at the beginning of an exam, and it takes me a few minutes before I can function. I almost always blank out at first—I never blank out at first. (15)

7 I am so tired from worrying about an exam, that I find I almost don't care how well I do by the time I start the test. I never feel this way—I almost always feel this way. (17)

8 Time pressure on an exam causes me to do worse than the rest of the group under similar conditions. Time pressure always seems to make me do worse on an exam than others do—Time pressure never seems to make me do worse on an exam than others do. (18)

9 I find myself reading exam questions without understanding them, and I must go back over them so that they will make sense. Never—Almost always. (23)

10 When I don't do well on a difficult item at the beginning of the exam, it tends to upset me so that I block even on easy questions later on. This never happens to me—This almost always happens to me. (26)

tional states under various stress conditions. Educational psychologists have studied test anxiety, or emotional states the student experiences under the stressful conditions of taking a test. Seymour Sarason and George Mandler (1952) believe that students fall into one of two groups: the anxious, or those for whom tests arouse anxiety and who make test-irrelevant responses such as worrying about failing and about their inadequacies, anticipating punishment, and blocking on questions—responses which lead to poor test performance; and those individuals who are without such tendencies and therefore improve their performance (p. 561). These investigators developed a questionnaire, the Test Anxiety Scale (TAS), to measure anxiety in test situations. In responding to the questionnaire the student reports such subjective reactions as worry before and during examinations, heart palpitations, uneasiness, and sweating. These findings emerged from the various studies: (1) Low-anxiety students perform better when challenged by the task and by the prospect that their performance will be assessed; (2) High-anxiety students perform worse under these same conditions; they perform better when they are not threatened with evaluation and faced with a challenging or difficult task.

Later research by Richard Alpert and Ralph Haber (1960) showed that anxiety does not always lead to poor performance. They claim that the TAS does not allow students to report how anxiety may actually enhance their performance. To correct this deficiency Alpert and Haber constructed the Achievement Anxiety Test (AAT), which consists of two sets of items: a *facilitating scale,* which allows the student to report how anxiety improves his test performance, and a *debilitating scale,* which describes how anxiety interferes with test performance. Table 6-1 lists the items (without the buffer items) of the two scales. By using both scales they found that they could make a better prediction of grade-point average than they could by using either scale alone.

Research on anxiety which uses anxiety tests and scales is mainly concerned with studying anxiety as a personality trait. Charles Spielberger (1966, p. 12) states that anxiety can also be a state. As such, it is the stimulus conditions which cause defenses to be set up to avoid the state. Subjectively, these states are feelings of apprehension and tension. As a personality trait, anxiety is an acquired disposition for the individual to perceive a wide range of objectively nondangerous conditions as threatening. The anxiety trait and the anxiety state are related to each other: The reactions typical of the anxiety state are experienced most often by individuals with the anxiety trait. When we refer to anxiety as arousal, we are referring to anxiety as a state. When we distinguish between students who tend to be anxious, and those who tend to be nonanxious, we are referring to anxiety as a trait.

In a series of studies on the relationship of arousal (or of the anxiety state) to complex learning, Spielberger (1966, pp. 361–96) observed these results: (1) High-anxiety students obtained superior test scores on a learning-recall test when relatively few recall errors were possible; low-anxiety subjects obtained superior test scores when relatively more recall errors were possible. (2) Of those students in the broad middle range of IQ, the low-anxiety students performed better than the high-anxiety students; high anxiety had no effect on the performance of low-ability students and tended to facilitate the performance of the very brightest students. In a follow-up study on the long-term effects of anxiety on academic performance, Spielberger found that the percentage of high-anxiety, able students who failed was four times greater than the percentage of low-anxiety, able students who failed. (3) In serial rote learning, low-anxiety students were superior in performance early in learning, while high-anxiety students were superior later in learning. (4) In the learning of concepts, high-anxiety, high-intelligence students performed better than low-anxiety, high-intelligence students; high-anxiety, low-intelligence students performed less well than low-anxiety, low-ability students.

On the basis of studies now available we cannot conclude that anxiety must always be avoided or reduced in teaching situations. Able students may profit more than less able students from anxiety. On occasion the teacher should deliberately increase anxiety, particularly for students with high IQs. Further study may reveal that increasing the anxiety of low-anxiety students of high IQ may result in performances which rival those of their anxious intellectual peers.

Frustration and arousal Frustration is a conflict situation in which the individual must complete one task or turn to another. In the classroom the student faces frustrating situations when either he wants to or feels that he must engage in activity which competes with his achievement of the instructional objective. Teachers face frustration when they must engage in activities which compete with the attention they could give to their teaching objectives. Current research on frustration (Lawson, 1965), interestingly enough, indicates that the frustrating (or conflict) situation may sometimes increase the individual's efforts to complete the task. When this occurs, the frustration becomes a challenge—the individual increases his determination to finish what he has started. Perhaps this increased vigor of response or rededication to the job has led the theorists to believe that frustration leads to aggression (Dollard et al., 1939).

The research question and, indeed, the question all of us want to answer is why frustration causes some individuals to pursue a task with renewed zeal and other individuals to surrender to other tasks which compete for their attention. Ian Waterhouse and Irvin Child (1953) designed a series of studies to help answer this question. They assigned college students complex and routine intellectual tasks. The complex tasks were those found on intelligence tests; the routine tasks required such performances as writing the letter *a* as many times as possible in two minutes. Subjects in a frustrated group were told from time to time that their performance was very poor; those in a neutral group were given the impression that their performance was realistically successful. To obtain information on possible competing responses, the students answered a questionnaire and reported their typical reactions to frustration. Illustrative statements were: "I tend to brood over my failures" and "I am inclined to be very critical of myself when I fail." The results of the questionnaire divided the students into high-interference and low-interference groups. When both groups were frustrated as described above, the effects were notably different: The performance of the high-interference group decreased, while the performance of the low-interference group increased.

Whether frustration assists students in achieving instructional objectives depends on their entering behavior. Frustration in almost every case will invigorate student behavior, but it will not necessarily cause the student to invest his effort in classroom tasks. It will elicit those responses in the student which has the greatest strength. Since frustration is part of the human condition and none of us escapes it, the teacher must find ways of channeling the effects of frustration toward achievement rather than toward either nonachievement or the achievement of alternative or irrelevant objectives. At present we know only that some individuals find achievement more difficult than others and that the teacher, like a good doctor, must adapt the treatment to the patient. For some students the difficult, the new, and the demanding will kindle what William James (1892, p. 51) has called their *pugnacity*. For the less pugnacious student the teacher must devote his efforts to strengthening the weaker task-relevant responses. In no case does the current research indicate that the teacher should retire either frustration or anxiety (if this were possible) from his repertoire of teaching procedures.

Summary The individual maintains an arousal level which avoids both boredom, or an absence of stimulation, and intense excitement, or a surplus of stimulation. Through curiosity and exploratory behavior, he seeks stimulation to maintain a suitable level of arousal. You saw examples of stimulus seeking in the behavior of monkeys solving mechanical puzzles in the absence of a food reward, in the behavior of individuals preferring incongruous to normal pictures, in the grooming behaviors of virginal chimpanzees, in the students' preferences for unknown items, and in the spontaneous activity of Montessori's school children. An impressive amount of evidence shows that we perform some acts only because they will produce relatively novel and unfamiliar situations and experiences. The degree of arousal and the kinds of tasks efficiently performed in high-arousal states vary from student to student. Some students find anxious and frustrating circumstances motivating. Others find them debilitating. The relationship between IQ and high arousal strongly suggests that when the student possesses the appropriate entering behavior in sufficient strength, high anxiety or high frustration will not impede and may even facilitate performance. When the prerequisite entering behavior is lacking or weak, however, the student may very well experience the punitive effects of increased anxiety and frustration without experiencing the benefits.

Expectancy

Expectancy is a momentary belief that a particular outcome will follow a particular act (Vroom, 1964, p. 17). Expectancies can range from the subjective certainty that something will occur to the subjective certainty that something will not occur. We may be aroused when there is a discrepancy between what we perceive and what we expected to perceive. We become angry when we perceive someone doing something we neither like nor expect. Miss Pegg smolders if Johnny colors when she expects him to read. When he colors his reading book, there is an even greater discrepancy between what Miss Pegg perceives and what she expects, and there is greater anger. Hebb (1966) tells us that the more intelligent we are the better able we are to detect discrepancy and the more emotional we become. He uses a mechanical analogy: "The more complex the equipment, the greater the number of things by which its operation may be disturbed, the greater the aberration from normal function may be, and the longer it may take to get it back in working order" (p. 239).

Discrepancies between perception and expectancies are sources of arousal. When we become overly familiar with our surroundings they lose their power to arouse us. This may be why we have the adage "there's no shoe like an old shoe," which reminds us not to sacrifice the familiar even though it no longer excites us. In any case, when the environment provides us exactly what we expect, we are no longer aroused by it. Hence we can sleep in a noisy environment of familiar sounds and suddenly awake at the sound of an unfamiliar footstep.

What determines whether we will be pleased or frightened by departures from our expectations? David McClelland (1953, p. 28) suggests that the size of the discrepancy determines the feeling we experience. A large discrepancy results in unpleasantness. A small discrepancy results in pleasantness. Keith Conners (1964) determined which nonsense shapes (see Figure 6-2) students found most esthetically pleasing. The students believed that they were subjects in an ESP experiment designed to find out if ESP could affect their esthetic preferences. In the experimental group the students first studied and drew one of the nonsense figures attached to the outside of the viewing box. This figure is called an *adaptation stimulus;* it is an anchor of expectancy—of what the students expect to see next. Then the students viewed the stimulus objects in random pairs. Adjacent figures were more similar (less discrepant) than figures farther apart. Preference was determined by how much time the student looked at one figure as compared with the time he looked at the other and by his verbally expressed preference. The graph, Figure 6-3, shows the students' preferences. Preference was highest when the size of the discrepancy was small (between shapes *A* and *B*) and lowest when the size of the discrepancy was large (between shapes *A* and *G*, for example). Conners' findings may explain our growing acceptance of modern abstract painting. The size of the discrepancy between what we see in the modern painting and what we expected to see narrows as we become more accustomed to visual abstraction. His study may also explain why we should not attempt to sweep the school with revolutionary innovation. When the size of the discrepancy between conventional and innovative

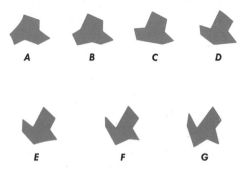

FIG. 6-2 Seven geometric shapes used as stimuli (after Conners, 1964, p. 460).

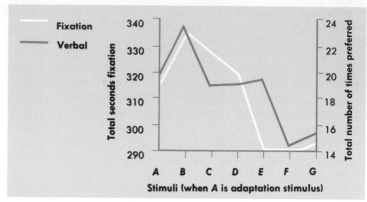

FIG. 6-3 Student preferences (measured in fixation time) for various sizes of discrepancy (afters Conners, 1964, p. 460).

practice is large, it may produce unpleasant reactions in both teachers and students. The findings on discrepancies may also explain adult reactions to adolescent fads and fashions. The discrepancies in adolescent dance, dress, and manners are small and pleasant for the adolescent. For the adult the discrepancies are large and sometimes shockingly unpleasant.

Valence—the individual's anticipated satisfaction, or his emotional preference for certain outcomes (Vroom, 1964, p. 15)—is associated with the concept of expectancy. Given two possible outcomes, the individual can prefer *X* to *Y*, *Y* to *X*, or remain indifferent to either outcome. More concretely, George can prefer a date with Harriet to a date with Hilda, a date with Hilda to a date with Harriet, or not care to date either girl. Desiring an outcome (valence) is not the same as enjoying an outcome once we attain it. The eyes are frequently bigger than the stomach. George may prefer Harriet to Hilda only to discover later that he does not enjoy Harriet. He may even discover that he enjoys an outcome he did not desire—that a date with Hilda is more satisfying. The anticipated satisfaction is called *valence*. The actual satisfaction is called *value*.

The vigor with which the individual acts is a product of both expectancy and valence. If a person is indifferent to an outcome (low valence) he will not act even though he is almost guaranteed success (high expectancy). We find students in our schools who expect little satisfaction in academic achievement (low valence) even though they have the ability which assures them academic success (high expectancy). We sometimes call them *underachievers*. We also find the reverse conditions of high valence and low expectancy: the students who want to achieve but are unable to do so. These students are unmotivated because they do not invest much effort in highly desired outcomes which they have little chance of attaining. Their anticipated failure produces only a polite modicum of effort.

Before summarizing the discussion of expectancy, we will consider a rather extensively studied type of expectancy and valence—the motive to achieve.

The motive to achieve The teacher must help the student who lacks the desire to achieve to acquire the desire or the motive. Exactly what we mean by motive to achieve will become clearer as we review a fascinating program of research in social psychology conducted by McClelland, John Atkinson, and their associates (McClelland et al., 1953; McClelland, 1955; Atkinson, 1958). We can define *achievement motivation* as the expectancy of finding satisfaction in mastering challenging and difficult performances. In education we sometimes call it the pursuit of excellence. In history and sociology we call it the Protestant Ethic (Weber, 1904).

McClelland (1965) listed twelve propositions for developing new motives in adults. These motives are based on his research on training programs designed to develop the achievement motive in such individuals as businessmen in India, where achievement motivation is not a part of the traditional culture. The following is a modified list of McClelland's propositions.

1 Educational attempts to develop a new motive will best succeed when the individual has many reasons in advance to believe that he can, will, or should develop a motive.

2 Educational attempts will best succeed when the individual understands that developing the new motive is realistic and reasonable.

3 The individual is likely to develop the motive when he can describe and clearly conceive the various aspects of the motive.

4 Change in thought and action will most likely occur and endure when the individual can link the motive to related actions.

5 The new motive is most likely to influence the thoughts and actions of the individual when he can link it to events in his everyday life.

6 The new motive will influence thought and action when the individual sees the motive as an improvement in his self-image.

7 The motive is likely to influence thought and action when the individual can see and experience the new motive as an improvement on the prevailing cultural values (e.g., Indian businessmen can see the motive to achieve as superior to the motive to withdraw).

8 The motive is likely to influence thought and action when the individual commits himself to achieving concrete goals in life related to the newly formed motive.

9 The motive is likely to influence thought and action when the individual keeps a record of his progress toward achieving goals to which he is committed.

10 Changes in motives are likely to occur in an atmosphere in which the person feels warmly but honestly supported and in which he is respected by others as a person capable of guiding and directing his own future behavior.

11 The more the setting dramatizes the importance of self-study and lifts it out of the routine of everyday life, the more changes in motives which are likely to occur.

12 If the new motive is a sign of membership in a new reference group, changes in motives are likely to occur.

McClelland's study of eighty-six businessmen in India over two- to three-year periods indicated that about two-thirds profit and one-third remain unaffected. Amount of profit was determined by a coding system which recorded whether each individual had shown unusual entrepreneurial activity, such as would result in receiving an unusual salary raise or promotion or in initiating a new business venture.

McClelland's course suggests that teachers may teach students how to develop the motive to achieve, especially those students who are notably deficient in the desire to meet challenges, to master, and generally to succeed. In such a course, the pedagogical problem is not only to accommodate the present entering behavior of the student but also to develop new entering behavior which, in turn and with time, will enable the students to accomplish advanced instructional objectives.

James (1892, p. 51) referred to achievement motivation as pugnacity and as ambitious impulses. His words are an appropriate way of ending our discussion of achievement motivation and teaching:

> Pugnacity need not be thought of merely in the form of physical combativeness. It can be taken in the sense of general unwillingness to be beaten by any kind of difficulty. It is what makes us feel "stumped" and challenged by arduous achievements, and is essential to a spirited and enterprising character. We have of late been hearing much of the philosophy of tenderness in education; "interest" must be assiduously awakened in everything, and difficulties must be smoothed away. *Soft* pedagogics have taken the place of the old steep and rocky path to learning. But from this lukewarm air the bracing oxygen of effort is left out. It is nonsense to suppose that every step in education *can* be interesting. The fighting impulse must often be appealed to. Make the pupil feel ashamed of being scared at fractions, of being "downed" by the law of falling bodies; arouse his pugnacity and pride, and he will rush at the difficult places with an inner wrath at himself that is one of his best faculties. . . . The teacher who never rouses this sort of pugnacious excitement in his pupils falls short of one of his best forms of usefulness.

Summary Expectancies can be a source of arousal, especially when there is a manageable discrepancy between what we see and what we expected to see. Instructional objectives are the expectancies that are the teacher's main concern. But he must also be concerned with the expectancies and valences of the student. The student must be made to desire instructional outcomes (valence) which he has a good chance of reaching (expectancy). The vigor with which the student pursues instructional objectives is a product of both expectancy and valence. The motive to achieve describes a particular relationship of expectancy and valence: the expectancy of finding satisfaction (valence) in mastering difficult and challenging performances. McClelland and his associates have been studying the conditions under which this motive best develops. Among these are the following conditions: The student gives reasons for developing the motive, understands that the motive is realistic, can link the motive to deeds and to daily events in his life, commits himself to concrete goals, keeps a record of progress, has honest and warm support, engages in self-study, and feels that he belongs to a successful group.

Incentives

Incentives are actual goal objects. For human beings they can be concrete or symbolic rewards. They incite, arouse, and move to action when they are associated with certain stimuli which signal their presence. For example, we are motivated by the various signs that we shall obtain money as well as by the money itself. Although Clark Hull (1952) and Kenneth Spence (1956) were primarily concerned with the development of drive theory (which we discuss briefly below), they also believed that some activities of the organism can be motivated by the goal object or incentive, itself. A rat will run a maze not only because it is hungry but also because it expects or anticipates food when it reaches the goal box. The mechanism which underlies this anticipation is too complex to discuss here. We observe, however, that the rat's mouth waters and its jaws begin to chew even before it obtains the food. And this anticipatory activity increases its running speed. The larger the incentive the more vigor we find in the rat's responses. The rat runs the maze faster when given several hundred food pellets than when given only a few. It presses a bar more frequently for a food mixture containing saccharine and less frequently for a mixture containing citric acid (Murray, 1964, p. 13). Similarly, we can expect the student to invest more effort for a goal or prize he really covets than for one in which he is only mildly interested. The vigor of his activity is affected by the nature of the incentive. Edward Murray (p. 9) also suggests these examples:

> A man may not feel particularly hungry when he smells the delicious aroma of a chicken frying on the stove. The smell, sight, or taste of the food is said to operate as an incentive. In social situations the motivating effect of the goal is much more apparent than that of internal factors. Motivation is aroused by incentive pay, by the sight of a pretty girl, and by a television commercial.

Albert Bandura (1962) has studied the relationship of incentives to imitative learning in children. The children, divided into three groups, viewed a film in which an adult model showed four novel aggressive responses. The first group saw the film model severely punished. The second group saw the model generously rewarded with approval and food. The third group saw the model receive no treatment (neither reward nor punishment) for his aggressive acts. The children were later placed in a situation in which they could imitate the model. The first group, which saw the model punished, made fewer aggressive responses than did the other two groups. The boys were more aggressive than the girls, especially in the first group. In terms of expectancy, the child's observation of who received rewards may have influenced his expectation of reward if he behaved in the same manner. In the second phase of this experiment the children in all three groups

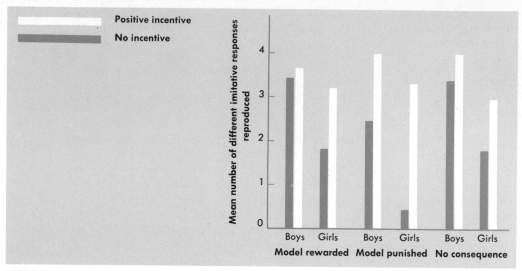

FIG. 6-4 Mean number of different imitative responses reproduced by children with and without incentives (after Bandura and Walters, 1963, p. 58).

were given attractive incentives for being aggressive. All previous performance differences were wiped out, including the sex difference. Figure 6-4 shows the difference between the incentive and no incentive performances.

Summary   Incentives are among the factors which increase the vigor of our behavior. They operate in two ways. First, they are goals or pleasant anticipations of repeating past experiences in the near future. Second, they strengthen responses which precede their delivery. Some evidence suggests that children identify with the adult who is rewarded in their presence and are alienated from the adult who is punished or left unrewarded.

Relationship of Arousal, Expectancy, and Incentives

We can now point out the relationship of these three motivational factors. In general, arousal is a product of learned expectancies. Past experience shows us that by making (or not making) certain responses under certain conditions we can attain valued goals. The smell of fried chicken stimulates our expectations of finding the chicken and consuming it. The combination of environmental stimuli and learned expectancies hastens our steps to the dining room. The goal object (the chicken) is the incentive because it influences future behavior by increasing the vigor of that behavior the next time. A completely novel incentive cannot motivate behavior. Once, however, we obtain an incentive we enjoy, we not only discover how to obtain it (a product of learning) but also learn to note the signs that its attainment is possible and perhaps even imminent. We then begin to make responses which bring us closer to the incentive. At Christmastime children become peculiarly aware both of the facial expressions of parents and of locked closet doors as indications of hidden treasures. They respond to these cues by discussing with their parents how their lives will be enriched by the anticipated gift if they receive it. The children even begin to improve their behavior if the rewards are associated with winning and maintaining parental approval. Under Christmastime conditions the children have learned to expect certain outcomes and these learned expectations motivate their behavior.

A Theoretical Model
We have presented the following view of motivation:

1 Motivation results in increased vigor of performance. Since the human organism is always active, the theoretical problem is not to explain how to arouse the individual from his torpor but how to increase the vigor of particular responses.
2 Arousal is the general state of alertness of the individual. Optimum levels of arousal avoid the extremes of monotony and intense stimulation.
3 Expectancy, as a motivational factor, is a momentary belief that a particular outcome will occur. Arousal may be a product of a small mismatch between what we see and what we expected to see. The discrepancy can be pleasant if it is in the direction of our expectancy. Expectancy depends on valence. The individual does what he wants because he expects to obtain something. Expectancy alone is not enough.
4 Incentives are goal objects which become associated with certain stimuli and responses. The associated stimuli (the smell of fried chicken associated with its later consumption) trigger off anticipations, and these learned anticipations motivate our behavior.

QUESTION 6-2

Mr. X. Seiting attempted to increase the vim and vigor of his students' efforts in studying logarithms. He particularly tried to pose challenging and difficult problems for his high-IQ students and interesting but easier problems for his average students. He occasionally gave both groups the opportunity to investigate alternate solution methods which they thought of. Which of the following classes of factors appears to be Mr. Seiting's chief motivational concern? (a) arousal; (b) expectancy; (c) incentives; (d) punishment.

After selecting your answer, explain the reasons for your choice and for your rejection of the alternatives.

After reading the next section of the chapter, you should be able to meet these objectives:

6-10 Define and illustrate the teacher's arousal function in terms of regulating arousal levels, attracting and holding student attention, and controlling anxiety levels through different teaching procedures.

6-11 Define and illustrate the teacher's expectancy function in terms of instructional objectives, immediate and remote objectives, changing expectancies, mismatching expectancies, and controlling the level of aspiration.

6-12 Define and illustrate the teacher's incentive function in terms of feedback of test results, praise and blame, grades, competition, and cooperation.

6-13 Define and illustrate the teacher's disciplinary function in terms of restitution, the ripple effect, teacher ineptness, instructional objectives, and the urban and suburban setting.

ON THE MOTIVATION OF STUDENTS

We have not reviewed the theory of and the research on motivation. The research which translates the theory into classroom practice, for the most part, does not now exist. At this point in the development of educational psychology we can only deduce from the available theory and data some general functions the teacher should perform to increase the motivation of the student. In describing these functions below we utilize the basic teaching model and the motivational concepts you have now learned. These are the teacher's motivational functions:

1 To engage the student in learning. This is the *arousal* function.

2 To describe concretely for the student what he will be able to do (his new capabilities) at the conclusion of the instruction. This is the *expectancy* function.

3 To provide rewards for present achievement in a way which stimulates future achievement. This is the *incentive* function.

4 To provide for the regulation of behavior. This is the *disciplinary* function.

The Arousal Function

Arousal, according to Hebb (1966, p. 209), is a general level of behavioral excitability. In education we prefer to define arousal as the student's general level of alertness or attentiveness. As teachers we may be faced with the problem of raising the level of arousal when the student is about to go to sleep or of lowering the level when the student is about to erupt emotionally. The student will perform best when he is neither sleepy nor frantic—when he is simply alert.

In the daily classroom routine the teacher must guard against monotony and boredom. He should always provide the student with enough to think about and to do. What the student does, however, must not be so regular and repetitious that it reduces his level of arousal. You will recall that, in the experiments on sensory deprivation in which the students spent several days lying on cots with nothing to do, their tolerance for the monotony and the lack of stimulation they were forced to endure was very short lived. Fowler suggests that curiosity is born out of boredom. Bored students invest considerable ingenuity and social deviancy in transforming a dull into an uncontrollably exciting classroom. The stimulation which the teacher fails to provide the students provide for themselves. James (1892; 1958 ed., p. 8) makes these suggestions to teachers who wish to attract and hold the attention of their students:

> If the topic is highly abstract, show its nature by concrete examples. If it be unfamiliar, trace some point of analogy in it with the known; if it be inhuman, make it figure as part of a story. If it be difficult, couple its acquisition with some prospect of personal gain. Above all things, make sure that it shall run through certain inner changes since no unvarying object can possibly hold the mental field for long. Let your pupil wander from one aspect to another of your subject if you do not wish him to wander from it altogether to something else, variety in unity being the secret of interesting talk and thought. The relation of all these things to the native genius of the instructor is too obvious to need comment here.

Teaching methods can capitalize on the student's need for new stimulation and on his propensities to be curious and to explore. We have referred to Montessori's method of observation and liberty. Bruner (1961) suggests that, when the student is allowed to approach learning as an act of discovery, he will engage increasingly in learning with the autonomy of self-reward. In Bruner's sense the student provides for his own stimulation and in this way performs his own arousal function. Robert White (1959) uses the term *competence motivation* to describe the child's "intrinsic need to deal with the environment" (p. 318). Competence motivation explains such acts as grasping and exploring, crawling and walking, attending and perceiving, talking and thinking, and manipulating and changing the surroundings. We have referred to such activity as curiosity and exploratory behavior.

Bert Kersh (1963) investigated the motivational effects of discovery learning. He provided high school geometry students with three ways to learn complex rules of addition. The directed-learning group used a programed learning booklet which reduced the material to a series of small steps. Each step contained the answers to the questions and the solutions to the problems. The guided-discovery group used a Socratic method which required each student to make inferences about the rules without help. A control group memorized the rules and obtained no explanation for them. Kersh found that the guided-discovery group used the rules (his measure of motivation) more often than did the directed-learning group. Kersh concluded that interest is a result of learning by discovery.

Torrance (1963) wanted to know which teaching conditions helped students to produce as many and as clever and unusual ideas as possible. The first of four groups of students used brainstorming procedures designed to facilitate the production of ideas by suspending initial discussion and criticism. This group was motivated to produce as many ideas as possible. The second group also learned the brainstorming procedures but was motivated to produce clever and unusual ideas. The last two groups did not learn these procedures, but instead were offered prizes on the basis of their performance. The third group was directed to produce as many ideas as possible, and the fourth group, to produce clever and unusual ideas. Torrance's results confirmed his expectations: (1) The special training in brainstorming produced more ideas than did the promise of prizes; (2) the directions to produce clever and unusual ideas produced more of these ideas than did the direction to produce as many ideas as possible. These findings indicate that the freer, or more open, conditions of brainstorming and originality of response produce greater response vigor, or motivation, than do the more closed conditions of responding for mere quantity and prizes.

Flanders (1951) investigated the relationship of personal-social anxiety and instructional method. He experimentally produced two learning climates designed to arouse different levels of anxiety. In the learner-centered climate the teacher's comments and interaction conveyed acceptance of and support for the students. The teacher used public standards of evaluation known to the students before they were invoked. In the teacher-centered climate the teacher's comments and interaction were directive and demanding, and the standards were private and unknown to the student. Anxiety was measured by increase in pulse rate and sweating, and the students could move a lever which recorded their positive and negative feelings. Flanders' results show the anxiety reactions students have to the use of rewards and punishment. Flanders discovered that the learner-centered students were more task-oriented, had less anxiety, and felt less emotional disturbance. The teacher-centered students felt more hostile, aggressive, apathetic, and generally more emotionally disturbed. Unfortunately, we have no comparable studies on the levels and types of anxiety produced by teachers who concentrate their efforts on the achievement of instructional objectives as contrasted with those produced by teachers who concentrate their attention on their interpersonal relations with their students.

Highly structured teaching situations are not necessarily debilitating for all students. Howard Kight and Julius Sassenrath (1966) used programed instruction to study the relationship of achievement motivation, anxiety, and teaching method. Programed instruction is the most highly controlled teaching situation we now have. These investigators found that students with high achievement motivation (we discuss this motivation below) or high test anxiety required less time to complete the program, made fewer errors, and remembered the material better than did students with low achievement motivation and low test anxiety. The authors suggest that students with high achievement motivation profit from the immediate knowledge of results provided in programed instruction. High-anxiety students find the highly structured teaching in programed instruction a less anxious situation than they find loosely structured teaching.

Summary of arousal function The arousal function is the teacher's effort to maintain the students' interest in learning. It involves the continuing responsibility of regulating the level of arousal to avoid both sleep and emotional eruption. To meet these requirements, the instruction must provide in the teaching situation a certain measure of freedom to wander from one aspect of the subject to another (in the words of James). Discovery-learning and brainstorming methods provide this freedom. Regulation of the level of arousal includes the control of anxiety and frustration. Not all students suffer the debilitating effects of anxiety and frustration; some evidently find them invigorating. The teacher must have sufficient knowledge of the entering dispositions of his students to provide the necessary increases and decreases in individual levels of arousal.

The Expectancy Function

The expectancy function requires the teacher to describe concretely for the student what he will be able to do when a particular class, lesson, or project is completed. In performing this function, the teacher must modify, substitute, or eliminate the student's expectations in such a way as to increase his efforts to accomplish the new instructional objectives.

Instructional objectives as expectancies Statements of instructional objectives must be concrete enough for the student to know exactly what outcomes the teacher expects. In making these statements, the teacher should avoid words like *appreciation, comprehension,* and *desire to understand.* The emphasis should be on *action*—some performance capability the student will acquire. For example, the teacher could begin his lesson with the vague and lofty pronouncement that his purpose is to develop in the students a deep understanding of and appreciation for human motivation. Students are accustomed to such abstract statements of instructional goals, and they have learned that they can ignore them without harmful consequences. Instead, the teacher could make this concrete statement: "At the end of today's lesson, when you are given various examples of human behavior, you will be able to identify those examples which are best explained by motivation rather than by habit." This latter statement provides the student with considerably more focus for his efforts and even with the promise that he will do something later he cannot do now.

It is also desirable to illustrate exactly what the objective means. In the example above, the teacher could describe two or more instances of human behavior which might or might not illustrate the concept of motivation. In one instance the teacher might describe how much energy Clyde expends on football and how little he expends on mathematics. In the other instance he might describe Hilda's ability to memorize poetry and to retain what she has learned. Which instance is the better illustration of motivation? The students might guess now, but the teacher can promise them that they will know later. If the illustrations of the objectives are phrased in terms of the students' present interests, the statement of the instructional objective should provide increased student motivation to achieve the objective.

The teacher's expectancy function requires him to select objectives which accommodate student entering behavior. To the extent that the teacher requires students to use skills and knowledge they now lack in the attainment of new skills and knowledge, he will produce the motivational effects of failure we will describe below. The teacher must make the students' expectancies the terminal behavior the instructional objectives promise. The teacher's repeated failure to deliver what he has promised will certainly undermine the confidence of the students in themselves and in the teacher. Students arrive at our classroom doors with different valences and different discrepancies. They are bored by and curious about different things. The teacher cannot impose on all children a uniform lesson plan or instructional procedure; these must be modified to accommodate individual students. I am not advising that the school and the curriculum simply dissolve before the sea of individual differences the student body represents. The school and the teacher should know what they want to teach, but they must remember that successful teaching requires accommodation to the present level of student capability.

Immediate, intermediate, and remote expectations   Instructional objectives represent the intermediate expectancies, or the outcomes the student can attain at the end of a lesson, session, project, and so on. In Chapter 2 we discussed task analysis, the process of reducing instructional objectives to their component subtasks. Subtasks represent immediate expectancies. Whenever the instructional objective (the major task) requires considerable effort and time on the part of the students, the teacher should concretely describe and illustrate the subtasks so that student effort does not wane along the way. The students ordinarily must have a continuing sense of accomplishment. Only the most advanced scholars in their laboratories and studies can sustain their efforts over long periods of time when they are faced with a paucity of results. Most of our students become more quickly impatient with error and slight gains.

Remote goals represent the student's long-range expectancies for home, family, friends, and career. The choice of these goals and the manner and the energy with which they are pursued largely reflect the student's basic beliefs about what will bring him satisfaction and happiness. In a democratic society the students can choose from myriad goals. Like all expectancies, remote goals influence the amount of energy we invest in various academic and nonacademic enterprises. The teacher who knows the remote expectancies the student cherishes (rightly or wrongly) can relate remote to immediate and intermediate expectancies. The inspiring teacher may be the one who convincingly relates what the student learns today to what the student deeply desires to do in his later life. The mass media develop in a student all kinds of expectations about the joys and adventure of adult life. Out of what he sees on television and reads in magazines, the student develops his remote expectancies (Cremin, 1965). The teacher must expend considerable effort in all phases of his teaching to impress upon the student the realization that the adult prerogatives he deeply desires require that he learn to do many things which he cannot do now but which he can learn to do with the proper expenditure of effort. Relating remote expectancies to instructional objectives may be a particularly burdensome task, unconvincing to the student and unrewarding for the teacher. Success in bridging the gap, however, whenever attained, becomes a source of motivation.

Changing expectancies Expectancies, we have said, are learned anticipations of the consequences of our behavior. They are indeed a product of our past experience. This fact suggests two ways in which expectancies can be modified: (1) The actual past experience of success and failure is the primary basis for predictions of the success and failure of our future efforts. The amount of effort students invest in academic, athletic, and social activities is largely determined by the amount of success and failure each realm of activity has provided them in the past. In this way success breeds success and failure breeds failure. Students thread their ways through gargantuan college catalogs and often select those courses—the so-called *snap* or *breeze* courses—which promise them the highest probability of success. To change their expectancies and to develop new ones, the students must have some solid base of success. Students who have never experienced academic success must be provided academic success at the level of their entering behavior before they will raise their expectancies to include more difficult outcomes in the future. (2) The teacher can also control a student's expectancy by telling him what the likelihood of success and failure will be. Our advising and counseling of a student often consist of this very function. We look at his previous grades, his general intelligence, and the courses and programs he desires to or must take, and we make some estimates of his probable success. The student, of course, will expend most of his energy where he has the greatest promise of success.

Since expectancy depends on valence, or anticipated satisfactions, the teacher must also find ways of increasing valence. Victor Vroom (1964, p. 23) suggests at least two ways of doing this: (1) When the student is unfamiliar with the possible outcomes he can attain, the teacher can give him information which increases his desirability for one outcome rather than for another. Teachers frequently point out to students how the particular execution of an assignment leads to better results than do alternative ways the students can think of. For example, by telling the student about the wide range of literary and personal expression possible through the use of certain literary and linguistic conventions, the teacher can increase the student's valence for acquiring the new verbal capabilities. (2) The teacher can also arouse appropriate motives. The fact that the student will be able to do something which he cannot now do and that he will do it well is often a great incentive.

Mismatching expectancies The discrepancy hypothesis states that a moderate, positive degree of discrepancy between what we experience and what we expect to experience can be a source of satisfaction. Hunt (1961, pp. 267–72) refers to the process of establishing a nondiscrepant situation—in which experience and expectation fit perfectly—as *matching*. For example, in the Berlyne experiment on incongruity (p. 142), a proper match would attach an elephant's head to an elephant's body. In the basic teaching model, a proper match would result in the instructional objectives, procedures, and materials fully accommodating the student's entering behavior. Hunt believes that a perfect match results in stultifying boredom. To avoid this the teacher has to introduce incongruity, complexity, and "surprisingness" into his lessons. New materials must have the proper blend of the familiar and the unfamiliar to attract and hold the attention of students. A study in a school setting (Gewirtz, 1959) supports the idea of increased motivation through mismatching. When children were given puzzles to solve, some were successful and some were not. Asked to select similar or different puzzles for their next trials, most of the unsuccessful children selected the same puzzles, while some of the successful children selected different puzzles. Television advertising exhibits considerable ingenuity in mismatching with Jolly Green Giants, Hawaiian punches, and Superman. Incongruity has been a major source of American humor from Charlie Chaplin to Charles Pierce. The tobacco industry has exploited the incongruity of a gentleman's offering a lady a Tiparillo and of the lady's contemplating acceptance of the offer. The discrepancy is kept within tolerable and even pleasing limits by the daintiness of the cigar, its ivory tip, the elegance and solidity of the gentlemen and the ladies and of the setting in which the proposal is contemplated. (In the early commercials the offer was never overtly made or accepted, but we were privileged to observe what the gentleman and lady were thinking.) The fact that we remember, sometimes with affection and humor and sometimes with humor alone, those teachers whose behavior we described as different, queer, hilarious, inspiring, and just plain interesting may attest to the motivational value of incongruity and mismatching.

Level of aspiration　　The effect of expectancy on student performance has been observed in several studies of level of aspiration, which, in the context of this chapter, we may call *level of expectancy*. In these studies students are asked how well they expect to do on their next performance. Then their actual performance is compared with their expected performance. In a very provocative study Pauline Sears (1940) divided elementary school children into three groups based on their grades and how successful they felt they were in school: (1) a success group with high grades and high feelings of success; (2) a failure group with low grades and little feeling of success; and (3) a mixed group who were successful in reading but unsuccessful in arithmetic. In the first phase of the experiment each child did ordinary reading and arithmetic assignments. After each assignment the child was asked how many seconds it would take him to do the next task. The amount of time the child indicated (a measure of his expectancies) was compared with the amount of time he took to complete the original task. This difference yielded a discrepancy score. Sears found that (1) the success group lowered their estimate of the amount of time it would take them to complete the next task, which amounted to a slight but realistic increase in their level of expectancy; (2) the failure group was erratic, setting their goals above, below, and at the same level as their original performance, with seven of twelve subjects in this group setting their goals higher and sometimes unrealistically high; and (3) the mixed group was more like the success group in reading (the school subject in which they had been more successful) and more like the failure group in arithmetic.

In the second phase the children performed similar tasks, which afforded them a second trial. Fifty percent in each group were told that they were very successful in their second trials, and 50 percent were told that they had done very poorly. How did this treatment affect the children? (1) The children who were told that they were very successful set goals which were realistic related to their past performance (low discrepancy scores). (2) The children who were told that they had done very poorly set very erratic goals—as the failure group had done in the first phase of the experiment.

A number of studies on level of expectancy have led to these conclusions:

1 Past success conditions students to make realistic increases in their expectancies.
2 Past failure, over long periods of time, conditions students to lower their expectancies, almost as if to guard themselves against failure by never expecting success.
3 Some students unrealistically raise their expectancies almost as if the hope of success alone would bring success.

Success, it seems, develops a modest self-confidence which often leads to more success. Failure results in more variable behavior—despair and resignation or an optimism which seems born out of defeat. This research supports the importance of the teacher's expectancy function: The student's every effort does not have to meet with success, but he must experience enough success to keep his wagon hitched to a star of reasonable height. By modifying students' expectancies in accordance with these findings, teachers can increase the vigor of student effort.

Jerald Bachman (1964) has found that a person's expectation of success is greatest when he thinks he has the appropriate training and when he has the freedom to use this training. On the basis of his findings Bachman speculates about the mechanisms which may explain why repeated failure reduces motivation. An individual may cope with failure by general dissatisfaction with the situation and eventually withdrawal; by lowering the estimate of his own ability and developing the feeling that he cannot perform a given task; by deciding that he has little control over the situation —which makes the situation, rather than his inability, responsible for the failure; and finally by discrediting or distorting the evidence of failure— which may be the mechanism employed by the undaunted optimists in Sear's study.

Summary The expectancy function requires the teacher to maintain or modify the student's expectation of success or failure in reaching the instructional objectives. It requires the teacher to describe concretely for the student what he will be able to do when a particular class, lesson, or project is completed. The teacher must relate intermediate expectancies to immediate and remote goals of the students to engage the student's full effort in learning. The teacher must sometimes change expectancies and, to increase behavioral vigor, deliberately mismatch them. Mismatched expectancies are a source of humor, and humor can be a source of motivation. Expectancies also concern the student's history of success and failure; the teacher may have to protect the student whose long history of failure has affected his levels of aspiration. Undoubtedly, a major source of motivation in any enterprise we undertake is the prior feeling and belief that we are equal to the task. The expectancy function requires the teacher to have sufficient knowledge of the past school failure and success of individual students to distinguish among realistic, pessimistic, and extravagantly optimistic expectancies. When there has been much failure, the teacher may have to provide much success.

The Incentive Function

The teacher rewards achievement in such a way as to encourage further effort on the part of the student. This statement describes the teacher's incentive function. The incentives are goal objects or symbols which the teacher uses to produce this increased vigor. They may be feedback of test results, spoken or written praise and encouragement, grades, or the fruits of successful competition. We shall discuss each of these below.

Incentives work their effects forward in time since they result in learned anticipations. Having obtained a particular goal object, the individual begins to associate the responses he made and the stimuli he met with every future approach to the goal. These responses and signs increase the vigor of his performance. The second time, the rat runs a little faster for the cheese in the goal box, the child hastens to the candy counter, and Sam's heart beats faster as he pulls his car into Carolyn's driveway. If Johnny solves a difficult problem in balancing chemical equations, in his later attempts to solve similar problems he makes responses and meets stimuli that assure him that he is on the right path. This learned anticipation of the correct solution increases the vigor of his efforts.

Feedback of test results At this point we wish to consider the motivational effects of performance assessment. Test results must be fed back to the student with sufficient frequency and in a form that will enable him to confirm his expectancies. Unconfirmed outcomes leave the student ignorant of his possible success and deny him the satisfaction of accomplishment. Continuous withholding of feedback can have very deleterious effects on student motivation and learning. American students ordinarily show keen interest in their test results. Results which somewhat exceed their expectations give them considerable satisfaction, which becomes a source of motivation for future learning. For learning and motivation purposes, testing should be more systematic and more frequent than it is in most schools. American schools are still influenced by the European practice of testing after long periods of time, sometimes from one to four years or more. The use of comprehensive examinations to assess student learning over long periods of time may encourage students to study materials in a way which guarantees their long-term retention. The more frequent testing in American education may motivate only short-term retention. Comprehensive examinations, however, are not a suitable substitute for the short-term feedback students need to bolster their efforts for continued study.

We may also arrange instructional materials and procedures in ways which permit students to develop checkpoints and standards for assessing their own achievement. In our discussion of curiosity and exploratory behavior, we referred to the discovery learning of Bruner, Kersh, and Montessori (p. 157). These studies indicate that we can teach students to generate their own instructions and strategies of learning. As students learn to engage in independent study and acquire skill in establishing their own standards —as any scientist, author, and artist must do—they have less need for feedback from the teacher or from a systematic program of tests. Our desire to produce independent scholars, however, should not obscure the fact that this achievement is frequently the result of long and dedicated teaching.

Praise and blame Elizabeth Hurlock (1924) made one of the earliest studies of the effects of incentives. In the first of the experimental sessions with elementary school children, the children took an intelligence test. Feedback on the test was handled in three ways: (1) Children in the praise group were told that their scores were very high and their papers very neat; (2) children in the blame group were told that their scores were very low and their papers sloppy; and (3) children in the control group received neither praise nor blame. In the second session these children were given another form of the same intelligence test. The scores for the second test showed that (1) the performance of both the praise and blame groups improved; (2) both groups did about equally well; and (3) both groups did better than the control group, which had received neither praise nor blame. In a later experiment (1925) Hurlock used three groups of children who took a short arithmetic test each day for five days. All groups (but one) worked in the same room and could witness all three experimental treatments: (1) Children in the praise groups were called by name before the class and praised for their work; (2) children in the blame group were publicly reproved for their work; (3) children in a third group were simply ignored; and (4) children in a control group worked in a separate room and received no praise or blame. Again Hurlock found that the performances of the praise and blame groups improved. She discovered, however, that continued blame over a five-day period reduced performance and continued praise increased performance. The control group did the worst, performing more poorly than even the children in the ignored group. Hurlock concluded that praise is a better incentive than blame because the effects of praise are more enduring. An alternative explanation of the results of the second experiment is simply that the reproved children stopped trying because their efforts were never rewarded (Cofer and Appley, 1965, p. 771).

In reviewing the praise-blame studies of Hurlock and others, Wallace Kennedy and Herman Willcutt (1964) suggest the need to control the entering behavior of the subjects in the experiments. For example, other investigators have found that praise does not help severe underachievers. Blame does not impede the performance of black students performing under black examiners. Finally, blame does not impede the performance of very bright adolescents. These later findings make it necessary for teachers to observe the effects that praise and blame have on various students. The teacher's incentive function requires him to use incentives which will increase student effort on subsequent tasks. The teacher must confirm the effectiveness with which he performs this function by observing the effects of the incentives he uses on subsequent student behavior.

Grades as incentives There have been several interesting studies of the effects of grades, written comments, and grading policies. Ellis Page (1958) conducted a most ambitious and provocative study involving 2,139 students in seventy-four classrooms. Cooperating teachers were asked to mark the objective tests of these junior and senior high school students in three ways: (1) the no-comment group received only their test scores and the equivalent letter grade; (2) the free-comment group received personalized comments which conformed to the teachers' own feelings and practices; and (3) the specified-comment group received the following stereotyped comments for each letter grade.

A   Excellent! Keep it up.
B   Good work. Keep it up!
C   Perhaps try to do still better.
D   Let's bring this up.
E   Let's raise this grade!

All groups received test scores and letter grades. The student subjects were totally naive; none of them was aware or suspected that he was an experimental subject. In the second phase of the experiment the students were given a second test to determine the effects of these three grading practices. Both the free-comment and the specified-comment groups did better than the no-comment group. The free-comment group did better (but not significantly better) than the specified-comment group. The F students who received the free comment showed the greatest improvement. The effects of the comments did not depend on student ability or school year. Page concluded that teachers should take the time to write encouraging comments on student papers.

Faculties frequently debate which grading policy most strongly motivates students to improve their performance. Lewis Goldberg (1965) has attempted

PERCENTAGE OF STUDENTS ASSIGNED EACH LETTER GRADE FOR FIVE GRADING POLICIES
(after Goldberg, 1965).

TABLE 6-2

GRADING POLICY	PERCENTAGE OF STUDENTS WHO RECEIVED				
	A	B	C	D	F
Strict	0.00	0.05	0.25	0.40	0.30
Lenient	0.30	0.40	0.25	0.05	0.00
Bimodal	0.20	0.30	0.00	0.30	0.20
Normal	0.10	0.20	0.40	0.20	0.10
Rectangular	0.20	0.20	0.20	0.20	0.20

to resolve this debate by studying the effects of five grading policies on college-student motivation. Students were assigned a grade on the first midterm examination on the basis of one of these grading policies: strict, lenient, bimodal, normal, and rectangular. Table 6-2 shows the percentage of students who received each letter grade. These percentages define each grading policy. The students were told that their course grades would be determined by the course examinations using these percentages: first midterm—10 percent; second midterm—40 percent; and final—50 percent. After the first midterm, only letter grades were reported to the students; individual test scores were withheld. Goldberg discovered no appreciable differences in performance on the second midterm as a result of the five different grading policies. He believed that his findings "should force proponents of a particular grading policy to make a thorough reappraisal of their beliefs. And, while instructors may wish to defend their own grading practice on *administrative* and/or *informational* grounds, they should now be wary of including *motivational* rationales as part of their arguments" (pp. 22–23). If grading policies do not produce different motivational effects, then teachers should emphasize giving that type of detailed feedback to students which does enhance their motivation and learning.

Competition In a competitive instructional situation, rewards are unequally distributed and given only to those students whose achievement is of recognized superiority. Traditional grading practices, for example, are competitive since relatively few students receive marks of distinction. Few receive scholarships, fellowships, and memberships in honorary societies. The rewards for the victors—high grades, choice colleges, and so on—have sometimes resulted in superior performance of dubious merit—when, for example, students take snap courses to maintain high grade-point averages rather than taking courses of recognized intellectual and vocational merit.

Competition and cooperation Research on competition and cooperation is inconclusive and does not furnish an adequate basis for determining the conditions under which competition aids individual student achievement. M. M. Gross (1946) investigated whether students would achieve and cheat more when they competed with themselves to surpass their previous levels of performance (the first group) or when they competed with each other (the second group). The experimenter provided the occasion for cheating by allowing the students to score their own daily tests, which gave them the opportunity to change their answers. In the first group the students kept their own progress records. Students in the second group were told how their scores compared with other scores in the class. Gross found (1) an equal amount of cheating in both groups, (2) equal levels of achievement, and (3) that bright students cheated less and achieved more than did the less bright students. However, competition probably had very little to do with the results of this experiment. The less able students cheated because this was the easiest way for them to obtain right answers. The daily feedback from the quizzes probably contributed more to the students' levels of achievement than did the competition.

Perhaps more to the point is the experiment of Morton Deutsch (1960) in which he compared the effectiveness of competitive and cooperative groups in solving puzzle problems and human-relations problems. The students in the cooperative groups had to arrive at joint solutions to the problems; they were rated as a group. Students in the competitive groups could work together but had to arrive at individual problem solutions; they were rated as individuals. Deutsch found that the cooperative groups surpassed the competitive groups in almost every respect: The communication was friendlier, more open, and more effective; the cooperative groups exhibited a greater diversity, coordination, and sharing of effort and responsibility; and they were more orderly and productive. In assessing these results, we must remember that Deutsch was comparing the effectiveness of competitive and cooperative groups. When Dorothy Marquart (1955) compared the relative effectiveness of group and individual solutions to puzzle problems, she discovered that the group was no more successful than the best individual problem solver in it. We should not generalize the results of group competition to individual competition.

James Coleman (1961) suggested that we substitute interscholastic competition in academic subjects for our present interscholastic competition in athletics. The intellectual should be able to contribute to his community and to the prestige of his school in the way the athlete now does. The student body, he contended, only rewards students who are members of a team which has done something to bring glory to old Alma Mater. Interscholastic academic competition would convert the present position of the adolescent scholar from one of opprobrious curveraiser to one of respected and adulated member of the student body. One worries, however, whether interscholastic competition for academic honors would sometimes have the same abrasive effect on the quality of academic performance that interscholastic competition has had on the quality of athletic performance.

James (1892) wrote that "to veto and taboo all possible rivalry of one youth with another, because such rivalry may degenerate into greedy and selfish excess, does seem to savor somewhat of sentimentality, or even fanaticism" (p. 50). The evidence we have examined does not indicate that we should try to eliminate competition from the school (if this were at all possible) any more than we should try to eliminate anxiety, frustration, and punishment. Students who enjoy challenge and risk may profit from the very same classroom conditions which make achievement difficult for students who are anxious and have low levels of expectancy. Rather than establishing conditions which favor one group over the other, it seems considerably more sensible to provide each student with his most congenial motivational environment. If time, energy, money, and resources make individual treatment impossible, we should recognize these limitations for what they are rather than espouse universal teaching prescriptions which inevitably prejudice the cause of large parts of the student body.

Summary   The incentive function requires the teacher to reward student achievement in such a way as to encourage further effort in the pursuit of instructional objectives. We have discussed the incentive value of test results, spoken or written praise and encouragement, grades, and competition and cooperation. The feedback of test results is a particularly useful incentive because it may not only increase student vigor but also play an important part in learning procedures and in performance assessment, two components of the basic teaching model. All these incentives can become punishment when improperly applied. When the feedback of test results shows the student that he has learned very little indeed, when spoken or written praise becomes reproof, when grades become further evidence of failure, and when competition becomes the final humiliation before one's peers, the use of these incentives leaves much to be desired. The misuse of incentives, which is often inadvertent, no more warrants their abolition from the classroom than does the fact that some students obtain high and others obtain low scores on IQ tests warrant their abolition. In one sense the classroom is a microcosm of the society in which it is embedded, and no modern industrial society, whatever capitalist, socialist, or communist labels it parades behind, has failed to find the use of incentives and competition an aid to social progress.

The Disciplinary Function

The disciplinary function requires the teacher to regulate behavior through the use of restitution and ripple effect. We shall review these two concepts here.

Restitution   Restitution requires the student to perform properly what he originally performed improperly. It combines the suppression of one response and the substitution of another. Terence restates in decent language what he originally blurted out in abusive language. In restitution, the substitute response must be rewarded. The teacher should approve Terence's demonstration of linguistic propriety. Restitution, which involves reward as well as suppression, is preferable to suppression alone because it focuses on learning new socially acceptable responses rather than on stamping out inappropriate responses. Restitution establishes a situation of response-competition (the inappropriate response competes with the appropriate response) in the hope that the rewarded appropriate response will eventually win out.

Any disciplinary technique involves two operations (Bandura and Walters, 1963, p. 189): the presentation of a punitive (aversive) stimulus (punishment) and the withdrawal or withholding of a positive reinforcer (reward). Bandura and Richard Walters state that disciplinary techniques differ in their emphasis on the punishment and reward components. When, for example, the emphasis is almost wholly on the withholding or withdrawing of love, the technique emphasizes the reward component. Bandura and Walters (p. 221) suggest that disciplinary techniques should emphasize rewards which are withdrawn or withheld until the child complies with adult demands or makes restitution. When disciplinary methods are used by warm and affectionate parents, children seem to develop self-control and the requisite amount of social conscience. Disciplinary methods which emphasize punishment often result in the avoidance of the person who does the punishing.

The ripple effect This effect describes the way students who witness a disciplinary technique used against their classmates are affected by the technique (Kounin and Gump, 1958). The metaphor *ripple* implies that the effects of the technique spread out in concentric waves from the disciplined student to his witnessing classmates. When Miss Pegg tells Leroy that she will make "an example of him," she is assuming that the rest of the class may profit by anticipating what happens when a certain deviant act occurs. She is causing the ripple effect.

The ripple effect can work to the teacher's advantage or disadvantage. Jacob Kounin, Paul Gump, and James Ryan (1961) have studied the effects on students of what they call *desist techniques.* An audience of children witnessed three desist techniques and were later asked to describe their reaction to each one. These were the techniques: (1) The teacher was punitive and grim. She said to the student, "Hey you, who do you think you are?" She pulled the student toward his seat and said, "Now sit down. If you ever do that again, I'll really make trouble for you." This technique emphasizes punishment, or the use of aversive stimuli. (2) The teacher using this technique was matter-of-fact. She said to the errant student, "Don't do that again. Please sit in your seat now." The "please" implied the use of a positive reinforcer, and the request to sit down specified the alternative response the student could make. (3) The teacher indicated awareness of the deviant behavior, but chose to ignore it. The student audience rated the various techniques as follows: (1) They like the third teacher best; (2) they thought the second teacher was the fairest; (3) they thought the first teacher was best able to keep discipline in a class of tough kids; (4) they believed that misbehavior would most likely occur for the third teacher; (5) they believed that the first teacher made too much of an issue of the misbehavior and produced the most discomforting reactions (ripple effect); and (6) most important of all, they believed that the students would pay more attention afterward to the second teacher than to the other two teachers. Since the major purpose of disciplinary techniques is to assist students to achieve instructional objectives, the matter-of-fact technique of the second teacher has much to recommend it.

William Gnagey (1965) suggests several ways in which the teacher can use the ripple effect to increase his control over the class:* (1) Use non-threatening techniques whenever possible to avoid negative reactions to the teacher and the lesson. (2) Make clear who the deviant is, what the misbehavior is, and the proper alternative. "Leroy, if you pull Harriet's hair again, you will remain after school for three weeks" is very clear as to deviant and deviation but does not specify an alternative behavior, an apology to poor Harriet. (3) Increase firmness (the I-meant-it quality) by lowering or raising your voice, moving close to the culprit, or staring him into compliance. (4) Focus attention on the learning task and not on teacher approval. Gnagey (pp. 10–13) illustrates this suggestion: (a) "I hear a noise in back of this room. We will never finish learning how to do square root if that din continues!" is preferable to (b) "I hear noise in the back of this room. Mrs. Cooper doesn't like noisy children in her room." Finally, (5) know your subject matter. Students are less inclined to misbehave when they are learning something if only because the learning supplies constructive competing responses. All of these techniques, because of the ripple effect, have beneficial effects on both the misbehaving student and his classmates.

QUESTION 6-3

Miss Dee Litefull spent considerable effort devising analogies between past and present historical events. In diplomacy she compared Queen Elizabeth I with President De Gaulle, St. Francis of Assisi with beatnik and hippie leaders, and the leaders of the Crusades with the leaders of the peace demonstrations. Which of the four motivational functions do Miss Litefull's analogies best illustrate? (a) Arousal function; (b) expectancy function; (c) incentives function; (d) disciplinary function.

After selecting your answer, explain the reasons for your choice and for your rejection of the alternatives.

SUMMARY

Motivation refers to factors which invigorate student behavior. For *invigoration* you may read *increased effort*. Motivation is closely related to entering behavior: When students are motivated, they make the strongest responses they have learned. No amount of motivation can trigger or direct responses the students have not learned.

The factors which produce motivation are grouped into three classes:

---

* It may be more precise to say *to arrange the conditions which cause* the ripple effect rather than *to use* the ripple effect. The latter is an abbreviated way of stating the former.

arousal, expectancy and incentives. These factors, of course, are interrelated and interdependent. Arousal is the general level of alertness of the individual. The optimum levels of arousal are related to stimulus seeking, anxiety, and frustration. Expectancies are momentary beliefs about the probability of the occurrence of particular results. Expectancies are often products of discrepancies, and they are closely related to valences—what the individual wants as well as what he expects. Incentives are goal objects which become associated with certain stimuli and responses; they trigger anticipations.

These factors (or classes) form a motivation model. From this model we derive the four motivational functions of the teacher. The arousal function requires the teacher to engage the student in learning. The expectancy function requires him to describe concretely what the student will be able to do at the conclusion of instruction. The incentive function requires the rewarding of present achievement in such a way as to encourage future achievement. Finally, the disciplinary function requires the teacher to use restitution and the ripple effect in regulating.

SUGGESTED READINGS

This book gives an introductory, well-written overview of motivational theory, research, and controversy:

MURRAY, EDWARD J., *Motivation and Emotion*. Englewood Cliffs, N.J.: Prentice-Hall, Inc., 1964. (paperback)

These books are for the serious student who wants comprehensive reviews and analyses of the vast research and theory on motivation:

BINDRA, DALBIR, *Motivation—A Systematic Interpretation*. New York: The Ronald Press Company, 1959.

BROWN, JUDSON S., *The Motivation of Behavior*. New York: McGraw-Hill Book Company, 1961.

COFER, CHARLES N., and APPLEY, MORTIMER H., *Motivation: Theory and Research*. New York: John Wiley & Sons, Inc., 1964. This is the *most* comprehensive.

These books are very provocative discussions of curiosity and exploratory behavior:

FOWLER, HARRY, *Curiosity and Exploratory Behavior*. New York: The Macmillan Company, 1965. (paperback) This is a good introductory review and synthesis of the research.

BERLYNE, DANIEL E., *Conflict, Arousal, and Curiosity*. New York: McGraw-Hill Book Company, 1960. This is a more advanced treatment.

For other aspects of motivation, as indicated by their titles, the following books are authoritative and challenging:

McCLELLAND, DAVID C., *The Achieving Society*. Princeton, N.J.: D. Van Nostrand Co., Inc., 1961.

SPIELBERGER, CHARLES D., *Anxiety and Behavior*. New York: Academic Press, Inc., 1966.

VROOM, VICTOR H., *Work and Motivation*. New York: John Wiley & Sons, Inc., 1964.

This stimulating discussion links theory and research to teaching practice:

SEARS, PAULINE S., and HILGARD, ERNEST R., "The Teacher's Role in the Motivation of the Learner," *Theories of Learning and Instruction,* ed. E. R. Hilgard, Part 1 of the 63rd Yearbook, National Society for the Study of Education, pp. 182–209. Chicago: University of Chicago Press, 1964.

This pamphlet gives some rather practical suggestions for discipline (based on the little available research):

GNAGEY, WILLIAM J., *Controlling Classroom Misbehavior.* Washington, D.C.: National Educational Association, 1965. (a pamphlet)

PART THREE

INSTRUCTIONAL PROCEDURES AND LEARNING

CHAPTER SEVEN

BASIC LEARNING CONDITIONS

This chapter describes the conditions necessary for the learning discussed in the remaining chapters of Part 3. These conditions are external—they exist outside the student in the stimulus situation—and as such are distinct from internal learning conditions—the student's entering behavior. Successful performance is the result of the happy confluence of external and internal learning conditions.

The chapter has two sections. The first defines learning and the learning event. The second (and major) section defines the basic learning conditions: contiguity, practice, reinforcement, generalization, and discrimination and punishment.

The chapter uses the language of the connectionist-reinforcement learning theories (Hill, 1963, pp. 27–30). Research based on these theories forms the major part of psychological knowledge.

Upon reading this section of the chapter, you should be able to meet these objectives:

7-1 Define learning in terms of change, reinforcement, and practice.
7-2 Distinguish learning from performance, native response tendencies, maturation, and temporary states of the organism.
7-3 Define the learning event in terms of stimulus, response, and learner, and provide illustrations of learning events.

BASIC CONCEPTS

This section defines learning and distinguishes it from performance, native response tendencies, maturation, and temporary states of the organism. The learning event comprises the learner, the stimulus situation, and the learner's response.

A Definition of Learning

Learning is a relatively permanent change in a behavioral tendency and is the result of reinforced practice (Kimble and Garmezy, 1963, p. 133). Reinforced practice is the cause of the learning. The learning actually occurs between the cause and the result. Figure 7-1 indicates the relationship between the three parts of the definition. We use the term *behavioral tendency* in the definition to keep the distinction between learning and performance. In Figure 7-1, the relatively permanent change in behavior refers to a change in performance. We can observe a performance, but we cannot observe learning. We infer that a person has learned when he can do something later which he could not do before. When Chuck shouts "Down!" his dog sits down. We know his dog has learned because he never before did anything at this command except stare soulfully at Chuck. Not everything we learn, however, results in a change of behavior or performance. A student may master all the knowledge in a textbook on teaching, but, before he teaches, he will not have the chance to change his performance by using this knowledge. If some day he is teaching a concept and he provides all the necessary illustrations, his learning will then affect performance. The learning, or change in behavioral tendency, however, occurred earlier.

When Chuck says "Paw!" his dog sits and presents his right paw as if to shake hands. For this performance he receives a morsel of food. How did his dog learn to perform what appears to be a most unnatural act for a dog? We cannot describe the full procedure, but it involved both internal and external learning conditions. His dog had to learn to sit when commanded

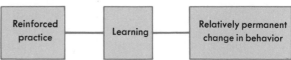

FIG. 7-1 The concept of learning (after Kimble, 1964).

to do so. This was necessary entering behavior or, if you like, a necessary internal learning condition. When his dog was sitting, Chuck uttered the command, "Paw," lifted the dog's paw, and shook it vigorously, trying not to knock the poor dog off balance. He then rewarded the dog with the choicest piece of meat. Chuck repeated this procedure several times a day for several days, and soon his dog cordially presented his paw whenever Chuck walked in the door. In terms of our definition of learning, the practice consisted of lifting his dog's paw and shaking it in response to the command over a period of several days. The reinforced practice consisted of the food reward Chuck presented each time he held the dog's paw. The change in behavior consisted of the dog's presenting his paw to Chuck. Now the dog may not present his paw to just anyone, and he may still prefer to bark at strangers who darken Chuck's door (learning does not change all performance). Still the behavioral tendency to raise his paw in greeting has been strengthened, and the actual performance of this act tells us that the dog has learned.

There are many obvious examples of human learning—learning to drive a car or to operate a typewriter, memorizing the lines of a play, acquiring new vocabulary. All these acts are new performances which we acquire with reinforced practice.

Some areas of behavior do not furnish examples of learning. First among these are the native response tendencies. We do not learn the knee jerk, the eye blink, breathing, and nausea. We once called these tendencies *instincts*. We can just as well call them *reflexes*. In any event, we are born with these capabilities, and we do not acquire them through practice and reinforcement. Some borderline behaviors may be a product of both instinct and learning. The best example is the tendency of newborn ducklings, at a critical period shortly after birth, to follow the first moving and quacking object they meet (Lorenz, 1937). Usually this object is their mother, but it is possible to get them to follow an artificial duck with a tape recorder inside which emits quacking sounds (Ramsay and Hess, 1954). This following behavior is called *imprinting;* once the ducklings have been imprinted with the artificial duck it is very difficult to get them to follow any other duck. We cannot ascertain at this time how much of this behavior is the result of instinct and how much the result of learning.

The second area of behavior which does not furnish examples of learning is maturation—growth tendencies which are relatively independent of specific learning conditions. Human and animal growth in height and weight is not learned behavior. The swimming of tadpoles and the flying of birds simply occur at the moment of anatomical maturation. But do we learn to walk? We cannot walk until our legs are strong enough to support our weight and we have developed the proper neural structures. But not every child walks the same way, and we can even distinguish between familiar and unfamiliar footsteps in adults. Similarly, the child cannot talk before proper vocal and neural development, but not all children speak the same language, and those who speak the same language do so in different ways. In other words, as in the case of native response tendencies, we do not have sufficient knowledge to make a clear distinction between learning and maturation.

The third area of behavior includes the temporary states of the organism due to fatigue, habituation, or drugs. If an endless line of visitors comes to his home the day Abigail gets married, the dog will certainly not raise his paw at every command and for every guest. The fatigue induced by repetition of a response disinclines its immediate repetition. But the resulting change in behavior is attributable to fatigue and not to learning. Habituation changes our behavior in the direction of reduced responsiveness. For example, many individuals fall asleep on the New York subways even with the usual screeching, rocking, and jerking of the trains. We also grow accustomed to the traffic moving below our apartment windows at night. Most likely we do not learn to ignore these and other irrelevant noises. Innate mechanisms automatically take over and produce the adaptation necessary for us to get our sleep or to pay attention to more relevant noises. Finally, drugs produce or inhibit behavior changes, usually just temporarily. After our return to normality, memory returns. Even with drugs, however, the case is not clear; it is possible that certain organic compounds or drugs can exert a positive influence on learning and memory.

This definition of learning states nothing about improvements in behavior. We can as easily strengthen potentially injurious behavioral tendencies as in the case of excessive smoking or excessive eating and drinking (see Dollard and Miller, 1950). Indeed, even pigeons can be trained to peck at each other at the sound of a buzzer and to soothe ruffled feathers at the flashing of a green light (Skinner, 1938).

The Learning Event

Which elements in a situation are essential for learning? Three elements together constitute the learning event (Gagné, 1970): the learner, the stimulus or stimulus situation, and the response. A *learner's* previous learning is his entering behavior, or his internal conditions of learning. A *stimulus* (plural: stimuli—to rhyme with pie) is an event in the environment; a stimulus situation is several events in the environment. A *response* is simply a part of our behavior. Rain is an environmental event—a stimulus—which leads to the responses of grabbing raincoats and opening umbrellas. A fall in temperature is a stimulus; the appearance of goose pimples is a response. Consider this statement: Lucille's lips pucker when she sees a lemon. The lemon is the stimulus. The pucker is the response.

One of the easiest ways to depict learning is as follows. When a stimulus is first presented, there may be no response. When it is presented the next time, there is a response. Miss Pegg shows the class a picture of a hyena and asks the class to name the animal. There is no response. She tells them that it is a picture of a hyena—she presents the stimulus. When she presents the picture a second time, everyone responds "hyena." This response indicates a change in the performance of these learners from the time before they were in the stimulus situation to the time after. From this change in performance we infer the occurrence of learning. Your behavior will presumably change as a result of reading this chapter. Before you read this chapter you may have defined learning as the acquisition of knowledge. After reading this chapter you may define learning as a relatively permanent change in a behavioral tendency as a result of reinforced practice. Your performance will have changed, and we will infer that you have learned.

By taking the learning event into consideration, we can plan instruction. A clear teaching plan should foresee which stimuli will result in the student's making which responses. Stimuli are all teaching materials and media —textbooks, films, lectures, programed lessons, television, discussion questions, and so on. The responses are the new performances the teacher expects the student to acquire. Considering how frequently instructors present materials to students without a clear conception of the new responses they expect the students to make, we can see how much clarity the use of the learning event introduces in instructional planning. In Chapter 2, we called the responses the instructor plans for *terminal behavior*—that behavior the teacher wants the student to show at the end of instruction. You will recall that in a detailed task analysis, the responses the student is expected to make lead to the terminal behavior.

From this discussion of learning, performance, response, and terminal behavior you can easily see that the terms overlap in meaning. In discussions of teaching, we almost always are referring to observable behavior changes, whether we call them learning, achievement, performances, responses, or terminal behavior. To develop a clear concept of learning, we distinguished between learning and performance or behavior. As teachers we can observe and measure achievement, performance, and behavior, but we can only infer the occurrence or non-occurrence of learning. In the ensuing discussion, therefore, even though we will refer to learning we ordinarily will mean achievement, performance, behavior, or response.

Summary Learning has been defined as a relatively permanent change in a behavioral tendency, the result of reinforced practice. Learning, an inferred state of the organism, should be distinguished from performance, an observed state of the organism. Learning events consist of stimuli, learners, and responses. In the chapters in Part 3 we will frequently refer to learning events.

Miss Pegg, a nursery school teacher, watched the children develop increased skill in movement. Leroy, who two months ago was unable to sit securely on the tricycle seat, has been peddling the tricycle with aplomb and peer approval for the last month. Which of the following best explains Leroy's change in behavior? (a) learning; (b) maturation; (c) native response tendencies; (d) habituation.

QUESTION 7-1

After selecting your answer, give the reasons for your choice and for your rejection of the alternatives.

Upon reading this section of the chapter, you should be able to meet these objectives:

7-4 Distinguish between internal and external conditions of learning.

7-5 Define contiguity in terms of occurrence of stimulus and response and describe its importance in various learning types.

7-6 Define practice in terms of repetition and describe its importance in various learning types.

7-7 Define reinforcement in terms of a procedure for presenting a reinforcer; give illustrations of the procedure.

7-8 Distinguish between positive and negative reinforcers and give illustrations of each.

7-9 Give illustrations of the trans-situational nature of reinforcers.

7-10 Define reinforcement in terms of a feedback procedure; list four feedback procedures and illustrate each.

7-11 Define extinction in terms of reinforcers and competing responses.

7-12 List the four major conditions of reinforcement and illustrate the major effects of each condition on learning.

7-13 Describe the importance of reinforcement as a condition for various learning types.

7-14 Define generalization in terms of a response to a new stimulus and illustrate this behavior.

7-15 Define discrimination in terms of a different response to two or more stimuli and illustrate this behavior; distinguish between S^D and S^Δ and provide behavioral illustrations involving both stimuli.

7-16 Give illustrations to show what is meant by overgeneralization and overdiscrimination.

7-17 Distinguish between escape and avoidance training and a punishment procedure; explain how punishment is related to intensity of shock, to a rewarded alternative, and to consummatory responses.

7-18 Describe and illustrate two psychological myths about the effects of punishment.

THE BASIC CONDITIONS

External conditions of learning—contiguity, practice, reinforcement, generalization, and discrimination—are important in the various learning types. In this section, we shall describe and illustrate each of these conditions and briefly relate each to the learning for which it is important. The chapters following this give more detailed consideration to these conditions and to their relationship to the various types of learning. Those chapters show that not all these conditions are equally important in each learning type. Whereas practice (for example, repetition) is important in simple learning, contiguity is important in both simple and complex learning.

Contiguity

One of the basic learning conditions is contiguity—the almost simultaneous occurrence of the stimuli and the responses. In the typical Pavlovian experiment the ringing of the bell—the stimulus—was contiguous with the salivation of the dog—the response. Miss Pegg presents a flash card which bears the word *cat,* and the children say "cat." The flash card is the stimulus, and "cat" is the response. One learning theory (Guthrie, 1952) holds that the only necessary condition for learning is contiguity, or the simultaneous occurrence of the stimulus and the response.* In planning your teaching you will often provide for such a simultaneous occurrence. When we teach the child to associate the word *doll* with the object, we must present the stimulus object at the time the child says "doll," the response. As teachers we are always interested in having the students build up associations between particular stimuli and responses. One of the necessary learning conditions for developing such associations is contiguity.

Contiguity is an important condition in most learning. Classical conditioning involves contiguity of the conditioned and the unconditioned stimulus. Operant conditioning involves contiguity of the response and the reinforcing stimulus. Skill learning involves contiguity in the occurrence of the various links in the motor chain. Concept learning involves contiguity in the presentation of examples and nonexamples. Principle learning involves contiguity in the recall of the component concepts. Finally, problem solving involves contiguity in the recall of the component principles.

Practice

The definition of learning refers to reinforced practice, another basic external condition of learning. Practice is the repetition of a response in the presence of the stimulus. Unless other learning conditions are ideally provided, we probably learn very little (of relative permanence) from the first response we make to a particular stimulus. We usually must practice or repeat *S-R* (stimulus-response) associations to retain them for relatively long periods. The current educational emphasis on cognition and meaningful learning has made practice or repetition an unpopular learning condition. To many educators practice recalls the monotonous drills required by the teacher in the country schoolhouse. Practice becomes less necessary when the student has the entering behavior particular instructional objectives require. For example, those of you who studied learning in introductory psychology have less difficulty with the concept than those who are studying it for the first time. The ease with which you learn new things is largely a result of what you know at the start. For relatively novel stimuli and novel responses more practice is required than for those which are familiar. If we were to ask you to learn pairs of associated words, such as sand—box, bed—rock, mind—matter, and we presented the words both in English and in French, most students would require much less practice with the English list than with the French list because they already know the single English words and must only learn the associations. For the French list, most students would have to learn the single words and the

* In Edwin Guthrie's theory, responses are conceived as movements (see Hilgard and Bower, 1966, pp. 74–106).

associations. Of course, the student whose entering behavior includes a knowledge of French would require less practice than the student who did not have this knowledge. The teacher's provision for student practice should not be based on personal preference or on philosophical grounds but on the student's need for practice to attain the instructional objective.

Practice is of diminishing importance as a condition as we move from simple to complex learning. In classical conditioning, operant conditioning, skill learning, and verbal learning, it is of crucial importance. In concept learning, principle learning, and problem solving, it is of minor importance if the other learning conditions are properly provided. Later discussions will describe the major ways in which practice may be changed: the amount (in time) of practice, the number of practice periods, and the distribution of practice.

Reinforcement: Its Nature

Reinforcement is a major condition for learning. You will see that we can vary reinforcement procedures to provide different effects. The effects, of course, are the learning types we want our students to acquire. Because of the breadth of the concept and because it is an important condition for learning, we give reinforcement extended treatment in this chapter.

In this section we discuss reinforcement as a procedure. First we consider the procedure of providing the reinforcing stimulus, and then we consider the somewhat more complex procedure of providing informational feedback. Finally we discuss extinction, the procedure of withholding a reinforcer or of giving opposing responses. In the following section we discuss the conditions of reinforcement: immediacy, frequency, amount, and number.

Overwhelming evidence supports this generalization: Reinforced responses tend to be repeated in given situations; nonreinforced responses tend to be discontinued. This statement, known as the law of effect, was first enunciated by the great American educational psychologist, Edward Thorndike (1911) as follows:

> Of the several responses made to the same situation, those which are accompanied or closely followed by satisfaction to the animal will, other things being equal, be more firmly connected to the situation, so that when it recurs, they will be more likely to recur; those which are accompanied or closely followed by discomfort to the animal will, other things being equal, have their connection weakened, so that, when it recurs, they will be less likely to recur.

Much of Thorndike's experimental work was done with cats. By pulling a string which in turn opened a door, they escaped from their cages and obtained rewards in the form of raw fish. The cats' response was pulling the string, and the satisfaction following this response was the fish or the freedom of life outside the cage. If the cat received a mild electric shock each time it pulled the string instead of receiving fish and freedom, it would be less likely to make the correct response. Thorndike's formulation of the law of effect did not include a description of what happens when responses are followed by neither satisfaction nor discomfort, a topic we will consider below.

In the reinforcement procedure, an organism is presented with a particular stimulus—a reinforcer—before or after it makes a response. In a given situation the organism will tend to repeat responses for which it is reinforced and to discontinue responses for which it is not reinforced. We can distinguish a reinforcer from other stimuli because it has this particular effect on behavior.

Many examples illustrate the use of the reinforcement procedure. Let us take as an example a reinforcer which follows the response. The dog raises his head and majestically presents a series of barks (a signal to Cliff that he intends to go outside). Cliff opens the door and his dog makes his exit. The door, according to our definition, is the reinforcer; opening the door, a procedure, is reinforcement; and the response being reinforced is the dog's barking by the door. In Thorndike's sense, opening the door is a satisfier. Several experiments have utilized similar procedures with human subjects. William Verplanck (1955) reports a study in which subjects, who were unaware of how their behavior was being influenced, were reinforced for making opinion statements. Opinion statements were those the subjects began with words "I think. . . ," "It seems to me. . . ," and "I believe. . . ," As reinforcement, the experimenters nodded their heads, smiled, paraphrased what the subject said, and made statements of agreement such as "You're right" and "I agree." The subjects tended to make more opinion statements as a result of the reinforcement. When the reinforcers were withdrawn or the experimenters disagreed with or failed to paraphrase the statements of the subjects, the number of opinion statements sharply decreased.

We can also provide the reinforcer before the response. Ivan Pavlov, the Russian psychologist, employed this procedure. He presented meat or meat powder to a dog to cause salivation. The meat powder was the reinforcer, and the salivation was the response. Later in this chapter, when we compare classical and operant conditioning, you will see that this difference in procedure is the chief distinction between two basic learning types.

In human behavior we can easily find examples of the procedure which presents the reinforcer after the response is made. Harriet, in the second grade, correctly spells *rat, bat,* and *fat.* For these responses she receives three gold stars, a practice conforming with the teacher's classroom policy. The responses are the correct spelling of the three words. The reinforcers are the gold stars. The procedure of presenting the gold stars after these correct responses is reinforcement. Tim punches Rodney in the mouth, and their classmates cheer. We have the response—the punch—and the reinforcer (for Tim, but not for battered Rodney)—the mob cheers of their classmates. The law of effect predicts that Harriet will continue to spell these words correctly and that Tim will probably throw more punches at Rodney and perhaps at others. It also predicts that Rodney will do everything in his power to avoid Tim's aggression.

Positive and negative reinforcers   We can distinguish between positive and negative reinforcers. James Holland and B. F. Skinner (1961, pp. 52–62) present many familiar examples of positive reinforcers. A funny television program is a positive reinforcer. Presenting the program is positive reinforcement. The teacher who dismisses the class when it is rowdy may increase the amount of rowdy behavior since dismissal may be a positive reinforcement for the rowdy children. Positive reinforcement is the procedure of presenting stimuli. The stimuli themselves (gold stars, cheers, and candy) are the positive reinforcers.

Many examples illustrate negative reinforcers and negative reinforcement. We close windows and doors to avoid hearing loud noises. The loud noises are the negative reinforcers. Closing the windows and doors is the procedure we employ to eliminate them—the procedure is negative reinforcement. We avoid seeing an ugly sight by turning our faces. We avoid wrong answers by giving right answers. Ugly sights and wrong answers are negative reinforcers. We also turn off television commercials or absent ourselves from the room to avoid hearing them. The commercials are the negative reinforcers. The various means of avoiding them are negative reinforcement. Negative reinforcement is the procedure of terminating stimuli. The stimuli which we try to terminate (noise, commercials, ugly sights, and so on) are the negative reinforcers.

Positive and negative reinforcers can be viewed as incentives (Skinner, 1953). A positive reinforcer is a positive reward. A negative reinforcer is a negative reward—a stimulus which gives us relief from an unpleasant state of affairs. Examples of positive reinforcers are praise, prizes, smiles, and money. Examples of negative reinforcers are the relief from noise which follows closing the window, the signal which marks the end of a dreary television commercial, the anesthesia which reduces or eliminates dental pain, and the laryngitis in the vocal cords of a nagging wife. Both reinforcers strengthen the responses which precede them. Skinner observes that if you give flowers to your girl after you have quarreled with her, you may very well strengthen her tendency to quarrel. Better to give her the flowers after she has been sweet to you. Jimmy faithfully practices his basketball because he receives the attention and the praise of the high school girls. He also knows that steady practice avoids the wrath of the coach (a negative reinforcer).

Skinner describes punishment as the removal of a positive reinforcer and the addition of an aversive stimulus. You not only take your flowers back but also slap your girl friend. This procedure produces emotional states (you can be sure), but it does not eliminate the troublesome response. Your girl may not continue to argue, but she also may not agree and she may very well cry. If you kiss her when she cries, she may very well cry more, and if your relationship survives this crisis you will probably face more quarrels and tears.

The control of behavior, in Skinner's formulation, is clearly outside the organism. In a later work, Skinner (1972) expanded upon this idea and extended it to the functioning of society in general. In describing the effects of environment on human behavior he wrote (p. 18):

> The environment not only prods or lashes, it *selects*. Its role is similar to that in natural selection, though on a very different time scale, and was overlooked [heretofore] for the very same reason. It is now clear that we must take into account what the environment does to an organism not only before but after it responds. Behavior is shaped and maintained by its own consequences. Once this fact is recognized, we can formulate the interaction between organism and environment in a much more comprehensive way.

The individual's expectation of obtaining a reinforcer and of avoiding aversive stimuli could account for the increased vigor of response which organisms often demonstrate as they approach attractive goal objects they have previously experienced.

Trans-situational reinforcers Reinforcers are trans-situational because they strengthen all or most learnable responses in a given species. A reinforcer which is effective in improving spelling will also be effective in improving arithmetic. Money is the best example of a trans-situational reinforcer. In modern urban society, in which we have little opportunity to assess the entering behavior of people we meet for the first time, we often say that "money talks." The amount of money one seems to have and to spend becomes the sole criterion of status and personal worth. In effect, we assign money a wide reinforcing value. To have money (or only to have the appearance of having money) is to carry within one's self trans-situational reinforcement. The fact that reinforcers are trans-situational spares the teacher the problem of finding a new reinforcer for each response. However, the reinforcers which students find rewarding are products of their past histories. Fortunately, students, as heirs of the same culture, have sufficiently common histories to react positively to about the same reinforcers. No matter how often dissident social elements condemn our bourgeois way of life, most of us continue to enjoy money, praise, status, and success.

Reinforcement as feedback In this procedure the student is given knowledge of his correct responses. Whereas the term *reinforcement* connotes the hedonic aspect of reward, the term *feedback* stresses the informational aspect of the teacher's function. When Harriet spells fat correctly, the teacher may give her gold stars (which may please Harriet no end), but the more important fact is that Harriet knows she has been correct in her spelling. Usually students expect reinforcers for their efforts, whether or not their efforts have paid off. Harriet might believe that she will obtain gold stars if she merely utters whatever letters come to mind. As yet we have no way of separating the reward function from the informational function. Until we devise such a procedure, we cannot dismiss the importance of reinforcement in school learning.

A study by Travers and his associates (1964b) illustrates various ways in which feedback may be provided. Elementary school children had to learn English equivalents of German words. The German words appeared on flash cards with two English words, and the children were to select the correct English alternative. The experimenters used four feedback procedures: If the child selected the correct alternative, he was told, "That's right"; when he was incorrect, he was told, "No, that's wrong." If the child selected the correct alternative, he was told nothing; if incorrect, he was told, "No, that's wrong." If the child selected the correct alternative, he was told, "That's right"; if incorrect, he was told, "No, that's wrong; [German word] means [English word]." If the child selected the correct alternative he was told nothing; if incorrect, he was told, "No, that's wrong; [German word] means [English word]." The results indicated that the last two procedures were superior to the first two. In interpreting these results, Travers observes that the last two procedures introduced more redundancy into learning the correct English equivalents—that is, the repetition of the English word increased learning.

In an earlier study Keith Van Wagenen and Travers (1963) investigated the importance of the student's making an overt response and being reinforced for it. In the typical classroom situation only one student responds, and the others remain observers. The investigators tried to determine whether the nonparticipating students, the observers, learned as much as the participating students, those who made responses and obtained direct feedback. In more technical language, they compared the effectiveness of direct learning with that of vicarious learning (the learning of the nonparticipants). They designed an ingenious classroom situation which allowed the teacher to interact with some children but not with others. They used the same materials described in the previous experiment, flash cards with German words and English alternatives. The teacher held up a card and said, "John, this word is *baum*." John had to select the correct English alternative. If he said "tree," the teacher said "Right"; if he made a wrong selection, the teacher said nothing. Van Wagenen and Travers found that the children who interacted with the teacher (the direct learning group) learned and retained more of the correct English words than the children who did not interact with the teacher (the vicarious learning group). The experimental procedure allowed the children in the direct learning group to respond only every fourth time because each such group was composed of four children and only one could respond each time. It was possible, therefore, to determine how well the children in the direct learning group retained items on which they interacted with the teacher and how well they retained items on which they did not interact. Figure 7-2a shows that the children learned more items when they actively responded and obtained feedback (the direct learning condition). Figure 7-2b shows how well the vicariously learned items were retained by children who learned one-fourth of the items directly (condition *A*) and by those who learned all the items vicariously (condition *B*). You can see little difference between the two groups. The child in the direct learning group benefited from being there only for those items on which he interacted with the teacher.

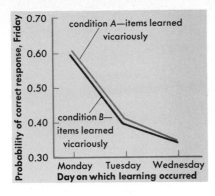

FIG. 7-2a   Test performance on Friday for direct learning group (after Van Wagenen and Travers, 1963).

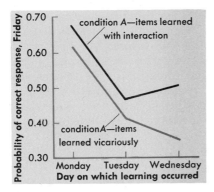

FIG. 7-2b   Test performance on Friday for vicariously learned items of direct and vicarious learning groups (after Van Wagenen and Travers, 1963).

Knowledge of the importance of supplying feedback has sparked several technological innovations, including programed instruction and computer-assisted instruction. Although the desirability of supplying feedback is amply supported by research, classroom observation quickly reveals the insuperable difficulties the teacher faces in attempting to provide feedback for twenty-five or more students. Patrick Suppes (1964, p. 83) describes the teacher's dilemma:

Let us suppose . . . that the class consists of only twenty-five children. If the class is working on this particular page [of a workbook containing problems] together, the teacher cannot hope to monitor the 250 problems being done, and, on the spot, have each child make appropriate corrections. Some of the elementary school mathematics teachers with whom I have worked have told me that in order to do a good job in the first and second grade it is necessary to spend at least one hour after each school day correcting the children's workbooks. Some of them have insisted that a more realistic estimate would be two hours. I have watched teachers who have gone through this laborious process of marking each child's work on each problem and requiring him to correct his errors the next day. . . . The impression of teachers who have tried this procedure has been positive, but I cannot cite any controlled data.

Suppes believes that technological methods will have to be introduced into the classroom to provide students with all the overt correction efficient learning requires.

Extinction   In this procedure a reinforcer is withheld to weaken a response. In the experimental laboratory, if an animal is not reinforced (with food) for pressing a bar which controls a feeding mechanism, the animal will press the bar somewhat more rapidly at first. Each nonreinforced occurrence, however, decreases the probability of the response. We can expect correct student responses which are not overtly reinforced to weaken or to become extinct. Unfortunately, we do not have the classroom research to support this assumption. In human learning, however, the situation is considerably more complex than it is in animal learning. The student can think he is right—that is, he can reinforce his own response—even when he is wrong. Or his response can be right, and he can think it is wrong. In the absence of reinforcement from the teacher, we cannot be certain that extinction will weaken correct responses, but we can suspect its operation in many cases. The teacher may also use extinction. If being informed of the incorrectness of his response is punishing and upsetting to the student, the teacher may reinforce the student's correct responses and ignore the incorrect responses. Admittedly, the procedure is risky because we do not know how the student will interpret the teacher's silence. Many students believe that no news is good news.

Another way to weaken or to eliminate a response is to make two responses incompatible. A husband who reinforces his wife when she makes life comfortable for him will find a decrease in the frequency of her outrageous demands on him. The husband's compliments presumably become incompatible with the wife's complaints. In the classroom, the teacher reduces the frequency of inattentive behavior by reinforcing the task-related responses of the student. If, however, in the adolescent classroom, the students obtain social reinforcers from their classmates for nonwork behavior, the teacher will find the management of the classroom difficult. The social reinforcers have become incompatible with the teacher's reinforcers. The teacher must control the reinforcers in the classroom in such a way as to make incompatibility of response work in favor of achieving instructional objectives.

Conditions of Reinforcement

Several conditions of reinforcement influence the strength of the response or the adequacy of the performance: (1) the immediacy of the reinforcer, (2) the frequency of the reinforcement, (3) the amount of the reinforcer, and (4) the number of reinforcers.

Immediacy of the reinforcer   Experimental studies show that the reinforcer must almost immediately follow the response if the organism is to associate the response with the stimulus. The delay should usually be no longer than one or two seconds. The case is not so clear in human learning because language can bridge the gap between response and reinforcement. One study actually disclosed that a delay in feedback and reinforcement was related to improved retention (Brackbill, Wagner, and Wilson, 1964). The experimenters required subjects to pair an English word with the correct one of two French words. The experiment used both informational feedback on the correctness of the choice and marbles and toys as rewards for correct responses. Some groups of children received a ten-second delay in feedback; and other groups, no delay. The groups with the delayed feedback retained more of the material after seven days than did the groups with the immediate feedback. This result is clearly inconsistent with the findings for animal learning. It is also possible that further findings may show that younger students require less delay than older students.

Learning efficiency often increases when the student receives feedback on the quality of his efforts. The importance of the student's receiving adequate feedback for his responses is not diminished by the uncertainty about how quickly the feedback should be provided. At no level of the educational system from preschool to graduate school is the absence or neglect of feedback pedagogically defensible. Unless the teacher makes systematic plans for feedback before moving on to new materials, he may easily ignore this important condition of learning. This then is a very practical reason for providing immediate feedback.

Frequency of reinforcement In partial reinforcement, the subject is rewarded only a fraction of the time for making responses. Evidence from extensive studies of partial reinforcement in animal learning indicates that responses resist extinction more when they have been reinforced on a partial rather than on a continuous pattern. Pigeons, for example, will continue to peck a disc when only one response in a thousand is rewarded. There have been extensive studies of various reinforcement procedures known as *schedules of reinforcement* (Ferster and Skinner, 1957). In some schedules the organism is reinforced for varying amounts of work or after varying amounts of time. In other schedules the organism is reinforced for fixed amounts of work or after fixed amounts of time. In general, responses on the variable schedules show more resistance to extinction than responses on the fixed schedules.

The applicability of these findings on partial reinforcement to teaching is questionable. The school curriculum, usually so crowded with instructional objectives, hardly leaves time to reinforce responses made even for the first time. It is true that, in the natural setting, responses we have already acquired are not reinforced each time we make them and yet they persist. In fact, dedication has been defined as the persistence of a response in the absence of reinforcement (Holland and Skinner, 1961). In the school setting, however, the findings on partial reinforcement do not excuse the teacher from reinforcing correct responses when they first occur. How often the teacher should reinforce these responses after they have been acquired is a question we cannot answer now.

Amount and number of reinforcers Response strength increases as the number of reinforcements of that response increases. When a limit is reached, however, each successive reinforcement adds smaller and smaller amounts of response strength. Since these limits hold in animal learning, we have every reason (and yet little supporting data) to believe that they hold and are reached sooner in human learning. The tedium often reported by students who have used teaching machines and programed materials is the result of more reinforcement of correct responses than they believe necessary. The amount of the reinforcer also affects behavior. In one study (Wolfe and Kaplan, 1941), a chicken ran faster to get four quarter-grains of corn than to get one whole grain, suggesting that the additional activity involved in consuming the four quarter-grains contributed something to the reward value. The applicability of this finding to teaching is uncertain, although it may puritanically suggest that our students will not appreciate what they learn unless we require them to expend the maximum effort.

Punishment

Solomon (1964) defines punishment as a stimulus the individual seeks to escape or avoid. Given a choice between punishment and no stimulus at all, the individual will choose no stimulus. Experimenters use three procedures in studying the effects of punishment: escape training, avoidance training, and a punishment procedure. For all procedures the experimenter may use an apparatus such as an alley runway, six feet long, with a start box (to contain a rat) at one end and a goal box at the other. In escape training the rat receives a shock as soon as the gate of the start box is raised; the rat quickly learns to run down the alley. In avoidance training the rat is given, for example, five seconds to reach the goal box after the start box gate is opened. He learns to run quickly enough to avoid the shock. In the punishment procedure the rat is first taught to run to the goal box to obtain food. After this behavior is well established, the rat is given a shock in the alley and goal box through an electrified grill. The rat quickly learns not to leave the start box. There is an interesting distinction between escape and avoidance training on the one hand, and the punishment procedure on the other hand. In the former case the rat is taught what to do, while in the latter case he is taught what not to do. You will later see interesting parallels in the control of human behavior.

According to Solomon, the effects of the punishment procedure differ according to the nature of the response involved. Moreover, to make even the crudest prediction of the effect of punishment on a response, you must know how that particular response was inserted in the individual's repertory of responses. Punishment, therefore, must be addressed to the entering behavior of the student. Let us consider the effects of punishment on responses previously established through positive reinforcers. Here the results of the punishment procedure depend largely on the intensity of the punishing agent. Solomon (p. 240) reports these findings:

As the intensity of shock applied to rats, cats, and dogs is increased from about 0.1 milliampere to 4 milliamperes, these orderly results can be obtained: (a) *detection* and *arousal*, wherein the punisher can be used as a cue, discriminative stimulus [Chapter 6], response intensifier, or even a secondary reinforcer: (b) *temporary suppression,* wherein punishment results in suppression of the punished response, followed by complete recovery, such that the subject later appears unaltered from his prepunished state; (c) *partial suppression,* wherein the subject always displays some lasting suppression of the punished response, without total recovery; and (d) finally, there is *complete suppression,* with no observable recovery.

The ambiguous results of many punishment experiments can be attributed to the different intensities and durations of punishment.

Evidence also shows that if the individual receives a shock together with positive reinforcement during reward training, the punishment procedure may actually strengthen the response. The association of reward and punishment produces stronger responses than the use of reward alone. Barclay Martin (1963) refers to an unpublished study which involved the rewarding and punishing of puppies. The reward-only puppies were petted and fondled by the experimenter. The punished-rewarded puppies were also petted and fondled, but, about five times a week, they were punished by switching, rough handling, and electric shocks. To test the effects of these two treatments, a human sat in a corner of the room and an observer recorded the amount of time the puppies spent near the human. The punished-rewarded puppies spent considerably more time near the human than did the reward-only puppies. This result is interesting because the usual effect of punishment is for the individual to avoid the punishing person and object. Martin suggests that the combination of reward and punishment may cause more arousal than reward alone and that occasional punishment may even heighten the anticipation of reward. The positive effects of punishment, however, would not prevail if the punishment were too intense and frequent, if it were not gradually introduced, and if the reward training which preceded the punishment were not sufficient. Martin's findings support the statement that disciplinary techniques should involve the combination of reward and punishment.

Punishment is extremely effective in producing compliance when the animal is offered a rewarded alternative to the punished response (Whiting and Mowrer, 1943). This procedure is used in housebreaking a dog. The dog learns to suppress urination and defecation inside the house (indoor stimuli) as long as these functions go unpunished outside the house (outdoor stimuli). This use of the punishment procedure, according to Solomon (1964), can produce a highly compliant animal. He has even observed that puppies raised in the laboratory, if punished by a newspaper swat for eating horsemeat and rewarded for eating pellets, will starve themselves to death when given opportunity to eat only the taboo horsemeat. They will readily eat the pellets when they are available. The use of punishment with a rewarded alternative is the basis of the disciplinary technique which we later describe as restitution.

We have now considered the effects of punishment on previously rewarded response. What are the effects of punishment on *consummatory responses*—responses necessary for biological survival, such as eating and sexual behavior? Contrary to ordinary expectation, these responses can be easily suppressed by punishment. Sexual behavior in males can be suppressed by weak punishment (Beach et al., 1956). Eating in dogs and cats can be permanently suppressed by even a mild shock delivered through the feeding dish or the feet (Masserman, 1943). The punishment may act as a conditioned stimulus warning the individual that punishment will ensue if he makes a particular response.

Solomon (1964) feels that the many psychological myths about the effects of punishment stem from two sources. First, there is the traditional emphasis in the psychology of learning, exemplified in the writing of both Thorndike and Skinner, that positive reinforcers (or satisfiers) are more effective than punishment in controlling behavior. For this reason no punishments were used in Skinner's *Walden Two* (1948). Second, there is the belief that, although punishment may effectively suppress undesired responses, the devastating side effects threaten the emotional balance of the individual. Solomon thinks this belief has been accepted at face value without supporting evidence (p. 250):

> Anyone who has tried to train a rat in a T maze, using food reward for a correct response and shock to the feet for an incorrect response, knows that there *is* a period of emotionality during the early training, but that, thereafter, the rat, when the percentage of correct responses is high, looks like a hungry, well-motivated, happy rat, eager to get from his cage to the experimenter's hand, and thence to the start box. Evidently going through a conflict is not a condition for neurosis. The rat is reliable, unswerving in his choices. Is he neurotic? Should this be called subservient resignation? Or a happy adjustment to an inevitable event? Is it a fixation, an evidence of behavioral rigidity? The criteria for answering such questions are vague today.

Summary   We have now considered the nature and the conditions of reinforcement. Discussing first the nature of reinforcement, we explained that reinforcers can be introduced before or after the desired response, can be positive or negative, and are trans-situational. As feedback, reinforcement is the procedure in which the student is given knowledge of his correct responses. Available evidence indicates that active responding combined with direct feedback is superior to passive responding with indirect feedback. Finally, we described extinction as a procedure in which a reinforcer is withheld to weaken a response or in which two responses are made incompatible. We next considered the conditions of reinforcement. Here we discussed the practical importance of immediate feedback, the efficacy of partial reinforcement, and the relationship of the amount and the number of reinforcers to student effort.

As a basic learning condition, reinforcement is important in most learning. In the form of the conditioning stimulus, it has major importance in classical conditioning. As the reinforcing stimulus, it has major importance in operant conditioning. As both kinesthetic and informational feedback, it plays a crucial role in skill learning. As feedback for the correct discriminations the student makes between examples and non-examples of a concept, it is important in concept learning. As feedback for the correct interrelating of concepts and principles, it is important in principle learning. It may be least important in problem solving since the correct solution generates its own feedback. In fact we may conclude that the importance of reinforcement diminishes somewhat in higher learning types since successful learning at these levels generates its own feedback. The student, in other words, when he undertakes some complex learning, knows the correct form of the class, relationship, or solution he seeks. Indeed, he achieves a large measure of scholarly independence when he knows what tests to apply to assess the adequacy of his own performance.

We can now turn to our last two conditions, or basic phenomena, of learning, what we shall call generalization and discrimination.

Generalization

Both generalization and discrimination are perhaps better defined as phenomena than as conditions of learning. They more properly refer to behavior which occurs under particular learning conditions than to the conditions themselves. We call them learning conditions because they are so closely associated with the basic conditions of contiguity, practice, and reinforcement and because they are basic to all learning. Many learning and educational psychologists prefer to describe even complex learning in terms of stimulus generalization and discrimination (see Glaser, 1962; Staats and Staats, 1963). Whatever your preference, it does appear that we can better understand all learning by understanding generalization and discrimination.

Frequently we observe that a child, when confronted with a new stimulus, makes a response he had previously learned to make to another stimulus. We call this behavior *generalization* (or stimulus generalization). When a child is told to call a particular color red, he is also learning to call other similar hues red. The child, however, does not make the same response to blue and yellow. When children learn not only that they have fathers but also that there are fathers of other children, fathers of fathers (or grandfathers), fathers of countries, fathers of inventions, and even fathers of various kinds of psychology, these children are generalizing. When Harriet discovers the similarity between *hat, sat, fat,* and *cat,* she recognizes other three-letter words ending in *at.* Harriet is generalizing. If we could not generalize, we would have to learn discrete responses for each discrete stimulus, and our behavior would appear to be something less than human.

Generalization gradients (curves) show that the tendency to generalize increases with the similarity of the new stimuli to the training stimuli. Figure 7-3 shows one such gradient. Experimenters trained pigeons to peck a disc illuminated with a green light. After they learned to peck at the green light, the experimenter gradually changed the color of the disc. In Figure 7-3, the arrow and the letters *CS* (for conditioned stimulus) indicate the

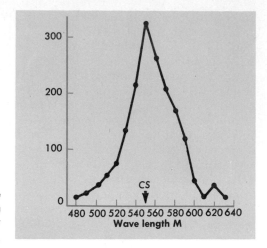

FIG. 7-3 A generalization gradient obtained from pigeons. The CS was a greenish light. The pigeon was tested to lights ranging from blue to red. Unpublished data, Norman Guttman and Harry I. Kalish (after Kimble and Garmezy, 1963, p. 145).

green light. The closer the hues are to green, the greater the frequency of pecking responses. Pigeons apparently see similarities among colors in much the same way as humans do.

Generalization is an important aspect of human behavior—either appropriate or inappropriate. Even our fear responses generalize. Although we feel pain (the prick of the needle with the anesthesia) for only a few moments in having a cavity filled, we generalize our fear responses to the dentist's waiting room, to his pretty and courteous receptionist, to the antiseptic smells of the inner offices, to all the implements lying on the tables, to the dental chair, and to white coats. Even the white coat of a waiter or a barber can conjure up memories of painful experiences at the hands of the dentist. Each of these examples illustrates what we commonly call *overgeneralization*.

Discrimination

In discrimination behavior the individual makes different responses to two or more stimuli. A child, for example, can learn to select the color red and not to select pink. To the extent that he learns to pick red and to ignore pink, he has learned to discriminate. Lewis Lipsitt (1961) studied discrimination learning of fourth grade children. The experimental apparatus included three windows with five different colored bulbs behind them. The children could press one of three buttons. If they pressed the correct button, the window light went out and a signal light went on. Incorrect response merely turned out the stimulus lights. Under one of the experimental conditions, the children were presented with the colors red, pink, and blue. Response to one of the buttons under these colors was rewarded (the signal light went on). Responses to the other two buttons were unrewarded (all the lights went out and no signal light went on). These children had to discriminate the right button from the wrong buttons. In terms of our definition of discrimination, the children were learning to make different responses to two or more stimuli.

As we become more discriminating, the environment exercises more control over our behavior. If the child learns to add when he sees a plus sign and to subtract when he sees a minus sign, these two signs (stimuli) exercise control over his behavior. When Hortense enters the Museum of Modern Art and is able to distinguish a painting by Picasso from one by Matisse and to point out to her companions the distinguishing characteristics, the stimuli of the paintings are controlling Hortense's behavior. When we ask a student to distinguish between two breeds of dogs and he correctly calls one a German Shepherd and the other a Collie, he can discriminate between these two breeds.

A useful way to describe discrimination learning is by the designations S^D and S^Δ. An S^D (ess-dee) is a discriminative stimulus—the occasion on which the response is reinforced. It is the go signal, like the green traffic light. In the S^Δ (ess-delta) situation, the response is not reinforced. It is the stop signal, like the red traffic light. We may visualize our behavior as being under the alternate control of S^Ds and S^Δs. Clarence likes Molly and always wants to be with her or at least to talk with her on the phone. He dials her number (S^D), and Molly answers (her voice is his reinforcer). He asks her for a date (S^D), and Molly accepts (more reinforcement). He continues to talk about the latest social scandals of the campus. Molly tells him that she is busy preparing for her midterm examinations (her mild complaint is an S^Δ). Clarence goes on to ask Molly what she thinks of the latest rock group to appear on campus. He receives no response (another S^Δ). With a slight tenseness in his voice, he asks Molly if she is serious about the date they have made (an S^D, but if he is not careful it could become an S^Δ). In a rather formal manner, she confirms her acceptance. Then she repeats that she is very busy (an S^Δ). This time Clarence notes the nature of the stimulus, and, with heart palpitating and the knowledge that a little love is better than none, he says good-bye (a possible S^Δ for Molly). Molly replies good-bye (a final S^Δ for Clarence).

It is also possible but not very useful for the teacher to analyze his teaching materials as patterns of S^Ds and S^Δs. We can, for example, analyze the print signals we have learned to use in reading in terms of these two stimuli. The new chapter headings, the paragraph indentations, the boldface type, and the capital letters at the beginning of sentences essentially represent go signals or S^Ds. The periods, the commas, and the ends of chapters and paragraphs represent stop signals or S^Δs.

It is more useful for the teacher to realize that teaching materials and methods provide stimuli (S^Ds) to which the students should respond and stimuli (S^Δs) to which the students should not respond. The teacher provides both types to develop the proper discriminations. When Daisy sees a plus sign (an S^D), she knows that she adds the adjacent numbers. When she sees a minus sign, she does not add the numbers if her directions are to add and not to subtract. In this instance the minus sign is an S^Δ. When teaching children the names of the capitals of the various states, we often find that the largest cities in those states are S^Δs. New York, Los Angeles, and Miami are incorrect responses to the question on capitals, while Albany, Sacramento, and Tallahassee are correct responses. The students eventually learn to discriminate between the stimuli *capital* and *largest city*. In teaching you the distinction between a positive and a negative reinforcer, we tried to supply S^Ds. The S^D for the positive reinforcer was the verb (and its equivalents) *present*. A positive reinforcer is a stimulus which is presented. The S^D for the negative reinforcer was the verb (and its equivalents) *terminate*. A negative reinforcer is a stimulus which is removed or terminated. In making this distinction, we make each verb an S^Δ for the opposite reinforcer, so that the word *present* is an S^Δ for the response *negative reinforcer*. These examples suggest the very fine-grain analysis of instructional procedures and materials the use of S^Ds and S^Δs makes possible. In our later discussion of programed instruction, we shall see the extensive use of these two stimuli.

Just as one can overgeneralize, so can one overdiscriminate. Making correct, even subtle, discriminations can be the mark of the scholar or the pedant, the gentleman or the dandy. The distinction in either case is sometimes difficult to make; it may depend on how useful the discriminations made prove to be. Sometimes old ideas parade under new names. The need for love becomes the need for succorance, and the need to give love becomes the need for nurturance. If the new terms add anything to the description of human behavior, individuals rarely agree on exactly what it is. Similarly, in the interests of courtesy to and comfort for one's guests, one should supply ample silverware for each place setting. When, however, the hostess supplies each guest with so many implements of silver that good taste becomes massive confusion, we have a case of overdiscrimination. A ring and cuff links are proper gentlemanly attire, but the dandy may include an array of jewelry, hair lacquers, ascots, and colognes which betray more than the usual discrimination in adornment.

Travers (1963, p. 123) refers to the tendency in the classroom to stress discrimination and to suppress generalization. He states that "many teachers will mark unusual metaphors and figures of speech as 'unclear' and will suppress generalization in the literary field. Despite the efforts to the contrary on the part of many school officials, the prosaic development of precise discriminations generally takes precedence as an objective over free, creative, and often undisciplined expression." The current emphasis on learning the basic structure of various subject matter and on creative thinking may often overlook the fact that generalizations must derive from the discriminations the student has learned. For purposes of motivation, however, but not necessarily for the acquisition of knowledge, we perhaps should allow the student his private avenues in the pursuit of some instructional objectives.

Summary The discussion of generalization and discrimination concludes the section on basic learning conditions and phenomena. We have postponed the discussion of other important learning phenomena, particularly retention and transfer, until we reach the description of the learning types with which they are most closely associated. In this section we have described contiguity, practice, reinforcement (both its nature and conditions), generalization, and discrimination. Contiguity, the almost simultaneous occurrence of stimulus and response, appears to be an important condition for most learning. Practice, the repetition of a response in the presence of the stimulus, diminishes in importance as we move up the hierarchy to complex learning. Reinforcement, as a procedure for introducing a stimulus or feedback, varies in importance in accordance with the nature of the reinforcer (as in the case of reward or information) and the conditions of reinforcement, as well as with the learning type. As an external condition of learning, it may diminish in importance as the student learns to generate his own reinforcers. Generalization and discrimination, as basic learning phenomena, can explain both simple and complex learning. In the description which follows of the two basic learning types, you will see generalization and discrimination at work. It is equally possible, and in the opinion of many educational and experimental psychologists entirely legitimate, to explain skill, verbal, concept, and principal learning in terms of generalization and discrimination. Whether such explanations are intellectual *tours de force* or the basis of distinctions useful for the teacher remains to be seen.

In the remainder of Part 3, we shall frequently refer to these basic learning conditions. As we discuss each learning type, we shall consider what conditions the teacher must arrange to facilitate the learning embodied in his instructional objectives. Since these conditions represent classes of external stimulus situations, you will see that they can be provided in many different ways. The next chapter considers the first two learning types, classical and operant conditioning.

You should now return to objectives 4–16 and determine how well you have achieved them.

QUESTION 7-2

Mr. Dromboski, in teaching the concept *dog* to children in the second grade, adopted this procedure. He used a series of pictures, exposing a pair of pictures each time. One picture always showed a dog. The other showed another animal, such as a fox, wolf, or coyote. Which of the following best describes Mr. Dromboski's procedure? (a) Reinforcement; (b) discrimination; (c) practice; (d) generalization.

After selecting your answer, give the reasons for your choice and for your rejection of the alternatives.

SUMMARY

Part 3 of this text considers the third component of the basic teaching model, instructional procedures. Each chapter in this part describes the procedures for providing instruction for the various learning types. The present chapter introduced you to the basic external learning conditions—those conditions outside the student in what is called the stimulus situation. Internal learning conditions are the student's entering behavior—the subject matter of Part 2 and the recurrent material of Part 3.

The first section of this chapter defined learning and the learning event. It distinguished learning from performance and from maturation, native response tendencies, fatigue, habituation, and drug effects. The second section described the external conditions of learning: Contiguity is the almost simultaneous occurrence of the stimulus and response. Practice is the repetition of the response in the presence of the stimulus. In the third condition, reinforcement, the organism is presented with a particular stimulus before or after it makes a response. Contiguity, practice, and reinforcement are classes of events. Particular instances of these conditions vary with the learning they are designed to produce. In school learning, for example, reinforcement is often a procedure for supplying the student feedback on the correctness of his responses. Extinction is a procedure of withholding a reinforcer to weaken a response or of making one response incompatible with another. This section also described two phenomena of learning: In generalization a response made to a new stimulus is one previously made to another stimulus. In discrimination, the individual makes a different response to two or more stimuli. Both generalization and discrimination are basic learning phenomena and have been employed in describing complex human learning. Punishment involves the suppression of an undesired response—the individual learns what not to do.

SUGGESTED READINGS

Several very important volumes on the psychology of learning, in hardcover and paperback editions, will help the serious student to find out about the research in this area:

HILGARD, ERNEST R., and H. BOWER GORDON, *Theories of Learning,* 3rd ed. New York: Appleton-Century-Crofts, 1966.

KIMBLE, GREGORY A., *Hilgard and Marquis' Conditioning and Learning.* New York: Appleton-Century-Crofts, 1961.

PAVLOV, I. P., *Conditioned Reflexes: An Investigation of the Physiological Activity of the Cerebral Cortex,* trans. and ed. G. V. Anrep. London: Oxford University Press, 1927.

SKINNER, B. F., *Science and Human Behavior.* New York: The Free Press of Glencoe, 1953.

Several volumes on learning were especially written for teachers, trainers, and other educators. These are among the leading volumes:

GAGNÉ, ROBERT M., *The Conditions of Learning.* New York: Holt, Rinehart & Winston, Inc., 1965.

HILL, WINFRED F., *Learning: A Survey of Psychological Interpretations.* San Francisco: Chandler Publishing Co., 1963.

TRAVERS, JOHN F., *Learning: Analysis and Application.* New York: David McKay Co., Inc., 1970.

TRAVERS, ROBERT M., *Essentials of Learning: An Overview for Students of Education*. New York: The Macmillan Company, 1963.

The following are general introductory texts on learning; some are programed:

GEIS, GEORGE L., STEBBINS, WILLIAM C., and LUNDIN, ROBERT W., *Reflex and Operant Conditioning*. New York: Basic Systems, Inc., 1965. A programed textbook.

HOLLAND, JAMES G., and SKINNER, B. F., *The Analysis of Behavior*. New York: McGraw-Hill Book Company, 1961. A programed textbook.

MEDNICK, SARNOFF A., *Learning*. Englewood Cliffs, N.J.: Prentice-Hall, Inc., 1964.

The following books discuss types or categories of learning and the problems associated with the classification of learning:

GAGNÉ, ROBERT M., *The Conditions of Learning*. New York: Holt, Rinehart & Winston, Inc., 1970.

MELTON, ARTHUR W., ed., *Categories of Human Learning*. New York: Academic Press Inc., 1964.

These books of readings emphasize the psychology of learning:

DE CECCO, JOHN P., ed., *Human Learning in the School*. New York: Holt, Rinehart & Winston, Inc., 1963.

HARRIS, THEODORE L. and SCHWAHN, WILSON E., eds., *The Learning Process*. New York: Oxford University Press, Inc., 1961.

STAATS, ARTHUR W., ed., *Human Learning*. New York: Holt, Rinehart & Winston, Inc., 1964.

CHAPTER EIGHT

CONDITIONING AND VERBAL LEARNING

This chapter describes and compares three basic types of learning: (1) classical conditioning (also called signal learning); (2) operant conditioning (also called stimulus-response learning); and (3) verbal learning (or verbal association). These types are not neatly separable and have similarities and differences. The first section compares operant and classical conditioning. The second section defines the nature and development of verbal learning. The third section describes both internal and external conditions which have effects upon verbal learning. And the fourth section explores the instructional implications of the material covered.

CONDITIONING

Upon reading this section of the chapter, you should be able to meet these objectives:

8-1 Describe the necessary learning conditions for classical conditioning and the order in which they are provided; distinguish between the nature of conditioned and unconditioned responses; give an illustration of classical conditioning.

8-2 Describe the necessary learning conditions for operant conditioning and the order in which they are provided; give an illustration of operant conditioning.

8-3 Describe the major distinction between classical and operant conditioning and give an illustration of this distinction.

In this section we shall look first at classical conditioning and then at operant conditioning. You will see that they are chiefly distinguished by the conditions under which they occur.

Classical Conditioning

The necessary entering behavior for classical conditioning is the unconditioned reflex—an inborn response to stimuli. It is unconditioned in the sense that it is unlearned. Many examples illustrate unconditioned reflexes in animals and humans: salivating of the dog at the sight of food, blinking of the eye in response to a puff of air, jerking of the knee in response to a tap below the knee, being nauseous in response to various noxious stimuli, being frightened and startled in response to loud noises, and so on. In human behavior, many of our emotional responses are the result of classical conditioning.

Pavlov exhaustively observed and measured the two external learning conditions necessary for this learning—contiguity and practice. The almost simultaneous presentation of two stimuli provides contiguity. One stimulus is called the *unconditioned stimulus,* and the other, the *conditioned stimulus.* In the familiar example of Pavlov's dogs, the dogs salivated at the sight of food. The food is the unconditioned stimulus. The conditioned stimulus could be any number of events. Pavlov used the ringing of a bell, the sounding of a tuning fork, or the flashing of a light. Originally each of these events is a neutral stimulus. It becomes a conditioned stimulus when it is paired with the unconditioned stimulus (food). In the typical classical-conditioning procedure the conditioned stimulus (the ringing of a bell) precedes the unconditioned stimulus (the food) by about one-half second, a very brief interval

The second external learning condition is practice. The pairing of the unconditioned (the food) and the conditioned (the bell) stimuli must be repeated. The amount of practice necessary depends on how strong the response to the unconditioned stimulus is. In any case the response to the conditioned stimulus (salivation in response to the ringing of the bell) becomes stronger with the number of pairings of food and bell. The result of the procedure, of course, is that the dog will salivate in response to the bell even in the absence of the food. Diagramatically, the procedure is this:

STIMULUS	RESPONSE

Food–(unconditioned)–salivation

Food + Bell .... salivation

Bell...(conditioned)...salivation

When the dog's response (salivation) is made to the bell, the response is called a *conditioned* response. The unconditional stimulus is called a *reinforcer* because it strengthens a new stimulus-response bond.

A favorite conditioning experiment involves the eye blink. When a puff of air reaches the pupil of the eye, the eye blinks. This is an unconditioned reflex—an inborn and not a learned behavior. In one variation of the procedure, a clicking noise is presented just one-half second before the air puff reaches the eye. This procedure satisfies the condition of contiguity. Repeated a number of times the air puff and the click meet the condition of practice. The air puff is the unconditioned stimulus, and the click is the conditioned stimulus. When the eye blink occurs in response to the click, the eye blink is the conditioned response.

To avoid oversimplification we should note that the conditioned blink (or response) is not the same as the unconditioned blink (or response). The unconditioned blink is a more rapid response and occurs in about one-fifth the time of the conditioned blink. We may learn an *anticipatory* blink, which occurs before the puff of air reaches the eye. Gagné (1970) refers to classical conditioning as *signal learning* because, in the example of the eye blink the conditioned blink anticipates the puff of air—it signals a puff of air to come. In other conditioned responses, both the rapidity and the magnitude differ from those of the unconditioned response. The dog's salivation is less in amount when the response is conditioned rather than unconditioned.

In human learning, it is difficult to find pure examples of classical conditioning. We learn to respond to signals, bells, buzzers, alarms, signs, and warnings through classical conditioning. Emotional responses, made originally to unconditioned stimuli, are often made to conditioned stimuli. Experiments show that the specific fears of children and adults are the result of classical conditioning (Dollard and Miller, 1950). The fear of water, for example, may be the result of falling into water and being temporarily submerged. The unconditioned fear of drowning becomes the conditioned fear of water.

Operant Conditioning

A somewhat more complicated learning type is called *operant conditioning* or instrumental learning. The necessary entering behavior is the availability to the organism of particular responses. A pigeon must be able to peck; a rat must be able to press a bar or lever, and a human being must be able to smile or scratch his head. These responses are called *operants* because they operate on the environment. When the pigeon pecks a disc, the rat presses a bar, or a dog scratches its head, it has changed the state of the environment by its response or operant. The objective of operant-conditioning procedures is simply to increase the frequency of the response—to have more pecking, pressing, and scratching.

Three external learning conditions must be provided in operant conditioning: reinforcement, contiguity, and practice. Fred Keller (1954, p. 6) gives this illustration of the conditions for this learning:

> This time our subject is a little girl, about seventeen months old, and the experimental situation is an ordinary living room, modified slightly to serve a laboratory purpose. Our observations begin as the little girl runs into the living room from the hallway and attempts to engage the attention of her mother, who sits by the window reading. Failing in her efforts, the child turns away. As her eyes wander over the room, they suddenly alight upon a new feature. Through a narrow gap between the sliding doors to the dining room, a small T-shaped handle projects itself. Just beneath the handle is a tin dish, easily within the child's reach. Approaching these objects quickly, but warily, the child touches the handle with her finger, and looks into the dish. As she does so, a small pellet of chocolate drops into the dish from a tube, the other end of which is out of sight in the dining room. Startled by this, the little girl momentarily withdraws from the dish, but returns to pick up the pellet and eat it. A few seconds later, she grasps the bar firmly and pulls it downward an inch or so, causing a second pellet to be discharged into the dish. From this time on, with rapidly growing efficiency, she operates this lever mechanism, eating each pellet as it comes, until the chocolate finally loses its appeal.

This description illustrates each of the external conditions of learning. First, the chocolate pellets are reinforcement, or, in Thorndike's terms, a satisfier. Second, contiguity is provided when the reinforcer is presented almost without delay once the girl responds by pulling the bar downward. Third, practice is provided since the girl pulls the bar several more times and is reinforced each time. The practice enables the girl to isolate the particular act which results in the reinforcement.

Operant conditioning is a more complex learning type than is classical conditioning, and we more easily find illustrations of it in human behavior. Gagné (1970) suggests these examples in the behavior of children: reaching and grasping for toys or other objects, smiling at particular people, posturing the body and limbs, vocalizing particular sounds and words. In adult learning, the pronunciation of unfamiliar foreign words is an instance of operant conditioning. Once the correct pronunciation is made (the operant), the correct response must be reinforced, the response and the reinforcement must be contiguous, and the response must be practiced under these conditions.

Diagrammatically, the procedure for operant conditioning is this:

R (pulling the handle) $\longrightarrow$ S (chocolate pellets)
S^D (chocolate pellets) $\longrightarrow$ R (pulling the handle)

In a later section of the book, when we discuss programed instruction, you will see how manipulating the reinforcement procedure allows us to produce varied and complicated responses, as in animal training acts. You will see, however, that in shaping a response we must still observe all conditions for operant conditioning.

Differences in Classical and Operant Conditioning

Gregory Kimble and Norman Garmezy (1963, p. 139) use these examples in comparing the two learning types. Example *A:* A dog is conditioned to lift his paw when he hears a bell. The bell is paired with an electric shock delivered to the dog by an electrode attached to its paw. Example *B:* The dog is trained to lift his paw at the sound of a bell. Again there is a shock to his paw, but the shock comes from a grill upon which the animal is standing. By lifting his paw the animal can avoid the shock. The first example illustrates classical conditioning. The second example, operant conditioning. In classical conditioning the bell and the shock are paired on every trial. In operant conditioning the dog can avoid the shock by lifting his paw. The difference then is in the reinforcement procedure: In classical conditioning the reinforcer (the unconditioned stimulus) occurs on every trial. In operant conditioning the reinforcer occurs only when the animal makes the correct response. In more precise language, we say that in operant conditioning the reinforcer is contingent (depends) upon the animal making the correct response. Whereas in classical conditioning the presentation of the reinforcer determines the response, in operant conditioning the response determines the presentation of the reinforcer.

The two basic learning types are classical and operant conditioning. They stand in the same relationship to complex learning as the electron and atom do to complex molecules. Because human learning is most frequently complex learning, we have difficulty finding pure examples of classical and operant conditioning. By understanding these simple learning types, however, we can easily observe how the conditions of learning relate to complex learning. Furthermore, familiarity with basic learning gives us the vocabulary we need to analyze complex learning in terms of the conditions and components the teacher can manipulate. Undoubtedly you will ask, as every student legitimately asks, "What does classical and operant conditioning tell me about how to teach?" Perhaps the most honest answer is that they tell you little. They do, however, contribute to the understanding of more complex learning.

QUESTION 8-1   Mr. I. M. Sternski has devised a disciplinary technique which he claims is very effective. Whenever a student breaks a classroom rule, a light flashes near the student's desk and he receives a relatively mild electric shock. On other occasions Mr. Sternski merely flashes the light without delivering a shock to the student. Which of the following best describes Mr. Sternski's technique: (a) classical conditioning; (b) operant conditioning; (c) both; (d) neither.

After selecting your answer, give reasons for your choice and for your rejection of the alternatives.

In this section, we shall describe the nature of verbal learning and its relationship to conditioning. In the following section, we shall describe the internal and external conditions necessary for verbal learning: meaningfulness, verbal mediation, instructions to learn, practice, reinforcement, and retention. Under retention we consider the processes of retaining and forgetting as explained by interference theory. Finally, we shall discuss the relationship between verbal learning and its measurement.

Upon reading this section of the chapter, you should be able to meet the following objectives:

8-4 Distinguish verbal learning from and relate it to *S-R* learning (operant conditioning) and skill learning.

8-5 Describe the materials and the three procedures used in the study of verbal learning and give examples of each.

The Nature of Verbal Learning

Since 1952, when John McGeoch and Arthur Irion published their second edition of *The Psychology of Human Learning,* investigators of human learning have shifted their emphasis from the study of animal conditioning to the study of verbal learning (Kausler, 1966; Mandler, 1967). As you will see in this section, however, the same basic learning conditions and processes are studied. Knowledge of their effects on human verbal learning has greatly expanded our general knowledge of human learning. Your skill in providing appropriate learning conditions for your students will be enhanced by your knowledge of human verbal learning. Research on verbal learning and language has revealed the close relationship of verbal learning to concept learning and to learning rules of grammar (Underwood, 1964a; Miller, 1962, 1965; and Mandler, 1967).

At its most basic level, verbal learning may be considered the process of forming verbal associations. Gagné (1970) uses this example: A child is presented with a three-dimensional object and told it is a tetrahedron. If the appropriate conditions are present, when the child sees this object the next time he will be able to say that it is a tetrahedron. At the most basic level, then, verbal learning is naming—attaching a name to an object. Later we shall refer to naming as *labeling* behavior. According to Gagné, verbal learning (at this level) is like skill learning in that it involves a chain of at least two links. The first link is the presentation of the object (the stimulus) and the observing of the object (the response). In the second link, the observing response results in certain internal stimuli which give rise to the verbal response—the utterance "tetrahedron." Gagné (p. 135) diagrams the simple act of naming:

$$Ss \longrightarrow R \quad \sim \quad s \longrightarrow R$$

   object   observing   tetrahedron   "tetrahedron"

The small *s*'s refer to internal stimuli.

The diagram indicates how verbal learning is related to basic *S-R* learning. The observing response which enables the child to distinguish one four-sided object from other four-sided objects is acquired through operant conditioning. The second link, which connects the internal stimuli to the actual utterance of the word, is also acquired through operant conditioning. As you will see shortly in the description of verbal development, both these links are necessary entering behavior for naming or labeling. You will also see that considerably more complex verbal associations are possible, involving longer chains and verbal hierarchies. Verbal learning resembles skill learning in that both involve the chaining of responses. In both chains each link is an individual stimulus-response association and acts as a stimulus for the next link. The major distinction between skill and verbal chains is the type of response. Skill chains involve motor responses; verbal chains involve syllable and word responses.

To give you a fuller conception of the nature of verbal learning, we shall now describe the materials and procedures used in its study.

Verbal Learning: Materials and Procedures

Materials The materials often used in research on verbal learning try to exclude meaning as an influence since the object is to study how individuals combine elements into the usual language structures (Deese and Hulse, 1967). The materials frequently do not consist of ordinary words, phrases, or sentences. A widely used verbal material is the nonsense syllable, invented by Hermann Ebbinghaus (1850–1909) in his early studies of memory. Originally, nonsense syllables consisted of a vowel between two consonants—for example, BAB, TUC, and YAB. Ebbinghaus (1885) found 2,300 consonant-vowel-consonant nonsense syllables in the German language. Using nonsense syllables eliminates meaningfulness as a factor in verbal learning. It was found later, however, that nonsense syllables as English words vary in meaningfulness (Glaze, 1928). Some nonsense syllables are easier to learn than others because they bear closer resemblance to English words. For example the nonsense syllables BIZ, SEN, and MAK are more meaningful than WEZ, XIY, and CIJ. To have stricter control over meaningfulness, recent investigators have used consonant syllables which contain no vowel, such as MHZ, KBH, and WDQ. Even these syllables differ in meaningfulness, however. For example, BKD and WHP are considerably more meaningful than MHZ and KBH. Despite all of our fears of meaningless rote learning, total meaninglessness is indeed a hard state to achieve.

Other materials are used in the study of verbal learning. Ordinary English words are often presented as a single list, as in serial learning, or as pairs of words, as in paired-associate learning. Occasionally both nonsense syllables and words are mixed.

Procedures We shall now briefly consider the three procedures used in presenting the materials: immediate free recall, serial learning, and paired-associate learning.

IMMEDIATE FREE RECALL   Here the subject is asked to recall what he has learned after one exposure to verbal material. Investigators may present the words one at a time and request the subject to recall as many words as possible in any order they occur to him. The verbal materials may consist of one or more lists. The words in the lists may be essentially unrelated or they may be closely associated (Deese, 1959). It is even possible to vary the order of the words in the list with each successive presentation of it (Waugh, 1961).

SERIAL LEARNING   Here the subject has less freedom in recall. He is expected to recall the words in the order in which they were presented. The usual method is to present the words one at a time and to have the subject anticipate the next word in the list—the serial anticipation method. When the complete list of words has been exposed, one trial is completed. If nonsense syllables are used, the subject must spell the item. If English words are used, he only pronounces the item. Later in the chapter we will consider the serial-position effect involved in serial learning.

PAIRED-ASSOCIATE LEARNING   This procedure is similar to learning the English equivalents of a list of foreign words. In the study of verbal learning, the verbal units in the pairs can be nonsense syllables, words, or both. This list of paired associates combines nonsense syllables and words:

CFY—KID
XBN—GAT
DSU—GAT
etc.

Later in our discussion you will see examples of lists in which only nonsense syllables or words are paired. The first word in the pair is called the *stimulus term* (CFY, XBN, and DSU). The second word is called the *response term* (KID, GAT, and CAT). Later you will also see that the factors which influence the learning of the response term do not always apply to the learning of the stimulus term.

Summary

In describing the nature of verbal learning we saw that it both resembles skill learning, because it involves chains of stimulus-response associations, and is distinct from skill learning, because it involves verbal rather than motor responses. Because each link in the chain is a stimulus-response association, operant conditioning must provide the necessary entering behavior. Materials used in the study of verbal learning are selected on the basis of their meaninglessness. The nonsense syllable permits the best control, but ordinary English words are also used. The three procedures used in the study of verbal learning are immediate free recall (the least structured procedure), and serial and paired-associate learning.

Meaningfulness

The first part of this section describes one internal condition that has major effects on verbal learning. Upon reading this portion of the chapter, you should be able to meet these objectives:

8-6   Describe two common views of rote learning in terms of verbal associations and discuss the possible intellectual worth of rote learning.

8-7   Define meaningfulness in terms of different verbal associations and, using three English words, illustrate your definition.

8-8   Describe the spew hypothesis in terms of experience and availability of verbal responses and illustrate your definition.

8-9   Describe the effect of meaningfulness on rate of learning and illustrate this effect.

8-10   Define retention and forgetting in terms of the amount of material and time.

8-11   Describe the effect of meaningfulness on retention and illustrate this effect.

Meaningfulness, among all the conditions of verbal learning, has the strongest influence over the rapidity of learning (Underwood, 1964b). Because of its importance we shall consider several aspects of meaningfulness: its relationship to rote learning; its empirical definition; the spew hypothesis; and its relationship to rate of learning and retention.

Rote and meaningful learning   Many slogans are able to galvanize educators into action, but no slogan has more revolutionary and dramatic appeal than this one: Down with Rote Learning! Up with Meaningful Learning! Benton Underwood (1964a, pp. 51–52) characterizes commonly held opinions of rote learning:

> Rote Learning! Let us imagine some free associations which these two words might elicit from people in psychological and educational circles, restricting the responses to those which meet standards of good taste. It is likely that the following would be among the most frequent responses: "dull," "Ebbinghaus," "narrow," "verbal learning," "sterile," "nonsense syllable," "memory drum," "serial list," and so on. Two notions might be culled from such associations. First is the notion that rote learning is closely associated with verbal learning, an association which is quite appropriate. The second notion is that rote learning is felt to be dull, narrow, sterile, and in a manner of speaking, deals with a form of learning that is almost intellectually demeaning.

This harsh image of rote learning undoubtedly has a long lineage. Mere verbal repetition, which requires students to memorize poetic passages from Shakespeare, Donne, Keats, and Browning, the great speeches of Jefferson and Lincoln, and the verses of patriotic songs, had fallen into considerable disrepute by the beginning of this century. The educational reformers of that time were quick to point out the rather obvious stupidity of having students recite with the bombast and dramatic gesture of the elocution teacher eloquent passages from Shakespearean soliloquies and Lincolnian public addresses. The students did not understand them, slavishly parrotted them, and soon forgot them. For the reformers, meaningful learning had to replace rote learning. Underwood (1959, p. 112) cites this extreme example of the former policy:

> . . . The student would memorize the multiplication tables in rote fashion. He would be supposed to acquire this knowledge over a period of time and as a consequence of having to use multiplication in contrived situations, such as, say, play store. Undoubtedly no practice of this policy has been quite this extreme, but it seems clear that there has been a marked de-emphasis of rote acquisition.

Definition of meaningfulness   The ambiguity of the words *meaning, meaningfulness, understanding,* and so on has caused several centuries of controversy in philosophical, educational, and, more recently, psychological circles. There are treatises on the meaning of meaning, on meaning as subsumption, on meaning as subjective interpretation of experience, on linguistic meaning, and on meaning as cognitive structure. You can take your choice of these and others still. From this potpourri we have chosen a definition consistent with the emphasis of this book on the importance of quantifying behavior as a means of studying it. Laboratory research on verbal learning, as distinct from armchair discussions of meaningfulness, has defined meaningfulness in terms of measurable behavior. Clyde Noble (1952), for example, defines it as the number of different associations elicited by a verbal unit—a nonsense syllable or an English word. This is how Noble proceeded. He gave college students a list of ninety-six words and asked them to write all the associated terms, things, places, and events they could think of in one minute. For example, given the word *king,* in one minute the student could record these responses: queen, King Cole, ruler, Sky King, kingdom, England, imperial, and kingfish. Noble selected his list partly from the Thorndike-Lorge (1944) list of the 20,000 most frequently used words in the English language. He also chose words which occurred very infrequently. His list, therefore, contained such words as *kitchen* and *army* (high-frequency words) and *lemur, grapnel,* and *stoma* (low-frequency words). Table 8-1 lists some of the words and indicates their frequency. The words at the head of the list evoked more associations from the students than did the words at the end. What Noble discovered (and Table 8-1 shows) is that the words with the highest number of associations are also the words which occur with the greatest frequency in the language. *Kitchen, army, money,* and *dinner,* for example, which head the list, occur with very high frequency. *Stoma, grapnel, flotsam,* and *carom* appear at the end of the list and also are not among the 20,000 most frequently used words.

When we define meaningfulness as the number of different associations elicited by a verbal unit we are defining it as *frequency* or *familiarity.* The more frequently a word occurs in the language, the greater its familiarity, and the greater the ease with which it can be attached to other words.

TABLE 8-1   MEANINGFULNESS OF WORDS AND FREQUENCY OF OCCURRENCE IN THE ENGLISH LANGUAGE (after Underwood, 1959, p. 114).

WORD	T-L	WORD	T-L	WORD	T-L
1. kitchen	AA	21. region	A	41. argon	—
2. army	AA	22. quarter	AA	42. sequence	6
3. money	AA	23. leader	AA	43. pallor	2
4. dinner	AA	24. mallet	3	44. tankard	1
5. wagon	A	25. kennel	6	45. bodice	2
6. office	AA	26. keeper	23	46. vertex	—
7. heaven	AA	27. fatigue	19	47. rostrum	—
8. jelly	19	28. unit	29	48. ovum	—
9. jewel	41	29. effort	AA	49. tartan	1
10. insect	40	30. quarry	11	50. endive	—
11. village	AA	31. quota	3	51. jetsam	—
12. garment	40	32. yeomen	11	52. lichens	7
13. zebra	2	33. zenith	4	53. percept	—
14. captain	AA	34. ordeal	5	54. capstan	—
15. typhoon	—	35. pigment	4	55. lemur	—
16. youngster	21	36. naphtha	1	56. nimbus	—
17. uncle	AA	37. pallet	2	57. carom	—
18. income	46	38. entrant	—	58. flotsam	—
19. zero	11	39. jitney	—	59. grapnel	—
20. hunger	37	40. rampart	4	60. stoma	—

Note: The sixty words are from Noble (1952); they are given in order of meaningfulness. The *T-L* column indicates the frequency of occurrence of that word in the Thorndike-Lorge count (1944). AA is most frequent, such words occurring more than one hundred times per million words. A words are those that occur from fifty to one hundred times per million. A number refers to the actual frequency per million. A dash indicates that the word does not occur in the 20,000 most frequently used words.

In this sense some words are more meaningful than others: *Kitchen* and *army* are more meaningful than *stoma* and *grapnel*. This definition lacks in pretentiousness what it gains in explicitness. For the experimental purposes for which it was invented, it has worked very well.

Spew hypothesis   This hypothesis, based on Noble's definition of meaningfulness, is as follows: The frequency with which words have been experienced determines their availability as responses in new associative connections (Underwood and Schulz, 1960). We have already shown how the words which occur most frequently in the language evoke the greatest number of associations. But even more strikingly, the order in which verbal responses are made to these words is determined by the amount of experience the subject has had with each response. An interesting experiment illustrates this point (Cromwell, 1956). Each subject was given eight blank cards and asked to write the names of eight different individuals who possessed the same first name. The experimenter gave the first name to be used. For example, if he gave the name *John,* each subject wrote down the names of eight Johns whom he knew. The eight cards were numbered so that the experimenter could determine later the order in which the names were written. Following this phase of the experiment the subjects ranked each of the eight people on these characteristics: (1) how well they liked the person; (2) how much contact they had had with the person; (3) how long it had been since they had seen the person; (4) how well they knew the person. Rue L. Cromwell was interested in how the order in which the names were written was related to frequency of contact. The correlation was 0.96, almost perfect. We can conclude that frequency of contact was related to the frequency with which the name was spoken and therefore to the various response strengths represented in the order in which the names appeared on the eight cards.

Meaningfulness and rate of learning A well-established principle is the following: The higher the meaningfulness, the more rapid the learning (Underwood, 1964b). Which of the following two lists, for example, would you find easier to learn?

LIST A
LWD—PANF
SPX—LEMUR
BDQ—GOYJO

LIST B
LWD—HORSE
SPX—FRENCH
BDQ—GO-GO

Most students would learn list *B* faster than list *A* because of the greater familiarity (meaningfulness) of the response terms in list *B*. Several studies supply the evidence upon which this principle is based. Using Noble's procedure for measuring meaningfulness, Kimble (1963) required students to learn eight different lists of different average levels of meaningfulness. Figure 8-1 shows the results of his study. List 1, which was the least mean-

FIG. 8-1 The relationship between ease of learning and meaningfulness of English words (Kimble and Garmezy, 1963, p. 222).

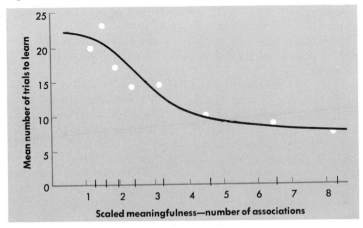

ingful, required between twenty and twenty-five trials (and considerable patience) to learn. List 8, the most meaningful, required between five and ten trials.

Rapid learning also results in slow forgetting, and slow learning in rapid forgetting (Underwood, 1949). This finding is contrary to the popular notion that students who learn rapidly forget just as rapidly, while the plodding student makes slower but surer progress. Although it would be pleasing to find the advantages more democratically distributed, the evidence is all in favor of the rapid learner.

Meaningfulness and retention   Before we can discuss this relationship, we must define *retention*. Retention refers to the amount of material remaining over a period of time. If we asked you to memorize five important dates in English history 1066, 1215, 1588, 1815, and 1914), and, if, several weeks later, we asked you to list these dates you might have forgotten one or two. Retention would refer to the three or four dates you could recall. *Forgetting* refers to the amount of material lost over a period of time. The total learning equals the amount of material retained plus the amount forgotten. Some individuals like to say that they have forgotten more than they learned in school and college. This, of course, is not possible. If you never learned one of the historical English dates you cannot, in all honesty, say that you have forgotten it. With regard to our formal education it may be more accurate to say that we have forgotten more than we have remembered (or retained). You should be aware of the distinctions in these definitions. It is quite possible that you have forgotten many dates which you once learned. We have all had the experience of cramming for examinations. As if the examination were a ritualistic act of purgation, shortly after it we find it quite impossible to recall the most obvious facts and ideas. There was more immediate recall than retention.

We can now examine the relationship between meaningfulness and retention. The principle is this: Not only is meaningful material more rapidly learned than meaningless material, but also it is remembered for longer periods of time. Figure 8-2 shows the retention of different materials over a period of one month. You can see that "substance with insight" (presumably more meaningful) was remembered longer than ordinary prose and nonsense syllables. Although the comparison is not made, we know that prose is remembered longer than lists of unrelated English words (e.g., fish, books, metal, geometry).

A study of how much course content was retained one year after the completion of a course in zoology (Tyler, 1934) classified materials on the basis of various examination questions. Table 8-2 lists the questions. You can see that retention of the first three questions, which dealt mostly with factual information, approximated retention of nonsense syllables and unrelated words in Figure 8-2. Retention of the last two questions, which required application of principles and interpretation, resembled retention of the more meaningful material in Figure 8-2. The retention of material in the zoology course probably represents the long-term outcome of many similar courses:

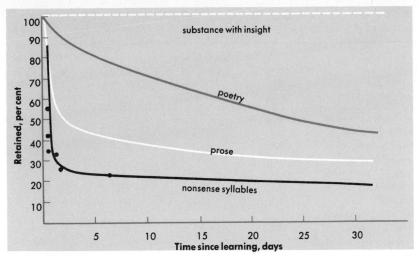

FIG. 8-2 Retention curves for different materials from five to thirty days (after Guilford, 1952, p. 408).

After one year much of the factual information is forgotten, but there is a gain in scores on questions dealing with conceptual material. The gain in retention of conceptual materials may reflect the student's continued use of this area of his knowledge. Tyler's study, unfortunately, has been used by some authors as a rationale for dispensing with the teaching of technical terms and information. In most disciplines such dispensation is neither feasible nor desirable. The teacher's function, we shall argue below, is not the elimination of unfamiliar course materials but the finding of procedures which make relatively unfamiliar materials relatively meaningful.

We shall now turn to another condition of entering behavior for verbal learning: verbal mediation.

Verbal Mediation

Upon reading the following portion of the chapter, you should be able to meet these objectives:

8-12   Define verbal mediation in terms of talking to yourself.
8-13   Distinguish between pictorial and verbal mediators by giving examples of each.
8-14   Describe the effect of verbal mediation on verbal learning.

Definition   Verbal mediation is talking to yourself in relevant ways when faced with something to be learned or a problem to be solved (Jensen, 1966). Most mediation is inaudible and unconscious. In fact, we are always slightly embarrassed when we are caught talking aloud to ourselves, al-

TABLE 8-2   A COMPARISON OF EXAMINATION SCORES DURING THE SEMESTER AND ONE YEAR LATER (after Tyler, 1934).

TYPE OF EXAMINATION EXERCISE	BEGINNING OF COURSE	MEAN SCORES TIME OF COURSE EXAMINATIONS	ONE YEAR LATER	PERCENT OF GAIN LOST ONE YEAR LATER
1 Naming animal structures pictured in diagrams	22.2	61.8	31.4	76.8
2 Identifying technical terms	19.7	83.1	66.5	26.2
3 Recalling information				
a. Structures performing functions in type forms	13.3	39.3	33.9	20.8
b. Other facts	21.4	62.6	54.1	20.6
4 Applying principles to new situations	35.2	64.9	65.1	Gain 0.7
5 Interpreting new experiments	30.3	57.3	64.0	Gain 24.8
Average for all exercises in the examination	23.7	74.4	63.3	21.9

though we all do it especially when the problems we are trying to solve are particularly difficult. In fact, when our problems "drive us out of our minds," we may ignore other people completely and talk aloud to the only person who understands us—ourselves.

An experiment by N. E. Miller (1935) shows how something you say to yourself can act as an internal stimulus for a public act. In this experiment the subject received a shock just after the letter T was presented but received no shock after the figure 4 was presented. Each time the T or the 4 was presented the subject had to say "T" or "four." In the next phase of the experiment the subject was presented with a series of dots. He was directed to think to himself of T when one dot was presented and to think to himself of 4 when the next dot was presented, and so on in an alternate manner. Every time the subject thought of T, he made the same physiological response that he made to the electric shock. He did not make this response when he thought of 4. This is another example of how our internal verbal behavior controls our public acts.

Pictorial and verbal mediators   Some mediators are pictorial rather than verbal. Gagné (1970) suggests the following example. If we require a student to learn the pair of words *hat—fix,* he can use a verbal or a pictorial mediator. He might think of Dick's hatband (a pictorial mediator) and learn the pair in this fashion: *hat—Dick's—fix.* The word *Dick's* also rhymes with *fix,* so it also acts as a verbal mediator. Another student might imagine a battered hat which needs fixing. In this case a purely visual image serves as the mediator. In Figure 8-3 Gagné gives examples of both verbal and pictorial mediators (or links) for learning the English equivalents of French

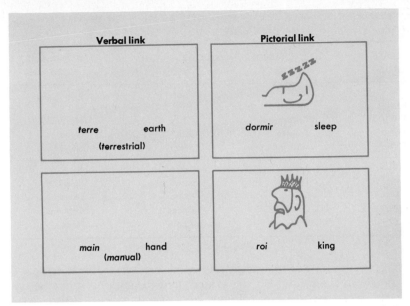

FIG. 8-3 Examples of verbal and pictorial mediators in learning English equivalents of French words (after Gagné, 1965c, p. 101).

words. The verbal links are English words similar to the French words, as in the case of *terrestrial* for *terre*. The pictorial links seem more peculiar and idiosyncratic but, on the whole, most people find that they work better than verbal links.

The effect of verbal mediation This effect was demonstrated in the classic study by Wallace Russell and Lowell Storms (1955). They wanted to find out exactly how verbal mediation could make learning easier. Table 8-3 lists the words and nonsense syllables they used in their study. Reading from left to right, note that the words above the line are all similar in meaning—for example, *wish—want—need.* The words below the line are not all similar in meaning. The words in the first two columns are similar, but the word in the last column is not—for example, *justice—peace—house.* Similarly, above the line we have *trouble—bad—good,* all similar in meaning, and below the line we have *thief—steal—sleep,* in which sleep is not similar in meaning to the first two words. To build the chains of associations above the line in Table 8-3 the following procedure was used. Given the word *stem,* the subject gave the first word he could think of—*flower.* Given the word *flower* next, he again gave the first word he could think of—*smell.* In this way the experimenters determined before the experiment proper the verbal associations the subjects had already formed.

In the experiment proper each subject had to learn two lists. The first list consisted of nonsense syllables paired with words in the second column

TABLE 8-3   NONSENSE SYLLABLES AND WORDS USED IN BOTH PARTS OF STUDY ON VERBAL
MEDIATION (after Russell and Storms, 1955, p. 290).

NONSENSE SYLLABLE	FIRST CHAINED WORD	SECOND CHAINED WORD	FINAL CHAINED WORD
CEF	Stem	Flower	Smell
DAX	Memory	Mind	Matter
YOV	Soldier	Army	Navy
VUX	Trouble	Bad	Good
WUB	Wish	Want	Need
GEX	Justice	Peace	House
JID	Thief	Steal	Sleep
ZIL	Ocean	Water	Doctor
LAJ	Command	Order	Cabbage
MYV	Fruit	Apple	Hand

of the table. For example, the subject learned CEF—STEM, DAX—MEMORY, and MYV—FRUIT. In the second list the subject had to pair the nonsense syllable with the word in the last column. For example, he learned CEF—SMELL, DAX—MATTER, and MYV—HAND. Now the question was: Would the subjects, in learning the second list, find the pairs above the solid line easier to learn than the pairs below the solid line? In other words, would mediators which were similar in meaning make learning easier than did mediators dissimilar in meaning? More concretely, would CEF—SMELL be easier to learn than MYV—HAND? The investigators' expectations were confirmed. In the second list the pairs above the line were learned in fewer trials than were the pairs below the line.

Types of verbal mediators   As yet we know comparatively little about the types of verbal mediators and their effects, even though this knowledge would be very useful for the teacher. One study classified mediators into single-step and multiple-step associations (Underwood and Schulz, 1960). Table 8-4 shows the word pairs the students learned; they were composed of nonsense syllables and three-letter English words. The table also lists the associations the students reported they used in learning these paired associates. Perusing the comments of the students, you will note a variety of mediators. Among others, the students used (1) letter identity, (2) sound identity, and (3) similar meaning. Each student used several types. If he tried to use only one, he would probably be quite unsuccessful since the word pairs require a shift. The study also showed that the multiple-step associations were not so useful as the single-step associations.

Summary   In addition to meaningfulness, verbal mediation is a condition of entering behavior necessary for verbal learning. Verbal mediation is talking to yourself in relevant ways when faced with something to be learned or a problem to be solved. Most mediation is inaudible and un-

TABLE 8-4

SINGLE-STEP ASSOCIATIONS For each association we will give the pair of items learned by the subject, and his reported association.

CFY—KID:	C and K similar in sound.
XBN—GAT:	GAT is odd word, X is odd letter.
DSU—CAT:	D to dog to CAT.
CFY—DOG:	C to cat to DOG.
XBN—RAT:	X suggested poison—poison RAT.
TPM—AND:	T associated with symbol (&) for AND.
RZL—SAT:	R to rum to SAT.
RZL—SAT:	R and s in alphabetical order.
DSU—BAN:	U—BAN (brand of coffee)
RZL—KID:	RZL suggested Russell; Russell is a KID.
CFY—THE:	remembered because first one in list.
KHQ—FAN:	KHQ to radio to radio FAN.
IGW—MAN:	W inverted looks like M, hence MAN.
IGW—MAN:	IG to IGnorant to IGnorant MAN.
RZL—BOY:	RZL looks like lazy; hence, lazy BOY.
RZL—CAT:	Z is hissing sound of CAT.

In some cases, a mediator would be used, but the subject could not report how he got from the mediator to the response. It is possible that these should be classed as no association:

IGW—AND:	IGW elicited International Geophysical Year; don't know how this suggests AND.
RZL—BAT:	made right out of R; just associated right with BAT.
TPM—PIG:	tympany to PIG.
OVJ—BAT:	OVJ became JOV and just tied BAT to it.
DSU—HAT:	DU means fraternity house; associated this with HAT.

MULTIPLE-STEP MEDIATION

RZL—BAT:	someone she knows on baseball team with initials R.Z.
DSU—HAT:	D is last letter in heaD; HAT goes on HEAD.
DSU—HAT:	Desilu Productions—to theater—to theatrical HAT.
DSU—HAT:	Desilu; Lucy wears HAT.
OVJ—MAN:	OVJ to OVA to woman to MAN.
TPM—AND:	TPM signifies time; AND is pause in time.
TPM—AND:	TPM to WPM—words per minute on typewriter; AND is word commonly written on typewriter.
IGW—FAN:	IGW to igloo to cold to FAN.

conscious. Mediators may be both pictorial and verbal, but pictorial mediators work better for most individuals. Some convincing evidence indicates that verbal mediation greatly facilitates verbal learning. We described some of this evidence in this chapter. Finally, we described different mediators: letter identity, sound identity, and similar meaning.

Before discussing the applications of the effects of meaningfulness and verbal mediation to teaching, we shall examine several external learning conditions: instructions to learn, practice, reinforcement, interference factors, and methods of measurement.

Several external conditions also influence verbal learning: (1) instructions to learn, (2) practice, (3) reinforcement, (4) interference, and (5) methods of measurement. Upon reading this portion of the chapter, you should be able to meet these objectives:

8-15   Distinguish between incidental and intentional learning in terms of instructions to learn and their relative effects on verbal learning.

8-16   Describe and illustrate the general effect of the amount of practice on the amount of learning.

8-17   Distinguish between massed and distributed practice in verbal learning and describe and illustrate the conditions under which each is more effective.

8-18   Define overlearning in terms of task mastery and describe and illustrate the conditions under which it is most effective.

8-19   Distinguish between whole and part practice and describe and illustrate the conditions under which each is more effective.

8-20   Describe the effect of reinforcement on verbal learning by comparing it with other conditions of verbal learning.

8-21   Distinguish between confirmation and prompting procedures and describe and illustrate the conditions for their effective use.

Instructions to Learn

Originally incidental learning was explained in terms of *set to learn*. Although set was an ambiguous concept, it described an apparent state of readiness induced by instructions given to the experimental subject (Gibson, 1941). Because of the ambiguity of the concept of set, the concept of *instructions to learn* has replaced set in discussions of incidental learning (McLaughlin, 1965).

Incidental versus intentional learning   The problem in both the laboratory and the classroom is to focus the attention of the student on particular stimuli among the deluge of stimuli which bombard him. Although students frequently do not learn what we intend to teach, they often incidentally learn other things and sometimes they learn things we would prefer they did not learn at all. The distinction between this intentional and this incidental learning is not sharp, but the effects of both have been the subjects of extensive laboratory research (see Postman, 1964). According to Leo Postman (1964), in incidental learning, the instructions do not prepare the student for a test on the materials. In intentional learning, the students are told before learning the materials that they will have a test. These two laboratory situations are not unlike classroom situations we all experience.

There are actually two types of incidental learning situations. In type *A*, the student is exposed to materials but is given no instruction to learn. After his exposure to the materials, he is given a surprise test. In type *B*, the student is directed to learn a specific task, but at the same time he is exposed to materials which are not covered in the directions. The test he is given tries to discover how much he learns of the tasks not covered in the directions.

The incidental-learning situation referred to as type *A* is illustrated in an experiment by Postman and Virginia Senders (1946). The students, Harvard and Radcliffe undergraduates, were given a thirty-five-word mimeographed selection from Chekhov's short story *The Bet*. The material was very detailed and had dramatic appeal. The subjects were divided into six groups. The experimenter told the students in the incidental-learning group (group *A*) to read the selection for purposes of timing because he was interested in their reading speed. Consistent with our definition of incidental-learning situations (type *A*), these students were exposed to material but given no instructions to learn. The experimenter gave the students in the other five groups specific instructions to learn, by telling them that the study was a memory experiment and that they were to read the selection carefully. After this general direction, the experimenter gave each of the remaining five groups a different task. Group *B* was told that it would be tested for general comprehension of the material, *C* for the specific sequence of individual events, *D* for details of content, *E* for details of wording, *F* for details of physical appearance. In general, the intentional learners obtained higher test scores than the incidental learners. Also, the directions varied in effectiveness. For example, the students who were told that they would be tested for details of content also did better on test items on general comprehension of the material. But the major result (the one you should remember) is that the students who were given directions to learn specific materials did better than the students in the incidental-learning situation, who received no directions to learn.

The incidental-learning situation referred to as type *B* is illustrated in the following situation (Postman, 1964). The subject is given a list of words, with each word in a different color. He is then instructed to learn the words. No mention is made of the colors. In another example of a type *B* situation, the subject is instructed to learn a series of words. Digits and geometric forms are exposed along with the words. In the two situations, the students are tested for their learning of the colors, digits, and forms rather than of the words.

It is important to note that the distinctions between incidental and intentional learning are quantitative and not qualitative. In a review of the relevant research, Barry McLaughlin (1965) concludes that incidental learning is usually a misnomer. No experimental evidence supports the belief in a distinct learning process which occurs without motive, self-instruction, or instructions to learn. He states (p. 374): "Whether such learning does occur is an unanswered, and perhaps unanswerable, question."

Practice

A second external learning condition for verbal learning is practice. Research on skill learning gives a fairly clear picture of the effects of practice. Research on verbal learning, however, has not resulted in the same degree of certainty about these effects. Even students and teachers question the value of practice in knowledge acquisition. The general rebellion against the Puritan Ethic on university and college campuses has made disreputable what many individuals have learned from their own experience and what laboratory studies almost without exception corroborate: The longer a person works at learning the more he will learn (Underwood, 1964b).

It is not practice itself but the conditions of practice which pose problems for the experimenter and the teacher. We shall consider first the effects of massed and distributed practice, then the effects of overlearning, and finally the effects of part and whole practice.

Massed versus distributed practice The learning of tasks can be concentrated into one time period or spread over several time periods. The familiar example of massed practice—the concentration of the learning in one time period—is the student cramming for examinations. All his study for a particular course is concentrated in one time period, usually a day or two before the examination. In distributed practice, periods of learning alternate with periods of rest.

Although not many teachers or students took the statement seriously, most textbooks in the past rather flatly reported that more learning resulted from distributed than from massed practice. The statement, of course, is a vast oversimplification because many conditions influence how much and how fast we learn. Practice is only one of these conditions. Despite the reiteration of the statement, however, teachers often ignored the necessity for review and students continued to cram for their examinations. Both students and teachers made a practical discovery which the textbooks ignored: Massed practice took less time than distributed practice. After all, distributed practice requires learning time plus spaced time. Massed practice requires only learning time. It is possible that the conditions under which distributed practice is superior to massed practice are so specialized that they are of little practical importance (Underwood, 1964b).

What are these special conditions? In reviewing ten years of research on the effects of massed and distributed practice on verbal learning, Benton Underwood (1961) arrived at this conclusion: The interval between practice periods (in distributed practice) must be shorter when error tendency is high than it must be when it is low. For example, in learning a list of paired associates, if the student tends to forget the response terms, the intervals of practice should be shortened; long intervals will result in forgetting. If the probability of forgetting is very high, massed practice should replace distributed practice.

Evidence also indicates that massed practice is better for immediate recall and that distributed practice is better for retention (Underwood, 1964). Everyone has observed that cramming for examinations often results in high test performance and in rapid forgetting after the test. Theoretically, distributed practice is beneficial because the intervals allow time for unwanted or erroneous responses to drop out or to become extinguished (Underwood, 1961).

Overlearning Overlearning is an example of massed practice. In this procedure the teacher requires the student to practice a task beyond initial mastery. For example, a teacher ordinarily does not require the child to discontinue the recitation of the alphabet after the child has turned in his first perfect performance. The teacher encourages the child to repeat this marvelous feat several more times not only to satisfy the child's exhibitionist cravings but also to calm his teacher's fears about the inevitability of forgetting. We overlearn many skills such as dancing, skating, typing, and bicycling. Certainly our reading, writing, and speaking skills are overlearned.

Overlearning can reach a point of diminishing returns (Kreuger, 1929). At this point additional practice increases retention only slightly—the effort surpasses the gain. As Figure 8-4 indicates, Kreuger used three degrees of

FIG. 8-4 Three degrees of overlearning and their effects on retention (after Kreuger, 1929, pp. 76–77).

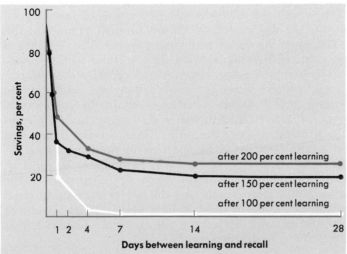

overlearning. In 0 percent overlearning, the subjects learned a list of nonsense syllables until they could recite them the first time without error. Strictly speaking, this is not overlearning but simply initial mastery of the task. In 50 percent overlearning, if the student required ten trials for original mastery, he would recite the list five more times. In 100 percent overlearning, he would recite the list ten more times. Figure 8-4 shows that there are striking gains for 50 percent overlearning and that 100 percent overlearning adds little to these gains.

Part versus whole practice   In the following chapter we shall describe the effects on skill learning of part versus whole practice. When verbal material is learned as a whole, the entire task is practiced once before any part of it is repeated. When the material is learned by parts, each part is learned before they are combined. One part method, the progressive-part method, requires practicing material by combining several units into fewer units (McGeoch, 1942). In this method parts 1 and 2 are mastered separately and then combined to form a whole. Part 3 is next learned separately, then practiced with parts 1 and 2, and so on, until all the parts of the original material have been combined. This is the way we often have memorized poetry of several stanzas. We master stanza 1. Then we master stanza 2. Next we recite stanzas 1 and 2 together. Then we master stanza 3. Next we recite together stanzas 1, 2, and 3. We continue this procedure until we have mastered all the stanzas of the poem. This method is time consuming but often very effective.

Studying the relative effectiveness of the part and the whole methods focuses attention on their relative efficiency: Which method requires less time for gaining mastery? In reviewing the most recent evidence, James Deese and Stewart Hulse (1967) conclude that the relative effectiveness of the part and the whole methods in verbal learning depends on the internal organization of the materials to be learned. If dividing the material into parts makes the task of learning the material simpler, the part method should be used. If, however, this division makes the task of learning the material more difficult, the whole method should be used. They use this example (p. 304). You must memorize two lists of words. List *A* contains these words: *north, man, red, spring, woman, east, autumn, yellow, summer, boy, blue, west, winter, girl, green, south.* List *B* contains these words: *north, east, south, west, spring, summer, autumn, winter, red, yellow, green, blue, man, woman, boy, girl.* Although both lists contain the same words, they differ in internal organization, with list *A* containing little apparent organization and list *B* being organized into directions, seasons, colors, and humans. You could easily learn list *B* by the part method because it divides easily into four parts and these parts easily recombine. In the case of list *A*, however, if you divide it into two parts by splitting it in the middle, you would have difficulty recombining the halves since no internal organization tells you which kinds of words belong where. Thus, the choice of the part or the whole method depends on the internal organization or structure of the materials to be learned.

Summary In an incidental learning situation, the experimenter does not provide instructions which prepare students for a test on the materials they are to learn. The students can be given no directions at all or they can be directed to learn one and be tested on another task. Intentional learning provides for the prior announcement of the test and the learning task. The differences between incidental and intentional learning are only quantitative. Because individuals can and do supply their own directions and motivation when these are not provided externally, in the strict sense of the term there may be no such phenomenon as incidental learning.

Because practice is the condition which describes the amount of work output, there is strong empirical support for the common sense observation that the longer a person works (practices) at learning the more he will learn. We have examined here three practice conditions: massed versus distributed practice, overlearning, and part versus whole practice. Evidence indicates that intervals for distributed practice must be shorter when the material is difficult and the probability of erroneous responses is high. If the likelihood of forgetting responses is very high, massed practice should replace distributed practice. Some evidence also indicates that massed practice is better for immediate recall and distributed practice is better for performance—a principle which may apply equally well to both skill and verbal learning. When we want our students to acquire secure mastery of materials and verbal skills, we can employ overlearning, which is learning beyond original mastery. Finally, the choice of the part or the whole method of practice must depend on the internal organization of the learning material. Some materials divide into parts and recombine into wholes much more easily than others. The part method can be used effectively with such materials.

We are now in a position to examine the effects of reinforcement on verbal learning.

Reinforcement

Another condition of verbal learning is the reinforcement of correct responses. Such reinforcement is often called *confirmation*—the student's correct responses are confirmed. This confirmation, of course, is a form of feedback, or knowledge of results. We provide confirmation in two ways. First, if the student is learning a list of words, we present him with a printed copy of the list after he has attempted to reproduce the words. Second, if the anticipation method of learning is used, the the student must guess the next word in the list and then be presented with that word within a limited time. The exposure of the correct word is a form of reinforcement, or feedback.

The current study of verbal learning places relatively little emphasis on the effects of reinforcement (Underwood, 1959). According to Underwood most of the verbal learning observed in the laboratory is not dependent on immediate reward. Only the informational feedback on the correctness of responses remains.

In the chapter dealing with programed instruction (see Chapter 12), we shall consider the relative effectiveness of what are called *confirmation* and *prompting procedures*. In a recent study, James Hawker (1964) made this comparison of the two procedures. Each student was to learn a list of paired associates, but each stimulus term had four response terms. He was to select the correct response term for each stimulus word. In the confirmation procedure, the student was presented with a set of items and required to push the switch under the response term he thought correct. If he were correct, the light over the response term would flash. In the prompting procedure the light over the correct response term flashed each time the student was presented with a new set of items. He was required to push the switch under that item and go on to the next set. In the prompting procedure the student had no opportunity to make errors. On a free-recall test, Hawker found no significant differences in numbers of correct responses. He did find, however, that prompting was more effective than confirmation in the first block of trials and also resulted in faster performances.

It appears then that, although confirmation can be a useful condition of verbal learning, it is possible to substitute other and sometimes more useful procedures for it. However, the student must be kept informed of the correct response whether this information is presented before or after he makes his response.

QUESTION 8-2 Mr. Werdee wants his students to distinguish between three land masses: a peninsula, an island, and a continent. He presents several drawings of each and directs his students to make the following associations: peninsula—finger; island—button; and continent—pfug. Each time they see a drawing they must respond with the word associated with the land mass. Which of the following conditions of verbal learning is Mr. Werdee particularly providing? (a) meaningfulness; (b) verbal mediation; (c) instructions to learn; (d) reinforcement.

After selecting your answer, give the reasons for your choice and for your rejection of the alternatives.

Inference Factors

Interference factors, unlike those conditions of verbal learning discussed above, are conditions of forgetting rather than of learning. First we shall define the major theory of forgetting, called *interference theory*. Then we shall examine two sources of forgetting—from associations learned later in time (retroactive inhibition) and from associations learned earlier in time (proactive inhibition). Next, we shall examine the effects of the amount of material learned and the serial-position effect. Last, we consider the effects of different tests.

Upon reading this portion of the chapter, you should be able to meet these objectives:

8-22 Define interference in terms of response competition and illustrate its effects on retention.

8-23 Distinguish between retroactive and proactive inhibition by describing and illustrating the conditions which result in each type.

8-24 Describe and illustrate the relationship between proactive inhibition and entering behavior.

8-25 Describe the effect of chunking on the retention of long verbal sequences and illustrate this effect.

8-26 Describe the serial-position effect in terms of what is retained and forgotten and illustrate this effect in the spelling of long English words.

8-27 Describe and illustrate the effects on retention of the five methods of measuring retention.

The theory of interference We have two consistent findings for verbal learning: Learning new associations causes one to forget old associations learned earlier in time and to forget the new associations as well. In effect, associations compete, with one association interfering with the retention of others. Interference is the competition of old and new responses which results in forgetting. We shall shortly examine some illustrations.

The theory that forgetting is the result of interference rather than of a mysterious fading away of traces in the brain originally came from a study of J. G. Jenkins and Karl Dallenbach (1924). These investigators studied the differences in retention following periods of sleeping and of waking. They required the two subjects in the experiment to recall lists of ten nonsense syllables after various periods of ordinary waking activity and after sleeping. The waking and sleeping periods were one, two, four, and eight hours in duration. With the self-sacrifice which has ennobled the scientific profession, the two subjects slept in the laboratory with the experimenter. Before they went to bed they learned the lists of nonsense syllables. Then they were awakened at the intervals indicated above. Apparently the subjects were not irritated with these interruptions of their slumber and, in spite of considerable drowsiness, were able to recall the lists. Only one interval (one hour, two hours, and so on) was used each night so that the subjects had to sleep in the laboratory for four nights. For the waking part of the experiment, the subjects returned to the laboratory during the day at the appropriate times (the same intervals as those used for the sleeping part) and were tested for recall of the lists. Figure 8-5 shows that recall after sleeping was considerably higher than recall after waking. The first two intervals show a similar drop in retention for both sleeping and waking, but the forgetting continues for the waking state in the later intervals. The experiment indicated that the intervening activity between learning and recalling the lists and not the mere passage of time was the cause of the forgetting. That teachers will ever gain sufficient control over the waking lives of their students to put these finding into practice seems very dubious.

Retroactive inhibition Many experiments deliberately introduce possible

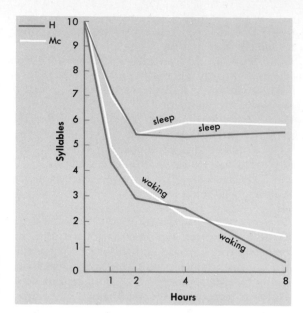

FIG. 8-5 Differences in retention after sleeping and waking periods. H and Mc are the two subjects in this experiment (after Jenkins and Dallenbach, 1924, p. 610).

sources of interference to observe their effect on retention. The sources of interference, as we saw earlier, are two: from associations learned earlier and from associations learned later. This is the design for observing the effects of associations learned later on associations learned earlier:

| Experimental group | Learn list *A* | Learn list *B* | Test list *A* |
| Control group | Learn list *A* | Unrelated activity | Test list *A* |

This design essentially repeats the experiment on retention after sleeping and waking. In terms of that experiment, the lists which the subjects learned are designated list *A*. The waking activity is equivalent to learning list *B*. The sleeping is equivalent to the unrelated activity of the control group. The recall after sleeping and waking is identical to testing list *A*. Using this design, we discover that the control group has better retention of list *A* than the experimental group because, for the experimental group, learning list *B* interferes with the retention of list *A*—the associations of the two lists compete. The control group eliminates this competition because it has a single list to learn. Interference which arises from associations learned later in time is called *retroactive inhibition*. Such interference, of course, is not retroactive in time (we cannot undo what has been done), but it is retroactive in effect—that is, in the effect it has on the recall of the materials learned earlier.

Proactive inhibition   The second source of interference is from associations

learned earlier in time. This source is called *proactive inhibition*. The
following experimental design illustrates it:

Experimental group	Learn list *A*	Learn list *B*	Test list *B*
Control group	Unrelated activity	Learn list *B*	Test list *B*

In these experiments the control group again shows greater retention than
the experimental group but for a different reason: Here the list learned
earlier interferes with the retention of the list learned later. As in retroactive inhibition, there is response competition, but the source of the interference has shifted. Early investigators believed that retroactive inhibition
was the major source of forgetting. Underwood (1957) uncovered an interesting flaw in the early research. He noticed that different studies of
forgetting reported very different amounts of forgetting, ranging from 25
percent to 80 percent, after one hour. The original forgetting curves of
Ebbinghaus were particularly discouraging because they seemed to indicate that after the first hour and certainly after one day our minds become
essentially tabulae rosae and forgetting is almost complete. In the studies
of retention which Underwood perused, subjects were required to learn
several different lists of nonsense syllables. Underwood discovered a very
clear relationship between the number of lists learned by the subjects and
the amount of forgetting reported by the investigator. Figure 8-6 shows
this relationship. When the subject learned a single list, he retained almost
80 percent after one hour. When he learned over twenty lists the retention rate resembled that in Ebbinghaus' studies, with less than 20 percent

FIG. 8-6 The percentage of material retained after one hour and the number
of lists previously memorized by the subject (after Underwood, 1957, p. 53).

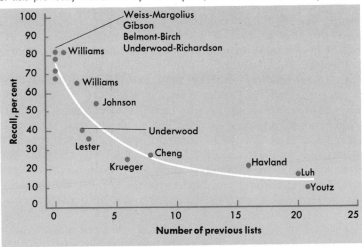

recall after one hour. We can be much less pessimistic today than we could have been in his day about how much we remember and how much we forget.

The major cause of forgetting appears to be proactive inhibition. In defending this assertion, Underwood (1964b, p. 146) states:

> Assume that a student, ten years of age, learns a given task and the retention of this task is tested one month later. The fact that proactive inhibition is assigned a major role in the cause of forgetting is based on the assumption that, during the first ten years of the student's life, he will have acquired more habits that will interfere with the task to be recalled than he will acquire during the one-month interval between learning and the retention test.

The emphasis on proactive inhibition stresses the importance in verbal learning of the student's entering behavior. The assessment of that behavior must include an appraisal not only of its status (the responses which are and are not available) but also of its potentially interfering effects on subsequent learning. More succinctly, not everything we have learned in the past makes it easier to learn new things in the present since learning is not an additive process, the simple accretion of knowledge; we are both the slaves and the masters of our previous learning. Underwood (1964b) goes on to suggest that some individuals may be able to resist interference better than others. Such a variable should also be included in the assessment of entering behavior.

Length of the sequence This refers to the amount of material presented to the student. The length of verbal sequences may vary from a simple sequence of two links *(dog—chien)* to long sequences which include all the lines of a Shakespearean play. Miller (1956) presents evidence that the span of immediate memory is about seven links (or bits of information). After seven links we recode the materials we are learning into chunks of information. Since the memory span is a fixed number of chunks, we can increase the amount of information we retain by building larger and larger chunks. Deese (1958) uses this example. You are asked to remember this number after a single reading: 0101101001101010110111001111011100. How much can you remember? Almost everyone would try to recode it. Most individuals would try to reorganize the series into sequences of three: 010—110—100—110, and so on. A more efficient method is to recode by assigning numerical names to groups of three numbers. For example, 100 could be coded as *four* and 110 as *five*. Using the second method, you would have fewer names than individual digits to remember. Nonsense syllables are harder to memorize than English prose because the prose is already organized into chunks; we must reorganize the nonsense material.

Serial-position effect This effect describes the fact that the easiest parts of a sequence (or list) to learn are the beginning and the end and the most difficult part is that just past the middle. Subjects recalling a list of

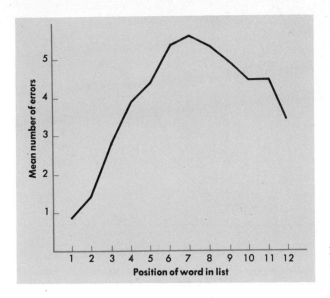

FIG. 8-7 The number of errors made at each position in a list of nonsense syllables in serial learning (after Hovland, 1938, p. 275).

twelve nonsense syllables, for example, make the greatest number of errors in about the seventh position. Jensen (1962a) found that spelling errors show the serial-position effect. That is, errors in spelling are generally more frequent in the middle of the word, with the fewest errors at the beginning and the end. Figure 8-7 shows the serial-position effect for nonsense syllables. Figure 8-8 shows the curve for English words of various length. You can see that the curves are very similar in shape.

Methods of Measurement

We shall now describe five methods of measuring learning. Figure 8-9 shows five retention curves for periods varying from twenty minutes to two days for the five methods of measuring retention. (We shall describe these below.) You should notice that the recognition method produces the highest and the anticipation method the lowest score. The curve for the savings (relearning) method should follow the pattern of the other curves and fall between the curves for the anticipation and reproduction methods. A methodological flaw in the study resulted in the distortion of this curve.

Reproduction This method (which you may have referred to as the *recall method*) requires the student to reproduce the material he has learned. You have taught the student five crucial dates of American history: 1776, 1789, 1849, 1860, and 1918. Using the reproduction method, on the midterm examination you require the student to list these dates and the associated events. Or, after a review of the history of verbal learning, you ask

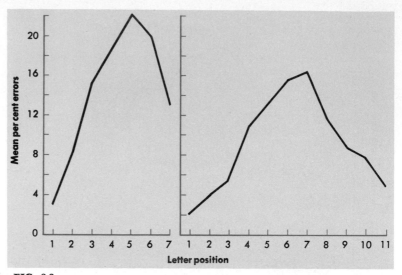

FIG. 8-8 Serial-position curves for errors in seven- and eleven-letter words. The curve for seven-letter words is based on a total of 1,546 spelling errors made on twenty-four words by 150 eighth graders. The eleven-letter curve is based on a total of 2,262 spelling errors made on forty-eight words by 89 junior college freshmen (after Jensen, 1962, p. 107).

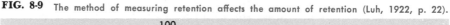

FIG. 8-9 The method of measuring retention affects the amount of retention (Luh, 1922, p. 22).

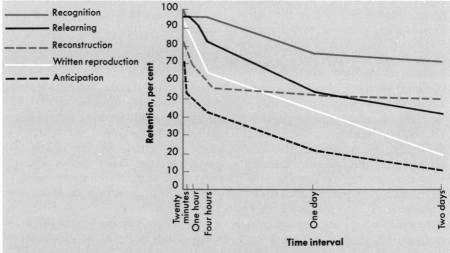

this question on an essay examination: List the psychologists who have made important methodological and theoretical contributions to the study of verbal learning. The essay examination, properly conceived, employs essentially the reproduction method: The student is required to reproduce what he has learned.

Recognition   This method requires the student to select from a series of items those which are the responses he has learned. Multiple-choice examinations are the most common examples of the recognition method. The student is presented with this test item: The (American) Civil War began in (1) 1776, (2) 1789, (3) 1849, (4) 1860, (5) 1918. The student recognizes (he selects) the correct response (1860).

Reconstruction   This method requires the student to unscramble a set of scrambled items. You ask the student to do the following: Arrange in proper chronological order the following historical events: (1) the French Revolution, (2) the American Civil War, (3) the American Declaration of Independence, (4) World War I, and (5) the California Gold Rush. By recalling the approximate dates for these events, the student can reconstruct the proper order.

Anticipation   This method, you have seen, is used in laboratory research on verbal learning. It requires the student to recall the next item in a series. Using a special mechanical contrivance which exposes one word at a time, the student must anticipate the next word in the list. If we use the dates instead of words, when the student sees 1776 he is expected to anticipate 1789. When he sees 1789, he anticipates 1849, and so on. After he learns the list of dates, you test him to find out how many he can recall in the proper order.

Savings   The savings (or relearning) method requires the student to learn a set of materials to mastery (an errorless performance) and then to relearn the materials. Using a fairly simple calculation, the teacher determines how much less time was required for relearning than for original learning. It is a somewhat surprising finding that relearning takes less time when the subject does not recognize the materials as being familiar.

Summary   Interference is the competition of old and new responses which results in forgetting. In retroactive inhibition what is learned later in time interferes with the retention of what was learned earlier. In proactive inhibition what was learned earlier in time interferes with the retention of what is learned later. From the standpoint of entering behavior, proactive inhibition is the major cause of forgetting. This conclusion is at odds with the traditional belief that what was learned subsequently (retroactive inhibition), rather than what was learned previously (proactive inhibition), was the chief source of forgetting. Present evidence also suggests that extinction is the process underlying interference. Concerning the amount of material (or length of the sequence or list), evidence indicates that we recode information we learn into chunks of information and thereby increase our capacity to retain bits of information. Finally, the serial-position effect describes the tendency to remember the material in the beginning and the end and to forget the material in the middle of a list.

These methods of measuring what material is remembered are also methods for learning verbal materials. For example, a student may learn through reproduction (or recall) but be tested by the method of recognition. Because recognition is a less demanding method of learning and testing, we can expect this student to perform better on a test of recognition than on a test of reproduction. This relationship between the method of measuring and learning is referred to in the statement, "methods of measurement affect what is retained."

INSTRUCTIONAL APPLICATIONS

In this section of the chapter we shall explore the relationship of external learning conditions to instructional procedures—methods of arranging the learning conditions in ways appropriate for the learning required by the instructional objectives. In contrast to internal learning conditions, which are the student's entering behavior, external conditions are the stimulus situation the teacher arranges. The proper confluence of entering behavior and external conditions enables the student to achieve the instructional objectives.

Conditioning

Upon reading this part of the chapter, you should be able to meet these objectives:

8-28 Define instructional procedures in terms of learning conditions, types, and objectives.

8-29 Illustrate a *class* of learning conditions by selecting a particular condition.

8-30 Describe and illustrate the advantages and disadvantages of using classical and operant conditioning as teaching models for various instructional objectives.

Can the basic learning types—classical and operant conditioning—also be translated into practical teaching procedures? We have the following, somewhat primitive examples. Mr. D. Termand wants the class to learn to come to attention when he assumes a typical teaching position behind his lectern. At first the students do not respond to this stimulus. Mr. D. Termand, lonely and ignored behind his lectern, is a neutral stimulus. He can become a conditioned stimulus by slamming his gavel against the lectern to make an impressively loud and disturbing noise. Our responses to very loud noises are largely unconditioned reflexes. One response is to attend at once to the loud noise. So, to produce a change in behavior from no attention to attention, Mr. Termand gets behind the lectern and within one-half second begins beating the gavel against the lectern. By pairing the noise of the gavel with his position behind the lectern, he provides contiguity of conditioned and unconditioned stimuli. By repeating this procedure for several days, he provides practice. Soon, either light taps of the gavel or the assumption of his pedagogical posture behind the lectern commands the students' instant attention.

The teacher also may analyze teaching materials in terms of unconditioned and conditioned stimuli. For example, before you read the section on reinforcement, you knew the meaning of the word *reward*. We could have defined learning as the result of rewarded practice. In this case, your response to the term reward would be unconditioned (you would not have been learning anything new about the word). However, by defining learning as the result of reinforced practice, we expected you to substitute *reinforcer* for *reward* and to realize that reward has a much broader meaning than does reinforcer, which refers to a particular procedure. If we gave you the statement: Learning is the result of _____ practice, eventually we would want you to respond "reinforced." When you did so, the statement would be a conditioned stimulus and your response a conditioned response. Much teaching involves substitute learning—substituting a foreign word for an English word, a more rigorous procedure for a less rigorous procedure, a technical term for a lay term, and so on. In planning your instruction you should analyze your materials and procedures in terms of unconditioned (previously learned) and conditioned (to be learned) stimuli. As in the case of discrimination learning, such a procedure provides a fine-grain analysis and organization of your materials and procedures. Such an analysis and such a construction of instructional materials were originally employed in programed instruction. The program frame was the stimulus; the student's response to the frame was the response; and the confirmation of the response was the reinforcement or feedback. Using this conception of the learning event, one could construct a series of frames and eventually a program. Many programers today continue to design programs in terms of basic phenomena of learning and, for example, refer to frames as representing generalization and discrimination sequences (Taber *et al.*, 1965, pp. 117–21).

We can now return to the original question about translating classical and operant conditioning into practical teaching procedures. The fact is that these translations or adaptations can be made, informally by the classroom teacher and formally by the educational researcher, with an important qualification: As teachers we should use classical and operant conditioning models only when our instructional objectives indicate that those learning types are required. The purpose of task analysis, you will recall, is to classify instructional objectives under various learning types. Most (but surely not all) instructional objectives of the school involve more complex learning than classical and operant conditioning and thus also require different learning conditions. There is no practical virtue, on the one hand, in reducing complex human learning to its most basic elements or, on the other hand, in conceiving of the simplest learning in terms of complex interrelationships; by a more precise analysis of our instructional objectives, we can distinguish several learning types, ranging from simple to complex, and can determine the appropriate learning conditions for each.

Verbal Learning

This part of the chapter deals with the instructional implications of the verbal-learning research we have examined.

Upon reading this portion, you should be able to describe and illustrate each of the following instructional steps:

8-31   Step 1: Describe for the student what you expect him to learn.
8-32   Step 2: Examine the instructional tasks and materials for their meaningfulness.
8-33   Step 3: Assess entering behavior for the availability of meaningful responses and verbal mediators.
8-34   Step 4: Provide appropriate practice conditions.
8-35   Step 5: Provide knowledge of correct results.
8-36   Step 6: Provide conditions which maximize retention.
8-37   Step 7: Use suitable methods of measurement.

STEP 1   **DESCRIBE FOR THE STUDENT WHAT YOU EXPECT HIM TO LEARN**

This step derives from the research on incidental versus intentional learning. The experiment of Postman and Senders (1946) showed that intentional learners obtained higher test scores than did incidental learners. In taking this step you should inform the students, prior to the time they begin to study, what aspects of their performance will be assessed. In effect, you should state for them the instructional objectives.

A classroom study by Ausubel and his associates (1957) illustrates the importance of telling students before they study what their tests will comprise. Students were given a passage of three or four pages on opiate addiction. In the first phase of the experiment the students were told that they would be tested on the materials at the end of the period. They were not told, however, that they would be retested two weeks later on the same materials. In the second phase of the experiment, which occurred the following semester, a second group of students was given the same passage to read. They were also told that they would be tested at the end of the period, and, in addition, that they would be tested two weeks later. They received this latter information after they had studied the passage. The results showed no significant differences in the scores of the two groups on either the immediate or the follow-up test. Telling your students what they will be tested on after they have studied does very little good.

We now need to look at an experiment in which students are told beforehand how their performance will be evaluated. It is a situation close to your hearts in that it involves student teachers and grades in educational psychology and student teaching. Merlin Wittrock (1963) informed one group of student teachers that the final course grade they received in educational psychology and student teaching would be determined by the amount of improvement in the performance of their high school students. A second group of student teachers did not receive this direction. The high school students of both groups were given tests to determine how much they knew about social studies, government, history, and English at the beginning of the semester, and they were tested later to determine how much more they knew at the end of the semester. The student teachers, therefore, were to be graded on the basis of the gains or the losses (a tragedy for everyone concerned) of their high school students. The experimental groups were the students of those teachers who received the direction. The control groups were the students of nondirected student teachers. The results were impressively clear: The students in the experimental groups did considerably better than those in the control groups, especially in English. Further evidence indicated that students in the control groups had more favorable attitudes toward their student teachers than did students in the experimental groups.

In taking step 1, two common instructional practices should be avoided. First, the practice of launching the instructional ship in uncharted waters with no destination specified can only diffuse the students' attention and cause them to attend to irrelevant and sometimes competing aspects of the instructional materials. Although we know that incidental learning occurs without specific direction, we also know that particular learning occurs more frequently and more easily when instructions on what to learn are explicit. Second, the practice, more common in colleges and high schools than in elementary schools, of teaching one set of materials and testing on quite a different and unrelated set should be avoided.

EXAMINE THE INSTRUCTIONAL TASK AND MATERIALS FOR THEIR MEANINGFULNESS

STEP 2

We defined meaningfulness as word frequency or familiarity—the more frequently a word occurs in the language, the greater its familiarity and, therefore, its meaningfulness. This definition suggests that some of the verbal materials you use in your teaching will be more meaningful than others. Studies have been made of the most frequently used words in the English language, and the resulting lists are available to the teacher (Thorndike-Lorge, 1944). Such lists are often used in the preparation of reading materials for the elementary grades. They can also be appropriately used in the preparation of verbal instructional material, both written and oral, at all educational levels.

One way of performing this step is to make a list of words which occur in the materials you will use and for which you do not plan to provide explicit instruction. These are words you are assuming to be in the students' entering behavior. A check of your list with a published word-frequency count will indicate the likelihood of the students' being familiar with the word. In this way you may discover that the students' entering behavior is below the level that you expected and that you will have to select more familiar words or provide instruction which will raise the level of entering verbal behavior.

STEP 3

ASSESS ENTERING BEHAVIOR FOR AVAILABILITY OF MEANINGFUL RESPONSES AND VERBAL MEDIATORS

In assessing the availability of meaningful responses, the teacher is attempting to make relatively meaningless materials meaningful. Or, if you prefer less technical language, the teacher is making unfamiliar materials familiar. The definition seems obvious—no one would expect otherwise of any competent teacher. Considerably less obvious are the procedures the teacher must use to perform this function. The performance requires two things: to assess the student's entering behavior to discover not only which responses are available but also their relative availability and to present the new (presently meaningless) materials in terms of meaningful responses now available to the student. As you learned in Chapter 3, the assessment of entering behavior involves testing the student's knowledge of material which is related to the new material you are about to introduce but for which you will not provide instruction. If the results of your testing indicate (and in most classrooms this would not be surprising) that the student lacks the prerequisite entering behavior, then you must teach the prerequisites first. Once the student has acquired the necessary entering behavior, you can proceed to the next step; that is, you can present the new materials in terms of meaningful responses—those which are available and relatively strong. The actual instruction you provide must bridge the old and the new meanings. Totally meaningless materials (if they exist) require considerably more time to learn. When the teacher does introduce highly novel materials (as in mathematics and some uncommon foreign languages), he should provide the additional time required for familiarization.

A teacher wants his students to learn the proper use of the colon and the semicolon in the writing of their weekly themes. He also wants to perform step 3 conscientiously. He first administers a short test to discover how skilled the students are in using these and other, more familiar punctuation marks. The test results indicate that the students have mastered the use of the period and the comma (if "mastery" of the comma is possible). He then gives them some reading material containing colons and semicolons and asks them to explain their use. In this way the teacher has assessed the entering behavior of the students and now has some information which he can use in planning his instruction. In introducing the use of the colon and semicolon, he reviews what the students know about periods and commas. He points out the similarities between the use of the colon and that of the period, and between the use of the semicolon and that of the comma. The semicolon, like the comma, is often used to separate phrases and clauses in a series, especially when the phrases are lengthy and when the clauses form complete sentences. In other words, the semicolon indicates less connectedness than does the comma. The colon is a more formal stop than the period. For example, lengthy quotations within a text are often introduced with a colon. The teacher gives several examples of the use of periods and colons and of commas and semicolons, carefully pointing out the similarities to capitalize on the knowledge of punctuation the students have already acquired. Later, of course, he must teach the distinctions in the use of the relatively unfamiliar punctuation marks. In any case, he has performed step 3: He assessed the entering behavior of his students to discover the relative availability of punctuation responses, and he presented the new material in terms of these responses. Of course, the familiarization function is not divorced from other functions the teacher must perform. Life, especially the life of the teacher, is never so simple as we can make it in textbook illustrations.

We can now consider the assessment of entering behavior for the availability of verbal mediators (the rest of step 3). This step consists of the following procedures: (1) determining which verbal and pictorial mediators may be useful for the instructional task; (2) assessing entering behavior to find out which of these (and others) may be available; and (3) supplying mediators which may be useful in the learning of the task.

Charles Spiker (1963) describes an experiment in which children learned to distinguish drawings of four faces through the use of verbal mediators. In the pretraining period, some of the children learned distinctive names for the faces, such as *wug* and *kos*. The other children learned similar names, such as *zim* and *zam*. In the experiment proper the children were asked to identify new examples of the four faces. Those children who had learned (in fact, overlearned) the distinctive names (mediators) were able to distinguish the faces more easily than were those who had learned similar names. The experiment showed that not any mediator will do, and, for a given task, some mediators are better than others. In the next chapter you will see how effectively mediators have been used in the teaching and learning of concepts.

PROVIDE THE APPROPRIATE PRACTICE CONDITIONS

STEP 4

In the performance of this step the teacher must (1) provide opportunities for the student to make the necessary responses, (2) schedule practice on a massed or a distributed basis, (3) determine the degree of mastery the student must attain, and (4) provide either part or whole practice. We described the experimental bases for making these decisions in the preceding section.

First, you can provide the student with the opportunity for making the responses he is expected to learn in several ways: recitation, discussion, and programed instruction. The recitation method is characterized by assignment, study, and report (Wallen and Travers, 1963, p. 483). In American public schools it is considered the traditional method of instruction, although little experimental evidence supports it. Recitation allows the individual student to practice overt responses. It may well be true that choral recitation, in which the whole class answers the teacher's question, leaves much to be desired. The difficulty with choral recitation, apart from its generally noisy, aspect, is that Elmer and Ella Mae may be able to hide their ignorance behind the impressive roar of their classmates. All the research we have on overt responding assumes individual monitoring of each student's responses.

There has been considerably more research done on the discussion method, especially the comparison of the relative effectiveness of the discussion and the lecture methods for the learning of factual information. Most of these studies find no significant differences between the two methods. The effect of the discussion method on the retention of learning has rarely been investigated. One study (Ward, 1956) found greater retention of material for students of high academic ability with discussion procedures and greater retention for students of low ability with the lecture method. The difficulty with group discussion is the same difficulty we find with choral recitation: There is little opportunity to monitor individual student responses. The discussion method has the further disadvantage of providing only limited opportunity for students to make overt responses: While one student talks, all the rest must listen. Unless the teacher provides oral instruction on a one-to-one basis, programed instruction is one of the few instructional procedures which provides each student in a group of students with the opportunity to respond and to obtain knowledge of results for each response.

Second, you must decide how to schedule the students' practice. Should you provide massed or distributed practice? The best practice schedule makes the most efficient use of the students' and the teacher's time and yields the greatest amount of learning and the longest periods of retention. The criteria are clear, but the procedures for meeting them are not. Certainly, when there is very little time for the learning of new material, massed practice is more efficient than distributed practice. In distributed practice, you recall, the teacher must allow for learning (practice) time and intervals between practice. When you are interested in having your students retain fairly large amounts of material for long periods of time, you should provide distributed practice. If you use a schedule of distributed practice, you must also decide what you will have the students do during the practice intervals. If the intervals are to be effective, the students cannot be occupied with learning related material, which only interferes with the retention of the practice material. The intervals can, of course, be occupied with the learning of relatively unrelated material or with recreational activities. One could even develop a rather valid argument for periodic recreational activities in the classroom to facilitate student learning.

If you plan your instruction in sufficient detail and with scrupulous respect for time, the practice of old material possibly can be combined with the introduction of new material. Travers (1963) suggests that the teacher utilize multiplication in the solution of daily problems in and out of school rather than simply drilling the student on the multiplication tables. The student has many opportunities to practice his reading skills in perusing material of his own choice as well as in reading class assignments. Practice, however, cannot be left to chance. Unless you arrange for practice in spelling, reading, writing, speaking, and playing the violin, there will often be no practice. Surveying the crowded school curriculum, one is often tempted to recommend a reform in which we teach a few things well, with practice, rather than myriad things poorly without practice.

Third, you must decide which instructional tasks should be overlearned, and you must allow the student to practice these tasks beyond mastery. The tasks scheduled for overlearning should be those which are mandatory entering behavior for the learning of a wide array of future tasks. Certain linguistic and mathematical skills and concepts must often be overlearned so that they can be automatically applied in more advanced learning. In this course in educational psychology it is mandatory that you overlearn the components of the basic teaching model. If you do not, your understanding of the course organization will certainly be poor. Overlearning can sometimes be provided by a spiral treatment of the particular learning task. That is, you can return again and again to the same task and require the student to practice it in continuously changing contexts.

Fourth, you must decide whether to require part or whole practice. You should base this decision on the structure of the learning material. Students can learn material which logically divides into parts and recombines into wholes by part practice. Other materials may require whole practice. The standard, again, is learning the most in the least amount of time. A poem with several stanzas, for example, has readily recognized parts and an overall structure in which the parts readily fit. An impressionistic essay, on the other hand, which tries to portray a general mood or attitude, may require reading and practice in its entirety since it lacks any discernible structure. Even impressionistic or existential poetry may defy profitable part practice.

PROVIDE KNOWLEDGE OF CORRECT RESPONSES

STEP 5

In this step you must provide prompting or confirmation (reinforcement) of correct responses. In prompting, you provide the correct answers before the student responds. In confirming, you provide the correct answers after the student responds. Some evidence indicates that prompting may be more effective than confirmation in early practice and that both procedures may be equally effective in late practice. With these and any other procedures, however, the student must have some means of discovering the correct answers and the opportunity to compare his own answers with them.

PROVIDE CONDITIONS WHICH REDUCE INTERFERENCE

STEP 6

In this step you must reduce the influence of factors which cause interference and forgetting. On the basis of the research we have considered, these general recommendations can be made: (1) The performance of this step requires the type of task analysis which reduces the major task to a series of component tasks. Such an analysis makes explicit for the teacher the steps the student must take and the order in which he must take them to master the task. In this sense, once the teacher has completed the task analysis, he has completed the major part of the sequence. (2) After the task analysis, the teacher must present the subtasks in such a way as to avoid interference. In the case of pro-active inhibition, interference results when the learning of an earlier subtask interferes with retention of a subtask learned later. Retroactive inhibition occurs when the learning of a later task interferes with retention of a subtask learned earlier. (3) The teacher must find those points in the material he presents which are frequently sources of interference or confusion. Our present knowledge of the effects of stimulus-and-response similarity should assist the teacher in identifying sequences likely to interfere with the retention of materials. (4) We know that highly dissimilar stimuli and responses prevent forgetting. Through the use of various devices, such as color, symbols, and drawings, the teacher may introduce dissimilarity into potentially confusing materials. An oversimplified example is the following: To aid students to learn and remember the differences between *ie* and *ei* in words like *receive, either, believe,* and so on, *ie* could be printed in red and *ei* in blue. Devices of this nature help to reduce retroactive inhibition. (5) The major source of forgetting is proactive inhibition—what the student has previously learned in our own and other classes. With a fairly standard curriculum for all students, we could identify sources of proactive inhibition. With so much diversity in the entering behavior of our students however, we must identify sources of interference for individual students. As in the case of assessing entering behavior for meaningful responses, research on proactive inhibition confirms our emphasis on the careful assessment of the entering behavior of the student as an important basis for planning instruction.

STEP 7

USE SUITABLE METHODS OF MEASUREMENT

You recall that the method of measurement affects how much is retained. How do you decide which method to use? The basis for this decision should be the standard of acceptability specified in the statement of the instructional objective. If the objective requires, under given conditions, that the student only recognize the correct response in a list of alternatives or reconstruct a list by unscrambling it, you should use only those methods of measurement. If the standard of acceptability requires recall, relearning, and anticipation, then you should use these more rigorous methods. Ordinarily we reserve the use of the relearning and anticipation methods for the laboratory, but we can easily adapt them to the classroom. You should also remember that each of these methods gives you a slightly altered picture of the effectiveness of your instructional procedures. For the most exacting tests of your procedures, for those moments in your career when you achieve supreme confidence in and a scientifically dispassionate view of your own teaching, you can use the more rigorous methods of measurement.

SUMMARY

In the first section of this chapter, we compared classical and operant conditioning. Both types of conditioning are methods for linking stimuli and responses. What distinguishes them are the reinforcement procedures.

The second section of this chapter dealt with the nature and the develop-

Miss Pegg wants her students to learn the French equivalents of the English names of anatomical parts (arm, elbow, leg, knee, and so on). Before requiring the students to recite the whole list of paired associates, she gives them extended practice on each pair of English and French words. Which of the following instructional steps is Miss Pegg performing? (a) Providing a statement of the instructional objective (step 1); (b) examining the task for its meaningfulness (step 2); (c) providing for knowledge of correct results (step 5); (d) providing conditions which reduce interference (step 6).

After selecting your answer, give the reasons for your choice and for your rejection of the alternatives.

---

ment of verbal learning. Verbal learning resembles skill learning in that it involves chains of stimulus-response associations. It is distinct from skill learning in that it involves verbal rather than motor responses. Verbal chains can vary in length from those which have only two links to those which have many. The materials used in the study of verbal learning vary from nonsense syllables, or relatively meaningless material, to words and phrases, or relatively meaningful material. Immediate free recall, serial learning, and paired-associate learning are the procedures used in this study. We can trace the development of verbal behavior through several levels—distinguishing human speech from other environmental sounds, naming objects in the environment, physically responding to internal verbal responses, confirming the response, linking words together, and, finally, forming verbal hierarchies.

The third section described the effects of several conditions of verbal learning. Meaningfulness and verbal mediation have powerful effects and are linked to entering behavior. Instructions to learn, practice, confirmation (or reinforcement), interference, and method of measurement also affect verbal learning and are linked to external conditions. Meaningfulness is based on the number of verbal associations elicited by a verbal stimulus. Verbal mediation is talking to yourself in ways which are relevant to something you are learning. Instructions to learn can vary from no instructions, as in the case of incidental learning, to explicit instructions, as in the case of intentional learning. Conditions of practice can also vary: We have massed and distributed practice, overlearning, and part and whole practice. We can provide reinforcement through confirmation or prompting. There are several sources of interference: Retroactive inhibition results from sources occurring later in time; proactive inhibition, from sources occurring earlier in time. There appears to be more interference due to proactive inhibition than to retroactive inhibition. Stimulus similarity within and between learning materials produces interference, and so does the serial-position effect. Finally, the method of measurement also affects how much is retained.

The fourth section described the instructional steps for providing verbal knowledge. These steps require the teacher to supply the students with statements of instructional objectives, to examine learning tasks for their meaningfulness, to assess entering behavior for meaningful and mediating responses, to provide appropriate practice conditions, to provide knowledge of correct results, to provide conditions which reduce interference, and to use suitable methods of measurement.

SUGGESTED READINGS

These are published symposia and books of readings on many aspects of verbal learning and the psychological study of language (psycholinguistics):

DE CECCO, JOHN P., ed., *The Psychology of Language, Thought, and Instruction.* New York: Holt, Rinehart & Winston, Inc., 1967.

GAGNÉ, ROBERT, *Conditions of Learning.* New York: Holt, Rinehart & Winston, 1970.

KAUSLER, DONALD H., ed., *Readings in Verbal Learning.* New York: John Wiley & Sons, Inc., 1966.

These articles explore the relationship of research on verbal learning to instructional practice:

UNDERWOOD, BENTON J., "Verbal Learning in the Educative Process," *Harvard Educational Review,* 29 (1959), 107–17 (also in De Cecco, 1964).

————, "Laboratory Studies of Verbal Learning," in *Theories of Learning and Instruction,* ed. E. R. Hilgard, Part 1 of the 63rd Yrbk. of the National Society for the Study of Education, pp. 133–52. Chicago, 1964.

These articles explore the relationship of verbal learning to concept learning, principle learning, and problem solving:

MANDLER, GEORGE, "Verbal Learning," in *New Direction in Psychology,* Vol. III, pp. 1–50. New York: Holt, Rinehart & Winston, Inc., 1967.

UNDERWOOD, BENTON J., "The Representativeness of Rote Verbal Learning," in *Categories of Human Learning,* ed. A. W. Melton, pp. 48–78. New York: Academic Press, Inc., 1964.

CHAPTER NINE

THE TEACHING
AND
LEARNING
OF
PSYCHOMOTOR SKILLS

In this chapter you will learn about a more complex type of learning—the acquisition of skills. We shall be concerned with motor skills as distinct from verbal skills. In the discussion which follows you will see how the simpler learning types and basic learning conditions contribute to the learning of skilled behavior.

The organization of this chapter is briefly as follows. In the first of the three major parts, you will learn what a skill is and how we acquire skills. In the second part, you will learn about the physical abilities which make it possible for us to learn a skill. Finally, in the third part, you will learn how to teach your students a skill. As in the previous chapters, we derive the instructional functions from basic theory and research on skill learning.

Upon reading the first part of this chapter, you should be able to meet these objectives:

9-1   Describe the two trends in skilled activity in the 1960s by referring both to the nature of the activity and to the change in research emphasis and illustrate these trends, using contemporary skills.

9-2   Describe the three characteristics of skilled activity in terms of chains, coordination, and response patterns and illustrate these characteristics, using a skill you will teach.

9-3   Define constancies in terms of behavior patterns and list the three ways in which we classify S-R chains.

9-4   Describe the three phases of skill learning in terms of their distinguishing characteristics and illustrate these phases, using a skill you plan to teach.

9-5   Describe the two aspects of contiguity important in skill learning and their relationship to whole and part-whole methods; illustrate how you would provide contiguity in a skill you plan to taech.

9-6   Describe three ways in which practice is important in skill learning and distinguish between distributed and massed practice and their advantages; illustrate how you would provide for practice in teaching your skill.

9-7   Distinguish between the two types and modes of feedback and provide illustrations of each; describe the effects of withholding and delaying feedback and provide an illustration of the effects of both procedures; define feedback as prompting and give an illustration of this procedure; describe the relationship of the two modes and the two types of feedback to stages of skill learning and provide illustrations of the relationship.

THE NATURE OF SKILL LEARNING

The Study of Skills

Research in the field of skills has had no pioneer who has shown a high degree of creativity, engaged in a wide variety of studies, or promulgated strong opinions which his followers could accept as dogma (Irion, 1966). No one, for example, has the stature of Ebbinghaus, Freud, Cattell, Binet, Thorndike, Hull, or Skinner. Arthur Irion (1966) suggests that the history of research on motor skills is largely the history of experimental psychology. Irion also suggests that the absence of dogma may have had beneficial effects since attention could center on research problems rather than ideological debates. An unfortunate effect of the absence of any great luminary figure and of a loudly trumpeted theoretical credo has been that research on motor-skill learning in the school setting is increasingly difficult to find. Although the field lacks any great pioneer A. T. Welford (1962) suggests that the scientific study of human skill began with Bessel, an astronomer, who, during the 1820s, studied the reaction times of himself and his colleagues to find out how they differed in their observations of star-transit times. But surely Bessel never intended to be the father of research on skill learning.

In the twentieth century we have seen a remarkable change in the specific skills which we learn. The change is largely the result of technological innovations and the earnest pursuit of leisure-time activities. Technology has introduced new machinery into the armed forces and industry at an increasingly rapid rate. We are now witnessing the rapid introduction of machinery into the home and the school. The use of this machinery requires the skills to build, install, repair, and properly operate it. Most of us feel that we do quite well if we learn only to operate the new gadgets with which industry either enriches or clutters our lives. We are indeed confronted with an impressive array of tape recorders, stereo–high-fidelity sets, dishwashers, sewing machines, musical instruments, duplicating machines, airplanes, automobiles and motorcycles, still and movie cameras, and slide projectors which promise to keep our lives busy and which require the learning of new skills. As new skills are introduced, old ones are retired; some of us painfully learned manual gear shifting only to have it replaced with automatic transmission. With the growth of leisure time we have turned with new zest to athletic and social activities, from the relatively uncomplicated bowling and badminton to the totally consuming golf and tennis. To swimming we have added water skiing, scuba diving, and even surfing. The composing of, rendering of, and dancing to rock music have become increasingly innovative if not always recognizably skillful. In our less social moments we (at least collectively) spend more time reading and writing than we once did.

These changes in human skills in modern society represent two major trends: a shift in emphasis from motor skills, performed while standing or in motion, to sedentary skills, and in research a shift in emphasis from skill learning and training in the armed forces to those in industry. Regarding the first trend, Paul Fitts (1962, pp. 77–78) notes the tendency today for skilled work to be done while the individual is seated. This is particularly true for both clerical and industrial jobs, and it is also true for the arts and crafts which occupy our time at home. In fact the increased concern (often more verbal than motor) with physical fitness, athletic activities, and weight control may partly reflect the increasingly sedentary nature of the jobs we perform and the hobbies we pursue. According to Fitts (1962, p. 78), the skills which are growing in importance are those in which the individual must keep track of several sources of information (stimuli), organize this information, and sort out the effects of his own earlier actions from the effects produced by outside agents. Flying an airplane is an example. The panel of dials, the position and feel of the plane, and the radio messages represent many sources of information. The effects of the pilot's manipulation of the controls must be separated from the effects produced by the aircraft itself and the effects of the atmosphere. Although flying an airplane may not be the best example, most skills performed when the body is at rest are easier to learn than skills performed when the body is in motion.

Regarding the second trend, Welford (1962) notes that the emphasis in applied research on skills is gradually shifting from the armed forces to industry. Large-scale developments in the scientific study of skills did not occur until World War II. During that time it became necessary to operate complicated military equipment, especially devices used in high-speed aircraft. These tasks became so complex that no amount of selection and training of military personnel could ensure adequate performance. Research had to uncover the factors which made the performance of the skill easy or difficult, especially when the skill had to be used under pressure, speedily, and with the adversary staring down the throats of our men. Now much of the applied research facilitates the operation of complex industrial electrical equipment.

The Definition of Skills

A skill has three characteristics: It represents a chain of motor responses; it involves the coordination of hand and eye movements; and it requires the organization of chains into complex response patterns.

Response chains   First, a skilled performance involves a chain of motor responses. Motor responses, as distinct from verbal responses, are muscular movements. The movements of the fingers, arms, legs, and toes are examples. Each movement can be viewed as an individual stimulus-response (*S-R*) association. A skill is a series or chain of such movements, with each link an individual *S-R* unit which acts as a stimulus for the next link. Gagné (1970, p. 124) uses this illustration, which involves the starting of a car engine by a novice driver:

S (start the engine)—*R* (looking forward and to the rear).
S (sight of clear road)—*R* (testing for gear in neutral).
S (gear in neutral)—*R* (turning the key to activate starter).
S (sound of motor catching)—*R* (release of key).
S (key released)—*R* (depressing the accelerator).

The *R*'s in the above example refer to the muscular movements or the motor responses. These responses must be executed in a particular sequence. If you depress the accelerator before releasing the ignition key, you create an impressive screeching noise to remind you of the proper *S-R* sequence. The releasing of the key (which is also a response) acts as a stimulus for the next response—the depressing of the accelerator.

The stimulation for each *S-R* link in a chain is partly kinesthetic. Kinesthetic stimulation is internal muscular tension, which we often refer to as the right "feel." When the golf club and baseball bat are properly positioned and swung, we experience certain feelings in the wrists and arms which tell us that our execution of the motor act is proper. When we first learn to shift, most of us rely on visual (or external) cues to tell us that the gear is in the proper position. After we become quite skilled at shifting, we rely almost entirely on kinesthetic stimulation and feedback to guide our shifting behavior. You will see below that this gradual change from reliance on external cues to reliance on internal cues characterizes most skill learning.

The amount of body movement involved in skilled behavior can vary considerably. Fitts (1964, p. 245) describes three categories: Some skilled behavior involves gross body movements, such as walking, running, jumping, swimming, balancing, and dancing. Other forms of skilled behavior involve only segments of the total anatomy, as in grasping, reaching, and manipulating objects with the fingers. Finally, for most of us today, skilled behavior often requires the manipulation of tools or objects or the control of machines, as in writing, typewriting, playing a musical instrument, sewing, driving a car, piloting an aircraft, playing tennis, tossing a ball, and doing assembly work.

Movement coordination   Second, you can view skilled behavior as the coordination of hand and eye movements (Bilodeau and Bilodeau, 1961). Frequently motor skills are called *perceptual-motor* skills to emphasize the coordination of perception (the eye) and motor acts (the hand). Swinging golf clubs, tennis rackets, and baseball bats requires high degrees of hand and eye coordination. In verbal skills, which we will consider in another chapter, the emphasis is on the tongue rather than on the hand or eye. Although we can use this distinction to separate the fields of motor learning and verbal learning, you will see that the two areas have much in common with each other and even with more complex learning types—the learning of concepts and rules (Fitts, 1964).

Response patterns   Third, you can view skilled behavior as the organization of *S-R* chains into large response patterns. When we discuss many complex human skills (piloting an aircraft, for example) we almost have to describe response patterns since there are so many individual *S-R* units and *S-R* chains. We sometimes describe the *S-R* chains which constitute the large response patterns as subtasks or subroutines. In swimming, for example, the arm strokes, the breathing, and the leg kicks are subtasks or subroutines. Each of these subroutines represents one or more response chains. Considerable evidence shows that the chains which make up complex human skills are hierarchically organized into larger response patterns; we must learn particular *S-R* units and *S-R* chains before learning others, and we must learn all the subordinate chains before we can perform a particular skill. The skill is the total response pattern. The timing, the anticipation, and the smooth flow of response which we observe in the accomplished musician, swimmer, and race car driver indicate that the learning of the *S-R* units and *S-R* chains has welded them into a single response pattern.

William Bryan and Noble Harter (1897, 1899) provided some of the earliest evidence for the theory that skills are hierarchical response patterns. They observed that as students became more skilled in learning and using the Morse code, the students seemed to hear and to tap patterns of dots and dashes for the individual letters directly. Later the students dealt with whole words and even short phrases. William Book (1908) observed the same development of response patterns in students learning to type. Book called the lowest level of the hierarchy the *letter association stage*. In this stage the student must look at each letter in the copy, say or think of the letter, mentally locate the letter on the keyboard, place the proper finger on the key, and again pronounce the letter or initiate the final letter-making movement. In the second stage, the syllable and word association stage, the student looks at words or syllables slightly ahead, uses an abbreviated mental spelling, and strikes off groups of letters and words. Finally, in the expert stage, the student reads the copy a number of words ahead of the movement of his hands, keeps his eyes continuously on the copy, initiates and directs his finger movements by the incipient or actual pronounciation of words, and centers his attention completely on the work. The third stage represents the highly organized response pattern which comprises the response chains learned in the two earlier stages.

Typewriting skill is unique in that it consists of a number of discrete acts rather than of a single unitary act. A study by M. A. Vince (1953) illustrated how continuous responses (or response chains) can be amalgamated into a single response pattern. Students had to learn a skill which involved drawing a line through a series of circles inscribed on a moving band. The students had to watch for the circles through a narrow slit. Figure 9-1 shows the basic pattern of circles. The direction of the pattern changed at the six corners, the student had to learn to anticipate each corner and to respond accurately in drawing the connecting line. Vince noted three stages in the learning of this skill. The students used a waiting response in the early part of the experiment, when the position of the next circle was not known and when a mistake had been made. In the early part they also used a predictive response, which led to overshooting at points where the direction of the pattern changed. At this stage the students had to learn the key points in the pattern. In the final stage the students learned to anticipate correctly the corners of the pattern—a task which involved accurate prediction and response to the slope of the line of the circles. Figure 9-2 shows the three stages of learning. The student could not learn this skill by responding to each circle separately. He had to develop a correct notion of the whole pattern of circles. As part of the

FIG. 9-1 Pattern of circles (after Vince, 1953).

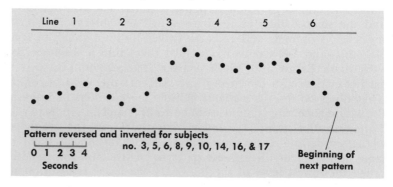

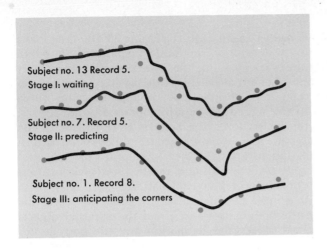

Subject no. 13 Record 5.
Stage I: waiting

Subject no. 7. Record 5.
Stage II: predicting

Subject no. 1. Record 8.
Stage III: anticipating the corners

FIG. 9-2 Learning stages (after Vince, 1953)

experiment the students reported their own thoughts as they were learning this skill. Almost all mentioned the pattern as being important. When one student was asked the number of circles she had seen, she stated, "They were more or less in units of four. I have just thought of that!" In this way she revealed her awareness of the pattern.

According to George Miller, Eugene Galanter, and Karl Pribram (1960, pp. 88–89), the student tackles the learning of a new skill with a verbal plan or strategy—a crutch he uses until he learns to walk. They refer to the look-remember-hunt-hit-check plan for typing:

> The entire pattern of movements, guided continually by perpetual feedback, can then be represented in other plans as if it were a unitary, independent act. The same procedure of welding these new unities together to form larger skilled units may repeat at the higher level, until eventually the typist is planning whole paragraphs and the aviator is planning whole trips, secure that when the time comes to execute the plan the subdivisions will be prepared to carry out orders in a rapid, efficient manner.

According to these writers, the plans of the beginner and of the expert may bring the same result, but they are different in nature. The expert's version of the plan is involuntary, inflexible, and usually locked in. The plan is often so automatic for him that he is unable to explain how he executes his performance. The beginner's plan is voluntary, flexible, and communicable. Until the beginner's plan becomes automatic, he is not free to work the skill he is learning into a larger plan—that is, into a more complex skill. The notion that complex skills (or plans) are the result of the learning of subordinate skills (or plans) is consistent with the idea of hierarchically organized response patterns.

Now that you know how to define a skill, we can turn to a fuller consideration of how skills are learned.

Classification of Skills

Fitts (1962, 1964) has developed a means for classifying skills. One basis for his classification is called *skill constancies*—uniform patterns found in highly skilled behavior. Constancies can be described as (1) gross body movements and (2) the extent of external pacing of the activity. Constancies also vary in the level of complexity. (Fitts (1962, p. 179) describes three levels.) Complexity refers to the varied relationships of body and objects, at rest and in motion. At the lowest level, the body is at rest prior to the beginning of the skilled action. The student initiates a behavior pattern which he carries out in relation to a fixed object. Examples of this level of constancy are driving a golf ball, threading a needle, and picking up a pencil. These constancies (or uniform behavior patterns) are fairly easy to describe and measure. At a more complex level, the student begins the skilled activity either when the body is in motion and the external objects are fixed or when the external objects are in motion and the body is not in motion but is set to go. The basketball forward is executed when the body is in motion; the batter in baseball is fixed (or set) when swinging at a pitched ball. The uniform patterns at this level are harder to describe. At the most complex level both the student and the external objects undergo change just prior to the execution of the skilled activity. Fitts suggests these examples: a man trying to keep his balance on the deck of a pitching ship and at the same time training his eyes (or perhaps a gun) on an aircraft flying overhead, and a football quarterback throwing a running pass. In both instances, both student and object are in motion before the performance of the skill. At this level it is very difficult to identify constancies.

We can also classify skilled activity in terms of certain *S-R*—chain characteristics—coherence, continuity, and complexity (Fitts, 1964, pp. 246–47). Chains are coherent to the degree that successive responses are dependent. Spoken English, walking movements, and the succession of notes in classical music are all highly coherent. Less coherent are the movement patterns involved in skating, swimming, and handwriting. Chains are continuous to the degree that the responses are continuous with few pauses in between. Steering a car is a continuous task. Hitting a baseball is a discrete task. Typing is also a discrete task—except that responses follow each other with great rapidity. Finally, the level of complexity of the *S-R* chains depends on the number of different stimuli and responses possible in a given block of time and space. Learning the English alphabet is less complex than learning the Chinese alphabet. Reading the instrument panel of an automobile is less complex than reading the panel of an aircraft.

Phases of Skill Learning

Fitts (1962, pp. 186–89) identified three phases—the cognitive, the fixation, and the autonomous—through which the student passes in learning a complex skill. The phases, of course, overlap; they are not distinct units. Moving from one phase to another is a continuous process.

In the *cognitive* phase the students attempt to intellectualize the skill they are to perform. In the terms of Miller, Galanter, and Pribram (1960), the students develop plans which guide the execution of the skill. During this phase, according to Fitts, the instructor and the students try to analyze the skills and to verbalize about what is being learned. The instructor describes what to expect and what to do. He describes procedures and gives information about errors, which occur with great frequency in this phase. In showing the importance of the proper instructional management of this phase, Fitts (p. 187) refers to the studies on pilot training made by A. C. Williams, Ralph Flexman, and their associates at the University of Illinois (see Williams and Flexman, 1949, and Flexman et al., 1950). They discovered that they could reduce from eight to four the average number of hours required to learn to solo by providing certain basic learning conditions. Relevant to this phase of skill learning, they developed a number of procedures to enhance understanding of flight problems and flight procedures. Among other learning conditions they gave knowledge of results (reinforcement), they established appropriate expectancies, and they talked through the maneuvers. In most adult learning this phase is short—lasting for hours or days.

In the *fixation* phase the correct behavior patterns are practiced until the chance of making incorrect responses is reduced to zero; the behavior becomes fixed. This stage lasts for days or months. At the most basic level the student is learning to link together the basic units of the chain. At a more advanced level he is learning to organize the chains into an overall pattern. Fitts (1962, p. 188) uses these examples. For the aircraft pilot, this phase extends from the first time he flies alone (the first solo) through the time he obtains a private license and perhaps through his first one hundred hours of flying. For the typist this phase extends from the point at which he learns the position of the different keys and how the fingers are used in striking them to the point at which he graduates from the first typing course and reduces errors to fewer than 1 percent.

Finally, the *autonomous* phase is characterized by increasing speed of performance in skills in which it is important to improve accuracy to the point at which errors are very unlikely to occur. In this phase the student also increases his resistance to stress and to the interference of outside activities which he is able to perform at the same time. This is the stage achieved by the expert, for whom the performance of the skill has become involuntary, inflexible, and even locked in. The available evidence indicates that performance can improve over millions of cycles of practice (Fitts, 1964, p. 165). Fitts refers to a study by E. R. F. W. Crossman (1959) which shows that gradual improvement may continue over several years of practice. Figure 9-3 shows the results of long periods of practice on an industrial task.

Basic Learning Conditions

Much research has been devoted to the conditions important in skill learning. The most important are contiguity, practice, and feedback (or knowl-

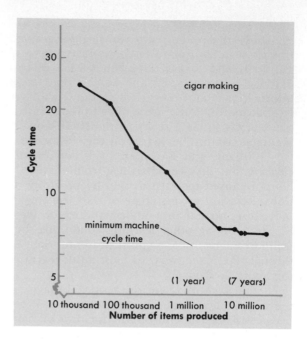

FIG. 9-3 Gradual improvement in the performance of an industrial task over several years of work (after Crossman, 1959).

edge of results). In this part of the chapter you will find out how each of these conditions influences skill learning. In the last part of this chapter, in which we develop a series of steps for the teaching of skills, we shall consider the practical implications of the research discussed in this section.

Contiguity We defined contiguity as the almost simultaneous occurrence of the stimulus and the response. At the basic level of skill learning contiguity is the simultaneous occurrence of the *S-R* units in the chains. At the higher levels of skill learning contiguity is the simultaneous occurrence of the chains which constitute the overall skill pattern. In lay terms, we often refer to contiguity as *timing, coordination,* or *proper order.*

Two aspects of contiguity are important in skill learning. One is the proper sequence of the *S-R* units and the chains. Unless these units and chains occur in the proper order we cannot perform the skill. Use of a little bizarre imagination shows what would happen if the novice driver, in stopping his car, failed to remove his foot from the accelerator before applying the brakes. Many lumpy foreheads remind us of the consequences of not observing the proper order for stopping a car: remove foot from accelerator and then gradually apply the brakes. Of course, the veteran driver learns to anticipate his stops and uses a pumping motion which alternately accelerates and decelerates the car by the careful application and release of pressure on the accelerator and the brakes. The sequence of *S-R* units here is more complex than that executed by the novice driver.

Training procedures for helping the student learn the *S-R* units and the chains in the proper order have been an area of research and even lively debate. The interest and the controversy have centered around whether the student should perform the entire skill or first practice the parts of the skill. The first procedure is called the whole method, the second is called the part (or part-whole) method. A study by F. J. McGuigan and Eugene MacCaslin (1955, p. 658) illustrates the two procedures. They were interested in teaching army recruits how to fire a rifle. This task has several subtasks which the trainee must learn.

In the *part training method,* the trainees received instruction on the first subtask (assuming proper postures). Then they received training on the second subtask (wrapping and looping the rifle sling) while practicing the first subtask. In this way contiguity was provided. Then they received instruction on the third subtask (moving the sight adjustment) while practicing the first two subtasks. This procedure was continued until all the subtasks were put together in their proper order for the act of firing. In the *whole training method,* the trainees first watched a half-hour demonstration of the entire sequence of subtasks. In the training periods which followed, they received instruction and practice on all the subtasks and on firing. In this particular study the investigators found that the whole method was superior to the part method. Their findings were consistent with those of an earlier study by Clyde Knapp and Robert Dixon (1952), who found that the whole method was superior to the part method in teaching students how to juggle.

Thomas Gilbert (1962a) suggests that a reversal of the part method may be the best training procedure. In Gilbert's reverse-contiguity (called *mathetics*) the trainee begins with the last subtask and works back to the first one. In rifle training, for example, you first teach the student to squeeze the trigger. Mastering this act should be reinforcing to the student and dispose him to learn the responses which lead to the proper firing of the rifle. You then teach him to control his breathing. As soon as he learns to hold his breath while firing, you allow him to squeeze the trigger again and thereby reinforce proper breath holding. You then teach him to align his sights on the target. When he does this, you immediately allow him to control his breathing and fire the rifle again. In this way the student works backward to the first subtask in our list. One may have some doubts about allowing untutored students the privilege of firing rifles, but one cannot deny that the act of firing has the major reinforcing effect in the learning of this skill. John Cox and Lynn Boren (1965) compared Gilbert's training method with a whole method of training and found that both methods were equally effective. They concluded that Gilbert did not consider that an adult human (unlike a rat) can hold a goal in mind and that this mental image of the goal can reinforce each response which he believes promotes attainment of the goal.

In summarizing the evidence on the part versus the whole method, James Naylor (1962) concludes that for skills which are not highly coherent, continuous, complex, or highly organized, using the part method to practice those parts in which the student is weakest is the most efficient procedure. For highly organized skills of moderate and high degrees of difficulty, the whole method is the most efficient procedure. Using Fitts's classification of skills, we conclude that the part method is the better one for teaching those skills in which the constancies are least complex—that is, those in which the body is at rest prior to the beginning of skilled action, as in driving a golf ball or threading a needle. When either body or external objects or both are in motion, the whole method is the better training procedure. We can also conclude that highly coherent, continuous, and complex chains may be learned better by the whole method.

The second aspect of contiguity important in skill learning is the need to execute the *S-R* links in the chains or the chains in the overall response pattern in close time succession (Gagné, 1970). If you recall that each link in the chain and each chain in the pattern acts as a stimulus for the subsequent responses, you see how delay can disrupt the performance of the skill. Delay is failure to present the stimulus needed for the next response in a series of responses. Because of the interdependence of the *S-R* units and chains in skill learning, the absence of contiguity can be seriously disruptive. Skilled professionals emphasize the importance of timing, which, in part, is the need for contiguity in the learning and performance of particular skilled activities. Some skills, of course, have delays built into their execution. Gagné (1970, p. 130) uses this example. In using a coin-operated machine we must learn to delay pulling the lever until we hear the coins fall into the coin box. But even here the pulling of the lever should be contiguous with the noise in the coin box; the lever must be pulled before someone else uses the machine.

Practice   A second condition of major importance in the learning of skills is practice, an external learning condition. Practice, we have said, is the repetition of a response in the presence of a stimulus. It sets the stage for corrective feedback and confirming reinforcement. In the learning of skills practice is a way of (1) rehearsing those particular subtasks which are only partially learned; (2) coordinating the subtasks so that they are performed in the proper sequence and with appropriate timing; (3) preventing extinction and forgetting of the subtasks; and (4) developing the skill to the autonomous stage of learning. Considerable evidence in skill learning proves that practice leads to perfect performance.

We can confidently assume that practice is a necessary condition for the attainment of a high level of performance in complex skills. The research presented here raises this question: Is it better to practice a task with as little interruption for rest as possible, or is rest beneficial to the learning and performance of skills? In more technical language, the issue is the relative benefits of massed and distributed practice. *Massed practice* provides little or no interruption for rest. If you reserve all your studying in a course for one study session before the final examination, you are massing your practice. *Distributed practice* allows for rest periods. If you reserve a period of time each week to study the material in each of your courses, you are distributing your practice (study) in those courses.

The classic experiment by Irving Lorge (1930) illustrates the two kinds of practice. Among other tasks, three groups of students had to learn to draw a figure using only a mirror image of the figure they were drawing—a task, of course, for which the students had little previous practice. The first group had twenty trials (attempts) to make the drawing with no rest between trials (massed practice). The two remaining groups were provided distributed practice. One of these groups had twenty trials with one-minute rest periods between trials. The other group had twenty trials with one-day rest periods between trials. The measure of performance was the amount of time required to complete the drawing on each trial. Figure 9-4 shows the results. On trials 3 and 4 the groups with distributed practice showed a very rapid drop in the amount of time per trial. The group with massed practice, however, showed no corresponding drop. Lorge's findings are typical of experiments which compare the effects of massed and distributed practice: The differences in favor of distributed practice are consistent and large.

Lorge's experiment raises another question: Does the length of the rest period make an important difference in the learning and performance of the skill? In his experiment a rest period of one minute had about the same effect as a rest period of one day (see Figure 9-4). Mary Kientzle (1946) performed an experiment to find at what point in time the rest period no longer pays off. She used a different task—printing the alphabet upside

FIG. 9-4 The effect of distribution of practice upon mirror drawing. Notice that, apart from the very first trials, there is almost a constant difference between the difference groups (after Lorge, 1930).

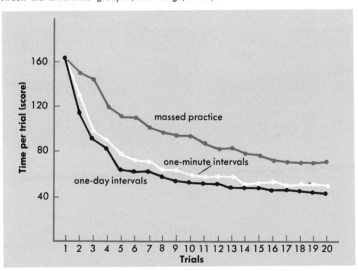

down so that when the paper was turned through an angle of 180 degrees the alphabet could be read from left to right in the usual manner. The rest periods varied from zero seconds (massed practice) to seven days. Figure 9-5 shows the effects of the different rest periods. You can see that after forty-five seconds there are few increases in performance. The sharpest gains are made between zero seconds and ten seconds. Confirming the findings of Lorge, this experiment makes it clear that a rest of a few seconds produces most of the maximum possible gain in distributed practice.

These experiments leave unanswered the following question: Which is more important—the practice (or work) or the rest periods? Gregory Kimble and Edward Bilodeau (1949) studied performance of a simple task to answer this question. They required students to overturn cylindrical blocks in a large board containing circular holes. Table 9-1 lists the four experimental groups, the various lengths of the work and the rest periods. These investigators found that shortening the rest period was much more important than lengthening the work period. But they also found that the length of the rest period must depend on the length of the work period. Furthermore, as James Deese (1958, p. 190) reminds us, we cannot arbitrarily decide how long the work periods must be, for this depends on the nature of the task. He suggests, for example, that it would not be wise to interrupt someone solving a puzzle before he had reached the solution.

These experiments leave one further question unanswered: What is the effect on learning and performance if the total amount of time is kept equal for all experimental subjects with some spending more time on practice and others spending more time at rest? Carl Duncan (1951) designed an experiment that compared these conditions. One group practiced continu-

FIG. 9-5 Mean gains under varied distributions of practice (after Kientzle, 1946).

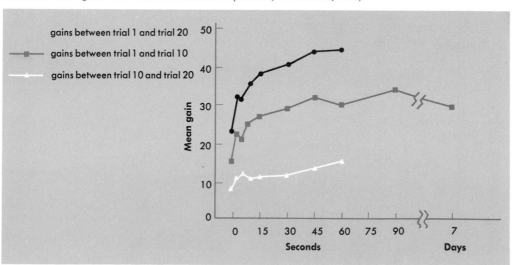

GROUP	WORK PERIOD, SECONDS	REST PERIOD, SECONDS
1	10	10
2	10	30
3	30	10
4	30	30

ously (massed practice), receiving three times as much practice as the other group. The other group periodically stopped for a rest period (distributed practice). Surprisingly enough, Duncan discovered that the group with distributed practice, even though it had only one-third as much practice, produced the better performance. He also discovered that after an equal period of rest for both groups the performance of the group with distributed practice remained superior.

Research on massed and distributed practice has raised one additional issue. An experiment by L. R. Doré and Ernest Hilgard (1938) raised the question of whether the distribution of practice affects learning or merely performance. Their experiment showed that almost all the inhibition which builds up during practice dissipates during the rest period so that the performance of both distributed-practice and massed-practice groups equalizes. Arthur Irion (1966) suggests however that the weight of modern evidence indicates that the distribution of practice affects performance and not learning, although he concedes that present evidence on the effects of distributed practice on learning and performance is not conclusive and that more complete evidence must await further research. These results do support the theory that learning and performance are not always the same.

We may conclude that for performance of motor skills some rest, or distribution of practice, is better than none. The effects of rest periods undoubtedly vary with different skills. It would be interesting to use Fitts's classification of skilled performances to find out what this variation may be. Later, you will see that the detrimental effects of massed practice do not occur in verbal learning so consistently as they do in skill learning. In verbal learning, the findings are much more complex and may even indicate no substantial difference in the effects of massed and distributed practice (see Chapter 8). In skill learning, however, we may conclude that distributed practice is superior to massed practice.

Feedback Our third basic condition for skill learning is feedback. In the discussion which follows you will see why the term *feedback* is more useful than the term *reinforcement* in the description of skill learning. Whereas reinforcement stresses the hedonic or reward effects of learning, feedback

emphasizes the informational aspect of learning. In the experimental literature, feedback is often called *knowledge of results*. We will use this definition: Feedback is the information available to the student which makes
possible the comparison of his actual performance with some standard performance of a skill.

John Annet (1964) distinguishes two types of feedback, intrinsic and
extrinsic. *Intrinsic* feedback is the information the student obtains through
his own actions. When, for example, he rolls the ball down the bowling
alley and knocks over ten pins, the effect of his actions (the knocking over
of all the pins) becomes intrinsic feedback. *Extrinsic* feedback is the information the teacher gives to the student about the effectiveness of his
actions. The bowling instructor may point out that the student is rolling
the ball with too much curve or that he is not giving enough spin to the
ball. As we move from the fixation to the autonomous stages of skill learning, we rely less on extrinsic and more on intrinsic feedback. In this way
our skill learning becomes self-evaluative.

Margaret Robb (1966) distinguishes between two modes of feedback—
external and internal. Information received through the external sensory
organs—that is, through vision, hearing, touch, smell, and taste—belongs
to the *external* mode. Information obtained from the internal receptor
organs, as in the case of kinesthetic feedback, is *internal* feedback. For
example, in the forehand drive in tennis, the student places his feet approximately shoulder-width apart and flexes his knees slightly. If the student determines the correctness of his position largely through vision—that
is, by looking at his feet and knees—he is using the external mode of feedback. But, if he relies on the feeling for the correct position without visual
inspection of this posture, he is using the internal mode of feedback. The
accomplished execution of a skill requires the student to rely more and
more in internal feedback (Fitts, 1951). Gagné and Edwin Fleishman (1959)
point out that only when internal feedback has been dependably sorted out
does the golfer execute a consistent swing.

Robb (1966) describes a study in which she controlled both the type and
the mode of feedback to observe the effects on the rate of learning a simple
arm-movement pattern. The major purpose of her study was to find out
whether the students relied mainly on internal feedback after this skill was
highly practiced. During their practice periods the students in the experimental groups received extrinsic feedback in the form of scores of their
practice performance and intrinsic feedback in the form of on-going information while performing the skill. Subjects in the control group were
trained only with internal feedback—that is, they were not allowed to use
vision in learning the arm-movement pattern. The final test in this study
required all students to perform the skill without visual (external) feedback. Robb found that the students in the experimental groups were able
to perform the skill as well as students in the control group. Through extensive practice, the experimental subjects had also learned to rely on internal feedback, even though they were not told to do so.

What evidence do we have that any feedback is important in skill learning? There are two major sources of such evidence: experiments in which feedback has been withheld and experiments in which feedback has been delayed. Some experiments, of course, study both effects. First we shall describe an experiment in which feedback was withheld. J. L. Elwell and G. C. Grindley (1938) taught students a coordinated movement of two hands by which they could direct a spot of light on the bull's-eye of a target. One hand regulated vertical and the other hand regulated horizontal movement. The amount of error in the movement of either hand was indicated by the amount of deviation of the spot of light from the bull's-eye—a form of intrinsic feedback. At a particular point in the experiment this feedback was withdrawn (the students could no longer see the target). Figure 9-6 shows the dramatic drop in performance at point B, at which feedback was withdrawn. The withdrawal of the feedback also affected motivation. Students expressed displeasure, became bored, lost keenness, and began to arrive late for experimental sessions. In discussing the results of their experiment, Elwell and Grindley stated that feedback not only has a directive effect in the learning of a skill but also can be conducive to the development of a conscious attitude to perform the skill with accuracy.

Whereas the Elwell and Grindley experiment showed the effects of complete withdrawal of feedback, several experiments show the effects of delaying feedback. One of the earliest of these was performed by Irving Lorge and Edward Thorndike (1935). Students had to learn to toss two wooden balls back over their heads at an unseen target of concentric circles. For one group the informational and motivational aspects of feedback were not separated since the students received money in proportion to the accuracy of their tosses. The feedback was extrinsic—announcements were

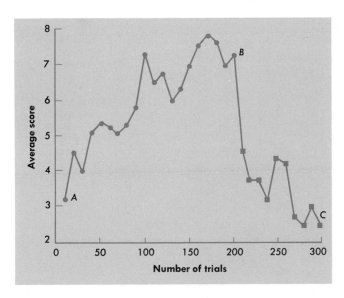

FIG. 9-6 Average of performance of ten subjects in Exp. I (feedback removed at B; after Elwell and Grindley, 1938, p. 45).

made to the students about the accuracy of their throws. Another group received no feedback; another received immediate feedback; and four groups received feedback after one, two, four, or six seconds. An additional group received feedback for a previous throw after they had made an intervening throw. Only this latter group and the group which received no feedback failed to show improvement. However, less improvement resulted from a four- to six-second delay than from a one- to four-second delay. A similar study by Joel Greenspoon and Sally Foreman (1956) considerably lengthened the periods of delay. The students had to draw three-inch, straight, horizontal lines while blindfolded and while their arms and hands were removed from the table. They had to draw fifty lines with thirty-second intervals between trials. They were given the following extrinsic feedback: If the line were more than $3\frac{1}{4}$ inches, they were told "long"; if less than $2\frac{3}{4}$ inches, they were told "short"; and if between $2\frac{3}{4}$ and $3\frac{1}{4}$ inches, they were told "right." Of the five groups, one received immediate feedback; another, no feedback; and three groups received feedback after delays of ten, twenty, or thirty seconds. Figure 9–7 shows the correct number of responses for the five groups. Increasing the length of delay of feedback reduced the rate of learning. Short delays of ten seconds or less seemed to have little effect. After ten seconds, the deterioration in performance was quite sharp.

Feedback also acts as a form of *prompting*–giving information to the student before or at the same time he makes his response. In the experiments we have described, most of the extrinsic feedback was supplied after

FIG. 9-7 Mean number of "right" responses of the control and experimental groups for successive blocks of five trials (after Greenspoon and Foreman, 1956, p. 227).

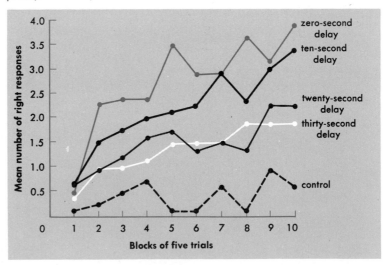

the student made his response. Annet reminds us that feedback really comes between responses. The fact that information comes before the next response in a series may be as important as the fact that information comes after the preceding response. In one study Annet (1946) showed that the advance information given to the students was more effective than feedback given after responses were made. In a number of maze-learning experiments, subjects had to learn a series of right-left choices presented on a moving paper band viewed through a slit in a screen. They traced the paths with a stylus. One group had to choose before seeing whether the choice would be correct. This group was entirely dependent on feedback. A second group was allowed to see the correct path before making their selection. Both groups were required to make two perfect runs. This task took the first group (with feedback) three to five times longer than it took the second. Providing sufficient advance instructional guidance to help students avoid mistakes in the first place has been a major concern of programed instruction (see Chapter 12). In any case, you must remember that feedback after the performance is only one way to present the student with the information necessary to carry out the desired actions. It may not always be the most efficient instructional procedure.

From these three experiments on the withholding and the delay of feedback you can see that feedback, as a form of reinforcement, affects motivation as well as learning. This was explicitly the case in the experiment by Elwell and Grindley in which the students' interest waned noticeably after feedback was withdrawn. Although experimentally it is difficult to separate the motivational and informational aspects of feedback (Postman, 1947), Alphonse Chapanis (1964) has made an attempt. He chose a very simple task (punching random digits into a teletype tape) which hardly required skill or informational feedback to learn. Three of his groups had counters in plain sight which they could use to record work output. In the case of only one of these groups was attention directed to the counter; they were told to record the numbers on the counter only for the purpose of attendance. Any differences in performance would have to be attributed to work incentive or to the motivational aspects of the available feedback. Chapanis found no significant differences among these three groups or between these groups and a control group, which had no counter available.

Annet (1964) believes that the following evidence supports the conclusion that the informational aspect of feedback is important in learning and the motivational aspect important in performance: (1) Both reward and punishment act as emphasizers since we recall quite readily responses which are either rewarded or punished; (2) emphasis (pleasant or unpleasant) on right responses is more effective than emphasis on wrong responses; (3) feedback increases effort and directs attention; (4) reward and punishment influence either beneficially or detrimentally the way the student tries to learn a skill; and (5) reported success and failure can both increase and decrease effort.

In summary, what may we conclude about the effects of feedback on the learning of skills? First, feedback is the single most important variable governing the acquisition of skills (Irion, 1966). Robert Ammons (1954) states that feedback is perhaps one of the most dependable and thoroughly tested principles in modern psychology. The principle holds for animals and men, children and adults, groups and individuals and for a wide variety of motor, monitoring, and other general-performance tasks.

Second, on the basis of the evidence presented in this chapter we may also conclude the following: (1) Extrinsic and external feedback are important in the early stages of skill learning, while intrinsic and internal feedback are important in later stages; (2) feedback should be immediate or very nearly immediate; (3) giving the student advance information on the performance of a skill may be more efficient than using only feedback for information; and (4) the motivational aspects of feedback may affect performance, or the amount of effort the student will invest in practicing the skill.

Summary

This consideration of feedback as a basic learning condition concludes our discussion of the nature of skill learning. In this part of the chapter we observed some modern trends which pertain to skill learning: (1) Emphasis is shifting from motor skills performed with the body in motion to less complex sedentary skills, and (2) the research emphasis is shifting from military to industrial skills.

In defining a skill we identified three characteristics: Skills are chains composed of *S-R* units, involve hand-eye coordination, and are hierarchically organized into response patterns. We described three basic conditions for the learning of skills: contiguity, practice, and feedback. Contiguity requires both the proper sequencing of the subtasks and their execution in rapid time succession. Depending on the skill, both the whole and the part-whole methods provide the necessary contiguity. In the case of practice, the evidence strongly favors some form of distributed practice in the performance of motor skills, but distributed practice may be superior to massed practice only in the performance and not in the learning of the skill. Finally the evidence shows that feedback is the single most important variable in skill learning.

You should now return to the list of instructional objectives for the first section of this chapter and determine how well you have achieved them.

QUESTION 9-1   In providing instruction in beginning swimming, Mr. Kinetic was particularly concerned that, in the early demonstrations of the skill, the student see the relationship among arm, leg, and foot movements and between these movements and breathing. About which of the following learning conditions was Mr. Kinetic most concerned? (a) reinforcement; (b) contiguity; (c) practice; (d) feedback; (e) discrimination.

After selecting your answer, give reasons for your choice and for your rejection of the alternatives.

Upon reading the following section of the chapter, you should be able to meet these objectives:

9-8 Indicate two ways in which entering behavior for skill learning can be described and give one illustration of each way.

9-9 Distinguish psychomotor abilities and skills and illustrate your distinction.

9-10 Distinguish the physical proficiency abilities from the notion of general physical ability by referring to the various areas of the former; define physical abilities in terms of hierarchical structures.

9-11 Distinguish the manipulative-proficiency abilities from the notion of general manual dexterity by referring to particular manipulative abilities.

9-12 Describe the relationship between psychomotor abilities and learning in terms of early and late stages of learning and illustrate how you would use your knowledge of this relationship for task analysis and for assessing entering behavior.

PSYCHOMOTOR ABILITIES

Entering Behavior

Successful learning of skills is determined not only by the external conditions of learning but also by the entering behavior of the student. In discussing his model of skill learning, Fitts (1964, pp. 259–60) describes the entering behavior of the student in this way:

> An adult, or even a child of a few years of age, never begins the acquisition of a new form of skilled behavior except from the background of many already existing, highly developed, both general and specific skills. Thus the initial stage of our model is not that of a random network but an already organized system [the student] possessing language skills, concepts, and efficient subroutines [skill subtasks] such as those employed in maintaining posture, walking, and manipulating. The number of such highly developed skills in an adult is certainly in the hundreds, each having its own executive program [plan] and library of subroutines, many of the subroutines being shared with other skills. Learning to swim provides a typical example of a skill that is already learned against a complex background of already existing habits.

In this statement Fitts emphasizes the fact that new skill learning must be built on old skill learning. The new learning consists largely of coordinating into a single pattern less complex skills that the student has already mastered. In swimming, for example, the student may have already learned proper breathing, arm movements, and leg movements in connection with other athletic activities. To learn to swim he must simply combine these three subroutines into an overall pattern. Indeed, one of the major characteristics of complex skilled performances is the response patterns which they comprise.

The entering behavior of the student, at the most basic level of skill learning, consists of the *S-R* units which constitute the links in the chain (Gagné, 1970, p. 128). The student must have previously learned the individual *S-R* connections or he will be unable to learn a chain on the first attempt. And, as indicated by Fitts, the student must also have acquired entire chains, which Fitts calls *subroutines*.

Definition of Psychomotor Abilities

We can also define entering behavior in terms of the student's psychomotor abilities, which have been identified and studied in an extensive research program by Fleishman and his coworkers (1962, 1964). According to Fleishman, a psychomotor ability is a general trait of the individual which is related to performance of a wide variety of skills. The distinction between ability and skill is fairly clear: A skill is performance of a specific task. For example, operating a turret lathe is a skill which depends on the basic psychomotor abilities of manual dexterity and motor coordination. These same abilities, however, are needed in other skills. Manual dexterity is needed in assembling electrical components, and motor coordination is needed in piloting an aircraft. Flying an aircraft and trouble shooting a circuit are skills. Reaction time, finger dexterity, and speed of arm movement are psychomotor abilities. These abilities change very little in the adult. At any given stage they are analogous to a wiring diagram that the individual brings with him to a specific task. This wiring diagram describes his psychomotor entering behavior.

Fleishman and his coworkers have identified several of these abilities. They can be roughly grouped into two classes: those which pertain to the area of physical proficiency and those which pertain to the area of manipulative skills.

Abilities in Physical Proficiency

Fleishman (1964) has identified fourteen physical abilities in five broad areas: strength, flexibility-speed, balance, coordination, and endurance. Further research will probably uncover others. The analysis of physical proficiency strongly suggests two hypotheses: There is no such thing as general physical ability; and there may be a hierarchical structure of ability in the various areas described above. The first hypothesis recalls those theories of intelligence which postulate several independent factors rather than a single *g* factor. The evidence which Fleishman and others have marshaled to support this conclusion has been considerably greater and more convincing in the area of physical ability than that which others have presented in the area of mental ability. The fact that there are physical abilities and not a unitary physical ability imposes upon the school and the teacher the responsibilities of properly assessing the physical entering behavior of the students and of establishing instructional objectives and designing instructional procedures which are appropriate for them. Differences in entering behavior may require the assignment of students to different sections and different remedial treatments. The often-popular policy of cultivating the star athletes and neglecting the rest of the school population seems particularly unwarranted in the light of our knowledge about the several physical proficiency abilities and the probability that most individuals have sufficient ability at least in some areas to warrant careful attention to the physical education of the entire student body.

The second hypothesis pertains to the hierarchical structure of physical ability. Fleishman (1964, p. 32) suggests that the hierarchy in Figure 9-8 may exist in the flexibility-speed area. The diagram indicates that the most general factor is general flexibility-speed, the ability of the muscles to endure strain and distortion with some emphasis on the rapid recovery from this strain, which allows an immediate repetition of the movement. Contributing to the general factor are two broad, second-order factors—extent flexibility and dynamic flexibility. Finally, there are the narrow third-order factors, and, in the case of one of these—speed of limb movement—fourth-order factors apply to the arms and legs. Such hierarchies, if supported by further research, have teaching usefulness since they make possible a careful analysis of the student's entering behavior for various instructional objectives which require more than one physical ability. For example, if the student lacks speed of limb movement, the teacher can predict that the student will have difficulty in tasks requiring dynamic flexibility and general flexibility-speed. If we could prescribe activities which would develop speed of limb movement in both arms and legs, we could provide the student with the entering behavior he needs for tasks requiring the broader physical abilities. Fleishman's research thus far does not indicate whether physical abilities are relatively static and genetic (they seem to be in the adult) or whether modification of them is possible.

FIG. 9-8 A possible hierarchical factor structure hypothesized to describe the flexibility-speed area (after Fleishman, 1964, p. 32).

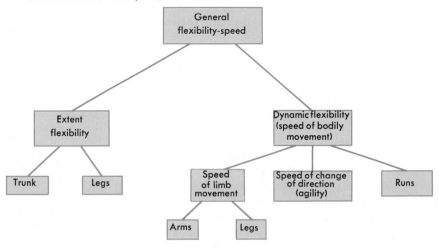

The manipulative abilities are necessary in the performance of particular laboratory skills. Walter Hempel and Fleishman (1955) found that these abilities, which contribute to the performance of fine manipulative skills, are quite independent of the physical proficiency abilities. Fleishman and his coworkers have identified eleven of these manipulative abilities. The tests of these abilities involve laboratory equipment. The reader can find illustrations and descriptions of the equipment and tests in Fleishman, 1964, pp. 16–26.

As with physical proficiency, in the area of manipulative abilities, the identification of several such abilities strongly supports the hypothesis that there is no general manual dexterity. A student may have fast reaction time and speed of arm movement and have poor finger dexterity and manual dexterity. We need no longer crudely classify students as the manually able and the manually disabled since the identification of several abilities permits a more precise assessment of entering behavior. Again, as in the case of physical education, the teacher can use the results of this assessment in two ways: He can predict how successful the student will be in learning skills which require various combinations of these abilities; and he can provide the remedial instruction which will enable the student to develop the abilities needed to perform the particular skills he is required to learn. The teacher, of course, uses this information about the student's entering behavior to achieve particular instructional objectives—the learning of particular skills. Accordingly, the statement of instructional objectives must include a task analysis which indicates exactly which manipulative abilities are required in the performance of the task. The teacher must try to obtain an appropriate match of the student's abilities and the abilities required by the skill.

Psychomotor Abilities and Learning

One of the most important findings in the research on skill learning is the following: As the student moves through the various stages of skill learning, the particular combination of abilities which the skill requires changes (Fleishman and Hempel, 1954, 1955). The combination of abilities required early in the training may be quite different from the combination required later. To study how these changes occur, Fleishman and Hempel (1955) had students practice on the discrimination reaction-time task illustrated in Figure 9-9. Figure 9-10 shows the results of this study. The percentages in the left margin indicate the contribution of each ability to the performance of the skill. You should note that the sizes of the labeled areas represent the percentage contributed by each ability at each stage (trial) of learning. As we move from the first to the fifteenth trial these percentages change for each ability. You can see, for example, that an ability called spatial relations contributes 36 percent in the beginning but only 11 percent at the end. Also, reaction time and rate of arm movement, which are barely represented in the initial performance of the skill, in-

FIG. 9-9 Discrimination reaction-time task. The subject throws one of four switches in response to rapidly changing light patterns. Score is the cumulative response time (after Fleishman, 1964, p. 19).

crease in importance, and, together, at the end of practice, contribute over 30 percent to the performance of the skill. Manual dexterity contributes in the beginning and at the end of practice, but decreases in importance during the middle part. Discrimination reaction time, which is a major factor in the performance of this task, increases in importance as practice continues.

Why do these changes occur? According to Fleishman and Hempel (1954), in the early stages of practice of the discrimination reaction-time task, the ability to learn the spatial relationships of the different stimuli to the different responses makes an important contribution to the performance of the skill. In this example, the different stimuli are rapidly changing light patterns. The different responses are throwing one of four switches. Once the students learn the spatial relationships to a sufficiently high degree, so that further improvement is neither necessary nor possible, other features of the task assume increasing importance. Rate of arm movement, in which the proper sequence of movements must be quickly completed, becomes the important ability.

The point is that the combination of abilities required later in practice differs from the combination required earlier in practice. Any prediction about the student's ultimate success based on the initial combination of abilities alone would be very misleading. As the ability requirements of the task change during practice, individual differences in these abilities affect the student's learning and performance. For example, we can predict that a student with good spatial ability but slow rate of arm movement will make much faster progress in the beginning than in the concluding phases of learning the discrimination reaction-time tasks. In assessing the entering behavior of the student the teacher must know all the abilities required by the practice of the skill so that he can determine where each student will make the most rapid and the slowest progress and so that he can supply the necessary help for the periods of slowest progress. Rarely can the student make the same rate of progress in all stages of skill learning.

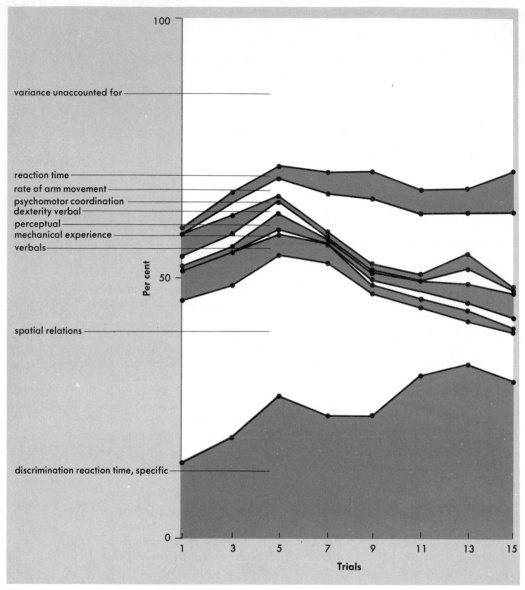

FIG. 9-10 Percentages of variance represented by loadings on each factor at different stages of practice on the discrimination reaction time task (after Fleishman and Hempel, 1955).

Our discussion of psychomotor abilities was related to our consideration of entering behavior in skill learning. First, the teacher must know that students use general and specific skills which they have already acquired, and that sometimes students have not acquired enough skills. To learn a new chain of *S-R* units, they must have previously learned each *S-R* link in the chain. In more complex skills, students must have learned the subtasks or chains which constitute the skill.

Second, psychomotor abilities also determine the extent of skill learning. These abilities are general traits related to performance of a wide variety of tasks. They fall into two classes: those that pertain to the area of physical proficiency (in which fourteen abilities have been identified); and those that pertain to the area of manipulative skill (in which eleven abilities have been identified). Research on these abilities strongly suggests that there is no general physical ability and no general manual dexterity. It is also possible that certain areas of physical ability are hierarchically organized. The teacher can use his knowledge of psychomotor abilities to obtain an appropriate match of the student's abilities and the abilities required by the skill. In arriving at this match, the teacher must be aware of an additional factor: Abilities required earlier in the learning of a skill differ from those required later. Any predictions about learning outcomes and any provision for instruction must be based on the variations in psychomotor abilities that different stages in skill learning require.

You should now return to the list of instructional objectives for this section and determine how well you have achieved them.

Upon reading the final section of this chapter, you should be able to meet these objectives:

9-13   List the four categories you can use in analyzing a skill; indicate

---

QUESTION 9-2

Mr. Potemkin, the tennis instructor, used the following screening test to determine which students he would accept for beginning tennis. He asked them to appear at the tennis courts for three consecutive days and to perform certain arm and foot movements typical of the initial steps in learning tennis. Which of the following statements is the best appraisal of this screening test?

(a) It is a suitable test of the entering behavior of the student and of the entering behavior required for this skill.

(b) It is less suitable as a screening device than as a careful observation of their performance of a skill they have already acquired.

(c) It is unsuitable as a screening device because it is unrelated to the entering behavior required by this skill.

(d) It is not so suitable as separate tests of each component ability required in tennis.

After selecting your answer, give the reasons for your choice and for your rejection of the alternatives.

---

how skills can be analyzed as *S-R* units; provide an illustration of both methods (using the categories and the *S-R* units). (Step 1)

9-14   Describe the three ways in which entering behavior can be assessed and illustrate your use of one of these ways. (Step 2)

9-15   Describe the two purposes for arranging preinstruction for skill components and illustrate how you would do this. (Step 3)

9-16   Describe the various ways in which skills may be presented and demonstrated and describe and illustrate the conditions under which each can be best employed. (Step 4)

9-17   Describe the various methods for providing for contiguity, practice, and feedback and indicate the basis for choosing each particular method; illustrate how you would provide for each of these basic learning conditions in a skill you will teach. (Step 5)

INSTRUCTION IN SKILLS

In this third (and final) part of the chapter, we shall deduce from our discussion of skill learning and psychomotor abilities the steps you should take in teaching skills to your students. Some of these steps, unfortunately, have less empirical support than others, but all are at least suggested by the basic research we have already described. To illustrate these steps we shall use a skill in a popular sport—the forehand drive in tennis.

STEP 1   **ANALYZE THE SKILL**

Your first teaching function is to do a task analysis of the skill you plan to teach. Frank Verducci (1967) made the following analysis of the forehand drive:

A   Body position: (1) The body is at right angles to the net with the left foot and shoulder toward the net; (2) the feet are placed approximately shoulder-width apart; (3) the knees are slightly flexed with the body weight carried on the balls of the feet.
B   Backswing: (1) The head of the racket moves back first with elbow close to the body; (2) as the racket moves back, the weight is shifted to the rear foot; (3) the racket head is brought straight back parallel to the ground; (4) the racket head is higher than the wrist; (5) the elbow is slightly bent; and (6) the eyes watch the ball.
C   Forward swing: (1) The forward swing is a continuous movement of the arm and racket; (2) the swing causes the path of the racket head to be a straight line pointing slightly upward; (3) the racket head should be even [with] or higher than the wrist throughout the forward swing; (4) throughout the swing, the arm is slightly bent and fairly close to the body; (5) the body weight shifts from the right to the left foot; (6) the body should rotate forward along with the shifting of the weight; and (7) the wrist should be fairly firm.
D   Position of the ball at impact: (1) The ball is opposite the forward foot at racket's length when impact occurs; and (2) the face of the racket is perpendicular to the ground.

Earlier you learned that skills can be described in terms of their constancies, continuity, coherence, and complexity. In the forehand drive, the constancies are the position and movement of the body and racket and the position and movement of the ball. The task analysis of the forehand drive clearly describes all these positions and movements. You can see that the execution of the forehand drive is more complex than that of the drive in golf because the tennis ball is in motion, and, under certain conditions, both the ball and the body are in motion. In any case, a task analysis of a skill must include a description of the relative position and movements of body and objects.

The sequences in which these movements are executed are as important as the movements themselves. These sequences can be described in terms of coherence, continuity, and complexity. The analysis of the forehand drive shows that it is a highly coherent skill—the proper execution of one movement is highly dependent on the proper execution of prior movements. At a basic level, for example, you can see that the forward swing depends on the backswing. But even within the forward swing, the positioning of the racket depends on the proper positioning of the arm, which, in turn, depends on the proper shifting and rotation of the body. The forehand drive is also a highly continuous task—with no pauses between backswing and forward swing and, as the task analysis states, with a continuous movement of the arm and the racket. Finally, this task analysis indicates that the forehand drive is not a complex task since the eyes must focus on only a single object—the ball. More complex tasks require a greater division of attention, as in the case of watching the instrument panel of an airplane. You can now see that a task analysis of a skill should include a description of coherence, continuity, and complexity.

Ernest Jokl (1966, p. 20) suggests that a task analysis begin with the observation of successful performers. He refers to an interview in which a professional basketball player analyzed the hook shot:

> Bradley's hook shot consists of the high-lifted knee of the Los Angeles Lakers' Darral Imhoff, the arms of Bill Russell of the Boston Celtics, who extends his idle hand far under his shooting arm and thus stabilizes the shot, and the general approach of Kentucky's Cotton Nash. Bradley carries his analysis of shots further than merely identifying them with pieces of these players. "There are five parts to the hook shot," Bradley explained. He picked up a ball and stood about eighteen feet from the basket. "Crouch," he said, whereupon he crouched and demonstrated the other moves. "Turn your head to look for the basket, step, kick, and follow through with your arms." Once, when he was explaining this to me, the ball curled around the rim and failed to go in.
> "What happened?" I asked him.
> "I didn't kick high enough," he said.
> "Do you always know exactly why you've missed a shot?"
> "Yes," he said, missing another one.
> "What happened that time?"
> "I was talking to you. I didn't concentrate. One of the secrets of shooting is concentration." [John McPhee, *The New Yorker*, January 23, 1965, p. 42.]

This informal description of the hook shot describes some of the constancies—crouching, turning the head, stepping, kicking, and following through. Except by implication, it does not describe the proper position of the arms and hands. For those constancies described, we have some idea of coherence and continuity. We see, that is, the order in which movements must be made and that they are essentially continuous. Also, since the eyes are focused on the basket (and attention is undivided), the task is not complex.

We may also analyze a skill in terms of *S-R* units, as we did in the example of the novice driver starting the car. An analysis of the forehand drive in terms of *S-R* units is as follows:

> *S* ("Position body to the net") *-R* (body positioned at right angle to net). . . *S* (sight of body at right angle) *-R* (feet placed shoulder-width apart). . . *S* (sight of feet in proper position) *-R* (knees slightly flexed). . . *S* ("Swing racket backward") *-R* (moving head of racket back first). . . *S* (sight of racket moving back) *-R* (shifting weight to rear foot). . . *S* (sight of moving ball) *-R* (beginning forward swing). . . and so on.

The analysis of a skill as a single chain of *S-R* units becomes difficult when body and objects move simultaneously, as in the forward swing. The analysis into *S-R* units is probably the best way of identifying the basic components of a skill, but it is not always the best way of showing their relationship. For the most thorough analysis of skills we should first identify the *S-R* units and then use constancies, coherence, continuity, and complexity to describe the relationship of the components.

STEP 2

ASSESS THE ENTERING BEHAVIOR OF THE STUDENT

Your second teaching function is to determine the adequacy of the student's preparation for learning the skill. This assessment of entering behavior can take three forms. First, if your analysis of the skill is in terms of chains of *S-R* units, you must determine whether the student has acquired all the links of the chains—all the specific *S-R* units. Since every link is the stimulus for the succeeding link, the absence of one link means that the skill cannot be performed. For example, in the forward swing, as the arm moves forward, the body weight shifts from the right to the left foot and also rotates to a forward position. A student who does not (or cannot) shift his weight from right to left foot will also fail to rotate his body. Or, if he does rotate his body without shifting weight, he will be in a most awkward position for hitting the ball and will miss it. In shifting the car gears, a student who does not know the position of an intermediate gear (such as second gear) will fail to reach the final gear in the proper sequence.

Second, if your analysis is in the form of component skills necessary for the learning of a complex skill, you must determine if the student has learned all the components. The forehand drive has several component skills: the proper grip of the racket, the proper basic stance, and the proper footwork. The absence of any of these prerequisite skills will make the learning of the forehand drive a difficult if not an impossible task.

Finally, in your analysis of entering behavior, you should assess the physical and manipulative psychomotor abilities of the student. We have already described the purpose and nature of this assessment so that our discussion here will be brief. This assessment must consist of a measurement of the psychomotor abilities of the student, an analyis of the abilities required by the skill or various components of the skill, and an attempt to bring the task requirements and the student abilities together in a way which makes learning possible. The results of this assessment will present the teacher with several courses of action: (1) When the student lacks or is underdeveloped in the necessary abilities, the teacher can provide him the opportunity to develop the abilities to the level necessary for learning the particular skill. An analysis of the abilities required in the forehand drive may indicate that speed of change of direction is an important ability in the advanced practice of this skill. If the student lacks this ability, the teacher can provide him with exercises which will develop it. (2) In this same situation the teacher may decide to abandon teaching the skill for which the student lacks the necessary physical abilities and to teach him those skills for which he is prepared. Students often choose this course for themselves when they invent ways of avoiding certain physical activities either by exercising choices which the curriculum gives them or by developing certain physical incapacities to evade curricular requirements. (3) Finally, the teacher can use the results of the assessment for planning his instruction. Knowing the student's level of psychomotor abilities and the ability requirements of the skill in various phases of learning, the teacher can predict where the student will have his greatest success and difficulty and consequently plan to assist him when he needs help.

ARRANGE FOR TRAINING IN THE COMPONENT UNITS, SKILLS, OR ABILITIES STEP 3

This step has two purposes: It provides the student with the opportunity to learn missing *S-R* links or component skills or to develop (as I stated in step 2) the prerequisite psychomotor abilities; and it provides the student with the opportunity to learn the skill components (or some of them) so well that he can focus his attention on the new aspects of the complex task he is learning. To illustrate the second purpose, the student who, in learning the forehand drive, continues his practice on grip, stance, and footwork to the autonomous stage of learning can give his undivided attention to arm, body, and racket position and coordination. In swimming, a student who has practiced kicking to an advanced stage of learning can devote his attention to breathing or to the coordination of all the component skills of swimming. It is more than coincidence that we practice those component skills we have learned best when we undertake the learning of a new complex skill. It is also good teaching practice to allow the student to develop mastery over skill components where and when he can as a way of moving him on to more complex performance.

DESCRIBE AND DEMONSTRATE THE SKILL FOR THE STUDENT

This step marks the actual teaching of the overall task or skill. According to Fitts (1964, p. 260), in skill learning the student usually listens to instructions, observes demonstrations, tries out different component skills which he already has available, and then somehow starts learning the new skill.

The purpose of describing and demonstrating the skill is to develop a plan for the execution of the task. In two studies (Guilford and Lacey, 1947, and Smode and Fitts, 1957) of instructors of aviation cadets and physical education students, all the instructors mentioned the importance of providing description and demonstration early in the training. In performing this step the instructors used movies, lectures, and demonstrations by experts, and had the students watch themselves in a mirror. They stressed the importance of these activities early in the skill learning. In another study, Dorothy Davies (1945) found that early verbal instruction helped students to learn archery. One group was given a description of the skill and methods for practicing it. A second group was permitted to learn by trial and error. The study continued over one semester, and the groups were provided an equal number of practice sessions. At the end of the semester Davies found that the group which had received instruction was far superior in performance. Students in the second group often adopted inadequate practice methods with which they laboriously persevered throughout the semester. The students in this group never learned the necessity of working on the components of the skill to raise their scores. Almost all their attention was on aiming the arrows at the target and chalking up points. Davies concluded that one of the chief advantages of verbal instruction is that it directs the student's attention to practice techniques more adequate than those he is likely to adopt by himself.

Verbal instructions should be at a minimum in the early stages of skill learning. Aileene Lockhart (1966) believes that most physical education teachers talk too much! She suggests that the initial explanation be brief and deal with the skill in general terms. Descriptions should direct the student's attention to only the essential aspects of a skill. To some extent the student must invent his own means for getting his muscles to carry out the skill the instructor describes and demonstrates. George A. Miller and his associates (1960) consider the following detailed description of a skill an example of bad teaching:

> On take-off the throttle should be opened slowly so that rudder control can be introduced smoothly to overcome the tendency of the plane to turn as a result of increased torque. Open the throttle continuously so that it is completed by the time you count to five; when you reach three start to apply some right rudder.

They explain that this description is bad teaching because it makes the student feel very busy. Although counting may work for some students, others may find that it interferes with their performance of other parts of the skill. One student found his own means. He pushed the throttle forward to the panel while keeping extended one finger of the hand on the throttle. When the extended finger hit the panel, he began to apply the right rudder.

The opportunity for the student to obtain feedback from his own movements is missing in descriptions and demonstrations. When the student's finger hit the panel, he received the feedback he needed. Robb (1966) found that students who passively watched a skilled performance of an arm-movement pattern and then engaged in active practice did not gain so much skill as another group which had continual active practice and visual feedback.

Several studies have examined the use of motion pictures in teaching various skills. Roy Priebe and William Burton (1939) used slow motion pictures of champions in teaching the high jump. Edward Ruffa (1936) used motion pictures to teach five track events to high school boys. Thurston Adams (1939) taught the tennis serve to college students in this way. Finally, Dale Nelson (1957) used a slow motion picture loop in teaching golf. These studies indicate that skills which involve gross body movements can be taught through the use of motion pictures. According to Lockhart (1966) the evidence strongly suggests that the chief value of motion pictures is in the early stage of learning and in the autonomous or final stage of learning. When the student has reached high levels of proficiency in skill practice, he is able to attend to details in the films which he would have ignored earlier. The chief advantage of the motion picture is that it reveals the elements of time and motion which are crucial in the performance of the skill.

Mark May (1946) found that to combine the advantages of demonstration and feedback the films should enable the students to participate verbally. May suggests a liberal pause between sentences of the commentary; this device allows the observers time to formulate their own verbal cues. In the group discussion immediately following the film, each student should review verbally and orally the directions he has heard. These directions should then be checked by running the picture a second time before the students begin their practice. Finally, each student must be given an opportunity to try his hand at the skill under the supervision of the teacher.

The student's own descriptions of the skill may be an important aid to learning. N. G. Ozolin (1958) allowed his experimental groups to learn the terminology connected with stunts by writing the words down and studying them. The control group gave no special attention to terminology. Ozolin found that the special training in terminology was especially helpful in the learning of the more complex exercises. Lockhart (1966) refers to an unpublished study by Bonnie Purdy in which student description or verbalization was the major variable. Students in both groups were learning beginning archery. Students in the verbalization group listened to instructions on correct address, position of bow arm and shoulder, and so on, and then repeated those instructions to a partner. Students in the other group simply practiced after listening to the instructor. Although the differences between the groups were not significant, the performance of the verbalization group fluctuated less than did that of the control group. One advantage of student verbalization is that the instructor can determine whether the student has received the directions as they were given. Joan Johnson (see Lockhart, 1966) discovered that students often form incorrect ideas of the movements in the beginning and use these ideas throughout practice. She also found that colorful words (for example, the racket *swishes*) were easily remembered and acted upon.

We can now summarize what you have learned about the description and demonstration of skills (step 4). Most instructors stress the importance of performing this step early in the learning of the skill. One of the chief advantages is that the student is directed to the most efficient means of practice in the beginning. It is important to remember, particularly in teaching beginning students, that verbal instruction should be kept to a minimum and should deal with only the most essential aspects of the skill. To a considerable extent the student must develop his own techniques and sources of feedback. The motion picture has the advantage of revealing time and motion in skill performance. The use of the motion picture must allow students to develop their own verbal descriptions, to review these descriptions, and finally to practice the skill under the teacher's supervision. In developing their own descriptions of the skill, the students stabilize their performance and give the teacher an opportunity to discover any erroneous interpretations before practice is underway. For most teachers, the danger is that they will say too much rather than too little. Beginning students need a set of specific directions with little or no analysis of the task or of the methods for performing it.

STEP 5

PROVIDE FOR THE THREE BASIC LEARNING CONDITIONS

In teaching skills, we combine the three learning conditions—contiguity, practice, and feedback—into a single step because we must usually provide them concurrently rather than sequentially. More simply, much of your success in teaching a skill will depend not only on how well you provide for each of these learning conditions but also on how skillfully you can combine them into a single teaching situation.

5a. Provide for contiguity To meet this condition you must teach the student proper coordination and timing. For proper coordination the student must learn the proper order, or sequence, of the units or subtasks of the skill. For proper timing, the adjacent units in a chain or adjacent subtasks in a hierarchy must occur simultaneously, without delay and unnecessary pauses. Previously we discussed three methods for providing contiguity: the whole method, the part method, and the reverse-part method of Gilbert. The decision on which method to use must rest largely on your analysis of the task and assessment of the entering behavior of the student. Highly organized skills have high coherence and continuity—that is, their components interact. For these skills the whole method is a means of simplification. Less highly organized skills have low degrees of coherence and continuity. For these skills part learning allows the student to become proficient in the subtasks. In considering the entering behavior of the student, you should realize that the whole method is better when your assessment indicates that the student will find the task difficult. When the student possesses the prerequisite ability, the part method will be more useful. The choice of method also should determine the conditions of practice. The whole method is more efficient with distributed practice; the part method is better with massed practice.

Instructors of aviation cadets and physical education students (Guilford and Lacey, 1947, and Smode and Fitts, 1957) stress the need for providing contiguity. They refer to it as the need for the student to develop coordination. In pilot training, the coordination of hand and foot movements is important. In learning to hit a golf ball, the coordination of body, shoulder, arm, and wrist action is important. In learning the forehand drive in tennis, the coordination of body, arm, and foot action is important. Coordination, of course, involves timing. These instructors stress the importance of the student's learning the proper timing both of movements which occur in sequence and of movements of the body in relation to external objects (the tennis ball). They also emphasize the importance of developing rhythm. Lawrence Lindahl (1945) found that identification of and training in the coordination of hand and foot movements in the use of a machine for slicing thin discs from tungsten rods reduced training time, improved both the quantity and quality of work, and reduced costly breakage in the machine in a few weeks.

5b. Provide for practice   In the opening part of this chapter we concluded that distributed practice was more useful than massed practice in the learning of psychomotor skills. Furthermore, we found that the effects of distribution are powerful and reliable, that there are optimum limits to the rest period, and that shortening the practice period is more important than lengthening the rest period. We also saw that massed practice may affect performance but not learning—that, after a suitable amount of rest after massed practice, what was originally lost in performance may be regained. We know very little about how the distribution of practice affects skills of varying constancies, coherence, continuity, and complexity.

The major teaching problem is scheduling the practice and the rest periods in ways consistent with these findings. Here, again, very little applied research has concentrated on how this can be done with skills taught in the school. The practice schedule must conform to the school schedule, which often routinely determines the amount of time to be spent on any course and, by necessity, the amount of rest, or time between student exposures to the same courses. Somehow the teacher must develop a practice schedule which meets the requirements of the task, the entering behavior of the student, the amount of time he has for direct tuition, and the schedule of the school. In addition, the taxpayer will be considerably concerned if he discovers that students are spending as much or more time at rest than on practice. At best, a rest period in the school means that the student is working on some task unrelated to the task he has been practicing. The absence of true rest periods may complicate the scheduling problems of the teacher who now finds himself juggling rest and practice periods for two or three tasks and finding intricate ways of interweaving them.

Here are some practical guidelines the teacher may use in determining the number and length of practice and rest periods. (1) The nature of the task should determine to some extent the length of the practice period. In teaching the forehand drive, we would find it unnatural to teach the backswing one day and the forward swing another day when the two movement patterns are so highly coherent. In teaching the breaststroke in swimming, we would not teach the movement of the right arm one day and the movement of the left arm the next day when the coordination of arm movements is so important in this maneuver. Possibly some highly complex tasks (like trouble shooting) cannot be rehearsed in one practice period and must be extended over two or more periods. The instructor then must find a dividing point which fits the school schedule but does not seriously disturb the learning of the skill. (2) During the rest periods students can practice tasks they have already learned in preparation for tasks they are beginning to learn. Of course, fatigue becomes a major concern when the skills involve gross body movement. In physical education rest must mean rest. (3) Provision can be made for students to practice on their own time and after school hours on schedules they develop with the instructor. Most complex physical and manipulatory skills require practice beyond that provided by formal instruction. (4) Massed practice is better than no practice at all. For learning, it may be equal in effect to distributed practice. The teacher may have to provide periods of massed practice when the school schedule does not permit distributed practice.

If your instructional objective requires the student to reach the autonomous phase of skill learning, a great deal of practice is required. Fitts (1962, p. 195) states the following:

> The importance of continuing practice far beyond the point in time where some (often arbitrary) criterion is reached cannot be overemphasized. . . . Individuals who have not had a great deal of practice beyond the stage of initial satisfactory performance probably do not experience the beneficial increase in resistance to stress, fatigue, and interference that comes from overlearning.

Although we have very little research on the effects of practice at the very advanced levels of skill learning, we do have the testimony of outstanding performers. Eva Bosakova, the Olympic gymnastic champion of Czechoslovakia, describes her practice periods, which began at the age of fifteen under the tutelage of her father:

> He prescribed daily thirty-minute periods of work on the beam, during which it was necessary to remain on the apparatus constantly in action, walking, hopping,

turning, and again walking without rest. I spent hundreds of hours and uncounted kilometers walking and running on the beam. . . . I constantly searched for new methods, elements, and dynamic combinations for my exercises. In the process I gained complete confidence, accustomed myself to unfamiliar movements, and lost all fear of falling. Each individual exercise period lasted more than one hour. During this time I went through my whole routine five to seven times. Afterward I worked on individual elements of the exercises and their connections, selected passages and their combinations. At the height of my career, it took me from about six to eight months to acquire mastery of a new exercise such as those prescribed for Olympic games. [Jokl, 1966, p. 19.]

Unless the instructor allows the student to develop a skill to the autonomous phase of learning, the necessary expenditure of time, effort, and energy may well deter the student from continued practice of the skill.

A considerable amount of research supports the beneficial effects of mental practice. Wilbur Twining (1949) compared three practice conditions for students learning to throw rope rings over wooden pegs. The first group threw 210 rings on the first and on the twenty-second day—this was the no-practice group. The second group threw 210 rings on the first day and twenty rings each day up to and including the twenty-second day—this was the live-practice group. A third group threw 210 rings the first day. After this they mentally rehearsed their first day's activity for fifteen minutes daily until the twenty-second day, when they again threw 210 rings. In group I no significant learning occurred. Group II showed 137 percent improvement, and group III showed 36 percent improvement. Mental practice was much better than no practice but not so beneficial as physical practice. Verdelle Clark (1960) obtained essentially the same results in teaching the one-hand foul shot in basketball. Instruction for the mental-practice group was restricted to the reading each day of mental-practice work sheets. They had to imagine each day that they were shooting five warm-ups and twenty-five foul shots. Clark found that physical practice was more effective than mental practice. However, consistent with the findings of Twining, he found highly significant gains in learning even with mental practice. Also mental practice was slightly more effective for the novice than for the varsity players. A recent study by John Jones (1965) lends further support to these findings. We may conclude that mental practice, which is a form of student verbalization, has beneficial effects on skill learning and that most of the benefits are derived in the early phases. In reviewing studies of mental practice, John Lawther (1966) claims these advantages: (1) It is a means of reviewing previous performance and planning the next trials; (2) it is a means of planning the order of movements in simple skills; (3) it reduces the amount of extinction in the next performance; and (4) it preserves mental alertness and mental set for a quicker start at the next practice session. Lawther also claims that mental practice is important at autonomous levels of skill learning (along with increased physical practice) to maintain awareness of feedback and precise adaptation to cues.

We shall consider briefly three further aspects of practice. First, Poppelreuter's law of practice states that the best results in skill learning occur when speed is retarded until a reasonable level of accuracy has been obtained and then is increased gradually. William Solley (1952) in subjecting this law to an experimental test found evidence to warrant this restatement: In skills in which speed is the predominant factor for successful performance, the most efficient results are obtained by early emphasis on speed; in skills in which both speed and accuracy are important, equal emphasis on speed and accuracy yields the best results. Second, Robb (1966) studied the effects of slow practice, in which students go through the movement pattern of a skill slowly before practicing at the standard rate. She found that this method hindered the students' learning of a simple skill. She concludes that slow practice should not be used in skills in which the timing requirements are important. Third, in the use of mechanical guidance with the student's cooperative effort, the teacher, in the practice of skills, guides the student through a rough approximation of the movement pattern he must learn. Although the studies of this method do not entirely agree, considerable evidence shows that mechanical guidance should be used only in the initial stages of practice and that it is best used with the very young, with the very old, or with students who have great difficulty in learning the skill (Ragsdale, 1950). It should probably not be used until the student has made some preliminary responses for himself. Excessive reliance on mechanical practice robs the student of the opportunity to use internal and intrinsic feedback.

In summary we may conclude that the teacher should make some provision for distributed practice within the framework of the school schedule and the available time the student has outside school. If feasible scheduling proves impossible, you are reminded that massed practice is better than no practice at all. It is very easy for a skill to go underpracticed. Without the proper provision for continued, strenuous practice, students never obtain the benefits of the autonomous stage of skill learning. Mental practice has beneficial effects, for different reasons, on both early and late stages of skill learning. We also have pointed out the limitations of emphasizing accuracy at the price of speed, of practicing slowly when timing is an important skill characteristic, and of providing mechanical guidance. Practice must remain an important element in planning programs for skill learning. Paul Hunsicker (1963) observes that even though students have different capacities for physical skills, they must all be pressed to improve the level of development they have attained.

5c. Provide for feedback   In the first part of this chapter we illustrated the primary importance of feedback in skill learning. The type of feedback most beneficial to the student depends largely on the phase of skill learning. Let us consider first the early phase, in which extrinsic and external feedback play the major roles. Since the teacher ordinarily provides extrinsic feedback, the early phase of skill learning requires close supervision. The teacher must point out discrepancies between the student's performance and a standard performance of the skill. In reporting their observations teachers frequently direct the attention of the student to external cues and discriminations in movements which the student tends to ignore. In the forehand drive, for example, the forward swing is executed with the racket head even with or higher than the wrist. The arm is slightly bent and held fairly close to the body. In providing extrinsic feedback the teacher reports to the student when the racket head falls too low and when his arm is too far from his body. In this early phase of learning the teacher must often demonstrate several times the proper execution of the movement and compare this execution with that of the student. The teacher combines the use of extrinsic and external feedback in early skill learning. When, for example, the student visually inspects the position of the racket head and the movements of his arm, he is relying on an external mode of feedback. The teacher should direct the student's attention to whatever external modes are available and useful. For example, by directing the student's attention to the racket's swish in the tennis serve, an auditory mode of feedback is employed.

As the student progresses through the fixation and the autonomous phases of skill learning, he relies on intrinsic and internal feedback. In using intrinsic feedback, he observes the effects of his movements. In the forehand drive, he observes the speed of the ball and the direction in which it moves. From the very consequences of his execution of the skill he is able to interpret flaws in movements, timing, and overall coordination. The student's increasing reliance on intrinsic feedback enables him eventually to take over the evaluation function performed by the teacher in the early phase of skill learning. In using internal feedback, the student loses his original self-consciousness and is less inclined to rely on visual inspection of his posture and movement for information on the acceptability of his performance. Instead he relies more and more on kinesthetic stimulation. He develops a feel for the correct movement of the tennis racket and of his arm. We do not have any direct way to develop each student's awareness of the feel for the proper movements (Robb, 1966). Whenever the proper movement is practiced, internal feedback is unavoidably provided. For this reason, specific devices for developing or strengthening the awareness of internal feedback appear to be unnecessary. As Miller and his associates (1960) suggest, the student must develop his own tactics for getting the proper movements into his muscles.

Summary

We have concluded this chapter with a description of the five steps you must take in teaching skills to your students. The first three are preparatory to the actual teaching of the overall skill. The first step requires you to analyze the skill in terms of *S-R* units and chains or in terms of a hierarchy of patterns of chains. These chains we have called *subtasks* or *component skills*. We may also analyze the skill in terms of constancies, coherence, continuity, and complexity. The most thorough task analysis combines the use of each of these methods. The second step requires you to assess the entering behavior of the student. Here again you are presented with a choice of analytical methods. You can assess entering behavior in terms of *S-R* units, of component skills (or subtasks), or of psychomotor abilities. In using the knowledge gained in the assessment of the student's psychomotor abilities, the teacher must also make an analysis of the abilities required by the skill the student is about to learn. Then the teacher must match student ability and task demands. The third step requires you to arrange for student practice of the components of the skill you are about to teach.

The actual teaching of the overall skill gets under way with the fourth step, which requires you to describe and demonstrate the skill and to help the student develop a plan for the execution of it. Both description and demonstration require that the teacher emphasize only the essential characteristics of the performance. Motion pictures are especially useful in demonstrating movement and timing. Whatever the form of the demonstration, it should eventually provide for student verbalization and later for student practice of the skill. The fifth step requires you to provide for three basic learning conditions. You can provide contiguity by a whole or a part method and even by a reverse-part method. Practice should ordinarily be distributed if it is feasible to arrange spaced practice sessions. Mental practice has distinct advantages over no practice and is a useful supplement to physical practice. Finally, the teacher has the responsibility of providing feedback. The need for extrinsic and external feedback in the early phase of skill learning imposes this immediate responsibility.

Return to the list of instructional objectives for part three of this chapter and determine how well you have achieved them.

SUMMARY

This chapter concerned the teaching and learning of skills. In the future we will have to learn different skills than those we have learned up to

---

QUESTION 9-3   In teaching his students the skill of rolling the bowling ball down the alley with the maximum striking accuracy, Mr. Tuition took the following steps. First, he analyzed the skill in terms of S-R units, constancies, continuity, coherence, and complexity. Second, he assessed the entering behavior of the students in terms of prerequisite S-R units, component skills, and psychomotor abilities. Third, he provided training in the component units, skills, and abilities. Then he used verbal instruction and films which described the skill and showed an expert rolling the ball down the alley. Finally, he taught the students the proper coordination and timing, using the whole method, and provided them with suitable practice schedules. Which of the following steps was *inadequately* provided for? (a) analysis of the skill; (b) assessment of entering behavior; (c) training in component skills; (d) description and demonstration; (e) basic learning conditions.

After selecting your answer, give the reasons for your choice and for rejection of the alternatives.

---

now, skills that are less complex and more sedentary in nature. Skilled behavior can be described and analyzed in a number of ways: as chains of *S-R* units, as hand-eye coordination, and as hierarchically organized response patterns. Skills can also be classified on the basis of constancies, coherence, continuity, and complexity. Skill learning has three phases: the cognitive, the fixation, and the autonomous. The basic conditions for learning skills are contiguity, practice, and feedback. Contiguity provides the proper sequence and timing of movements. Distributed practice is usually better than massed practice, but massed practice is better than none. The importance of the different types and modes of feedback varies with the nature of the skill and the phase of learning.

The second section dealt with entering behavior and psychomotor abilities. New skill learning is based on old skill learning and often requires coordinating into a single pattern less complex skills. Psychomotor abilities, as distinct from skills, are individual traits important in the performance of several skills. There is no general physical ability or manual dexterity but rather a number of relatively distinct abilities for each of these general areas. Abilities required early in learning may differ from those required later in learning—a fact teachers must consider in assessing entering behavior.

The third section dealt with instruction in skills. First, you must analyze the skill you will teach in terms of constancies and sequences of movements (coherence, continuity, and complexity). You may also (although it is not always practical) analyze the skill as a single chain of *S-R* units. Second, you must assess the entering behavior of the student in terms of specific *S-R* units, component skills, and psychomotor abilities. Third, as preinstruction, you must provide training in component units, skills, and abilities to allow the student to acquire missing links or parts and to learn these links and parts so well that he can concentrate on their coordination. Fourth, you must describe and demonstrate the skill so that the student can develop his own plan for its execution. Verbal instructions are usually combined with live or filmed performance in this step. Finally, you must provide for contiguity, practice, and feedback. In providing contiguity you can use the whole, the part, or the reverse-part method. You can use either distributed or massed practice and even mental practice. The type and mode of feedback varies with the phases of skill learning. Whereas extrinsic and external feedback are important in early skill learning, intrinsic and internal feedback are important in late skill learning.

SUGGESTED READINGS

Unlike other topics we have considered, the teaching of skills suffers from a dearth of literature. The most serious recent discussions of the basic research are in the following articles and books:

BILODEAU, EDWARD A., ed., *Acquisition of Skill*. New York: Academic Press Inc., 1966. The chapters are on the history of skill research, selective learning, individual differences, mechanisms of motor responding, facilitation and interference, information feedback, retention, tracking behavior, cybernetic theory, and motor skills and verbal learning.

FITTS, PAUL M., "Factors in Complex Skill Learning," in *Training Research and Education,* ed. R. Glaser, pp. 177–98. Pittsburgh: University of Pittburgh Press, 1962.

———, "Perpetual-Motor Skill Learning," in *Categories of Human Learning,* ed. A. W. Melton, pp. 244–85. New York: Academic Press Inc., 1964.

FLEISHMAN, EDWIN A., "The Description and Prediction of Perceptual-Motor Skill Learning," in *Training Research and Education,* ed. R. Glaser, pp. 137–76. Pittsburgh: University of Pittsburgh Press, 1962.

IRION, ARTHUR L., "A Brief History of Research on the Acquisition of Skill," in *Acquisition of Skill,* ed. E. A. Bilodeau, pp. 1–46. New York: Academic Press Inc., 1966.

In the field of physical education, the following books and articles report research or are based on research:

ESPENSCHADE, ANNA S., *What Research Says to the Teacher: Physical Education in the Elementary Schools.* Washington, D.C.: National Education Association, 1963.

FLEISHMAN, EDWIN A., *The Structure and Measurement of Physical Fitness.* Englewood Cliffs, N.J.: Prentice-Hall, Inc., 1964.

HUNSICKER, PAUL, *What Research Says to the Teacher: Physical Fitness.* Washington, D.C.: National Education Association, 1963.

PATERSON, ANN and EDMOND C. HALLBERG, eds., *Background Readings for Physical Education.* New York: Holt, Rinehart & Winston, Inc., 1965. See especially Sec. 3, "Psychological Backgrounds," pp. 211–321.

"A Symposium on Motor Learning," *Quest,* Monograph VI (Spring 1966). A publication of the National Association for Physical Education of College Women and Men.

The chief research journal in physical education is the *Research Quarterly.*

CHAPTER TEN

THE TEACHING AND LEARNING OF CONCEPTS AND PRINCIPLES

In this chapter you read about more complex learning types. The learning of concepts and principles is more complex because it requires as entering behavior the previous learning as well as an extension of that learning. You will see, therefore, that the basic learning conditions of contiguity, reinforcement, and practice still apply to the learning of concepts and principles. You will also see that skill and verbal learning are necessary prerequisites.

The chapter has three sections. The first deals with the nature and uses of concepts and principles. We shall define *concept* and *principle,* their relationship to levels of intellectual development, and, primarily in the context of the school and classroom, their uses. The second section deals with the learning of concepts. Here we describe seven steps for teaching concepts. The third section deals with the learning of principles. This brief resume of the steps for concept and principle teaching should reveal the close similarity of their learning conditions.

THE NATURE OF CONCEPTS AND PRINCIPLES

In this section of the chapter you should learn what a concept is and what a principle is, their relationship to level of intellectual development, and their important uses in school learning.

The Nature of Concepts

Upon reading the first section of this chapter, you should be able to meet these objectives:

10-1   Define concept in terms of a class of stimuli and give three examples of concepts in the subject areas you plan to teach.
10-2   Define attribute in terms of concepts and designate the attributes of your three illustrative concepts.
10-3   Define attribute value in terms of attributes and designate the attribute values of your three illustrative concepts.
10-4   Give the number of attributes of your three illustrative concepts.
10-5   Define attribute dominance in terms of obviousness and designate the relative dominance of the attributes of your three illustrative concepts.
10-6   Distinguish among conjunctive, disjunctive, and relational concepts in terms of the relationship of their attributes and give two examples of each type of concept.

Here we will define and illustrate a concept, describe the characteristics of concepts, and distinguish among three types of concepts.

What is a concept?   A concept is a class of stimuli which have common characteristics. These stimuli are objects, events, or persons. We ordinarily designate a concept by its name, such as book, war, and student, or beautiful women, dedicated teachers, and hallucinatory drugs. All these concepts refer to classes (or categories) of stimuli. Some stimuli do not refer to concepts: Elizabeth Taylor, Miss Pegg (the elementary school teacher), Tolstoy's *War and Peace,* the Vietnam War, and the annual Tournament of Roses. These are particular (not classes of) stimuli, persons, or events. A concept is not a particular stimulus but a class of stimuli. The difference is between all beautiful women and Elizabeth Taylor. The concept *beautiful women* includes (undoubtedly) Elizabeth Taylor, but it includes many other women as well. The concept *beautiful women* excludes all ugly women and even plain and unfetching women. In this chapter, when we talk about concepts, you should remember that we are not referring to particular stimuli but to classes of stimuli.

Concepts are not always congruent with our personal experience, but they represent human attempts to classify our experience at least crudely. Not all of us agree on who the beautiful women are, although there is considerably less argument about including some women than there is about including others. The concept is a very broad one, and it can include women of varied sizes, colorations, and shapes. Similarly, the concept *book* may include something as monumental as the *Oxford English Dictionary* or something as trivial and flimsy as a comic book. The concept *state* can include Luxembourg and China and, in another sense, Rhode Island and Texas. A student may be an individual who grows a beard, strums a banjo, smokes marijuana, and occasionally attends class. He may also be an individual who dresses plainly, visits the library frequently, carries books, and studies regularly. In classifying both individuals as students we have to ignore the nonessential characteristics of their behavior and concentrate on only the essential ones. Romantic artists and educators have lamented the fact that the classification of the stimuli of our environment destroys the fine nuances of nature and feeling. They argue that what we feel is good whether we or others call it love or passion. We cannot argue with the romantics about the appreciation of the nuances of experience. We can and will insist, however, on the need for all of us to classify the confusion of our world and to render it more amenable to our control and satisfaction.

Concept attributes An attribute is a distinctive feature of a concept and thus varies from concept to concept. For example, let us use a laboratory concept, *blue squares,* which has two attributes: color and form (or shape). Color, of course, can vary from concept to concept and, therefore, qualifies as an attribute. We can indeed have blue circles, blue triangles, and blue parallelograms. We can even have chartreuse octagons! A more ordinary concept is *lake.* The chief attribute which distinguishes a lake from an ocean and sea, on one hand, and from a pool and pond, on the other hand, is size. A lake is usually smaller than an ocean or a sea and usually larger than a pool or a pond. There are undoubtedly other attributes of *lake* (river drainage, fresh water, and so on), but size is one of its major attributes. Size qualifies as an attribute because it can vary from concept to concept.

Attribute values Values are the particular variations an attribute many undergo. We have established color as an attribute. It may have several values: red, white, blue, maroon, and fawn. Similarly, form may have several values: rectangular, trapezoidal, square, and circular. Concepts vary in the number of values their attributes have. Some concepts have attributes with only two values. A human being (a concept) can be a man or woman, dead or alive, and married or single. Other concepts may have attributes with a range of values. The color of an orange (the fruit) can vary from red-orange to orange-yellow. The color, however, must not vary so much that we confuse an orange with a lemon or grapefruit. Fortunately, when an attribute has a wide range of values, we can use other attributes to identify the concept in question. In identifying an orange, for example, we also observe the attributes of shape, size, and texture.

Number of attributes The number of attributes varies from concept to concept. *Blue squares* has only two attributes—color and form. *Small blue squares* has three attributes—size, color, and form. An *orange* has four attributes: color, size, form, and texture. Some very complex concepts have a dozen or more attributes. Making a list of the attributes for the concepts *democracy* and *human rights* may require the exhaustive consideration of long treatises. As the number of attributes increases, the difficulty of learning the concept increases. Scanning the values of a dozen attributes, for example, is strenuous and time consuming. Bruner and his associates (1956) suggest that, when operating under ordinary time pressures, the individual tends to reduce the amount of strain involved in perusing several attributes by reducing the number of attributes to which he attends. He can do this by attending to some attributes and ignoring others or by combining a large number of attributes into a smaller number of patterns. We shall use the concept of *tort* below to show how the teacher can reduce the number of attributes to be learned in complex concepts.

Dominance of the attributes Dominance refers to the fact that some attributes are more obvious than others. We know that physical location is more dominant (or obvious) than the attributes of color and form. Also color-form concepts such as *red squares* are more dominant than number-color concepts such as *one red*. Thus, dominance refers to the concept as well as to its attributes. Dominant concepts have dominant attributes. James Archer (1962) studied the effects on concept learning of increasing or decreasing the obviousness of attributes. In the high-obvious condition he used figures which were recognizably different in height and shape, and in the low-obvious condition he used figures which were about the same in height and shape. He found that when the attribute of size or shape was both important for recognizing the concept and obvious, the mastery of the concept was easy. Mastery of the concept was most difficult when the attributes were not obvious. In a similar experiment Lee Sechrest and Judith Kaas (1965) used triangles of various shades of red (dark, medium, and light), of various heights (short, medium, and tall), and of various sizes thin, medium, and fat). The cards which displayed these triangles had borders of one, two, or three lines. Thus each of the four attributes had three values. The students had to learn the concept *bif*. *Bif* was a light red, fat triangle. In learning this concept they could ignore the attributes of height and the number of lines in the border. The experimenters found that when they used cards which had similar attribute values (for example, light red and medium red), the students had increased difficulty learning the concept. When they used dissimilar values (light red and dark red), the students learned *bif* more easily. John Wallace (1964) discovered that students learn concepts with dominant attributes with significantly fewer examples than are needed to learn concepts with obscure attributes.

Through your own experimentation you will discover the variation in dominance of the attributes of the concepts you plan to teach. Informally, teachers observe that students usually attend to certain points in their description of a concept but ignore other points that are equally important. In learning the concept *state capital* children may attend to the attribute of location (usually near the center of a state) and ignore size (the fact that capitals are often small cities). Teachers must give aural or visual emphasis to attributes which are obscure and yet important in identifying the concept. In defining concepts teachers traditionally resort to vocal inflection, hand and arm gesticulation, underscoring, diagraming, drawing, and so on, to make obscure attributes obvious. Unless this emphasis is provided, the student will learn some attributes and not others and, thereby, fail to learn the complete concept.

Types of concepts Attributes combine in three different ways to produce three types of concepts: conjunctive concepts, disjunctive concepts, and relational concepts. We shall now define and illustrate each of these. Our examples are simple and experimental rather than "real." Experimental concepts such as *three green circles* show the process of concept learning in clear relief.

CONJUNCTIVE CONCEPTS In a conjunctive concept the appropriate values of several attributes are jointly present. Figure 10-1 shows an array of cards which illustrate various concepts. One of these concepts is *three dark gold circles*. It is a conjunctive concept because it has three attributes (number, color, and form) and each attribute has a particular value (respectively,

FIG. 10-1 An array of concepts with four attributes, each exhibiting the three values of color, shape, and number. (Bruner and associates, 1956, p. 42).

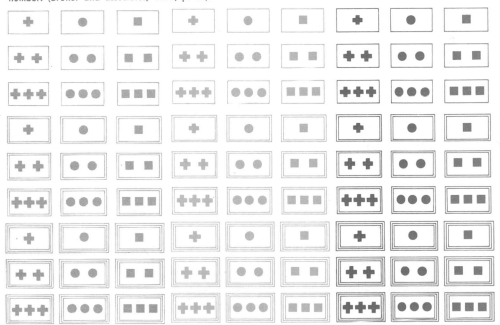

three, dark gold, and circle). How many cards in Figure 10-1 are examples of this concept? In only three cards are the appropriate values (three, dark gold, and circle) of each attribute jointly present. Another conjunctive concept is *one gold*. The attributes are number and color and the values are one and dark gold. How many examples of this concept can you find in Figure 10-1? Most concepts which come readily to mind are conjunctive concepts. Dog, for example, has attributes of color, size, shape, texture, and behavior. The values of these attributes indeed vary—from those of the fawn-colored Great Dane to those of the white miniature poodle. The classification of a particular animal as a dog requires the joint presence of the appropriate value of each attribute. Despite the considerable variation in values which exist in the attributes of *dog*, most of us can readily distinguish dogs from cats, horses, cows, and other domesticated animals. Conjunctive concepts are often the easiest to learn and to teach because of the additive quality of their attributes and values. More simply, attributes and values are added together to produce a conjunctive concept. The student must simply learn a list of attributes and appropriate values.

DISJUNCTIVE CONCEPTS   A disjunctive concept is one that can be defined in a number of different ways. In such a concept, attributes and values are substituted for one another. *Two figures and/or two circles* is a disjunctive concept. You can see that the attributes are form and number and that the value of the number remains the same. The concept is disjunctive because the value of the form can change—it can be a circle or any form. How many cards in Figure 10-1 illustrate this concept? A much more difficult disjunctive concept is *three dark gold circles or any constituent thereof*. In Figure 10-1 fifty-seven cards illustrate this concept. These cards include three figures, dark gold figures, circles, three dark gold figures, dark gold circles, or three circles. A more ordinary example of a disjunctive concept is a *strike*—a pitch which crosses the plate between the batter's knees and shoulders or a pitch which the batter strikes at and misses. In football the *extra point* after a touchdown is made by successfully kicking the ball between the goal posts or by carrying or by catching the ball over the goal line. In baseball a *walk* occurs when four balls have been pitched or when a pitched ball strikes the batter. Disjunctive concepts are often difficult to learn because of the seemingly arbitrary equivalence of their attributes. Disjunctive concepts are, in effect, rules which the student must learn to apply to equivalent stimulus situations. But the situations are not equal or equivalent until given the label. Most of our thinking tends to be conjunctive—the inclusion of stimuli in one class excludes them from other classes. As teachers we must often invest greater effort and ingenuity in the teaching of disjunctive concepts than in the teaching of conjunctive concepts.

RELATIONAL CONCEPTS   A relational concept is one that has a specifiable relationship between attributes. In Figure 10-1 the following concepts are relational: (1) all cards containing the same number of figures and borders; (2) all cards containing fewer figures than borders; and (3) all cards containing fewer borders than figures. The number of figures and the number of borders are the attributes of these three concepts. The statement of the relationship of these attributes describes the concepts. As in the case of disjunctive concepts, each of these descriptions is a rule which can be used to select cards from the array in Figure 10-1. Bruner (1959) suggests that income tax brackets after deductions are relational concepts: They depend on the relationship between the number of dependents and the net amount of income. *Distance* and *direction* are relational concepts. Distance specifies the relationship between two points; it refers to the separation of these points. *Direction* also specifies a relationship between two or more points; it refers to the movement from one to another point. Carroll (1964) discusses several relational concepts which are difficult for students to learn: time, many, few, average, longitude, mass, and weight. Relational concepts are more difficult to learn than conjunctive concepts. Since the concept does not adhere in the attributes themselves but in the particular relationships of the attributes, it is easy for the child (and even the adult) to become confused. For example, both the concept *distance* and the concept *direction* have as their attributes points in space and time. What distinguishes them is the difference in the relationship of the same attributes.

Summary   Thus far in this chapter we have discussed the nature of concepts. You have learned that concepts are distinguished by their attributes and the values of their attributes. You have also learned that some concepts have more attributes than others and that some attributes are more dominant or obvious than others. Concepts with a few obvious attributes are easier to learn than concepts with several obscure attributes. As a teacher you must determine the number and relative dominance of the attributes of the concepts you teach and use this information in planning your instruction. Important attributes which lack dominance must be given special emphasis. Large numbers of attributes can be reduced by ignoring some and focusing attention on others or by combining the attributes into a smaller number of patterns. Identifying the type of concept you are teaching makes clear the relationship of the attributes and the possible level of difficulty of the concept. Conjunctive concepts are generally (but not always) easier to learn than disjunctive or relational concepts. The student, of course, should learn the same relationship of the attributes which you used in identifying the type of concept with which you are dealing.

The Nature of Principles

Upon reading this portion of the chapter, you should be able to meet the following objectives:

10-7   Define principle in terms of concepts and other principles and give three examples of principles in the subject areas you plan to teach.

10-8   Express your three principles as if-then statements.

10-9   Indicate the relationship between the teaching of concepts and principles and the student's level of intellectual development by describing two concepts and principles you plan to teach at each level.

10-10 Demonstrate the relationship between concept learning and pre-school experience by using a particular concept.

10-11 Illustrate six uses of concepts in school learning in terms of reducing environmental complexity, identifying objects, reducing the need for constant learning, providing direction for activity, facilitating instruction, and serving as stereotypes.

What is a principle? A principle is a statement of the relationship between two or more concepts. Principles are sometimes called rules or generalizations (Gagné, 1966, 1970). These are some examples: (1) Four plus ten equals fourteen; (2) all men are created equal; (3) learning is the result of reinforced practice; (4) three-dimensional objects have six sides; and (5) the active voice is used when the subject performs the action of the verb. These statements and phrases are not principles: (1) Hortense likes Harry; (2) Harry claims he is stronger than any boy at Horatio High; (3) evergreen trees; (4) the Democrats won the last election; and (5) who's afraid of Virginia Woolf? The first set of statements qualifies as principles because the sentences state relationships among concepts. The first sentence, for example, states the relationship among five concepts: *four, plus, ten, equals,* and *fourteen.* The second statement relates four concepts: *all, men, created,* and *equal.* Count the concepts in the three remaining statements. The second set of statements is not a set of principles: *Hortense* and *Harry* are not concepts. *Likes* is a concept, put the statement describes no relationship between this and any other concept. *Evergreen trees* is not a principle; it is a concept. In the last statement, *afraid* is the only concept; *who's* and *Virginia Woolf* refer to particular individuals. For practice in stating principles, try to convert the second set of statements into principles.

It is sometimes helpful to think of statements of principles as if-then statements. For example, if you add four and ten, then you obtain fourteen; if you are a man, then you have been created equal (to all men); if there is reinforced practice, then learning results; if an object has six sides, then it is three-dimensional; and if the subject performs the action of the verb, then you use the active voice. The advantage of phrasing a principle as an if-then statement is that the statement then indicates the proper ordering of the component concepts. Only the proper arrangement of the concepts results in satisfactory learning of principles.

Now that we have defined concepts and principles, we shall briefly consider their relationship to the student's intellectual development.

Intellectual Development and Concepts and Principles

In the sections which deal with the teaching of concepts and principles, we shall consider the prerequisite behavior for learning them in terms of less complex learning. Here we want to focus on that aspect of entering behavior which pertains to intellectual development as described by Piaget and to preschool concept learning.

Limits imposed by developmental periods   The learning of concepts and principles requires the student to engage in what Piaget calls *abstract thought.* According to Piaget the child's stage of development determines the level of thought of which he is capable. In the context of school learning we should not expect children from the ages of 7 to 11 (the period of concrete operations) to have the adult's capacity for abstract thought (formal operations). You recall the chief characteristics of the two periods: In the period of concrete operations, the child's thinking is oriented toward concrete objects in his immediate environment; he relinquishes the physical attributes of objects one by one, and each grouping remains an isolated organization. In the period of formal operations, the child's thought concerns the possible as well as the real. He is capable of hypotheticodeductive and propositional thinking.

What implications do these periods of intellectual development have for the teaching and learning of concepts and principles? The child in the period of concrete operations can learn concepts which require the classification of concrete objects and events. In acquiring new concepts he can employ his rudimentary concepts of time, space, number, and logic. His intellectual operations or groupings of this period show the characteristics of closure, associativity, reversibility, and identity. The child in the period of formal operations can handle principles as well as concepts since principles, as if-then statements, are a form of propositional and hypotheticodeductive thinking. If-then statements require the student to think of possible combinations of concepts and, in the period of formal operations, he can consider these combinations in an orderly and systematic way. It would appear therefore that the younger child, in the period of concrete operations, is not ordinarily capable of engaging in all aspects of scientific thought which the older child, in the period of formal operations, often can engage in with considerable skill. Although teaching can contribute to the development of abstract thought in both periods of development, the rigors of abstract thought required in the learning of concepts and principles must be reserved for older children.

Preschool concept learning   In assessing the entering behavior of the younger child we must also be aware that much of his learning occurs before he begins his formal education and that the elementary school depends on this previous learning to a large extent. For the most part the child learns concepts from direct experience, and, since this experience is always limited, he learns them incompletely. Carroll (1964, p. 195), to illustrate this point, reports that children often have incorrect or incomplete concepts for *tourist* and *immigrant:*

> . . . All tourists may be obviously American whereas all the immigrants may be obviously Mexican. . . . The tourist may be well dressed, the immigrants poorly dressed, and so on. If the natural environment is like a grand concept-formation experiment, it may take the child a long time to attain the concepts *tourist* and

immigrant; indeed, the environment may not be as informative as the usual experimenter since the child may not always be informed, or reliably informed, as to the correctness of his guesses. No wonder a child might form the concept that a tourist is a well-dressed person who drives a station wagon with out-of-state license plates!

The school must take these incomplete concepts with which the child enters his formal education and add all the relevant and eliminate all the irrelevant attributes. In school, if not in his direct experience, the child can learn that Americans emigrate to other countries and become both immigrants and foreigners in their newly adopted lands.

As yet we have no studies of the concepts and principles with which most American children enter school and of the concepts they should learn first and those they should learn later. Several studies are underway which promise to provide some of this information. Project Talent (Flanagan, 1964) has developed a comprehensive battery of tests which measures conceptual development in areas such as general information, English, verbal memory, arithmetic computation and reasoning, introductory and advanced mathematics, and spatial visualization. The International Study of Achievement in Mathematics (Husén, 1967), by comparing outcomes of educational systems in twelve countries, gives us some indication of the level of mathematical development we can expect in our students. Continuation of these studies and inauguration of others will be invaluable in planning the curriculum of the elementary school.

Gagné (1970) suggests that when the child enters kindergarten he may know these concepts: *above* and *below, on top of, underneath, next to, the middle one, start, stop, go, come, sit, stand,* and so on. He may not know concepts such as these: *the one before, the next one, double, like, unlike,* grapheme-phoneme correspondences, and number names for quantities. In the case of disadvantaged children we must be especially careful to avoid unwarranted assumptions about what they have and have not learned.

Uses of Concepts and Principles

Let us now consider the various ways in which concepts are useful in the student's education and one way (as stereotypes) in which they are not always useful but are at least influential.

Concepts reduce the complexity of the environment You recall that concepts are not particular stimuli, but classes of stimuli. If we were forced to respond to each stimulus we encountered as unique, the complexity of the world would overwhelm us. This complexity is especially evident with the present knowledge explosion, which forces us to develop efficient categories of information to spare ourselves the distraction of fine detail. The fact that we can group events into classes is an important source of mastery over our environment. Bruner and his associates (1956, p. 1) point out that there may be more than seven million distinct colors and that we see a fair proportion of them in one week. If we had to respond to each of these colors individually, we would be reduced to intellectual impotence:

> Consider only the linguistic task of acquiring a vocabulary fully adequate to cope with the world of color differences! The result of this seeming paradox is achieved by man's capacity to categorize. To categorize is to render discriminably different things equivalent, to group objects and events and people around us into classes, and to respond to them in terms of their class membership rather than their uniqueness. . . . In place of a color lexicon (dictionary) of 7 million items, people in our society get along with a dozen or so commonly used color names. It suffices to note that the book on the desk has a "blue" cover. If the task calls for finer discrimination, we may narrow the category and note that it is in the class of things called "medium blue."

Archer (1966, p. 46) suggests that reducing the complexity of the world takes on the character of motivation or striving. The individual tries not only to reduce complexity in chaotic environments but also "to seek and search out peculiarities and differences in the elements in its environment in order to optimize its environmental complexity." Archer also believes that this motivation to reduce environmental complexity is related to age and intelligence. He uses this example. When a child learns that his pet is a dog, his tendency is to classify all four-footed animals as dogs, whether they be cats, horses, or cows. At a later age, however, the child becomes more sensitive to the differences which make dogs dogs and cats cats. At this point the child shows a need to appreciate differences in his environment as well as to reduce the complexity of his environment. Archer suggests that the highest levels of intellectual sophistication are reached when the individual can with ease both reduce environmental complexity and appreciate the subtle differences among the elements within his environment—a feat accomplished frequently by the artist.

The learning of concepts and principles, therefore, enables the student to grasp, in an array of environmental stimuli, similarities and differences which he would otherwise have great difficulty coping with. Education, in this sense, gives the student environmental mastery which he would otherwise lack.

Concepts help us to identify the objects of the world around us This use is closely related to the first use we have described. Identification involves placing an object in a class and, therefore, reducing the complexity of the environment. Identifications are never absent from our experience. Bruner (1956, p. 12) reminds us that we even classify sounds as "that sound which comes from outdoors at night" or "those porcupines chewing on an old tree stump." Archer (1966) believes that this use also takes on the character of a drive—the child is tempted to try out his concepts and to identify as many dogs as he can. This use can be extended in that concepts that the child first learns affect the nature and extent of the concepts he subsequently learns. Archer (1966, p. 47) writes:

Until the child is able to specify his concept of "dog" he will probably have considerable difficulty distinguishing between dogs and cats. However, until he has successfully differentiated the two concepts of "dog" and "cat" he will probably have considerable difficulty distinguishing foxes, wolves, hyenas, and domesticated dogs. And, of course, the real world will not leave him alone; after our imaginary child has finally figured out all of these beasts, it will be his misfortune to encounter a Tasmanian tiger.

The use of concepts to identify objects in the world around us points out the importance of concepts as entering behavior. As Gagné (1970) suggests, concepts and principles may be related to the world and to each other in hierarchical fashion; if the child does not learn concepts and principles low in the hierarchy, the learning of those higher in the hierarchy becomes difficult or impossible.

Concepts and principles reduce the necessity of constant learning We do not have to be taught *de novo* that the object before us is a mammal. Once we have learned the attributes of mammals, we can apply the concept *mammal* over and over again without further learning. In the schools, concepts and principles, by reducing the necessity of constant learning, enable the student to progress through a discipline and to acquire increasing amounts of knowledge. As we grow older, however, we may develop a resistance toward breaking old patterns of thought to learn new ways of organizing knowledge (Bayley, 1966).

Concepts and principles provide direction for instrumental activity By using concepts and principles we know in advance the actions we can take; placing the object or person in the right class enables us to arrive at important decisions. This use is probably very important in problem solving, which is discussed in the following chapter. In problem solving, it is possible that we try different classes for an object until we find one that it fits in and one that solves the problem.

Concepts and principles make instruction possible The steps described for the teaching of concepts and principles are largely embodied in a set of verbal instructions. These instructions would not be possible if the student had not already learned some concepts and principles. As we move from elementary school to high school to college and finally to the university graduate school, instruction becomes increasingly verbal because the assumption is made (and often warranted) that the student has mastered concepts and principles and that the words which refer to them are sufficient for evoking them when their recall is important. Specific words arouse concepts and principles in our students and save us the effort of covering all the old territory to introduce a new area of knowledge. The atmosphere of the graduate school appears very rarefied to the unsophisticated because the great store of concepts at the command of graduate professors and students reduces the need to deal with the concrete environment. When the layman refers to the "ivy tower" and the "unrealism" of the university, he fails to understand the complex relationship of concepts and concepts, of principles and principles, and of both concepts and principles to environmental stimuli.

Of course, teachers and students may lose sight of the fact that the great value of concepts is that they refer to the concrete environment. Gagné (1965c, p. 189) writes:

> Learning can become ververbalized, which means that concepts learned are highly inadequate in their references to actual situations. . . . The danger of verbal superficiality, and the necessity of avoiding it, is recognized in a number of educational doctrines. "Learning by doing" is one of these. Another is the recognition of the importance of the laboratory and the demonstration in science teaching. The concepts of science deal with the real world and therefore must be based on "operations" that are equally concrete.

In the following chapter, when we discuss inductive and deductive teaching and what we currently call *discovery learning,* we shall discuss also the value of carefully anchoring the learning activities of our students in concrete experience. Here we wish only to point out that concepts and principles can become an obstacle to instruction when the student has an inadequate grasp of them and does not know their relationship to the concrete environment.

Concepts can be stereotypes   Frederick McDonald (1965) defined a stereotype as a rigid or inaccurate concept impervious to experience. In discussing stereotypes we are not talking about a use of concepts so much as we are referring to the responsibility of the teacher to take the incomplete social stereotypes with which the child enters school and make these concepts complete or, at least, adequate. If the child excludes members of some races, religions, and nationalities from the general concept *human being,* some instruction is strongly indicated. Or, if the child lists the attributes of one race as intelligent, socially responsible, sanitary, and achieving and the attributes of another race as stupid, irresponsible, dirty, and lazy, the teacher can provide a wider array of positive and negative examples for both races than the child may have experience before. Certain emotional auras surround many of our concepts and principles, and these auras seem less amenable to new learning than do those which, as teachers, we often prefer. The concepts of *motherhood, children, God,* and *brotherhood,* for example, are not cold lists of attributes. The emotional aspect of our concepts may be a product of early classical conditioning and consistent reinforcement, as in the case of our fears and appetites, and therefore they may be difficult to extinguish. In the North and in the South we all know very well that there are dirty white men and clean Negroes, but many of us continue to exclude these examples from our concepts of *white man* and *black man.* The teacher can present information to the student in objective and relatively impersonal ways and hope that the student will incorporate the new positive examples into a more accurate concept than he now has. In the final analysis, however, concepts (even stereotypes) reside in individuals and are always idiosyncratic. Carroll (1964, pp. 183–84) writes:

> Concepts . . . reside in particular individuals with particular histories of experience that lead them to classify those experiences in particular ways. My concept of "stone" may not be precisely your concept of "stone" because my experiences with stones may have included work with pieces of vitreous rock that you may have seldom seen. To a large extent, how I sort out my experiences is my own business and may not lead to the same sorting as yours.

In attempting to improve the social stereotypes of our students we must always remember the great range of personal experience and entering behavior which those stereotypes represent. Complex social concepts and principles often result from opinion and not from information. The overzealous teacher can find himself in the untenable position of trying to get the student to surrender his own for the teacher's own stereotypes.

Summary

In this section we have considered the nature of concepts and principles, their relationship to the intellectual development of the student, and their uses in school learning. Among the uses of concepts, we have considered stereotypes or concepts based on a nonrepresentative array of examples.

First, we defined a concept as a class of stimuli which have common characteristics. Concept attributes are distinctive features of a concept and vary in value, number, and dominance. The value is the particular variation an attribute may undergo. The number of attributes varies from concept to concept. Dominance is the fact that some attributes are more obvious than others. Attributes combine in various ways to produce three types of concepts: conjunctive, disjunctive, and relational. In a conjunctive concept the appropriate attribute values are jointly present. In a disjunctive concept the appropriate values of one attribute or another attribute or both are present. A relationship concept has a specifiable relationship among attributes. A principle is a statement of the relationship between two or among more than two concepts. This relationship can often be expressed as an if-then statement.

Second, the teaching and learning of concepts must be related to the student's level of intellectual development. In teaching concepts during the period of concrete operations (ages 7 to 11), the teacher must remember that the child's thinking is oriented toward concrete objects in the immediate environment, that the child relinquishes the physical attributes of objects one by one, and that each grouping (or schema) remains an isolated organization. In the period of formal operations, the older child is capable of hypotheticodeductive and propositional thinking. Although the teaching of concepts can and does occur during both periods, the teaching of principles proceeds more easily during the later period. Because the child's school learning of concepts is limited by his preschool learning, the school must often provide corrective experience to exclude irrelevant and include relevant attributes. A comprehensive national survey of school achievement promises to provide teachers with information on which concepts students should learn first and which they should learn later.

Third, we suggested several educational uses of concepts and principles: (1) Concepts reduce the complexity of the environment. (2) Concepts help us to identify the objects of the world around us. (3) Concepts and principles reduce the necessity of constant learning. (4) Concepts and principles provide direction for instrumental activity. (5) Concepts and principles make instruction possible. Finally, the teacher must sometimes provide corrective experience for an additional use of concepts: stereotypes. As concepts, stereotypes can sometimes be changed when the student is provided with a wider array of positive and negative examples than those which he has previously experienced.

Use the key which follows in classifying the items below: **QUESTION 10-1**

Key **(a)** attributes
(b) attribute values
(c) conjunctive concept
(d) disjunctive concept
(e) relational concept
(f) principle

1 two long-haired students
2 several
3 two dogs and/or cats
4 color, size, shape, and weight
5 two, red, enormous
6 a concept refers to a class of stimuli

After selecting your answers, give the reasons for each one.

THE TEACHING OF CONCEPTS

Upon reading this section of the chapter, you should be able to describe and illustrate each of the following instructional steps:

10-12 Step 1: Describe the performance expected of the student after he has learned the concept.
10-13 Step 2: Reduce the number of attributes to be learned in complex concepts and make important attributes dominant.

10-14   Step 3: Provide the student with useful verbal mediators.
10-15   Step 4: Provide positive and negative examples of the concept in terms of appropriate number and realism.
10-16   Step 5: Present the examples in close succession or simultaneously.
10-17   Step 6: Provide occasions for student responses and the reinforcement of these responses.
10-18   Step 7: Assess the learning of the concept.

We shall now describe the teaching of concepts as a series of seven steps which conform to the four components of the basic teaching model. Steps 1 and 2 pertain to instructional objectives. Step 1 requires a statement of the objective, and step 2, a type of task analysis. Step 3 provides the student with the appropriate entering behavior. Steps 4 through 6 are specific instructional procedures for concept teaching, and step 7 deals with performance assessment.

STEP 1

DESCRIBE THE PERFORMANCE EXPECTED OF THE STUDENT
AFTER HE HAS LEARNED THE CONCEPT

In the case of concept learning, the expected performance is the correct identification of new examples of the concept. For the concept *direct object,* this could be the expected performance: When given new examples of direct objects in English sentences, the student will correctly identify them. You will note that this description of terminal behavior requires a performance quite different from rattling off this definition: A direct object is a noun or pronoun which receives the action of a verb. The student might very well memorize the definition and fail to identify direct objects. And, conceivably, the student could correctly identify direct objects and not give a very good definition. We shall discuss later the advantages of learning the concept and learning the definition of the concept. The point here is that the description of the expected behavior should not include the requirement that the student give a definition of the concept.

Describing terminal behavior has two purposes. First, the teacher has a means for assessing the adequacy of the performance and for determining the need for further instruction. The teacher at a given point in time may not desire that the students be completely able to identify and use the concept. In the beginning, for example, the teacher may be quite satisfied to have the students recognize direct objects only in simple English sentences. Later he may want the students to recognize direct objects in compound sentences in both dependent and independent clauses. Still later he may want the students to use direct objects in various sentence contexts. The prior description of the students' expected performance clearly indicates to the teacher and to the students the degree of adequacy the students are to attain at a particular time. Second, the students have a way of assessing their own performance and of determining when their learning is complete. The students' self-assessments then become a way of generating their own reinforcement.

In this step what you learned about the values, number, dominance, and relationship of attributes can be put to pedagogical use. This step requires you to make an analysis of the concepts you decide to teach your students. The determination of the values and the number of attributes can be made before instruction is underway. The determination of the dominance of the attributes requires experimentation on your part and observation of which important attributes students are likely to ignore. After you have made these determinations, you must devise procedures for teaching the concept. Two general procedures reduce the number of attributes of complex concepts: You can ignore some of the attributes and focus on those you think most important, or you can code the attributes into fewer patterns.

Carroll (1964) lists the attributes of one complex concept—*tort. Tort* is a legal term which refers to a wrongful act, injury, or damage for which a civil action can be brought. A careful analysis of the various laws and decisions relating to torts shows that the concept has these attributes: (1) battery; (2) false imprisonment; (3) malicious prosecution; (4) trespass to land; (5) interference to chattels; (6) interference with advantageous relations; (7) misrepresentation; (8) defamation; (9) malicious intent; (10) negligence; (11) causal nexus; (12) consent; (13) privilege; (14) reasonable risk by plaintiff; and (15) breach of contract. To discover the relative dominance of these attributes, we would have to allow the students to examine various civil actions, some of which involved torts and others which did not. By observing how the students applied the concept, we could discover which attributes in the list they favored and which they ignored. These observations would tell us on which attributes additional emphasis was necessary.

Beyond considering the number and the dominance of the attributes, we would have to determine their relationship. In as complex a concept as *tort,* the relationship of the attributes is both conjunctive and disjunctive. In the above list the first eight attributes are disjunctive in that a tort can have any or all of these attributes. That is, a tort can be a battery, a false imprisonment, a malicious prosecution, a trespass to land, an interference to chattels, an interference with advantageous relations, a misrepresentation and/or a defamatory act. The next two attributes (9 and 10) are also disjunctive: The act (whichever it is) can be done with malicious intent and/or with negligence. And the last four attributes (12, 13, 14, and 15) are disjunctive. The act can be done without the plaintiff's consent or without privilege on the part of the plaintiff or without reasonable risk by the plaintiff or it can be an act which is not a breach of contract. Attribute 11 (causal nexus) indicates that the wrongful act must be the cause of the injury claimed by the plaintiff. The concept is also conjunctive because the attributes can be grouped as follows: Attributes 1 through 8 refer to the wrongful act; attributes 9 and 10 refer to the motivation or irresponsibility of the defendant; attribute 11 indicates the causal relationship of the first ten attributes to the last four attributes; and the last four attributes (12 through 15) specify the agreements and responsibilities of the defendant and the plaintiff before or during the act. The conjunctive grouping of the attributes of *tort* suggests the way the teacher could code them and thereby reduce them in number. The first eight attributes could be coded (grouped) under types of acts; the next two under motivation and irresponsibility of the defendant; and the last four under prior and concurrent responsibilities and agreements of defendant and plaintiff. With this grouping, the students would have only four patterns of attributes (if we call attribute 11, causal nexus, a pattern) to remember. Alternatively, the teacher could ignore some attributes and concentrate on others. Some acts, for example, may qualify as torts more often than other acts. Misrepresentation may occur much less frequently than battery. Also, the absence of a breach of contract may be much more important than the absence of privilege on the part of the plaintiff since contracts are so common in legal proceedings. The choice of which attributes to ignore requires that the teacher have considerable familiarity with the concept and its ordinary uses. For a complete understanding of the concept, the student would have to learn all the attributes listed.

STEP 3

PROVIDE THE STUDENT WITH USEFUL VERBAL MEDIATORS

The teacher should ascertain the child's knowledge of the words used as attributes and attribute values and his knowledge of the relational words that are necessary. In this step you can see how verbal and concept learning are related. Considerable evidence indicates that the learning of certain names or labels (as verbal mediators) facilitates the student's learning of a concept. Some studies even indicate the type of verbal association which can be most helpful.

Wittrock, Keislar, and Stern (1963, 1964, and 1965) have shown how verbal mediators can be provided. To illustrate the materials used in their studies, we will discuss first the experiment of Carolyn Stern (1965), who was interested in finding out whether giving children the class cue (explained below) was better than giving them the name of an example of the concept. Figure 10-2 illustrates the material Stern used for two of the concepts, *mammal* and *tree*. The figure indicates that the children had to match the picture in the top row with one of the pictures in the bottom row. One group of children received the class label as a verbal mediator. That is, they were told that the picture in the top row was a mammal or a tree. The other group received the name of the example of the concept. They were told that the picture in the top row was a dog, a horse, a rabbit or a maple, a palm, a fir. After this training period the children took various tests in which they had to identify new examples of the concepts, new concepts of the same type, and a new category of concepts. Stern found that the students who learned the class labels did better than the other group in tests on a new set of concepts. Both groups did equally well in tests which measured their ability to identify new instances of the concepts.

FIG. 10-2 Sample sequence of slides from the eight-concept program (after Stern, 1965, p. 237).

In an earlier study with somewhat more conclusive results (Wittrock, Keislar, and Stern, 1964), kindergarten children were given three months of pretraining in which they learned the French names of two common objects and animals; they also learned that each French name had an initial *la* or *le* sound, and that *la* and *le* stood for *articles*. After the pretraining, the children were presented with a picture and asked to match it with one of five pictures (as in the Stern experiment). The children were divided into four groups each of which was given a different verbal mediator or no mediator at all. Group 1 was given no mediator. These children were merely told, "Something you have learned will help you find the right answer." Group 2 was given a general mediator. They were told that recalling the article would help them find the right answer. Group 3 was given the class mediator (as in the previous Stern experiment). They were told, "The top picture is a *la (le)* word. Find a *la (le)* picture on the bottom which goes with it." Group 4 was given a specific mediator: "The name of the top picture is [French word]." The class mediator represented an intermediate amount of instructional guidance—more guidance than that provided by the general mediator and less guidance than that provided by the specific mediator. The results showed that the children who received the class mediator (intermediate guidance) retained the concepts longer and recognized more new examples of the concepts. In a later study (Wittrock and Keislar, 1965), the class mediator and the specific mediator were equally effective in teaching concepts like those in Figure 10-1. Both studies rather effectively dispute the popular myth that young children can learn concepts best with little or no instructional guidance.

The first and second steps we have described for the teaching of concepts primarily concern the first component of the basic teaching model. Both steps involve decisions about what you will teach and what the students will learn. More simply, these steps concern instructional objectives. The third step primarily concerns entering behavior. In this step we establish the verbal associations (if they are not already learned) necessary for learning the concept. We are beginning to realize that verbal learning and concept learning have much in common (Underwood, 1966). Gagné (1970) uses the concept *edge* to illustrate this point. The student must be able to respond *edge* when the teacher points to three different edges. The responses are what enable the teacher to ascertain whether the student has the appropriate verbal response available. In the experiment by Wittrock and his associates (1964), the appropriate verbal associations (*la* and *le*) were taught so that there was little doubt that the students would use them in their concept learning. The following steps for the teaching of concepts primarily concern the external conditions of learning and relate particularly to the third component of the basic teaching model.

STEP 4

PROVIDE POSITIVE AND NEGATIVE EXAMPLES OF THE CONCEPT

In discussing this step, we shall use the word *example* rather than *instance* or *exemplar* since *example* is used more frequently in discussions of teaching. A positive example of a concept is one which contains the attributes of the concept. A negative example is one which does not contain one or more of the attributes. Positive examples of the concept *bird* are robin, canary, hummingbird, and snowy egret. Negative examples are dog, cat, snake, fly, bee, and even bat. The research on concept learning indicates that provision of positive and negative examples is a major condition of learning. We can even say that the use of positive and negative examples is a necessary condition for the learning of concepts.

Psychologists have developed various models to depict and explain how the student utilizes positive and negative examples in learning a concept. To describe one of these models, we must consider some of the conditions under which concepts can be learned. If, in teaching the concept *dog,* you are using cards which bear drawings of various breeds of dogs, you can present the cards in three different ways. You can present one card (bearing a drawing of a German shepherd), tell the student that this is an example of a dog, and leave that card in view as you present positive and negative examples of dogs. You can present a series of positive and negative examples with no positive example remaining in view. You can leave every card, both positive and negative examples, in view as you present them. Under all three conditions you inform the student immediately of the correctness or incorrectness of his responses. Our question concerns how the student uses the examples you present. Solis Kates and Lee Yudin (1964) suggest that the student's implicit responses may follow this sequence: (1) He makes a guess; (2) he tests his guess against the current example and the shown or remembered example; (3) he retains his guess if it agrees with the shown or remembered example; (4) he changes his guess if it does not agree; and (5) he may possibly change his method of arriving at guesses about the correct concept.

You can also view the student's learning in terms of discrimination and generalization. In learning the concept *dog,* the student must discriminate between the cards which bear drawings of dogs and those which bear drawings of other animals. He is discriminating among the attributes which define the concept and the attributes which do not. Since *dog* is a conjunctive concept, we can say that by discrimination the student is learning what to exclude from his list of dog attributes. He excludes, for example, beaks, feathery tails, wings, and certain feline characteristics. If his discrimination learning is successful, he is able to distinguish among dogs, cats, birds, cows, jackals and so on. But he must also learn to apply his list of dog attributes to a wide variety of breeds of dogs—from the small, ingratiating schnauzer to the rather bulky Saint Bernard. That is, the student must be able to generalize. By generalizing he learns what to include in his list of dog attributes. Thus, through the processes of discrimination and generalization (exclusion and inclusion), the student learns the attributes of dogs or, if you like, he learns the concept *dog.* By presenting the student with positive examples (to be included in his concept) and with negative examples (to be excluded), we facilitate his making the proper discriminations and generalizations.

How many positive and negative examples? Gagné (1970) suggests that you use enough positive examples to represent the range of the concept you are teaching. He uses the concept *edge* to illustrate his point. *Edges* are parts of (1) three-dimensional objects, such as books, desks, and chairs; (2) flat, thin objects, such as a piece of paper, a handkerchief, and a bedsheet; and (3) drawn two-dimensional pictures, as in the case of the figures in this book. In teaching the concept *edge* you must present positive examples of these three edges. If you present examples of only two the student's concept will be inadequate. To be certain that you represent the entire range, you must consider the various attributes and attribute values of the concept and the relationship of these attributes. Then you must select those positive examples of the concept which you will present to the student.

We must be less explicit about the number of negative examples you should use. This number will be an outgrowth of your experience in teaching the concept, which should reveal the negative attributes the student incorrectly includes in his concept. Using Gagné's example once more, we see that the student must distinguish an edge from the side of a three-dimensional object, from the corner, the top, and the curved surface. All negative examples of the attributes which usually confuse the students should be presented and, if necessary, explained.

Relative merits of positive and negative examples Although we can learn a concept with all positive or all negative examples, the degree of concept mastery and the amount of time and effort involved often discourage us from limiting ourselves to only one type. Kenneth Smoke (1933) compared the merits of learning concepts from only positive examples and from both positive and negative examples. One concept was *mib*—a triangle with a line extending at right angles from its shortest side. The positive examples of mib contained all the necessary attributes. The negative examples violated one, and only one, attribute (the line might extend from the longest side of the triangle, for example). Although Smoke discovered no difference in the amount of time it took students to learn the concept with positive examples alone or with both positive and negative examples, most subjects preferred having both. Smoke believes that the negative examples discouraged snap judgments and prevented the students from coming to erroneous conclusions. A later study by LeRoy Olson (1963), which used materials from physics on reciprocal motion and levers, confirmed the findings of Smoke. Janellen Huttenlocher (1962) allowed students to learn a conjunctive concept with positive examples only, negative examples only, or a mixture of positive and negative examples. She controlled the amount of information, so that each example contained the same amount. (This control was lacking in the two previous studies.) Huttenlocher found that students learned the concept better in the mixed series than in the positive series. The series which contained only negative examples was the most difficult to learn. Roy Braley (1963) compared the merits of teaching an easy concept with all negative examples and of teaching a relatively difficult concept with all positive examples. Examples of the two concepts were presented side by side so that each student could learn both. Surprisingly enough, Braley discovered that the students learned the more difficult concept much more rapidly than they learned the easier concept. He concluded that it is difficult for students to use information they gain from negative examples until they have acquired some reasonably well-defined positive representation of the concept. The use of negative examples alone places a considerable burden on the memory of the learner. He must remember all the attributes he has seen in the negative examples and then eliminate the irrelevant attributes as he progresses toward the solution of the problem. Such *exclusion strategies,* as Braley calls them, are used in trouble shooting by mechanics, who must locate a malfunction by eliminating one by one the systems which are functioning properly. If you recall how frequently mechanics arrive at the wrong conclusion and make an unnecessary repair, you will begin to see how difficult this elimination process can be.

In support of Braley's conclusion, Yudin and Kates (1963) studied the value of using negative examples when the student had before him at all times a positive example of the concept. With the provision of this positive example (called a *focus instance*), they found no differences in concept learning under these three conditions: when the subjects were shown (1) all positive examples, (2) all negative examples, and (3) a mixed series of positive and negative examples. Negative examples, they concluded, help in concept learning only when some positive example accompanies the negative ones. Finally, Arnold Buss (1950) found that the example the students use determines what they learn. If the students practice on negative examples, they learn these better than positive examples and vice versa.

Realism of the examples   Since Alexis de Tocqueville wrote on the topic, considerable fear has been expressed that the American student will learn abstractions in rote fashion and that these abstractions will have little or no relevance to his experience. Even before John Dewey, American education had a pragmatic bent. Teachers have tried to overcome the isolation of the classroom by packing their students into wagons and buses and sending them into the real world outside. These fears about insular classrooms are warranted to some extent. There is not much possibility that children will memorize definitions which have no relevance to their experience as long as the school attempts to broaden and inform that experience. Yet it is always possible that concept learning will be so divorced from the stimuli to which it refers that it becomes empty verbalism. Cronbach (1963) used this example. The teacher might define sea chantey as a "rhythmic song, sung in chorus by a ship's crew." For a child who has never heard a sea chantey, this definition would convey only a pallid image. Preferably, the teacher would (and most music teachers do) provide recordings of sea chanteys (positive examples) and related songs (negative examples) and have the students make the proper discriminations. It is probably unnecessary, however, to put the children on the bus, head for the nearest wharf, and, by some laborious prearrangement, have the local college choir, dressed in crew garb, sing sea chanteys to the children. The children might very well miss the whole point of the field trip and learn more about the ship and the crew than about sea chanteys. The decision to go on a field trip should not be based on cognitive factors alone because motivational benefits are also possible. Klausmeier and William Goodwin (1966) suggests that one trip to the turkey farm to see hundreds of turkeys with the same attributes is not better than showing pictures of two turkeys, two hens, and so on. The teacher should not avoid teaching about both turkeys and hens even though they are similar and potentially confusing concepts.

Possibly realistic situations present us with more information that we can easily handle. Travers and his associates (1964a) prove that drawings or animated moving pictures which show only the important attributes of the concept are considerably more effective than direct experience. Travers (1964) points out that human beings have only a limited capacity to use information. When the brain receives more information than it can use, it compresses that information—discarding some of it and attending to those parts of it which are most useful. In visual displays the boundaries of objects provide more information than do other parts. Consequently, line drawings and cartoons are powerful (even if artificial) transmitters of information. Travers (1964, p. 4) criticizes the emphasis on realism in the design of instructional materials, particularly educational films:

> The nervous system cannot deal with the environment in all of its wealth of detail. It handles it by simplifying it, and it is through such simplified inputs and the resulting perceptions and conceptualizations that man learns to cope with a very complex universe. Through simplified presentations in learning situations, the teacher can be sure that the compression process is effective. When this is done the selection of the important element of the message is not up to the learner, who may fail. The separation is made for him. Unfortunately, some producers of instructional movies are, at the present time, doing precisely the reverse. Movies are being produced with visual displays highly embellished with color and complex artistic adornments, and the sound channel is cluttered up with music and other sound effects. The evidence seems clear that such a procedure is not the way to transmit information effectively.

Melvin Marks and Charles Ramond (1951) suggest that the real situation may disrupt or inhibit awareness of those elements which are necessary for concept learning. They state (p. 428), "We know that people do better in school problems than in real-life problems. Perhaps the academic halls have an atmosphere conducive to analysis."

Summary What can we say about the number, type, and realism of the examples used in teaching concepts? The presentation of a mixed series of positive and negative examples is usually more effective than the presentation of a purely positive or a purely negative series. Presentation of only negative examples makes concept learning extremely difficult. As for number, you should present enough positive examples to represent the range of attributes and attribute values of the concept. In the case of negative examples, you should present at least enough of these to eliminate irrelevant attributes which students are likely to include as part of the concept. Finally, direct experience or realistic examples are usually not preferable to simplified presentations of the concepts, such as line drawings, cartoons, diagrams. and charts. These presentations help achieve the effects of step 2 above, which directed you to simplify the learning of the concept by focusing on its major attributes.

PRESENT THE EXAMPLES IN CLOSE SUCCESSION OR SIMULTANEOUSLY

In this step we are concerned with the order in which the examples as a whole and the types of examples (positive and negative) are presented to the student. The learning condition which this step seeks to provide is contiguity—the almost simultaneous presentation of the examples of the concept. A study by Kates and Yudin (1964) indicates the presentations you can make: *successive presentation,* in which one example is shown at a time and removed after twenty seconds; a *focus condition,* in which two examples are presented together—the focus example (which is always positive) and the new example (which is positive or negative); and *simultaneous presentation,* in which each new example is shown with all the previous examples remaining in view. They found that simultaneous presentation was better than the focus condition, which, in turn, was better than successive presentation. Apparently, simultaneous presentation is superior because the student does not have to rely upon memory for previous examples. Other research tends to support this conclusion and to indicate the superiority of procedures which keep in view the examples presented earlier (Dominowski, 1965). Successive presentation is probably the most common teaching practice, however, because our teaching habits sometimes prompt us to focus the student's attention on one thing at a time. It is a very simple matter, however, to plan our verbal, visual, and auditory presentations so that the student has available all the information he needs to learn the concept. In teaching the concept *dog,* we should leave in view pictures of cats, birds, horses, and dogs while presenting new picutres. In this way we maximize contiguity and reduce the information load on the memory. The evidence is less conclusive about the order of the types of examples. Should the positive examples or the negative examples come first in a mixed series of examples? Carl Hovland and Walter Weiss (1953) found that the order did not affect learning efficiency. More recently, however, Huttenlocher (1962) found that a series of negative examples followed by positive examples facilitated concept learning.

PROVIDE OCCASIONS FOR STUDENT RESPONSES AND THE REINFORCEMENT OF THESE RESPONSES

It is somewhat misleading to call this a *step* because response and reinforcement are integral parts of steps 4 and 5. By including them in our list however, we are able to give them more detailed consideration and to remind you of their importance. In concept learning reinforcement primarily provides informational feedback, which enables the student either to separate positive and negative examples and to compose his list or to define the relationship of the various attributes. We know that the consistency with which reinforcement is provided affects the learning of concepts (Rhine and Silun, 1958). Some evidence indicates that 100 percent reinforcement speeds the learning of the concept more than partial reinforcement does (Carpenter, 1954). Delaying the reinforcement even by as little as forty minutes impairs the learning of concepts (Sax, 1960).

The type and the intensity of the feedback (reinforcement) affect concept learning. In his study, Wallace (1964) used two types of negative feedback—auditory and verbal. These examples illustrate the three levels of intensity of verbal feedback: mold—"Wrong!"; moderate—"Wrong, I didn't think it would be this hard!"; and strong—"Most college students get this one very quickly. I don't understand why you can't get it!" Auditory feedback was provided by the ringing of a doorbell attached to a muffin pan and placed in a large galvanized tub. Auditory feedback also varied in intensity from mild to moderate to strong. Wallace found that the more difficult concepts (as compared with the easier ones) were learned with fewer examples when the intensity of the feedback was strong. Also, mild verbal feedback was less effective than mild auditory feedback. Wallace suggests that auditory feedback may be more effective than verbal feedback because it is relatively impersonal and does not discourage guesses about which the student is relatively uncertain. In a previous experiment Sechrest and Wallace (1962) found that negative verbal feedback discouraged what they call *hypothesis spewing*—making more than one guess in learning a concept. Of course, if the student views any verbal feedback as punitive, he may not even venture his first guess. If he suspends all overt guessing, he receives less feedback, and it will take him longer to learn the concept.

Shifting the mode of response also inhibits concept learning. Nancy Wilder and Donald Ross Green (1963) asked students to observe the growth of two plants, one in the sun and the other in poor light, over a two-week period, without discussing the changes with their fellow students. After two weeks, the plants were placed side by side, and the students were asked to describe their differences. One group drew pictures of the differences. A second group wrote about them. After forty minutes, the students were presented with two begonia plants which had been grown under the same conditions, and they were again asked to describe the differences. At this point the students were divided into four groups: Group I wrote their descriptions both times; group II wrote the first time and drew the second time; group III drew both times; and group IV drew the first time and wrote the second time. They found that shifting the response mode from writing to drawing (or the reverse) inhibited the expression of the concept.

Further occasion for reinforcement is provided in practicing the concept beyond the original learning situation. While studying other animals the student can be reinforced for the correct identification and use of the concept *dog*. After he has applied the concept to a variety of new examples, he has thoroughly learned the attributes and can, from that point, reinforce his own use of the concept.

In summary, student responses and reinforcement of these responses are crucial learning conditions for concept learning. The primary purpose of reinforcement is to provide informational feedback to the student on the correctness of his responses. Since this feedback is crucial, any inconsistency, delay, or failure to provide it will impair student learning. However, because the student knows which terminal behavior he must acquire, he can to some extent monitor his own learning. Since reinforcement has motivational aspects, negative verbal feedback may impair concept learning by discouraging the student from making early guesses which can be confirmed. The teacher should remember to focus on the reinforcement of the student's responses and not on the student. The mode of the response should not be shifted, at least in the early learning of the concept. It is quite possible, however, that the shift from spoken to written responses is less inhibiting than the shift from drawing to writing or writing to drawing. Various mechanical and electronic devices may maintain consistency of response mode and informational feedback better than we can now do under ordinary classroom conditions. These same contrivances may also provide students with more occasions for reinforced practice than we can now provide.

ASSESS THE LEARNING OF THE CONCEPT

STEP 7

In this step you are providing both contiguity and reinforcement. Whereas the previous step emphasizes discrimination (or the distinction between positive and negative examples), this step emphasizes generalization, or the ability of the student to make the conceptual response to a new but similar pattern of stimuli. In teaching the concept *dog,* for example, you might have shown pictures of Dalmatians, Saint Bernards, poodles, German shepherds, English Bulls, and terriers. In this step then you present a picture of a sad-faced cocker spaniel. If the student is able to identify the new example of a dog, he has learned the concept. To provide reinforcement the student must be informed about the accuracy of his response.

Here you should present several new positive and negative examples of the concept and ask the student to select only the positive examples. You can now show pictures of basset hounds, Doberman pinschers, Weimaraners, and otterhounds (all dogs) along with pictures of wolves, foxes, jackals, and bobcats. The available evidence does not indicate whether this step is necessary for concept learning. It is important in concept teaching because it is our means for assessing the student's performance (the fourth component of the basic teaching model). It also provides the student with additional opportunities to make responses for which he can obtain his own or the teacher's reinforcement or both.

Some experimental evidence indicates that students can learn to identify concepts without being able to define them correctly. Donald Johnson and Charlene O'Reilly (1964) taught students the difference between a gunkle bird and a bunkle bird (two laboratory concepts) by having them learn that all gunkle birds had black tails. The cards which the students were shown contained pictures of birds with several other attributes of different values: red, yellow, and blue wings; orange, green, as well as black tails; pointed, long, and hooked beaks. In the pictorial group, the students had to classify as gunkle or bunkle birds a series of pictures of birds with these attributes. The verbal group had to classify verbal phrases which decribed birds with the same attributes as those in the pictures. The third group, a pictorial-definition group, had to classify the same pictures used by the first group, but they also were asked after every five cards, "How do you tell a gunkle bird?" The first and second groups were asked this question only after they had completed their examination of all the cards and phrases. Johnson and O'Reilly found that the pictorial-definition group gave twice as many good definitions as did the pictorial group. They also found that the classification task was learned fastest by the verbal group. The investigators concluded that a small amount of practice of the definition, even when the students are not told how good the definition is, improves the quality of definitions. The researchers also argue that if thorough concept learning includes the ability to use the concept in communication, special attention should be given to learning the definition. The teacher cannot assume that the student's ability to define the concept follows from his ability to identify the concept. We should also recall that some concepts in science, mathematics, and other disciplines are difficult to describe in words. It is probably most necessary to provide special training for concept definition when that definition is particularly difficult to formulate.

Summary: An Illustration of Concept Teaching

To summarize the seven steps for concept teaching, we shall describe how Miss D. Voted taught her students the concept *tourist*. Miss Voted (step I) began her lesson with these words: "Today I want to teach you the concept *tourist*. By the end of the lesson you should be able to identify quickly any examples of *tourist* which I present to you." Miss Voted had analyzed the concept (step 2) and decided that it was a simple conjunctive concept with three attributes—activity, purpose, and residence. Each attribute had a particular value: For activity, it was travel and sightseeing; for purpose, it was pleasure; for residence, it was keeping the same permanent residence. These were the attributes and attribute values the students had to learn. Miss D. Voted thought of other attributes such as mode of travel, mode of dress, passports, and visas, but she decided that these were not major attributes and that their introduction could confuse the students. She then made certain that her students had the necessary verbal association (step 3). She wrote the word *tourist* on the board and asked the students to say the word; they did so with impressive choral response. Next, Miss D. Voted presented her positive and negative examples of *tourist* (step 4). Her examples were verbal descriptions printed in large letters on large cards which all the students could see and read. Each card was left in view after it was presented (step 5). Before presenting each card she reminded the students that they were looking for a *class* of people. Her first card bore these words: Mr. Phog lives in San Francisco but he is on vacation and he is visiting Rome to see friends and the city. Miss Voted asked, "Is Mr. Phog a tourist?" The class in complete unison responded "yes." Miss Voted smiled and said they were correct. She then presented a second card which bore these words: Mr. Michael Angelo left Italy in 1898 and has raised his children in the United States. Is he a tourist? The students shouted "no." Harriet Smart added that Mr. Angelo was an immigrant. Miss D. Voted smiled, and the children knew they were right and that Harriet was right and smart. She then presented a card which described an American visiting another country; the students recognized this person as a tourist. Miss D. Voted also presented several negative examples, such as commercial pilots who flew between cities and countries, ambassadors and envoys who retained their original citizenship and residences but who were not traveling primarily for pleasure, Americans who changed their permanent residence to other countries, and even a man without a country. She had several more positive examples of *tourist*, such as individuals moving within a country to sightsee and visit friends, people moving from one country to another for the same purpose, and even people moving from one region of the world to another, as in the case of the jet set. Each time she presented a card she waited for the students to indicate whether the description referred to a tourist, and she told them in each case whether they were correct. By the end of her presentation, all the cards were in view.

Miss D. Voted was now ready to proceed to the next step (7). She presented a new positive example of tourist. It was Mr. Angelo and he was returning to Italy to visit friends and relatives, to sightsee, and to relax along the Adriatic Sea. Is Mr. Angelo a tourist? The class (with a few students remaining silent) said "yes," and Harriet added "definitely!" Miss Voted said they were correct. She then presented several new positive and negative examples of *tourist*, using different nationalities, different regions, and different purposes for travel. She threw in a few more examples (for Harriet) of individuals who were both tourists and immigrants at different times in their lives. Then Miss Voted asked the students to write a definition of a tourist. She asked them to keep in mind how a tourist is different from an immigrant. In evaluating these definitions Miss Voted simply

---

In presenting cards which contained positive and negative examples of *tourist*, Miss D. Voted left each card in view after it was presented. Why did she do this? **QUESTION 10-2**

(a) To keep the students aware of their expected performance.

(b) To provide the students with useful verbal mediators.

(c) To provide contiguity in the presentation of the material.

(d) To verify the students' learning of the concept.

After selecting your answer, give the reasons for your choice and for your rejection of the alternatives.

---

compared her list of attributes with those attributes contained in the students' definitions. She reinforced all correct definitional responses and indicated all inaccuracies. Finally, she reminded her students of the original instructional objective. She then administered a test of terminal performance which contained several new positive and negative examples of *tourist*. She immediately scored the tests, and the students discovered that they all did very well and that Harriet obtained a perfect score.

THE TEACHING OF PRINCIPLES

Upon reading this section of the chapter, you should be able to describe and illustrate each of the following instructional steps.

10-19   Step 1: Describe the performance expected of the student after he has learned the principle.
10-20   Step 2: Decide and indicate which concepts or principles the student must recall in learning the new principle.
10-21   Step 3: Assist the student in the recall of component concepts.
10-22   Step 4: Help the student to combine the concepts in the proper order.
10-23   Step 5: Provide for practice of the principle and for reinforcement of student responses.
10-24   Step 6: Assess the student's learning of the principle.

We shall now describe the teaching of principles as a series of six steps which conform to the four components of the basic teaching model. Steps 1 and 2 pertain chiefly to instructional objectives. Step 1 requires a statement of the objective, and step 2 requires a task analysis. Step 2 also specifies the prerequisite entering behavior, while step 3 assists the student in the use of the appropriate entering behavior. Steps 4 and 5 provide the essential learning conditions of contiguity, practice, and reinforcement. Step 6 pertains chiefly to performance assessment.

For the sake of brevity we shall use a single principle in the illustration of these steps: The plural of most nouns is formed by adding *s* to the singular form of the noun. (We shall not worry for the moment about the plural form of nouns that end in *s, sh, ch, x,* or *z.*)

STEP 1

DESCRIBE THE PERFORMANCE EXPECTED OF THE STUDENT AFTER HE HAS LEARNED THE PRINCIPLE

As in the case of concept learning, this step allows the student to monitor his own performance and to generate his own reinforcement. For our principle, the statement could be as follows: When given the singular form of several English nouns, you will form the plural by adding *s*.

STEP 2

DECIDE AND INDICATE WHICH CONCEPTS OR PRINCIPLES THE STUDENT MUST RECALL IN LEARNING THE NEW PRINCIPLE

In this step, you must analyze the principle to determine what the component concepts are, and you must assess the entering behavior of the student to determine whether he has mastered these concepts. For our illustrative principle, the student needs to know these concepts: *plural, most, nouns,* formed by adding, *s,* and *singular form.* Unless the student has mastered each of these, he cannot learn the relationship the principle specifies. Supporting evidence for the necessity of knowing component concepts is found in an experiment by Howard Kendler and Robert Vineberg (1954). The component concepts were *size* and *shape.* In the first part of the experiment the students were taught in three different ways: Group 1 learned the two component concepts; group 2 learned one of the two component concepts (shape); and group 3 learned neither of the component concepts but learned instead two irrelevant concepts. In the second part of the experiment they had to learn a principle, or compound concept. They were presented with a large gray triangle and a small orange circle and required to sort several cards which bore similar figures by matching them with the triangle or the circle. For example, if they were presented with a card with a large orange square, they were to match it with the large gray triangle because both figures are the same in size (large) and in shape (with straight lines). A card with a small black crescent was to be matched with a small orange circle because both figures are the same in size (small) and shape (with curved lines). Group 1 took an average of twenty-three trials to learn the test concept, while the next best group (group 2) took almost twice this number, and group 3 (which had learned neither component concept) took four times as many trials!

Your performance of step 2 in principle teaching is complicated by the fact that the learning of one principle is often dependent on the prior learning of another principle. There are, in effect, hierarchies of principles. Gagné (1970) states, "In hierarchies of principles two or more principles may be prerequisite to the learning of a superordinate principle. Once the latter is learned, it may combine with another principle to support the learning of still another higher-level principle, and so on. A hierarchy may be called a structure of organized knowledge about a topic." Gagné and his associates (1961, 1962, 1963) have found that the order in which topics are presented figures prominently in the students' achievement of the instructional objectives.

Figure 10-3 is a hierarchy of principles in the topic of nonmetric geometry. The student has to learn not simply to recognize points, lines, and curves, but also to show that the existence of each of these entities is dependent on the application of certain principles. The figure is interesting because it depicts how concepts are organized into principles and how principles are interrelated. Gagné (pp. 151–52) explained Figure 10-3 in these words:

> At the lowest level, the boxes numbered VI and V represent *concepts* that must be known at the start. VIa is the concept *separation (of entities into groups).* VIb is *point.* Va is *set of points*—a new name for what most uninstructed students would simply call a "line." Beginning with these fairly simple concepts, which must be acquired in the manner described for type 6 [concept] learning, the

learner is ready to attain a new set of interrelated *principles.* First he learns to identify and draw a straight line (IVa), which is a set of points extending indefinitely in both directions. Later, he learns the principle which defines *line segment,* namely, that part of a line which consists of two points and the set of points between (IIIa). Then, he learns to identify and draw a *ray,* the set of points formed by a point on a line and one of the half lines made by this point (IIIb). Later still, he learns to define and make a *triangle;* this is made up of three points not on the same straight line, and the line segments that join these points (IIa). Picking up another thread of principles that build on each other, the student has also learned about *intersections* of lines and parts of lines (IVb, IIb, IIc). Finally, putting together these ideas of a *triangle* and of *intersections* he comes to learn principle Ia, which enables him to state that the intersection of a triangle and lines or parts of lines is 0, 1, or 2 points. If he has indeed mastered these principles, one building on the other, he is able at this stage to provide examples of intersections of lines with triangles that form sets of 0, 1, or 2 points, and to justify the drawing he makes.

Such a drawing must not "look" right; the learner will be able at this stage to say why it is right.

Gagné goes on to say that determining the prerequisites for any given principle may be accomplished by asking the question: What does the student have to know in order to be instructed in this principle? Knowing principle IIc, for example, means being able to deal with intersections of sets of points whether these are line segments, rays, half lines, or indefinitely extended lines. Principle IIc is a superordinate principle made up of lower-order principles.

Task analysis reminds us of the necessity of analyzing our subject matter before presenting it to the student. In the case of component concepts, it is necessary to determine which concepts we expect the student to know before we try to teach him the principle. In the case of higher-order principles, it is necessary to determine beforehand the lower-order principles the student must know. Step 2 requires the teacher to ask and answer the question: What does the student have to know in order to be instructed in this principle? Hierarchies of concepts and principles may become research areas for educational psychologists. If such research is successful, it could tell the teacher the proper sequence in which to present the concepts and the principles he teaches. In the absence of this research it is necessary for each of us to do some practical experimentation to find which sequence works best. For example, no sequence has been determined for introducing the principle on the formation of the English plural. Ordinarily this principle is taught as part of the instruction on nouns and noun forms. Should it follow or precede instruction on the formation of possessives or on the singular and plural verb forms? It is very likely that it should precede instruction on these latter principles because it can contribute more to their learning than they can to the learning of our illustrative principle. But we really do not know the best sequence until we experiment with alternative sequences and find out which works best.

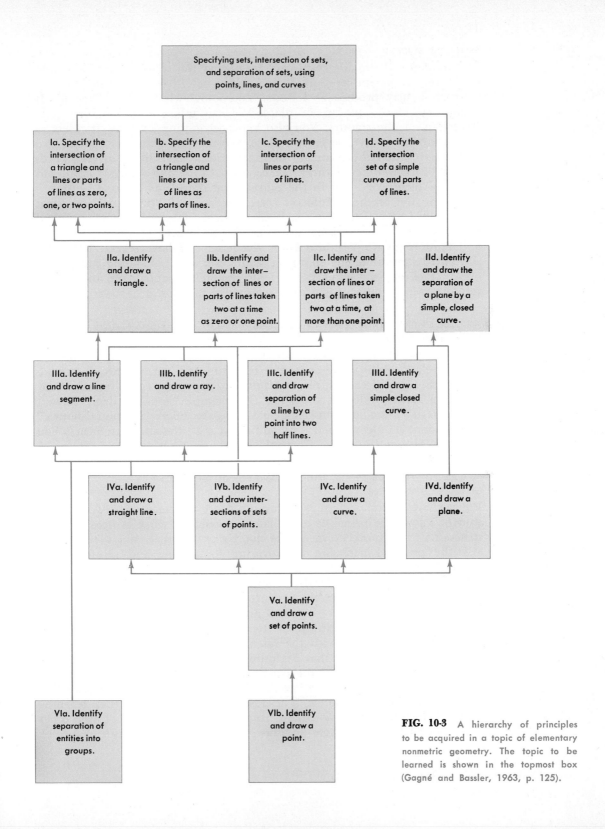

FIG. 10-3 A hierarchy of principles to be acquired in a topic of elementary nonmetric geometry. The topic to be learned is shown in the topmost box (Gagné and Bassler, 1963, p. 125).

STEP 3   ASSIST THE STUDENT IN THE RECALL OF COMPONENT CONCEPTS

In this step you provide contiguity by having the student simultaneously recall the component concepts. In the case of our illustrative principle, this instruction may proceed as follows: You know what singular means. It means one object, person, or place. We can talk about one book, one American, or one country. You also know what plural means. It refers to more than one object, person, or place. We can talk about two books, two Americans, or all the countries in the world. I have listed several words on the board [*mother, fathers, teachers, dog, cats, and houses*]. Point out which of these words are in the plural form. [Students respond appropriately, and the teacher reinforces correct responses.] You also know what nouns are. I have listed five words on the board [*show, boy, girl, run,* and *fat*]. Point out which of these words are nouns [again appropriate response and reinforcement]. You also know the letter *s.* I have several letters on the board [several letters in upper and lower case, including more than one *s*]. Pick out the letter *s.* [Students respond appropriately and obtain reinforcement. Similar instruction is provided for *most.*]

STEP 4   HELP THE STUDENT TO COMBINE THE CONCEPTS
IN THE PROPER ORDER

In this step you also provide contiguity of concepts and contiguity for the proper relationship of the concepts. The student's learning requires guidance here. It is not enough to ask him to order the concepts properly. Your questions must guide the ordering. For example, you say this: "Now I want you to tell me how you change most singular nouns into plural nouns." The student should respond, "By adding an *s* to the singular form." You respond (with enthusiasm), "Correct!"

STEP 5   PROVIDE FOR PRACTICE OF THE PRINCIPLE AND FOR REINFORCEMENT
OF STUDENT RESPONSES

We may well assume, if steps 1 through 4 are properly enacted, that the student knows the principle and that no further practice is necessary. Instructional conditions, however, are not always optimal, and there is usually the practical necessity of providing for review and reinforcement beyond the original learning situation. In the case of plurals, students have the opportunity to identify plurals in their reading and to form them in their writing. Of course, the instructor must monitor the students' practice and reinforce correct responses and point out incorrect ones. Reinforced practice of a principle is particularly crucial when the learning of one principle interferes with the retention of others. Doris Entwisle and W. Huggins (1964) found that beginning engineering students who studied voltage principles first and the corresponding current principles immediately afterward retained less of what they learned than when they studied the voltage principles alone. The researchers also found that learning several principles of electric circuits interfered with retention of each other and caused forgetting. These findings suggest the need for both proper sequencing of the subject matter and reinforced practice of potentially confusing principles.

ASSESS THE LEARNING OF THE PRINCIPLE

Here we must refer to step 1 to remind ourselves what performance we selected as our instructional objective. Our objective indicates that it is not enough to give the student a list of positive and negative examples of plural nouns and to ask him to choose the plurals. The objective requires the student to form the plural when given the singular form. Therefore, you say to the student, "Show me how you form the plurals of the list of words I have given to you." Gagné (1966) emphasizes the importance of requiring the student to demonstrate or show the teacher his grasp of the principles. Using the principle of work (work = force × distance), Gagné (p. 86) writes:

> I do not mean to imply by this [demonstration] a single measure of performance such as the question which verbally says to the student "demonstrate work in the following situation" and then describe the situation. Instead, it seems to me that there are a number of different questions that might be asked in order to determine whether a student has learned a principle. One might say, "What is the work done in pushing a body of 1000 grams a horizontal distance of thirty centimeters?" or "Show how to calculate the work done by a force of fifty pounds pushing a trunk along a floor for ten feet." Any of these questions may be considered to reflect what is meant by "demonstrate."

Again, as in step 4, you can use verbal mediators to elicit the definition. You ask, "How do you form the plural of singular nouns?" The student should respond, "By adding *s* to the singular form." To be certain that the student has not given a rote definition, you should test further to determine how well he has acquired the new principle. In the case of our example, you present the student with a list of singular nouns and ask him to form their plurals. The student has learned the principle before this step; the verification is primarily an opportunity for the instructor to ascertain how well the new capability has been established.

In teaching the principle of the formation of plural nouns by adding *s* to the singular form, Mr. Punctilious, at one point in the instruction, gives the students these words: *space ships* and *box cars*. He then requests the students to give him the singular forms of these words. Why does Mr. Punctilious do this? **QUESTION 10-3**

  (a) He is describing the expected terminal performance.
  (b) He is deciding which concepts the student must recall.
  (c) He is assisting the students in the recall of component concepts.
  (d) He is helping the students to combine the component concepts in the proper order.
  (e) He is requiring the students to demonstrate the principle.

After selecting your answer, give the reasons for your choice and for your rejection of the alternatives.

SUMMARY

The first section of the chapter dealt with the nature and uses of concepts and principles. A concept was defined as a class of stimuli which have common characteristics. Each concept has attributes—distinctive features which vary from concept to concept. Attributes, in turn, have values which describe the particular variations the attributes may undergo. The number of attributes varies from concept to concept. In general, the more attributes the concept has the more difficult it is to learn. The dominance, or obviousness, of attributes also varies. When relevant attributes are not dominant and irrelevant attributes are dominant, the concept becomes more difficult to learn. Attributes combine in three different ways to produce three types of concepts. In a conjunctive concept the appropriate values of several concepts are jointly present. In a disjunctive concept the appropriate values of one attribute or another or both are present. A relational concept has a specifiable relationship between attributes. Conjunctive concepts are easier to learn than disjunctive and relational concepts. A principle is a statement of the relationship of two or more concepts or principles. These statements often take an if-then form. It is necessary to relate the teaching of concepts to the student's level of development and to his preschool learning. Finally, there are many uses of concepts in school learning, ranging from those uses which reduce complexity and the need for constant learning to those misuses of concepts as stereotypes.

We described seven steps for the teaching of concepts: Step 1 requires the description of the student's expected performance after he has learned the concept (the first component of the basic teaching model). Step 2 requires the teacher to reduce the number of attributes to be learned by ignoring some and emphasizing others or by reducing a large number of attributes to a few patterns. Step 2 also requires the teacher to make all relevant attributes dominant. Step 3 requires the teacher to provide the student with useful verbal mediators to prepare him for concept learning. Steps 2 and 3 pertain mainly to the entering behavior of the student.

The remaining steps deal with procedures for teaching concepts when the entering behavior is adequate (component 3 of the basic teaching model). Step 4 requires you to provide positive and negative examples of the concept. You must present enough positive examples to represent the actual range of the concept you are teaching. The presentation of a mixed series of positive and negative examples is more effective than the presentation of a purely positive or a purely negative series. Simplified examples are often more effective than realistic examples, which often present more information than the student can easily handle. Step 5 requires the teacher to provide contiguity by presenting the examples in close succession or simultaneously. For step 6 you provide occasions for reinforced practice beyond the original learning situation. The type and intensity of the reinforcement (feedback) affect concept learning. Shifting the response mode may inhibit concept learning. For step 7, you assess the student's learning of the concept.

Six steps were described for the teaching of principles. Step 1 requires the teacher to describe the performance expected of the student after he has learned the principle (component 1 of the basic teaching model). Step 2 deals with entering behavior. Here the teacher decides and indicates which concepts or principles the student must recall in learning the new principle. Because there are hierarchies of principles, the learning of a higher-order principle requires the prior learning of a lower-order principle.

The next three steps deal with the third component of the basic teaching model. In step 3 you provide contiguity by assisting the student in the recall of component concepts. In step 4 you help him to combine the concepts in the proper order. Step 5 provides reinforced practice. The remaining step verifies, extends, and preserves the original principle learning.

SUGGESTED READINGS

These three books of readings deal particularly with the subject matter in this chapter. For the most part these readings report actual research or comprise theoretical discussions upon which the research is based.

ANDERSON, RICHARD C., and AUSUBEL, DAVID P., *Readings in the Psychology of Cognition.* New York: Holt, Rinehart & Winston, Inc., 1965.

DE CECCO, JOHN P., *Psychology of Language, Thought, and Instruction: Readings.* New York: Holt, Rinehart & Winston, Inc., 1967.

HARPER, ROBERT J. C.; ANDERSON, CHARLES C.; CHRISTENSEN, CLIFFORD M.; and HUNKA, STEVEN M., *The Cognitive Processes: Readings.* Englewood Cliffs, N.J.: Prentice-Hall, Inc., 1964.

These fairly recent articles and books deal with the various theories and research on concept and principle learning:

BRUNER, JEROME S., GOODNOW, JACQUELINE J., and AUSTIN, GEORGE A., *A Study of Thinking.* New York: John Wiley & Sons, Inc., 1956.

HUNT, EARL B., *Concept Learning: An Information Processing Problem.* New York: John Wiley & Sons, Inc., 1962.

GAGNÉ, ROBERT M., "The Learning of Principles," in *Analyses of Concept Learning,* eds. H. J. Klausmeier and C. W. Harris, pp. 81–96. New York: Academic Press, Inc., 1966.

KENDLER, HOWARD H., "The Concept of the Concept," in *Categories of Human Learning,* ed. A. W. Melton. New York: Academic Press, Inc., 1964.

REITMAN, WALTER R., *Cognition and Thought: An Information Processing Approach.* New York: John Wiley & Sons, Inc., 1965.

No entire volume deals with the teaching of concepts and principles, but these various chapters and articles do:

GAGNÉ, ROBERT M., *Conditions of Learning.* New York: Holt, Rinehart & Winston, Inc., 1965, Chaps. 5 and 6.

KLAUSMEIER, HERBERT J., and HARRIS, CHESTER W., eds., *Analyses of Concept Learning.* New York: Academic Press, Inc., 1966. See Part III (on learning-teaching processes) and Part IV (on concepts in various subject matter fields).

Much of the research on concept and principle teaching and learning is published in the *Journal of Educational Psychology.*

CHAPTER ELEVEN

PROBLEM SOLVING, CREATIVITY, AND DISCOVERY LEARNING

In this chapter we consider the methods for teaching the most complex kind of human learning—*problem solving*. We shall view problem solving as a form of principle learning in which lower-order principles are applied in the learning of higher-order principles. In this view, successful problem solving results in the acquisition of new knowledge just as does the successful learning of concepts and principles. Although this chapter emphasizes problem solving as a gain in substantive knowledge, we shall also consider techniques of problem solving which are sometimes called *creative thinking, critical thinking,* and *learning by discovery.* One of the major issues the latter part of the chapter considers is the following: Are there techniques of problem solving independent of particular subject matter and disciplines and, if there are, can you teach them to students?

The chapter has four major sections. The first describes the nature of problem solving. Here we recall our definition of learning and introduce the concepts of *habit family hierarchies* and *transfer of learning*. The second section describes and illustrates five steps you can take in teaching problem solving. Later in the chapter you will see that these five steps illustrate learning by guided discovery. The third section describes the nature of creativity and the teaching conditions which foster it. We define creativity as creative abilities, the learning of original responses, and problem solving. The fourth section defines and illustrates a widely discussed concept of teaching procedures—*learning by discovery*. Learning by discovery is compared with expository teaching for its value in achieving various instructional objectives.

THE NATURE OF PROBLEM SOLVING

Upon reading this section of the chapter, you should be able to meet these objectives:

11-1   Define and illustrate problem solving in terms of the definition of learning given in Chapter 7.
11-2   Describe and illustrate the differences and similarities in problem solving and principle learning.
11-3   Define habit family hierarchies in terms of divergent and convergent mechanisms and distinguish between simple and compound hierarchies.
11-4   Define mediated generalization in terms of increased strength of members of hierarchies and illustrate the process by using an example of verbal mediation in a problem solution.
11-5   Distinguish between reproductive and productive thinking in terms of habit family hierarchies.
11-6   Define transfer of learning in terms of two tasks and distinguish between and illustrate the differences between (a) positive, (b) negative, and (c) zero transfer.
11-7   Define and illustrate problem solving in terms of transfer of learning.

Problem Solving as Learning

In Chapter 7, we defined learning as a relatively permanent change in a behavioral tendency which results from reinforced practice. We also described the learning event as consisting of the learner, the stimulus situation, and the response. You will see that both the definition of learning and the description of the learning event apply to problem solving. To understand this point consider the matchstick problems invented by George Katona (1940). The physical stimulus situation consisted of unusual geometric forms made with matches or pencils and paper. Figure 11-1a is an example of one of these geometric forms. The numerical designation beneath the figure indicated that the student had to solve this problem by reducing five squares to four squares and by moving only three matchsticks. The student was also told that the squares were equal in size and

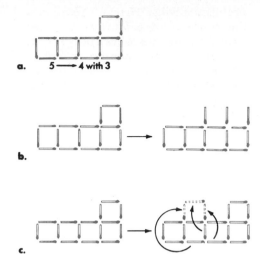

a.   5 —→ 4 with 3

b.

c.

FIG. 11-1 a. An example of a matchstick problem. b. Unacceptable solution to the matchstick problem. c. Acceptable solution to the matchstick problem (after Katona, 1940, pp. 58–60).

that the new figure had to consist of equal squares of the same size as those in the original figure. The student was then given three alterations of the figure which did not constitute solutions. It was not permissible (a) to take away any matchsticks from the table, (b) to form figures which were not squares or to have unused lines, or (c) to have duplication of sides—each square could have only four sides. Figure 11-1b shows an unacceptable solution. In this learning event the stimulus situation consisted of the various physical and verbal stimuli which we have described. To these stimuli the student was to make the acceptable response shown in Figure 11-1c. In solving the problem the student needed to realize that there was no requirement that all figures have sides in common as they did in the original.

Now we can apply our definition of learning. When the student solves these and similar problems, we can infer a change in behavioral tendency, especially because he could not solve the problems when he was originally presented with them. We also know that the change in behavioral tendency which results from successful problem solving is more permanent than the changes which result from the less complex forms of learning we discussed earlier. With very little practice we can remember how to solve matchstick problems after relatively few trials and long periods of time. When we discuss learning by discovery, you will see, however, that reinforced practice adds considerably to the long-term retention of problem solutions and to their wide application to new and similar problems. We can, therefore, think of problem solving as a form of learning.

Problem Solving and Principle Learning
Problem solving (sometimes called rule learning) is closely related to principle learning (Gagné, 1964, 1970) since it combines two or more previ-

ously learned principles (rules) into a higher-order principle. And, like concept and principle learning, problem solving represents acquisition of substantive knowledge Gagné (1964) uses this example. A beginning algebra student is given a problem—multiply X^2 and X^3—which he has not seen before. To solve this problem he must have learned two principles: Multiplying a number by n means adding that number n times, and an exponent r represents multiplying the number by itself r times. The combination of these principles produces the solution to the problem and the learning of a higher-order principle: To multiply identical variables with exponents, multiply the variable by itself the number of times represented by the sum of the two exponents. If a student obtains the right answer to this problem, we usually infer that he has learned the higher-order principle without requiring him to state it. We confirm our inference by having him solve other problems of the same class—problems which involve multiplying variables with exponents.

Solution of the matchstick problems also implies the proper application of two principles and the learning of a higher-order principle. One principle refers to the double function of particular sticks—one stick can serve as the side of two squares. The other principle is that the original figure can be loosened by creating holes in it. The higher-order principle is that to make fewer squares with the same number of matchsticks create holes in the original figure and give particular sticks double functions. The student's successful solution of a number of matchstick problems indicates that he has learned the higher-order principle.

This discussion of problem solving as the learning of higher-order principles distinguishes between problem solving as the acquistion of knowledge and problem solving as the learning of some very general techniques which can be applied to a wide variety of problems. As much as we would like to believe in some general problem-solving strategies of wide applicability, the research we have available does not convince us of their existence. We shall discuss some of that research in the latter part of the chapter when we consider the general topics of creativity and discovery learning.

Habit Family Hierarchies

Several theories suggest how problem solving occurs in the individual. Since the theory of Irving Maltzman (1955) is consistent with our view of problem solving as complex learning, we shall give you a simplified version of this theory. A basic principle in it is that of stimulus and response hierarchies. Figure 11-2a shows such a hierarchy. S is a stimulus.

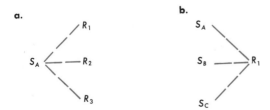

FIG. 11-2 a. A divergent mechanism. The stimulus has varying tendencies to elicit the alternative responses. b. A convergent mechanism. The alternative stimuli have varying tendencies to elicit a given response (after Maltzman, 1955, Figs. 1 and 2).

R_1, R_2, and R_3 are three responses to this stimulus. The figure indicates that R_1 is stronger (higher in the hierarchy) than R_2, which, in turn, is stronger than R_3. A stronger response is more likely to occur in the presence of the stimulus. For example, if the word *table* represents S, three responses in order of strength might be *chair* (R_1), *legs* (R_2), and *floor* (R_3). *Chair* is a more dominant response than the other two and therefore occupies the highest position in the hierarchy. It is quite possible that in a given situation, however, *floor* is the correct response. Maltzman describes this situation as a *divergent mechanism*—a hierarchy of responses which are made to a given stimulus and in which the correct response is low in the hierarchy. Figure 11-2a depicts a divergent mechanism. A *convergent mechanism*, Figure 11-2b, is a hierarchy in which various stimuli exhibit varying strengths in eliciting the same response. The words *book* (S_A), *pen* (S_B), and *future* (S_C) can all elicit the same response, *student*. But S_A *(book)* has the strongest tendency to elicit this response, and it therefore occupies the highest position in the hierarchy.

Convergent and divergent mechanisms combine to produce habit family hierarchies, as in Figure 11-3. S_A (an external stimulus) elicits three responses (in the divergent mechanism) of varying lengths. These responses, in turn, are connected with three stimuli which have varying tendencies to elicit a given response (in the convergent mechanism). R_{GA} is the problem solution. In Maltzman's theory these habit family hierarchies combine to produce compound habit family hierarchies. In other words, habit family hierarchies vary in strength and occupy greater or lesser positions of dominance, just as responses and stimuli vary in dominance. In Figure 11-4, S_A has the power to arouse its own habit family hierarchy and also the hierarchies of stimuli S_B and S_C. R_1 becomes a member of a convergent mechanism because it can be aroused by S_A, S_B, and S_C. We now have a hierarchy of habit family hierarchies or a class of classes of stimulus-response relationships. Maltzman believes that problem solving may involve the selection of habit family hierarchies as well as the selection of specific response sequences within a hierarchy.

Mediated generalization In solving a problem, the individual is in this situation: Initially, the correct response is low in a single hierarchy or the correct habit family heirarchy is low in a compound hierarchy. The strength of the correct response or hierarchy must increase for the individual to solve the problem. According to this theory, the originally dominant but incorrect response or hierarchy will gradually be extinguished as

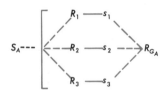

FIG. 11-3 A habit family hierarchy produced by a divergent and a convergent mechanism (after Maltzman, 1955, Fig. 3).

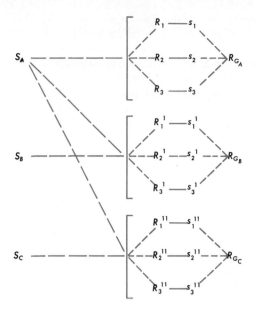

FIG. 11-4 A compound habit family hierarchy produced by a combination of habit family hierarchies (after Maltzman, 1955, Fig. 4).

a result of repeated failures to solve the problem. In the meantime, through a process of mediated generalization, the strength of responses low in the hierarchy will increase in strength. In mediated generalization, effects upon one member of a hierarchy may influence other members and finally increase the strength of the initially weak but correct member. The effects we refer to are the effects of reinforcement. Through mediated generalization, when one member of a hierarchy is reinforced all individual members of that hierarchy receive added strength.

To illustrate somewhat more clearly what Maltzman means by mediated generalization, we shall describe an experiment by Judson, Cofer, and Gelfand (1956) in which these researchers used the *two-string* (or two-cord) *problem*. To solve this problem the student must tie together the free ends of two strings suspended from the ceiling to the floor of a corridor. The distance between the two strings is such that the student cannot reach one string if he is holding the other. The solution of the problem requires the student to tie a weight to the end of one string to convert it into a pendulum. By swinging this string, he can catch it while holding the stationary string. He then ties the two strings together and solves the problem.

In this experiment the students were divided into four groups. Three groups memorized lists of words before presentation of the problem, while the fourth (control) group was simply presented with the two-string problem. The lists varied in their relevance to the solution to the problem. Group *A* learned the following list: *rope, swing, pendulum, clock, time.* Group *B* learned only one word from this list, *rope,* and this word was imbedded in the following list: *hemp, tie, twine, package.* Group *C* also learned the word *rope,* but it appeared as the last word in this list: *hemp, twine, tie, package, pendulum.* The learning of these lists, of course, meant that these words, as responses to the problem, were reinforced. But the associations among the words were also reinforced. In the list for group *A,* therefore, the reinforcement of *rope* also meant the reinforcement of the association of *rope* with *swing* and *pendulum.* In the lists for groups *B* and *C,* the word *rope* was primarily associated with words which denoted tying or binding. If each of these lists represented a response hierarchy, the effect of reinforcing one word (or member) would be to reinforce other members (or words) of the hierarchy. This exemplifies what Maltzman means by mediated generalization—the spread of effect from one member to another member of the hierarchy. By reinforcing *rope* in the list for group *A,* we also reinforce *swing* and *pendulum.* The results of this study showed that students in group *A* produced more solutions to the two-string problem than did students in the other three groups.

A further experiment by Arthur Staats (1957) shows how the status of various responses in the student's habit family hierarchy influences his attempts to solve problems. Staats also used the two-string problem. Before presentation of the problem the students were asked to list all the different ways in which they could use a screwdriver, balsa wood, and a piece of string. Staats observed which students gave *weight* responses to the word *screwdriver* such as fishing sinker, ballast, and paperweight. Staats found that only seven out of sixty-one students gave verbal weight responses. Consistent with Maltzman's theory however, after solving the problem by tying a screwdriver to the end of one string and swinging this string as a pendulum, the students frequently responded to the screwdriver as a weight. The problem-solving experience had increased the strength of the weight response in their response hierarchies. Some evidence in this study also indicated that the stronger the weight response the less time it took the student to solve the problem.

Productive and reproductive thinking On the basis of his formulation Maltzman distinguishes between reproductive and productive thinking. In reproductive thinking the student is presented with a succession of problems belonging to the same class. The solution of a series of algebraic problems which require essentially the same operations is an example of reproductive thinking. Another example is the solution of anagrams of the same class. In anagram problems the letters of a word are presented in scrambled form and must be unscrambled to discover the word. If all the anagrams belong to the same category, such as words ending in particular suffixes or beginning with particular prefixes or belonging to the same part of speech, the solution involves reproductive thinking because it elicits various responses of the same habit family hierarchy. This habit family hierarchy becomes dominant in the compound habit family hierarchy because, as we have seen, its response members are reinforced and the responses belonging to different hierarchies are extinguished. The student might still fail to solve a particular algebraic problem or anagram, however, if the particular response within the hierarchy were very low in dominance.

In productive thinking (sometimes called creative thinking), the habit family hierarchy of low dominance must gain strength in the compound hierarchy and the dominant incorrect hierarchies must be extinguished for the solution to be attained. For example, when the student is presented with his first matchstick problem, the tendencies to use matchsticks for only single functions and to create new figures without holes must be extinguished before he can solve the problem. At the same time the initially weak but correct hierarchies (double functions for sticks and loosening the figure by making holes) must gain strength through the reinforcement of their individual response members. Thus productive thinking is more complex and therefore more difficult than reproductive thinking. Reproductive thinking involves primarily the response members of a single hierarchy. Productive thinking involves response competition among several hierarchies. Both types of thinking, however, remain forms of learning.

Later in the chapter, in the discussion of creativity, we shall distinguish between divergent and convergent thinking (Guilford, 1959) by their products—the types of responses made to various test stimuli. In this formulation, divergent is similar to productive thinking, and convergent to reproductive thinking. The chief distinction between the two formulations is that Maltzman describes a learning process—how these types of thinking occur—while Guilford focuses on the responses—what these types of thinking produce. Also, Guilford, at least in his original formulation of these types of thinking, attributes their origin to variations in personality traits rather than to learning experiences—there seem to be convergent and divergent individuals who exhibit their respective modes of thought.

We have viewed problem solving as principle learning and in terms of habit family hierarchies. We shall now take another view of this most complex type of learning.

Transfer of Learning

We can also view problem solving as a form of transfer of learning in which experience in one task influences performance on another task. Ellis (1965, p. 3) uses this example:

American visitors to England occasionally report that they experience difficulty in driving on the left side of the street because of their established habit of driving on the right. What happens in some instances is the tendency to revert momentarily to driving on the right or to vacillate between right and left, even though the rules of driving in England are clearly understood. In a similar vein, a common experience of individuals who begin to drive a car with automatic transmission, after having driven cars with standard transmission, is to attempt to depress a nonexistent clutch pedal. In both these situations we see that earlier learned habits, or modes of responding, can affect performance on some subsequent task that in a general way describes transfer of learning.

Transfer of learning may take three forms: (1) Positive transfer occurs when the previous performance benefits the performance on the subsequent tasks. There is positive transfer from pedaling tricycles to pedaling bicycles and from roller skating to ice skating. (2) Negative transfer occurs when the previous performance disrupts the performance on the second task (as in Ellis' two examples). (3) Zero transfer occurs when the previous performance has no effect on the performance of the second task. As far as we know, improving your bowling skills will have no effect on the improvement of your skill in writing novels, except, perhaps, that the time you spend bowling be should be spent writing.

Unfortunately, we have considerably more research on negative transfer than on positive transfer. An example of negative transfer in human problem solving is the experiment of Birch and Rabinowitz (1951). They too used the two-cord (or two-string) problem (see p. 436). In this experiment only two objects could be used as weights—an electrical switch and an electrical relay. To influence the solution of the problem, they divided the students into various groups and gave two of the groups different pre-problem experiences. They gave group *A* the task of completing an electrical circuit on a breadboard by using a switch. Group *B* had to complete an identical switch by using a relay, which is simply another type of switch. Group *C* (the control group) consisted of engineering students who had a wide variety of experience in solving circuit problems. The students in the other groups had little or no experience with wiring. After completing the wiring of the circuits, the students were presented with the two-cord problem. The experimenters observed which object—the switch or the relay—the students in the various groups used for making the pendulum. The results were truly impressive. Almost all the students who used the switch in the preproblem experience used the relay to make the pendulum. The reverse was true for the students who first used the relay. The engineering students used the switch and relay with equal frequency.

This experiment demonstrates the effects of negative transfer of prior experience. Later in the chapter you will see how the wise choice of prior experience can aid in the solution of problems through positive transfer. The instructional steps for problem solving described in the following section of this chapter are designed to enhance positive transfer. We can also explain the results of this experiment in terms of habit family hierarchies. The preproblem experiences with relays and switches reduced the dominance of certain hierarchies and increased the dominance of others.

Problem solving as transfer of learning If we consider the second task in a series of two tasks as a problem, we can view problem solving as transfer of learning. In Figure 11-5 Rudolph Schulz (1960) depicts the experimental operations which define transfer. In this design, if either the experimental or the control group performs reliably better on task *B* (which represents the problem and problem solution), transfer of learning has occurred. The transfer is positive when the experimental group is superior in performance and negative when the control group is superior. Zero transfer

	Task A	Task B	
Experimental group	X	X	Reliable difference
Control group		X	

FIG. 11-5 Operations for defining transfer (after Schulz, 1960, Fig. 1).

occurs when both groups perform at about the same level. Schulz uses the detour problem to show how his design for transfer of learning can be used in explaining problem-solving behavior. Figure 11-6a diagrams the detour problem. The O is the organism or student. The solution of the problem is G (goal). The student attempts to solve the problem by using response A, a direct approach, but the barrier prevents this response from solving the problem. The solution to the problem lies in making response D, the detour approach, which circumvents the barrier.

Figure 11-6b shows the design for transfer of learning as it applies to the detour problem. Task A consists of the student's making his customary direct approach to reach the goal (using A to reach G). Task B involves learning to use the detour approach to reach the goal (using D to reach G). Research on detour problems shows that the student's tendency to make response A must be extinguished before he can make the new response D. In theory, response A initially occupies a higher position in the habit family hierarchy which includes response D. Similarly, in the matchstick problems, the student's tendency to create figures without holes must be extinguished before he arrives at the problem solution.

Both Katona (1940) and Gagné (1964) emphasize that a major distinction between problem solving and other learning is that problem solving has high generalizability, or transferability. In problem solving the single solution to the single problem is not important. The correct solution must be an abstraction from the products of responding and not the responses themselves. More simply, we are interested in the student's solving a type of problem rather than in his solving single problems. The measurement of how much learning has occurred in problem solving is the student's ability to solve new problems of the same class. Not the solution of one detour or matchstick problem but the solution of a series of these problems

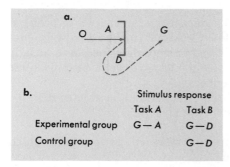

a.

b.

	Stimulus response	
	Task A	Task B
Experimental group	G — A	G — D
Control group		G — D

FIG. 11-6 a. Typical detour problem. b. The transfer applied to the detour problem (after Schulz, 1960, Figs. 2 and 3).

is the test of successful learning. Successful solutions of similar problems is the evidence for positive transfer of learning as well as for successful problem solving. Successful problem solving should result in immediate transferability.

Summary

The first section of this chapter described problem solving as complex learning. Using learning as the basic concept, we have viewed problem solving in three interrelated ways. First, we said that problem solving involved the application of lower-order principles to form higher-order principles. Then we saw that these principles form habit family hierarchies whose response members vary in strength and which can also themselves vary in strength as parts of compound habit family hierarchies. In discussing habit family hierarchies, we considered the influence of verbal mediation (as mediated generalization) on problem solving. Finally we saw that successful problem solving can be described as positive transfer of learning. The principles relevant to the solution of the problem are transferred.

QUESTION 11-1 Four educational psychologists were discussing the chief purpose of teaching problem solving in the school and discovered that they had four different viewpoints. Which viewpoint best represents the chief purpose of problem solving described in this chapter? Psychologist A believed that the chief purpose was the acquisition of knowledge of wide applicability. Psychologist B believed that the chief purpose was learning and using the techniques of problem solution. Psychologist C believed that the chief purpose was the learning and transfer of skills, verbal associations, and concepts. Psychologist D believed that the chief purpose was the development of the ability to transfer skills acquired through school problem solving to the solution of personal and community problems.

After selecting your answer, give the reasons for your choice and for your rejection of the alternatives.

INSTRUCTION FOR PROBLEM SOLVING

Now that you have developed some basic concepts and principles of problem solving, you are prepared to learn about the steps you must take in providing instruction for problem solving. The five steps described here include all four components of the basic teaching model. We shall describe these steps and the supporting research evidence.

Upon reading this section of the chapter, you should be able to describe and illustrate each of the following instructional steps:

11-8   Step 1: Describe for the students the terminal performance which constitutes the solution of the problem.

11-9 Step 2: Assess the students' entering behavior for the concepts and principles they will need to solve the problem.

11-10 Step 3: Invoke the recall of all relevant concepts and principles (including the use of advance organizers).

11-11 Step 4: Provide verbal direction of the students' thinking, short of giving them the solution to the problem.

11-12 Step 5: Verify the students' learning by requiring them to give a full demonstration of the problem solution (using other problems of the same class).

The Pendulum Problem

To make the description of the steps easy to learn we shall use for illustration a problem devised by Norman Maier (1930) in his research on human reasoning, which he began at the University of Berlin. The problem is similar to the two-string problem but considerably more complex and difficult. Here is Maier's (1930, p. 118) description of it:

> Your problem is to construct two pendulums, one of which will swing over this point [cross indicated on the floor as shown in Fig. 11-7] and one of which will swing over this other point [another cross indicated]. These pendulums should be so constructed that they will have a piece of chalk fastened to them which will make a mark (which can be seen) on the points on the floor just indicated. Naturally you must have something to hang the pendulums to. That is for you to worry about. Otherwise do anything you want to. This material is at your disposal [see below]. That chair, however, is not to be a part of your construction; you may use it for a work bench or a place of meditation, or anything you wish so long as it is free when you are through. Ask anything you wish. I'll be glad to assist you in building, only you must tell me what to do.

This was the basic description given to all students in the experiment. Later you will see that some groups of students received additional instruction.

The students were provided with the following materials: two long poles, two shorter poles, one table clamp, two burette clamps, two pieces of wire, and several pieces of chalk. The material was scattered around a table. Figure 11-7 shows these materials properly assembled. The problem solution consisted of placing the long pole against the ceiling and holding it in place by clamping two other poles together in such a manner that they were able to reach from floor to ceiling. One pole was wedged against the ceiling and formed a T with the vertical pole. The pendulums could then be hung from both ends of the pole wedged against the ceiling. A piece of chalk fastened to each burette clamp (see detail in Figure 11-7) formed the pendulum weights. The pendulum was made just long enough to allow the chalk to touch the floor. The structure, Maier tells us, was very simple and stable and required even one less pole than was given.

Although Maier did not observe all the steps for instruction in problem

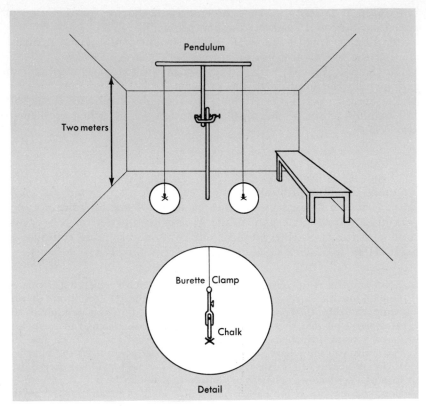

Pendulum

Two meters

Burette | Clamp

Chalk

Detail

FIG. 11-7 The solution of the pendulum problem (after Maier, 1930, p. 123)

solving, which we are about to describe, he did observe most of them, and, in any case, his problem, as described above, is still useful for illustration.

STEP 1

DESCRIBE FOR THE STUDENTS THE TERMINAL PERFORMANCE WHICH CONSTITUTES THE SOLUTION OF THE PROBLEM

This step corresponds to the first component of the basic teaching model. Maier fulfilled this function when he presented the students with the above statement of the problem. In effect, he told the students that they had to create two pendulums which would swing over the designated chalk marks on the floor. This statement, of course, does not tell them how to solve the problem but only what the solution must consist of. Later in the chapter you will see that instruction in problem solving is a form of guided discovery. It stops short of giving the students the problem solution; the students must construct the solution on their own. In one sense then, they discover the solution. The description of the students' terminal performance fulfills two learning conditions: The students' attention is directed to those aspects of the materials which will lead to a particular solution, and they will know when they have solved the problem and thereby generate their own reinforcement for successful moves and for the final solution.

ASSESS THE STUDENTS' ENTERING BEHAVIOR FOR THE CONCEPTS AND PRINCIPLES THEY WILL REQUIRE IN THE SOLUTION OF THE PROBLEM

This step fulfills the requirements of the second component of the basic teaching model by requiring the teacher to analyze the problem he presents to his students to determine the lower-order principles the students must know to solve the problem and to find out whether the students know them. The pendulum problem involves the application of three principles: the pendulum principle, which involves making a plumb line with the burette clamp and the piece of chalk; making long poles out of short poles by using the table clamp; and placing one pole against the ceiling and wedging it in place with one or two other poles. This is the higher-order principle (rule or problem solution): In the absence of hammer and nails, two pendulums can be constructed by extending the length of poles by using a clamp and by using the extended poles to wedge another pole against the ceiling. The higher-order principle, as you can see, simply states the relationship of the three component principles. The student whose entering behavior does not include one or more of these principles will fail to solve the problem. Figure 11-8 shows some of the solutions which did not work because collapsible structures were constructed. Although all these unacceptable solutions used the pendulum principle, most of them failed to use the wedging principle.

INVOKE THE RECALL OF ALL RELEVANT CONCEPTS AND PRINCIPLES

This step is the usual provision for contiguity. It is not enough that the students have learned these principles and that they are a part of their entering behavior. They must recall these principles in the presence of the problem and discover the relationship between them (the higher-order principle) which will result in the problem solution. In a part of the experiment we did not describe, Maier did provide for the recall of the three principles by actually demonstrating each one. He used a burette clamp, pencil, and a piece of wire to make a plumb line; he held a piece of cloth against the wall of a doorway by pressing the side of a flat board against it and kept this in place by wedging another board horizontally between the flat board and the other wall of the doorway; and he used a table clamp to combine two poles to make a longer one. Not all the groups in Maier's experiment witnessed these demonstrations. Even with the demonstrations, the problem proved to be very difficult for most students.

Per Saugstad (1957), in replicating Maier's study found that the demonstration of the principles was not enough because the students failed to see the wide applicability of the principles demonstrated. He points out that even though the students may have known the principle of wedging

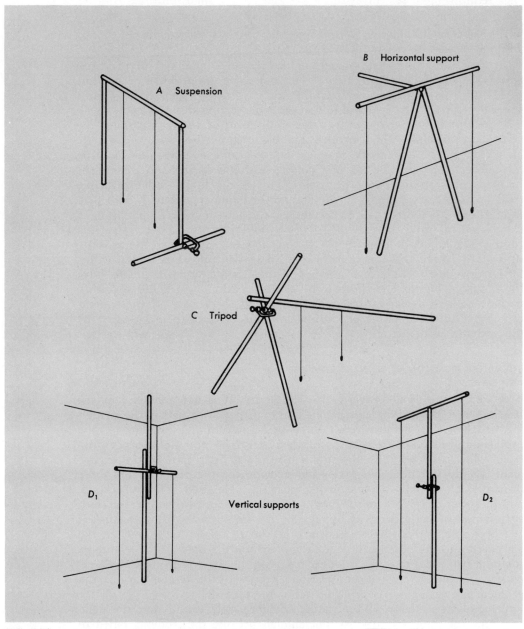

FIG. 11-8 *A, B,* and C are three incorrect approaches to the solution of the pendulum problem. D_2 represents the solution as Maier depicts it in Fig. 11-7. D_1 is another possible solution (after Weaver and Madden, 1949, p. 335).

they still were faced with finding a second flat surface (the ceiling). In fact, Maier did direct the attention of one group to the ceiling, and this group had more problem solutions than the others did. Using a different problem, Saugstad showed that the students who had learned the principles and had them available for application were best able to solve the problem. The problem was to put out a candle placed on one table while standing behind another table. The student had available six hollow glass tubes, a rod, and a lump of putty. The only possible solution was to put the glass tubes end to end around the rod and make the joints airtight with the putty. The student could then kneel down, direct the blowpipe at the candle flame, and by blowing through it, blow out the candle. The solution required the application of three principles: The glass tube had to conduct a stream of air blown through it; the putty had to provide an airtight and possibly a watertight conduit; and the rod had to support objects hung from it when held in a horizontal position. Saugstad administered an availability test to find out which students could recall these functions. In this way he was not only assessing the entering behavior of the students but also determining which students could recall the principles. The availability test consisted of the presentation of the glass tube, the lump of putty, and the rod. The students were required to list all the functions of these objects they could think of. He found that thirteen students listed all the functions necessary for the solution of the candle problem. All thirteen later solved the problem.

Of course, for step 3, the teacher must do more than administer a test to determine which principles are already known. By questions and demonstrations he can help the student recall the principles. Although Maier made his demonstrations to invoke recall, the students had not learned two of the principles (extension and wedging) well enough to apply them in the problem solution.

Advance organizers   The use of advance organizers may be a convenient means of invoking recall of relevant principles (Ausubel, 1960, 1963, 1965a, 1968). Although Ausubel has developed a unique theoretical framework for the definition and function of advance organizers, in the context of this chapter we may view them as a particular form of verbal mediation. Advance organizers are concepts or principles introduced before the presentation of the main body of instructional material. They are chosen for their usefulness in explaining and organizing that material. In his early study of advance organizers, Ausubel (1960) used a specially prepared passage on the metallurgical properties of plain carbon steel. He used two groups in his experiment. The experimental group was given the benefit of the advance organizers in the form of a written passage which they read before they were given the passage on carbon steel. Some of the basic principles (advance organizers) taught prior to the reading of the passage were the major similarities and differences between metals and alloys; their respective advantages and limitations; and the reasons for making and using alloys. The control group received instead an introductory passage of historical material which did not contain these advance organizers. Ausubel found that the experimental group which had the benefit of prior explanation of the relevant principles was more successful in the retention of the material on carbon steel than the control group was.

Using more provocative materials with college seniors, Ausubel and Mohamed Youssef (1963) investigated the effect of advance organizers on learning material on Buddhist and Zen Buddhist doctrines. The experimental group was provided with comparative advance organizers—two short introductory passages which pointed out the chief differences and similarities in Buddhist and Christian doctrines and Buddhist and Zen Buddhist doctrines. Instead of these advance organizers, the control group was given two "nonideational introductory passages of a historical and biographical nature" (p. 333) about Buddhism and Zen Buddhism. Following these introductions, both groups studied the new materials on Buddhism and Zen Buddhism. Both groups then took multiple-choice tests on the oriental doctrines. The results showed that the organizers aided the learning and the retention of the Buddhism but not the Zen Buddhism passage.

Ausubel contends that the procedure of using advance organizers may reverse traditional teaching practice, in which students are required to learn the details of new and unfamiliar material before they have acquired an adequate body of relevant subsumers (concepts and principles). Ausubel reminds us that, if the student lacks the necessary concepts and principles, the teacher should supply them. The student cannot acquire higher-order principles unless he has already learned the component principles.

For his example of the successful use of advance organizers, Ausubel (1968, pp. 153–154) refers to Boyd's famous *Textbook on Pathology*. Boyd devotes the first half of the book to a discussion of several principles which are used to organize the material in the latter half of the book. For example, he discusses the different categories of pathological processes and their principal causes and characteristics; the various kinds of etiological agents in disease; the interaction between generic and environmental factors in the development of pathological processes; types of humoral and tissue resistance to disease; and the general relationships between pathological lesions and clinical systems. In the second half of the book he discusses the pathology of separate organs. Most textbooks in this subject, according to Ausubel, consider only the major kinds of pathological processes occurring within various organs and organ systems and omit consideration of the more general principles. Ausubel argues for more highly organized instructional material with thorough cross referencing of all related principles. In the context of this chapter, advance organizers are important because of their usefulness in evoking previously learned concepts and principles in the learning of new principles and in problem solving.

STEP 4   **PROVIDE VERBAL DIRECTION OF THE STUDENTS' THINKING, SHORT OF GIVING THEM THE SOLUTION TO THE PROBLEM**

The direction to which we refer is illustrated by the verbal directions Maier (1930, p. 120) gave to two of his experimental groups. This is verbal direction *A,* the direction to use parts:

I'm going to give you a problem to solve. You will have to construct something. [Problem was then given.] Before you start on the solution I should like to show you three separate things, each of which will involve a principle. If you combine the ideas which I thus give you in the right manner, you will have the best solution to the problem. Try to use them; they are the solution in three separate parts. You do not have to use them, but only by using them will you get the most satisfactory solution. So try to use them.

This is verbal direction *B:*

I should like to have you appreciate how simple this problem would be if we could just hang the pendulum from a nail in the ceiling. Of course, that is not a possible solution, but I just want you to appreciate how simple the problem would be if that were possible. Now that it is not possible the problem is, as you may find out, quite difficult.

Table 11-1 shows the five groups in Maier's (1930) experiment and the type of instruction they received. Maier discovered that, with the exception of one student, only those students in group V (and only eight of the twenty-two in this group) were able to solve the problem. The demonstration of the three principles, the direction to use them, and the direction about suspending pendulums from the ceiling were all necessary for the problem solution.

Further evidence for the importance of channeling the thinking of students for problem solving is provided in an experiment by Hilgard and his associates (1953). They used Katona's (1940) card tricks to compare methods of instruction for their effects on transfer of learning. One of the card tricks required the use of four red cards and four black cards. The student was shown how to arrange them so that as he played them alternately from the top and from the bottom of the deck, they would appear alternately red and black on the table; that is, they would turn up in this order: *R-B-R-B-R-B-R-B.* This trick was called four red, four black, skip one. The solution required the cards to be arranged in the following order: *R-R-B-R-R-B-B-B.* Two groups of students were taught in different ways. The memorization group was simply given the order of red and black cards (the solution),

DESCRIPTION OF EXPERIMENTAL GROUPS IN MAIER (1930) STUDY   **TABLE 11-1**

	INSTRUCTION
Group I (control)	Statement of problem
Group II	Statement of problem and demonstration of three principles
Group III	Statement of problem, demonstration of principles, and verbal direction A (to use parts)
Group IV	Statement of problem and verbal direction B
Group V	Statement of problem, demonstration of principles, and verbal directions A and B

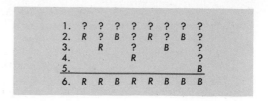

FIG. 11-9 Scheme for determining correct order of cards (after Katona, 1940, p. 264).

and they memorized the order. They then arranged the cards in the pre-scribed order and performed the trick.

The understanding group was presented with the written scheme in Figure 11-9. The question marks refer to the cards still held in hand. Row 1 contains only question marks because none of the cards has been dealt. The first time through, the alternate cards have to be red and black as in row 2. The four question marks in row 2 indicate that four remaining cards are held in hand and are unknown. The first of the remaining cards has to be red since the last card in row 2 was black. The third card must be black. This information is recorded in row 3. There are still two question marks. In row 4 red is assigned to the first question mark. In row 5 black is assigned to the last question mark. In row 6, these operations are simply summarized, and you have the solution indicated above. After the student was shown how to use this scheme, he was asked to repeat the solution with pencil and paper and then arrange the cards in the pack and do the trick. Later he was given a similar task to set the stage for the transfer experiments which followed. (The task was eight spades, skip one—solution: A-5-2-7-3-6-4-8.)

The major question was which of the groups would do better when presented with similar but novel problems (transfer of learning). Hilgard found that the understanding groups had the advantage throughout. Table 11-2 shows the highly significant superiority of this group. The significance of this experiment is that it shows the importance of providing that instruc-tion which guides the student toward the solution of problems. You should note however that in this experiment the guidance did not include the solution of the problem except in the first demonstration of the use of the written scheme. Hilgard notes that the understanding method is not an unmixed blessing. Large numbers of errors were made by students in these groups because they grew impatient with the understanding method and adopted the rote method, made careless errors, and were confused because of their partial understanding. He found also that overnight retention was equally good for both groups. Only in transfer was the understanding group definitely superior.

STEP 5   VERIFY THE STUDENTS' LEARNING BY REQUIRING THEM TO GIVE
A FULL DEMONSTRATION OF THE PROBLEM SOLUTION
(USING OTHER PROBLEMS OF THE SAME CLASS)

Here you must simply recall our discussion of transfer of learning. We pointed out that the major distinction between problem solving and other

GROUP	N	TASK 4 THREE RED, THREE BLACK; SKIP ONE	TASK 5 FOUR RED, FOUR BLACK; SKIP TWO	TASK 6 TEN SPADES; SKIP TWO
Memorization	30	3	1	1
Understanding	30	16	7	10
Probability of this difference arising by chance		0.0003	0.03	0.003

learning is that problem solving has high transferability. Once the higher-order principle has been learned, the student should be able immediately to solve new problems to which the principle applies. Both in research on problem solving and in classroom instruction this important step is omitted. However, since it represents the fourth component of the basic teaching model, it is vitally important for assessing the adequacy of the student's learning and the instruction.

Summary

In the second section of this chapter we have described a series of steps you must take in teaching problem solving. The steps, as you have seen, correspond to those of the basic teaching model. You have seen the importance of describing the terminal behavior for the students (step 1). You have also seen the importance of analyzing the problem to find out what the prerequisite concepts and principles are for its solution and to assess the students' entering behavior to see if they know what they must (step 2). The next two steps (3 and 4) deal with the third component of the basic

---

In aiding the students' solution of the two-string problem, Miss Methodical provided these   **QUESTION 11-2**
learning conditions: (a) She administered a test which contained questions about the pendulum principle and the dual functions of heavy objects, one of which is to serve as a weight. (b) She demonstrated for the students how the strings could be swung in an arc to reduce the distance between them. (c) She told them how Tarzan could rescue Jane by swinging on a vine over a chasm that separated them. She diagrammed Tarzan's procedure on the board. (d) She asked the students to solve new and unfamiliar problems which involved the application of the weight and pendulum principles. (e) She indicated that the problem would be solved when the student held string A in one and string B in the other hand.

Arrange these learning conditions in the proper order.

After determining the order, give your reasons for the order you have chosen.

---

teaching model and are particularly crucial in teaching problem solving. These steps describe the guidance the teacher must provide short of giving the students the solution to the problem. Step 3 requires invoking recall of relevant principles, and step 4 requires that you provide guidance in the combination and application of these principles for the solution of the problem. The last step (5) requires that you assess the performance of the students to see whether they can transfer their learning to new and similar problems.

INSTRUCTION FOR CREATIVITY

Upon reading this section of the chapter, you should be able to meet these objectives:

11-13   Define and illustrate creative abilities in terms of flexibility, originality, and fluency.

11-14   Distinguish (and illustrate the differences) between divergent and convergent thinking.

11-15   Define tests of creative abilities in terms of response production and indicate the degree of correlation of these tests.

11-16   Define and illustrate creativity as the learning of new responses.

11-17   Define and illustrate creativity as problem solving.

11-18   Distinguish (and illustrate the difference) between presented and discovered problems with known and unknown methods of solution.

11-19   Define brainstorming in terms of free association and deferred evaluation and list its effects in terms of (a) problem solving, (b) quality of solutions, (c) effects on creative abilities; describe and illustrate its use in invoking recall of concepts and principles in problem solving.

11-20   Describe and illustrate the use of research skills and creative reading in creative problem solving.

11-21   Describe and illustrate the ways in which the teacher can reward creative achievement.

This section of the chapter considers the nature of creativity and the procedures you can adopt to foster it in your students. Creativity is currently a very popular subject in educational and psychological circles. Considerable research on creativity in the early 1960s resulted in studies of the creativity and intelligence of creative artists and scientists, of the creative process as manifested in artistic and scientific achievement, of creative (as well as critical) thinking, and of the relevance of all this to educational practice. Many educators believe that the school should foster creativity in every child. They also feel that the school may unwittingly stultify creative development, as illustrated by the following anecdote told by a dean of a midwestern university (Guilford, 1950, p. 448):

> An old, experienced teacher and scholar said that he tried to encourage original-
> ity in his students. In a graduate course, he told the class that the term paper

would be graded in terms of the amount of originality shown. One school teacher in the class was especially concerned about getting a high mark in the course. She took verbatim notes, continuously and assiduously, of what the learned professor said in class. Her term paper, the story goes, was essentially a stringing together of her transcribed lecture notes, in which the professor's pet ideas were given prominent place. It is reported that the professor read the term paper himself. When the school teacher's paper was returned, the professor's mark was *A,* with the added comment, "This is one of the most original papers I have ever read."

The anecdote illustrates the pitfall of all subjective judgment, including the teacher's—that we call original or creative those opinions and contributions most congenial to our own.

The Nature of Creativity

So much confusion surrounds the term *creativity* that it is most difficult to discuss and use it. Ausubel (1963a, pp. 99–100) believes that we should use it to refer to "rare and unique talent in a particular field of endeavor." He further states: "Creative achievement . . . reflects a rare capacity for developing insights, sensitivities, and appreciations in a circumscribed content area of intellectual or artistic activity." According to Ausubel, the creative individual who embodies this capacity is, by definition, an uncommon individual, much rarer than the intelligent person.

The following discussion on the nature of creativity will focus on three aspects: creative abilities, the learning or acquisition of these abilities, and their development and use in problem solving. For practical reasons the discussion will consider a low degree of creativity. To some extent everyone has the capacity for creative behavior, but few individuals will make scientific and artistic contributions which will achieve historical distinction.

Creative abilities   These abilities can be defined as the means the individual has for expressing whatever creativity he possesses. Guilford (1950, 1959, 1962) maintains that these abilities are somewhat general and can be applied to a variety of tasks. They are not associated with particular subject matter or disciplines. According to Guilford these abilities together constitute creative thinking. The distinctive aspect of creative thinking is divergent thinking, which is characterized by, among other things, flexibility, originality, and fluency. *Flexibility* is illustrated in Guilford's Unusual Uses Test by the divergent responses made to the word *brick.* The student is given this word and asked to list all the uses he can think of in eight minutes (Guilford, 1959). One student responds: build a house, build a barn, build a school, build a church, build a chimney, build a walk, and build a barbecue. All these responses belong to the same class of uses (construction) and show little flexibility or divergency. Another student responds: make a door stop, make a paperweight, throw it to a dog, make a bookcase, drown a cat, drive a nail, make a red powder, and use for baseball bases. The latter responses show more flexibility and, therefore, according to Guilford, give evidence of more divergent or creative thinking. *Originality* is illustrated by Guilford's Plot Title Test. A short story is presented, and the student is told to list as many appropriate titles as he can to head the story. One story is about the capture of a missionary by cannibals. The princess of the tribe wins a promise for his release if he will marry her. The choice is clear—death or the princess. The missionary refuses marriage and is boiled alive. One student responds with these titles: Defeat of a Princess, Eaten by Savages, The Princess, The Missionary, and Boiled by Savages. The second student responds: Pot's Plot, Potluck Dinner, Stewed Parson, Goil or Boil, A Mate Worse Than Death, He Left a Dish for a Pot, Chaste in Haste, and a Hot Price for Freedom. Guilford calls the responses of the second student more original (clever) than those of the first student. *Fluency* simply refers to the quantity of output. When asked, for example, to produce a list of items of information of a certain kind, some students produce many more items than others do. The sheer volume of output increases the probability that some responses will be divergent. Guilford contrasts *divergent* and *convergent* thinking. Divergent thinking produces a variety of responses. Convergent thinking produces the single correct answer.

James Gallagher (1964) showed how the questions a teacher asks determine the kind of thinking the student does. In teaching *Hamlet* the teacher may ask, "Explain why Hamlet rejected Ophelia." The student may go through this convergent thinking process in answering this question: Hamlet became disillusioned with all women. Ophelia was a woman. Hamlet rejected Ophelia. The teacher, however, could stimulate divergent thinking by asking these questions: What other ways could Hamlet have used to trap the king? What other courses of action might have been open to Hamlet's mother? Suppose Polonius had not been killed; how would that have modified or changed the eventual outcome of the play?

According to Getzels and Jackson (1962), divergent thinking tends to be stimulus free, while convergent thinking is stimulus bound. To illustrate this point these researchers asked students to respond to a picture of a man reclining in an airplane seat on his return from a business trip or professional conference. The stimulus-bound student constructed this story (p. 39):

> Mr. Smith is on his way home from a successful business trip. He is very happy and he is thinking about his wonderful family and how glad he will be to see them again. He can picture it, about an hour from now, his plane landing at the airport and Mrs. Smith and their children all there welcoming him home again.

The less inhibited, stimulus-free (and presumably more creative) student constructed this story (p. 39):

> This man is flying back from Reno, where he has just won a divorce from his wife. He couldn't stand to live with her anymore, he told the judge, because she wore so much cold cream on her face at night that her head would skid across the pillow and hit him in the head. He is now contemplating a new skidproof face cream.

In both cases the student had four minutes to produce his story. Whereas the first student produced a story of a very conventional family reunion, the second student produced a much more modern story about weird incompatibility and divorce. The latter story shows more divergent thinking than the former story does.

Creativity and learning The major educational question concerns the possibility of developing whatever creative abilities the student may have. Before we can engage in programs designed to produce this result, we must know whether training (or teaching) can increase creativity. Maltzman and his associates (1958, 1960) carried out a series of experiments based on the assumption that training could increase originality. Maltzman preferred the term *originality* to creativity because he could define originality simply in terms of unusual or uncommon verbal responses without engaging in the debate over whether these responses were creative or only bizarre. In these experiments the learning conditions were arranged to increase the student's output of original responses. In theory, Maltzman tried to raise a response low in the student's response hierarchy to higher positions in the hierarchy. In one experiment he used the five different groups and training conditions summarized in Table 11-3. All the groups began their training with a twenty-five–word list called the *training list*. These words evoked relatively few different responses in a period of free association during which the student had to respond as quickly as possible with the first word which came to mind. At the end of the training all the groups were given a test list of the same length and with the same kind of words to find out if the experimental treatment had increased the originality of the responses. All groups were also given Guilford's Unusual Uses Test.

The types of training for the five groups varied. Group C (the control

A DESCRIPTION OF THE TRAINING PROCEDURE FOR CONTROL AND EXPERIMENTAL GROUPS IN AN EXPERIMENT ON ORIGINALITY TRAINING (after Maltzman et al., 1960) — **TABLE 11-3**

	GROUP	FIRST LIST RECEIVED	TRAINING PROCEDURE	LAST LIST RECEIVED
CONTROL	C	Training list	None	Test list
	C_R	Training list	Training list five times and gave same response	Test list
	X	Training list	Training list five times and gave different response	Test list
EXPERIMENTAL	X_H	Training list	Five lists of uncommon words	Test list
	X_L	Training list	Five lists of common words	Test list

group) received no training. Group C_R was presented with the training list five additional times and asked to give the same responses each time—a treatment obviously designed to inhibit original responses. The three experimental groups were treated as follows: Group X was also given the training list five additional times, but this group was to give different responses each time. Group X_H was given five new lists of high-frequency (common) words and asked to respond to each word as quickly as possible. Group X_L received five lists of low-frequency (uncommon) words and asked to respond as quickly as possible. Maltzman found that group X had the highest originality scores—members of this group gave the greatest number of uncommon responses to the words in the test list. Group X_L did next best. As you might expect, group C_R was the least original. Group X also did best on the Unusual Uses Test. On the basis of this research we can conclude that asking students to produce different responses to the same stimulus does increase originality. To the extent that this procedure is effective, we can say that originality is one form of learned behavior. Through learning, as defined in this experiment, it is possible to increase student originality.

Creativity and problem solving   Many writers discuss creativity as creative thinking or problem solving. Torrance and his associates (1960), for example, define creative thinking as the process of "sensing gaps or disturbing or missing elements; forming ideas or hypotheses concerning them; testing these hypotheses; and communicating the results, possibly modifying and retesting the hypotheses." Gagné (1970) also considers creativity to be a form of problem solving which involves intuitive leaps, or a combining of ideas from widely separated fields of knowledge. Gagné (p. 228) gives this example:

> An excellent example of such inventiveness is provided by the kinetic theory of gases. What was known, on the one hand, was a set of principles concerning the behavior of gases, the relations among the variables of temperature, pressure, and volume. On the other hand there were the laws of motion, the effects of force in imparting acceleration to objects of specified mass. The stroke of genius in this case was one of hypothesizing that the gas was composed of particles (molecules) that had mass and whose reactions to force could therefore be considered to obey the laws of motion.

The consequences that follow from this single new synthesizing idea, a remarkable higher-order rule, permit the confirmation of the theory. But the central idea itself was arrived at by putting together subordinate rules from two widely disparate systems of organized knowledge. A problem of this magnitude had to be solved by combining two sets of rules that originally seemed to have only the remotest connection with each other.

The autobiographical sketches in a volume edited by Brewster Ghiselin (1955) provide several examples of these intuitive leaps of genius. In one selection, the French mathematician, Jules Henri Poincaré, describes this experience (p. 36):

For fifteen days I strove to prove that there could not be any functions like those I have since called Fuchsian functions. I was then very ignorant; every day I seated myself at my work table, stayed an hour or two, tried a great number of combinations and reached no results. One evening, contrary to my custom, I drank black coffee and could not sleep. Ideas rose in crowds; I felt them collide until parts interlocked, so to speak, to make a stable combination. By the next morning I had established the existence of a class of Fuchsian functions, those which come from the hypergeometric series; I had only to write out the results, which took but a few hours.

Unfortunately, in reading these accounts, individuals have emphasized (1) the emotional aspects of the experience—the sudden illumination, the heightened excitement, the esthetic appeal of an idea which has suddenly taken shape, and (2) the accidents of the experience—the drinking of black coffee, the musing under the apple tree, and the simple bathing in a bathtub, as in the case of Archimedes. What is not emphasized often enough are two other factors: These insights which suddenly bridge seemingly unrelated bodies of knowledge can only occur in individuals who have acquired the prerequisite knowledge, and they are often the result of concentrated effort over long periods of time. Creativity, at this level, is advanced problem solving. It is very doubtful that any teacher could deliberately foster such creativity. Although brilliant professors often have brilliant students who carry on for them, whatever the alchemy of these relationships may be, they are not within the grasp of most students and most teachers. When we discuss the fostering of creativity in the next section of the chapter, we are not outlining a program which will create Poincarés or Hemingways.

Instruction for Creativity

In this section, *fostering creativity* refers only to the development of the creative abilities described earlier. That is, the teacher can provide certain conditions which will increase the flexibility, fluency, and originality of the student's solutions to various problems. This term does not refer to ways for developing genuinely new knowledge and new discoveries. In effect, in this section of the chapter, we are viewing creativity as high-order problem solving which may require instructional supports in addition to those already described for the problem solving discussed in the first half of the chapter. The distinction here between the two types of problem solving is not a very clear one, but it may be clear enough to use as a basis for presenting some of the educational research on creativity.

Classify the kind of problems you present to students Getzels (1964) distinguishes between presented problems and discovered problems. Presented problems are those which are given to the student. Discovered problems are those which exist and must be discovered by the student. Getzels also distinguishes between known and unknown methods of solving problems. Using this classification scheme, he believes that creative thinking begins with situations in which the problem is presented but the method of solution is unknown to the student. From here we can move to the situation in which both the problem and the method of solution are unknown to the student and all of humanity. The less that is known in the problem situation the more the student must create. In the first half of this chapter we limited our consideration to those situations in which the problem is known but the solution is unknown only to the student, not to others. In Getzels' scheme, this would be the lowest level of creativity. It may very well be that the auxiliary problem-solving conditions outlined here apply primarily to those situations in which the student knows neither the problem nor the standard method of solving it. Surely, under such conditions, the student requires considerable assistance from the teacher even though the exact nature of that assistance may not be clear. In any case, you can classify the problems you expect your students to solve by using the scheme developed by Getzels.

Provide for the development and use of problem-solving skills A body of research indicates the usefulness of certain techniques and skills in creative problem solving. The most popular technique is *brainstorming* (Osborne, 1957), which had its first flowering in the business world but has now made its way into the classroom—especially the college classroom. As used in the classroom, after the problem has been presented, the teacher requires the students to list as many solutions as they can think of. Any evaluation of these ideas is deferred until all the solutions are listed. The technique is a form of free association, except that it is often used with groups and it is ideas rather than words that are freely associated. Sidney Parnes and Arnold Meadow (1959, 1960, 1961, 1962) have made the most extensive study of the possible usefulness of brainstorming for problem solving. Their findings can be briefly summarized: (1) Training in brainstorming increases creative problem solving; (2) brainstorming produces more problem solutions than do methods which penalize bad ideas in some way; (3) more good ideas are produced with brainstorming than with conventional techniques; (4) extended effort to produce ideas (the latter part of the brainstorming sessions) leads to an increased number of ideas and proportions of good ideas; and (5) students in creative problem-solving courses (which include brainstorming) obtain higher scores in Guilford's tests of creative abilities than do students who have not had these courses.

Contrary evidence disputes some of these findings. Donald Taylor and his associates (1958) found that individuals who worked in groups using the brainstorming technique actually produced ideas which were considerably inferior in quantity and quality to the ideas produced by individuals who worked alone. Torrance (1961) found that directions to produce as many ideas as possible without regard to quality resulted in fewer responses than did directions to produce interesting, clever, and unusual ideas.

These somewhat conflicting findings make it difficult to determine under what conditions you should use brainstorming. Although originally devised as a method for producing large numbers of ideas by postponing to a later time the evaluation or criticism of them, brainstorming may be useful in ways which better fit the context of this chapter. It may be a way of assessing the entering behavior of the student since the responses he emits first are probably those which have the greatest strength in his response hierarchy. Persistence in brainstorming, at least theoretically, could ultimately evoke responses of comparatively low hierarchical strength. Brainstorming may also be a way (not necessarily the best way) of invoking recall of concepts and principles necessary for the solution of a problem. It is difficult to understand, however, how this technique can be successful when the students lack the knowledge necessary for the problem solution or when the responses have so little hierarchical strength that they require explicit reinforcement to be successfully applied. Deferring evaluation of the ideas also defers reinforcement. And, by dredging up several ideas when only one or two are useful in solving a given problem, brainstorming may increase the student's difficulty in selecting those ideas which apply to the problem solution. By a combination of proactive and retroactive inhibition the useless ideas interfere with the retention of the useful ideas. Where the teacher finds a great dearth of ideas, however, brainstorming may enable students to pool what little knowledge they have and proceed together from there.

Teaching certain basic *research skills* may be a second technique for fostering creativity. This technique is consistent with Torrance's definition of creative thinking as forming and testing hypotheses. Torrance and R. E. Myers (1963) taught a course in educational research to gifted sixth grade students. The students learned some basic methods of research in the behavioral sciences, including the formulation and testing of hypotheses. The course took several days. On the first day the students played the guessing game "What Is in the Box?" After they arrived at the solution, they outlined the steps of the research process which had led them to it. On ensuing days they participated in three kinds of research projects—historical, descriptive, and experimental. Finally, they carried out an experiment of their own. After these experiences the students were given a test on the basic research principles they had been taught. Although Torrance and Myers report no data, they concluded that the students had a good grasp of basic principles.

Creative reading is another useful problem-solving skill. Torrance and Judson Harmon (1961) have provided some evidence that students can be taught to read creatively with the proper directions and the encouragement to use these directions. In this study, students received these directions (or particular set to read) (p. 208):

When you read, it is important that you think about the many possible uses of the information which you are reading. It is especially important that you think of various ways in which the information could be used in your personal and professional life. In reading, do not just ask, "What is the author saying?" Also ask, "How can I use what the author is saying?" Do not stop with just one use. Think of as many uses as you can of the important ideas presented. Jot down some of their uses for future reference or action. It may take some practice before you are really successful in assuming this set, or attitude, toward your reading, but do not be discouraged. By the third day, you should find it easy to assume this set.

This study also divided students into two groups and asked them to read research reports. One group was to read the reports critically, the other creatively. The critical group had to think of (1) the defects in the statement of the problem and their importance; (2) the underlying assumptions of the hypotheses studied; (3) the procedures for collecting and analyzing data; (4) the conclusions and interpretations of the findings; and (5) a critical appraisal of the worth of the research. The creative group had to think of (1) new possibilities suggested by the statement of the problem; (2) other possible hypotheses related to the problem and its solution; (3) improvements which could have been made in the collection of the data; (4) other possible conclusions and interpretations of the findings; and (5) an appraisal of the possibilities stemming from the findings. Students in both groups were later required to perform a research project of their own. Those in the creative group were judged to have produced more new and creative ideas of their own than did students in the critical group. No report indicates whether the creative group also produced more bad ideas. The import of these findings and others like them is that teachers should encourage students to suspend their critical functions and to use instead various creative functions. One can well imagine that a student who read the reports both critically and creatively (asking himself both sets of questions) could gain more than students in either group.

The utilization of certain reading sets and research skills may have the distinct advantage of helping the student to identify with the researcher and the writer and to begin to see the many alternatives available in making scientific and literary decisions. The consideration of alternatives, of course, can considerably complicate the learning of any subject matter, and it is often reserved for advanced college classes, gifted students, or the graduate schools. The primary consideration, however, must be the entering behavior of the student. A student who learns what is happening in *Hamlet* may be in the position to see how it could have all been different and even less tragic. When encouraged to think creatively about the play, a student who has not learned what is happening can only impose his less informed and poetic fantasies upon those which Shakespeare has woven with considerably more skill. No one stands to gain—Shakespeare, the student, or even the teacher, who must hear all over again a version of Shakespeare which is more like *Peanuts* than *Hamlet*.

Reward creative achievement   The teacher may not reinforce creative achievement because he fails to recognize it, despises the behavior which accompanies creativity in his students, or is overawed by any classroom manifestation of creativity. Torrance (1960, 1965) lists five ways in which the teacher can encourage and reward creative achievement. You, as the teacher, should (1) treat unusual questions which the children ask with respect; (2) treat unusual ideas and solutions with respect; (3) show children that their ideas have value; (4) provide opportunities and give credit for self-initiated learning; and (5) provide chances for children to learn, think, and discover, without threat of immediate evaluation.

We have now concluded the third section of this chapter. You can see that we have been less explicit about the nature of creativity and instruction for creativity than we have been about the nature of and the instruction for other types of learning. Part of the difficulty is that creativity represents a new area of concern and research in American education and psychology. Few well-defined theoretical ideas or terms bind together the little research we presently have. This scientific confusion makes it difficult to apply the findings on creativity to teaching. Whether the teacher implements any of the suggestions for creative teaching which this chapter contains ought to be a decision based on the requirements of the learning situation and not on purely ideological grounds.

QUESTION 11-3

Three psychologists are discussing creativity and express three somewhat divergent views. Match the psychologist (and his view) with the alternatives below. Psychologist A: Divergent and convergent thinking seem to reflect typical and consistent patterns of cognitive behavior found in two different groups of individuals. Psychologist B: Creativity manifests itself in sensing gaps and missing elements. Psychologist C: By instructing students to think of new and even unique associations for various words, we can increase the number of unfamiliar associations.

(a) Creative abilities
(b) Creativity as learned behavior
(c) Creativity as problem solving

After selecting your answers, give the reasons for each one.

LEARNING BY DISCOVERY

Upon reading this section of the chapter, you should be able to meet these objectives:

11-22   Define discovery learning in terms of instructional guidance and in terms of giving or not giving the principle and the problem solution; distinguish (in these terms) between guided and unguided discovery.

11-23   Define inquiry training in terms of strategies and tactics and describe and illustrate the presentation and practice phases; distinguish (and illustrate the differences) between questions of information and verification and experimental questions.

11-24 Describe four teaching strategies in terms of three levels of thought (informational, inferential, and predictive).

11-25 Define expository teaching in terms of instructional guidance and in terms of the teacher's giving or not giving the principle and problem solution and distinguish between expository teaching and discovery learning.

11-26 List four advantages (Bruner's) for discovery learning in terms of intellectual potency, intrinsic motivation, techniques of discovery, and information storage.

11-27 Describe the instructional conditions under which, in the studies of Corman and of Gagné and Brown, problem solutions were most successful.

11-28 Describe four areas in which (according to Wittrock) discovery learning may be helpful.

11-29 List the advantages of expository teaching by referring to the selecting and organizing of subject matter and the learning of concepts and principles.

11-30 Describe the mixed method (Johnson and Stratton) by referring to the methods it includes and its effectiveness.

11-31 Describe and illustrate how programed instruction as represented by the Ruleg system is a form of expository teaching.

11-32 List unsupportable claims about discovery learning in terms of learning subject matter, developing creative and critical thinking, making the great discovery, and available research.

11-33 Describe the conditions under which discovery learning should be used by referring to the components of the basic teaching model.

In this final section of the chapter we shall consider some methods of problem solving which involve considerably less guidance than do the procedures we have already described. These methods, which often show remarkable variation, collectively bear the name *learning by discovery*. This section has the following parts: (1) a definition and examples of discovery learning; (2) a definition of expository teaching; (3) the rationale for and research on discovery learning; (4) the rationale for and research on expository teaching; and (5) a critique of discovery learning.

Definition and Examples of Discovery Learning

Unfortunately there has been considerable confusion over whether learning by discovery refers to (1) a method of teaching, (2) a method of learning, or (3) something you learn (Wittrock, 1966). Even when there is agreement that it is something you learn, it is not clear whether this "something" refers to specific principles or problem solutions, the ability to solve many problems by the application of a single principle, a structure of knowledge in a given discipline, the technique of discovery, or simply interest in the satisfaction of the creative urge (Cronbach, 1966a, pp. 88–90). You can take your pick of these and many other outcomes.

In order to perform some useful pedagogical function with regard to discovery learning, we will adopt a particular definition of it. Discovery learning refers to those teaching situations in which the student achieves the instructional objective with limited or no guidance from the teacher. The chief characteristic is the amount of guidance the teacher provides (Kersh and Wittrock, 1962). Wittrock (1963) developed a useful scheme for classifying the amounts of instructional guidance the teacher may provide in problem solution: (1) The teacher may give the principle and the problem solution—a situation which we later call *expository teaching;* (2) the teacher may give the principle which applies but not give the problem solution; (3) the teacher may not give the principle but give the problem solution; and (4) the teacher may give neither the principle which applies nor the solution to the problem—a situation which we shall describe as *unguided discovery*. Between expository teaching, in which the principle and solution are both given, and unguided discovery, in which neither the principle nor the solution is given, we have an intermediate area often described as *guided discovery*. The procedures which we examined for problem solving fall into this intermediate zone. The teacher assists in the recall and the application of the relevant principles—in this sense he gives the principles but not the solution of the problem. Unfortunately, discussions of discovery teaching often fail to make Witttrock's distinctions and the term is often identified solely with the teaching situation which we described as unguided discovery.

Teaching strategies Other research programs have attempted to enlarge the teacher's role in discovery learning and even to provide special training for the teacher to enact this role. Taba and her associates (1964b), using a social studies curriculum for the elementary schools, studied the effects of various teaching strategies on thought processes. The curriculum was organized as series of basic ideas the children were to learn and apply in a variety of contexts. Taba's major objective was to teach thinking rather than substantive knowledge. She classified thinking (or thought) as occurring at three levels: The first and lowest level is the grouping and labeling of information; the second level is interpreting information and making inferences; and the third and highest level is predicting consequences. Taba believed that these levels describe specific thought processes the student must master in sequential order. When introducing new subject matter, the teacher must recycle the student through the three levels of thought.

The teacher employs four teaching strategies in this recycling process: (1) He provides focusing, which establishes both the topic and the particular angle for its treatment. For example, the teacher makes this statement: "If the desert had all the water it needed, what would happen?" In this way the teacher focuses the ensuing discussion. (2) The teacher extends the thought at the same level. He does this by giving or seeking information or by providing elaboration or clarification on already established thought levels. (3) The teacher lifts the thought to a higher level. He may do this, for example, by asking why something occurs—in this case giving information (the first level) is raised to explanation (the second level). (4) Finally, the teacher controls thought by assigning a cognitive task for the student to perform. In effect, this final strategy constitutes an expository rather than a discovery mode of teaching. The teacher is classifying information, making inferences, and predicting consequences.

In Taba's program the emphasis is on the acquisition of techniques of problem solving, not on the acquisition of substantive knowledge. Taba allowed the teacher to perform a variety of functions in response to the student's needs as evidenced in the quality of verbalized thought. Unfortunately, Taba employed her techniques almost exclusively with groups, so that we do not know how the effectiveness relates to variations in the entering behavior of the students. In any case, you now have an example of discovery learning. The method provides less instructional guidance than do the steps for teaching problem solving, as described earlier in this chapter.

Definition of Expository Teaching

Using Wittrock's classification of teaching methods (1963, p. 469), we may define expository teaching as the situation in which the teacher gives both the principles and the problem solutions. In contrast to his role in discovery learning, the teacher presents the student with the entire content of what is to be learned in final form (Ausubel, 1963a, 1968); the student is not required to make any independent discoveries. The usual verbal instruction of the lecture hall exemplifies expository teaching. It is sometimes called *deductive teaching* because the teacher often begins with a definition of the concepts or principles, illustrates them, and unfolds their implications. Although expository teaching is a widespread and traditional teaching practice in our schools and colleges, it has attracted very little research (Carroll, 1964). Ausubel (1963a, 1968) believes that the reason for the lack of research is that expository teaching has been identified with rote learning. The students, presumably, can only memorize the lectures by constant review and repetition. Indeed, it is possible to present a body of material so poorly that unless the students commit it to rote memory (as in the case of nonsense syllables), they have no way of remembering it. Expository teaching, however, can present a rich body of highly related facts, concepts, and principles which the students can learn and transfer. Textbooks are examples of expository teaching, and, as you very well know, they can vary in their methods of teaching subject matter and in their organization of that subject matter.

As in the case of discovery learning, it is probably difficult to find pure examples of expository teaching. In most classes we find a combination of lectures (or teacher explanation) and discussions or lectures and laboratory and field work. In these situations, although most of the instruction is under the direct guidance of the instructor, much of it is the more or less independent effort of the student.

Perhaps the most eloquent defender of learning by discovery is Bruner. In an early article, "Art of Discovery," Bruner (1961) claimed four advantages of discovery learning. First, discovery learning increases intellectual potency. The student acquires information in such a way that it is readily available in problem solving. Second, discovery learning increases intrinsic motivation. It strengthens the student's tendency to carry out his learning activities with the autonomy of self-reward or the reward of discovery itself. Third, discovery learning teaches the student the techniques of discovery. Solving problems through discovery develops a style of problem solving or inquiry that serves for any task—or almost any task—one may encounter. The student improves his technique of inquiry by engaging in inquiry. Finally, discovery learning results in better retention of what is learned because the student has organized his own information and knows where (in his own storage system) to find the information when he needs it. We shall examine some of Bruner's claims below.

Research on discovery learning has provided information on the effects of different types and amounts of instructional guidance. Bernard Corman (1957), using Katona's matchstick problems, studied the effects of various amounts of guidance on the learning, application, and verbalization of the principle and the method required to solve the problems. He used three degrees of guidance: providing no information, some information, and much information about the relevant principle and method. He obtained, in general, the following results: (1) As the amount of information about the principle increased, the successful learning (simple acquisition) of the principle increased; (2) although the amount of information did not affect the verbalization (writing) of the method, students who received information about the principle (either some or much) verbalized the principle better than did students who received no information; (3) giving information was more effective than withholding it as far as application of the principle to new matchstick problems was concerned, although this effect varied with the level of student ability, the difficulty of the problems, and the amount of information (much or some) provided about the principle. Corman concluded that guidance facilitated the learning and application of principles and methods and that withholding guidance could impede problem solutions.

In a study by Gagné and Larry Brown (1961) hints were given about the solution of the problem rather than about the method of solving the problem. The students learned, through programed instruction, two principles involved in the solution of number-series problems. All students received an introductory program which began with the following item (p. 315):

Here is a series of numbers: 1 3 5 7 9 11 13 _____ _____.
What are the next two numbers in this series? _____ _____.

In the introductory program all students learned the prerequisite principles (term value and term number) for the solution of various number-series problems. Then the students were divided into three groups: (1) The rule-and-example group was given the correct formula for the solution of the number-series problems with which they were presented and a number of examples of the rule—a teaching procedure known as the Ruleg system (see below). (2) The discovery group, after a few introductory number-series items, was abruptly asked to state the principle for the solution of these problems. If they needed hints, they were directed to the next cards, which focused their attention on important relationships between the numbers and provided progressively more complete guidance. (3) The guided-discovery group began with the same introductory problems and was taken through a series of steps which helped them state a general principle for the solution of the problems. As measures of terminal performance, a problem-solving test was administered which comprised four new number-series problems for which the students had to find the correct formula. Records were kept of the amount of time needed to solve each problem, the number of hints employed on the test, and the incorrect answers. The best performance scores were obtained by the guided-discovery group, the worst by the rule-and-example group, with the discovery group falling between the other two. Gagné and Brown concluded that what is learned is more important than how it is learned. They state (p. 320):

> Discovery as a method appears to gain its effectiveness from the fact that it requires the individual learner to reinstate (and in this sense, to practice) the concepts he will later use in solving new problems. To the extent that the GD (guided discovery) program was able to identify these concepts, it could then provide systematic practice in their use, and thus lead to a performance superior to that attained otherwise. The practice provided by the R&E [rule-and-example] program, in contrast, did not *require* the use of these essential concepts (although it permitted it). Accordingly, it led to distinctly inferior problem-solving performance.

Other (and most) experiments on discovery learning have stacked the cards against expository teaching (Cronbach, 1966a). Kersh and Wittrock (1962) observe that most of these studies provide opportunities for reinforced practice following the treatment period. With sufficient amounts of reinforced practice, almost any teaching method will work. Cronbach (1966a, p. 90) believes that discovery teaching is seldom superior to expository teaching for putting across single principles. He continues to hope, however, that discovery learning "has special power to make a practicing intellectual out of the student." To confer this benefit, discovery teaching requires a long-term effort with intellectually respectable subject matter. Wittrock (1966) suggests that learning by discovery may prove to be effective in the learning of concepts and subject matter which have been organized into learning structures. It may also be effective in applying concepts to the learning of new concepts, in developing originality, and in teaching the techniques of discovery. He acknowledges, however, that his statements are hypotheses which await experimental verification.

Ausubel (1963a, p. 19) provides one of the best defenses of expository teaching:

> The art and science of presenting ideas and information meaningfully and effectively—so that clear, stable, and unambiguous meanings emerge and are retained over a long period of time as an organized body of knowledge—is really the principal function of pedagogy. This is a demanding and creative rather than a routine and mechanical task. The job of selecting, organizing, presenting, and translating subject-matter content in a developmentally appropriate manner requires more than the rote listing of facts. If it is done properly it is the work of the master teacher and is hardly a task to be disdained. . . . Beginning in the junior high school period, students acquire most new concepts and learn most new propositions by *directly* grasping higher-order relationships between abstractions. To do so meaningfully, they need no longer depend on current or recently prior concrete-empirical experience, and hence are able to bypass completely the intuitive type of understanding reflective of such dependence. Through proper expository teaching they can proceed directly to a level of abstract understanding that is qualitatively superior to the intuitive level in terms of generality, clarity, precision, and explicitness. At this state of development, therefore, it seems pointless to enhance intuitive understanding by using discovery technics.

To these advantages Carroll (1964) adds others. Expository teaching is more popular in our schools today because it is more efficient and takes less time than discovery learning. When combined with practice, it is very successful in teaching concepts and principles. Expository teaching offers the student the best opportunity to obtain an organized view of the discipline he is studying because the teacher can organize the field much more effectively for learning than the novice student can. In discovery learning the concern to teach the techniques of discovery overrides the concern for learning the unifying principles of a discipline.

We have pointed out that there is little research on expository teaching. We have already noted Ausubel's use of advance organizers in expository teaching (p. 448). Donald Johnson and Paul Stratton (1966) compared several methods of expository teaching with the usual inductive method of teaching concepts in three expository programs, one discovery program, and one mixed program set up as follows: (1) Students were given definitions of terms, similar to those one finds in the dictionary although each term was related to a higher-order class. Then the students were required to write their own definitions of the terms. (2) The term was used in sentences which were part of a short story. After reading the story, the student was asked to complete a sentence which required the use of the term. (3) Students were given synonyms for the new term—"alacrity means eagerness" and "altercation means squabble." (4) In the classification approach, students were given examples of objects and events and were asked to classify them. The students had to discover the correct categories. (5) A mixed problem was constructed out of materials in the four preceding approaches. This is an example of instruction using the mixed method (p. 51):

> To chide someone is to talk to him to get him to correct his mistakes. Chide means to criticize or reproach. Thus a mother might chide her children for fighting with each other. An example might be a group of fellows poking fun at a boy with dirty clothes. Now write in your words what chide means. [This was followed by one block of synonyms for matching and one block of events for classification, with correct answers.]

The students who were taught with the mixed method did better than those in all the other groups. The experimenters (p. 53) concluded that the "superiority of the mixed program supports the common practice of teachers and textbooks."

Programed instruction is a form of expository teaching, especially when the Ruleg sequence is used (Glaser, 1966). In the Ruleg sequence, the student is presented with an explicit statement of the rule (or principle) followed by one or more carefully chosen examples. He is then presented with one or more incomplete examples, which act as prompts to reduce the possibility of incorrect responses. The incomplete examples also provide the student with the reinforcing activity of directly employing the rule. In comparing the Ruleg system with discovery (or inductive) teaching and learning, Glaser (1966, p. 16) states:

> This philosophy leads to the rejection of inductive presentation. With a rule-example sequence, the student can recognize and apply a rule with proficiency, and often it seems hazardous and slow to approach a rule through induction or through incidental learning. With rule and then example, the student adopts the expert's carefully chosen statement of a rule rather than using his own, more fallible induction-derived statement. The limited range of exemplars in most teaching and textbook situations may make it possible for the student to induce what is essentially an incorrect rule but one which happens to fit all the examples presented. This is another possible source of danger in the inductive process.

The rule-example technique is very frequently used in teaching. The teacher provides the student with a general statement of the principle and then offers a series of illustrations. Glaser suggests that this procedure is widely used because it leads to rapid reinforcement for both teacher and student.

Critique of Discovery Learning

An eloquent indictment of learning by discovery has been made by Ausubel (1963a, p. 139):

> Learning by discovery also has its own elaborate mystique. Its legitimate uses and advantages have been unwarrantedly extrapolated to include both educational goals and levels of intellectual maturity, levels of subject-matter sophistica-

tion, and levels of cognitive functioning for which it is ill-adapted—and for reasons which derive from sheer dogmatic assertion; from pseudonaturalistic conceptions about the nature and conditions of intellectual development; from outmoded ideas about the relationship between language and thought; from sentimental fantasies about the nature of the child and the aims of education; and from uncritical interpretations of the research evidence.

Ausubel believes that the adherents of discovery learning make several unsupportable claims. Among these are the following: that the discovery method is the best method for transmitting subject matter; that problem solving is the primary goal of education; that there can be training in the techniques of discovery; that every child can become a critical and creative thinker; that expository teaching is authoritarian; and that discovery methods are unique generators of motivation and self-confidence. Ausubel believes that the primary purpose of teaching is to present in some systematic way an organized body of knowledge. The organization should be explicit and given in explicit form to the student. He does not believe that you can teach creative thinking and critical thinking outside the context of a specific discipline. Such thinking, he contends (p. 158), can only be learned by "adopting a precise, logical, analytical, and critical approach to the teaching of a particular discipline, an approach which fosters appreciation of the scientific method in that discipline."

Gagné (1970) also repudiates the notion that a discovery method of learning if constantly used will finally result in the individual's making the great discovery. He wrote (p. 229):

So far as any present evidence is concerned, such a proposition is wishful thinking at best; at worst, it is mere verbal sophistry. The use of discovery as a method of learning rules, as we have seen, may lead to individual capabilities that are highly effective from the standpoint of generalizability, applicability, and retention. In other words, this method of learning may generate a solid basis of intellectual skills in the individual. Furthermore, because it is a method rich in reinforcement value, the solving of problems within structures of intellectual skills to be learned may create a love of learning, a "thirst for knowledge" in the individual learner. But it is a vastly different thing to suppose that this kind of learning will necessarily predispose the individual to become a "creative" thinker, capable of making a great contribution to science or art.

Cronbach (1966a, p. 91), at the conclusion of his consideration of experiments on discovery learning, addresses remarks to his fellow educational psychologists which can be appropriately heeded also by students of educational psychology and prospective teachers:

The educational psychologist is torn between two responsibilities. His responsibility as educational specialist is to give schools advice on matters where the evidence is pitifully limited. His responsibility as scientist is to insist on careful substantiation of claims for each educational innovation. In education, unfortunately, there is a great furor about whatever is announced as the latest trend, and the schools seem to career erratically after each Pied Piper in turn. This giddy chase keeps them almost beyond earshot of the researcher standing on his tiny, laboriously tamped patch of solid ground, crying in a pathetic voice, "Wait for me! Wait for me!"

Within the framework of this book and the basic teaching model it is possible to offer this critique of discovery learning. Intrinsic to our concept of teaching is the assumption that the selection of teaching procedures must be based on prior statements of instructional objectives and a description and assessment of the prerequisite entering behavior. The complex interrelationship among objectives, students, and procedures should make all a priori claims about the universal suitability of particular instructional procedures for all objectives and all students immediately questionable.

It seems highly preferable that our selection of teaching procedures be guided by the instructional objectives and the entering behavior of the student. The instructional objectives tell us what is to be learned and the type of learning involved. Descriptions of entering behavior tell us what the students need to know and what in fact they do know as they embark on the instruction which will lead them to achieving the objectives. Once we know the type of learning and the entering behavior, we can select instructional procedures which accommodate the necessary internal and external conditions of learning. Finally, with performance assessment, we have a ready source of feedback on the degree of success of our own and the students' efforts, and we can proceed to make the necessary adjustments among these instructional components. In practice the teacher may very well discover that purely expository or discovery methods of teaching cannot accommodate or provide all the learning conditions necessary for reaching particular instructional objectives. Indeed, a mixture of the two methods to produce guided-discovery teaching may often be the most suitable instructional method. For the teacher the realistic and scientifically sound question should always be "For what purposes and for which students and under what learning conditions should I employ any one method or combination of methods of instruction."

Summary

We have now completed our discussion of discovery learning, the fourth section of this chapter. There we defined learning by discovery and compared it with expository teaching. We presented two examples of relatively unguided discovery teaching. And we looked at the rationales for both expository and discovery teaching and considered some of the available research. The conclusion we arrived at is that a mixture of the two methods (or guided discovery) will often prove to be more practical and effective than strict adherence to one method. The particular mixture we arrive at ought to be determined by the objective requirements of the instructional situation: the instructional objectives, the entering behavior of the student, and the materials and procedures required by the external learn-ing conditions. The step sequences described for the teaching of concepts, principles, and problem solving represent a mixture of expository and discovery teaching based on at least one view of the objective requirements of instructional situations.

363

Which of the following combinations of conditions, concerning instructional objectives and entering behavior, describes the best conditions for the use of discovery learning? **QUESTION 11-4**

(a) When the instructional objective pertains to basic, skill, or verbal learning and entering behavior shows the prerequisite learning.

(b) When the instructional objective pertains to the learning of techniques of discovery and expository teaching has proven unsuccessful.

(c) When the instructional objective pertains to concept or principle learning or to problem solving and the assessment of entering behavior indicates that the students have the prerequisite entering behavior.

(d) When the instructional objective pertains to the development of originality (or creativity) in problem solving and the assessment of entering behavior indicates de-ficiencies in knowledge of prerequisite principles.

(e) When there is no explicit instructional objective and assessment of entering be-havior indicates that students have little exploratory and manipulative motivation.

After selecting your answer, give the reasons for your choice and for your rejection of the alternatives.

SUMMARY

The first section of this chapter considered the nature of problem solving. Three interrelated conceptions of problem solving were described. First, as the most complex type of learning we consider in this book, problem solving is the application of lower-order principles to attain higher-order principles. Thus, like the other forms of learning considered in Part 3 of this book, problem solving results in the true acquisition of knowledge. Second, we viewed problem solving in terms of the habit family hierarchy whose response members, in this case, are principles which vary in response strength. Principles can also be hierarchies embedded in compound habit family hierarchies. Finally, we viewed problem solving as positive transfer of learning in which the second in a series of two tasks serves as the prob-lem. The transfer view underscores an important characteristic of this type of learning: Successful problem solving results in learning of high gen-eralizability and transferability—in learning of higher-order principles of wide applicability.

The second section dealt with the steps you should take in teaching problem solving. Like the step for the previous learning, these steps cor-respond to the components of the basic teaching model. First, you should describe for the students the terminal performance which constitutes the solution to the problem (instructional objective). Second, you must assess their entering behavior for the concepts and principles required in the problem solution. Third, you must invoke recall of all relevant concepts and principles. In this step, which deals with instructional procedures, you can use advance organizers—concepts and principles which mediate the problem solution. Fourth (also a part of procedures), you should provide verbal direction of the students' thinking, short of giving them the solution to the problem. Fifth (as part of performance assessment), you should verify the students' learning by requiring them to give a full demonstration of the problem solution, using other problems of the same class.

The third section dealt with instruction for creativity. In describing the nature of creativity, we examined creative abilities and the tests of these abilities, creativity as learned behavior, and the relationship between creativity and problem solving. In considering instruction for creativity, we provided several guidelines (but not steps): (1) classifying the kind of problems you present to students, (2) providing for the development and use of problem-solving skills, such as brainstorming, research skills, and creative reading, and (3) rewarding creative achievement.

The fourth section dealt with learning by discovery. Discovery learning was defined as those teaching situations in which the student achieves the instructional objective with little or no help from the teacher. Two examples of discovery learning which provided minimal guidance—inquiry training and teaching strategies—were described. We then considered the rationale and research on discovery learning, and we saw that the results are quite inconclusive although, under certain conditions, it may be an effective means of learning concepts, originality, and discovery techniques. We also considered the rationale of and the research on expository teaching. Earlier, we defined expository teaching as the situation in which the teacher gives both the principles and the problem solutions. Expository teaching, in the opinion of several educational psychologists, has much to recommend it, particularly for the clarity and organization with which subject matter can be presented, the certainty of its results, and the time it saves both teacher and students. Some of the research reported in this chapter (Corman, Gagné and Brown, and Johnson and Stratton) also suggests that discovery teaching and expository teaching can usefully combine to produce a general method of teaching, *guided discovery*. We pointed out that programed instruction is a type of expository teaching. Critiques of discovery learning suggest that it has become a pedagogical mystique (Ausubel), that it will not, as claimed, predispose individuals to become great discoverers (Gagné), and that it is far from being an educational panacea (Cronbach). Rather than reject or accept discovery learning on a priori grounds, you should use a much sounder and more scientific basis for your decision: "For what purposes and for which students and under what learning conditions should I employ any one method or combination of methods of instruction?"

This chapter also concludes Part 3 of this book. Our concern here has been the design of instructional procedures appropriate for the internal and external learning conditions. The basic learning conditions were described as well as the special conditions required by the types of learning considered in the various chapters: classical conditioning, operant conditioning, skill learning, verbal learning, concept learning, principle learning, and problem solving.

SUGGESTED READINGS

These books of readings contain some of the major theoretical discussions and research on problem solving:

ANDERSON, RICHARD C., and AUSUBEL, DAVID P., *Readings in the Psychology of Cognition.* New York: Holt, Rinehart & Winston, Inc., 1965.

AUSUBEL, DAVID P., *Educational Psychology: A Cognitive View.* New York: Holt, Rinehart & Winston, Inc., 1968.

DE CECCO, JOHN P., *Human Learning in the School: Readings in Educational Psychology.* New York: Holt, Rinehart & Winston, Inc., 1963.

————, *Psychology of Language, Thought and Instruction: Readings.* New York: Holt, Rinehart & Winston, Inc., 1967.

HARRIS, THEODORE L., and SCHWAHN, WILSON E., *Selected Readings on the Learning Process.* New York: Oxford University Press, Inc., 1961.

The articles in these collections of particular relevance to the contents of this chapter are the following (the journal citations for these articles are given in the list of references at the end of the book):

DUNCAN, CARL P. (1959), "Recent Research on Human Problem Solving" (in De Cecco, 1963).

MAIER, NORMAN R. F. (1930), "Reasoning in Humans. I. On Directions" (in Harris and Schwahn).

MALTZMAN, IRVING (1950), "Thinking: From a Behavioristic Point of View" (in Anderson and Ausubel and in De Cecco, 1967).

SCHULZ, RUDOLPH W. (1960), "Problem Solving and Transfer" (in Anderson and Ausubel, 1965).

These books and articles on problem solving include the material of this chapter but often give a more intensive discussion:

GAGNÉ, ROBERT M., "Problem Solving," in *Categories of Human Learning,* ed. A. W. Melton, pp. 294–317. New York: Academic Press Inc., 1966.

KATONA, GEORGE, *Organizing and Memorizing: Studies in the Psychology of Learning and Teaching.* New York: Columbia University Press, 1940.

WERTHEIMER, MAX, *Productive Thinking,* 2nd ed. New York: Harper & Row, Publishers, 1959. This book examines thinking from a view which is much more cognitive than that of this chapter.

This book gives an excellent summary of the theory and research on transfer of learning, with implications for teaching:

ELLIS, HENRY, *The Transfer of Learning.* New York: The Macmillan Company, 1965 (paperback). Also contains several major research articles.

Of the several books and articles on creativity and creative thinking the following may be of particular interest to prospective and active teachers:

GETZELS, JACOB W., "Creative Thinking, Problem-Solving, and Instruction," in *Theories of Learning and Instruction,* ed. E. R. Hilgard. The Sixty-third Yearbook of the National Society for the Study of Education, Chicago, 1964.

——, and JACKSON, PHILIP W., *Creativity and Intelligence.* New York: John Wiley & Sons, Inc., 1962.

MALTZMAN, IRVING, "On the Training of Originality," *Psychological Review,* 67 (1960), 229–42 (also in Anderson and Ausubel and in De Cecco, 1963).

PARNES, SIDNEY J., and HARING, HAROLD F., eds., *Source Book for Creative Thinking.* New York: Charles Scribner's Sons, 1962.

TAYLOR, CALVIN W., and BARRON, FRANK, *Scientific Creativity: Its Recognition and Development.* New York: John Wiley & Sons, Inc., 1963.

TORRANCE, E. PAUL, *Guiding Creative Talent.* Englewood Cliffs, N.J.: Prentice-Hall, Inc., 1962 (paperback).

——, *Education and the Creative Potential.* Minneapolis: University of Minnesota Press, 1963.

——, *Creativity: What Research Says to the Teacher,* Pamphlet No. 28 of the Department of Classroom Teachers and American Research Association (NEA) Washington, D.C., 1963.

These books and articles contain research on and discussions of discovery learning:

AUSUBEL, DAVID P., *The Psychology of Meaningful Verbal Learning.* New York: Grune & Stratton, Inc., 1963.

BRUNER, JEROME S., "The Act of Discovery," *Harvard Educational Review,* 31 (1961), 21–32.

——; OLIVER, ROSE R.; GREENFIELD, PATRICIA M., et al., *Studies in Cognitive Growth.* New York: John Wiley & Sons, Inc., 1966.

KEISLAR, EVAN, and SHULMAN, L. M., eds., *Learning by Discovery.* Chicago: Rand McNally & Co., 1966.

KERSH, BERT Y., and WITTROCK, MERLIN C., "Learning by Discovery: An Interpretation of Recent Research," *Journal of Teacher Education,* 53 (1960), 571–75 (also in De Cecco, 1967).

CHAPTER TWELVE

INSTRUCTIONAL TECHNOLOGY

This chapter deals with instructional technology in both of its modern meanings. The first section is about programed instruction. Here you will learn how to prepare for program writing, how to write the program, and how to try out and revise the program. The available research is the basis for most of the recommendations made. Here we also describe the various programs and the standards for the selection of commercial programs. Upon completing this section you should have developed some competence in the programing of materials for your major teaching areas. The second and third sections of the chapter are shorter. In the second section you learn about instructional media, particularly the selection and use of films and television programs, and also about computer-assisted instruction and a wide array of audiovisual materials. In the third (and final) section you learn about flexible scheduling. Here we consider the use of modules and modular units in place of the traditional class periods; models of team teaching for content areas, grades, and teaching staffs; and nongraded instruction.

Upon reading the introduction to this chapter, you should be able to meet these objectives:

12-1 Point out and illustrate the similarities and differences between the two types of instructional technology.

12-2 Describe the source of the influence of instructional technology in the schools.

DEFINITIONS OF INSTRUCTIONAL TECHNOLOGY

The development of a modern educational technology has been either heralded as the necessary ingredient of an educational revolution which will lift the schools out of the Dark Ages and into twentieth-century enlightenment or castigated as a movement which can only reduce teachers and students to robots in the manner described by our more pessimistic science fiction. The dispute often fails to distinguish between two meanings of *instructional technology* (Lumsdaine, 1964). One meaning refers to the detailed application of the psychology of learning to practical teaching problems. Francis Mechner (1965) uses this analogy: In the same way that an aeronautical engineer believes that he can design an airplane by applying a few basic physical principles and a little art and intuition, the educational technologist believes that he can build in the student a complex repertory of knowledge or behavior by applying a few basic principles of learning psychology in addition to a little art and intuition. Arthur Melton (1959) observed that educational technology is based on the assumption that the psychology of learning encompasses all forms of relatively permanent behavioral changes which result from experience, including, of course, the experiences of the child in school. In the first part of this chapter, in which we describe how to program materials, we are applying the psychology of learning to practical teaching problems. In other words, we are describing educational technology in this scientific sense. The programs which such a technology produces are often called the *software* to distinguish them from the machines, or *hardware,* into which the programs are fed. The second meaning of educational technology refers to the application of engineering principles in the development of electromechanical equipment used for instructional purposes. Examples of these devices are motion pictures, tape recorders, teaching machines, and computers—the educational hardware.

The two meanings of instructional technology interact in the design and use of equipment to provide control over the learning situation, a rich array of stimulus material (for example, through motion pictures), and interaction between the responses of the learner and the presentation of instructional material (Lumsdaine, 1964). When we organize instruction, as in the case of team teaching, flexible scheduling, and instructional systems, we must combine our application of the psychology of learning with electromechanical engineering to produce the desired results. In fact, H. A. Bern (1967) suggests that the educational psychologist of the future may be a psychologist-engineer.

American business has entered the educational scene to hasten the development of instructional technology particularly for the purpose of providing the hardware which the future educational markets will demand. In its acquisition of many of the major textbook publishing companies, the business community is also manifesting its interest in educational software. Francis Keppel (1967) observed that the American educator is not accustomed to having business knocking at his door. In fact, according to one popular stereotype (and there are many), the teacher long ago retreated behind his classroom door to protect a hide too sensitive and submissive to have allowed him to function successfully in the more aggressive and remunerative business world. Now, the business world is invading his classroom.

Upon reading the following section of this chapter you should be able to meet these objectives:

12-3   Describe and illustrate each of the following steps in the preparation of a program: (a) select a unit or topic; (b) prepare a content outline; (c) define your objectives in behavioral terms; (d) construct a test of entering behavior; and (e) construct a test of terminal behavior.

12-4   Describe and illustrate each of the following steps in the writing of a program: (a) present material in the form of frames; (b) require active student response; (c) provide for confirmation or correction of student response; and (d) provide careful sequencing of the frames.

12-5   Point out and illustrate the differences and similarities between frames and lesson plans.

12-6   Describe and illustrate the informational conditions under which overt responding facilitates learning more than covert responding does.

12-7   Describe and illustrate the differences between prompting and confirmation procedures and indicate the advantages of each.

12-8   Describe and illustrate the two major purposes of prompts.

12-9   Define and illustrate fading in terms of prompts.

12-10   List the two factors which determine frame sequencing.

12-11   Describe and illustrate each of the following steps in the tryout and revision of the program: (a) write the original draft; (b) edit the original draft; and (c) try out and revise the draft.

12-12   Point out and diagrammatically illustrate the similarities and differences in these three types of programs: (a) linear, (b) branching, and (c) adjunct autoinstructional.

PROGRAMED INSTRUCTION

A Definition

Figure 12-1 presents three frames, or units, of a program which teaches the use of a symbolic notation for describing and analyzing behavioral contin-

1

Your being born <u>was not</u> a response event for you. That is, it <u>was not</u> an action you initiated.

Your throwing your rattle out of your crib, however, <u>was</u> an action initiated by you. It <u>was</u> a response event for you.

CHECK each sentence below that describes a response event for the person or animal named in the sentence (note that there is no limit to the number of sentences you can check):

- ☐ a. Clara dyed her hair red.   **a**
- ☐ b. Herman died of old age.
- ☐ c. The dog has fleas.
- ☐ d. The cat meowed.   **d**

2

When you hit someone, it (☐ is ☐ is not) your action.   **is**
It (☐ is ☐ is not) your response event.   **is**

When the other person hits you back, it (☐ is ☐ is not) **is not**
your response event.

CHECK each sentence below that describes a response event for the person or animal named in the sentence:

- ☐ a. Philip ran fast.   **a**
- ☐ b. Gregory was run over.
- ☐ c. Alice cheated on the exam.   **c**
- ☐ d. Mary was reprimanded for cheating.
- ☐ e. The canary lost all its feathers.
- ☐ f. The parrot said, "Polly wants a cracker."   **f**

3

The sentence, "The officer gave Mr. Smith a summons," <u>describes</u> the officer's giving the ticket, but it merely <u>implies</u> Mr. Smith's speeding or going through the red light.

Does the sentence describe a response event for
Mr. Smith? ☐ yes ☐ no   **no**

CHECK the statements below that describe, not merely imply, response events for <u>you</u>:

- ☐ a. You solved a hard math example.   **a**
- ☐ b. Your teacher gave you a good grade
       in math.
- ☐ c. You are a doctor.
- ☐ d. You are studying to be a doctor.   **d**

FIG. 12-1 Some examples of program frames (after Mechner, 1965, p. 491)

gencies (Mechner, 1961, 1965). If you inspect these frames you will see some of the major characteristics of programed instruction: (1) The material is broken down into small steps (or frames); (2) frequent response is required of the student (for example, the student must make six responses in the second frame); and (3) there is immediate confirmation of right answers or correction of wrong answers for each response the student makes. An additional characteristic, which you cannot observe, is that (4) the content and sequence of the frames were subjected to actual tryout with students and were revised on the basis of the data gathered by the program author. These four factors are the major characteristics of programed instruction and of programed materials. The programed materials, as distinguished from programed instruction, or the actual use of the materials, are simply the educational materials from which the students learn (Jacob et al., 1966). A *program* accepts the responsibility for the management of the learning situation. According to Arthur Lumsdaine (1964), the program tries to see to it that the student does learn, and it takes the blame for the student's failures. A program can be distinguished from a lesson plan or a book. A book is only a source of materials to which the student exposes himself. There is little or no predetermined interaction between the book and the reader in the form of required responses and feedback. A lesson plan is often a skeletal outline of materials and activities the teacher will use in teaching. The actual instruction is something related to but apart from the lesson outline. A program, however, is the actual instruction. The student's success or failure depends on the program. Nearly all students are capable of learning when properly programed materials are made available.

The first section of this chapter teaches you how to write and revise a program. Program writing has three major stages: (1) preparation, (2) the actual writing, and (3) tryout and revision.

Preparation

Select a unit or topic   The selection of a topic can be guided by several factors. First, select subject matter with which you are thoroughly familiar. Unfamiliarity will result in misleading and inaccurate materials and will interfere with your learning how to program the materials. Second, restrict yourself to a very small area of subject matter. Robert Filep (1961) suggests that, if you intend to teach English grammar, you should restrict yourself to something as manageable as the agreement between verbs and such pronouns as "each," "either," and "nobody." Third, choose subject matter that is easy to program. Jerome Lysaught and Clarence Williams (1963) suggest that it is easier to write a program on algebra than on the dynamics of political power. The tendency of the beginning programer is to select too wide a topic. The development of a program and the administration of it to the student are usually very time-consuming activities.

Prepare a content outline   This outline should cover all the material you plan to teach (Klaus, 1961). It is frequently the product of a careful examination of a number of textbooks and reference sources. An experienced teacher also has the use of his notes, textbooks, and the assignments he has used in conventional instruction. If you have not taught the material you are about to program, you should consult an experienced teacher who can supply knowledge, specific examples, and interesting illustrations which may be very useful in your program. One of the chief criticisms of programed materials is that they have been published before adequate editing of the manuscript for accuracy and clarity of subject matter and presentation (Soles, 1963). Occasionally an individual with some unpolished programing skills and with little knowledge of the subject matter has accepted the responsibility of writing a program. The results can be and have been disastrous. The chief advantage of the teacher as programer is that he can combine his knowledge of the subject matter with his new knowledge about programed instruction.

Define your objectives in behavioral terms We described the importance of and ways for stating these objectives in Chapter 2. The writing of objectives involves both task description and task analysis. Task description, you recall, is the description of the terminal behavior. Task analysis examines the component behaviors the student must acquire in the process of reaching the terminal behavior. Peter Pipe (1966) suggested that it is better to state your objectives in general rather than in behavioral terms. The general statement is an instructional goal. You then analyze this goal by asking yourself what behaviors are needed to attain it. Pipe suggested that you continue the analysis of behavior until you have reached the probable level of entering behavior.

Construct (and administer) a test of entering behavior The construction of this test requires you to determine the necessary prerequisite behaviors which you will recall but not provide instruction for in your program. The prerequisite behaviors are the bases for writing the items for the test of entering behavior. If you administer such a test to your students early in the development of your program, the test results should indicate at what points your programing must begin. You should write several items for each entering behavior to be certain that the student does not answer an item correctly by only making a lucky guess. In dealing with a group of students you may discover considerable variability in entering behavior. One possible way of handling this problem is to develop a program with branches. The program can direct students with more adequate entering behavior than others to skip the introductory frames of the program and to turn to the advanced frames.

Construct (and administer) a test of terminal behavior This test, based on your original task description, is used for performance assessment, the fourth component of the basic teaching model. The items should be scrambled and should not follow the order in which the terminal behaviors were acquired in the program. Pipe (1966) suggested that you administer the test to your students before they study the program. In this way you can discover whether any students have already acquired the behaviors your program teaches. Material which the student already knows should be deleted from the program. In the administration of your entering and terminal tests, the ideal result (and the one you can least expect) is that all students obtain a perfect score on the test of entering behavior and obtain a zero score on the test of terminal behavior.

Summary   The preparation of a program consists of the five steps you should take before you begin writing it:

1   Select a unit or topic.
2   Prepare a content outline.
3   Define your objectives in behavioral terms.
4   Construct (and administer) a test of entering behavior.
5   Construct (and administer) a test of terminal behavior.

Program Writing

With the preparatory stage behind you, you are ready to begin the actual construction of a program. We will now describe the five steps for the preparation of your program. The material we present in this section is largely based on research on linear programs.

Present the material in frames   A frame is a small segment of subject matter which calls forth particular student responses (Taber et al., 1965). As a programer your task is to provide those stimuli necessary to evoke the student responses which must be acquired as steps toward the terminal behavior. Not only is a frame a unit of subject matter, such as a sentence or paragraph of a chapter, but also it is constructed to call forth particular responses and, eventually, specific terminal behaviors. There are four essential parts of a frame (Klaus, 1961): the stimulus and the stimulus context; the cues or prompts necessary to produce the response reliably; the response (s) the stimulus evokes; and enrichment material which makes the frame more readable or interesting or which recalls previously learned materials to facilitate student response. The frames in Figure 12-2 illustrate the essential parts. In each frame the stimulus and the stimulus context are the words which precede and follow the blank. The blank, of course, provides for the student's response. You should also note that the stimulus context is a familiar one—the flashlight, the flashlight bulb, and the glow of a hot wire. The stimulus material of the frame and the response which the student makes to this material constitute an *S-R* relationship. In programed materials, the new stimulus material is gradually introduced while the cuing (prompting) with familiar material is gradually withdrawn. In this manner, the student's behavior comes under the control of the new

1. The important parts of a flashlight are the battery and the bulb. When we "turn on" a flashlight, we close a switch which connects the battery with the _____.

   Response: bulb

2. When we turn on a flashlight, an electric current flows through the fine wire in the _____ and causes it to grow hot.

   Response: bulb

3. When the hot wire glows brightly, we say that it gives off or sends out heat and _____.

   Response: light

FIG. 12-2 Beginning frames from a physics program (after Skinner, 1958, p. 973).

subject matter. Later frames in the program illustrate this procedure (Figure 12-3). In frame 29 you see that the term *filament* now substitutes for the less technical *fine wire*. The additional technical term *incandescent* is evoked in new stimulus contexts to describe in more technical language hot objects which emit light.

You should also note in Figures 12-2 and 12-3 that each frame presents a relatively small segment of material. You should present only enough material to elicit a single response. The size of the segment may vary, however, in different parts of the program. Nathan Maccoby and Fred Sheffield (1961) found that (1) short steps are more effective than large steps for initial learning, and (2) the progressive lengthening of steps leads to the best performance on the test of terminal behavior. In Figure 12-4, Scott Parry (1964) shows how a sequence of frames remedies the difficulties of a single frame.

Require active student response An essential part of the frame is the response the student is asked to make. Stuart Margulies (1964) formulated the critical-response rule for the construction of frames: The student can be expected to know only that portion of the material to which he has responded correctly. He cannot be expected to learn information which he does not use in making an immediate response. Margulies used the example

29. A nearly "dead" battery may make a flashlight bulb warm to the touch, but the filament may still not be hot enough to emit light—in other words the filament will not be _____ at that temperature.

Response: incandescent

31. When raised to any temperature above 800 degrees Celsius, an object such as an iron bar will emit light. Although the bar may melt or vaporize, its particles will be _____ no matter how hot they get.

Response: incandescent

FIG. 12-3 Later frames in a physics program (after Skinner, 1958, p. 973).

in Figure 12-5. The student could be expected to learn that delivery takes ten days but not expected to learn how much time it takes for labeling or for packing and assembling.

It is important that the student be required to make the critical response. Holland (1960) altered the normal version of a program by choosing different response words which had little relationship to the critical content and which could be supplied by observing trivial cues. Figure 12-6 shows a normal and an altered frame. In the posttest, Holland found 18.3 percent error on the program with normal frames, and 39.4 percent on the program with altered frames, which was about the same amount of error obtained when the students read complete sentences without responding. Interestingly enough, the students made fewer errors on the program with the altered frames than on the program with the normal frames. Figure 12-7 shows the results of Holland's study. The absence of errors made during the study of a program can mislead the programer into believing that the students are learning more than they are. By making trivial responses they are learning very little.

Holland (1965b) in another study found that he could obliterate 68 percent of the words in a program without altering the error rate. In his black-out technique, a black crayon is used to mark out all parts of a frame not needed for answering correctly. Figure 12-8 shows the application of this technique to six frames of a monetary program. The removal of the blacked-out material failed to increase the error rate.

If you analyze the terminal behavior in sufficient detail, you will be able to indicate clearly the critical responses the student should make. The responses in the frames always depend on some important part of the sub-

ENGLISH GRAMMAR

In studying **qualifiers** and **modifiers**, this little rule will help you distinguish between **adjectives** and **adverbs**:
Adjectives are words which _____ whereas _____ are words which modify.

Responses: qualify, adverb

Adjectives are words which **describe** (or tell more about) nouns or pronouns.
　　John has brown **eyes.**
In this sentence, the word _____ describes the noun **eyes.**
Therefore, the word **brown** is a(n) _____.[1]

Responses: brown, adjective

[1] Sequence expanding this concept follows.

Now let's meet another part of speech: the adverb. Adverbs tell more about, or _____, verbs, adjectives, or other adverbs.

Response: describe

John runs quickly.
In this sentence, the word **quickly** tells more about the word **runs,** which is a _____. Therefore quickly is a(n) _____.[2]

Responses: verb, adverb

[2] Sequence expanding this concept follows.

As you have seen, adjectives and adverbs are the parts of speech used to _____, or tell more about, other words.

Response: describe

Adjectives are used to describe _____.
Adverbs are used to describe _____.

**Responses: nouns and pronouns;
verbs, adjectives, adverbs**

FIG. 12-4 A faulty frame (top), which is corrected by a sequence of five frames (after Parry, 1963, p. 4).

It requires seven days to pack and assemble material after the request is made. It requires three days to label the material for delivery. How long is the time between request and delivery? _____

Response: 10 days

FIG. 12-5 A program frame (after Margulies, 1964, p. 7).

ject matter, such as understanding a new illustration, recognizing important details of the subject matter, or acquiring a new term.

The location of the response blank may also be a source of difficulty. Robert Horn (1963, p. 4) argued that the blank should appear as close to the end of the frame as possible because this position spares the student the awkwardness of flipping his eyes back and forth, "skidding around inside frame after frame looking for the relevant material." It is often helpful at first to write the frame in question form because the question focuses the attention on the form of the required response. It is, of course, entirely permissible that a frame remain in question form. And it is sometimes desirable to use multiple-choice alternatives rather than fill-in blanks.

Whether the responses in programed material should be *overt* or *covert* has been the subject of considerable inquiry. Unfortunately, these terms have shifted in meaning and "one man's overt is frequently another man's covert" (Cummings and Goldstein, 1962). Perhaps the most useful distinction is illustrated in a study by John Krumboltz and Ronald Weisman (1962). Here students who made overt responses wrote down their answers

FIG. 12-6 A normal frame and an alteration of it (after Holland, 1965a, p. 79).

If a previously reinforced response is no longer reinforced, it soon occurs (1) _____ frequently. This is called (2) _____.

Responses: (1) less; (2) extinction

If a previously reinforced response is no longer _____, it soon occurs less often. This is called extinction.

Response: reinforced

INSTRUCTIONAL TECHNOLOGY

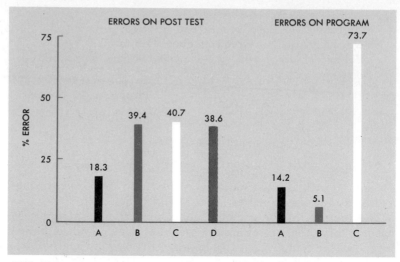

FIG. 12-7 Percentage of errors on posttest and in the program for four experimental versions. Program A is the normal program, with response determined and dependent upon critical content; program B has responses determined, but answers relatively unrelated to critical content; program C has responses relatively undetermined, but dependent upon critical content; and program D has only complete statements with no responses (after Holland, 1965b, p. 3).

on sheets of paper. Students who made covert responses mentally composed a response to each blank in the frame before turning the page to the correct answer. Although the findings on the relative benefits of overt and covert responding have not always been consistent, Richard Anderson (1967) points to two conclusions which have considerable empirical support: (1) Overt responses facilitate learning when the responses are relevant to the content of the lesson, and (2) overt responses should be required in the learning of unfamiliar and technical terms. A study by Krumboltz and Charles Kiesler (1965) supports the first conclusion. Two studies support Anderson's second conclusion. Allana Cummings and L. S. Goldstein (1962) found that overt responding was better than covert responding when students were required to make long, intricate, and unfamiliar responses. In a later study Eigen and Margulies (1963) discovered that an overt-responding group learned about twice as many difficult nonsense syllables as did a covert-responding group. Both groups learned about the same number of the easy nonsense syllables.

The reason overt responding facilitates learning is not clear at present. Ernest Rothkopf (1966) suggests that test questions (and we may include the frames of a program) control what he calls *mathemagenic behaviors*—covert and overt behaviors of the student in the instructional situation which give birth to learning. Mathemagenic behaviors include reading,

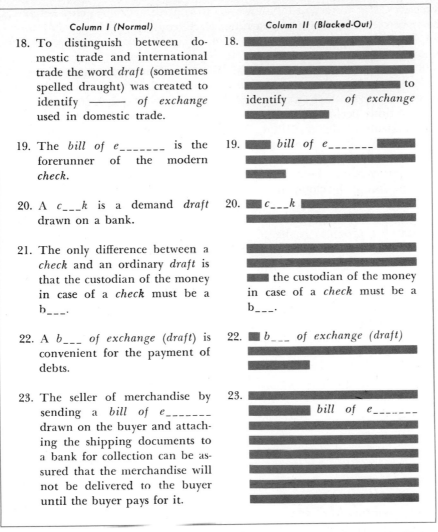

Column I (Normal) | Column II (Blacked-Out)

18. To distinguish between domestic trade and international trade the word *draft* (sometimes spelled draught) was created to identify ——— *of exchange* used in domestic trade.

19. The *bill of e_____* is the forerunner of the modern *check*.

20. A *c___k* is a demand *draft* drawn on a bank.

21. The only difference between a *check* and an ordinary *draft* is that the custodian of the money in case of a *check* must be a b___.

22. A *b___ of exchange (draft)* is convenient for the payment of debts.

23. The seller of merchandise by sending a *bill of e_____* drawn on the buyer and attaching the shipping documents to a bank for collection can be assured that the merchandise will not be delivered to the buyer until the buyer pays for it.

FIG. 12-8 Normal and blacked-out items from ponetary program. Material covered in blackout version can be omitted without influencing the subject's ability to answer correctly. Item 18 can be answered because of previous item (after Holland, 1965a, p. 83).

asking questions, inspecting an object, keeping the face oriented toward the teacher, and mentally reviewing a recently seen motion picture. They also include looking out of the classroom window, yawning, turning the pages of a textbook without reading, writing notes to a student in a neighboring seat, and sleeping either in class or in a library carrel. Some of these behaviors, you can see, are quite unrelated to the achievement of instructional objectives. If it were possible, however, to control mathemagenic behaviors, the control could facilitate learning. Such control, Rothkopf has found, can be obtained through the insertion of questions in reading passages. In one study students were asked to read a very long (34-page, or about 9,000-word) passage of high factual content. After every three pages, the student was directed to answer two questions and, if he chose, to check the correct answers which were supplied. Students who had the benefit of the questions performed better on a posttest than students who read the passages without the questions. The beneficial effects occurred only when the questions followed the relevant text segment and only when they were inserted fairly frequently. Questions, according to Rothkopf, profoundly affect mathemagenic behaviors which, in turn, affect how much we learn.

In the initial development of your program, overt responding is a practical necessity. The complete written record of student responses becomes a major basis for program revision. A conventional standard used in the revision of a program is the 10 percent error rate, which requires you to revise a program frame until 10 percent or less of your students respond incorrectly to it. Parry (1963), however, cautions against an overly stringent application of this rule. He suggests several situations in which the purpose of the frame is best served by an erroneous response by more than 10 percent of the students: (1) when incorrect or unwanted responses already exist as a result of previous learning; (2) when new learning is best accomplished after the student has responded incorrectly; (3) when the student's appetite is whetted if he is occasionally asked to guess a response; (4) when an occasional slow-down frame forces the student to read more carefully and to avoid the temptation to respond before reading; (5) when the student is asked for an opinion; and (6) when a branching frame determines whether the student requires review before proceeding with the new frame sequences.

Provide for confirmation or correction of student responses You have seen in the preceding examples of frames that the correct response to the frame always appears. Providing the correct response, with which the student compares his own response, has been a standard characteristic of programed instruction. When the student discovers that his response is correct, he obtains confirmation; when it is incorrect, he receives correction. The practical necessity or efficiency of immediate confirmation has never been adequately studied. It does appear that early programers failed to distinguish between the motivational and informational aspects of immediate knowledge of results. Krumboltz and Weisman (1962) found no difference in test performances of students who were supplied the correct answer all the time and of those supplied the correct answer only part of the time. They suggested that supplying the correct response may be more important later than earlier in the program, when most of the prompts for the correct responses are withdrawn. The tight sequencing of program frames, so that one frame interlocks with those which precede and follow it, provides a source of informational feedback apart from that provided by the printed answers.

Use prompts to guide student responses Prompts are cues provided in the program frame to guide the student to the correct response. They are supplementary stimuli in that they are added to a frame to make the frame easier but are not sufficient in themselves to produce the response (Markle, 1964). Figure 12-9 shows two prompted frames (2 and 3) and one unprompted frame (1). In frame 2 the number of dashes serves as a prompt by indicating the number of letters in the correct response. In frame 3, the letter *P* serves as a prompt for the correct response.

There has been lively debate and considerable research on the relative merits of prompting and confirmation (see Cook, 1963, and Holland, 1964). A simplified statement of the issue is this: Is it better to prompt responses so that errors are avoided in the first place or to correct erroneous responses after they are made? J. Oliver Cook and his associates (1956, 1958, 1960, 1963) argue in favor of prompting and against needless trial and error.

Prompts have two basic purposes: They guide the student to the correct response without overcontrolling his behavior, and they prevent the student from making unnecessary errors. These purposes suggest that you must avoid both overprompting and underprompting in writing your frames. A common source of overprompting is the *copying frame,* in which the student is asked to make a response given in the frame. Figure 12-10 shows a copying frame. In it the student need only copy the important word to respond correctly. The copying frame is a means for producing the response the first time and is useful as an introductory frame. Since it displays the full response, however, it is not a form of prompting. Julian Taber and his associates (1965) believe that copying frames are overused by many programers. Susan Markle (1964) believes that they can be an insult to students. The chief disadvantage is that the student can make correct verbatim

FIG. 12-9 Frames with prompted and unprompted responses (after Markle, 1961, pp. 2–3).

Frame 1   The capital of France is _____.

                              Response: Paris

Frame 2   The capital of France is _ _ _ _ _.

                              Response: Paris

Frame 3   The capital of France is P_____.

A *compound* word is made up of *two words*. The word *ball-room* is made of two root words, *ball* and *room*, so ballroom is a _____ word.

Response: compound

FIG. 12-10   A copying frame (after Taber et al., 1965, p. 95).

responses which he conceptually does not understand. Margulies (1964) shows how a copying frame can be improved. In Figure 12-11, frame 1 is the copying frame, and frame 2 is the improved version. The use of copying frames tends to make a program dull and to reduce the amount of student learning. It is not uncommon that students respond correctly to all the frames in a program and still fail to answer correctly questions on the test of terminal behavior. Such a result is usually the result of over-prompting and of the liberal use of copying frames.

The use of prompts to guide student responses requires you to withdraw these prompts so that the student can eventually achieve the terminal behavior without supporting cues. The gradual removal of prompts is called *vanishing*, or *fading*. Figure 12-12 shows how the letter prompts for the word *manufacture* are gradually withdrawn. In this example the dashes could be replaced with a solid line, thereby vanishing the dashes as formal prompts.

Provide careful sequencing of the frames   The sequence, or order, in which your frames appear depends upon two factors: the description and analysis of the behaviors your program intends to teach, and the conditions neces-

FIG. 12-11   Revision of a copying frame (after Margulies, 1964, p. 7).

Frame 1   All Gaul was broken into THREE divisions. Thus Gaul consisted of t_ _ _ _ parts.

Response: T(hree)

Frame 2   Gaul was divided into parts occupied by the Celts, the Belgae, and the Aquitani. Into how many parts was Gaul divided? _____

Response: Three

Frame 1   Manufacture means to make or build. Chair factories manufacture chairs. Copy the word here.

- - - - - - - - - -

Frame 2   Part of the word is like part of the word *factory*.
Both parts come from an old word meaning *make*
or *build*.

m a n u _ _ _ _ u r e

Frame 3   Part of the word is like part of the word *manual*.
Both parts come from an old word for *hand*. Many
things used to be made by hand.

_ _ _ _ f a c t u r e

Frame 4   The same letter goes in both spaces:

m _ n u f _ c t u r e

Frame 5   The same letter goes in both spaces:

m a n _ f a c t _ r e

Frame 6   Chair factories _ _ _ _ _ _ _ _ _ _ chairs.

FIG. 12-12   Withdrawal of prompts (after Skinner, 1958, p. 972).

sary for the learning required by the various tasks. The sequences described
in Part 4 of this book should guide your ordering of the program frames.
Figure 12-13 shows how Mechner (1965) developed a sequence of frames
for teaching students how to diagnose Lead 1 tracings in an electrocardio-
gram as ischemia, injury, or infraction. In effect the students were learning
three classes of patterns, or tracings; or, we can now say, they were learning
three concepts. Figure 12-13 shows not only the program frames but also
the relationship of the frames to the prior task analysis which Mechner
made and to the learning principles which he selected as the bases for frame
construction and sequencing.

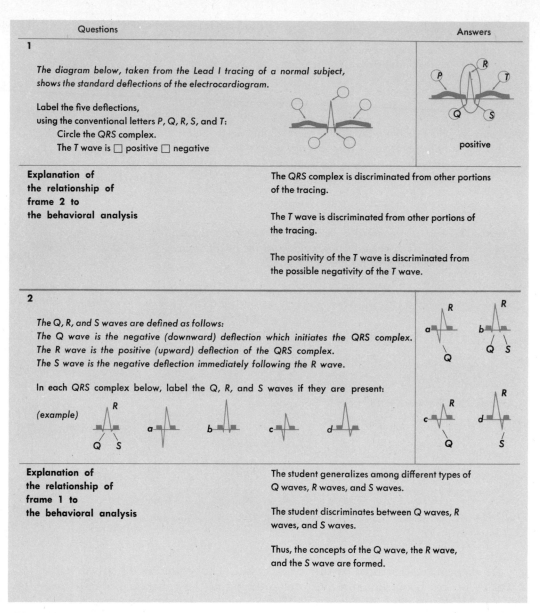

Questions	Answers
1 The diagram below, taken from the Lead I tracing of a normal subject, shows the standard deflections of the electrocardiogram. Label the five deflections, using the conventional letters P, Q, R, S, and T: Circle the QRS complex. The T wave is ☐ positive ☐ negative	positive

Explanation of the relationship of frame 2 to the behavioral analysis	The QRS complex is discriminated from other portions of the tracing. The T wave is discriminated from other portions of the tracing. The positivity of the T wave is discriminated from the possible negativity of the T wave.

2

The Q, R, and S waves are defined as follows:
The Q wave is the negative (downward) deflection which initiates the QRS complex.
The R wave is the positive (upward) deflection of the QRS complex.
The S wave is the negative deflection immediately following the R wave.

In each QRS complex below, label the Q, R, and S waves if they are present:

(example)

Explanation of the relationship of frame 1 to the behavioral analysis	The student generalizes among different types of Q waves, R waves, and S waves. The student discriminates between Q waves, R waves, and S waves. Thus, the concepts of the Q wave, the R wave, and the S wave are formed.

FIG. 12-13 Program frames for reading electrocardiograms and their relationship to the behavioral analysis (after Mechner, 1965, pp. 469–71).

It is even possible to develop frames which engage the student in problem solving and discovery learning. Kersh (1964, 1961) developed a programed-discovery procedure which prescribed conditions under which the student would engage in searching behavior and which specified occasions for the teacher to give verbal approval to the student for the searching behavior he exhibited as he progressed through the program. Martin Covington (1967) developed a program which fostered originality in visual and other types of problem solving.

All the basic learning conditions—discrimination, generalization, contiguity, practice, and reinforcement—can be embodied in the frame sequences. Frame sequences, of course, can also provide for review and testing whenever these are necessary. One of the major advantages for educational psychologists in studying programed instruction is the freedom allowed in manipulating the basic learning conditions.

Summary We have now described these five steps for the preparation of your program:

1 Present the material frames.
2 Require active responding.
3 Provide for confirmation or correction of responses.
4 Use prompts to guide student responses.
5 Provide careful sequencing of the frames.

Tryout and Revision

We have divided the third stage of program development into three steps. The first requires that you develop the first draft of the program while working quite closely with your students. The second step requires that you edit the program on the basis of the original tryout with these students. The third step requires that you revise the program on the basis of terminal-test performance and student responses to the program frames.

Write the original draft At this stage you should not try to produce highly polished frames. After you have written from fifty to one hundred, you should try them out on five to ten students. Thomas Gilbert (1960, p. 480) suggests that you work closely with each student in this stage of program development. Find out where the student makes his mistakes and what you can do about it. Revise the frames or frame sequence until the student learns from them what he is supposed to learn. Gilbert suggested that the first tryouts should occur before you have developed the program very far.

Edit the original draft Markle (1964) has developed a checklist for the first drafts of the program. This is an abbreviated version: (1) Frames should be written clearly in good English. (2) What is said should be correct. (3) The response required of the student should be relevant to the purpose of the frame. If the student is to learn to do something, you should make him do it rather than talk about doing it. (4) If you use a multiple-choice question, the alternatives should be feasible answers. (5) Frames should contain sufficient context to make clear what is being presented and what is wanted. (6) You should not include more points than the student can respond to in one frame. (7) You should eliminate irrelevant material. (8) In concept teaching, you should provide a representative sample of illustrations and provide for negative examples as well. (9) You should make liberal use of thematic prompts and sparing use of formal prompts. (10) You should make the steps (frames) toward mastery as large as the student can reasonably be expected to handle. Let testing tell you when the step is too large. (11) The testing should tell you how much practice and prompting to provide.

Try out and revise After this editing, you have what Pipe (1966) calls a *fledgling* program to try out. It should be neatly typed and carefully duplicated. You will need about fifteen to forty or more students—but use as many (or as few) as you have. When you administer your program this time, resist any impulse to intervene. The program must now assume the full instructional responsibility. You can supply the students with paper which bears numbered blanks. On these they can check the frames which give them difficulty and give a description of the difficulty. You can also record any questions they ask while studying the program. After finishing the program, the students should take the test of terminal behavior. The students' response records will reveal which frames were missed. From these records you can make a list of common errors. If you group the items of the test by subunits, you can also determine which sections of the program were ineffective. High error rates on particular frames or particular sections indicate a need for revision. The conventional standard has been the 10 percent error rate. Finally, if you require the students to annotate their copies of the program, their comments can also guide your revision.

Summary We have now described three steps for the tryout-and-revision stage of your program development:

1 Write the original draft.
2 Edit the draft.
3 Try out the edited draft and revise it.

Frame Sequencing

In this part of the chapter we will distinguish among two types of sequences: linear and branching. Skinner and his associates (1958, 1961) invented the linear sequence. Norman Crowder (1963a, b) created the branching sequence. Sidney Pressey (1963, 1964), who is not sure that either linear or branching programs do anything but make the printed page more difficult

FIG. 12-14 Diagram of a linear sequence.

to read, has argued for adjunct, or auxiliary, practice materials to accompany conventional texts.

Linear sequences   In this type of sequencing all students read and respond to the same frames. The sequence is linear in that there is a single line or path for all students to follow. Figure 12-14 diagrams a linear sequence. Each circle represents a frame. The student proceeds from one frame to the next until he completes the program. Most linear sequences use the constructed (or fill-in) response. Most of the frames we used as illustrations in the previous part of this chapter are frames of linear programs. Many new programs, however, use both constructed and multiple-choice responses. The frames in Fig. 12-13 (Mechner, 1965), for example, use both forms of response. In fact, the appearance of the correct response in the list of alternatives in a multiple-choice question acts as a useful prompt (Markle, 1964). Although most linear sequences use shorter frames than those used by the branching sequences we describe below, the single-sentence or short frame is not an essential characteristic of linear sequences. Markle (1964) developed a linear sequence on programing which contained frames which were paragraphs or longer in length. Even the major characteristic of linear sequences—the use of the single path—is no longer rigidly prescribed. Lysaught and Williams (1963) show many ways in which a linear sequence can be modified into a multipath program. An interesting variation is the linear sequence with criterion frames. These frames test entering behavior at various points in the program to determine whether the student should go through the sequence of frames which follows. If this is not necessary, the student is directed to a subsequence, which will move him quickly to an advanced point in the program. Figure 12-15 is a diagram of a linear sequence with a criterion frame and a subsequence.

Branching sequences   In this format the student proceeds to the next frame until he makes an error. The errors branch him to supplementary material designed to give him remedial instruction. The best-known branching technique was developed by Crowder (1960) and is called *intrinsic programing*. It consists of rather long frames which often appear as pages in an ordinary textbook. The student reads the page (or frame) and then responds by selecting the correct alternative in a three-alternative multiple-choice item. Each alternative is associated with a page number which directs the student to another frame. Figure 12-16 diagrams an intrinsic program. In this diagram the main sequence (if you make no errors) is: frames 1, 5, and 14. Depending on the errors you make in answering the multiple-choice items, you are branched along various paths. Frame 1 has two branches, frames 9 and 13. Frame 1 has two branches, frames 10 and 18.

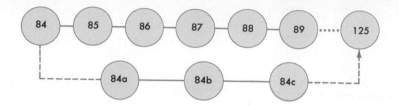

84. Let's see if you have had some experience with the Greek alphabet. Write out the first five letters of that alphabet in proper order—use Greek letters and equivalent English spellings (small letters, not caps).

84. alpha—α
beta—β
gamma—γ
delta—δ
epsilon—ϵ

If right, go on to item 84a. If you made an error, or if you are not sure of Greek letters, go to item 85.

FIG. 12-15 Diagram of linear program with criterion frame. Frame 84 is the criterion frame (after Lysaught and Williams, 1963, p. 80).

Adjunct Autoinstruction

Pressey, in numerous articles, argued for a less drastic alteration of the learning situation than that produced by programed instruction. These articles compare the relative advantages of conventional and programed instructional materials. This procedure, called *adjunct autoinstruction,* inserts programed or testing materials into a textbook, laboratory manual, or other materials whenever these supplementary materials are needed. Pressey argued (1964, p. 363) that the textbook writer or the teacher ought to be heard first:

> In a well-organized book, written at a level suitable for its users, elucidative autoinstruction might well be most effective and integrative if placed at the end of each chapter. Or there might be clusters of autoinstructional items at whatever places in the chapter they seem to be needed. Experienced teachers will know fairly well (and informal experimenting and check-up "quizzes" will show more definitely) when and where such material is needed; points where it is needed can be located with greater precision in such subjects as arithmetic and science.

In Pressey's opinion, the conventional instructional materials should carry the main burden of instruction, and the programed materials should tackle only that material which is potentially difficult and confusing. His emphasis on the need to organize well the initial presentation of subject matter is consistent with Ausubel's notion of advance organizers, or the presentation

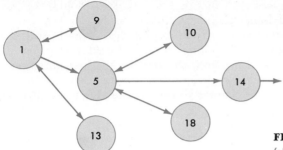

FIG. 12-16 Diagram of a branching (intrinsic) sequence (after Lysaught and Williams, 1963, p. 82).

of the basic principles of the subject matter followed by its detailed treatment. Pressey objects to the fragmentation of material which occurs when it is broken into frames. In one informal study, Pressey (1964) rewrote all the content material in a 1,100-word program by Holland and Skinner (1961) into a succinct statement of 360 words. This abbreviated statement was read in a median time of one and one-half minutes compared with the twenty-three minutes needed to read the original program. The students who merely read the short statement did as well on an essay test as students who had been through the Holland-Skinner program. There is considerable practical appeal in Pressey's suggestion for adjunct autoinstruction in that it permits the combination of both an expository and a programing style of teaching. To some extent we have adopted adjunct programing in this book by embedding questions within the text at points where they may be most useful for the reader.

Summary You have seen that the two types of sequences—linear and branching—can combine in various ways to meet the requirements of the

---

Inspect the following frames and answer the questions below.* **QUESTION 12-1**

Frame 1 Pegasus had two _____.

Frame 2 Like a bird, Pegasus had two _____.

Frame 3 Pegasus had two _ _ _ _ s.

Place an X after each of the following steps which these frames illustrate.

(a) Present the material in the form of frames. _____

(b) Require active student response. _____

(c) Provide for confirmation or correction of student response. _____

(d) Use prompts to guide student response. _____

(e) Provide careful sequencing of the frames. _____

After placing your X's, give reasons for your choices and for your rejection of the alternatives.

---

* The frames are from Markle, 1964, p. 70.

---

instructional situation. It is possible, in other words, to add branches to linear sequences and to add linear sequences to the branching sequences. You have also seen that adjunct autoinstruction provides a way of shifting between expository and programed teaching procedures. At this phase in the development of programed instruction, the overlap in these three programs may be more significant and useful than their lines of demarcation.

Upon reading this section of the chapter you should be able to meet these objectives:

12-13   Define the instructional media in terms of electromechanical devices.

12-14   Point out and illustrate four distinctions between new and traditional media.

12-15   List three new media.

12-16   List nine sources from which you obtain information about available media.

12-17   Define instructional systems design in terms of a comparison of alternatives and of performance criteria.

12-18   Point out the differences and similarities of the basic teaching model and the instructional system illustrated in Figure 12-18.

12-19   Describe and illustrate the conditions under which films and television facilitate learning as much or more than direct instruction.

12-20   Point out the relationship between the control of realism and the facilitation of student learning.

12-21   Describe the three machine capabilities of computers for instruction.

12-22   List three limitations in CAI in the accommodation of individual differences in entering behavior.

THE INSTRUCTIONAL MEDIA

In the first section of this chapter the emphasis was on instructional technology as the science of instruction. Our concern was with the design of instructional materials rather than with the media or machines into which these materials are fed. To oversimplify the distinction, the first section of the chapter dealt with the software of instruction, while the second section will deal with the hardware. This distinction is useful in organizing the materials of this chapter. In actual practice, however, the design of instructional materials and the design of the media and machines which convey these materials must be a joint enterprise. The materials and the media influence each other and produce an instructional tool recognizably different from their isolated constructions. The interaction of materials and media is a relatively new area of research and will require considerably more inquiry before we can predict and control the effects for our instructional practices.

What Are the Instructional Media?

A medium is a middle condition. Instructional media are the electromechanical devices which act as middle conditions between the student and what he is to learn. An instructional medium is simply a means of transmitting instruction. It is not the substance of that instruction. In an age enamored of technology, it is important to keep in mind that the instructional medium serves as the channel of instruction. What passes through that channel is the substance of instruction.

We can make the distinction between the old, or traditional, media and the more recently developed media (Erickson, 1965). Several traditional media still make important contributions to the instructional process. First, models or mockups are simplified representations of real things. A globe, for example, is a model of the earth. We also have take-apart models of the human torso and the major human organs. Geometric models are increasingly used in the teaching of mathematics. Second, graphic materials are nonpictorial in nature. Examples are maps, graphs, cartoons, diagrams, and charts. Third, the motion picture combines motion, sound, and realism. Increasingly popular is the 8mm single-concept film ready for insertion into its own projector. Fourth, projected still pictures, such as slides and filmstrips, are useful media. Transparencies are used with the overhead projector and are usually made by the teacher. Microscope slides are particularly useful in the teaching of the life sciences. Fifth, the opaque projection materials use a special projector which reflects light from the surface of the picture or object onto a projection screen. Sixth, tape recordings have become the chief aural instructional medium.

Carlton Erickson also describes the new media: First among these is television. As a medium television has three aspects: It is a composite of auditory and visual presentation; it can reach an audience of unlimited size; and it can transmit program content without delay from the point of origin to the point of reception. Television uses several of the older media. For example, a telecast may consist of a motion picture or videotape recording of a laboratory demonstration which uses slides, models, and transparencies. The second new medium is the teaching machine, which is designed for autoinstruction. The original teaching machines were rather overelaborate page turners for the various pages of programed material. They also provided a way of masking the correct response until the student made his own overt response. Interest in machine teaching has shifted from these devices to computer-assisted instruction, which we describe below. Third, Erickson points out the increasing popularity of the instructional kits, which contain a variety of carefully related materials including objects, models, motion pictures, filmstrips, tape recordings, student leaflets, programed materials, apparatus assembles, and workbooks.

Selection and Use of the Media

As a teacher your practical problem is to select from this rather formidable array of media those which are most useful in reaching your instructional objectives. Rather than outlining a series of steps you should take in the selection of appropriate media, we shall describe several bases for your selections: information about available media, an analysis and design of an instructional system, and knowledge of the research findings on the use of the media.

Information about the available media Colleges, universities, and local school systems are developing large educational technology centers, which serve as depositories for the many media of instruction. Unless the media are immediately available, the tendency of the teacher is to use other instructional materials. Erickson (1965) has compiled a list of general references which can be helpful in finding out which media are available. From these various sources and others you can find which media are available or can be produced for your use. A sound basis for selection and use lies in systems analysis and research findings.

Systems analysis and design When you increase the number of objectives you try to reach, the amount of material and the array of media you utilize, and the number of students and teachers involved in a total operation, you usually need comprehensive and detailed planning. Getting the best equipment in the best place for the best people at the best time and at the best price becomes a rather monumental problem. With its emphasis on efficiency and productivity in the competitive market, industry has probably given more serious consideration than has any other group to the systematic planning of complex operations which involve people, machines, materials, and the ultimate delivery of a product of precise specifications. The armed services, as well, are often faced with a situation in which men must be trained for the performance of complex tasks in very short periods of time, especially during national emergencies. Here also the systematic planning of instruction is a more critical issue than it is in our schools. In our schools and colleges, however, there is increasing competition for the students' time as we try to crowd the acquisition of increased knowledge and skill into the traditional time limits set on education and as the schools compete for their share of the tax dollar. Because of this additional pressure, we must improve the effectiveness and efficiency of instruction.

Instructional systems design is the application of various methods and tools for the purpose of predicting and comparing the value, effectiveness, and cost of alternative courses of action involving teachers, students, and machines (Meals, 1967). We can inspect each aspect of this definition more closely. First, the systems designer or analyst, as he is called, must select the best alternative. Donald Meals (1967) uses this example. The choice between a language laboratory and conventional instruction involves obtaining information on all the following factors: how rapidly linguistic skill is acquired in the laboratory, the cost and availability of the software, the required amount of teacher training, the amount of maintenance required for the equipment, and so on. One likely outcome of this particular systems analysis is the consideration of those additions to the language-laboratory facilities which would make them useful for other courses. The important point, however, is that the school does not make the decision to install a language laboratory until all the system pieces have been assembled and compared. A second element of the definition deals with performance criteria. On what basis does the systems analyst decide that one alternative is better than another? His criteria are usually effectiveness, efficiency, and cost.

Effectiveness depends on how well the students acquire the terminal behaviors. For efficiency, the system can be designed to speed the learning of the student if the time saved can be effectively used in the attainment of other desirable instructional objectives. Cost is determined on the basis of what are called *performance budgets* (Mauch, 1962). Such a budget tells how much it costs to teach students particular subject matter and skills. For example, it might determine that it costs fifty dollars per year per student to teach mathematics. James Mauch observes that the typical school budget is an object (not a performance) budget. It shows us what education buys (books, chairs, the time of the teacher) not what education does (provides instruction in mathematics, science, and history). The performance budget enables the systems designer to make comparisons of and clearer choices among instructional alternatives. Third, the definition implies that systems analysis and design combine knowledge and skill from many disciplines, including mathematics, economics, and industrial and electrical engineering. The systems analyst, according to Mauch, provides a bridge between science and technology, on one side, and education, on the other.

Under the auspices of Michigan State University, a study was made of procedures and costs for the full range of media in instructional systems (see Barson, 1965). This study developed a model for the analysis and design of these systems. Figure 12-17 shows the complex interrelationship which is possible among functions, materials, media, and personnel. It may simplify your understanding of the flow chart if you think of its application to a course you will be teaching. In this case you will be the instructor. In analyzing and designing your course, you will meet with such individuals as a design coordinator, an evaluation specialist, an instructional specialist, an audiovisual specialist, a media specialist, and the technical supervisor. Inspection of Figure 12-17 quickly reveals that the model is in many respects identical to the basic teaching model and to the procedures for the development of programed materials. Added, of course, are the services of the various specialists who can assist in areas in which the teacher is deficient in knowledge and skill. With enough knowledge, the instructor (that is, you) could carry out alone the entire analysis and design. The various specialists are merely convenient ways of segmenting the general teaching function. In the future, as educational technology (in both senses) grows, it is likely that instructional planning will stretch beyond the single classroom and teacher and include a much wider range of factors and personnel.

Research on the instructional media   Knowledge of research on the media is the third basis you have for the selection of media appropriate to your instructional objectives. Private and Federal grants have brought a considerable increase in research on instructional media. Between 1918 and 1950 there were over 200 experiments on instructional films (Hoban and

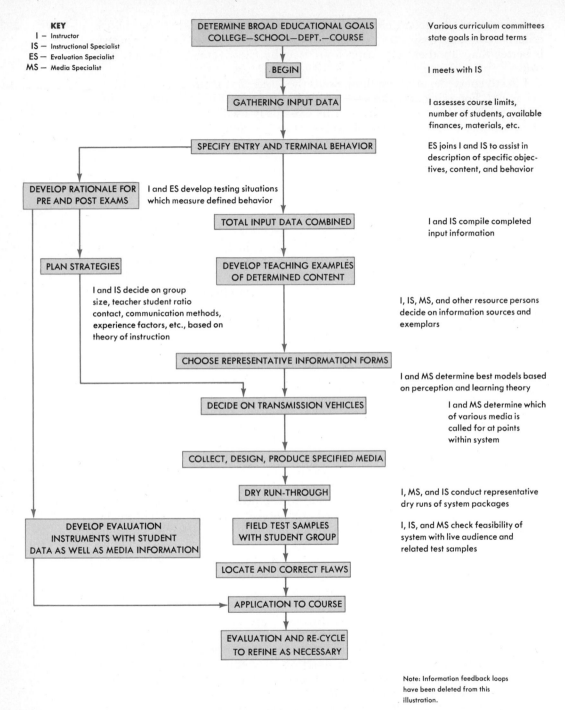

KEY
I — Instructor
IS — Instructional Specialist
ES — Evaluation Specialist
MS — Media Specialist

DETERMINE BROAD EDUCATIONAL GOALS
COLLEGE—SCHOOL—DEPT.—COURSE

Various curriculum committees
state goals in broad terms

BEGIN

I meets with IS

GATHERING INPUT DATA

I assesses course limits,
number of students, available
finances, materials, etc.

SPECIFY ENTRY AND TERMINAL BEHAVIOR

ES joins I and IS to assist in
description of specific objectives, content, and behavior

DEVELOP RATIONALE FOR
PRE AND POST EXAMS

I and ES develop testing situations
which measure defined behavior

TOTAL INPUT DATA COMBINED

I and IS compile completed
input information

PLAN STRATEGIES

DEVELOP TEACHING EXAMPLES
OF DETERMINED CONTENT

I and IS decide on group
size, teacher student ratio
contact, communication methods,
experience factors, etc., based on
theory of instruction

I, IS, MS, and other resource persons
decide on information sources and
exemplars

CHOOSE REPRESENTATIVE INFORMATION FORMS

I and MS determine best models based
on perception and learning theory

DECIDE ON TRANSMISSION VEHICLES

I and MS determine which
of various media is
called for at points
within system

COLLECT, DESIGN, PRODUCE SPECIFIED MEDIA

DRY RUN-THROUGH

I, MS, and IS conduct representative
dry runs of system packages

DEVELOP EVALUATION
INSTRUMENTS WITH STUDENT
DATA AS WELL AS MEDIA INFORMATION

FIELD TEST SAMPLES
WITH STUDENT GROUP

I, IS, and MS check feasibility of
system with live audience and
related test samples

LOCATE AND CORRECT FLAWS

APPLICATION TO COURSE

EVALUATION AND RE-CYCLE
TO REFINE AS NECESSARY

Note: Information feedback loops
have been deleted from this
illustration.

FIG. 12-17 A flow chart of procedures for analysis and implementation of newer media of communications (after Barson, 1965).

Van Ormer, 1950). Almost all the studies on instructional television occurred between 1954 and 1964 (see MacLennan and Reid, 1964). There has been very little research on media other than films and television. The research in this area can be classified as follows (Greenhill, 1964): comparisons of the benefits of and the attitudes toward instructional films and television versus direct (face-to-face) instruction; studies of other uses of instructional films and television; and research concerned with production variables. We review each of these areas, emphasizing instructional television (our major current medium), and then discuss the media in connection with production variables.

DIRECT INSTRUCTION VERSUS FILMS AND TELEVISIONS By far the greatest amount of media research has tried to discover the relative benefits of face-to-face and televised instruction. One of the earliest studies (Carpenter and Greenhill, 1955) compared the effectiveness of direct and televised instruction in the teaching of psychology, chemistry, and the psychology of marriage. This study was later extended (1958) to include the teaching of elementary business law, meteorology, music appreciation, and introductory sociology. In both studies the researchers were unable to find significant differences between televised and face-to-face instruction. In one interesting phase of this extensive study, 626 chemistry students alternately experienced both types of instruction. Students with direct instruction were randomly assigned to the front, middle, and rear portions of the lecture hall. After experiencing both treatments, both groups were taught chemistry in the lecture hall. After one week and a half, the students were given the option of remaining in their present lecture seats or moving to the television classrooms. Thirty-two percent moved to the television classroom. About 50 percent of those who moved had been assigned seats in the rear of the lecture hall. When asked why they moved, they mentioned close-up views of the television screen, the greater comfort of the rooms, and the lack of distraction. Those remaining in the lecture mentioned the lack of color and the narrow field of view of television as reasons for staying.

A study of Robert Dreher and Walcott Beatty (1958) compared student achievement and attitudes under three conditions: face-to-face instruction, on-campus television instruction, and off-campus (at-home) television instruction. The subjects taught were psychology, economics, basic communication, and creative arts. In general they found no signifiant differences in achievement for any of the conditions or subject matters. Students with high grade-point averages did significantly better with television than with face-to-face instruction in the psychology course. Students with low grade-point averages did significantly better with televised instruction in both psychology and economics. Students with high IQs in the televised course gained more than did students of comparable ability in face-to-face instruction. Regarding attitude, off-campus students tended to be favorable to television instruction, while on-campus students tended to be disapproving; the face-to-face students were least critical of their courses.

Glenn Macomber and Laurence Sigel (1960) compared the relative effectiveness of televised instruction and instruction in small and large groups. The subject areas were human behavior, air science, animal biology, and American government. Tests which measured the acquisition of subject matter showed no significant differences in the scores of students under the three instructional conditions. In two of the courses, the students were more favorable in attitude toward the face-to-face instruction than toward televised instruction. They also tended to rate the same instructor more favorably in the face-to-face situation than in the televised situation. Generally, high-ability students were less favorable toward instructional television than low-ability students were. In both this study and the one by Clarence Carpenter and Leslie Greenhill, there was a growth of acceptance of instructional television over a period of two or three years. After this time, the students tended to be less concerned with television per se and reacted more to the quality than to the medium of instruction. Hence, the researchers found significant course-to-course variation in attitude. The studies by Macomber and Sigel and by Dreher and Beatty both indicated that the professors found instructional television less preferable than face-to-face instruction. They believed that certain intangible educational goals could not be achieved and that both student and instructor were lost in an impersonal electronic world. Shepard Insel and his associates (1963) found that television instruction evoked more other-dependent (than self-dependent) responses in students, as indicated by their description of effective and ineffective teaching incidents in televised and direct instruction.

A wealth of evidence supports the conclusion that there is no significant difference in amount learned from direct and from televised instruction. The decision to use instructional television, therefore, must rest on other bases. One of the advantages of television is its distributive powers. Instruction can be provided in many places at the same time. When instruction is carefully designed and employs a wide range of human talent and instructional media, distinct advantages may result from extending the benefits of this instruction to as many students as may profit by it. Frequently, too, a school must choose between offering the televised course or no course at all in a particular subject or skill. Finally, distinct economic advantages can result from using televised rather than direct instruction.

OTHER USES OF INSTRUCTIONAL FILMS AND TELEVISION Greenhill (1964) notes substantial research on the use of television for purposes other than the presentation of subject matter. He describes these additional uses: (1) Television is used for the observation of demonstration teaching. The evidence indicates that trainees gain as much from televised as from direct observation, although they tend to prefer the direct observation. One practical advantage of televised observation is that it permits analysis and discussion of the teaching while it is occurring. The major disadvantage is that classroom conversations are often not adequately picked up by microphones. At Stanford University (see Allen, 1963) videotape is used to record demonstrations by the teacher trainees. When these videotapes are later played back, the teacher, the trainees, and others who can profit from the demonstration analyze and discuss the tapes. (2) Television is used for in-service training and professional training. The research indicates that such training can be effectively provided. (3) Television is used for the teaching of motor skills. For this to be effective, the conditions of skill learning which you learned in a previous chapter must be observed.

PRODUCTION VARIABLES The third research area concerning the use of television and films deals with production variables—variations in the organization and presentation of program content (Greenhill, 1964). Unfortunately, there has been very little research in this area, although the need and the possibilities for it are great. Such research could make important contributions to educational technology as the science of education. Illustrative of studies on production variables is the series of investigations by George Gropper and A. Lumsdaine (1961) on the use of instructional television in the teaching of high school physics and body chemistry. In one study, they taught lessons on heat and on nuclear reaction to junior high school students. Each lesson was presented by conventional television instruction and by a televised programed presentation. In the programed presentation, the television teacher paused long enough to allow students to write down their responses. During the pause, a question mark appeared on the screen. All students took an immediate and a delayed test of terminal behavior. These were the results: (1) The programed presentation resulted in significantly higher achievement than did the conventional television instruction; (2) the high-ability students in the programed course had sigficantly higher scores than high-ability students in the conventional course did; (3) low-ability students in both groups performed equally well on the immediate posttest, but low-ability students under conventional instruction scored significantly higher on the delayed posttest than the programed students did. For the lesson on nuclear reaction, two of the five comparisons made significantly favored the programed group. A later experiment in which students were taught how movies work supported these findings on active responding. One group saw a version of the televised lesson which required active response; the lecturer supplied the correct answer after the students responded. The second group saw the lesson without active responding. On both the delayed test and the immediate posttest, the active-response group obtained significantly superior scores.

Research on the use of various instructional media indicates that increasing amounts of both audial and visual information do not lead to greater learning. We have already referred to the research of Travers and his associates (1964a) on the amount of realism desirable in teaching the attributes of a concept. On the basis of their findings they conclude that the major purpose of using visual media is "not so much to bring the pupil into close touch with reality, but to help students become more effective in dealing with reality." They point out that the brain can use much less information than our information channels can transmit to it. Most of the stimuli which bombard our senses never really enter into our perception or memory. In emphasizing realism in teaching, the danger is to bombard

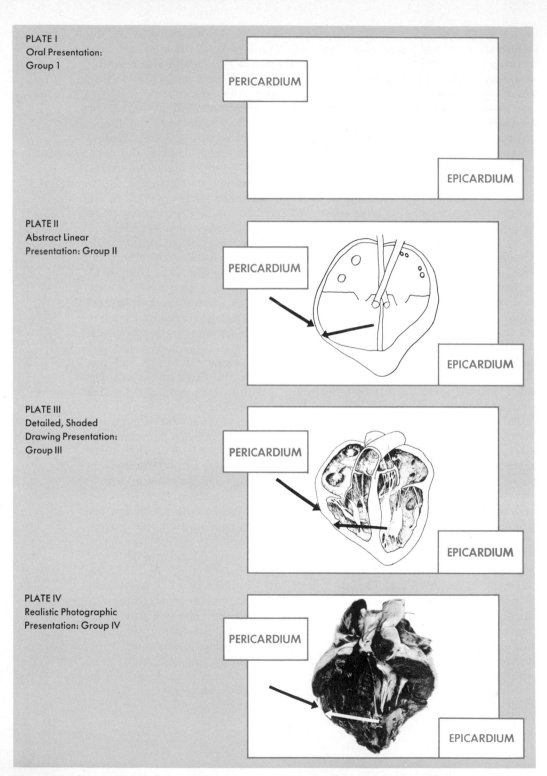

PLATE I
Oral Presentation:
Group 1

PERICARDIUM

EPICARDIUM

PLATE II
Abstract Linear
Presentation: Group II

PERICARDIUM

EPICARDIUM

PLATE III
Detailed, Shaded
Drawing Presentation:
Group III

PERICARDIUM

EPICARDIUM

PLATE IV
Realistic Photographic
Presentation: Group IV

PERICARDIUM

EPICARDIUM

FIG. 12-18 Three types of visual representation varying in degree of detail and realism (after Dwyer, 1967, opposite p. 156).

the student with more information than he can possibly utilize and to distract his attention from the major aspects of the concepts and principles he is learning. A study by Francis Dwyer (1967) with college freshmen compared the relative effectiveness of three types of visual representation which were shown as they were mentioned in an oral presentation: (1) abstract linear representations (see Figure 12-18, Plate II) of the form and relative locations of the parts of the heart; (2) detailed, shaded drawings (Plate III) representing the parts of the heart; and (3) realistic photographs (Plate IV) of the parts of the heart. A control group received instruction with no accompanying illustrations. To measure student achievement, Dwyer used a heart-model test, a terminology test, a drawing test, and a comprehension test. A total criterion test combined scores on these individual tests. Dwyer found that the abstract linear representations and the detailed shaded drawings were equally effective and that both of these were significantly more effective than the oral presentation alone and the realistic photographic presentation. Interestingly enough, the realistic photographic presentation was no more effective than was the oral presentation alone. Dwyer's findings remind us that instructional visual materials must be designed with experimental knowledge of the effects of various production variables. Rampant color, the existential realism of European motion pictures, and other excesses, whatever their artistic appeal, are not sound bases for the development of visual materials for instruction.

Computer-Assisted Instruction (CAI)

The computer has made its impact on industry and government and is making its impact on the school. In handling more and more information about more and more students, the schools need the capabilities of information storage and retrieval which are required by industry and government. The first impact of the computer on education will no doubt be in the area of clerical and accounting efficiency.

The computer's impact on instruction will be felt much later because its relationship to teaching and learning requires a great deal of research, some of which must await the fuller development of empirically based theories of teaching. In Chapter 1 we described the computer-based teaching model of Stolurow and Davis (1965). In the absence of a theory of teaching, such models help us launch the necessary research by suggesting the interrelationship of important teaching variables. Use of the computer as a highly adaptive teaching machine weakens the distinction between software and hardware. In computer-assisted instruction there can be no sharp division of functions. According to their definition, a teaching machine must have three capabilities: in a given subject area, it must have at its disposal a number of different programs; when specifying a program for each student, it must make use of the student's entering behavior, general ability, and personality characteristics; and it must be able to change programs during the course of instruction. The computer, of course, is the only machine with these capabilities, and a machine with these capabilities is far different from the metal boxes which industry first marketed as teaching machines.

Ronald Gentile (1967) describes some of the devices used in CAI. In the area of visual communication, (1) typewriters ask a question under computer control and answer a question under student control; (2) film projection devices, on the basis of student responses, select films, present auditory and visual materials, and automatically score student responses; (3) displays superimposed on films highlight certain aspects of the films; (4) with cathode-ray tubes a pen can be used for drawing curves or indicating answers on a screen. These answers can then be evaluated by the computer; and (5) random-access slides and films are available. The area of auditory communication presents many unsolved problems. However, two devices have been developed: In compiled speech, the computer has random access to prerecorded phrases which can be arranged on the basis of student response (for example, the computer can tell the student a chemical formula); in synthetic speech, the computer uses a set of rules to convert stored speech sounds into meaningful speech patterns.

Considerably more progress has been made with the technical development of CAI than with the problem of writing instructional programs. The chief unsolved technical problem is how to reduce the cost sufficiently to prevent bankruptcy of local school districts. As in the case of the general development and use of the instructional media, the temptation has been to dazzle the student with an array of visual and auditory stimuli which serve more to impress him with the capabilities of the computer than to provide him with the necessary instruction. Although, as Stolurow and Davis point out, CAI promises the best means yet for providing for variation in student entering behavior, Gentile (1967) indicates that several realistic considerations make provision for such individual differences a difficult educational feat. First, how we should provide for individual differences is rarely specified. There are many kinds of differences, and not all of them can be accommodated by allowing the computer to generate sequences on the basis of student response. Second, we need a classification of individual difference variables, especially in terms of learning variables. Third, the elimination of individual differences by any teaching method is an unrealistic expectation because of prior differences in student verbal abilities and mental sets. Finally, adaptation to individual differences must prove to be superior to teaching which is aimed at the group mean.

At several universities and research facilities there is extensive research on CAI (see "CAI—System and Projects," 1966). Figures 12-19, 12-20, and 12-21 show two intructional terminals and one computer laboratory. The computer laboratory can operate 200 instructional terminals located in one or more school districts. The older student is seated at a teletypewriter upon which he can compose his answers. The computers in the laboratory type feedback messages and expository material. The younger student can receive auditory, visual, and written materials from the remote computers. He can respond through use of the teletypewriter keyboard or by touching the television screen.

FIG. 12-19 A computer laboratory which can simultaneously operate 200 instructional terminals located in one or more school districts.

FIG. 12-20 Student reading feedback from a remote computer to an instructional terminal (photo courtesy of System Development Corporation).

FIG. 12-21 Student at an instructional terminal located in a classroom (photo courtesy of RCA Instructional Systems)

All these facilities and equipment, we must remind you, are much more sophisticated than any theory of teaching we presently have. The temptation in a technological society is to allow our fantastic machines to determine our research problems and our educational practice. It is far more important that we subordinate the machines to the theoretical and practical instructional problems which, undoubtedly, the machines can help us solve.

Summary

You now have an introductory knowledge of the old and the new media of instruction. With an increasingly wide array of media from which to choose, your problem is to find adequate bases for decision. Three bases for the selection and use of the media were suggested: (1) The first basis is availability. Several sources of information on available media, along with the names of manufacturers who will make media that you specially request, are listed in Erickson, 1965. (2) The analysis and design of instructional systems show you how to develop a course of instruction with full utilization of a wide range of media and media specialists. (3) Finally, and most importantly, the research on the effectiveness of the media, although much of it is preliminary and inconclusive, now furnishes a fairly solid basis for instructional decisions. Conclusive evidence shows no significant differences in student achievement in televised or face-to-face instruction. The decision to use or not to use televised instruction must clearly rest on other grounds. The need to combine overt responding with viewing and listening to the presentation of lessons has rather convincing research support. However, in our rush to portray all of life on television, in motion pictures, and on slides, we must remember that too much realism impedes student learning. Simplified representations of objects often teach more than the objects themselves. The use of computer-assisted instruction and simulation techniques requires considerably more research. Both activities enable researchers to deal with a complex array of teaching and learning variables. At this time and for the next several years we should view both simulation and computer-assisted instruction as very promising areas of research but not as practical innovations for the school.

QUESTION 12-2 As a teacher you want to select the best instructional procedures and materials and those which yield the best performance in terms of achievement, money, and time. Given these standards, which of the following innovations could you adopt to give you the highest probability of meeting them? (a) instructional television (including videotapes); (b) systems analysis and design; (c) computer-assisted instruction; (d) instructional films, with careful control of information input; (e) instructional kits and low-cost items.

After selecting your answer, give the reasons for your choice and for your rejection of the alternatives.

In the introduction to this chapter, we made a distinction between the two meanings of instructional technology. One meaning refers to the detailed application of the psychology of learning to practical teaching problems. The second meaning refers to the application of engineering principles to the development of electromechanical equipment used for instructional purposes. The two aspects interact in the design and use of instructional equipment, materials, and procedures. A major influence on the schools for the adoption of instructional technology is business and industry.

The first section of the chapter dealt with programed instruction, particularly the preparation, writing, tryout, and revision of programs. Programed instruction includes reducing material to small steps, requiring student response, providing immediate confirmation or correction, and trying out and revising materials. In the preparation of the program there are five steps: selecting a unit or topic, preparing a content outline, defining objectives in behavioral terms, and constructing and administering tests of entering and terminal behavior. In the program writing there are also five steps: presenting the material in the form of frames, requiring active student responses, providing confirmation or correction of student responses, using prompts to guide student responses, and providing careful sequencing of materials. The use of prompts requires vanishing or fading. In the tryout and revision of the program there are three steps: writing the original draft, editing it, and trying it out and revising it. There are two types of programs. The linear sequence provides a single path for all students to follow. In the branching sequence the student branches to supplementary material when he makes an error. Adjunct autoinstruction inserts programed or testing materials into a textbook, laboratory manual, or other materials whenever these supplementary materials are needed.

The second section of the chapter dealt with instructional media. Instructional media are the electromechanical devices which act as a middle condition between the student and what he is to learn. The traditional media include mockups, graphic materials, motion pictures, projected stills, and magnetic tape recordings. The new media include television, teaching machines, and instructional kits. Three bases for the selection of media were described: information about available media, an analysis and design of an instructional system, and knowledge of the research findings on the use of the media. In computer-assisted instruction there is no sharp distinction between hardware and software. CAI involves the use of typewriters, film projection, superimposed displays, cathode-ray tubes, and random-access slides.

SUGGESTED READINGS

Because of the lively current interest in most of these topics, almost a superabundance of literature is available.

In the area of programed instruction and the instructional media, several collections of theoretical discussions and research reports make excellent references for the student who wishes to probe more deeply than this chapter. The most authoritative collections are the following two:

GLASER, ROBERT, ed., *Teaching Machines and Programed Learning, II: Data and Directions.* Washington, D.C.: Department of Audiovisual Instruction, National Education Association, 1965.

LUMSDAINE, ARTHUR A., and GLASER, ROBERT, eds., *Teaching Machines and Programmed Learning: A Source Book.* Washington, D.C.: Department of Audiovisual Instruction, National Education Association, 1960.

The following less comprehensive collections include major papers and statements of important theoretical issues:

DE CECCO, JOHN P., ed., *Educational Technology: Readings in Programmed Instruction.* New York: Holt, Rinehart & Winston, Inc., 1964 (paperback).

OFIESH, GABRIEL D. and MEIERHENRY, WESLEY C., eds., *Trends in Programmed Instruction.* Washington, D.C.: Department of Audiovisual Instruction, National Education Association and the National Society for Programmed Instruction, 1964 (paperback).

SMITH, WENDELL I. and MOORE, J. WILLIAM, eds., *Programmed Learning.* Princeton, N.J.: D. Van Nostrand Co., Inc., 1962 (paperback).

The following books on how to program materials are particularly sound and useful:

LYSAUGHT, JEROME P. and WILLIAMS, CLARENCE M., *A Guide to Programmed Instruction.* New York: John Wiley & Sons, Inc., 1963.

MARKLE, SUSAN MEYER, *Good Frames and Bad: A Grammar of Frame Writing.* New York: John Wiley & Sons, Inc., 1964 (paperback).

PIPE, PETER, *Practical Programming.* New York: Holt, Rinehart & Winston, Inc., 1966 (paperback).

TABER, JULIAN I.; GLASER, ROBERT; and SHAEFER, HALMUTH H., *Learning and Programmed Instruction.* Reading, Mass.: Addison-Wesley Publishing Co., Inc., 1965.

For excellent summaries and reviews on the research on programed instruction, the instructional media, and related topics see the following articles:

ANDERSON, RICHARD C., "Educational Psychology," *Annual Review of Psychology,* 18 (1967), 103–64.

LUMSDAINE, ARTHUR A., "Instruments and Media of Instruction," in *Handbook of Research on Teaching,* ed. N. L. Gage, pp. 583–682. Chicago: Rand McNally & Co., 1963.

——— and MAY, M. A., "Mass Communication and Educational Media," *Annual Review of Psychology,* 16 (1965), 475–534.

For reading on flexible scheduling, team teaching, and nongraded instruction, see the following books:

BAIR, MEDILL and WOODWARD, RICHARD G., *Team Teaching in Action*. Boston: Houghton Mifflin Company, 1964.

BROWN, FRANK B., *The Nongraded High School*. Englewood Cliffs, N.J.: Prentice-Hall, Inc., 1963.

BUSH, ROBERT N. and ALLEN, DWIGHT W., *A New Design for High School Education*. New York: McGraw-Hill Book Company, 1964.

GOODLAD, JOHN I., and ANDERSON, ROBERT H., *The Nongraded Elementary School*. New York: Harcourt, Brace & World, Inc., 1963.

PART FOUR

PERFORMANCE ASSESSMENT AND RESEARCH

CHAPTER THIRTEEN

HOW TO CONSTRUCT YOUR OWN TESTS

This chapter has two major sections. The first describes the nature of performance assessment, distinguishing between criterion-related and relative standards of achievement. We consider four standards which tests of student performance should meet: validity, reliability, objectivity, and efficiency. The second section describes the planning, construction, administration, scoring, and evaluation of your tests. Here we consider procedures and guidelines which, if followed, will help your tests reach the standards described in the previous section.

Upon reading this section of the chapter you should be able to meet these objectives:

13-1 Define and illustrate performance assessment in terms of auxiliary and terminal performances.

13-2 Describe and illustrate the relationship of performance assessment to other components of the basic teaching model.

13-3 Distinguish and illustrate the differences between absolute, criterion-related and relative standards of performance.

13-4 Describe and illustrate the disadvantage of using relative standards in performance assessment.

13-5 Describe and illustrate three important results of using absolute and criterion-related standards.

13-6 Define and illustrate validity in terms of instructional objectives and test items.

13-7 Define reliability in terms of consistency.

13-8 Describe and illustrate three ways in which reliability and validity are related.

13-9 Define objectivity in terms of scoring and illustrate its use in scoring essay and objective tests.

13-10 Define efficiency in terms of time and illustrate the comparative efficiency of essay and objective tests.

BASIC CHARACTERISTICS OF PERFORMANCE ASSESSMENT

The first section of the chapter describes the nature and purposes of performance assessment and of the tests used in this assessment. Here we introduce some basic concepts—absolute, relative, and criterion-related standards of assessment; validity, reliability; objectivity; and efficiency. We shall describe, illustrate, and interrelate these concepts.

Performance Assessment: Definition and Uses

Performance assessment is the process of measuring the student's auxiliary and terminal performances during and at the end of instruction (Glaser, 1962). Auxiliary performances are behaviors which must be acquired at the lower levels of a learning structure before the terminal performances are acquired at the higher levels. In the teaching of a principle, for example, the teacher must determine whether the student has acquired the component concepts, as auxiliary performances, before proceeding with the instruction which arranges these concepts in the proper relationship for the learning of the principle. Terminal performances, you already know, refer to the end products of instruction—usually verbal performances (Chapter 2). The emphasis on the measurement of both auxiliary and terminal performances means that you should not think of performance assessment as occurring only at the end of a unit or a course. The assessment can occur whenever the teacher or the student needs information about the adequency of the student's present learning for subsequent instruction. In programed instruction, for example, a test, or criterion, frame can occur whenever it is necessary to determine whether the student has acquired essential auxiliary behavior. Similarly, each frame in a program can be considered a test item which provides feedback to the student on the adequacy of his performance.

Three uses can be made of the information, or feedback, obtained through performance assessment. In Chapter 1 (Figure 1-2) you saw that performance assessment has feedback loops to the other three components of the basic teaching model. These loops describe the three uses of the feedback. First, you use the feedback to determine how well the student has achieved the instructional objective (or terminal performance). If the student has reached the standard of acceptability the instructional objective states, the instruction has been successful and you can proceed to new instruction. Second, you use the feedback to determine the adequacy of entering behavior. This use is appropriate either during the course of instruction, when you are measuring auxiliary behavior, or at the end of instruction, when you are determining why the instruction was unsuccessful. Third, you use the feedback to determine the adequacy of your instructional procedures, particularly when you compare the effectiveness of one with another procedure. Thus, performance assessment, the fourth component, is an important basis for making appropriate modifications in one or all of the remaining components of the basic teaching model.

Criterion-Related, Absolute, and Relative Standards

We will distinguish between three types of standards which can be applied when interpreting test scores: absolute, relative, and criterion-related. Then, we will distinguish between the characteristics that are necessary and desirable for tests used with each standard.

Absolute and criterion-related standards describe the precise amount of end-of-unit or end-of-course competence the student is expected to attain. His achievement determines whether he proceeds to the next unit or course of instruction. A test using these standards provides explicit information about what the student can or cannot do. If, for example, the instructional objective required the student to identify all statements of theories of learning when presented with positive and negative examples of such statements, before you would permit him to proceed to the next unit of instruction (for example, the identification of statements of theories teaching), you would expect him to achieve a specified performance.

The relative standard compares the performance of one student with that of other students in his group. Tests based on the relative standard tell us that one student is more or less proficient than another but do not tell us how proficient either student is with respect to a specified standard. For example, relative standards indicate that Suzanne identified more positive examples of statements of educational philosophy than Joy did and that Joy identified more than Bill did. This information, however, does not tell us whether Suzanne correctly identified 100 percent, 90 percent, or only 25 percent of the examples. Similarly, Joy ranked only second. Furthermore, with the relative standard, the student proceeds to the next unit or course of instruction even though his level of performance may fall considerably below a specified standard of mastery.

The chief shortcoming of performance assessment based on relative standards is that the student can proceed to the next instructional objective and unit of instruction before he has mastered the prerequisite entering behavior. Dorothy Adkins (1958, p. 234) describes some of the practical effects of using the relative standard:

> Consider, if you will, the hundreds of hours devoted to instruction in English by the time a person becomes a college senior. Then ponder his inability to write. Turn to arithmetic . . . and later to algebra and geometry. Then reflect upon the ineptitude of a typical college student in solving the most elementary equation or even adding a column of figures. Recall the idiosyncrasies in spelling which confront you in personal correspondence. Contemplate the current reading hubbub, by no means without foundation. Shudder at the prevalent superstitions and gullibility of the American public.

Adkins believes that what is needed is a curriculum revision which divides each area of subject matter into units arranged according to difficulty, with tests for each unit based on a specified standard. A particular unit would require each student to achieve a stipulated degree of mastery; after that, he would proceed to the next higher unit. Adkins describes (p. 237) what would happen if we adopted such a practice:

> In 1984, we may be able to say to an employer or to a university that John Doe has mastered mathematics unit 1728, English grammar 642, spelling 1021, physics 303, and so on. The personnel officers will by that time have conducted studies to enable them to predict from such data his relative chances of success as an outerspace radiological isotopist or as a student in a modern household engineering curriculum.

The use of a specified standard has three important instructional results. First, the standard which the performance of all students must meet is the standard of acceptability specified in the instructional objective. The meeting of this standard is the prerequisite for the introduction of new instructional objectives and materials. Second, all students must meet the standard of acceptability not in a single objective but in all objectives. Presumably you will adopt as instructional objectives only those performances you deem worthy of student achievement. If an objective lacks value, let us say to subsequent learning, then it is highly questionable that you should expend on it your own and your students' time. Once you embark on instruction for a particular objective, the ordinary assumptions are that you expect all students for whom you provide instruction to achieve mastery of the terminal performance and that instruction will continue until all achieve mastery. This, of course, is a most rigorous demand on both teachers and students, but anything less rigorous condemns much instruction to aimless futility. Third, the use of specified standards alters some conventional procedures in test construction. When using the relative standard, we construct our tests so that students achieve high, average, and low scores. We are disappointed if everyone receives a perfect or high score because we seek a distribution or spread of scores as a basis for assigning letter grades. To obtain this distribution we include items of high, average, and low difficulty. When using specified standards, we construct our tests so that all students who achieve the instructional objective obtain appropriate scores. We retain even very difficult and very easy items if they are relevant to the terminal performance. Since each terminal performance becomes entering behavior for subsequent instruction, we continue to provide instruction for those students whose scores indicate that they have not attained a minimum standard of acceptability. Both absolute and criterion-related standards provide for the establishment of levels of acceptable performance before a test is administered. These methods do not rely on the performance of individuals in the group but require that definitions of acceptable performance levels be determined before a test is given or, at least, before the score distribution is known and examined.

Absolute standards are based on mastery or perfect student performance. The only acceptable performance level is 100 percent. This procedure requires, of course, that the instructor define terminal performances explicitly and consider the appropriate entering behavior for subsequent instructional sequences.

Criterion-related standards are similar to absolute standards in that they require the explicit definition of terminal behaviors, usually in reference to the entering behaviors necessary for the next sequence of instruction. There is, however, a fundamental difference: criterion-related standards may be set at any level up to 100 percent. Criterion-related standards are established by considering the nature of the content, the objectives for a sequence of instruction, entering behaviors necessary for the next sequence of instruction, and difficulty of the items. One of the procedures for establishing performance criteria for multiple-choice items was described by Leo Nedelsky (1954). Before deciding which of the types of standards to apply to classroom or other tests, a teacher should examine and consider carefully the implications of the various procedures. Table 13-1 contains some of the characteristics and implications for each of the three types of standards we have discussed.

We shall now turn to the consideration of four concepts which deal with the tests used in performance assessment more than with the process itself.

Validity

A committee designated by the American Psychological Association, the American Educational Research Association, and the National Council on Measurements in Education (A.P.A., 1966) has defined the types of validity which should be used in assessing the usefulness of tests for a particular purpose. These types of validity are known as content validity, criterion-related validity, and construct validity. The first of these, content validity, is usually of most importance to classroom teachers and is the one on which most of the rest of our discussion will be based. Both criterion-related and construct validity are more important when considering tests such as aptitude batteries and intelligence tests. The relationship to those measures

TABLE 13-1   COMPARISON OF PERFORMANCE STANDARDS

CRITERION-RELATED	ABSOLUTE	RELATIVE
Difficult to establish	Difficult to establish	Relatively easy to establish
Requires clear and explicit definition of instructional and testing objectives	Requires clear and explicit definition of instructional and testing objectives	Permits the least definition of instructional and testing objectives
Allows all or any number of students to pass or fail	Allows all or any number of students to pass or fail	Generally requires a specified number of students to be classified in each letter grade or other category
Allows direct comparison of students from class to class or year to year with reference to a specifically defined level of performance	Allows direct comparison of students from class to class or year to year with reference to a specifically defined level of performance	Allows performance comparisons based only on how high or how low one group performed in relation to another
Performance is judged in terms of how well or poorly students do in terms of how they should do	Performance is judged in terms of how well or poorly students do in terms of how they should do	Allows judgments only in terms of comparing one student or group of students with another
Requires intense scrutiny of every item	Requires intense scrutiny of every item	Allows inclusion of items which may not have been carefully examined and which may be hastily and uncarefully written

will be shown in a later chapter. In this section we will give a basic definition of them.

Content validity tells us whether the items in a test are constructed around appropriate content. For example, a test in chemistry would deal with topics which were clearly related to the facts, concepts, and principles which were presented in the course; the test would not contain extraneous filler material. Further, the test would be constructed to measure those particular facts, concepts, and principles which were clearly relevant for the intended instructional sequence, and they would be balanced in proportion to the importance of the material and the emphasis which was placed on it during the instructional phase. Content validity is determined by inspection of the test items and by relating them to an outline of the material which is intended to be measured. Such an outline is known as a test blueprint or table of specifications and will be discussed in a subsequent section of this chapter. For the moment you should remember that content validity is determined by comparison of the actual test items in relation to the content and intellectual processes which the test writer intended to measure.

The central problem in constructing a content valid test is to engage the student on the test in the sample performance the instructional objective requires. Consider this example. This is the instructional objective: When presented with a list of statements of theories of teaching, theories of learning, and philosophies of education, the student will select from the list only the theories of teaching. Is the following item a valid test of this objective?

> Write *TT* (for theory of teaching) after each of the following statements which describes a theory of teaching:
> *A   (A short description of Herbart's methodology).
> B   (A short description of Combs' and Snygg's theory).
> C   (A short description of Dewey's pragmatism).
> D   (A short description of Thorndike's learning theory).
> *E   (A short description of Carroll's model for school learning).

This item is valid because it requires the student to engage in exactly that performance described in the instructional objective—to select from a list the appropriate statements (in this case, *A* and *E*). For this same objective compare the validity of the following item:

> Match the names of the men below with the theory or philosophy of education they formulated:
> *Key:* A   William James
> B   John Dewey
> C   Arthur Combs
> D   Edward Thorndike
> E   Lawrence Stolurow
> F   John Carroll
> 1   Theory of teaching *(E, F)*
> 2   Theory of learning *(D)*
> 3   Philosophy of education *(B, C)*

This item, besides containing certain intrinsic difficulties, is less valid than the preceding item because it does not require the student to engage in the performance described in the objective—namely, with his knowledge of the characteristics of theories of teaching, to select only those statements which describe such theories. A student with little or no knowledge of these characteristics could answer the second item correctly.

The definition of content validity in terms of terminal performances reveals that we are dealing with direct validation—the obvious validity of appropriate items. The first item above, which contains statements of theories of teaching, is obviously more valid than the latter item, which contains only the names of the theorists. An item with content validity requires the student to perform operations on the content he has learned. Surely one of the great advantages of explicit statements of instructional objectives is that the teacher can validate his tests directly by comparing the test items with the instructional objectives. Ebel (1972, p. 440) believes, "The persistent difficulties that plague our efforts to measure some outcomes of education are less attributable to limitations of measurement than to uncertainty about what is to be measured." Ebel (p. 443) further states:

> If one is willing to accept as a definition of what a test is measuring a simple description of the tasks that the test requires the student to perform, then what a test appears to measure and what it really does measure will be practically identical. For example, the question, "What is the sum of ⅕ and ⅙?" appears to measure and really does measure (beyond his ability to read), the student's ability to add two particular common fractions. The tasks in most classroom tests of educational achievement can be described as obviously and sensibly as this one if one is willing to settle for an obvious, common sense description.

The definition of test validity in terms of instructional objectives indicates that it is more closely related to absolute and criterion-related than to relative standards of performance. An explicit statement of an instructional objective, you recall, specifies a minimum standard of acceptable performance. When the student fails to meet this minimum standard, the teacher considers it a failure to achieve the objective. The items on the test and the uses made of test performance must be compatible with a predetermined standard. Whether the items are of high, average, or low difficulty is less important than their content validity. Having the students all achieve a specified score level is more important than obtaining a distribution of scores. When all or some students receive scores which indicate below-standard performance, the need for further instruction is clear.

Criterion-related validity and construct validity have less direct usefulness to the classroom teacher, but the terms are likely to be encountered in reading descriptions of validation procedures used by researchers or commercial test publishers. Briefly, criterion-related validity refers to the validity of a test with respect to some external criterion. In content validity, we were concerned with the measurement of specific outcomes of instruction as defined with specific instructional objectives. In criterion-related validity, we are concerned with the prediction of a behavior related to the one being tested directly. For example, we may wish to estimate the achievement level of a group of entering students, in which case we would administer an aptitude test. The external criterion against which the test would be validated would be performance in school subjects. Or, we might be interested in job performance such as that exhibited in a secretarial position. In that case we would administer a secretarial aptitude test and relate the results to on-the-job performance as measured by some independent measure.

Construct validity is more difficult to assess and more difficult to understand completely. Basically, construct validity is established by making inferences about things which cannot be observed directly from things which can be observed directly. For example, we cannot observe intelligence directly, and, in fact, there are competing theories about its nature as we discussed in Chapter 4. When establishing construct validity, the investigator develops a test which he thinks measures the factors in which he is interested and, through a complex procedure involving detailed statistical and logical analysis, determines the validity. Construct validity is generally determined by making inferences from observable entities to nonobservable entities. Tests which rely heavily on the establishment of construct validity are those measuring such things as intelligence, motivation, personality factors, and so on.

Reliability

A reliable test measures terminal performances consistently. On a highly reliable test we expect the student to obtain about the same score on the second administration of the test as he did on the first. We expect, that is, the same consistency of performance for a reliable test as we do for a reliable individual. When tests and individuals are unreliable, we expect erratic, unpredictable, indeed, very inconsistent performance.

At least three factors influence the degree of test reliability. First, if the items are too easy, too difficult, or ambiguous, they will yield highly unreliable scores. Second, if the students vary considerably in personal behavior—in alertness, energy, emotional balance, and so on—the reliability of the scores will be reduced. Third, if the person who scores the test assigns scores on the basis of momentary considerations rather than on the basis of standards uniformly applied to all test papers, the scores will lack reliability. The first and third factors are discussed at further length in the section on test construction.

Reliability and validity are closely related. First, for a test to have validity it must also have reliability. Validity pertains to what a test purports to measure. Reliability pertains to how consistently a test measures. If a test fails to measure with consistency, then it cannot purport to measure anything at all. A rubber yardstick which changes its length as you apply different amounts of tension to its ends is neither a reliable nor a valid measure of length or distance. A test of terminal performance which yields different results when administered to the same students a second time, so that we are never clear about their relative levels of achievement, is neither reliable nor valid. Second, the converse of this relationship between reliability and validity is not true: A test may be reliable without being valid. It is entirely possible and not amusing for a teacher to construct a test which gives about the same scores to the same individuals in successive retests without the teacher's knowing what the test attempts to measure. A teacher who assesses performance of unstated and unknown instructional objectives may some day construct a test of known reliability and unknown validity—a state of instructional affairs no one should emulate. Third, it is possible that by improving the reliability of your test you reduce its validity. Some terminal behaviors are more easily measured than others. Verbal learning, which requires the learning of a list of single or associated terms, is easier to measure than concept and principle learning, which require the student to demonstrate his knowledge. Adequate performance assessment, however, requires you to measure all the learning your instructional objectives embrace and not only those types for which you can easily construct reliable test items.

Objectivity

In an objective test the scores are free of subjective judgments (Gorow, 1966, p. 16). Objectivity is difficult to attain whether the items are cast in objective or essay form. Responses to items in the objective form, for example items on multiple-choice and true-false tests, are often the subject of heated debate between instructor and student and even among subject matter experts. It is possible to obtain colleague and expert agreement on particular responses and, in this way, to improve the quality of the test. Responses to essay questions are scored subjectively because there is usually little recourse to expert agreement and because each response is usually read, interpreted, and scored somewhat in its own terms.

Ebel (1972, p. 372) believes that when experts disagree on the correct answers to objective questions, the fault usually rests with the item. Several factors may reduce the objectivity of various objective items: (1) The item may fail to specify all the conditions and qualifications necessary to make one and only one response correct; (2) the item may pertain to opinions and theories about which there is little agreement; and (3) the item as originally conceived may be satisfactory but its written expression may be faulty. We discuss ways of improving the objectivity of objective and essay tests in subsequent sections.

Objectivity is closely related to reliability. Inconsistency in scoring a test leads to low reliability. This inconsistency occurs most easily in the scoring of essay tests when momentary considerations replace uniform standards of judgment. Inconsistency can also occur in the scoring of objective tests when answers are incorrectly scored, when the response key is altered in the process of scoring the papers, and when the choice of the right answer shifts with the winds of controversy.

Efficiency

An efficient test is one that yields a large number of independent scorable responses per unit of time (Ebel, 1972, p. 371). An efficient test, therefore, makes the best use of the instructor's and the students' time. Items cast in the objective form, such as multiple-choice items, are time consuming to prepare. They are efficient to use, however, because they can be administered to successive classes and scored very quickly by hand or machine. The essay test is often more efficient when a separate examination must be prepared for several classes and when the likelihood of reusing the examination is slight. Thus, part of the decision of whether to use essay or objective items in any particular examination or program depends on the most efficient use of time and energies. If more time is available before the examination and can be used to construct good items, while only a limited amount of time is going to be available for scoring and analyzing the results, it would be appropriate to use objective items. If, however, there is a limited amount of time in which to prepare items but a great deal of time available for scoring and studying results, essay items might be more appropriate.

In most school situations the time following test administration is short, and the teacher is under considerable pressure to produce scores and grades soon after examinations are administered. In terms of the student's time the essay test is less efficient than the objective test because the student must spend most of his time in writing rather than in reading. The typical student can read about ten times as fast as he can write (Ebel, 1970, p. 371). Even objective items which involve interpretation of explanatory materials and problem solutions are less efficient than items involving factual information. Ebel reminds us, however, that these item types are not interchangeable. The instructional objective may dictate the use of a less efficient but more valid item. There must be a balance between validity and efficiency as well as between validity and reliability.

Summary

Performance assessment is the process of measuring the student's auxiliary and terminal performances during and at the end of the course of instruction. Feedback from performance assessment shows how well the student has achieved the instructional objective, the adequacy of his entering behavior, and the effectiveness of the instructional procedures. The measure-

---

Read the instructional objective and multiple-choice item below and answer the true-false **QUESTION 13-1** questions which follow.

Instructional objective: When presented with a list of numerical problems requiring various arithmetic operations, the student will select only those problems requiring multiplication.

Item   Circle the letters of those problems which require multiplication.

(a) $34 + 43 + 116 =$
*(b) $782416 \div 42 =$
(c) $7333 - 333 =$
*(d) $823 \times 843 =$
*(e) $(34 + 113) \times 2 =$

Now answer these true-false statements by circling T for true and F for false.

T F (1)   This item is valid for this instructional objective.
T F (2)   This item measures a relative standard of achievement.
T F (3)   This item is probably reliable.
T F (4)   This item is objective.

After selecting your answers, give the reasons for your choices.

---

ment of achievement involves the use of absolute, relative, or criterion-related standards. Absolute and criterion-related standards describe the minimal level of mastery the student is expected to attain. The relative standard compares the performance of one student with others in his group. Four concepts are basic to test construction and use: Validity is the degree to which a test measures appropriate terminal performances; reliability is the consistency with which a test measures these performances; objectivity is freedom from subjective judgments in the scoring of the test; and efficiency refers to the number of independent scorable responses per unit of time. The four concepts are related, and the construction of the test requires the teacher to strike a balance among them.

You should now return to objectives 1–10 and determine how well you have achieved them.

Upon reading this section of the chapter you should be able to meet these objectives:

13-11   Describe the relationship between task analysis and test preperation.

13-12   List and illustrate four rules for the preparation of tests.

13-13   Describe and illustrate differences and similarities of essay and objective tests.

13-14   Describe the appropriate conditions of the use of essay and objective tests.

13-15   Describe and illustrate types of desirable and undesirable essay questions.

13-16   Construct two essay questions which follow the guidelines.

13-17   Score two essay questions by following the guidelines.

13-18   Distinguish and illustrate differences between free-response and limited-response items.

13-19   Construct two completion items which follow the guidelines.

13-20   Define and illustrate distractors, specific determiners, and item stems.

13-21   Construct five true-false items which follow the guidelines.

13-22   Construct two matching items which follow the guidelines.

13-23   Recast a matching item of your own as a multiple-choice item.

13-24   Construct five multiple-choice items which follow the guidelines.

13-25   Construct two key-list multiple-choice items which measure principle learning or problem solving.

13-26   Describe and illustrate the relationship between key-list items and long-term retention.

13-27   Describe the best arrangement of items for limited and generous time limits.

13-28   Illustrate properly written directions for a test containing multiple-choice items.

13-29   Describe three characteristics of efficient test administration.

13-30   Describe and illustrate how you can prevent or handle three forms of cheating.

13-31   Describe and illustrate the bad effects of cheating on subsequent student achievement.

13-32　Describe how you would score a test in terms of a key, assignment of points, and correction for guessing.

13-33　Describe and illustrate how you would apply the criteria of validity, reliability, objectivity, and efficiency to the evaluation of a test.

13-34　Define item analysis in terms of discrimination and difficulty indices.

13-35　Determine the difficulty index and discrimination index for particular test items.

13-36　Describe and illustrate the use of these indices in the revision of an item.

13-37　Describe the ways of improving reliability of tests based on relative, absolute, and criterion-related standards of achievement.

HOW TO CONSTRUCT AND REVISE YOUR TESTS

This section deals with the planning, construction, administration, scoring, and evaluation of essay and objective tests. The guidelines are procedures for incorporating in the body and the use of the test the basic characteristics of performance assessment: validity, reliability, objectivity, and efficiency. First, we shall consider four rules to follow in planning the test. Second, we shall compare the characteristics and uses of objective and essay examinations. Third, we shall consider the construction and scoring of the essay test. Fourth, in the longest portion of this section, we shall deal with the construction of the objective test. Fifth, we consider matters concerned with the use of the test: preparing the test copy, giving the test, scoring the test, and evaluating and revising the test. You are also taught how to do an item analysis as one method of assessing the quality of the objective tests you construct.

Planning the Test

Julian Stanley and Kenneth Hopkins (1972, p. 172) present four rules which you should follow in planning a test:

1　Adequate provision should be made for evaluating all important outcomes of instruction.
2　The test should reflect the approximate typical emphasis of the course.
3　The nature of the test must reflect its purpose.
4　The nature of the test must reflect the conditions under which it will be administered.

We shall now consider each of these rules.

Adequate provision should be made for evaluating all important outcomes of instruction　In the context of the basic teaching model, this means that you must construct items which assess achievement of important instructional objectives. Since ordinarily there are many objectives, to simplify your task you should use one of the two systems for the classification of behavior described in Chapter 2.

Tables 13-2 and 13-3 show how the use of a chart or grid can simplify the classification of objectives. Table 13-2 employs Gagné's behavior categories. Table 13-3 employs four of the major categories of the *Taxonomy* and also uses course content rather than statements of instructional objectives. The use of such charts increases the likelihood that the important objectives and content are covered in the test.

The test should reflect the approximate proportion of emphasis of the course If the test covers a large amount of material and the time for administration is short, as in a final examination in a course, it will be necessary to sample from the content. Sampling procedure is a critical component of test construction. The preparation of a grid or chart like those

TABLE 13-2   AN ILLUSTRATION OF CHART PLANNING OF TESTS, BASED ON GAGNE'S CLASSIFICATION OF LEARNING TYPES (see Chapter 2). EMPTY CELLS WILL CONTAIN NUMBERS, INDICATING NUMBER OF ITEMS FOR EACH OBJECTIVE AND LEARNING TYPE

INSTRUCTIONAL OBJECTIVES	SIGNAL LEARNING	STIMULUS-RESPONSE LEARNING	CHAINING	VERBAL ASSOCIATION	MULTIPLE DISCRIMINATION	CONCEPT LEARNING	PRINCIPLE LEARNING	PROBLEM SOLVING
1 Define and illustrate performance assessment in terms of auxiliary and terminal performances.								
2 Describe and illustrate the relationship of performance assessment to other components of the basic teaching model.								
3 Distinguish and illustrate the differences between absolute and relative standards of performance.								
4 Describe and illustrate the disadvantage of using relative standards in performance assessment.								
5 Describe and illustrate three important results of using absolute standards.								
6 Define and illustrate validity in terms of instructional objectives and test items.								
7 Define reliability in terms of consistency.								
8 Define objectivity in terms of scoring and illustrate its use in scoring essay and objective tests.								
9 Describe the relationship between task analysis and test preparation.								
10 Construct two essay questions which follow the guidelines.								

COURSE CONTENT	OBJECTIVES *				
	Knowledge	Comprehension (Translation, Interpretation, Extrapolation)	Application	Analysis	Total
I Perception, symbolization, and the methods of science	5	5			10
II The cell—structure and function; cell principle; spontaneous generation and biogenesis	5			5	10
III Sexual reproduction in animals and plants; human reproduction and sex hormones	4	6			10
IV Cellular reproduction; mitosis	4	6			10
V Meiosis; chromosomes and genes	3	3	4		10
VI Monohybrid cross		4	6		10
VII Dihybrid cross		3	3		10
VIII Blood group inheritance; heredity in man		4	6	4	10
IX Linkage and crossing-over	3	3	4		10
X Sex determination and sex linkage	1	1	2	6	10
Total	25	35	25	15	100

* Based on Bloom, 1956.

shown in Tables 13-2 and 13-3 will be helpful in determining if all the most important aspects have been covered and if undue emphasis has been placed on one or more portions of the content. In Table 13-3 the figures which appear in the various cells denote the number of items which will be devoted to each topic within a particular behavior class. For example there will be ten items on various aspects of the cell—five in the category of knowledge and five in the category of analysis. The subtotals for each behavior class indicate that the test items have their strongest emphasis on comprehension and their weakest emphasis on analysis. These emphasis, according to Stanley and Hopkins (p. 185), should reflect the relative amount of emphasis each objective has received in the actual teaching of the course. The same course may receive different emphases from two teachers, one teacher stressing the simple acquisition of knowledge and the other stressing the application of knowledge to practical problems. The assignment of test items to the various objectives, topics, and behavior categories must reflect these differences, particularly if the test is to be given to all the classes.

Following these two rules will improve the validity of your tests. A test cannot be valid unless the items are relevant to the instructional objectives and materials and to the learning they embody. Unless you take deliberate steps to provide the proper relevance and emphasis, your tests will lack validity.

The nature of the test must reflect its purpose Here you must determine whether to employ an absolute, relative, or criterion-related standard of achievement. If your purpose is to determine whether the student has achieved the level of mastery specified in the instructional objective or the prerequisite level of entering behavior (an absolute or criterion-related standard), it is not important to include items which will yield a wide range of scores. Your purpose is to determine the present status of the student's behavior in relation to the specified standard and not in relation to other students in his group. If your purpose is to compare the performance of the student with others in his group (a relative standard), then you must include items which will distribute the scores from high to low. Following this rules provides both validity and reliability. To be valid, a test must actually measure what it was designed to measure. For the relative standard, one of the best ways of improving test reliability is to include items which yield a wide range of scores.

The nature of the test must reflect the conditions under which it will be administered Ebel (1972, pp. 97–121) has identified several conditions about which the teacher must make decisions. First, you must decide how frequently you can test. Ebel believes it is safe to say that few classes are overexposed to good tests. The basic teaching model indicates that performance assessment, or testing, is an integral part of the teaching process and that it should occur during as well as at the conclusion of instruction. Second, you must decide how many items to include in the test—based on the amount of available time, on the number of instructional objectives, and on the amount of content covered. These items must, of course, be distributed according to the plan you have developed by following the procedure described previously. Although the longer examination often has greater validity and reliability, an examination lasting more than three hours is often impractical. Third, you must decide in which format you will give the test. You should present objective examinations in the form of a printed booklet. You can save space by printing multiple-choice items in double columns rather than across the page. Whether you use fixed-response or free-response examinations each student should receive his own copy of the test. Although there have been some attempts to administer tests by visual projection (Curtis and Kropp, 1965) the cost of materials, the tediousness for the teacher, and the sources of distraction for the student discourage its use.

After this initial planning stage, you must decide whether to use an objective or an essay test. The basis for this decision should be your knowledge of the respective characteristics of these tests and the appropriate conditions for their use, the subject matter of our next topic.

Objective and Essay Examinations: Characteristics and Use

Ebel (1972, pp. 123–44) has ably described the following differences and similarities of objective and essay tests:

DIFFERENCES

Objective Tests	Essay Tests
1 Requires student to choose among two or more alternatives.	1 Requires the student to plan his own answer and express it in his own words.
2 Consists of many rather specific questions requiring only brief answers.	2 Consists of relatively few, more general questions which call for extended answers.
3 Students spend most of their time reading and thinking.	3 Students spend most of their time in thinking and writing.
4 Quality is determined by the skill of the test constructor.	4 Quality is determined largely by skill of the grader reading.
5 Is relatively tedious and difficult to prepare, but easy to score.	5 Is easy to prepare, but relatively tedious and difficult to score.
6 Offers freedom to the test constructor to demonstrate his knowledge and values but limits the student in his expression.	6 Offers freedom to the student to express his answers individually and freedom to the scorer to score preferentially.
7 States student's tasks and the basis for judgment more clearly.	7 States student's tasks and basis for judgment less clearly.
8 Permits and occasionally encourages guessing.	8 Permits and occasionally encourages bluffing.
9 Distribution of scores is determined by the test.	9 Distribution of scores is controlled largely by the grader-reader.

SIMILARITIES

1 Both tests can measure almost any important instructional objective that any written test can measure.
2 Both tests can encourage students to learn concepts, principles, and problem solving.
3 Both tests involve the use of subjective judgment.
4 Both tests yield scores whose value is dependent on objectivity and reliability.

On the basis of these differences and similarities, Ebel (pp. 144–145) describes the conditions for the appropriate use of objective and essay tests. Use essay tests under the following five conditions:

1 The group to be tested is small and the test should not be reused.
2 The instructor wishes to do all possible to encourage and reward the development of student skill in written expression.
3 The instructor is more interested in exploring the student's attitudes than in measuring his achievements. (Whether an instructor should be more interested in attitudes than achievement and whether he should expect an honest expression of attitudes in a test he will evaluate seem open to question.)
4 The instructor is more confident of his proficiency as a critical reader than as an imaginative writer of good objective test items.
5 Time available for test preparation is shorter than time available for test grading.

Use objective tests under these conditions:

1 The group to be tested is large or the test may be reused.
2 Highly reliable test scores must be obtained as efficiently as possible.
3 Impartiality of evaluation, absolute fairness, and freedom from halo effects are essential.
4 The instructor is more confident of his ability to express objective test items clearly than of his ability to judge essay test answers correctly.
5 There is more pressure for speedy reporting of scores than for speedy test preparation.

Use either objective or essay tests for the following purposes:

1 Measure almost any important educational achievement which a written test can measure.
2 Test understanding of ability to apply principles.
3 Test ability to think critically.
4 Test ability to solve novel problems.
5 Test ability to select relevant facts and principles, to integrate them toward the solution of complex problems.
6 Encourage students to study for command of knowledge.

Now that you can describe the similarities and differences in the characteristics and uses of objective and essay tests, we can turn to their construction.

Constructing and Scoring the Essay Test

Types of essay questions C. C. Weidemann (1933, 1941) identified ten types of essay questions, which he arranged in order from simple to complex. These questions begin with (1) *what, who, when, which,* and *where,* (2) *list,* (3) *outline,* (4) *describe,* (5) *contrast,* (6) *compare,* (7) *discuss,* (8) *develop,* (9) *summarize,* and (10) *evaluate.* Ordinarily it is undesirable to start with the words in (1) and (2) because they require simple verbal associations which can be more easily tested with objective items (Thorndike and Hagen, 1969, p. 80). It is also generally undesirable to begin an essay question with *discuss* when the question fails to provide a basis for or the limitations or focus of the discussion. Additional words which adequately

Item: What, if anything, developed in 1955 with respect to relations between Egypt and Soviet Russia?

    A A Russian military force invaded Egypt.

    B Egypt accused members of the Russian embassy of spying and broke off diplomatic relations.

    C Soviet Russia supported Egypt's demand for independence from Britain.

    D The Egyptian government arranged to buy arms from the Soviet Union.

Alternatives are the options provided from which the student is to make the correct choice. *Distracters* are incorrect alternatives, in this case choices *A, B,* and *C. Specific determiners* are unintended clues to the correct answer. In the above statement this clue is the generality of statement *D,* as compared with the specific events named in the alternatives. Another common specific determiner is the incorrect use of articles—for example, the use of *an* when one or more of the incorrect alternatives begins with a consonant. The *stem* is that part of the item which introduces the alternatives—in the item shown above, it is a direct question.

True-false items   These items permit only one of two responses. The usual responses are true or false, but they can also be right-wrong, correct-incorrect, yes-no, same-opposite (Stanley and Hopkins, pp. 226–227). Consider the following items, which appear in both the true and false forms (Ebel, p. 174). True form:

Item **A:** The mercantile system requires legislative support.

Item **B:** All eclipses involve shadows.

False form:

Item **A:** The mercantile system requires corporate income taxes.

Item **B:** If light rays could not be bent, eclipses could not occur.

Stanley and Hopkins (pp. 228–29) have gathered several illustrative items in which alternative responses are not true or false. Here are three items from a test on English grammar (Greene, 1939):

```
                         1. a
Item A:  Ted is              industrious man
                       2. an
                           1. has
Item B:  My father              no money.
                         2. hasn't
                               1. himself
Item C:  I want everyone to help
                             2. themselves
```

Stanley and Hopkins (pp. 230–32) list fifteen rules for composing true-false items: (1) Avoid specific determiners. Statements are generally false when they contain these words: *all, always, never, nothing, impossible, inevitable,* and so on. Statements are generally true when they contain these words: *some, sometimes, often, frequently, may, generally, as a rule, usually,* and so on. You may use these words however if you carefully balance their appearance in the true and the false statements. (2) Avoid a disproportionate number of either true or false statements. (3) Avoid the exact wording of the textbook. (4) Avoid trick statements which are false only because of a petty insertion. (5) Limit each statement to a single point. (6) Avoid double negatives. (7) Avoid ambiguous statements which give rise to two or more interpretations only one of which may be true. (8) Avoid unfamiliar, figurative, or literary language. (9) Avoid sentences with complex structure. (10) Avoid qualitative language whenever possible—words such as *few, many, large, young, old, important,* and so on. *More than* and *most* are permissible because they are parts of quantifiable statements. (11) Avoid using statements of commands, which cannot be true or false. (12) Make the main clause true and the reason true or false if you are testing for the truth of falsity of a reason. (13) Require the simplest method of indicating the response. Stanley suggests that the student write *T* and *F, Y* and *N* rather than *True* and *False, Yes* and *No.* The student can also be directed to circle or underline the correct response or even to use + and −. (14) Arrange the statements in groups of about five per group so that scoring can be completed with more ease. (15) Use true-false statements only for items that are unambiguous and lend themselves to this form distinctly. Here are three examples (Stanley and Hopkins, 1972, p. 232) of undesirable items. Which rules do they ignore?

Item A: The gas xenon is generally inert.
Item B: As it ages, pure copper turns brown because it oxidizes.
Item C: Poe wrote *The Gold Bug* and *The Scarlet Letter.*

Item *A* ignores the first, *B* the twelfth, and *C* the fifth rule. Here are improved versions of these items:

Item A: The gas xenon forms compounds with most elements.
Item B: As it ages, pure copper turns green because it attracts green algae.
Item C: Poe wrote *The Gold Bug.*

Matching items Another form of limited-response items is the matching item, in which the student must match the elements in one column with those in another. Norman Gronlund (1965, p. 135) lists several examples of column relationships which teachers in several fields considered important.

COLUMN A	COLUMN B
Men	Achievements
Dates	Historical events
Terms	Definitions
Rules	Examples
Symbols	Concepts
Authors	Titles of books
Foreign words	English equivalents
Machines	Uses
Plants or animals	Classification
Principles	Illustrations
Objects	Names of objects
Parts	Functions

Gronlund observes that matching items use visual materials when, for example, the item requires the student to match words with pictures and names of places with map locations.

Here is an example of a matching item (Gronlund, p. 134):

	COLUMN A	COLUMN B
(G)	1 Name of the *answer* in addition problems.	A Difference
(A)	2 Name of the *answer* in subtraction problems.	B Dividend
(D)	3 Name of the *answer* in multiplication problems.	C Multiplicand
(E)	4 Name of the *answer* in division problems.	D Product
		E Quotient
		F Subtrahend
		G Sum

Gronlund (pp. 136–38) describes several rules for composing matching items: (1) Use only homogeneous material in a single matching item. The previous item illustrates homogeneity in two ways: Column *A* concerns only names of answers to problems in arithmetic, and column *B* lists only plausible names for these answers. (2) Include more elements in the second than in the first column and tell the students that they can use each of these elements once, more than once, or not at all. (3) Keep the list of elements to be matched brief and place the shorter elements in column *B*. (4) Arrange words in alphabetical order and numbers in sequence. (5) Indicate in the directions the basis for matching the elements. (6) Place all elements for one matching item on the same page. Gronlund (p. 136) gives this example of a faulty matching item. Which rule does it ignore?

Directions: On the line to the left of each achievement listed in column *A*, write the letter of the man's name in column *B* who is noted for that achievement. Each name in column *B* may be used once, more than once, or not at all.

		COLUMN A		COLUMN B
(A)	1	Invented the telephone	A	Alexander Graham Bell
(B)	2	Discovered America	B	Christopher Columbus
(C)	3	First United States astronaut	C	John Glenn
		to orbit the earth	D	Abraham Lincoln
(F)	4	First President of the United	E	Ferdinand Magellan
		States	F	George Washington
			G	Eli Whitney

This item largely ignores the first rule. The elements are a motley collection of inventors, explorers, and presidents. It is better to have one matching item for each of these categories. An even better solution to the problem would be to make this matching item a series of multiple choice items, each of which has distractors more plausible for the stem.

You can also cast the matching item as a multiple-choice item to determine how well the student can relate concepts and principles. Here is an example (Berg, 1965, p. 75):

> Key: 1 The entry in column A is an example of the opposite entry in column B.
> 2 The entry in column A is synonymous with the opposite entry in column B.
> 3 The entry in column A and its opposite entry in column B are parallel (terms which are subpoints under the same topic).

	COLUMN A	COLUMN B	
Item A	Villein	Serf	(3)
Item B	Baptism	Sacrament	(1)
Item C	Middle Ages	Medieval period	(2)

As can be seen from this example, this form of item usually requires a fairly complex set of instructions, and should, therefore, be used discriminately and only in instances where it is absolutely required.

The multiple-choice item Despite the fact that it is the most difficult item to write, test specialists favor the multiple-choice item. Practice has shown that a multiple-choice test composed of one-half the number of items on a true-false test has equal reliability. Compared with true-false items, the multiple-choice item tends to distinguish better between high and low achievement, is less subject to ambiguity and misinterpretation, and can be answered correctly by chance less frequently (Ebel, p. 188). The multiple-choice item includes an item stem in the form of a complete or incomplete question or statement and usually four or more alternatives (or options). In the case of four alternatives, three are distractors and one is the correct answer. Here is an example of a multiple-choice item (Ebel, pp. 219–20):

> Item: What is the principal advantage of a battery of lead storage cells over a battery of dry cells for automobile starting and lighting?

A   The storage cell furnishes direct current.
B   The voltage of the storage cell is higher.
*C The current from the storage cell is stronger.
D   The initial cost of the storage cell is less.

Here the distracters are true statements, but only one of these statements
(C) explains the preference for the storage cell. The stem, of course, is a
complete question.

Ebel (pp. 191–210) lists nine suggestions for composing multiple-choice
items: (1) Before writing the item make an explicit statement of the idea
the item will embody. You can also select key statements, especially those
which clearly define concepts and principles, from good instructional materials. (2) Write the item in the way which will allow greater success for
those students who have achieved greater mastery of terminal behavior than
for those students who have achieved less mastery. (3) Prepare the original
draft in such a way as to make revision and assembly convenient. It is best
to begin with a pencil draft of each item on a separate sheet of paper. In
preparing the alternatives, you should write the correct answer first and
then vary randomly the place of the correct answers among the alternatives.
(4) Write the stem as a question or incomplete statement which has a concise answer and plausible alternatives. A direct question is usually better
than an incomplete statement because it more clearly defines the problem
and indicates the teacher's purpose. Here is an example of a concise stem
question with concise alternatives (Ebel, p. 198):

Item: Who were the Huks in the Philippines?
   A   A tribe of primitive head hunters.
  *B   A Communist-supported rebel group.
   C   Wealthy Philippine landowners and industrialists.
   D   Members of the minority party in the Philippine legislature.

Ebel's next suggestion: (5) Make the correct answer thoroughly correct,
express it clearly, and avoid specific determiners which will betray the answer to the alert but unknowledgable students. Here are two examples of
items which fail to avoid specific determiners (Ebel, pp. 200–201):

Item A: When used in conjunction with the T-square, the left vertical edge
         of a triangle is used to draw:
    *A   Vertical lines
    B   Slant lines
    C   Horizontal lines
    D   Inclined lines

Item B: How did styles in women's clothing in 1950 differ most from those
         in 1900?
    A   They showed more beauty.
    B   They showed more variety.
    C   They were easier to clean.

*D They were easier to live in, work in, move in, and were generally less restrictive.

The irrelevant cues in both of these items would allow students who knew little or nothing about T-squares and clothing styles in 1950 to select the correct answer. In item *A,* the irrelevant cue is the appearance of *vertical* in both the stem and the correct answer. In item *B,* it is the greater length and detail of the correct answer. (6) Make the distractor thoroughly wrong and yet plausible to the student who knows a little but not enough. Victor Noll (1965, pp. 152–53) illustrates how distracters can vary from being plausible to being absurd:

Item A: The capital of the United States is
    *A Washington   C Chicago
     B New York   D St. Louis
                     E Los Angeles

Item B: The capital of the United States is
    *A Washington   C Reno
     B Atlantic City   D Milwaukee
                     E San Antonio

Item C: The capital of the United States is
    *A Washington   C Tokyo
     B Rome   D Paris
                     E London

Item D: The capital of the United States is
    *A Washington   C China
     B wheat   D air
                     E birds

The plausibility of the alternatives determines the difficulty of the item. If the alternatives are implausible, they serve no useful purpose and consume the students' valuable reading time during the examination. In effect, items *B, C,* and *D* are one-alternative items because their distractors are implausible. One-alternative items hardly function as test items! (7) Write the item as clearly, simply, and correctly as possible. (8) Modify the item, if necessary, so that 50 percent of the students will answer correctly. (9) Arrange for a colleague to review your original draft. The reviewer should try to answer each question and should check his choices against the answer key.

Multiple-choice items can assess concept learning, principle learning, and problem solving. In the following example (Heenan, 1961, p. 183), the student must be able to identify an example of Epicurean philosophy, an example of Thomistic (Aquinas) philosophy, and a particular attribute of Epicurean philosophy. The item begins with a quotation from a philosophic work.

Quotation: The senses at first let in particular ideas and furnish the yet empty cabinet, and, the mind by degrees growing familiar with some of them, they are lodged in memory, and the names get to them. . . . In this manner the mind comes to be furnished with ideas and the language, the materials about which to exercise its discursive faculty. And the use of reason becomes daily more visible, as these materials giving it employment increase.

Item A: The above quotation reflects the philosophic position of the
    A Empiricists
    B Scholastics
    C Platonists
    D Realists
  *E Epicureans

Item B: Which of the following men would be most inclined to accept this quotation as a true statement?
    A Plato
    B Socrates
    C Descartes
    D Locke
  *E Aquinas

Item C: The school characterized in this paragraph believes that the source of our ideas is
    A divine revelation
    B experience
    C faith
    D study
  *E unknown

The next item requires the student to demonstrate his knowledge of a principle which involves the relationship between two concepts, mean and standard deviation:

Item: Sam made a score of 74 on an English achievement test which had a mean of 50 and a standard deviation of 10. Helen made a score of 50 on a different English achievement test which had a mean of 40 and a standard deviation of 5. Assuming that both tests are valid measures of knowledge of English, which of the following statements is most likely correct?

    A Sam knows more English than Helen.
    B Helen knows more English than Sam.
  *C They both know about the same amount of English.
    D If their IQs are the same, they know about the same amount of English.

The following item also requires the student to demonstrate the relationship between concepts he has learned:

Mean is to *standard deviation* as *median* is to
*A semi-interquartile range
B percentile range
C quartile
D percentile band
E average deviation

The next item requires the student to engage in problem solving, the application of principles (Nelson, 1961, pp. 126–27):

Items 10–16 are concerned with the following series of statements concerning the electrical condenser shown in the diagram [Figure 13-1]. The outer coating is connected to the earth, as shown, by means of a copper wire. Evaluate each statement (items 10–12) and reason given according to the key below.

Key: 1 The statement given is true and the reason given is accepted as correct and supports the statement.
2 The statement given is true and the reason given is true but it does not support or contradict the statement, i.e., is true but irrelevant.
3 The statement given is true but the reason given is either false or contradicts the statement.
4 The statement is false and the reason is not accepted as correct.
5 The statement is false but the reason is accepted as correct.

Item 10: If the inner coating of the jar is charged negatively, the outer coating becomes charged positively *because* positive charges flow from the earth to the coating along the wire. (3)

Item 11: If the inner coating of the jar is charged positively, the inner coating becomes charged negatively *because* unlike magnetic poles attract. (2)

Item 12: If the inner coating of the jar is charged negatively, the outer coating becomes charged negatively *because* like charges repel one another. (5)

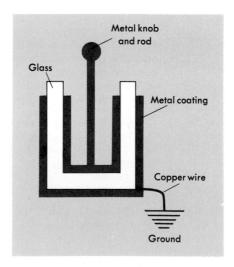

FIG. 13-1 An electrical condenser (after Nelson, 1961, p. 126).

Such an item is sometimes called a *key-list* multiple-choice item. To the previous suggestions for composing multiple-choice items, Harry Berg (1965, p. 75) adds three more suggestions for key-list items: (1) Avoid basing too many items on a single key—the key must provide appropriate alternatives for each item. (2) Make the alternative in the key broad and significant enough for nearly all students to understand. A student should not miss items only because a part of the key contains highly specialized knowledge. (3) Tell the student that the alternatives in the key can apply to one, more than one, or none of the items.

A study by Morris Weitman (1965) showed that the more a multiple-choice item relied on principle learning and problem solving rather than on verbal association (rote memory), the better the item distinguished between long-term and short-term retention. The measure of long-term retention was the number of items that medical students answered correctly on a final examination in physiology given at the end of the spring quarter and, several weeks later, at the beginning of the fall quarter. Weitman classified the thirty-one test items on the degree of dependence on rote memory, calling one class items with strong emphasis on rote memory and the other class items with weak emphasis on rote memory. A key-list item, although not used in this examination, is an example of an item with weak emphasis on rote memory. Weitman discovered that the items which distinguished long-term retention (items which the students answered correctly in both the spring and the fall) were those items with weak emphasis on rote memory. This finding is consistent with our knowledge of concept learning, principle learning, and problem solving—forms of learning which suffer fewer of the effects of interference than verbal learning does.

Preparing the Test Copy

After you have constructed your objective test items, you must assemble the fruits of your labor and present them to your students in some printed form. First, you must decide how to arrange the items. Gilbert Sax and Theodore Cromack (1966) studied the effects of four arrangements of test items: easy to hard items (*E*), hard to easy items (*H*), an interspersion of easy and hard items (*M*), and a random arrangement of items (*R*). Using these four conditions one group was given thirty minutes, the other about fifty minutes, to complete an examination. Table 13-4 summarizes the re-

EFFECTS OF FOUR ARRANGEMENTS OF TEST ITEMS (after Sax and Cromack, 1966, p. 310) **TABLE 13-4**

	THIRTY-MINUTE GROUP				FORTY-EIGHT-MINUTE GROUP			
	E	H	M	R	E	H	M	R
Mean	37.83	21.39	27.00	29.12	47.54	45.58	42.65	42.02
S. D.	8.33	8.34	9.40	8.53	10.58	15.47	12.23	13.07
N	72	70	68	66	50	45	49	47

sults. You can see that the students obtained significantly higher average scores on form *E* (easy to hard) than on the other forms. You can also note that the students in the thirty-minute group obtained the lowest scores on form *H,* in which the hard items preceded the easy items. You can further note that, when the examination time was extended (from thirty to forty-eight minutes), the advantage of form *E* was comparatively less. Finally, mixing easy items with difficult items to produce what is sometimes called a *motivational test* apparently has no advantage over randomly arranging the items. The conclusion of this study is that you should arrange your items in order of ascending difficulty (easy to hard) unless you allow generous amounts of examination time. You should also group all items of the same format together. That is, you should not intersperse matching items with multiple-choice item, true-false with completion, and so forth. In addition to making the instructions more difficult to prepare it can lead to errors which are due to confusion rather than lack of knowledge.

After deciding how to arrange the items, you should provide the students with adequate directions and read aloud the directions. If you vary the item form, you must provide a new set of directions for each form. For younger students who are unaccustomed to objective tests, it is desirable to follow the directions with a sample item which you answer for them.

Next, you must consider the actual format in which the items will appear on the printed page. The format should be one which both teacher (as scorer) and students find clear and convenient. If you do not use a separate answer sheet, you should provide an answer column in the right or left margin of the page. True-false items should appear in groups of five to avoid an overwhelming and confusing solid page of words and letters. To conserve space, multiple-choice items can appear in two columns. The alternatives for these items should not appear in paragraph form; they should be listed, as in the illustrations above.

Administering the Test

Efficient administration of the test should include the following: (1) careful organization and efficient distribution of all the test materials, (2) brief directions and brief answers to questions raised by students, and (3) a record of time on the blackboard to help the students pace their efforts. By following these suggestions, you give the students the maximum time for answering all the test questions. Ebel (p. 238) suggests that the following notation appear on the blackboard:

> No more than _____ minutes remain for you to work on this test. If you have not reached item _____ you are working too slowly.

The numbers for completing these statements should be changed about every fifteen minutes. As for the questions about test items which students raise in the course of taking the test, it is advisable to let these interruptions occur as quietly and infrequently as possible and that the teacher give only that help which increases the student's understanding of the task but does not give him an unfair advantage in answering the question.

Preventing cheating   One of your major responsibilities in administering the test is the prevention of cheating. Ebel (p. 239) lists a number of activities which illustrate cheating:

1   The side-long glance at a fellow student's answers
2   The preparation and use of a crib sheet
3   Collusion between two or more students to exchange information on answers during the test
4   Unauthorized copying of questions or stealing of test booklets in anticipation that they may be used again later on
5   Arranging for a substitute to take an examination
6   Stealing or buying copies of an examination before the test is given or sharing such illicit advanced copies with others.

What can you do to prevent cheating and what should you do when it occurs? Ebel (p. 240) makes the following suggestions: (1) Establish clearly that when cheating occurs it will be punished by a failing grade, loss of course credit, and suspension or dismissal from school; (2) safeguard the security of the test while it is written, duplicated, and stored; (3) use alternate forms of the test when students must sit close together; and (4) take seriously your proctoring duties during the examination period. When the teacher finds a student cheating, his examination materials should be collected and the results of the examination should be voided, made up, or possibly replaced with a failing grade. The use of honor systems, in which one student reports the cheating of other students, is frequently unsuccessful because, as Ebel (p. 241) states, "The honor sought by the honor system thus must be purchased at the price of another kind of honor, that of loyalty to one's close associates. It is not surprising that systems of this kind sometimes break down."

Failure to prevent cheating may have several deleterious effects on student achievements: (1) cheating occurs with impunity, honest achievement goes unrecognized or punished and reduces student motivation to achieve; (2) there is no way to assess validly and reliably what the student has and has not learned; and (3) ingenuity in devising ways to cheat becomes more important than attainment of the instructional objectives.

Scoring the Test

You should observe two major practices in scoring objective tests. First, you should prepare an answer key. The key may be simply an answer sheet which you have filled out or, if you use a commercially made sheet, it may be a cardboard stencil or template which fits over the answer sheets. Second, you should ordinarily assign one point for each correct answer, with no allowance for fractional credit. Giving different weights to different items in a test or to different correct and incorrect alternatives in a particular item usually does not improve the validity or reliability of the test (Ebel, pp. 233–36).

You may wish to correct students scores for the effect of possible guessing, but we do not recommend it for most classroom tests and situations. Rather than penalizing students for guessing, it seems more reasonable to encourage them to make rational guesses based on what they do know. In any case, students will generally retain about the same position in the score distribution whether or not a correction for guessing formula is applied to the scores (Ebel, p. 251). Therefore, if you are applying relative standards, there will be little if any change in the decisions you would make. If you are using criterion-related standards, you will already have built in a "correction for guessing" when the standards were set.

If you do decide to use the correction for guessing formula, it should generally be applied only when some students have omitted a fairly large number of items (Stanley and Hopkins, p. 145). In other circumstances it probably will have very little effect on the scores. Further, the formula can, under some circumstances, "overcorrect" and penalize students unduly for incorrect answers. A safe rule to follow is to use the formula only when you are certain that students are guessing wildly. Under those circumstances it would be wise to study the test itself to see if it has flaws which require guessing and/or examine the instruction to determine why it is necessary for students to guess wildly on items about which they presumably should know something. We present the correction formula below and provide two illustrations of computations to show you how it works. When studying this formula be sure to note that omitted items are distinct from incorrectly marked ones—that is, you do not count omits as incorrect.

$$\text{Score} = R - \frac{W}{n - 1}$$

where R = number of correct reponses
$\quad\quad\,\, W$ = number of incorrect (not omitted responses
$\quad\quad\,\, n$ = number of alternatives for an item

For an item which has only two alternatives, as in the case of true-false items, $n - 1$ becomes $2 - 1$. For an item with four alternatives $n - 1$ becomes 3. For example, if a test contains one hundred multiple-choice items, each with four alternatives, and Frank answers fifty items correctly and fifty items incorrectly, his corrected score is determined as follows:

$$\text{Score} = 50 - \frac{4 - 1}{50} = 50 - \frac{50}{3} = 33.34$$

If, however, Frank answers fifty items correctly and omits fifty items, his correct score is

$$50 - \frac{0}{3} = 50 - 0 = 50$$

Criteria   To determine the quality of your test, you must use the four criteria discussed in the first section: validity, reliability, objectivity, and efficiency. Three of these criteria require your own prima facie judgment: The test has validity to the extent 'that the items assess the terminal performances described in the instructional objectives. The test has objectivity to the extent that a colleague in your discipline would assign the same scores to a set of responses. The test has efficiency to the extent that it makes the best use of the students' examination time and of the time you have available for preparing the test and for scoring the test. Reliability is a little more difficult to establish than the other crieria for a good test. Most teachers do not attempt to establish the reliability of their tests, because the statistical procedures are too complex. However, the basic procedures require only straightforward arithmetical calculations, and the results could be useful to a teacher in assessing the quality of her tests.

Item analysis   There are ways you can improve the reliability of your tests, even if you do not know the reliability as computed from standard formulas. The techniques we describe here for assessing and modifying item discrimination and difficulty will normally affect the reliability of a test. In fact, it can be shown that these operations affect reliability directly. We refer to the techniques to be described as *item analysis* techniques because they provide data on the internal structure of the test and on how the items function individually and in relation to the test as a whole. These techniques are very important considerations in the serious analysis of tests, and you can learn how to use them and actually apply them to your tests.

Item analysis involves determining the level of item discrimination and difficulty. Item discrimination reflects the degree to which an item distinguishes between the high scorers and the low scorers. Item difficulty indicates the percentage of students who answer the item correctly. The formulas and illustrations of item discrimination and difficulty below will be clear once you consider a simple procedure for item analysis.

Before you can determine item discrimination and difficulty, you should take these steps: (1) arrange the tests in order of scores, from high to low; (2) form a group of high scorers by separating the upper 25 percent or more of the papers; (3) form a group of low scorers by separating the lower 25 percent or more of the papers; (4) for each group count the number of times the group chooses each alternative; and (5) record these counts on a copy of the test. Here is an example of this procedure; the upper- and lower-scoring groups each contain one hundred students.

Item: The first premier of Lower Slabovnia was

    A   George Washington (hi = 5; lo = 16)
  *B   Petroff Mehalovich (hi = 27; lo = 18)
    C   Sergei Potemkin (hi = 56; lo = 40)
    D   Ivan Tito (hi = 12; lo = 26)

The figures appearing after the alternatives are the number of high-scoring (hi) and low-scoring (lo) students choosing each alternative. Originally you should record these numbers as tally marks which you will later sum.

With this information you can now determine discrimination and item difficulty. The formula for item difficulty is

$$\text{Diff.} = \frac{R}{N} \times 100$$

where Diff. = the difficulty index (a percentage)

R = the number of high-scoring and low-scoring students who chose the correct response

N = the total number of students in both groups

For the item above

$$\text{Diff.} = \frac{27 + 18}{200} \times 100 = 22.5 \times 100 = 23 \text{ percent}$$

We now know that 23 percent of the sample, comprising 200 papers, chose the correct alternative. The formula for item discrimination is

$$D = \frac{R_{hi} - R_{lo}}{0.5N}$$

where D = the discrimination index (a decimal fraction)

R_{hi} = number of high-scoring students who answered correctly

R_{lo} = number of low-scoring students who answered correctly

$0.5N$ = one-half the number of papers in the sample

For the item above

$$D = \frac{27 - 18}{100} = \frac{9}{100} = 0.09$$

Frequently the difficulty and discrimination indices are recorded next to the item number as follows:

The first premier of Lower Slabovnia was

A George Washington (hi = 5; lo = 16)
*B Petroff Mehalovich (hi = 27; lo = 18)
C Sergei Potemkin (hi = 56; lo = 40)
D Ivan Tito (hi = 12; lo = 26)
Diff. = 23% $D = 0.09$

What do these indices tell you about the quality of your test items? Generally speaking, if you are using a relative standard, you can follow these guidelines: (1) The closer the difficulty index is to 50 percent, the better the reliability of the item. You should reject or revise very easy and very difficult items. Very easy items are those which almost all the students answer correctly; very difficult items are those which almost all the students answer incorrectly. (2) The closer the discrimination index is to 0.40 and above, the better the reliability of the item. Items between 0.30 and 0.39

probably require minor revisions, those between 0.20 and 0.29 require somewhat more revision, and those below 0.19 require major revision if they
are retained at all (Ebel, p. 399). If you are using absolute standards, these
criteria for items may be inappropriate. In this instance, you strive to gear
the instructional procedures so that most, if not all, students obtain a
perfect score. Under these circumstances the optimum difficulty index would
be 1.00 (100 percent). Similarly, when using absolute standards, you are
not trying to discriminate between high- and low-scoring students so the
optimum value of the discrimination indices would be 0.00. When using
criterion-related standards, you will find that the situation becomes a little
more complex, and you must judge the item values in relation to the
specific content of the items. For some items a very high difficulty value
may be appropriate, while for others a low value might be quite acceptable.
The general rule to follow in this case is to use the item analysis data as a
guide in evaluating whether students understood each item and whether
there is evidence that any of the rules for item construction have been
violated.

Item analysis provides the basis for the revision of items. Ebel (1965,
p. 368) shows how revision of an item improves its discrimination and reduces its difficulty:

What, if any, is the distinction between climate and weather?

    A There is no important distinction. (1–6)
    B Climate is primarily a matter of temperature and rainfall, while
       weather includes many other natural phenomena. (33–51)
 *C Climate pertains to longer periods of time than weather. (43–30)
    D Weather pertains to natural phenomena on a *local* rather than a
       national scale. (23–13)
Diff. = 38%   D = 0.58

The item is not difficult because considerably more than half (63 per cent)
of the students answered it correctly. The item discriminates poorly because
about the same number of high-scoring (43) and low-scoring (30) students
answered it correctly. The following revision improves both item difficulty
and discrimination. The revision portions of the item are in italics.

What, if any, is the distinction between climate and weather?

    A There is no important distinction. (2–22)
    B *Climate is primarily a matter of rainfall, while weather is primarily a*
       matter of temperature. (3–25)
 *C Climate pertains to longer periods of time than weather. (91–33)
    D *Weather is determined by clouds, while climate is determined by*
       winds. (4–20)
Diff. = 38%   D = 0.58

The revised item is now more difficult, and more discriminating. Although
fewer students chose the correct answer, most of these were high-scoring

students (91). The revision of the second alternative reduced its attractiveness for both high-scoring and low-scoring students. With this revision, however, most of the low-scoring students switched to the first and fourth alternatives, while most of the high-scoring students switched to the correct alternative—thus making the item more discriminating. This general procedure for revision can be used when you are applying either relative or criterion-related standards. With items in a relative standard test, you can apply the value limits described previously in a more straightforward manner. With criterion-related standards, you must use more judgment when applying the value limits.

Improving reliability   There are several ways to improve the reliability of tests based on relative standards of achievement. First, you can lengthen your tests by adding items which are of the same average difficulty and discrimination and which are based on similar content. Second, you can increase the discrimination of the individual items. Third, you can include items of about 50 percent difficulty and exclude very difficult or very easy items.

It is difficult to assess the reliability of tests based on absolute standards of achievement. In such tests all students who have achieved the instructional objectives are expected to answer all items correctly. For each item the difficulty index is 100 percent and the discrimination index 0.00. In preparing such a test it is necessary that any variation in item difficulty reflect only variations in task difficulty and not irrelevant variations in the items. The quality of these tests is almost entirely a product of how well the instructional objectives have been stated—the specificity of the terminal behaviors, of the conditions under which they must be performed, and of the standards of acceptable performance.

Summary

We have now completed our consideration of the construction and revision of essay and objective tests. In planning the test it is important to make adequate provision for evaluating all instructional objectives if the test is to have the necessary validity. The two major tests are objective and essay. Their characteristics to a large extent determine their appropriate use. Although the essay test is easier to prepare, it is harder to grade with reliability and objectivity. Although the objective test is harder to prepare, it is easier to grade with reliability and objectivity. Both tests can measure almost any important instructional objective that a test can measure. The guidelines for the preparation of essay tests in general suggest a prior determination of the learning you are assessing and a clear and unambiguous delineation of the task the student should perform. The scoring of the test usually requires the preparation of model answers used in grading all the papers. There are several types of objective items: completion, short answer, true-false, matching, and multiple choice. The preparation of these items requires the observance of the particular guidelines described. All these items, particularly multiple-choice items, require you to provide plausible distractors, to avoid specific determiners, and to provide an adequate description of the task in that part of the item which *precedes* the response. Key-list multiple-choice items can assess the higher types of learning. After the construction of the items particular care must be exercised in the preparation of the test copy, in the test administration, in the prevention of cheating, in the scoring, and in the test evaluation. The scoring of the test should not ordinarily require correction for guessing or differential weighting of items. The evaluation of the test requires an assessment of the test's validity, reliability, objectivity, and efficiency. An easy way to estimate test reliability, based on internal test standards, is item analysis. Through item analysis you can determine item difficulty and discrimination and revise items accordingly. By adding items of average difficulty and high discrimination, you can improve the reliability of tests based on relative standards. For tests based on absolute standards, test reliability depends on how adequately you state instructional objectives.

QUESTION 13-2

In this multiple-choice item (Ebel, 1965, p. 372), the numbers following the alternatives show the number of high-scoring and low-scoring students who chose each one. Read the item and these data and answer the questions which follow:

Item   A workman lifts planks ot the top of a scaffold by pulling down on a rope passed over a single fixed pulley attached to the top of the scaffold. The rope will break under a load of 500 pounds, and the workman weighs 200 pounds. What is the heaviest load the workman can lift with the pulley?

   A   100 pounds (hi = 1, lo = 6)
 *B   200 pounds (hi = 35, lo = 42)
   C   400 pounds (hi = 32, lo = 23)
   D   500 pounds (hi = 32, lo = 29)

1   Assuming that there are one hundred high-scoring and one hundred low-scoring students in your sample, determine (a) the difficulty index and (b) the discrimination index.
2   Is this item easy or difficult?
3   Is this item a good or poor discriminator?
4   How could alternatives C and D be made less atractive to the high-scoring students?

SUMMARY

This chapter has considered the nature and purposes of performance assessment and the construction and revision of tests.

Performance assessment is the fourth component of the basic teaching model. As the process of measuring the student's auxiliary and terminal performances during and at the end of instruction, it is the basic source of feedback on the adequacy of the student's entering behavior and on our instructional procedures. When the instructional objectives specify the minimum level of mastery the student must attain, they employ an absolute standard of achievement. When you compare the performance of one student with others in his group, you are using a relative standard of achievement. All measures of performance should have validity, reliability, objectivity, and efficiency. A valid test actually measures the terminal performances described in the objectives; a reliable test accurately or consistently measures these performances; an objective test is scored with freedom from subjective judgment and according to the consensus of expert opinion; an efficient test makes optimal use of the available time teachers and students can devote to testing.

Test construction and revision are the major content of this chapter. The planning of the test requires careful provision for validity—that is, for the assessment of all stated objectives and for the appropriate emphasis on each objective. The classification of objectives, through either Gagné's or Bloom's system, is one way of assuring adequate coverage of instructional objectives. Objective and essay tests have both differences and similarities. What the objective test gains in reliability and ease in scoring, it loses in difficulty of preparation and in validity. The use of essay questions requires a clear statement of the tasks the student should perform, the provision of adequate time for answering the questions, and scoring practices which assure consistent and unbiased judgment. Objective items are either free-response or limited-response items. We provided guidelines for the preparation of completion items, true-false items, matching items, and multiple-choice items in this chapter. The key-list multiple-choice item offers a convenient way to assess principle learning and problem solving. Suggestions were made for the preparation of the test copy, the administration of the test, and the prevention of cheating. In scoring the test, ordinarily you should allow one point for each correct answer. Correction for guessing is generally not advisable, but may be used in some instances when students have omitted a fairly large number of responses. The evaluation of the test involves judgments about its validity, reliability, objectivity, and efficiency. Item analysis is an objective means of determining reliability when the test is based on a relative standard. The results of the item analysis can be the basis for revising items for optimal levels of difficulty and discrimination.

SUGGESTED READINGS

BLOOM, BENJAMIN S., HASTINGS, THOMAS J., and MADAUS, GEORGE F., *Handbook of Formative and Summative Evaluation of Student Learning.* New York: McGraw-Hill Book Company, 1971.

EBEL, ROBERT L., *Educational and Psychological Measurement and Evaluation.* Englewood Cliffs, N.J.: Prentice-Hall, Inc., 1972.

GRONLUND, NORMAN E., *Measurement and Evaluation in Teaching.* New York: The Macmillan Company, 1965.

NOLL, VICTOR H., *Educational Measurement* (2nd ed.). Boston: Houghton Mifflin Company, 1965.

THORNDIKE, ROBERT L., ed., *Educational Measurement* (2nd ed.). Washington, D.C.: American Council on Education, 1971.

The following soft-cover texts are especially useful for the construction of classroom tests:

GOROW, FRANK F., *Better Classroom Testing*. San Francisco: Chandler Publishing Co., 1966.

LINDEMAN, RICHARD, *Educational Measurement*. Chicago: Scott, Foresman & Company, 1967.

WOOD, DOROTHY ADKINS, *Test Construction*. Columbus, Ohio: Charles E. Merrill Books, Inc., 1960.

The following book contains a collection of papers which provide a very good discussion of criterion-related measurement:

POPHAM, W. JAMES, ed., *Criterion-Referred Measurement*. Englewood Cliffs, N.J.: Educational Technology Publications, 1971.

CHAPTER FOURTEEN

CHARACTERISTICS
OF
STANDARDIZED TESTS

The major purpose of this chapter is to introduce you to the nature of four types of standardized tests: intelligence, achievement, creativity, and personality and interest tests. Because teachers deal with tests frequently, the concepts in this chapter should be well understood. The proper use of standardized tests should be based on knowledge of how the results can be interpreted and applied. The first section of the chapter deals with the special characteristics of standardized tests—those which pertain to constructing, administering, and scoring the test and establishing the test norms. We then describe several uses of these tests. The second section distinguishes four types of standardized tests—general intelligence tests, achievement tests, tests of creativity, and personality and interest tests. In the next chapter, we shall deal with the interpretation of standardized test scores. We shall begin our discussion in this chapter with the principles of standardized test construction.

Upon reading this first section of the chapter you should be able to meet these objectives:

14-1   Describe four characteristics of standardized tests and point out an example of each characteristic when given a standardized test and its accompanying manuals.

14-2   Describe the similarities and the differences of standardized and classroom tests by referring to each of the characteristics in objective 14-1.

14-3   Describe and illustrate five uses of standardized tests.

Standardized tests, like all tests, have four basic characteristics: validity, reliability, objectivity, and efficiency. They also have special characteristics —the procedures they use to enhance these general test qualities: systematic methods of item construction and testing, uniform procedures of test administration and scoring, and the use of test norms in score interpretation. Standardized tests share the same uses with all tests—the assessment of entering behavior and terminal performance. Their special character, however, makes them particularly useful in the evaluation of new instructional programs and procedures, in the assessment of learning over the long haul, in the general assessment of student achievement and ability, and in the diagnosis of entering behavior for classroom purposes. We shall now consider each of these characteristics and uses.

Characteristics of Standardized Tests

The *standardization* of a test involves the development of uniform procedures for each administration and scoring of the test. The authors of these tests design procedures which minimize the possibility that variations in scores are due to variations in test procedures. Variations in scores should be the result of student performance and not of the conditions of testing. These tests also employ systematic methods of test construction and interpretation.

Constructing the tests   The reliability and validity of the tests are determined by tryout. Objective measurement determines the difficulty level of each item and of the test as a whole. Anastasi (1961, p. 25) describes the method used in the first successful intelligence scale:

When Binet and Simon prepared their original, 1905 scale for the measurement of intelligence . . . they arranged the thirty items of the scale in order of increasing difficulty. Such difficulty . . . was determined by trying out the items on fifty normal and a few retarded and feebleminded children. The items correctly solved by the largest proportion of subjects were, *ipso facto,* taken to be the easiest; those passed by a relatively few subjects were regarded as more difficult items. By such a procedure, an empirical order of difficulty was established This early example typifies the objective measurement of difficulty level in psychological test construction.

Test reliability is determined by observing the consistency of scores obtained by the same individuals when given the same test a second time or an equivalent form of the test. Test validity is determined by the use of external standards of whatever the test is designed to measure. A standardized test of juvenile delinquency would distinguish between two groups of boys, those who have and those who have not been arrested for juvenile offenses. If the test succeeded in distinguishing between these two groups, we could say that it had met its standard of validity or that it was a valid test of juvenile delinquency, or at least of those who had been caught (King et al., 1961). Similarly, a standardized test of medical aptitude would distinguish between two groups of students, those who would successfully complete medical training and those who would not. If the test succeeded in distinguishing between these two groups we could say that it was a valid test of medical aptitude. Standardized tests of intelligence distinguish with considerable success among students who are above or below average in school achievement and who score above or below average on other intelligence tests. These distinctions (or predictions) are never perfect however because success in school or out is not determined by IQ alone.

Administering the tests   We have observed that the directions for administering the tests are standardized—they are uniform conditions which must be provided whenever the test is used. Directions for administration—usually both general and specific—are contained in the manuals which accompany all standardized tests. The general directions describe the proper physical or classroom conditions and time limits the examiner must provide throughout the test. The specific directions describe what the teacher (or test administrator) must tell the students for particular parts of the test. Directions for the administration of the Stanford Achievement Test (Kelley et al., 1964, p. 7) illustrate general directions:

1   Before beginning a test, the examiner should see that the desks are cleared and that each pupil has one or two sharpened, soft-lead pencils. Special electrographic pencils are needed only if IBM answer sheets are used. . . . PENS SHOULD NOT BE USED. A supply of extra pencils should be at hand. Scratch paper should be provided for use with the arithmetic tests where indicated.
2   When administering the test, the examiner should have a blank copy of the test booklet and of an answer sheet (if an answer sheet is being used) for demonstrating, along with these "Directions of Administration."
3   A natural classroom situation should be maintained as far as possible.
4   Provision should be made to insure quiet and freedom from interruptions of any kind. This may be accomplished best by posting on the door of the room a sign reading, "Testing. Do Not Disturb."

Additional general directions pertain to the kind of assistance the examiner can provide individual students during the course of the examination, adherence to time limits, and the required number of testing sessions.

This test also provides specific directions for particular parts. Here are the specific directions for the test on arithmetic computation (Kelley et al., 1964, p. 13):

> Before distributing the test materials, SAY: "I shall give you a test booklet again. Do not open it until I tell you to do so."
>
> Pass out the booklets, answer sheets (if they are being used), and scratch paper, making sure that each pupil receives his own booklet and answer sheet.
>
> THEN SAY TO THE CLASS: "Now open your booklet to test 6, Arithmetic Computation, which starts on page 17. Fold the booklet back so that only page 17 is showing." See that the pupils do this.
>
> "Now find the answer spaces for test 6. Then look at the top of the page of your test booklet where it says 'DIRECTIONS.'" Hold up a booklet and point to the proper place.
>
> "The directions say: 'Work the example in each box. Then look at the possible answers at the right side of the box and see if the answer is given. If it is, fill in the space at the right on your answer sheet (if you have one) which has the same letter as the answer you have chosen. If your answer is *not* given, fill in the space which has the same letter as the letter beside the NG (which means "not given"). Use a separate answer sheet for figuring.'" Pause.

Further specific directions pertain to working through a sample item, giving the start signal, recording the starting time, giving the signal to stop, and collecting the test materials. The instructions for administering individual intelligence tests, to be discussed in a later section, are substantially more complex than the examples just cited.

Scoring the tests Directions for scoring the tests are also standardized—they are uniformly followed every time the test is scored. Frequently the test publisher provides special scoring keys or even a centralized scoring service using machine scoring. In the scoring directions for the intermediate battery of the Stanford Achievement Test (Kelley et al., 1964, Form W, Sheet 1a), these are some of the scoring rules provided:

1 Do not attempt to score these tests without using the keys. The keys are provided to make the scoring objective and at the same time quick, convenient, and accurate.

2 The score for each test is the number of correct responses.

3 No part or fractional credit is given for any item. Each item is counted as right, wrong, or omitted.

4 When an answer obviously has been changed by a pupil, the final response is the one which should be scored.

5 Sample items are never scored.

6 The number right will be the number of marks appearing through the holes. The score (number right) should be checked in the *upper* row of the conversion table *at the end of each test*. The number appearing directly under the value checked is the pupil's *grade score* on the test.

Other scoring rules pertain to the use of the scoring key, the time used in scoring, the transfer of grade scores, and checking for accuracy.

Establishing test norms Standardized tests are based on relative standards of performance. An individual's score has meaning only when compared with the scores others have obtained. A *norm* is the score which indicates average, or normal, performance. For example, if the average child of six can identify correctly ten objects in a picture vocabulary test when he is given a word and asked to select the associated picture (for example, find the picture of the chair), the six-year-old norm for this test is a score of ten. If the average child of eight can identify fifteen pictures correctly, then the eight-year-old norm is a score of fifteen. By using norms we can determine how close a child's performance is to the performances of children in his own age and grade group. These tests, then, use relative standards rather than criterion-related standards.

Establishing norms requires the use of a *standardization sample*—a representative sample of the type of student for whom the test is designed. For example, in developing the Pictorial Test of Intelligence, Joseph French (1964, p. 10) uses 1,830 children between the ages of three and eight. In selecting these children, he was careful to represent the various regional areas of the United States (Northeast, North Central, South, and West); communities of various sizes, ranging from over 1 million to under 2,500; and six parental occupational levels, from the professional and technical to the laboring and service.

Comparison of standardized and classroom tests The similarities of the two types of tests are easy to identify: (1) They are both means of performance assessment; (2) they both use the same types of test items; and (3) they both require validity, reliability, objectivity, and efficiency. The differences of the two types are only of degree: (1) It is possible that the classroom test may have more content validity because it is more carefully adapted to your own instructional objectives and subject matter. In an effort to measure the achievement of objectives common to the majority of American schools, standardized tests may fail to measure achievement of objectives unique to your course or school or they may measure achievement of objectives for which no formal instruction is provided. (2) The quality of the test items on the standardized test is usually superior because they are prepared by test specialists and are revised on the basis of actual tryout and item analysis. These advantages result in tests of high reliability, often between 0.80 and 0.95 (perfect reliability is indicated by a value of 1.00, Gronlund, 1965, p. 223). (3) The procedures used in administering and scoring standardized tests are carefully described, and they are standardized (made uniform) for each administration of the test. (4) A very significant difference is the use of norms in the interpretation of the test. The student's score on a standardized test is compared with those of the national sample, whereas his score on classroom tests based on the relative standard compares his performance only with those of other students in the class (a local norm). (5) Finally, publishers of standardized tests prepare test manuals, which report data on test validity and reliability and provide directions for test administration. To help in the evaluation of standardized tests, the

Mental Measurements Yearbook (Buros, 1972) provides critical reviews of standardized tests which are currently available. Each test is reviewed by measurement experts who frequently have some training or experience in the content field of the tests they review. Such information is usually not available for classroom tests.

Summary

Test standardization is the development of uniform procedures for the administration and scoring of the test. In constructing standardized tests, validity, reliability, and difficulty are determined by objective measurement. The uniform conditions provided in the administration and scoring of the test increase the likelihood that variations in scores are the result of variations in student characteristics and performance and not the result of variations in test conditions. The use of standardization samples establishes test norms which provide the basis for the interpretation of individual and group scores. Although standardized and classroom tests share the same major characteristics, it is likely that standardized tests have greater reliability and classroom tests greater validity for local curricula. Standardized tests are useful for general assessment of student ability and achievement, diagnostic classroom assessment, and assessment of school programs and intructional procedures either on a short-term or a long-term basis.

The next section describes particular types of tests and provides illustrations of them.

QUESTION 14-1

The Performance Assessment Corporation developed a test to measure knowledge of various drugs and their medical uses and effects. In developing this test the authors were careful to control the difficulty level of the items. They made careful observations of score consistency, prepared and tested procedures for scoring and administering the test, and carefully chose their standardization sample and reported the test norms. In the fuller standardization of this test, which of the following tasks must be done? (a) establishing and reporting test validity; (b) establishing and reporting test reliability; (c) establishing and reporting scores and scoring objectivity; (d) listing which rival tests are superior to the test being marketed; (e) providing more efficient means of test administration.

After selecting your answer, give the reasons for your choice and for your rejection of the alternatives.

TYPES AND EXAMPLES OF STANDARDIZED TESTS

We will distinguish four types of standardized tests: intelligence, achievement, creativity, and personality and interest tests. In this section we shall consider same examples of intelligence achievement, special aptitude, and personality tests.

Types of Tests

Standardized tests are classified on the basis of the aspects of behavior they sample. Anastasi (1968) discussed tests in terms of three major categories or functions: tests of general intellectual development, tests of separate abilities, and personality tests. We discuss these various types of tests in subsequent sections of this chapter. Under tests of general intellectual development Anastasi described both individual and group tests. Within this category of tests, we find examples ranging from infant to adult levels, from verbal to nonverbal or culture-fair tests, and tests designed to measure weaknesses or strengths in specific aspects of intellectual functioning. Within the category of tests of separate abilities, we find measures of special and multiple aptitudes, achievement tests, and tests useful in predicting or evaluating occupational success. Personality tests include measures of interest and attitudes, self-perception, and more complex tests known as projective techniques.

Intelligence Tests

Upon reading this portion of the chapter, you should be able to meet these objectives:

14-4   Distinguish among the three types of intelligence tests: individual tests, group tests, and test batteries; point out the assets and limitations of each type; illustrate appropriate uses of each type.
14-5   Describe (in terms of correlation and percentage agreement) the relationship between IQ and school achievement; illustrate how narrowing or broadening the sample affects these correlations.
14-6   Distinguish and show the relationship between general-factor and multifactor tests of intelligence.

In this part of the chapter we discuss the measurement of intelligence at some length. There are several reasons why the discussion of intelligence deserves extensive treatment. First, the use of intelligence tests is very widespread in American education, and any informed teacher must know their nature, assets, and limitations. In fact, a great deal of the controversy which surrounds the tests pertains to their use and not to the tests themselves. Second, an impressive amount of educational research has attempted to establish relationships between scores students achieve on intelligence tests and scores these same students obtain on a host of achievement, special aptitude, personality, and attitude tests, and on other inventories. Third, the student's IQ has been the basis for many educational decisions on grade and track placement, on majors or courses of study, and on placement in advanced study in high school and college; and it has also been the basis for predictions about ultimate academic success (or failure) and even about success (or failure) in one's career or profession. Fourth, intelligence tests are major diagnostic devices for separating the bright and the dull (sometimes the very bright and the very dull) students. Fifth, intelligence tests within the last several years have been linked very closely to the study of creativity and, consequently, have been subjected to a new kind of criticism. Whereas the old (and still current) argument is that the tests are prejudicial to race and social class, the more recent argument is that they are prejudicial to the bright, nonconformist student. The final, but not the least important, reason for the lengthy treatment of these tests is that they represent a very sophisticated level of psychological and educational measurement, and they have been emulated again and again in the development of other psychological and educational instruments.

Types of Intelligence Tests

Both the general-factor and the multifactor theories of intelligence have produced a number of tests and test batteries which differ in their administration and physical form. The administration of these kinds of tests requires specialized training in theoretical foundations of intelligence and much practice in administration and interpretation. For these reasons classroom teachers do not often administer them but use results obtained by clinical or school psychologists. In terms of administration, you can distinguish between two major types of intelligence tests designated as individual and group tests. The individual tests, as the name implies, are administered by a psychologist or trained teacher to a single child at a time. The testing period is approximately one hour, and, during this time, the examiner records the answers which the student (or examinee) makes orally. The examiner also records any significant behavior he observes during the test administration. Throughout the examination the student is required to do little if any writing. Group tests are paper and pencil tests. They are administered by a teacher or counselor to large or small numbers of students or to a single student if the occasion arises. Frequently the tests require less time than the individual tests; this saving in time and money has favored their use over that of the individual tests. Test batteries consist of several tests, which often must be administered over two or more sessions. We shall now describe and compare particular individual and group tests and test batteries.

The individual tests   Among the individual tests of intelligence, the Stanford-Binet Scales are the best known. The first edition of this test appeared in 1905 and was largely the work of Alfred Binet, the French psychologist, who devised it to identify mentally deficient school children. The three major revisions of the Binet Scales made in 1916, 1937, and 1960 by L. M. Terman, of Stanford University, and Maud E. Merrill are formally known as the Stanford Revisions of the Binet-Simon Intelligence Scale.* The 1960 revision was standardized on a stratified sample of 4,498 subjects aged 2½ to 18 years. These tests have been based from the beginning on a theory of

* Simon was Binet's collaborator; the name of the 1905 test was the Binet-Simon Scale. Other American revisions, by Goddard and Kuhlmann, preceded those of Terman and Merrill.

general intelligence. Binet intended to develop an instrument which measured a student's general intelligence by sampling a variety of intellectual activities. We should not be surprised to learn, then, that every effort, such as Thurstone's, to isolate group factors on the basis of these scales has failed. Test items, however, differ in the extent to which they measure the general factor g. The following lists name the various parts of the test for older children and show which parts measure g to a high and which to a low extent.

HIGH g FACTOR

1 Definitions of abstract words
2 Arithmetical reasoning
3 Differences among abstract words
4 Essential differences
5 Proverbs
6 Sentence building
7 Verbal absurdities
8 Vocabulary

LOW g FACTOR

1 Enclosed box problem
2 Memory for stories
3 Papercutting (visual imagery)
4 Plan of search
5 Problems of fact
6 Repeating digits (forward order)
7 Repeating digits (reverse order)
8 Reproducing a beaded chain from memory

Inspection of these lists should suggest two generalizations. First, items which are low in g are less complex than items high in g. The low-g items involve space perception and spatial relationships (as in the plan of search), visual imagery, and rote memory. Second, items which are high in g involve the acquisition and use of language and of the concept of numbers. These items involve acquisition and use of vocabulary; verbal analysis of a situation; comprehension of similarities and differences; verbal and numerical concept formation; and analysis, synthesis, and reorganization of verbal and nonverbal materials (Freeman, 1962, pp. 225–26).

The other widely used tests of individual intelligence are the two Wechsler Scales: the Wechsler Adult Intelligence Scale (known as the WAIS, pronounced to rhyme with base) and the Wechsler Intelligence Scale for Children (known as the WISC, pronounced to rhyme with brisk—see Wechsler, 1949).* The first form of WAIS appeared in 1939, but the 1955 revision (see Wechsler, 1955) is currently in use. The WISC, which appeared in

* The Wechsler Preschool Performance Scale of Intelligence (WPPSI) is not included because research has shown a low relationship between performance and later IQ scores.

1949, is for children from 5 to 15. The WAIS is for older subjects. For adults, the WAIS is more extensively used than the Stanford-Binet Scale, which is not intended for them. Like the Stanford-Binet Scale, both the WAIS and the WISC are based on a general-factor theory of intelligence. Wechsler hoped, however, that, by combining verbal and nonverbal material, he would develop an instrument which was more diagnostic of both intellectual and personality functions than the former scale. Hence, the Wechsler Scales are divided into two groups of subtests—verbal and performance.

There are six verbal subtests: the information test, which covers a wide range of facts which most individuals in American society can be expected to know (for example, Who discovered America?); the general comprehension test, which depends upon the possession of practical information and the use of past experience (What do you do if you find a letter with stamp and address on it?); the arithmetic reasoning test; the analogies test; the test of memory span for digits; and the vocabulary test of forty words arranged in order of difficulty. Three of the above tests, you will recall, are high in the general factor of intelligence: arithmetic reasoning, similarities, and vocabulary.

There are five performance subtests: a digit-symbol test requires the subject to match symbols with digits—a test of speed, accuracy, and visual memory; a picture-completion test requires the subject to note a missing detail—for example, the nose in a picture of a face; a block-design test requires the subject to copy by the proper arrangement of nine cubes several designs of increasing complexity; picture-arrangement test requires the arrangement of cards into series which tell a story; and an object-assembly test requires the correct arrangement of the pieces of a disassembled object, such as a hand or an animal.

The Wechsler Scales yield three scores—verbal, performance, and a combination of these—which become the full-scale IQ. Has there been any real gain in adding the performance tests? Recall our earlier definition of intelligence: the capacity for verbal and numerical reasoning. Inspection of the list indicates that the performance tests may be low in g (general intelligence). For the WAIS, the performance scores and the verbal scores are moderately related. For the WISC, these relationships are considerably lower. For children of normal intelligence, scores on the Stanford-Binet have more relationship to the verbal than to the performance scores of the WISC. It appears that, as a measure of intelligence, we can put less trust in the performance subtests than in the verbal subtests. Even as a diagnostic device the Wechsler has not fulfilled its purpose, perhaps for the simple reason that a test based on a theory of general intelligence can reveal deficiencies only in general intelligence and not in independent intellectual factors.

The group tests The schools commonly use group tests of intelligence, which have many of the characteristics of individual intelligence tests. First, like the Stanford-Binet and the Wechsler Scales, they are based on a theory of general capacity and on the assumption that the measurement of this capacity requires a sampling of a variety of mental activities. Group-test items, therefore, closely resemble individual items: verbal analogies, word meanings, disarranged sentences, sentence completion, arithmetic problems, information, picture arrangement, absurdities, and so on. Second, the arrangement of items usually runs from easy to difficult so that almost every student is able to obtain some correct responses. Third the ages and the grade levels of the students determine the items and their level of difficulty. For example, at the kindergarten level the times are nonverbal. At the college level they are almost entirely verbal and numerical. Finally, the raw score is converted into a mental age, which in turn, is converted into an IQ. Unlike the scoring on the individual tests, the scoring on the group tests is rigid and objective and allows no qualitative judgment. The scoring of individual tests, while allowing subjective judgment, conforms to specific criteria. Table 14-1 lists the more commonly used group tests of general intelligence, along with their grade levels and their correlations with school achievement tests. The dates following the names of the scales are those of their latest revision. The grade level list shows that one test has different scales for each grade level (the California Test), whereas another has a single scale (the Terman-McNemar). The others fall within this range. The correlations, ranging from 0.42 to 0.87, suggest how well you can predict student performance on school achievement tests. These decimal numbers are called *coefficients of correlation;* * they express the degree of correspondence between intelligence scores and other scores and grades. To estimate the degree of correspondence between test scores, you should square the coefficient. Take, for example, the coefficient 0.42. By squaring it you obtain

TABLE 14-1   MAJOR GROUP INTELLIGENCE SCALES FOR ELEMENTARY AND HIGH SCHOOL

NAME OF SCALE	GRADE LEVELS (FOR USE IN)	CORRELATIONS WITH SCHOOL ACHIEVEMENT TESTS
California Test of Mental Maturity (revised annually)	2 to 12 and adults (twelve scales)	0.42 to 0.81 (fair to good)
Henmon-Nelson Tests of Mental Ability (1957)	3 to 6, 6 to 9, 9 to 12, college (four scales)	0.64 to 0.85 (average to good)
Kuhlmann-Anderson Tests (1952)	K, 1, 2, 3, 4, 5, 6, 7 to 8, 9 to 12 (nine scales)	0.60 to 0.80 (average to good)
Lorge-Thorndike Intelligence Tests (1952)	K to 12 (five scales)	0.76 to 0.87 (good)
Terman-McNemar Test of Mental Ability (1949)	7 to 12 (one scale)	0.54 to 0.66 (average)

* See Chapter 15 for a fuller explanation of coefficients of correlation.

0.17; for 0.87, you obtain about 0.78. By converting these decimals to percentages, you know that the range of agreement between the IQ scores and scores on school achievement tests is from 17 percent to 78 percent. Since each of these scales correlates differently with school grades, educational achievement tests, and performance in various subjects, schools and teachers should clearly know their purposes for administering a test and select that scale which best meets their requirements.

Currently on the market are several group scales for college students. Table 14-2 lists the tests now in general use, the types of scores, the performance predicted, and the correlations. These college scales have a high degree of technical precision and interscale correlation. Presently their chief drawback is their inability to distinguish among the middle 60 percent of students. The homogeneity of this middle group, the lack of test refinement, and the social-emotional factors which influence academic achievement account for the lack of successful predictions. Thus we must consider more than these test scores in selecting college freshmen. Students' school grades, scores on standardized achievement tests, and teacher ratings are useful for this purpose.

How do the individual and group tests of intelligence compare in merit? The individual tests still maintain their primacy. In the evaluation of the group tests, the major standard is how well their scores correspond to scores on the Stanford-Binet. When we are concerned with the case study of an individual student, the personally administered and scored test gives us more information than an IQ score. The number and variety of the student's responses, his ingenuity, strategy, and style in tackling and solving problems are open to observation and are reported; they furnish important clues to the way he functions mentally. Because the group tests of intelligence leave so much to conjecture, teachers and schools must consider

MAJOR GROUP INTELLIGENCE SCALES FOR COLLEGE FRESHMAN   **TABLE 14-2**

NAME OF SCALE	TYPES OF SCORES	PREDICTED PERFORMANCE (CRITERIA)	CORRELATION
Scholastic Aptitude Test (SAT, revised annually by College Entrance Examination Board)	Verbal and two mathematical	Freshmen average	0.45
College Qualification Test (CQT, 1955–58)	Verbal, numerical, total, science, social studies	First-semester grades in junior college	0.26–0.67
Cooperative School and College Ability Tests (SCAT, 1955–57)	Verbal, quantitative, total, and breakdown for subject area	Freshmen grades	0.43–0.68
Henmon-Nelson (1961)	One score only	First-term grades	0.54

other factors as well as scores on these tests in making instructional decisions.*

The multitest batteries Not all psychologists accept a theory of general intelligence. In fact, American educational psychologists have almost eagerly jettisoned this theory. Those psychologists who follow in the tradition of the Thurstones and Guilford have attempted to devise tests which measure presumably independent intellectual components. Their assumption is that a battery of several tests will predict student achievement in school and college better than the individual and group tests we have already described. These psychologists also claim that such tests can predict success in nonverbal skills, such as mechanical and clerical skills, and can even predict occupational success. If these claims are true, such prophetic batteries would, of course, be an enormous boon to our school psychologists and school counselors. They could decide to keep Sally out of physics, Harold out of music, and Eric where he belongs, in mathematics and science. They could assign Ralph to premedical training, Gertrude to nursing training, and Marvella to homemaking. The counselors could optimistically assume that every child has his aptitudes and every aptitude its niche.

Of the seven multitest batteries in current use perhaps the most popular and complete is the Differential Aptitude Tests (DAT). In preparing this battery researchers tested a sample of 47,000 boys and girls in grades 8 through 12. The DAT include these eight tests: verbal reasoning, numerical reasoning, clerical speed and accuracy, spelling, and language usage. The authors of the DAT also made follow-up studies of 1,700 individuals who were tested in high school to find out how well the battery predicted their educational and vocational careers. Quinn McNemar (1964) carefully perused the 4,096 correlations in the manual for the DAT test battery. With such exhaustive correlational studies the DAT should have been the answer to the prayer of every counselor. McNemar, however, reached these conclusions: (1) Verbal reasoning is the best single predictor; the language-usage test is a close second. (2) Numerical ability, a test of simple arithmetic operations, is the best predictor of achievement in school mathematics; verbal reasoning, however, correlates better than numerical reasoning with grades in science. (3) The remaining five tests do not distinguish different patterns of academic achievement or occupational choice. General level of performance alone indicates those students who go on to study science, medicine, and engineering and those who become salesmen, beauty operators, and stenographers. The final ironic note is that beauty operators and stenographers do better on the tests of space relations and mechanical reasoning than do musicians and carpenters! The other test batteries do not fare better than the DAT. On the basis of considerable test information we may conclude that multitest batteries and multifactor theories of intelligence do not predict school achievement or occupational choice any better than the old-fashioned tests of general intelligence. Moreover, we

* If you recall that intelligence is the capacity for numerical and verbal reasoning, you will realize that school achievement is not the only criterion used in developing these tests. The tests are based on *construct validity*.

should not forget the advantages of giving one test rather than a battery: It takes less time, costs less money, and offers fewer scores to consider.

Upon reading the next portion of the chapter you should be able to meet these objectives:

14-7 List and illustrate four types of standardized tests.

14-8 Define a test battery and provide an illustration of your definition, using the ITED.

14-9 Illustrate the following characteristics of standardized achievement tests by referring to the ITED: (a) relationship of items to test objectives; (b) establishment of test validity; (c) establishment of test norms.

14-10 Define three factors measured by the Guilford creativity tests, by describing a test for each factor.

14-11 Define creativity in terms of problems, hypotheses, and testing (Torrance's definition) and, by referring to Torrance's creativity tests, illustrate how they correspond to his definition.

14-12 Describe the limitation in the use of creativity tests for instructional purposes.

14-13 List five common personality and interest inventories.

Achievement Tests

Achievement tests are often survey batteries—series of short tests which cover basic areas of educational achievement. These are among the best-survey batteries:

> California Achievement Tests, grades 1–4
> Iowa Tests of Educational Development, grades 9–12
> Metropolitan Achievement Tests, grades 1–12
> Sequential Tests of Educational Progress (STEP), grades 4–14
> SRA Achievement Series, grades 1–9
> Stanford Achievement Test, grades 1–12

The successive levels of these batteries often measure the same basic skills at increasing levels of difficulty.

Iowa tests of educational development The ITED (1963, 8th ed.) illustrates the major cheracteristics of standardized achievement tests. It is a battery of nine tests with the following titles:

1 Understanding Basic Social Concepts
2 Background in the Natural Sciences
3 Correctness and Appropriateness of Expression
4 Ability to Do Quantitative Thinking
5 Ability to Interpret Reading Materials in the Social Studies
6 Ability to Interpret Reading Materials in the Natural Sciences
7 Ability to Interpret Literary Materials
8 General Vocabulary
9 Uses of Information

The heart of the battery are tests 5 through 7, which deal "not so much with *what* the pupil has learned, in the sense of specific information, but rather [with] how well he can *use* whatever he has learned in acquiring, interpreting, and evaluating new ideas, in relating new ideas to old, in applying broad concepts and generalization to new situations or to the solution of problems" (SRA, 1962, p. 6). These three tests, therefore, measure concept learning, principle learning, and problem solving.

Objectives which the items measure are stated. For example, here are some of the objectives for items in test 7, dealing with literary interpretation (SRA, pp. 27–28):

A To understand the significance of specific words or phrases in the light of the literary context.
B To understand the relationships among the ideas and the function of individual ideas in relation to total context.
C To evaluate the author's purpose, point of view, and attitudes.
D To become aware of the style and literary techniques used in the development of the passage and appreciate its mood, tone, and emotion.

Table 14-3 contains some of the items which measure these objectives.

TABLE 14-3 **SAMPLE ITEMS FOR TEST 7 OF THE IOWA TEST OF EDUCATIONAL DEVELOPMENT**
(after SRA, 1962, pp. 29–30)

It's easy enough to talk of Master Jim, after a good spread, two hundred feet above the sea level, with a box of cigars handy, on a blessed evening of freshness and starlight that would make the best of us forget we are only on sufferance here and got to pick our way in cross lights, watching every irremediable step, trusting we shall manage yet to go out decently in the end—but not so sure of it after all—and with dashed little help to expect from those we touch elbows with right and left. Of course, there are men here and there to whom the whole of life is like an after-dinner hour with a cigar: easy, pleasant, empty, perhaps enlivened by some fable of strife to be forgotten before the end is told—even if there happens to be any end to it.

1 The writer thinks that the lives of most people are
   (1) gay
   (2) uncertain and lonely
   (3) difficult but successful
   (4) easy and empty

2 The phrase "two hundred feet above the sea level," in the first sentence, suggests
   (1) loneliness
   (2) safety
   (3) hardship
   (4) adventure

3 The tone of this passage is
   (1) cheerful
   (2) thoughtful
   (3) angry
   (4) amused

4 The passage is unusual particularly because of
   (1) the thought expressed in it
   (2) its strong emotion
   (3) the way in which the thought is stated
   (4) its purpose

5 What is the writer apparently trying to do?
   (1) defend Jim directly
   (2) complain about life in general
   (3) defend Jim indirectly
   (4) condemn Jim's conduct

ITEM	OBJECTIVE
1	B
2	A
3	D
4	D
5	C

The manual clearly describes both general and specific procedures for test administration. A sample item precedes each test, and the answer is marked on the answer sheet in a way which the student can easily follow. The test may be scored manually or by machine. The items are multiple choice in form, there is no correction for guessing, and the score on each test is the number right, with one point for each item. Scores are converted into standard scores, a procedure described below. To facilitate score interpretation, each student's score are profiled by using the chart in Figure 14-1. If the student follows the directions in the left margin, he plots his percentile scores. These kinds of scores are discussed in the next chapter which deals with score interpretation.

To establish the validity of the battery, the ITED manual (SRA, 1962) reports, among others, the following correlations:

VARIABLE X	VARIABLE Y	CORRELATIONS
Composite score on ITED	Grade 9 grade-point average	0.73
Composite score on ITED	Cumulative grade-point average through grade 12	0.63
Composite score on ITED	Henmon-Nelson Tests of Mental Ability	0.84
Composite socre on ITED at grade 12	College freshmen grades	0.61

It appears that the ITED is as good a predictor of success in college, as measured by freshmen grades, as are high school grades and IQ. It might even be a *better* predictor of this success than high school grades and IQ. The reliability of the various tests are usually very high, between 0.88 and 0.92.

In establishing norms for the ITED, the test authors used 51,098 students in 136 school systems in thirty-nine states. The population to which the norms apply includes all students in grades 9 through 12 in the public high schools of the continental United States. The number of schools in each geographical region used for establishing norms was proportional to the percentage of school population for each region.

According to the test authors (see SRA, 1963, p. 7), the ITED has two purposes: (1) to enable teachers and counselors to keep acquainted with the achievement of each student and to use this knowledge in designing instruction and (2) to provide the school administrator with an objective basis for assessing the total educational offering of the school.

Tests of Creativity

One form of special aptitude test is a test of creativity. In Chapter 11, we discussed creative abilities and thinking and briefly alluded to creativity tests. Here we consider these tests in greater detail.

HOW TO PROFILE YOUR SCORES

To compare your scores with the scores of the national student group used to develop these tests, use the profile on this sheet in the following way:

1. Place the name and score portions of your *PRESSCORE* in the space provided for each or copy your scores onto the blank space if you are not to use the *PRESSCORE* here.

2. Put a dot on each line opposite the number on the chart corresponding to the one shown in the *shaded* box under each test score. For example, if the number in the box under Test 1 is 65, you should make a dot on the first up-and-down line opposite the number 65. In the same way make a dot for each of the other scores on the lines just below the boxes in which the percentile score numbers appear. Then connect the dots with a solid line. This is your profile.

INTERPRETING YOUR PROFILE

The numbers you have plotted are percentiles. A percentile score tells what percentage of students at your grade level had lower scores than the one corresponding to that position on the chart. For example, a percentile score of 80 means that 80 percent of a very large and typical group of high school students at your grade level received lower scores. The 50 percentile line is printed boldly to indicate the point—called the *national median*—that separates the upper 50 percent of this group from the lower 50 percent.

Your teacher may also want to know how your scores compare with those of other students of your school in your grade. This will require drawing a *dotted line* profile that is based on ten numbers that your teacher will put on the board. Label this profile "school average."

As you look at your profile, it probably does not go straight across the chart. Instead, it has peaks and valleys. It is by noting these high and low positions that you can learn of your strengths and weaknesses in view of (1) your other scores, (2) the national median, and (3) the school average percentiles.

Discuss this report with your teachers and parents. Ask yourself, "Has my educational development been good, fair, or average?" "In what areas am I weakest, and how can I strengthen these areas?" Try to set a fair standard for improving your scores. Your teachers can be of help in this. Remember that a well-educated person is one who has equally high scores on all the *Iowa Tests*.

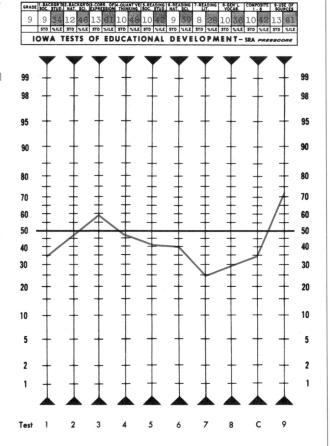

FIG. 14-1 A sample profile of scores for the Iowa Tests of Educational Development. From *Iowa Tests of Educational Development, How to Use the Test Results.* Copyright © 1962, 1953, 1949, University of Iowa. Reprinted by permission of Science Research Associates, Inc.

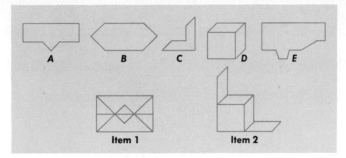

FIG. 14-2 Sample items from the Hidden Figures Test. The problem: Which of the simple figures is concealed within each of the two more complex figures? (after Guilford, 1959, p. 475).

Guilford's tests According to Guilford (1959), creative thinking is divergent thinking. Whereas convergent thinking produces the single correct answer, divergent thinking produces a variety of responses. Flexibility, originality, and fluency are the three factors which constitute creative, or divergent, thinking. Guilford has developed several tests of creativity to define and investigate these factors. In addition to the Brick Uses Test, the Hidden Figures and Match Problem Tests measure flexibility. The Hidden Figures Test requires the examinee to use parts of one figure in new ways to produce parts of another figure. In Figure 14-2, for example, the student must recognize the simpler figure within the structure of a more complex figure by assigning new functions to particular lines. The Match Problem Test requires the relocation of a specified number of matches to form a specified number of squares. Figure 14-3 shows one match problem and its solution. If the examinee tries to keep the squares the same size, he will fail to solve the problem. The measure of his flexibility is his ability to produce squares of varying size.

One test of originality is the ability to produce novel titles in the Plot Title Test. Another is the Symbol Production Test (Guilford, 1959). The examinee produces a pictographic symbol to stand for a noun or verb in a number of short sentences. A third test requires the student to write punch lines for cartoons. In a modification of this test, Getzels and Jackson (1962, p. 43) gave students a sheet of paper with a printed, single-lined border and the title "Playing Tag in the School Yard." The students were to draw any picture they could imagine for this theme. Figure 14-4 is an example which was given a high score for creativity, while Figure 14-5 was given a low score.

FIG. 14-3 A sample item from the Match Problem Test. The problem: Take away four matches in a and leave three squares, using all the remaining matches. b is the solution (after Guilford, 1959, p. 474).

468

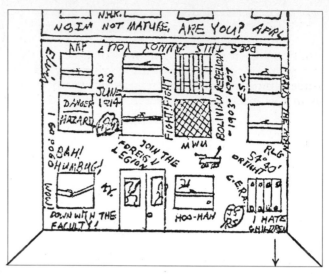

"Playing tag in the school yard"

note: *It is ghosts who are playing tag.*

FIG. 14-4 The drawing of a student given a high score for creativity (after Getzels and Jackson, 1962, p. 46).

"Playing tag in the school yard"

FIG. 14-5 The drawing of a student given a low score for creativity (after Getzels and Jackson, 1962, p. 48).

There are several tests of fluency. The student may be asked to list as many associations as he can think of for a list of stimulus words (see Maltzman et al., 1960). Or he may be asked to list words which are opposite in meaning to the stimulus words (*short* for *long*). In another test the student must rapidly form phrases or sentences when given initial letters, as in this example (Guilford, p. 474):

W_____ c_____ e_____ n_____.

One subject may write "We can eat nuts," while another subject, with more creativity, may write "Whence came Eve Newton?"

Flanagan's ingenuity test   In this test, part of a large battery, the student must think of "ingenious and effective ways of doing things" (Flanagan, 1957, p. 51). The student is presented with a verbal problem, is asked to think of a solution, and then must find his solution among the listed alternatives. In other problem solutions the student must supply the missing letter in two or more words, which in turn make complete sentences. Anastasi (1961, p. 419) classifies this test as a test of originality and notes a fairly high degree of correlation between Ingenuity Test scores and ratings for originality in high school art classes.

Torrance tests of creative thinking   Torrance (1966) has developed a series of verbal and figural tests of creativity. He defines creativity (p. 6) as follows:

> A process of becoming sensitive to problems, deficiencies, gaps in knowledge, missing elements, disharmonies, and so on; identifying the difficulty; searching for solutions, making guesses, or formulating hypotheses about the deficiencies; testing and retesting these hypotheses and possibly modifying and retesting them; and finally communicating the results.

Whereas Guilford's emphasis is on creative aptitudes or traits, Torrance tries to emphasize "creative thinking processes." Torrance uses Guilford's factors, however, to score the problem solutions produced for his tests. There are the following five verbal tests:

1   Ask-and-guess activities. The student is presented with a drawing in response to which he is to (1) ask all the questions he can think of, (2) list all the possible causes of the action he can think of, and (3) list as many consequences of the action as he can think of.
2   Product improvement. The student is presented with a drawing of a toy and asked to list the most clever, interesting, and unusual ways of changing the toy to make it more fun to play with.
3   Unusual uses. As in the case of Guilford's Brick Uses Test, the student is given the name of an object and asked to list as many interesting and unusual uses as he can think of.

4 Unusual questions. Using the same object, the student must think of unusual questions about particular aspects of the object.
5 Just suppose. The student is presented with an improbable situation to think about, and he must list all the exciting things that might happen if this event occurred.

There are the following three picture tests:

1 Picture construction. The student is presented with a colored, curved shape and asked to think of a drawing he could make to incorporate this shape. Then he sticks the shape to a blank sheet of paper and adds pencil or crayon lines to complete the drawing.
2 Picture completion. The student must make interesting objects and pictures out of simple, incomplete nonsense figures and entitle each drawing.
3 Parallel lines. The student must make drawings of objects out of several pairs of straight lines and entitle each drawing.

Reliability and validity Results of the tests of creative abilities or thinking raise some question about exactly what is being measured and how the scores on the various tests are related. The common characteristic of creativity tests is that the student must produce answers rather than select them from a set of choices presented to him. Also, he is asked to produce multiple responses rather than just one response (for example, all the uses of a brick he can think of). Since creativity is a pervasive capacity of the individual, we expect that the individual who scores high on one test will score high on all the other tests of creativity. Thorndike (1963) indicates that the correlations among tests of creativity range from near zero to as high as perhaps 0.40. These test data show a modest core running through the various tests which provides the degree of correlation that does exist, but this core appears to play only a minor role as far as success on any given test is concerned. Scores on tests which purportedly measure various factors of intelligence correlate more highly than the creativity test scores. If we tried to use the creativity tests to identify children who should receive special instruction to foster the development of extraordinary creative potential, we would face the serious problem of selecting some and excluding other children simply because of the particular tests of creativity we used. There is also the question of the validity of the tests—are they really measuring creativity? Ausubel (1963, p. 100), perhaps somewhat wryly, suggests that "high scores on tests that purportedly measure divergent thinking also reflect the influence of such contaminating factors as verbal fluency and glibness, uninhibited self-expression, and deficient self-critical ability."

Despite these limitations, many of which are recognized by the test authors, there are strong indications that the study of creativity and the development of creativity tests will continue. Anastasi (1961, p. 420) writes:

One point appears to be fairly clear at this time. . . . Investigations of scientific talent are becoming increasingly concerned with creative abilities. Interest has shifted from the individual who is merely a cautious, accurate, and critical thinker to the one who displays ingenuity, originality, and inventiveness. Thus creativity, long regarded as the prime quality in artistic production, is coming more and more to be recognized as a basis for scientific achievement as well. It is also likely that in the years ahead we shall see many new kinds of tests. The traditional emphasis on understanding and recall that has characterized intelligence and aptitude tests will probably give way to a more comprehensive approach with greater concentration on productive thinking.

There are at least two reasons for this: (1) The teacher usually has his hands full if he is to do a satisfactory job in areas of intellectual development, and (2) investigations into student personality characteristics usually require competence and training distinctly different from those possessed by the classroom teacher. When it appears, on the basis of informal observation, that the source of the pupil's difficulty may lie in this domain, the teacher should seek assistance from the school counselor or psychologist. The use of instruments for assessing personality by persons without proper training may result in real harm to the child.

Personality Tests and Interest Inventories

As indicated earlier, personality tests measure a great variety of traits, processes, motives, and interests. Although we have placed personality tests and interest inventories in the same subsection of this chapter, they have quite different characteristics. Interest inventories indicate the extent to which the expressed interests of a student coincide with the expressed interests of persons who are engaged in specific occupations. They are not intended to tell whether a student "should" enter a specific vocation. For example, a student may be interested in many of the same things in which an artist is interested but have very little artistic talent. It would be a serious error to guide him in the direction of an artistic career. Personality tests are designed to measure factors related to how individuals function in their daily living and are generally based on complex theories. They require clinical training for correct interpretation. Among the most frequently used personality tests and interest inventories are the following:

The *Kuder Preference Record* (Kuder, 1953) is designed to direct the examinee's attention toward occupational areas which appear to be promising in the light of his general preferences. It gives scores in eight areas of general interest: mechanical, computational, scientific, persuasive, artistic, literary, musical, and social service. The manual contains a classification of occupations based on these interest areas.

The *Strong Vocational Interest Blanks* (Strong, 1951) yield scores which direct the examinee's attention to particular occupations or families of occupations. An examinee's pattern of scores is compared with patterns of specific occupational groups. Horace, for example, may show interest patterns which closely resemble those of psychologists, ministers, and vocational counselors, but which are very dissimilar to those of physicists, senior accountants, bankers, and morticians.

The *California Psychological Inventory* (Gough, 1957) measures the personality characteristics of nondisturbed individuals—those characteristics important for social living and interaction. The test has four measures, those which assess (1) poise, ascendancy, and self-assurance; (2) socialization, maturity, and responsibility; (3) achievement potential and intellectual efficiency, and (4) intellectual and interest modes.

The *Study of Values* (Allport, Vernon, Lindzey, 1960) is designed to show the relative strengths of an individual's values in six areas: theoretical, economic, esthetic, social, political, and religious.

The *Minnesota Teacher Attitude Inventory* (Cook, Leeds, and Callis, 1951) measures those attitudes of teachers (or prospective teachers) which indicate how well they will get along with students and how satisfied they are with the teaching vocation. It consists of 150 statements with which the examinee can strongly agree, agree, be undecided or uncertain, disagree, or strongly disagree.

For prospective teachers, the usefulness of personality tests is somewhat dubious. Richard Lindeman (1967) believes that investigation of personality problems lies outside the teacher's province (p. 109):

> There are at least two reasons for this: (1)The teacher usually has his hands full if he is to do a satisfactory job in areas of intellectual development, and (2) investigations into student personality characteristics usually require competence and training distinctly different from those possessed by the classroom teacher. When it appears, on the basis of informal observation, that the source of the pupil's difficulty may lie in this domain, the teacher should seek assistance from the school counselor or psychologist. The use of instruments for assessing personality by persons without proper training may result in real harm to the child.

Ordinarily, in designing the proper conditions for instructions, personality probes and assessments are unnecessary and unfruitful.

Summary

We have described four types of standardized tests: intelligence, achievement, creativity, and personality and interest tests. The Stanford-Binet was used to demonstrate the kinds of items found in individual intelligence tests. The Iowa Tests of Educational Development (ITED) show the major characteristics of standardized tests in the construction of the items, the procedures for administration and scoring, the study of their validity and reliability, and the establishment of norms. Tests of creativity are special aptitude tests which frequently measure flexibility, fluency, and originality. Although the tests themselves may be considered measures of creative ability (Guilford), they can also be viewed as measures of creative-thinking processes (Torrance). Personality tests are primarily instruments for clinical diagnosis and treatment. We briefly described some common personality and interest inventories.

The Performance Assessment Corporation constructed a test to measure the number and quality of different solutions students could produce for a series of social problems presented to them. Most likely this is a test of (a) general intelligence; (b) multiple aptitudes; (c) special aptitude; (d) achievement; (e) personality.

After selecting your answer, give reasons for your choice and for your rejection of the alternatives.

SUMMARY

Test standardization is the development of uniform procedures used in each administration and scoring of a test. Such standardization increases the probability that variations in scores are the result of variations in student performance and not the result of test conditions. In the construction of the test, systematic procedures are used for increasing validity and reliability. To establish test norms, a standardization sample, representative of the type of students for whom the test will be used, is carefully selected. In many cases, while classroom tests may have more content validity, standardized tests may have more reliability. Teachers may use standardized tests for general assessment of student ability, general assessment of student achievement, diagnostic assessment in the classroom, assessment of school programs and instructional procedures, and assessment of school learning over the long term.

Achievement and creativity tests are among the five types of standardized tests. Achievement tests are often survey batteries or series of short tests covering basic areas of educational achievement. The ITED battery illustrates the major characteristics of standardized tests. Statements of instructional objectives indicate those classes for which the test is valid. The manual describes both specific and general procedures for test administration and for scoring. Norms have been carefully established. The validity of the battery has been checked against scores on other standardized tests and against level of school achievement. The common characteristic of creativity tests is that the student must produce answers. While the Guilford tests emphasize the measurement of the creative attributes of individuals (fluency, flexibility, and originality), the Torrance tests attempt to measure creative-thinking processes. At present the reliability and validity of creativity tests limit their classroom usefulness. Personality tests are primarily instruments for clinical diagnosis and treatment and are ordinarily not useful for classroom purposes. Interest inventories direct attention to particular occupations or families of occupations.

SUGGESTED READINGS

Several excellent texts in both hard and soft cover discuss educational tests and measurement. The following hard-cover texts emphasize the psychological theory underlying tests and measurement:

ANASTASI, ANNE, *Psychological Testing* (2nd ed.). New York: The Macmillan Company, 1961.

CRONBACH, LEE J., *Essentials of Psychological Testing* (2nd ed.). New York: Harper & Row, Publishers, Inc., 1960.

FREEMAN, FRANK S., *Theory and Practice of Psychological Testing* (3rd ed.). New York: Holt, Rinehart & Winston, Inc., 1962.

MEHRENS, WILLIAM A. and LEHMANN, IRVIN J., *Measurement and Evaluation in Education and Psychology*. New York: Holt, Rinehart & Winston, Inc., 1973.

STANLEY, JULIAN C. and HOPKINS, KENNETH D., *Educational and Psychological Measurement and Evaluation*. Englewood Cliffs, N.J.: Prentice-Hall, Inc., 1972.

THORNDIKE, ROBERT L. and HAGEN, ELIZABETH, *Measurement and Evaluation in Psychology and Education* (2nd ed.). New York: John Wiley & Sons, Inc., 1969.

CHAPTER FIFTEEN

HOW TO INTERPRET TEST SCORES

In this chapter you are introduced to some basic statistical concepts important in score interpretation: the normal curve, measures of central tendency, measures of variability, derived scores, and measures of correlations. Although this section introduces you to the computation of these statistics, the emphasis is on their use in the interpretation of test scores. Several of the methods described for dealing with test scores are applicable to teacher-made tests, although most teachers make little or no use of some of the more detailed methods. The interpretation of scores depends as much on knowledge of the characteristics of tests as it does on knowledge of the ways that scores are computed.

THE INTERPRETATION OF TEST SCORES

Upon reading this section of the chapter, you should be able to meet these objectives.

15-1   List and illustrate three characteristics of the normal curve.

15-2   Define central tendency and illustrate three measures of central tendency.

15-3   Compute the mode, median, and mean of a short series of scores and indicate the appropriate use of each measure.

15-4   Define variability and illustrate two measures of variability.

15-5   Compute the range and standard deviation of a short series of scores.

15-6   Distinguish and illustrate the difference between a raw and a derived score.

15-7   Define percentile rank in terms of percentage standing and illustrate your definition with specific examples of percentile ranks.

15-8   Illustrate the relationship of particular percentile ranks to cumulative percentages and to the standard deviations of the normal curve (use Chart 1).

15-9   Compute the z score from given raw scores and illustrate how it may be used in comparing scores from different tests.

15-10   Define the T, AGCT, and CEEB scores in terms of the z score.

15-11   Define deviation IQ scores in terms of the z score and illustrate the importance of knowing standard deviations in using IQ scores.

15-12   Define and illustrate age-grade scores by using examples of these scores and illustrate one appropriate use and other inappropriate uses.

15-13   Define correlation and illustrate two measures of correlation.

15-14   Distinguish among positive, negative, and zero correlations by using coefficients illustrating each one.

15-15   Compute the product-moment and rank-difference coefficients of correlation for a short series of scores.

One of your teaching responsibilities will be the interpretation of test scores. To make this interpretation you must have an elementary knowledge of descriptive statistics. This chapter section, therefore, presents the following statistical concepts: the normal curve, measures of central tendency, measures of variability, derived scores, and measures of correlation. Although this section shows you how to compute these statistics, the emphasis is on their use in the interpretation of test scores.

The Normal Curve

As a distribution of scores, the normal curve has three characteristics: (1) Most of the scores cluster in the middle of the curve; (2) the curve is bell-shaped, combining both concave and convex curves; and (3) it is symmetrical, with 50 percent of the scores in each half of the curve. Not all symmetrical curves are "normal." There are very precise mathematical characteristics present in a normal distribution which are based on the laws of probability. For practical purposes, however, it is permissible to treat data as if they were normal, provided that the curve is symmetrical and generally bell-shaped. Truly "normal" curves rarely result from real data, especially when the number of students tested is small. Nonetheless, the statistical procedures we discuss in this chapter and in Chapter 17 assume that there is a normal distribution.

Figure 15-1 is an example of how scores cluster in a normal curve. Each of the squares represents a single score. If you count only the squares completely under the curve, you will see that the two highest columns each contains fifteen squares. Each of the two adjacent columns, to the right and left, contains fourteen squares. The columns become shorter as we move away from the middle until there is one or fewer than one score per column at the extreme ends of the curve. Figures 15-2 and 15-3 are two more examples of normal curves. Figure 15-2, a distribution of IQ scores, shows a normal curve superimposed on the columns of scores. Although the fit is not perfect, the distribution of column scores closely approximates the normal curve. In Figure 15-3 you see the distribution of scores on a personality test which measures the tendency of college women to dominate or to submit in personal relationships. The distribution of scores is nearly normal because the scores cluster in the middle and the curve is bell-shaped and symmetrical.

When the distribution of scores is not normal, we say the curve is *skewed*. In Figure 15-4, for example, the curve is skewed because most of the scores cluster on the right. Figure 15-5 shows another skewed curve, with the majority of scores clustering on the left. The direction in which the "tail" of the curve points indicates the direction of skew. If it points to the left we say the curve is skewed to the left, and vice versa. More often, we say the curve is negatively skewed if the tail points to the left and positively skewed if it points to the right.

FIG. 15-1 A normal curve. Consider each square under the curve as the score of one student. Most of the scores, you see, cluster in the middle.

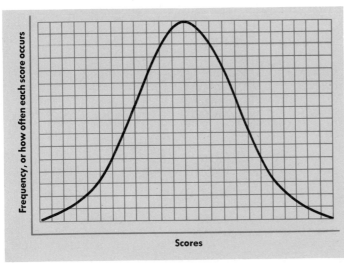

478

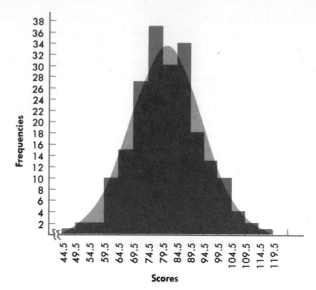

FIG. 15-2 Distribution of scores on a test of intelligence (after Garrett, 1958, p. 104).

FIG. 15-3 Distribution of scores on a personality test (after Anastasi, 1958, p. 32).

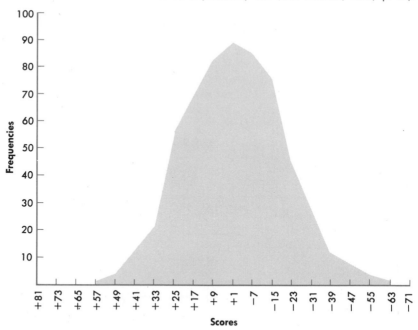

The scores may also cluster too much or too little in the middle of the curve. Figure 15-6 is an example of a distribution in which the scores spread out too much. In Figure 15-7 the scores are too peaked in the middle of the curve. Although both these curves show a middle clustering of scores and symmetry, they are not bell-shaped.

In consructing standardized tests, the authors often collect items that will result in a normal distribution of scores for the population of students for whom the test is designed. If, in the preliminary tryouts of the test, the authors discover too many high or low scores they replace easy with difficult or difficult with easy items. This procedure helps insure that the resulting distribution of scores will be closer to normal. In Chapter 13 we mentioned that the use of relative standards of achievement encourages selection of items which cluster around a difficulty value of 0.50. This

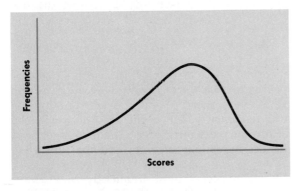

FIG. 15-4 A negatively skewed curve.

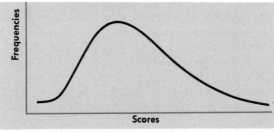

FIG. 15-5 A positively skewed curve.

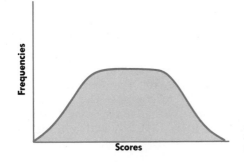

FIG. 15-6 A curve with too much flatness to be a normal curve (a platykurtic curve).

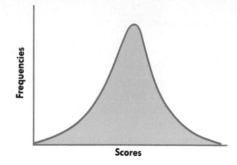

FIG. 15-7 A curve which is too peaked to be a normal curve (a leptokurtic curve).

value helps insure curves that are symmetrical; it helps insure that the number of students who score high will be about the same as the number who score low, and that most scores will be near the middle of the distribution.

Measures of Central Tendency

A fourth characteristic of the normal curve is that all measures of central tendency represent the same point on the curve. Central tendency is the inclination of scores to cluster about a point somewhere between the extremes. The *measure* of central tendency is the point around which the scores cluster. These points, in ordinary discourse, are called *averages,* and we can distinguish three types: the mode, the median, and the mean.

Mode The mode is the score which occurs most frequently in a group of scores. Consider these ten scores: 14, 12, 10, 20, 19, 16, 18, 12, 22. The mode is 12, since 12 is the score which occurs twice, or more frequently than any other score in the group. A group of scores may have one or more modes. Consider the following scores: 14, 12, 10, 12, 16, 14. The distribution is bimodal because it has two modes: 12 and 14.

How useful is the mode? It is convenient to use because it is determined by mere inspection of a series of scores. It is misleading, however, when we use it to represent a typical score, which it may not be. In a group of fifty students, for example, the mode may be 35. If, however, forty-five of the students scored below 35, the mode is a misleading indication of the group's central tendency.

Median The median is the midpoint in a distribution of scores. If there are an odd number of scores, it is the middlemost score. If there are an even number of scores, the median is a point between the two middlemost scores. Consider this series of scores: 4, 6, 8, 10, 16. The median is 8, the middlemost score. Table 15-1 shows you how to compute the median for an even and an odd number of scores. When particular scores are obtained by more than one student, the median is more difficult to determine (see Tate, 1965, pp. 47–48).

TABLE 15-1

Formula: $\text{Mdn.} = \dfrac{X_1 + X_2}{2}$

(for an even number of scores)

Mdn. = the median of scores on one test
  X_1 = the higher of the two middlemost scores
  X_2 = the lower of the two middlemost scores

Problem: Compute the median of the raw scores on the natural science test in Table 15-9.
  Step 1:   Arrange the scores in ascending order, from low (22) to high (72).
  Step 2:   Find the two middlemost scores by counting up to the tenth and eleventh scores.
     You should obtain $X_1 = 51$; $X_2 = 50$.
  Step 3:   Substitute the numbers in the formula, as follows:

$\text{Mdn.} = \dfrac{51 + 50}{2} = 50.5$

For an odd number of scores, perform step 1 above, and find the middlemost score by counting from the top or the bottom of the distribution.

The median is particularly useful for two reasons: (1) It is easily understood and determined, and (2) it is the measure of central tendency least affected by extremes. Consider the average of these salaries: $50,000, $20,000, $15,000, $13,000, and $12,000. The median salary is $15,000. The arithmetic average salary (obtained by adding the salaries and dividing by five) is $22,000. The median is more representative of this group of salaries because it is less affected than the arithmetic average by the extremely high salary of $50,000.

Mean   The mean, or arithmetic mean, is the sum of a group of scores divided by the number of scores. Table 15-2 shows you how to compute the mean.
   The mean is the most useful measure of central tendency for the following reasons: (1) It can be used in the computation of other statistics, as you will see below; and (2) it tends to give a more accurate measure of central tendency than the median and the mode do. Ordinarily one should use the mean unless there are good reasons not to.

Measures of Variability

Whereas measures of central tendency describe the clustering of scores, measures of variability describe the spreading out of scores. Consider the following situation, in which knowledge of two measures of central tendency is an insufficient basis for making instructional decisions. A geometry teacher has two classes each with three students (in a highly enlightened school district). On the basis of average IQ scores for the classes, he wants

TABLE 15-2   HOW TO COMPUTE THE MEAN

Formula: $M = \dfrac{\Sigma X}{N}$

M = the mean of scores on one test
Σ = to add these scores (Σ is pronounced "sigma")
X = the raw score
N = the number of students who have scores

Problem: Compute the mean for the raw scores on the natural science test, in Table 15-9.
  Step 1:   Add the scores to obtain ΣX.
    You should obtain 971.
  Step 2:   Count the number of scores to obtain N.
    You should obtain 20.
  Step 3:   Substitute the numbers in the formula, as follows:

$$M = \frac{971}{20} = 48.55$$

---

to determine whether he should use the same instructional procedures and materials in both classes. Here are the IQ scores, means, and medians for both classes:

CLASS A		CLASS B	
Elizabeth	101	Ron	150
Ken	100	Thelma	100
Connie	99	Marjorie	50
$M =$	100	$M =$	100
Mdn. =	100	Mdn. =	100

If the teacher pays little attention to individual IQ scores and bases his decision on these measures of central tendency, he may decide to teach both classes in the same way. Inspection of the spread of the scores in these two classes quickly indicates, however, the possible disastrous consequences of this decision. The scores in class *B* are much more spread out (variable) than the scores of class *A*. In class *B*, anything the teacher could add to Marjorie's knowledge of geometry would bore Ron, and probably Thelma, to tears, and he could not significantly add to Ron's knowledge without hopelessly befuddling Marjorie and probably Thelma as well. The teacher needs some new measures—ones which describe the variability ("spreadoutness") as well as the clustering of the scores. Two of these measures of variability are the range and the standard deviation.

Range   The range is the difference between the highest and the lowest scores. In the preceding illustration, for class *A* the range is 2; for class *B*, the range is 100. The range indicates at once that there is fifty times more variability in class *B* than in class *A*. On the basis of the range alone, one

could decide to make different accommodations for entering behavior. The
range is a useful statistic because it is easily understood, easily determined,
and an accurate estimate of variability when scores are normally distributed.
Its chief advantage is that it does not tell us about the amount of variability of the intermediate scores, which, as fate has it, constitute about two-
thirds of the scores in a normal distribution.

Standard deviation   The standard deviation, the most important measure
of variability, is defined by the operations used to compute it. Table 15-3
describes these operations. Unlike the range, which is based on only two
scores, the standard deviation is based on all the scores in the group. In
the table the standard deviation is computed for class *A*, which has three
students—Elizabeth, Ken, and Connie. It is 0.812. The standard deviation
for class *B* is about 40. You can see again that the IQ scores in class *B*
are fifty times as variable as they are in class *A*. The greater the value of
the standard deviation, the greater the variability of the scores. Table 15-4

HOW TO COMPUTE THE STANDARD DEVIATION   **TABLE 15-3**

Formula: $s = \sqrt{\dfrac{\Sigma(X - M)^2}{N}}$

s = the standard deviation of one set of scores
Σ = the sum of
X = one raw score
M = the mean of this set of scores
N = the number of students with scores
$\sqrt{}$ = the square root of

Problem: Compute the standard deviation of the following threee scores: 101, 100, 99.

Step 1:   Prepare four columns of figures as follows:

X	M	(X − M)	(X − M)²

Step 2:   List the scores under column X, and determine M (M = 100).
Step 3:   Subtract the mean from each score to obtain figures for column X − M, as
follows:

X	M	(X − M)	(X − M)²
101	100	1	1
100	100	0	0
99	100	−1	1

Step 4:   Square each of the differences in column X − M to obtain the figures in column
(X − M)², as shown above.
Step 5:   Add column (X − M)² to obtain $\Sigma (X - M)^2$. $\Sigma (X - M)^2 = 2$.
Step 6:   Divide by the number of students who have scores (N = 3).
Step 7:   Substitute the numbers in the formula, as follows:

$$s = \sqrt{\frac{2}{3}} = \sqrt{0.66}$$

Step 8:   Take the square root of 0.66 to obtain s = 0.812.

Step 1: Arrange the scores in ascending order, from low to high.

Step 2: Find the two scores which mark the middle two-thirds of the scores by counting off one-sixth of the scores from the top and one-sixth from the bottom.

Step 3: Find the difference between these two scores and divide by 2. This quotient is the estimated standard deviation.

Problem: Using the short method, estimate the standard deviation of the scores on the reading test in Table 15-9.

Step 1: Arrange the scores in ascending order, from 26 to 80.

Step 2: Find the two scores which mark the middle two-thirds (69 and 38).

Step 3: $s = \dfrac{69 - 38}{2} = 15.5.$

(With the formula in Table 15-3, $s = 17.68$.)

---

describes a method of estimating the standard deviation. Although this method is not as precise as the method shown in Table 15-3, it provides an estimate which is sufficiently accurate for use with most classroom tests, and it is certainly better than no estimate at all.

The relationship of standard deviation to the normal curve is of major importance in the interpretation of test scores. In considering this relationship, make frequent reference to Chart 1, which is on the inside of the back cover of this book. In referring to Chart 1, note the following:

1   About 68 percent of the scores fall between $-1s$ and $+1s$.

2   About 34 percent of the scores fall between the mean (the center line in the curve, marked 0) and either $-1s$ or $+1s$ from the mean.

3   About 84 percent of the scores fall between $-3s$ and $+1s$.

4   The solid vertical lines mark the various standard deviations.

5   Deviations below the mean are preceded by a minus sign, above the mean by a plus sign.

We shall make frequent use of standard deviation in the discussion of the statistics below.

Derived Scores

In the interpretation of standardized test scores you must distinguish between raw and derived scores. The *raw score* is the number of items a student answers correctly on a test. If you have used the formula for correcting for guessing or have weighted the items, the results of scoring and applying the appropriate formula is the raw score. The *derived score* is a raw score that has been transformed to facilitate interpretation. In this section we shall consider several types of derived scores: percentile rank, standard scores, deviation IQ scores, age scores, and grade scores.

Percentile rank   One of the easiest ways of interpreting scores is to rank them from high to low, assigning a rank of 1 to the highest score. The significance of the rank depends on the number of scores in the group: A rank of 1 in a graduating class of three students is not so impressive as a rank of 1 in a class of 300 students. The percentile rank, the most widely used derived score, avoids this limitation. It expresses the student's score in terms of the *percentage of the group* the student has scored above. If a student has a percentile rank of 45, his score exceeds the scores of 45 percent of the group. If another student has a percentile rank of 88, his score exceeds the scores of 88 percent of the group. The percentile, itself, is any one of ninety-nine points which divides a set of scores into one hundred groups of equal size. The highest rank is 99 since no individual can score above himself, and the lowest rank is 1 since no individual can score below himself.

Percentile ranking is the most popular way of reporting scores on standardized tests. They are computed easily and are relatively easy to interpret. There are, however, precautions to take when interpreting percentile ranks. Chart 1 (on the inside of the back cover) shows the relationship of percentile rank to the normal curve. Note that percentile ranks are the same as cumulative percentages. A percentile rank of 84, for example, indicates that the student has scored above 84 percent of the students in his group and that his score lies one standard deviation ($+1s$) above the mean. A percentile rank of 50 means that the student has scored above 50 percent of his group and that his score lies at the mean. It does not mean that the student answered 84 percent of the items correctly.

Given the standard deviation for the student's score, you can estimate his percentile rank. Referring to Chart 1, if you know that a student's IQ score lies halfway between $+1s$ and $+2s$, you can estimate that his percentile rank is about 93. Similarly, if you know that his score falls at $-2s$ on the curve, you can determine that his percentile rank is 2. These relationships hold only for the case in which the distribution of scores is normal. For distribution with other shapes these relationships can be different.

Percentile ranks cannot be compared directly from test to test for the same student. Nor is it easy to compare the relative achievement levels of different students on the same test, especially if the students have widely different ranks. For example, the difference between ranks of 55 and 58 is not the same as the difference between ranks of 93 and 96 even though there is the same difference of 3. This occurs because the scores tend to lump together in the middle of the distribution. Chart 1 shows that the intervals between sets of points vary. For example, the interval between the ranks of 5 and 10 is much greater than the interval been the ranks of 45 and 50. Serious error is avoided if you interpret the scores by saying that one student (or group of students) is higher than another but do not say that he is X times higher. Because these intervals are not equal it is not legitimate to add, subtract, or divide them. If you wish to combine the percentile ranks you must reconvert them to raw scores.

Standard scores   The basic standard score is the z score, which is computed in Table 15-5. The z score is very useful in the interpretation of test scores. Referring to Chart 1, you can see that a z score of 0 indicates that the raw score is at the mean. A negative z score means that the raw score is below the mean; a positive z scores means that it is above the mean. A z score of +3.00 indicates that the score is very high, +3s above the mean.

The use of the z score facilitates the comparison of two or more scores. Consider the situation in which Connie obtains a raw score of 36 on an English test and 80 on a science test. Let us assume the following means and standard deviations for these tests:

	ENGLISH TEST	SCIENCE TEST
Class mean	32.3	75.3
Standard deviation	9.2	15.4
Connie's raw scores	36	80

Does the higher score indicate that Connie is twice as good in science as she is in English? By using the standard deviations, we may be able to answer this question. For the English test, a score of 41.5 lies at +1s (32.3 + 9.2). For the science test a score of 90.7 lies at +1s (75.3 + 15.4). It appears in both cases that Connie's raw scores lie about midway between

---

TABLE 15-5   HOW TO COMPUTE z AND T SCORES

Formula: $z = \dfrac{X - M}{s}$

z = a standard score
X = one raw score
M = the mean of a set of scores
s = the standard deviation of this set of scores

Problem: Connie took a test on the interpretation of English literature. She obtained a score of 36. The class mean was 32.3 and the standard deviation 9.2.
Compute Connie's z score.
Step 1: Find the class mean (M = 32.3).
Step 2: Find the standard deviation (s = 9.2).
Step 3: Substitute numbers in the formula, as follows:

$$z = \frac{36 - 32.3}{9.2}$$

$$z = 0.40$$

Compute the T score:
Step 1: Find the z score (z = 0.40).
Step 2: Multiply the z score by 10.
Step 3: Add 50.

$$T = (0.40 \times 10) + 50$$
$$T = 54$$

---

the mean and one standard deviation above the mean, indicating that her levels of achievement in science and in English are about the same. By using the z score, however, we obtain a better comparison. Using the formula in Table 15-5, we discover that her z score in English is 0.40, in science 0.30. It now appears that Connie is slightly better in English than in science. If you want to avoid decimals, you can use the formula for the T score, also in Table 15-5. You discover then that her T score in English is 54, in science 53, indicating the slightly higher level of her English achievement.

Standard scores can be computed using any mean and standard deviation you choose. The computation follows the same steps illustrated for the T scores except that you insert the new mean and standard deviation. For example, ITED standard scores are computed using a mean of 15 and standard deviation of 5. To see how this works, compare the following formula to the one shown for computing T in Table 15-5: ITED score = $15 + 5z$. Chart 1 also shows other standard scores in common use, the AGCT score and the CEEB score. The AGCT score is obtained on the Army General Classification Test, the CEEB score is obtained on the College Entrance Examination Board tests. Like the T score, they are based on the z score, except for established means and standard deviations, as indicated here:

	MEAN	STANDARD DEVIATION
T score	50	10
AGCT score	100	20
CEEB	500	100
ITED	15	5

The interpretation of these scores is the same as that of the z scores from which the were derived. A T score of 65 indicates that the student is 1.5 standard deviations above the mean; an AGCT score of 130, a CEEB score of 550, and an ITED score of 22.5 have the same meaning. These scores are based on relative standards and describe student performance in terms of the scores obtained by others who took the test.

By referring to Chart 1 you can see the relationships among standard deviations, percentile ranks, and various types of z scores. This chart shows the relationships for a normal distribution. As the distribution deviates from normality, some of these relationships change. Only the general relationships are important. Standard scores generally provide the most precise and reliable way of reporting and comparing scores. A disadvantage is that they are slightly more tedious to compute than percent scores or percentile ranks, and they are not as easily interpreted by students and parents.

Deviation IQ scores Both the Stanford-Binet and the Wechsler Intelligence Scales now use means and standard deviations which are constant from age to age. In the Stanford-Binet scale the mean is 100 and the standard deviation is 16. To find a student's IQ you multiply his z score by 16 and then add 100. The Wechsler tests, as shown in Chart 1, use a mean of 100 and a standard deviation of 15. Almost all modern IQ tests use means of 100, but their standard deviations range from 5 to 20. To properly interpret a student's IQ it is not enough to know his IQ score; you must know the test and the standard deviation of that test. An IQ score of 105, obtained on a test with a standard deviation of 5, equals an IQ score of 115, obtained on a test with a standard deviation of 15. Both scores are one standard deviation above the mean. Similarly, a student with an IQ score of 110, obtained on a test with a standard deviation of 5, has scored above a student with an IQ of 125, obtained on a test with a standard deviation of 15. The former student's score falls two standard deviations above the mean, while the latter student's score falls somewhat short of this point. Most modern IQ tests now provide tables which transform raw scores into derived IQ scores.

Age and grade scores Standardized achievement tests often use age or grade scores for test interpretation. Table 15-6 is an example of age and grade norms. The norms are based on scores attained by the standardization sample at particular grade and age levels. Note, for example, that a standard score of 123 is equivalent to a grade score of 3.1 and an age score of 8–4. For the grade scores, the school year is divided into nine months. A grade score of 3.1 means the first month of grade 3. A grade score of 5.8

TABLE 15-6   AGE AND GRADE SCORES FOR COMPREHENSION SUBTEST OF THE IOWA SILENT READING TEST (Greene and Kelley, 1943, p. 15)

STANDARD SCORE	GRADE EQUIVALENT	AGE EQUIVALENT
109		6–5
114	2.0	7–1
118	2.5	7–8
123	3.1	8–4
128	3.8	9–0
132	4.3	9–7
136	4.9	10–1
139	5.3	10–6
140	5.4	10–8
141	5.6	10–10
144	6.0	11–2
148	6.5	11–9
152	7.1	12–4
157	7.9	13–3
162	8.7	14–4
167	9.8	16–3
172	11.1	18–6

refers to the eighth month of the fifth grade. For the age scores, the calendar year is used. An age score of 8–4 simply refers to the fourth month of the eighth year of age. A score of 18–6 refers to the sixth month of the eighteenth year. Table 15-6 informs us that a standard score of 123 should be the average level of reading comprehension of a child of eight years, four months and in the first month of the third grade.

Age or grade scores have much public appeal because they are based on two ordinary assumptions: (1) that most students of the same ages and grades have about the same amount of knowledge and skill and (2) that students who have achieved above their age and grade levels are equal in achievement to students in advanced grades. Howard Lyman (1963, pp. 125–26) points out the limitations of these assumptions. First, we cannot assume that curricula are uniform throughout the nation. Some students know more or less because they have been taught more or less in general or in particular subject matters and skill areas. This variation in curricula undoubtedly results in considerable variation in achievement and makes the establishment of normal achievement a precarious endeavor. Second, age or grade scores assume that the student learns at a uniform rate throughout the school year and ceases to learn during the summer vacations. The rate of learning, as you saw in Part 3, is influenced by a great many conditions, some of which pertain to the entering behavior and others to the particular type of learning. The student may learn certain arithmetic concepts more rapidly than he improves his reading skills. Third, the age or grade scores of different standardized tests often give conflicting results because they use different standardization samples and give different emphases to the same subject matter. A standardization sample which includes a higher proportion of urban schools does not produce the same age-grade scores as one which includes a higher proportion of rural or consolidated schools. Fourth, the relative level of the score does not correspond to the relative level of achievement. A high score on one subtest of the same battery may actually be lower than a low score on another subtest. Lyman (p. 126) uses this example: A grade score of 8.5 in reading may equal a percentile rank of 60, while a grade score of 8.2 in arithmetic may equal a percentile rank of 98, even though both tests are in the same battery.

Some of these limitations of age or grade scores are overcome if you use them to compare the achievement of your students with their own groups. For example, if Dubbie, in the third month of the fifth grade, obtains a reading score equivalent to grade 5.6, we may consider his reading to be above average. If, however, most of Dubbie's classmates are reading at grade level 6.6, Dubbie's reading is one grade level below the average for his group. Similarly, the average grade score in reading for the seventh grade in an urban school may be 5.1. If Clarence, in the seventh grade of that school, reads at a level equivalent to a grade score of 6.3, he is reading above the average for his group. Even these kinds of interpretations must be made with some caution. Large differences in age or grade scores may be due to very small differences in raw scores. The popular appeal of age and grade scores has led teachers and parents to put too much faith in them. For example, it is a misinterpretation to say that Chad, who is in the fifth grade and scored at grade level 7.7 on a reading test, "can read as well as seventh graders." This merely tells that Chad scored at a level achieved by the average of students at grade level 7.7 who took the test. Note that these scores are norm-related. They are not based on a criterion which defines the level of performance appropriate for a given grade level. When the curricula and the students of your school differ significantly from the student sample and curricula used in

A scatter diagram showing a correlation of −1.00. A regression line connects the points.

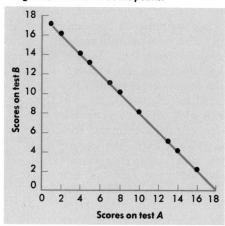

A scatter diagram showing a correlation of +1.00.

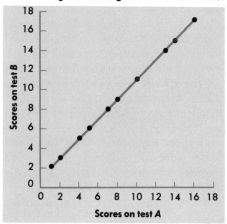

A scatter diagram showing a correlation near 0.

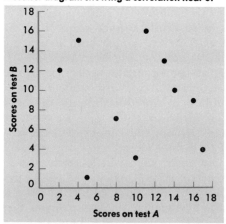

FIG. 15-8   Three scatter diagrams.

the standardization of the test, comparing the performance of your students with the test norms rather than with the performance of their own group results in misleading interpretations.

Measures of Correlation

Correlation is the relationship between two sets of test scores. For example, you may wish to know the relationship of your students' IQ scores to their biology achievement scores, or the relationship of their reading comprehension scores to their scores on a test measuring ability to interpret English literature.

Coefficients of correlation are numbers which describe the degree of relationship which exists between the test scores. These numbers can range from +1.00, through 0, to −1.00. A coefficient of +1.00 describes a perfect *positive* correlation. A coefficient of −1.00 describes a perfect *negative* correlation. A coefficient of 0 (or near 0) indicates little or no relationship between the test scores. Figure 15-8 shows examples of these coefficients of correlation. These figures are known as *scatter diagrams*. The points represent pairs of scores, one score on test *A*, the other score on test *B*. Each point occurs where the two scores coincide. A line is drawn through the points. If all the points fall in a straight line, we have either a perfect positive or a perfect negative coefficient of correlation. In a near 0 correlation, no straight line will pass through or near many of the points. Coefficients of correlation are seldom perfect. Figure 15-9 is a scatter diagram of scores on spelling and arithmetic tests. The coefficient of correlation is 0.73.

FIG. 15-9 A scatter diagram of scores on two tests, showing a correlation of 0.73 (after L. Tyler, 1963, p. 18).

Children	Spelling	Arithmetic
Elaine	20	20
Martha	18	25
Bill	15	19
Jim	15	20
Edna	14	19
Harry	14	20
Marie	14	18
Joe	13	19
Lucy	13	18
John	10	16
Grant	8	15

The closer the coefficients are to +1.00 and −1.00, the greater is the relationship between the pairs of test scores. The closer the relationships are to 0, the less relationship there is. A coefficient of −0.87 shows a higher degree of relationship than does a coefficient of +0.72. A coefficient of +0.32 shows a higher degree of relationship than a coefficient of −0.10. The degree of relationship is shown by the size of the correlation and not by the sign (plus or minus) of the coefficient.

Tables 15-7 and 15-8 show two methods of computing coefficients of cor-

---

TABLE 15-7   **HOW TO COMPUTE THE PRODUCT-MOMENT CORRELATION**

Formula: $r = \dfrac{\Sigma\,(X - M_x)\,(Y - M_y)}{(N)\,(s_x)\,(s_y)}$

r = this coefficient of correlation
Σ = sum of
$X - M_x$ = differences between each score on test x and the mean of that test
$Y - M_y$ = differences between each score on test y and the mean of that test
N = the number of pairs of scores
s_x = the standard deviation of test x
s_y = the standard deviation of test y

Problem: Compute r for these pairs of test scores:

	TEST A	TEST B
Elizabeth	50	60
William	60	80
Connie	70	90
Dub	80	70
Thelma	90	100

Step 1:   Prepare four columns of figures for each test, as follows:

	TEST A				TEST B			
	X	M	$(X - M_x)$		Y	M	$(Y - M_y)$	$(X - M_x)\,(Y - M_y)$
Elizabeth	50	70	−20		60	80	−20	400
William	60	70	−10		80	80	0	0
Connie	70	70	0		90	80	10	0
Dub	80	70	10		70	80	−10	−100
Thelma	90	70	20		100	80	20	400

Step 2:   To obtain $\Sigma\,(X - M_x)\,(Y - M_y)$ multiply columns $(X - M_x)$ and $(Y - M_y)$ as indicated above; then add these products:
$\Sigma\,(X - M_x)\,(Y - M_y) = 700$

Step 3:   Determine the standard deviation for each test by using Table 15-3:
$(s_x = 14.14;\ s_y = 14.14)$

Step 4:   Substitute the numbers in the formula as follows:

$r = \dfrac{700}{(5)\,(14.14)\,(14.14)} = 0.70$

Formula: $rho = 1 - \dfrac{6\,(\Sigma D^2)}{N\,(N^2 - 1)}$

rho = this coefficient of correlation
Σ = sum of
D = the difference between the student's rank on test x and that on test y
N = the number of pairs of scores

Problem: Compute *rho* for the five pairs of scores in Table 15-7.
          Step 1: Prepare columns of figures for each test as follows:

	X	Rank	Y	Rank	D	D^2
Elizabeth	50	5	60	5	0	0
William	60	4	80	3	1	1
Connie	70	3	90	2	1	1
Dub	80	2	70	4	−2	4
Thelma	90	1	100	1	0	0

Step 2: Assign rank for each test as indicated above.
Step 3: To obtain D^2, find the difference between the ranks for each student and square the difference, as indicated above. To obtain ΣD^2, add the figures in column D^2. (6)
Step 4: Substitute the figures in the formula as follows:

$$rho = 1\,\frac{6\,(6)}{5(5^2 - 1)} = 1 - \frac{36}{5(24)} = 1 - \frac{36}{120} = 1 - \frac{3}{10} = \frac{7}{10}$$

$rho = 0.70$

---

relation. The product-moment coefficient is the more widely used and the better method. It is a more sensitive measure of relationship than the rank-difference coefficient because the ranking of the scores in computing the latter coefficient reduces the effect of the individual score on the resulting coefficient. By preserving the score value, the product-moment coefficient remains sensitive to the amount and direction (positive or negative) of correlation. The rank-difference method should generally be used when the available data are expressed as ranks and when raw scores have not been recorded. If there are tied scores, you divide their rank by the number of scores. For example, in Table 15-8, if there were two scores of 50 in column X, you would divide the sum of the rank of 5 + 4 by 2 and assign each of these scores a rank of 4.5.

Correlation coefficients are often misinterpreted. They only indicate the extent to which two things appear to be related. They do not describe cause and effect. The use of correlation coefficients in psychological and educational research and the limited significance of findings based on them are topics considered in the following chapter.

The following questions are based on Tables 15-9 and 15-10.

TABLE 15-9   RAW SCORES OF TWENTY OF YOUR STUDENTS ON STANDARDIZED SCIENCE AND READING TESTS AND THEIR IQ SCORES

NAME OF STUDENT	(RAW SCORE) NATURAL SCIENCE TEST	(RAW SCORE) READING TEST	IQ
Thelma	52	74	115
Dub	65	52	121
Connie	22	26	89
William	40	38	98
Maynard	35	41	111
Elizabeth	72	80	130
James	51	56	103
Helen	46	40	93
Kristi	62	69	108
Julia	31	45	84
Fred	28	37	95
Annette	54	64	106
Howard	50	51	113
Rheba	39	48	90
Rudy	61	75	127
Kenneth	57	61	104
Ronald	59	54	101
Russell	55	46	97
Dorothy	44	33	99
Hazen	48	57	94

TABLE 15-10   MEANS AND STANDARD DEVIATIONS FOR FICTITIOUS STANDARDIZED TESTS, LISTED FOR EACH GRADE

GRADE	SCIENCE TEST		READING TEST	
	M	s	M	s
4	30	5	33	4
5	35	7	35	4
6	40	7	38	5
7	45	9	42	7
8	50	10	45	8
9	52	9	49	9
10	54	8	55	10
11	55	9	60	12
12	56	7	65	14

How do the means and the medians of your eighth grade class compare with the national **QUESTION 15-1**
means?

   Science test: $M = 48.55$; Mdn. $= 50.5$. Reading test; $M = $ _____; Mdn. $=$
_____. Science test (using Table 15-10): national $M = $ _____; reading test
(using Table 15-10): national $M = $ _____.

   Now answer the question above.

How do the standard deviations of your class compare with the national standard de- **QUESTION 15-2**
viations?

   Science test: $s = $ _____. Reading test: $s = 17.68$. Science test (using Table 15-10):
national $s = $ _____; reading test (using Table 15-10): national $s = $ _____.

   Is your class more variable than the national sample?

Using Chart I and the norms in Table 15-10, find the percentile scores for the following **QUESTION 15-3**
students:

   Science test: William _____; Howard _____; Elizabeth _____
(approximately); and Maynard _____ (approximately).

   Reading test: Dub _____ (approximately); Fred _____; Julia _____
_____; and Kenneth _____.

Using Table 15-10, determine the grade-level score of these same students: **QUESTION 15-4**

   Science test: William _____; Howard _____; Elizabeth _____;
Maynard _____.

   Reading test: Dub _____; Fred _____; Julia _____; Kenneth
_____.

Do you believe that the percentile or grade-level scores convey more valid information **QUESTION 15-5**
of the achievement of these students? Why?

How many of your students score at or below the sixth-grade mean of the science test? **QUESTION 15-6**
_____; reading test? _____. How many score at or above the tenth-grade mean
of the science test? _____; reading test? _____.

QUESTION 15-7   Determine the relationship between IQ scores and the test scores, using the designated coefficients.

    (a) IQ scores and science scores (use product-moment correlation).

    (b) IQ scores and reading scores (use rank-difference correlation).

    (c) Which students are achieving below-average scores for their general intelligence level?

    (d) Which students are achieving above-average scores for their general intelligence level?

QUESTION 15-8   Russell, a high school senior, has an IQ of 100. He has a choice of two colleges. At Rolling Hills College the freshman class has a mean IQ of 115 and a standard deviation of 7. At Pacifica State College the freshman class has a mean IQ of 115 and a standard deviation of 12.

    (a) What percentage of the class will Russell exceed in IQ level at Rolling Hills? _____; at Pacifica State? _____.

    (b) Based on these data, which college should you advise Russell to attend?

SUMMARY

The interpretation of standardized test scores requires at least an introductory knowledge of statistical concepts. The normal curve is the basis for these scores. The curve describes a distribution of scores in which most of the scores cluster in the middle. It can be distinguished from skewed, overly peaked, or flat curves. Central tendency is the inclination of scores to cluster at a point somewhere between the extremes. The mean, generally, is the most useful measure of central tendency. Measures of variability describe the spreading out of scores. The standard deviation is the chief measure of variability. A derived score is a raw score that has been transformed to facilitate interpretation. The most popular and useful derived score is the percentile rank, a way of expressing a student's score in terms of the percentage of his group he has scored above. The basic standard score is the z score, which is expressed in standard deviation units. The T score, the AGCT score, and the CEEB score are all modifications of the z score. Deviation IQ scores use means and standard deviations which are constant from age to age. To make a proper interpretation of a student's IQ, you must know the standard deviation of the particular test which yielded his score. Age-grade scores, despite their popularity as derived scores, give misleading interpretations of student achievement unless the students are compared with their own groups. Measures of correlation describe the relationship between two sets of test scores. The product-moment correlation is a more sensitive measure of this relationship than the rank-difference correlation is. The significance of measures of correlation for educational research is considered in the chapter which follows.

SUGGESTED READINGS

In addition to the books listed at the end of Chapters 13 and 14 the following books are excellent treatments of the material in this chapter.

ANASTASI, ANNE, *Psychological Testing*, 3rd ed. New York: The Macmillan Company, 1968.

LYMAN, HOWARD B., *Test Scores and What They Mean*. Englewood Cliffs, N.J.: Prentice-Hall, Inc., 1963. (paperback)

TYLER, LEONA E., *Tests and Measurement*. Englewood Cliffs, N.J.: Prentice-Hall, Inc., 1968. (paperback)

The following programed texts are very useful for descriptive statistics:

AMOS, JIMMY; BROWN, FOSTER; and MINK, OSCAR G., *Statistical Concepts: A Basic Program*. New York: Harper & Row, Publishers, Inc., 1965. (125 pp.)

ELZEY, FREEMAN F., *A Programed Introduction to Statistics*. Belmont, California; Wadsworth Publishing Co., Inc., 1965, 1966. (276 pp.)

GOTKIN, LASSAR G., and GOLDSTEIN, LEO S., *Descriptive Statistics: A Programed Textbook*, Vol. 1. New York: John Wiley & Sons, Inc., 1964. (221 pp.)

Several hard-cover texts for descriptive and inferential statistics are listed at the end of Chapter 17.

CHAPTER SIXTEEN

HOW TO USE TEST SCORES

The purpose of this chapter is to show you some of the ways in which test scores can be used by the classroom teacher. In previous chapters we have discussed ways in which you can improve the quality of your own tests and talked about how you can interpret scores obtained from a variety of tests. In this chapter we provide a discussion of the ways in which the scores can be used to evaluate student progress, assess instructional effectiveness, and assist in planning for instructional and curricular changes. We begin in the first section with a discussion of methods which should be useful to you in assigning marks and grades to your students. In the second section, we discuss how results of standardized tests can be used to assess the educational progress of your students. In the third section, we describe the relationships which have been found to exist between factors of importance in school learning, such as intelligence and creativity.

Upon reading this section of the chapter you should be able to meet these objectives:

16-1 Describe and illustrate (in terms of various official roles) five uses of marks in making decisions.

16-2 Distinguish and illustrate the differences between marks based on achievement and those based on three nonachievement factors; describe and illustrate the hazards in marking on nonachievement factors.

16-3 List and illustrate measures of performance other than tests; illustrate how you would assign weights to these measures as well as to the tests.

16-4 Distinguish between percentage and letter-grade marking systems and describe and illustrate the ambiguity of giving and interpreting percentage grades below 100 percent.

16-5 Describe and illustrate the relationship between the assignment of letter grades and marking on the curve.

16-6 Describe the relationship between marking and the design of instruction.

16-7 Describe and illustrate reporting in terms of achievement, checklists, and parent-teacher conferences.

MARKING AND REPORTING

The tests you construct are a major basis for assigning students their marks. Marks are easily defined as measures of the achievement of instructional objectives. Reports are the means teachers and schools use to convey information about achievement to students and others. In this section of the chapter we shall briefly deal with the use and the importance of marks and reports, the general and specific bases for their assignment, the differences between absolute and relative marking systems, and two types of reporting —the report card and teacher-parent conferences.

Use and Importance of Marks and Reports

In a society which places increasing emphasis on educational progress, marks and reports have become the bases for crucial decisions about the educational and occupational destiny of the student. Consider how marks are the bases for the following decisions: First, the student uses marks to appraise his own educational accomplishments, to select major and minor areas of study, and to decide whether to terminate or to continue his formal education. Second, teachers and counselors use marks for similar decisions: to assess past accomplishments, to assess present ability, and to help the student make educational and vocational plans for the future. Third, parents use marks to determine which (if not all) of their children they should send to college and to estimate the probability of success any one child might have in advanced study and paritcular vocations. Fourth, school and college administrators, faced with limited educational facilities, use marks as the basis for admission to advance study and as indications of the student's progress after admission. Finally, employers use marks in selecting the applicant most likely to perform best the service they require. Part of the hue and cry over marks and marking systems stems from the major role marks desirably and undesirably play in the lives of our students.

Marks can also serve as incentives or positive reinforcers. In Chapter 6 you saw how incentives can increase motivation by raising the anticipation of reaching a desired goal. Incentives can yield learned expectancies. A student who has learned to expect good marks for competent performances will approach most educational tasks with more vim and vigor than will the student who has learned to expect poor marks for inadequate performances. Marks, therefore, not only convey information for crucial decisions but also provide important motivational influences.

The Bases of Marks

In terms of performance assessment, the basis for the assignment of marks is the student's achievement of the instructional objectives. A valid mark indicates how well the student has achieved the terminal performances described in the instructional objectives. A reliable mark is an accurate measurement of the achievement of terminal performances. A mark can be no more valid or reliable than the measures of achievement upon which it is based.

Unfortunately all teachers do not agree that achievement of instructional objectives should be the exclusive basis for marking. Instead, they use several other bases. First they often base grades on the student's attitude, or citizenship, or desirable attributes of character. A student who shows a cooperative attitude, responsible citizenship, and strength of character receives a higher mark than a student who shows a rebellious attitude, underdeveloped citizenship, and weakness of character. Second, teachers often base marks on the amount of effort the student invests in achieving instructional objectives, whether or not these efforts meet with success. Conceivably, the student who expends more effort and does not succeed may receive a higher mark than does a student who expends less effort and does succeed. Third, teachers base marks on growth or how much the student has learned, even though this amount falls short of that required by the instructional objective.

There are many hazards to not using achievement as the exclusive basis for marking. First, if the mark is no longer a valid and reliable measure of the achievement of instructional objectives, it becomes very ambiguous in meaning and a shaky basis for making important educational decisions. Most of the decisions based on students' marks assume that they are measures of achievement: decisions about academic advancement, concentration of study, vocational career, and termination of formal education. It is indeed possible and not unlikely that the teacher will mark on the basis of non-achievement factors even though others will use the marks as measures of achievement alone. Second, the other bases for marking almost always involve highly subjective judgments or vague goals. It is entirely possible that fostering a cooperative attitude, responsible citizenship, and strong character is a worthwhile instructional objective if it can be explicitly stated and consciously pursued. Unfortunately, however, our estimate of student co-operation, citizenship, and character is highly impressionistic and often reflects little more than the fact that particular students accept or reject in varying degrees our beliefs, values, and classroom control. It is equally difficult to estimate the total amount of effort the student has invested in his work since much of this effort does not occur under our observation; we do not systematically record those observations we can and do make, and so much effort can be superficial busy-work which never accomplishes stated objectives. In lieu of an objective basis for measuring effort, the teacher often resorts to subjective judgment with all the attendant bias we have described. He could, however, with the use of reliable pretests and posttests measure growth or increased knowledge rather than the present attainment of instructional objectives. In one sense the teacher is measuring growth when he measures the student's auxiliary performances. Measures of student progress or growth, however, assume that this development is moving in some identifiable direction, which must be toward one or more instructional objectives. In terms of the basic teaching model, it is possible to alter the objectives if the original choices prove unfeasible for the present level of entering behavior and the available instructional procedures. At this point, however, it is incumbent upon the teacher to establish new objectives and not simply to settle for instructional goals vaguely described as progress and growth.

Although achievement of instructional objectives appears to be the only solid basis for marking, the scores which students obtain on your tests should not be the sole means of measuring their achievement. Ebel (1972, p. 348) wrote:

> Exclusive reliance on tests, for example, may give an unfair advantage to students who have special test-taking skills and may unfairly handicap students who give the best account of their achievements in discussions, on projects, or in other situations. But irrelevant accomplishments, such as mere glibness, personal charm, or self-assurance, should not be mistaken for solid command of knowledge. Nor should much weight be placed on vague intangibles or subjective impressions that cannot be quantified reliably.

You should require additional demonstrations of terminal behavior: oral reports, classroom discussions, homework, term papers, term projects, laboratory reports, and so on. The use of several measures of achievement raises the question of how much influence, or weight, each measure should have on the final grade. For example, a course in educational psychology may have these measures of student achievement: (1) weekly quizzes, (2) the midterm examination, (3) the final examination, (4) an oral teaching demonstration project, and (5) a written project requiring a detailed design of instruction based on the basic teaching model. You may conclude that some of these measures of achievement—for example, the oral and written projects

—are more valid than other measures—for example, the quizzes and examinations. In line with this decision you may assign the following weights:

Weekly quizzes	10 percent
Midterm examination	15 percent
Final examination	20 percent
Oral project	25 percent
Written project	30 percent

With these weights the quizzes and examinations will account for less than half of the grade—45 percent. The use of this weighting requires the teacher to multiply the total points accumulated for each of these measures by the percentage assigned to that measure.

For this weighting to have its intended effect on the grades, you must distinguish between the effective and the possible range of scores for each measure. (Thorndike and Hagen, 1969, pp. 577–78). On a multiple-choice test of one hundred items, the possible range of scores is 100. After scoring the test, however, you may find that about two-thirds of the students scored between 25 and 75, making the effective range only 50. If this test were the final examination, and, as the above weighting scale indicates, you assigned to it a weight of 20 percent, you should know that 20 percent of an effective range of 50 will carry less weight than 20 percent of 100. Similarly, if you assign 100 possible points to the oral and written projects and you score these projects in such a way that you use the full possible range of scores, each project will have twice the weight of a one hundred-item final examination with an effective range of only 50. If to the weight contributed by the greater range of scores you added the weight contributed by the larger percentages, the projects would far outweigh the influence of the final examination on the students' grades. You must remember, therefore, that the weight of each achievement measure is a combination of its percentage weight and its range of attained scores.

Three Marking Systems

The marking systems currently used are based on the three types of standards defined in Chapter 13: absolute, criterion-related, and relative standards. The absolute system is based on 100 percent mastery. Percentages below 100 represent less than mastery. The grade is based on the percentage of mastery. For example, a grade based on a percentage less than 70 or 60 is considered too imperfect and, therefore, a failing grade. It is sometimes called the *absolute system* because it assumes the possibility of the student's achieving absolute perfection. According to the definition of absolute standards of achievement, 100 percent could simply mean that the student has attained the standard of acceptable performance specified in the instructional objective. With the absolute standard, it is harder to explain the meaning of any percentage below 100 since the student achieves or does not achieve (all or none) the required standard. A grade of less than 100 percent could indicate the percentage of the total number of instructional objectives a student has achieved at some point during or at the end of the course. Criterion-related standards do not rely on absolute mastery of every objective. Instead, they depend on criteria established by the teacher who has considered the number and kind of objectives which must be met before the next stage of instruction can be entered. In this way criterion-related standards are more meaningful because they can recognize differential levels of competence and achievement and allow some students to achieve above the minimum performance required for all students. Teachers who use percentage grades rarely adopt either of these interpretations, and their grades, despite their deceptive arithmetical appearance, convey no clear information about student achievement.

The more popular marking system consists of the assignment of letter grades: *A, B, C, D,* and *F. A* denotes superior, *B* good, *C* average, *D* fair, and *F* failing or insufficient achievement. It is sometimes called the *relative system* because the grades are intended to describe the student's achievement relative to that of other students rather than to a standard of perfection or mastery. An ordinary but by no means universal assumption of this marking system is that the grading should be on the curve. The curve in question is the normal curve, which Chapter 15 discusses. A teacher who grades on the curve ordinarily expects to give the largest percentage of *C*'s, smaller percentages of *B*'s and *D*'s, and the smallest percentages of *A*'s and *F*'s. It is by now a notorious fallacy that the curve determines the percentages for each grade. The normal curve, you will see, merely describes a particular distribution of scores. Which points in that distribution we assign the letter grades to is a policy decision made by teachers and administrators. A lenient teacher may give considerably more *A*'s than a strict teacher. A teacher may decide that one class has earned more superior or failing grades than another class which, in turn, has earned more average and good grades. Undoubtedly, if faculties and school districts adopted uniform percentage assignments for each of the five letter grades, they could quiet some of the present criticism directed against the inequities of this marking system. One way in which these objections could be corrected is through the use of criterion-related standards. Criterion-related standards can be established for several performance levels. The teacher can also set criterion-related standards for the assignment of letter grades.

Despite the rather obvious limitations of validity, reliability, and interpretation, reform of these marking systems has had only temporary appeal. Reforms advocating the elimination of marks have failed because students, teachers, counselors, parents, administrators, and employers believe they enjoy distinct advantages in knowing the student's marks. Many know that marks mislead them, but many believe that some simplified knowledge of the student's achievement is better than no knowledge at all. Reforms advocating either more simplified or more complicated reports of student achievement, such as simple pass or fail or lengthy verbal and arithmetic descriptions, have also failed. The simplified forms do not tell us enough, even though we do not want to be burdened with too much information about the student. The complicated forms break on the rocks of practicality and familiarity.

As viewed here, the marking system is something external to the design of instruction. It has been created largely for use outside the teaching situation. For the careful design of instruction the teacher must have more detailed knowledge of entering behavior and terminal performance than marks usually convey. As a public record marks have obvious utility. As a means of assessing entering behavior and the effectiveness of instructional procedures they have obvious limitations.

Reporting

The most popular method of reporting marks is the report card. Most modern report cards contain grades and checklist items (Stanley, 1964, p. 329). The grades describe the level of achievement, and the checklists describe other areas such as effort, conduct, homework, and social development. Figure 16-1 shows the report card used in the elementary schools of Berkeley, California.

Because the report card does not convey all the information parents sometimes seek and to improve the cooperation between parents and teachers, schools often use parent-teacher conferences. The teacher invites the parents to the school for a short interview. The conferences allow the teacher to provide fuller descriptions of the student's scholastic and social development and allow parents to ask questions, describe the home environment, and plan what they may do to assist their children's educational development. There are inherent weaknesses in the conferences, and ordinarily they should supplement rather than replace the report card (Gronlund, 1965, p. 378).

Summary

Marks are the bases for important decisions made by students, teachers, counselors, parents, school administrators, and employers. They can also serve as incentives for increased motivation. The most solid basis for marking is on the achievement of the instructional objectives. Attempts to base marks on attitudes, effort, and character development lead to subjective judgments and contaminate the meaning of the grades. In termining the student's achievement, you should rarely rely exclusively on tests. The inclusion of other measures of achievement may involve the weighting of each measure. Two marking systems are in current use: grading by percentages and grading by letters. Grading by letters, the more popular practice, is usually based on a relative standard which compares the achievement of one student with others in his group. The report card is the conventional method for reporting grades, and the schools sometimes supplement this report with parent-teacher conferences.

File Copy

BERKELEY UNIFIED SCHOOL DISTRICT

PUPIL PROGRESS REPORT — — **ELEMENTARY LEVEL**

PUPIL'S
NAME _____ SCHOOL _____ GRADE _____
(Last)   (First)

Checks in the appropriate columns below indicate how well your child has progressed during the particular report period.

	PERIOD I				PERIOD II				PERIOD III			
	EXCELLENT PROGRESS	SATIS-FACTORY PROGRESS	WORKING BELOW CAPACITY	SPECIAL LEARNING PROBLEMS	EXCELLENT PROGRESS	SATIS-FACTORY PROGRESS	WORKING BELOW CAPACITY	SPECIAL LEARNING PROBLEMS	EXCELLENT PROGRESS	SATIS-FACTORY PROGRESS	WORKING BELOW CAPACITY	SPECIAL LEARNING PROBLEMS
LANGUAGE ARTS												
READING ....(Text Level_____)					(Text Level_____)				(Text Level_____)			
COMPREHENSION												
VOCABULARY												
PHONICS & OTHER WORD ATTACK SKILLS												
READING OUTSIDE OF BASIC TEXT												
SPELLING ....(Text Level_____)					(Text Level_____)				(Text Level_____)			
ASSIGNED WORDS												
SPELLING CORRECTLY IN WRITTEN WORK												
ORAL LANGUAGE												
WRITTEN LANGUAGE												
HANDWRITING												
SKILLS OF WRITING												
CONTENT OF WRITTEN WORK												
LISTENING SKILLS												
ARITHMETIC ....(Text Level_____)					(Text Level_____)				(Text Level_____)			
LEARNING & MAINTAINING PROCESSES												
SOLVING PROBLEMS												
SOCIAL STUDIES - Including Geography, History & Civics												
SCIENCE												
HEALTH FACTS & ATTITUDES												
PHYSICAL EDUCATION												
MUSIC												
ART												
BEHAVIOR & ATTITUDES												
BEGINNING & FINISHING WORK PROMPTLY												
FOLLOWING DIRECTIONS												
DOING WORTHWHILE WORK INDEPENDENTLY												
DEVELOPING SELF CONTROL												
OBSERVING CLASS & SCHOOL RULES												
GETTING ALONG WELL WITH OTHERS												

ATTENDANCE   □ SATISFACTORY   □ FREQUENTLY ABSENT / □ FREQUENTLY TARDY   □ SATISFACTORY   □ FREQUENTLY ABSENT / □ FREQUENTLY TARDY   □ SATISFACTORY   □ FREQUENTLY ABSENT / □ FREQUENTLY TARDY

COMMENTS (Period I) __/__/__   COMMENTS (Period II) __/__/__   COMMENTS (Period III) __/__/__
DATE   DATE   DATE

TEACHER _____

TEACHER_____   TEACHER_____   PRINCIPAL_____

PARENT_____   PARENT_____   GRADE PLACEMENT NEXT YEAR _____

FIG. 16-1 Report card used in the elementary schools of Berkeley, California. The first two written reports are presented to parents during fall and spring teacher-parent conferences. The final report is mailed home.

QUESTION 16-1 Mr. Fairminded decided to weight the various measures of achievement in his biology course as follows:

Laboratory experiments	15 percent
Collection and classification of specimens	10 percent
Term project	25 percent
Class discussion	5 percent
Three midterm examinations	15 percent
Final examination	30 percent

Mr. Fairminded determined the number of points he would allot to experiments, projects, and discussion and used the full range in scoring these activities. The number of points allotted to examinations was simply the number of items on the exams. How would you evaluate his weighting procedure? (Choose one.)

   (a) It seems fair enough.
   (b) He has failed to consider the effective range of scores on the activities.
   (c) He should not allow the exams to determine 50 percent of the grade.
   (d) The exams may account for more or less than 50 percent of the students' grades.
   (e) He would be better off to exclude class discussion as a basis for the grade.

After selecting your answer, give the reasons for your choice and for your rejection of the alternatives.

Upon reading this portion of the chapter you should be able to meet these objectives:

16-8   List five ways in which standardized tests can be useful in assessing educational achievement levels.

16-9   Contrast the use of general assessment procedures with the use of diagnostic assessment procedures.

16-10   Distinguish between the uses appropriate for tests of ability and tests of achievement.

USES OF STANDARDIZED TESTS

Standardized tests can be used to assess entering behavior and terminal performance. They can also be used to determine the relative effectiveness of various school programs and innovations. Consider the following general uses of standardized tests.

General assessment of student ability   Intelligence tests, which measure general ability, are one type of standardized test. They help us to predict how well the student may do in particular grades and courses, to compare his actual with his potential achievement, and to assign him to various tracks and programs in which instruction is differentiated on the basis of general ability. Aside from the benefits, we shall also consider the limitations of IQ tests in educational decision making. IQ is an important but not the single factor accounting for successful school achievement; we can make other useful assessments of entering behavior based on the period of intellectual development and on the available detailed descriptions of pre-requisite learning sets, abilities, and styles.

General assessment of student achievement Many standardized achievement tests are batteries which measure achievement in many skill and subject areas. The primary II battery, for grades 2 and 3, of the Stanford Achievement Test includes eight tests: word meaning, paragraph meaning, science and social science concepts, spelling, word-study skills, language, arithmetic computation, and arithmetic concepts. The advanced battery, for grades 7 through 9, also includes eight tests: paragraph meaning, spelling, language, arithmetic computation, arithmetic concepts, arithmetic aplications, social studies, and science (Kelley et al., 1964, p. 2). Both batteries provide considerably more breadth of measurement than most classroom tests. The macrocosmic view of student achievement, which the standardized test provides, has several uses: We can compare the student's general level of achievement with his general level of ability (IQ); we can make decisions to promote him to a new grade or to retain him in an old grade on the general level of his achievement; and we can use this general profile of achievement when we counsel him about future courses of study and vocational plans. The second use, promotion to the next higher grade level, requires data in addition to test scores.

Diagnostic assessment in the classroom The teacher can use the standardized test for detailed assessment of entering behavior. The Gates-MacGintie Reading Tests (1965), for example, measure reading vocabulary, comprehension, and speed and accuracy at various grade levels. By indicating relative strengths and weaknesses in those three areas of reading skill, they tell the teacher which objectives he must emphasize in the reading instruction of particular students. The student who has developed more speed and accuracy than comprehension requires different instruction than the student who has developed comprehension at the price of speed and accuracy. Similarly, with the use of the Stanford Achievement Tests for the intermediate level, we may find that Gus is better in word and paragraph meaning than he is in spelling, language usage, and punctuation. This assessment may indicate that Gus is more skillful in reading than in writing and that the emphasis for him must be on those instructional objectives which stress writing. The use of standardized tests indicates those instructional objectives which the student should pursue most intensively.

Assessment of school programs and instructional procedures Before we permanently adopt or reject any educational innovation, it is wise to determine the relative success of the new and the old programs and practices. If, for example, you want to determine whether instructional television is more effective than conventional instruction in teaching tenth grade algebra, you must find some common means of measuring achievement for both types of instruction. Possibly you could administer a standardized test of algebra at the beginning and again at the end of the course and determine the relative level of achievement for both types of instruction. Standardized tests are often chosen for these evaluations because of their high reliability and because, in theory at least, of their high validity—their measurement of all important course outcomes. Although this research has many pitfalls, the difficulty is not in the standardized tests but in the uses to which they are put. In such research the use of standardized tests is warranted only when both types of instruction pursue identical objectives, when the tests are valid measures of these objectives, and when the only variations in entering behavior, instructional procedures, and instructional content are those specifically isolated for study.

Standardized tests are also a mean of comparing the general achievement level of various schools, districts, and regions throughout the nation. However, not all large-scale assessment programs attempt to distinguish between individual units in the measured population. For example, the National Assessment of Educational Progress (NAEP) does not report results by individual schools or districts but rather attempts to assess the educational achievement level of persons at several age and grade levels (Womer, 1970). To accomplish the goal of assessing the level of national educational achievement, the NAEP staff has developed a carefully validated set of criterion-related test exercises and periodically administer these to representative samples of children and adults across the nation. National and international assessments are a valuable source of knowledge for individuals who want to improve whatever weakness may exist in particular school curricula.

Assessment of school learning over the long haul This assessment is the measurement of cumulative gains in student achievement which result from programs lasting several months or years. For example, what are the cumulative gains in language and cultural proficiency from the beginning of study of a foreign language in the elementary school through high school and college? Carroll (1965, p. 249) notes an unfortunate dearth of studies on how student performance improves over a long term:

> Most educational research studies are what we may call "snapshot" studies of school learning: They look at particular aspects of the school learning process for a relatively brief moment. We need also "panoramic" studies that would examine all interrelated aspects of educational growth over a major part of the years in school by significant numbers of pupils.

Carroll also points out that the new curricula in science, social science, language, and mathematics emphasize long-term learning. To make an assessment of such learning it will be necessary to develop valid stan-

Upon reading this section of the chapter you should be able to meet these objectives:

16-11   Describe (in terms of correlation and percentage agreement) the relationship between IQ and school achievement; illustrate how narrowing or broadening the sample affects these correlations.

16-12   Describe stereotypes of bright and dull children and show the relationship of these stereotypes to life expectancies; physical, intellectual, and social development; and occupational level.

16-13   Describe stereotypes of IQ differences for males and females and show the relationship of these stereotypes to the data on arithmetic reasoning, other skills and aptitudes, and school achievement.

16-14   Describe the stereotypes of artists or other creative individuals; indicate the shortcomings of the Getzels-Jackson study of IQ and creativity; and describe the probable relationship between IQ and creativity.

16-15   List the alleged limitations of the notion of general intelligence and the use of IQ tests and show how these allegations are related to misconceptions of g, narrow interpretations of democracy and equality, and personal emotional bias.

16-16   List the practical limitations of IQ tests and show how these could be reduced by the appropriate analysis of intellectual processes; indicate how IQ becomes a better predictor of school achievement as we increase our precision in describing entering behavior and as we improve the quality of instruction.

RELATIONSHIPS BETWEEN INTELLIGENCE AND OTHER FACTORS

School Achievement and IQ

In this part of the chapter, we shall frequently refer to intelligence and intelligence test scores as *IQ*. IQ, or Intelligence Quotient, originally referred to a score on the Stanford-Binet which was obtained by applying a formula no longer used. The use of the abbreviation IQ, however, has been retained by psychologists, educators, and laymen, as a convenient way of referring to intelligence or to a score on an intelligence test. In the latest revision of the Stanford-Binet (1960), scores are converted into IQ by referring to tables in the test manual.

A persistent question arising from the use of intelligence tests in this: How much trust can teachers place in IQ as a means of predicting the student's scholastic success or failure? Philip Vernon (1958), the noted English educational psychologist, examined some interesting correlations of IQ and achievement. He reports that by combining the information we obtain from intelligence tests, English and arithmetic tests, and teachers' estimates of ability, and by correlating all this information with school performance over a period of two to five years, we obtain a correlation of 0.86 for a whole age group. For the correlation of intelligence test scores and school performance, again for whole age groups, the correlation is 0.80. These are impressive amounts of agreement—from 64 to 74 percent. For groups which are narrower in range than the whole age group, the amount of agreement decreases. For example, college freshmen do not represent the whole age group of eighteen-year-olds. Similarly, we would expect lower correlations between intelligence test scores and reading scores for one fourth-grade class than for all fourth-grade classes in an urban school system. We know enough about the problems of school integration to recall that groups of fourth-graders are not identical the city over.

In Table 16-1 Donald Ross Green shows how correlations change as we narrow our sample from a population of twelve classes in four schools to one class in a single school. The reading scores in the table are called *grade-equivalent scores*. A score of 6.4 means that the student is reading at the level of the average sixth-grader in the fourth month of the school year. For a student in the fourth grade, this may be a very high level of reading

TABLE 16-1   GRADE-EQUIVALENT READING SCORES AT THE BEGINNING OF THE FOURTH AND FIFTH GRADES (after Green, 1964, p. 9)

	GROUP I DRAWN FROM TWELVE CLASSES IN FOUR SCHOOLS Reading Score			GROUP II DRAWN FROM ONE CLASS IN ONE SCHOOL Reading Score	
IQ	FOURTH GRADE	FIFTH GRADE	IQ	FOURTH GRADE	FIFTH GRADE
118	6.4	7.5	118	6.6	7.5
115	3.6	4.1	118	6.4	7.5
113	5.4	6.2	116	6.7	7.5
111	2.9	4.1	116	5.5	6.1
Range	3.5	3.4	Range	1.1	1.4
108	4.9	5.1	115	4.7	5.8
105	3.0	3.3	113	5.0	5.4
105	5.8	6.5	110	5.0	7.3
100	3.6	4.1	108	4.1	5.3
Range	1.3	1.0	Range	3.6*	0.5
97	3.4	4.5	106	4.5	5.1
92	3.5	3.4	98	4.1	4.8
91	3.1	3.7	98	3.1	3.5
81	1.3	1.7	77	4.0	6.6
Range	2.1	2.8	Range	0.5	0.5
Correlation with IQ	0.70	0.74		0.71	0.35

* Because of this increase in range there is no drop in the fourth-grade correlation coefficient.

(depending on the school he is in). Note the differences in range between the highest and lowest scores. In group I, for children in the fourth grade with IQs between 111 and 118, the range is 3.5; in the fifth grade the range is 3.4. In group II, however, for children in the fourth grade with IQs between 116 and 118 (itself a narrower range), the range is 1.1; for the fifth grade it is 1.4. Further perusal of the correlations between IQ and reading scores for the two groups shows a similar trend. We expect the lower overall correlation of 0.35 for fifth-graders in group II because the group is drawn from one school. The corresponding correlation for group I is 0.74. This latter correlation is much closer to Vernon's correlation of 0.86 for a whole age group, although group I, of course, does not represent a whole age group.

As Vernon points out, however precise our tests of intelligence may become, their use as screening devices will inevitably result in error. Even if we combine the test scores with other sources of information, we still make mistakes in the selection of students for various educational niches. Using the best criteria we have, let us select the top 20 percent of a group of one hundred high school graduates for college. The typical result of this selection in Table 16-2, shows that we would exclude six students who would succeed and that we would include six who would fail.

Vernon does not find convincing the frantic assertion that too large a part of our talented youth does not go to college since the correlation between IQ and success in college is about 0.75. However, if we used IQ alone as our basis for admission to college, about 40 percent of our students would be unsuitable. If we selected only those students with IQs of 125 and above (the upper 5 percent), about 25 percent would still fail. Also, if we sent the upper 75 percent to college, those with IQs of 90 and above, we would exclude 2 percent who may have succeeded. We would also include many who would be far happier in vocational schools than in college.

Tests of general intelligence enable educators to reduce the amount of error in their academic prophecies. The tests' value, in this respect, is unquestionable. Alone, though, they are not a sufficient basis for making predictions of school and college success for success is not the result only of intelligence. Even if it were, IQ scores of children fluctuate sufficiently to complicate the matter further. These fluctuations, which we shall discuss later, combined with the changing values and interests of the developing

PREDICTION OF COLLEGE SUCCESS (after Vernon, 1958, p. 97)   TABLE 16-2

	SUCCESSFUL IN COLLEGE	UNSUCCESSFUL IN COLLEGE	TOTAL
Selected on the basis of tests and previous grades	14	6	20
Rejected on the basis of tests and previous grades	6	74	80
Total	20	80	100

child and adolescent and with a confused social milieu to make unreliable all but short-range predictions based on many sources of information.

In summary, although IQ on the average accounts for less than 50 percent of the variation in academic performance, no other single factor accounts for so much variation. In this sense, IQ is our best predictor of school achievement, even though more than half of the variation remains unexplained. Even more sobering is the fact that IQ correlates more with high school than with college grades, and more with college than with graduate school grades (Lavin, 1965, p. 58). Our original question concerned how much trust the teacher can place in IQ as a predictor of school achievement (as measured by grades and grade-point average). The answer is, of course, limited faith. Obviously other factors, such as the choice of instructional objectives and procedures based on careful assessments of the students' entering behavior, can significantly affect student achievement. Also, other aspects of entering behavior, such as learning sets, learning ability, and learning styles (which we have already considered) and motivation and socioeconomic status (which we consider in the following two chapters), affect the future success or failure of the student. We will consider what particular use the teacher can make of IQ in the last part of this chapter.

Individual Differences and IQ

In Chapter 3 you learned that the psychology of individual differences is largely the study of group differences. The individual enters this study only to the degree that his particular attributes (IQ, sex, height, and so on) fit the groups being compared. When we refer to an individual's IQ we are describing his relative position in a group. We are not describing, as in the case of entering behavior, the relationship of his specific previous learning to specific instructional objectives or, as in the case of personality, the relationship of one attribute to his other attributes.

In this part of the chapter we shall discuss three areas of individual differences—gifted and retarded students, male and female students, and creative and noncreative students—and relate these differences to IQ. As in the previous part, we will reserve for the concluding section of this chapter discussion of the practical implications of this body of information in the assessment of entering behavior and the selection of instructional procedures.

Brilliance and dullness   Many individuals have scores which fall at the ends of the distribution of IQ. Those with IQs of 120 and above are often referred to as *gifted,* although this term is occasionally reserved for the very superior students, who have IQs of 140 and above. Those with IQs below 80 are described as *mentally retarded.* Several other appellations fit individuals in these groups: talented, mentally superior, mentally deficient, mentally defective, and so on. American school practice has been to use labels which are more innocuous than descriptive if only because we believe that every child should have an opportunity to appear average or normal.

The schools often eschew the use of such terms as genius, mental defective, moron, imbecile, and idiot for the use of the more neutral, compassionate, and ambiguous names. The advantake of using IQ, without any label attached, is that it is both clear and neutral.

The 1938 revision of the Stanford-Binet shows the distribution for IQs listed in Table 16-3. It is based on a sample of 3,184 native-born, white American children. The actual mean for this sample was 101.8. About two-thirds of the children obtained scores between 129 and 85, or from high average to low average.

The widespread occurrence of mental deficiency in the population has stimulated considerable research (Blackman and Heintz, 1966) focused on the biological or congenital origin of mental deficiency and on the requirements for training programs which will give deficient children the maximum amount of economic and social independence. Much descriptive research attempts only to identify these children. As a group they appear to be below average in physical, social, and intellectual development. They have more physical and sensory defects than does the population as a whole. They have greater susceptibility to disease and shorter life spans. They tend to be below average in all mental functions but especially in verbal and numerical reasoning. For tasks which are monotonous and repetitive, they show the patience of Job. Institutionalization often causes further decreases in IQ, but with proper training and guidance many of them learn to accept and enjoy a fairly restricted occupational and social life.

For the mentally superior children, the description is almost an exact correspondence in reverse. This group appears to be above average in physical, social, and intellectual development. They are healthier and they live longer than average. They achieve a greater degree of social and occupational success. Contrary to the popular stereotype, they suffer from less

IQ DISTRIBUTION (Merrill, 1938, p. 650)   **TABLE 16-3**

IQ	PERCENTAGE	CLASSIFICATION
160–69	0.03	
150–59	0.2	Very superior
140–49	1.1	
130–39	3.1	Superior
120–29	8.2	
110–19	18.1	High average
100–9	25.5	
90–99	23.0	Normal or average
80–89	14.5	Low average
70–79	5.6	Borderline defective
60–69	2.0	
50–59	0.4	
40–49	0.2	Mentally defective
30–39	0.03	

mental illness than do the intellectually deficient. By far the most distinguishing characteristic of the intellectually superior is their ability to handle verbal and numerical abstractions in almost all contexts. This alone greatly enhances their chances of educational and occupational success. The most extensive study of intellectually superior children was Terman's Stanford Gifted Children Study, which was carried out over a thirty-five-year period, with a sample of 1,528 individuals. Despite its methodological limitations, it indicates their degree of success (Terman and Ogden, 1950). The gifted group excelled in college degrees, graduate degrees, grades, and academic honors. These individuals obtained five to eight times as many Ph.D. degrees as did a comparable sample of college graduates. Table 16-4 indicates the occupational success of gifted men in California in comparison with all California males.

One of the most significant comparisons of the Terman study was that of the 150 men rated most successful with the 150 men rated least successful in adult achievement. The most conspicuous differences between these two groups were the superior educational and vocational level of the parents of the most successful men. Over 50 percent of the most successful group had fathers who had graduated from college, against 15 percent of the least successful group. More than twice as many of the most successful men had fathers who were in the professions.

Despite the somewhat convincing nature of the Terman study and other studies of the mentally superior individuals, popular stereotypes of the genius and the curve-raiser persist. The very superior individual, in the top 0.03 percent of the IQ distribution, will hardly seem ordinary to most of us no matter how hard he tries to conceal his intellectual capacities.

In relation to education, is the usual public school environment rich enough or free enough to satisfy the intellectual demands of these individuals? Increasingly, many public school educators are accepting the fact that their schools are not the answer to all the needs of the heterogeneous American population. For students at either end of the IQ continuum, the

TABLE 16-4   OCCUPATIONAL CLASSIFICATION OF GIFTED MEN AT THE AGE OF 35
(after Schiller, 1934, p. 67)

OCCUPATIONAL GROUP	PERCENTAGE OF GIFTED MEN ($N = 724$)	PERCENTAGE OF EMPLOYED MALES IN CALIFORNIA (1940) ($N = 1,878,559$)
I. Professional	45.4	5.7
II. Semiprofessional and higher business	25.7	8.1
III. Clerical, skilled trades, retail business	20.7	24.3
IV. Farming and other agricultural pursuits	1.2	12.4
V. Semiskilled trades, minor clerical	6.2	31.6
VI. Slightly skilled trades	0.7 ⎫	17.8
VII. Day laborers: urban and rural	0.0 ⎭	

very special educational environment they require is often not within the organizational or financial means of the general public school. Rather than water down or enrich the curriculum for a few, special agencies with both private and public support can often more efficiently and effectively meet the needs of the child of exceptionally high or low mentality.

Sex and IQ   More significant than differences in male and female intelligence, according to Anne Anastasi (1958, p. 453), is the immense amount of overlap. She reminds us of Samuel Johnson's reply when asked whether man or woman was more intelligent: "Which man, which woman?" This view challenges our stereotypes of men and women. In fact, much evidence points to the wide individual differences found within each sex. For example, Figure 16-2 shows the distribution of scores of an arithmetic reasoning test for 189 boys and 206 girls in the third and fourth grades. The median for the boys is 40.39; for the girls, 35.81. There is a 28 percent overlap—that is, 28 percent of the girls reach or exceed the median of the boys. The median is an average: It is the midpoint in a distribution of scores, the point above and below which an equal number of scores occur. By overlap, we mean the common area occupied by the two curves. If the overlap were 100 percent, the two curves would be identical (they would occupy the same area).

Keeping in mind the great degree of overlap, we can compare the performance of the two sexes in various physical and mental activities. Table 16-5 summarizes these comparative data. Advantage in the major intellectual functions (verbal and numerical reasoning) is well divided between the females and males. Whereas the girls have the verbal advantage, the boys have the advantage in numerical reasoning. In the light of these intellectual differences it is interesting to compare performance of

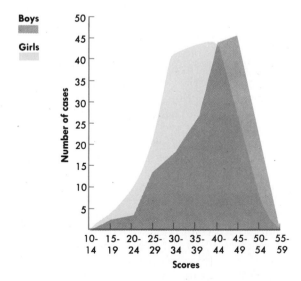

FIG. 16-2 Distribution of boys and girls on a test of arithmetic reasoning (after Anastasi, 1958, p. 455).

TABLE 16-5   SEX COMPARISON OF VARIOUS FUNCTIONS (after Anastasi, 1958, pp. 470–78)

SKILL, PROCESS, OR FUNCTION	THE FAVORED SEX
Gross bodily movement	Males, of all ages
Manual dexterity	Females, of all ages
Perception of details (speed of)	Females
Spatial orientation (Witkin et al., 1954)	Males
Word fluency and mechanics of language	Females
Vocabulary, verbal comprehension and verbal reasoning	Females (but a smaller difference than in word fluency and mechanics)
Memory of verbal material	Females
Memory of numbers and geometric forms	About the same
Mental imagery—vividness	Females
Spatial and mechanical aptitudes	Males
Numerical aptitude—computation	About the same
Numerical aptitude—reasoning test	Males
Artistic and musical aptitudes—esthetics	Females
—skills	About the same

the sexes on the standardized achievement tests and their school performance. On the standardized achievement tests the boys surpass the girls in those subjects requiring numerical reasoning, spatial aptitudes, and the retention of certain information in such subjects as history, geography, and science. The girls surpass the boys in subjects which require verbal abilities, memory, perceptual speed, and accuracy. These differences in test performance are consistent with the differences in aptitudes reported in Table 16-5.

In actual school performance, however, the girls consistently surpass the boys. That is, the girls obtain better school grades, whether the subject is language, literature, arithmetic, science, history, and so on. When compared with boys receiving the same achievement test scores, girls even surpass boys in school grades. This difference in school performance persists throughout high school and college. Anastasi suggests several reasons for the superior school performance of the girls. Their superior verbal ability gives them the advantage both in responding to instruction and in testing, both of which, of course, are predominantly verbal. Also, girls tend to be more docile than boys—less resistant to school routine and more resistant to out-of-school distractions. The predominance of women teachers in elementary school enables the girls to identify more quickly with school and also predisposes the school to adapt more quickly to girls than to boys.

Paradoxically, career and success belong to the men rather than to the women. Despite the superior academy ability and achievement of the women, vocational achievement is virtually a male monopoly. In the Terman studies of gifted children, the adult careers of the women were very undistinguished. A very small number engaged in university teaching, creative writing, art, and research, but two-thirds of those with IQs of 170 and above were office workers or housewives. Follow-up testing also indicated that the mean IQ of the women tended to drop at a faster rate than that of the men.   **517**

The picture is fairly clear. The stereotypes of the American woman as housewife, mother, companion, and social catalyst make it difficult for the American female of intellectual ability and aspirations to distinguish herself in the professional or semiprofessional world without the risk of losing some of her femininity in the eyes of her would-be male competitors and her conservative female friends. It is not at all uncommon in the American high school and college to see the girl of superior intellectual ability and of average physical appearance displaying more interest in social than in academic achievement. The last veil which the American woman must surrender for her full emancipation is the one that now hides her intellectual capacities.

Creativity and IQ   The most recent challenge to the concept of general intelligence has come from studies on creativity. Guilford raised the standard of battle in 1950, when he stated that to fathom creativity we must look beyond the bounds of intelligence. He predicted that the correlations between scores on tests of intelligence and on tests of creativity would be moderate or low. The highly intelligent would probably not be highly creative, and the highly creative would not be highly intelligent. A series of creativity studies conducted in the 1960s reached conclusions which tend to support Guilford's prophecy.

Jacob Getzels and Philip Jackson (1962) published a study on creativity and intelligence which has particular relevance to education. Creativity tests were administered to a sample of 533 students with an average IQ of 130. No intelligence tests were newly administered, but previous scores on the WISC, the Henmon-Nelson, and the Stanford-Binet, which had been recorded by the schools, were used. On the basis of the creativity and intelligence tests, the authors made a selection of smaller samples for intensive study. They selected the top 20 percent of students on the creativity measures and the top 20 percent on the IQ measures. Those students who were in the top 20 percent on both the IQ and creativity measures were excluded from the study. The high creatives were compared with the high IQs on total scholastic achievement, motivation for achievement, perception by teachers, personal values, imaginative production, career aspirations, and family background.

Of major concern for this chapter are the relationships which these authors found between intelligence, creativity, and achievement. Table 16-6

COMPARISON OF IQ, CREATIVITY, AND ACHIEVEMENT (after Getzels and Jackson, 1962, p. 24)   **TABLE 16-6**

	TOTAL POPULATION (N = 449)	HIGH IQ (N = 28)	HIGH CREATIVITY (N = 24)
IQ (mean)	132.00	150.00	127.00
School achievement	49.91	55.00	56.27

reports some of these data. The authors were elated to find that a difference of 23 IQ points between the high-creative group and the high-IQ group was not reflected in the average school achievement of the two groups. On the basis of this evidence the authors felt they were free to conclude that creativity is equal to or more important than intelligence in determining scholastic achievement.

Although some circles have heralded this study as a great break-through in our notions about IQ and creativity, others have criticized its many shortcomings. First among these shortcomings, the authors failed to administer an intelligence test at the time they administered the creativity tests. Reliance on test scores of previous years and different scales leaves the study open to many sources of uncontrolled variation. Second, and more seriously, the authors deliberately excluded from their study students who were in the top 20 percent on both the creativity and intelligence tests, as if they were already committed to the belief that both these qualities could not be found in the same individual. Third, the authors failed to report the basic correlations between creativity, intelligence, and achievement. In the absence of this information, McNemar (1964, p. 879) suggests that we assume the difference between mean creativity scores for the two groups to be the same as the mean difference for IQ, about 23 points. If we make this assumption, we arrive at exactly the opposite conclusion: The high-IQ group did as well in school achievement as the high-creative group despite the mean difference in creativity. A replication of the study which corrected these and other defects did not support the findings of Getzels and Jackson (Yamamoto, 1964).

Many more replications of the faulty design of Getzels and Jackson not quite surprisingly have led to the same conclusions. Paul Torrance (1962), for example, suggests that by using tests of intelligence we fail to identify 70 percent of the top fifth of the creative school children. He strongly implies that the correlations between intelligence and creativity are low and that the creativity tests, better than the intelligence tests, identify the gifted. Other writers with the same bias suggest that we identify creativity in preschool children in order to foster its growth and prevent its early extinction.

The lack of valid tests on creativity has surely hampered research on this topic. The ultimate validity of any creativity test must be based on whether it measures the actual creativity prized by our society. Thus far, the makers of creativity tests have not put these measures to such a test. McNemar (1964) suggests that, rather than an inimical relationship between creativity and intelligence, we may expect high positive correlations. In literary, architectural, and scientific work the relationship between creativity and IQ can be depicted as an inverted triangle. At high levels of IQ we find wide ranges of creativity. As we move down the triangle to average and lower IQ, we would find very narrow ranges of creativity. McNemar concludes that having a high IQ is not a guarantee of being creative; having a low IQ means creativity is impossible. In summary, then, we have little reason to

Summary   We have now concluded our discussion of individual differences in IQ as they relate to the gifted and the retarded, to male and female students, and to creativity. We have seen that having a high IQ is not a guarantee of success and happiness, but it is certainly not a handicap for occupational and social success (for women no less than for men) and for creative achievement in the liberal and scientific disciplines. Much of this part of the chapter has attempted to dispel popular stereotypes held by teachers, students, and laymen regarding the disadvantages of having a high IQ.

Your child has an acute attack of appendicitis and you must select one of three doctors: **QUESTION 16-2**
Doctor A, who received all As in medical school; Doctor B, who received both As and Bs; and Doctor C, who obtained a C average in medical school. You can obtain no further information and you must make an immediate decision. Which one do you choose?

Indicate your reasons for choosing a particular doctor and for rejecting the other two.

SUMMARY

In this short chapter we have described some of the uses to which teacher-constructed and standardized tests can be put. We have tried to point directions rather than provide concrete answers for all situations in which these measures might be useful. By describing different situations and procedures we have led you through examples of several of the ways in which achievement and ability tests can be used. By raising some conflicting points of view, we hope we have stimulated your thinking so that you will not accept interpretations of test data at face value but will examine conclusions in the light of knowledge about appropriate and inappropriate uses of test results.

SUGGESTED READINGS

The references which have been provided at the end of Chapters 13, 14, and 15 will provide useful, detailed information on the topics discussed in this chapter.

CHAPTER SEVENTEEN

HOW TO EVALUATE RESEARCH IN EDUCATIONAL PSYCHOLOGY

The major purpose of this chapter is to introduce you to the nature, use, and evaluation of research in educational psychology. In dealing with the nature of this research, the first section describes six steps which lead from the most basic to the most applied research on human learning. Summaries of actual investigations illustrate each of these steps. This section also distinguishes among and relates various variables, problems and hypotheses, experimental and control groups, and experimental and correlational studies. The section concludes with the consideration of several uses of research in educational psychology. The second section illustrates how to evaluate reports. It describes six steps, extending from the preliminary reading of the report to the evaluation of its conclusions. It emphasizes the problems of sampling and the sources of sampling bias. The third section deals with the statistical analysis of data. Here we distinguish between research and null hypotheses and discuss levels of statistical significance. We describe the nature, computation, and use of three tests of statistical significance: the *t* ratio, the *F* ratio, and the chi square. The section concludes with a brief consideration of nonparametric tests and factor analysis.

Upon reading the first section of this chapter you should be able to meet these objectives:

17-1 Distinguish between basic and applied research in terms of rigor and relevance.

17-2 Describe the research continuum in terms of six steps leading from basic to applied research.

17-3 Identify experimental studies of learning in terms of one or more of these steps.

17-4 Distinguish between and show the relationship of independent and dependent variables and provide examples of each.

17-5 Define hypothesis in terms of independent and dependent variables and give two illustrations of hypotheses.

17-6 Distinguish between and show the relationship of experimental and control groups and provide illustrations of each.

17-7 List and define five factors (apart from sampling) which require experimental control.

17-8 Distinguish between and show the relationship of experimental and correlational studies and identify examples of each.

THE NATURE AND USE OF RESEARCH IN EDUCATIONAL PSYCHOLOGY

This chapter section introduces you to some of the basic concepts in educational research necessary for your evaluation and use of research reports. The primary theme is the relationship between basic and applied research. In developing this theme we shall consider the following topics: the differences in methodological and theoretical rigor and in the educational relevance of basic and applied research; six steps on the research continuum stretching from the most basic to the most applied research on learning; the distinction between independent and dependent variables; the definition and use of hypotheses; the distinction between and use of experimental and control groups; and the relationship of experimental and correlational studies. We conclude this section with a brief consideration of the uses of research in educational psychology.

Basic and Applied Research

Research in educational psychology is both basic and applied (Cronbach, 1966; Gilbert, 1962; Hilgard, 1964; Melton, 1959; and Wittrock, 1967). Hilgard (1964) makes the following distinctions between them. Basic (or pure-science) research is pursued without regard for the immediate applicability of the results to practical situations. Although the investigator may ultimately be interested in the application of his findings, he does not allow this interest to determine his choice of problem, theory, and research procedures. Basic research is more interested in methodological and theoretical rigor than in practical relevance. Applied research is pursued primarily to develop instructional techniques and products which will have immediate classroom use. Although the early phases of applied research may occur in laboratory classrooms, the research purpose is the engineering of specific products which will be tested (or proved) later under ordinary classroom conditions. Applied research is more interested in educational relevance than in methodological and theoretical rigor.

Although this distinction helps us to separate basic and applied research, it is also useful to think of them as occupying different points on a single continuum. Contrary to popular misconceptions, the psychology of learning is a product of both basic and applied research and often the result of a single research program. In repudiating popular misconceptions, Melton (1959, p. 105) writes:

> These and many other false implications will be avoided if it is remembered that basic and applied research lie on a single continuum, and that the variable involved is the freedom of the investigator in the manipulation of independent variables. Obviously the more constraints one places on the freedom of the investigator to manipulate variables, the more restricted will be the information gained from the research. Much basic research that goes on in our laboratories of psychology in universities suffers constraints, such as the nonavailability of subjects other than college sophomores or the limitation of subject availability to one hour, which act to limit the scientific process and restrict the generality of findings; on the other hand it is not difficult to conceive of a truly basic research effort on concept formation which would be conducted entirely in a school setting.

As an illustration of the laboratory constraints Melton refers to, Gilbert (1960, pp. 484–85) tells this anecdote:

> This friend tells the story of his last venture into the laboratory investigation of human learning when some years ago, as a newly produced experimental psychologist, he set about to study human avoidance conditioning, presumably because there was an old hand-shock grid cluttering the laboratory. He was well equipped in the classical tradition. He had a theory (something about an inscrutable mediating between light and shock). He had a group of male college sophomores, carefully matched for sex and education. He had an experimental design, a properly conservative two-tailed t test. And to complete the Galilean picture, he had a standardized source of uncontrolled variation: a wholly mysterious set of instructions designed to startle the most self-satisfied mediator out of its hypothetical existence. The first of the sixty scheduled sophomores proved too unsophisticated for such a high-level setting. When the experimenter threw the switch which flashed a light and pulsed a shock, the subject blandly kept his hand on the grid. Trial after trial the shock intensity increased without a twitch from the indifferent hand when, on the final trial, with the current at a searing maximum, the subject's steady fingers began to smoke. At this point, the experimenter's fine consideration for scientific control gave way to understandable

human curiosity, and he asked the subject why he didn't move his hand. The subject's reply provided perhaps the finest opportunity for scientific discovery since Skinner's first automatic food-magazine broke down. The subject simply said, "I thought you were studying how much *guts* I had!" My friend thereupon canceled the schedules of the remaining fifty-nine sophomores, and today he is productively engaged in the investigation of the eating and defecating behavior of hooded rats. Alas, he may have foregone the opportunity to provide us the first systematic and quantitative methodology for the study of human courage.

At the applied end of the continuum, research in educational psychology has often suffered from different constraints: the insistence on developing procedures and products which will immediately revolutionize the modern classroom. In lamenting the serious lack of basic educational research, Cronbach (1966b, p. 540) writes:

> But today's proudest educational ideas, as practiced in the shiniest of suburban schools, seem to be little more effective than the stereotyped programs that the majority of American schools have been running off in their sleep for a generation or more. To be sure, the research literature reports that this or that innovation is an improvement; over and over you will find the phrase, "The new method produces greater learning than the old; the difference is statistically significant." This telltale phrase usually means that the difference is not large enough to impress the naked eye, and that statistical analysis had to be invoked to dispel the suspicion that the difference occurred by chance. Educational improvements that really make an impact on the ignorance rate will not grow out of minor variations of teaching content and process. Effective educational designs, worth careful development and field trial, can emerge only from a deep understanding of learning and motivation.

Consistent with Cronbach's position, Wittrock (1967, p. 17) defines educational psychology as the "scientific study of human behavior in educational settings." Such a study, he believes, combines basic and applied research but emphasizes basic research:

> As scientists, we [educational psychologists] should attempt to describe, understand, predict, and control behavior in education. That is, educational psychology should invest most of its resources into its most important activity—basic research aimed at control and understanding of the problems and phenomena of instruction in schools. Research explicitly aimed at the production of useful knowledge is an activity defensible in its own right, with its own important *products*—functional relations, generalizations, and theories.

The Research Continuum

Hilgard (1964, pp. 405–10) distinguishes six research steps, which he describes as points on the continuum leading from the most basic to the most applied research on learning. Figure 17-1 shows these steps.

Step 1. Research on learning with no regard for its educational relevance, e.g., animal studies; physiological, biochemical investigations. Learning in

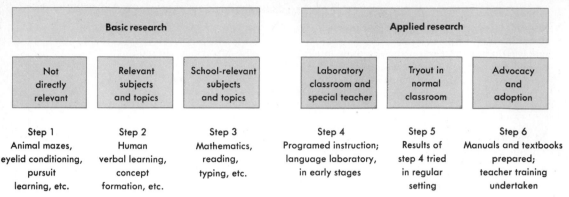

Basic research			Applied research		
Not directly relevant	Relevant subjects and topics	School-relevant subjects and topics	Laboratory classroom and special teacher	Tryout in normal classroom	Advocacy and adoption
Step 1 Animal mazes, eyelid conditioning, pursuit learning, etc.	Step 2 Human verbal learning, concept formation, etc.	Step 3 Mathematics, reading, typing, etc.	Step 4 Programed instruction; language laboratory, in early stages	Step 5 Results of step 4 tried in regular setting	Step 6 Manuals and textbooks prepared; teacher training undertaken

FIG. 17-1 Steps in research on learning—pure research to technological development (after Hilgard, 1964, p. 406).

the flatworm and learning in the rat with transected spinal cord classify here.

Step 2. Research on learning which is not concerned with educational practices but which is more relevant than that of step 1 because it deals with human subjects and with content that is nearer to that taught in school, e.g., nonsense-syllable memorization and retention. The principles being tested are likely to be theoretical ones, such as the relative importance of proactive and retroactive inhibition.

Step 3. Research on learning that is relevant because the subjects are school-age children and the material is school subject matter or skill, though no attention is paid to the problem of adapting the learning to school practices, e.g. foreign-language vocabulary learned by paired-associate method with various lengths of lists and with various spacing of trials.

Step 4. Research conducted in special laboratory classrooms, with selected teachers, e.g., bringing a few students into a room to see whether or not instruction in set theory or symbolic logic is feasible, granted a highly skilled teacher.

Step 5. A tryout of the results of prior research in a "normal" classroom with a typical teacher. Whatever is found feasible in step 4 has to be tried out in the more typical classroom which has limited time for the new method and may lack the special motivation on the part of either teacher or pupil.

Step 6. Developmental steps related to advocacy and adoption. Anything found to work in steps 4 and 5 has to be "packaged" for wider use and then go through the processes by which new methods or procedures are adopted by those not party to the experimentation.

Research in educational psychology, according to Hilgard, has been deficient in steps 4 and 5. Educational psychologists have conducted most of their investigations in the area of steps 1 and 2 and then have made inferential leaps to step 6. Research is needed all along the continuum.

Examples of research steps The following examples of research on learning roughly correspond to the six steps described by Hilgard. In summarizing these research studies we have included some terms and expressions which you have not yet encountered in this book: for example, t-ratio, p value, one-tailed and two-tailed tests, and F test. While you are reading the summaries of the studies, the meanings of these terms may become apparent. The meanings of these terms and explanations of the statistical tests to which they refer will be explained in the section following this one. After reading about these statistical tests it would be profitable for you to come back and reread the studies to see how the tests were used in drawing inferences about the experimental results.

The first study, the formation of learning sets in rats, illustrates step 1. In reading Study I (which you should do at the conclusion of this paragraph), note that the authors are not concerned with the educational relevance of the problem or findings. Note also that the use of animal subjects extends previous animal experimentation and also locates this study at that end of the research continuum farthest from classroom application. Although you know from Chapter 3 that learning sets are useful means of describing entering behavior, this particular study would have to progress several additional steps before classroom application was possible. The next step would be to study learning sets in children (a step that has been taken).

THE FORMATION OF LEARNING SETS IN RATS (Koronakos and Arnold, 1957)

STUDY I

Problem   These investigators refer to the previous studies of Harlow and his associates (1950) which demonstrate the formation of learning sets in primates. They also refer to previous studies of rats which show that at least some rats have the ability to generalize and transfer. The purpose of this study is to investigate the formation of learning sets in rats.

Procedure   The subjects were twenty experimentally naive rats, ten males and ten females. The rats had to learn to push open two doors, one in each of two chambers, to obtain a food reward. The unlocked door in each case was the one door among five which bore a design different from those on the other doors. In one case, for example, the unlocked door bore an X, while the four locked doors bore plus signs. The rats also had to select the X among a second set of five doors. Each animal had ten trials a day. The correct door never appeared in the same position twice in succession and never was in the same position as the second door. When the rat chose the correct door 80 percent of the time, it was given the next oddity problem (given four circles and one triangle, choose door with triangle).

Results   Figure 17-2 shows the performance of the only five rats to reach the 80 percent standard on all seven oddity problems. Each point represents the mean performance on the first ten trials. The figure shows that the rats accelerated their rate of learning; they solved later problems more quickly than earlier ones. By problem 6 they were right about 70 percent

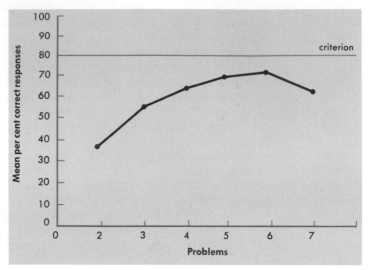

FIG. 17-2 Response curve of the five rats which reached the accepted standard of performance. Note the rise in the curve with successive problems. Each point represents mean performance on the first ten trials for problems 2 to 7 (after Koronakos and Arnold, 1957, p. 12).

of the time on the first ten trials. Analysis of the performance of individual rats showed great variation in performance but the same general pattern of improvement in the ability of the rats to solve later problems.

Discussion The investigators state that the results indicate that rats as well as primates form learning sets. They also state that an alternative explanation of their results is that the problems varied in difficulty and that their presentation in descending order of difficulty yielded these results. Although no objective study was made of problem difficulty, they state that it does not appear reasonable that the results could be entirely explained in this way.

The second study, transfer between paired-associate and serial learning, illustrates step 2. In reading Study II note that the author is not concerned with the educational relevance of the problem and findings. Two characteristics of this study, however, bring it one step nearer to what is taught in the classroom: (1) It deals with human subjects, in this case college students; and (2) it deals with language or verbal learning. Even though the actual learning materials used in the study are not relevant to the classroom, the study could be conducted with verbal materials used in the classroom in teaching particular verbal skills or subject matter.

Problem   Jensen investigated the differences between learning a list of paired associates and learning a serial list (see Chapter 9). He reviewed the traditional conception of serial learning, according to which it is a form of stimulus-response learning. The stimulus for each successive response, in this theory, is the item which immediately precedes it in the list. Research, however, has not supported this theory because only a negligible amount of transfer has been found in going from a paired-associate (PA) to a serial list, even though the lists are composed of the same elements. The paired-associate list, of course, is acquired through stimulus-response learning. Jensen hypothesized that there would be more transfer from the PA to the serial list under conditions which make it easy for the subject to carry over his set for PA learning to the serial task.

Procedure   Jensen used 171 college juniors and seniors as subjects. They were divided into three groups: (1) the odd group learned pairs 1-2, 3-4, 5-6, 7-8; (2) the even group learned pairs 2-3, 4-5, 6-7, 8-9; (3) the control group did not learn a PA list. All three groups learned the serial list. Both the PA and the serial lists contained the same items. Jensen facilitated the learning of the odd group by making the first items in the serial list the first items they had learned as paired associates.

Results   Table 17-1 shows that the odd group learned the items of the serial list significantly faster than the even and control groups did. "Trials to criterion" refers to the acceptable standard of performance, in this case three successive trials without error. Using the *t* ratio (explained below) as the test of significance, he found that the odd group did significantly better than the even group and the control group ($p < 0.001$). The even and control groups did not differ significantly from each other ($p < 1.00$).

Discussion   The findings support Jensen's hypotheses that the paired-associate set facilitates serial learning, that, without this set, the subject adopts a strategy peculiar to serial learning; and that serial learning does not occur as a chain of *S-R* connections.

SUMMARY OF DATA FOR SERIAL LEARNING FOR EXPERIMENTAL AND CONTROL GROUPS   **TABLE 17-1**
(after Jensen, 1962, Fig. 1)

GROUP	TRIAL 1 ERRORS		TRIALS TO CRITERION		PERCENT ERRORS	
	M	S.D.	M	S.D.	M	S.D.
Control	7.83	1.10	24.98	7.73	43.79	7.31
PA (odd)—Serial	5.70	1.49	16.50	6.91	36.69	9.90
PA (even)—Serial	7.02	1.48	22.48	8.40	42.87	9.01

The third study, the role of grapheme-phoneme correspondence in the perception of words, illustrates step 3. In reading Study III note that the authors are concerned with the educational relevance of their research—they are searching for the critical unit of language for reading in English. Three characteristics of this study illustrate step 3: (1) It is the outgrowth of the cooperation of a subject-matter specialist, in this case a linguist (Hockett), and of research psychologists; (2) although the particular subjects in this experiment were not school-age children, the authors could easily replicate the study using these children; and (3) it concerns an important skill taught in the schools—reading. This study remains, however, an example of basic research because the investigators pay no attention to the problem of adapting the learning to classroom conditions.

STUDY III

THE ROLE OF GRAPHEME-PHONEME CORRESPONDENCE IN THE PERCEPTION OF WORDS
(Gibson, Pick, Osser, and Hammond, 1962)

Problem   The letters in the English alphabet do not always correspond to English phonemes (see Chapter 5). This study investigates the critical unit of language for reading in English. The hypothesis is that this reading unit is comprised of spelling-to-sound correlations. It is not defined by speech alone or by writing alone. By simultaneous exposure to graphic and phonemic stimuli, a child who learns to read well forms useful spelling-to-sound correlations. The hypothesis is based on the work of Charles Hockett in discovering the rules by which pronunciation can be predicted from spelling. The specific hypothesis for this study is: Skilled readers will discriminate pseudowords constructed according to rules of spelling-to-sound correlations better than words that are not constructed according to these rules.

Procedure   The subjects were twenty-one college students in a class on the psychology of language. Two types of pseudowords, using the same letters, were constructed: those observing and those ignoring the spelling-to-sound rules. Examples of the former words are *dink, vuns,* and *glox.* Examples of the latter words (using the same letters), are *nkid, nsuv,* and *xogl.* In random order fifty pseudowords were flashed on a screen, and the students were told to write what they saw.

Results   Figure 5-3 shows that students scored consistently higher on those pseudowords with spelling-to-sound correspondences. Using the Wilcoxon Matched Pairs Signed Ranks Test, the experimenters found that the difference between the two types of words was significant ($p < 0.01$, two-tailed).

Discussion   Results show that a letter group with high spelling-to-sound correlation is reproduced more accurately than an equivalent letter group of low spelling-to-sound correlation. The proper unit for analyzing the reading process is not the alphabet letter but the spelling pattern as it relates to the phonemic pattern. Skilled readers perceive *superforms,* which are compounded from their simultaneous hearing, speaking, and reading of words.

It is more difficult to find illustrations which demonstrate the remaining three steps because the conditions of applied research can vary considerably. The following examples are rough approximations of the step characteristics they illustrate.

The fourth study, programed instruction versus usual classroom procedures in teaching boys to read, roughly illustrates step 4. The study has more classroom relevance than the previous studies because it is directly concerned with the practical problems of reading instruction. In reading Study IV note that the first more than the second phase illustrates step 4. There are three characteristics of the first phase: (1) The instruction occurs in a special laboratory classroom equipped with the necessary instructional media; (2) the use of programed instruction provides highly skilled instruction; and (3) the skill which is taught, certain aspects of reading, is one taught in school. If the study were more typical of step 4, it would use fewer students, live instruction by a highly skilled teacher, and omit the second phase, which more properly illustrates step 5.

PROGRAMED INSTRUCTION VERSUS USUAL CLASSROOM PROCEDURES IN TEACHING BOYS TO READ (McNeil, 1964)

STUDY IV

Problem   John McNeil refers to previous studies which show that girls are more successful than boys in beginning reading. Since the inferior performance of the boys may be due to the differential treatment they receive from female teachers, McNeil proposes the use of programed instruction as a method of eliminating this treatment. His hypothesis is that boys will do better than girls in beginning reading under programed instruction but will lose this superiority when taught by female teachers.

Procedure   The experiment had two phases, programed reading instruction and live reading instruction using female teachers. McNeil used 130 kindergarten boys and girls in the first phase and followed many of these pupils through the second phase. A pretest measured their knowledge of letter words and their ability to recognize configurations of letters, the content of the programed instruction lessons. Lessons were projected on a large screen in the form of questions. Each child sat in an individual laboratory-type booth equipped with headphones through which he heard a taped commentary. The pupil answered questions by pushing one of three buttons; a green light followed his response if correct, a red light is incorrect. Unlike the situation in the typical reading classroom, the boys and girls had equal opportunity to respond and obtain encouragement. A posttest (covering some of the knowledge and skills of the pretest) followed the first phase. In the second phase, seven female teachers provided live instruction in reading in typical classroom environments. A posttest also followed this phase.

Results   Table 17-2 shows that the boys' achievement was superior to the girls' following programed instruction but inferior to the girls' following

TABLE 17-2 ACHIEVEMENT ON WORD-RECOGNITION TEST FOR FIRST AND SECOND PHASES
(after McNeil, 1964, p. 116)

| | FOLLOWING PROGRAMED INSTRUCTION | | FOLLOWING INSTRUCTION BY FEMALE TEACHER | |
	M	S.D.	M	S.D.
Boys (N = 49)	26.4	9.0	31.7	11.0
Girls (N = 44)	23.6	8.4	38.3	11.9
	$t = 2.24$		$t = 2.75$	
	$p < 0.05$		$p < 0.01$	

live instruction. Also pupils reported that the boys received more disciplinary comments than the girls under live instruction.

Discussion Boys learn to read better than girls under programed instruction but not under live female instruction. Programed instruction may improve the performance of boys because it reduces peer-group interaction and the number of opportunities to display male aggression.

The fifth study, teaching capitalization with a programed text, illustrates step 5. The study has more classroom relevance than the previous studies (with the exception of the second phase of Study IV) because it occurs in typical classrooms. In reading Study V note the following characteristics which illustrate step 5: (1) The experimentation occurs in a regular classroom with regular pupils; (2) we do not know for certain but we may assume that the investigators are using a revised and not the original version of the program even though they indicate that more revision is necessary; and (3) the program is teaching a skill which these pupils must ordinarily learn. If the study were more typical of step 5, we would know more about the original versions of the program, its success and failures in a laboratory classroom, and the effects of substituting carefully designed live instruction for programed instruction. The second phase of Study IV illustrates two characteristics of step 5: moving from the laboratory to the average classroom and using regular rather than expert instruction.

STUDY V

TEACHING CAPITALIZATION WITH A PROGRAMED TEXT
(Schutz, Baker, and Gerlach, 1962)

Problem The purpose of the study is to evaluate the experimental application of a self-instructional program designed to teach elementary students how to capitalize words acceptably. This evaluation should uncover problems programed instruction poses in the typical elementary classroom.

Procedure The subjects were thirty-six fourth and fifth grade pupils attending summer school. The children varied widely in general level of ability and achievement. After taking a standardized test on capitalization as a pretest, the pupils were taught how to use a program. They were then

(after Schultz et al., 1962, p. 360)

	GRADE 4		GRADE 5	
	M	S.D.	M	S.D.
Pretest	4.3	1.5	5.9	1.5
Posttest	4.8	1.5	7.2	1.3
Difference	0.5		1.3	

given the experimental linear program with which they worked from eleven to sixteen days, for a total of about five to eight hours.

Results Table 17-3 shows the means and the standard deviations for the two grades on the pretest and posttest. The average (mean) gain for the fifth grade pupils is significant ($p < 0.01$) but for the fourth grade pupils it is not. When the investigators inspected individual test scores, they saw that some pupils performed far above and other pupils far below average.

Discussion The significant effect in the fifth grade can be attributed to particular individuals. The results suggest these inferences for the investigators: (1) The program contains some ambiguous, misleading, and otherwise faulty items; (2) because the program failed to teach capitalization rules well for some students, the revision requires changes which insure that each pupil can state a rule before applying it to a novel situation; and (3) the program does not control for entering behavior, particularly reading vocabulary.

The sixth study, the effect of changes in programed text format and reduction in classroom time, illustrates step 6. The study has complete classroom relevance because this training prepares the students for a job they must soon perform. In reading Study VI, note the characteristics which illustrate step 6: (1) The author is taking steps in developing the program for serious adoption in an industrial training program; (2) the material has been packaged, and it is now being modified to save time and improve learning and attitudes; and (3) previous experimentation shows that the programed material provides at least minimal achievement of instructional objectives. If the study were more typical of step 6, the author of the materials and the original investigator of their use would not be the same individual who tries out the material in this step, and the materials would be used by trainees of other companies.

EFFECT OF CHANGES IN PROGRAMED TEXT FORMAT AND REDUCTION IN CLASSROOM TIME ON THE ACHIEVEMENT AND ATTITUDE OF INDUSTRIAL TRAINEES (Hughes, 1962)   STUDY VI

Problem In the original program designed to teach the maintenance of a data-processing system, John Hughes found three disadvantages: (1) The student had to turn the page to find the correct answer to a frame; (2) the student wrote answers in the tests, which therefore could not be reused; and (3) frequent repetition of written answers was boring and fatiguing for the student. By introducing certain program modifications, Hughes seeks improvement in (1) learning achievement, (2) trainee attitude, and (3) speed of program completion.

Procedure   Hughes used two groups of subjects, seventy men who used the original program and served as a control group and 129 men, studying at a later period, who used the new program and served as four experimental groups. Both programs were linear and dealt with the names and functions of data processing units—data flow, bit coding, types of computer words, and program steps. The live instructor had only to keep a record of time for program completion. The time for working on the program was reduced from fifteen to eight hours. The treatments of the four experimental groups differed as follows: Group I found the correct frame answers on the next page of the text and wrote all the answers in the text; group II found the correct frame answers on the next page of the text and wrote all the answers on a separate pad; group III found the answers on the back of the page and wrote all the answers on separate answer pads; and group IV found the correct answers on the back of the page and wrote only 17 percent of the answers on a separate pad (only those answers required by the drawings). All groups received an achievement test and a questionnaire which asked about their reactions.

Results   Table 17-4 shows means and standard deviations for achievement. Hughes found no significant differences among means but he did find significant differences among standard deviations: The standard deviation for experimental group I was significantly greater than those for the other classes ($p < 0.01$), when Hughes used Bartlett's test of homogeneity of variance. Also, the standard deviation for experimental group II was significantly greater than that for group III ($p < 0.02$). Using the F test, Hughes found that reducing the amount of classroom time reduced uniformity of achievement and produced more pronounced individual differences among students. He also found that the reduction in classroom time had a negative

TABLE 17-4   ACHIEVEMENT TEST SCORES FOR ALL GROUPS (after Hughes, 1962, p. 47)

EXPERIMENTAL CONDITION	NUMBER OF CLASSES	NUMBER OF STUDENTS	M	S.D.
Control	6	70	95.1	4.0
I	2	33	93.7	6.8
II	2	28	94.3	4.8
III	3	44	95.0	3.6
IV	2	24	95.3	3.3

effect on the attitudes of the trainees, although in the main they preferred programed to conventional instruction.

Discussion Variability in achievement is greater with the new than with the original program because the reduction in classroom time provides less time to master the subject matter. However, it is possible to reduce presentation time by 47 percent without affecting mean achievement. Also it is not necessary to write out the answers, and, although the correct frame answers are in plain view and enable the student to cheat, this location of the answer does not reduce achievement.

The last three studies (IV, V, and VI) illustrate that we are dealing with a research continuum rather than discrete types of research. Many research studies you may try to classify may embrace more than one step. You have seen, for example, that Study IV covers steps 4 and 5, Study V covers steps 4 and 5, and Study VI covers steps 5 and 6.

Types of Variables

In designing, communicating, and reading research in educational psychology it is useful to distinguish between independent and dependent variables. There are three characteristics of an *independent variable:* (1) It is the variable manipulated by the experimenter; (2) it is the presumed cause of the experimental effects; and (3) it is the basis for predicting the experimental effects. The previous studies provide many examples of independent variables. Consider these:

INDEPENDENT VARIABLES

Study I	Successive trials on oddity problems
Study II	Making the first items in the serial list the first items on the PA list
Study III	Pseudowords which observed and ignored grapheme-phoneme correspondence
Study IV (first phase)	Use of programed instruction to teach reading
Study V	Use of programed instruction to teach capitalization
Study VI	Differences in program format and reduction in classroom time

By comparing the variables in these studies, you can observe that the independent variables of the first three (basic) studies are more precisely defined than the variables of the last three (applied) studies. Programed instruction in the last three studies refers to several independent variables, including the various characteristics of the program and the conditions under which it was used. In all six cases, however, the independent variables are those manipulated by the experimenter, are the presumed cause of the learning, and are the basis for predicting what would probably happen.

A *dependent variable* has two characteristics: (1) It is the presumed effect of manipulating the independent variable, and (2) it is the effect which is predicted. The previous studies provide many examples of dependent variables. Consider these:

DEPENDENT VARIABLES

Study I	Performance of the rats in solving the oddity problems
Study II	Transfer of learning to the serial list
Study III	Performance of the student in reading two types of pseudowords
Study IV (first phase)	Knowledge of letter words and skill in recognizing letter configurations
Study V	Performance on a standardized test on capitalization
Study VI	Performance on a test of knowledge of computer functions and reactions to a questionnaire on attitudes

Perusal of this list of dependent variables should reveal that they are terminal performances which result from the manipulation of the independent variables in the previous list. In the three applied studies the dependent variables are mostly test performances, while in the three basic studies they are mostly performances the experimenters directly observe.

The dependent variables of one study may be the independent variables of another. In Study IV, for example, we could reverse the position of the independent and dependent variables and study the effect of various levels of reading achievement on the use of programed verbal materials. In this case reading achievement becomes the independent variable and the programed materials the dependent one. Similarly, in Study VI, we could study the effects of trainee attitude on their ability to learn programed materials and thereby reverse the relationship of the two variables.

Hypotheses

A hypothesis is a statement of the probable relationship between independent and dependent variables. Consider these examples of hypotheses:

1 *If* conditions make it easy for the student to carry over his set for PA learning to the serial task, *then* there will be more transfer from the PA to the serial list (Study II).

2 *If* pseudowords constructed according to spelling-to-sound rules are presented to skilled readers, *then* they will recognize them more quickly than words not constructed according to these rules (Study III).

3 *If* boys are taught beginning reading through programed instruction, *then* they will read better than girls (Study IV).

These examples should reveal the following characteristics of hypotheses: (1) They are declarative sentences which specify relations between variables; (2) the independent variables follow the "if," while the dependent variables follow the "then"; and (3) they contain clear implications for objective measurement.

Fred Kerlinger (1965, p. 22) described three reasons why hypotheses are essential in scientific research. First, they are the working instruments for theory. Because they can be deduced from theory and from other hypotheses, they become the chief means of theory building. Second, they can be tested for their truth or falsity. Acceptance of the relationship that the hypothesis expresses must rest on the obtained facts. Third, hypotheses are powerful tools for advancing human knowledge because their probable truth or falsity rests outside the experimenters' attitudes and opinions. In summary, we could not have a theoretical and objective science without the use of hypotheses. Kerlinger writes (p. 28): "The scientist cannot tell positive from negative evidence unless he uses hypotheses."

Experimental and Control

Several of the previous studies used experimental and control groups. An experimental group is one in which the independent variable is manipulated. The control group is a comparison group which receives no special treatment or a treatment distinct from that of the experimental group. Consider these examples:

STUDY	EXPERIMENTAL GROUPS	CONTROL GROUPS
II PA and serial learning	Odd group with PA set and even group without PA set	Group which did not learn PA list
IV Boys and reading	Boys under programed instruction	Girls under programed instruction; girls and boys under female instruction
VI Training for computer maintenance	Groups I through IV distinguished by programing format mode of response, amount of learning time	An earlier group who studied the program in the original form and who had more learning time

You can see from these examples that the characteristics of control groups can vary from experiment to experiment. In Study II the two experimental groups each operate with a different set in learning the serial list. The control group is the only one of the three groups which did not learn the PA list. In Study IV, first phase, the boys are the experimental group because the hypothesis tells us that the major relationship investigated is the relationship between the reading achievement of boys and programed instruction. Although the girls receive the same instruction, they serve primarily as a comparison, or control, group. In the second phase, in the comparison of the achievement of the boys under programed and female instruction and in the comparison of their achievement, with the achievement of the girls under these two conditions, the boys in the second phase act as a control for the boys in the first phase, who, indeed, are the same boys. Similarly, in Study V, the pupils act as their own controls when their preprogram capitalization skill is compared with their postprogram skill. In Study VI, the major comparison is between the four groups who use the modified program and have less time and the earlier group who used the original program and had more time. The author calls the original group the control group because they provide the major comparison. The four experimental groups differ in the degree to which their learning conditions are modified. Group I, for example, studies the same program as the control group did but is given less time for study. Group IV, on the other hand, is also given less time but they do not write most of the answers to the frames and can see the correct response when they turn the page.

The primary purpose for using control groups is to eliminate rival hypotheses as alternative explanations of the experimental results. Campbell and Stanley (1963, pp. 175–76) have identified several factors which, left uncontrolled, can effect the dependent variable as much or more than the independent variable. Among these factors are the following:

1 History or the unique events which may occur between a pretest and posttest and affect the results, e.g., an antimachine riot breaking out during an experiment on teaching machines. A repetition of the experiment without these events occurring may produce quite different results.

2 Maturation or the development of changes within the student occurring largely as a result of time. In a reading experiment, for example, some improvement between pretest and posttest may be due to the collateral reading the student does independently of the experiment. Also students grow over time more bored, older, and more tired.

3 Testing or the effect of pretesting on the experimental results. The process of measuring may change what is measured. On intelligence and achievement tests, but particularly on attitude and personality-adjustment tests, students taking the same or alternative form of the test do better the second than the first time.

4 Instrumentation or the decay of the measuring instrument over time. In scoring answers to essay tests, for example, the scorer may shift his standards during different scoring periods or the observer or interviewer may shift their emphases in using their schedules.

5 Reactivity or the increase of the students' sensitivity to the desired experimental outcomes through the use of the pretest. Students ordinarily try to divine the experimenter's intent. The types of roles students assume when they know they are experimental subjects are often unrepresentative of the school situation.

Some other uncontrolled causes of experimental effects described by Campbell and Stanley are considered below under sampling and sampling bias. In examining the design and conclusions of educational research, you should try one or all of these factors as alternative explanations for the experimental results.

Experimental and Correlational Studies

In Chapter 14 we considered the distinction between experimental and correlational studies and their relative usefulness in providing for entering behavior. We can define correlational studies as follows: They investigate the relationship of two or more variables as they exist in nature. Here is a fictitious example (suggested by Campbell and Stanley, p. 235) of a correlational study:

> Dr. I. See decides to study the relationship between the amount of education of school superintendents and the length of their tenure in office. He is also interested in the relationship between the amount of their education and the quality of their schools. He finds these positive correlations: (1) that the greater the amount of education of the superintendents, the higher the quality of the schools, and (2) [that] the longer the tenure of the superintendents, the higher the morale of the schools. Dr. I. See concludes that the education of the superintendents and the stability of their tenure *cause* better schools and higher morale. This study examines the relationship of four variables: amount of education, quality of the schools, length of tenure, and level of morale. It is a correlational study.

Chapter 14 pointed out that correlational studies *suggest* causes of behavior, while experimental studies *isolate* causes. The six studies summarized earlier in this chapter are experimental studies; they isolate causes of learning. It is true that Dr. See's study suggests that the education and the stability of superintendents results in better schools and higher morale. It also suggests that better schools with higher morale may attract the better-educated superintendents and hold them longer than the less fortunate schools do, a conclusion which reverses that of Dr. See. This study is useful because it suggests both hypotheses, both of which will require subsequent research. The chief function of correlational studies in educational psychology is to survey several hypotheses to recommend experimental studies of the more promising. Experimental studies are generally more expensive than correlational studies, which can perform the useful function of screening out the less promising independent variables.

Uses of Research in Educational Psychology

The previous quotations of leading educational psychologists suggest several uses of educational research: (1) the development of theories of teaching, (2) improved teaching materials or products, and (3) improved teaching practice in all four components of the basic teaching model.

538   Concerning the first use, Wittrock (1967, pp. 17, 20) argues strongly for basic research in educational psychology to build an organized body of knowledge:

> I suggest that in our methodology we emphasize the following practices: (1) use as laboratories for research those situations and subjects which sample the phenomena we strive to study; (2) use sophisticated apparatus to control carefully the presentation of stimuli and the recording of responses; (3) use designs and analyses that will evidence interactions among treatments and groups of individuals; (4) in "true experiments," obtain data about treatments which differ from one another conceptually; and (5) test theoretical approaches to instruction.

Kerlinger (1964, p. 12) also believes that the development of theory should be the basic aim of research in education. Theories, he contends, have wider applicability and usefulness than nontheoretical findings do. Kerlinger states:

> Theories, because they are general, apply widely to many phenomena and to many people in many places. A specific relation, of course, is less widely applicable. If, for example, one finds that test anxiety is related to test performance, this finding, though interesting and important, is less widely applicable and less understood than if one first found the relation in a network of interrelated concepts that are parts of a theory.

The next two uses, dealing with improved products and practices, can be outgrowths of the basic research described by Wittrock and Kerlinger or of applied research which has an almost solely practical emphasis. Much of the early research on instructional films and television and on programed instruction and teaching machines focused directly on improved products and practices without considering the theoretical base for such research. Indeed, much more educational research has focused on practice than on theory building. As mentioned before, Hilgard (1964) believes that there may be too much research in educational psychology at steps 2 and 6 and too little at steps 4 and 5. Indeed, there are very few examples of learning research which progress from the development of products under laboratory-classroom conditions to their careful tryout and revision under conventional classroom conditions. It may very well be that we need a greater coordination of research efforts all along the research continuum (Gilbert, 1962).

Ebel (1967, p. 81) gives three reasons why basic research will not improve the educational process: Its past record of performance is poor, there are serious basic difficulties which indicate that the future will not improve this poor performance, and the educational process is not a natural phenomenon, such as has rewarded scientific study in fields like physics and biology. In arguing for applied research, Ebel (p. 84) asserts, "Let us also push, and rather more strongly, the kind of survey research that provides data crucial to the decisions we must make. Let us not worship pure science and basic research unrealistically and irrationally."

Hilgard's research continuum is an easy resolution of the two positions, one emphasizing basic research, the other emphasizing applied research. Gilbert (1962, pp. 569–70) emphasizes the coordination of efforts of basic and applied investigators:

> If scientists working in a midwestern university create the basis for developing an efficient means for controlling stuttering, the presence of a similar scientist in an educational development program could make the difference in whether the developmental activities began to produce an engineered product now or in ten years . . . the presence of an exploratory [basic] research operation in a developmental setting may be the determining factor in whether or not these scientists work on problems relevant to education.

Gilbert convincingly argues that coordinated efforts keep basic research focused on educational problems and applied research focused on the fruitful use of laboratory findings.

The reading and evaluation of research reports, the major focus of this chapter, also have three practical uses. The reports can (1) suggest further research which must be undertaken before classroom application is possible; (2) indicate which research may be undertaken in a particular school to find out which modifications must be made of practices and products before they can be adopted for local use (step 6 in the research continuum); and (3) suggest changes in procedures and products that can be immediately implemented. In all three cases you, as the consumer of these reports, should keep abreast of the present state of knowledge and know how to proceed in proposing either an extension of the research or the immediate implementation of its findings in your school and classroom.

Summary

Basic research is concerned with theoretical and methodological rigor, while applied research is concerned with practical relevance. They occupy different points on a single continuum, stretching from research on animal learning to the modification of packaged instructional materials for local use. Hilgard has identified six steps on this research continuum from the most basic to the most applied research. We provided an example of a study for each step. Educational psychologists may conduct their research in one or several of these six areas. The variable manipulated by the experimenter is the independent variable. The presumed effect of this manipulation is the dependent variable. The dependent variables of one study may be the independent variables of another. Hypotheses are statements of the probable relationship between independent and dependent variables. In an experimental group, the independent variable is manipulated. The control group is a comparison group which receives no or different treatment. The use of control groups eliminates rival hypotheses as alternative explanations for the experimental results. Correlational studies investigate the relationship of two or more variables. They are useful in suggesting hypotheses for later experimental studies. There are several uses of research in educational psychology, extending from the development of teaching theories to improved teaching practices in the four components of the basic teaching model.

QUESTION 17-1 An educational psychologist has assessed under laboratory conditions the effects on student behavior (as indicated by an achievement test) of a film on drug usage; he now intends to assess its effectiveness in public school classrooms. On the basis of this brief description answer the following questions:

(a) At which of Hilgard's six steps does his intended research (in public schools) occur?

(b) What is the independent variable in the intended study?

(c) What is the dependent variable in the study under laboratory conditions?

(d) State the hypothesis in the form of an if-then statement.

Upon reading this section of the chapter you should be able to meet these objectives:

17-9 Identify the four major parts of the research report (statement of problem and hypotheses, description of procedures, results, and conclusions) when given examples of these reports (step 1).

17-10 Distinguish between adequate and inadequate descriptions for each part (step 2).

17-11 Evaluate the sampling procedure by indicating uncontrolled sources of sampling bias (step 3).

17-12 Describe how the standard error of the mean is a measure of sampling error.

17-13 Evaluate the validity and reliability of the procedures by referring to the original hypotheses and the correct application of procedures and instruments (step 4).

17-14 Check the analysis of data for adequate and clear reporting of results and the correct choice of significance tests (step 5).

17-15 Evaluate the conclusions in terms of alternatives which fit the data and in terms of this fit with previous research and ordinary experience (step 6).

EVALUATION OF THE RESEARCH REPORT

Your use of educational research depends largely on your skill in assessing the research reports appearing in educational and psychological journals. This chapter section deals with the four major parts of these reports; it describes their major characteristics and the steps you should take in assessing each part. As the summaries of the six preceding reports indicate, most reports have four major parts: (1) a statement of the problem and hypotheses; (2) description of the procedures, including the selection and use of subjects and materials; (3) a description of the results, including the analysis of the data; and (4) a statement of the conclusions drawn by the investigator. This section also deals with sampling as it pertains to acceptable research procedure. Sampling is the selection and assignment of subjects to experimental and control groups. We reserve extended consideration of the analysis of data for the following chapter section, which deals with statistical inference and tests of significant differences.

READ THE ENTIRE REPORT AND IDENTIFY THE FOUR MAJOR PARTS

Most research reports do not label their major parts as distinctly as the six preceding summaries do. They often provide statements of problems and hypotheses, for example, without using these designations. The parts may not be clearly distinct; descriptions of hypotheses may appear under procedures, and descriptions of results may include the inferences the investigator draws from the results. To identify the major parts of these reports, you must know their typical characteristics.

The problem Although this first part of the research report shows the greatest amount of variation in the journals, it is possible to identify the following characteristics. First, the description of the problem states the purpose of the study and sets the stage for the reader. The author delimits his study and focuses attention on the particular area of investigation. Second, this section may be very long or very short. In dissertations and lengthy investigations it tends to be long and detailed. In many journals, in which space must be conserved and the authors can assume considerable background knowledge of the reader, it may be very short. Third, this section should ask or at least imply a question about the relationship between variables. In Study II, for example, Jensen asks about the transfer effects of PA learning on subsequent serial learning. In Study VI Hughes asks about the possible effects of changes in programing format and of the reduction of time. Fourth, and most important, this section should contain statements of subproblems or hypotheses. These statements require greater linguistic precision than the general problem statement. Finally, there should be a review of the previous research.

Procedures There are two parts to this section of the report: a description of the selection and assignment of subjects and a description of the methods of collecting data, including materials, apparatus, tests, and so on. A description of subject selection should include who the subjects are, from what population they are selected, why they are selected, and how they are selected and assigned. The assignment of subjects involves questions about proper sampling and the proper formation of experimental and control groups.

Results The third part of the report describes the findings of the investigation. This part usually has the following aspects: It summarizes the data as means and standard deviations, and it reduces the data to tables and graphs, as illustrated in the six studies. The summaries of Studies I and III present the data as graphs, while those of the remaining studies present the data as tables. This part has one further characteristic: It provides a statistical analysis of the data to determine the significance of the results.

Conclusions In this part the investigator interprets his results. Usually we expect him to provide the following elements: how the data confirm or disconfirm the hypothesis; the limits imposed on his conclusions because of his procedures; alternative conclusions which can be drawn from his data; and the implications his study has for further research and for school use.

STEP 2

INSPECT THE REPORT FOR ADEQUATE DESCRIPTIONS

A report should include adequate descriptions of the hypotheses, previous research, methods of data collection, and selection and assignment of subjects.

Adequately stated hypotheses have these characteristics: The independent variables are described in terms of the procedures used in introducing them; the dependent variables are described in terms of the measuring instruments used to assess terminal performances as experimental effects; and the relationship of the hypotheses to their theoretical base and to previous research is carefully delineated. Because adequate descriptions of hypotheses often require investigators to describe methods of data collection, you may find statements of hypotheses in the procedure section rather than in the problem section of the report. In Studies II and III the statements of hypotheses fulfill all the necessary requirements.

The review of the research should be adequate enough to serve two purposes: to state the theoretical rationale of the problem and to inform the reader of what research there now is and how the investigator plans to extend this knowledge. Jensen, in Study II, carefully explains the theoretical rationale for his hypothesis to show the inadequacies of a stimulus-response explanation of serial learning. Because publishing costs have risen so rapidly, many journals do not provide the authors the space they need for an adequate review of the literature.

The description of methods of data collection must be adequate enough to allow you to evaluate their appropriateness for the problem and the hypothesis and their appropriate application. They should answer most of your questions about how the data were collected and enable you to distinguish between those collection methods and alternative procedures. In the six previous studies you can find detailed descriptions of methods. In Study VI, for example, Hughes describes the exact modifications he made in the program format. In Study III, Gibson and her associates describe the formation and the use of the pseudowords.

Finally, there must be adequate description of the procedures employed in the selection and assignment of subjects. We have already considered what this description must consist of. The previous summaries briefly describe the experimental subjects—rats, college students, elementary school children, and industrial trainees. The five studies using human subjects are not good illustrations of adequate descriptions of sample selection and assignment because, for the most part, they used intact classes. The problem of sampling is often a serious one in studies which deal with human subjects. More often than not the experimenter must use those subjects who are available to him rather than work with a random or specially selected sample. In interpreting results from these studies caution must be exercised in generalizing to groups which may have different characteristics.

EVALUATE THE SAMPLING PROCEDURE

To perform this function you must distinguish between a population and a sample. A *population* is any group of students or scores alike in one or more ways. A *sample* is any group of students or scores less than the total number in that population. Consider the following examples:

POPULATIONS	SAMPLES
All college students	Students in Harmony Haven College
All elementary school children	Elementary school children in California
Nannette, Opal, Patience, and Charles	Nannette, Patience, and Charles

POPULATIONS	SAMPLES
Students in Harmony Haven College	Members of the football team at Harmony Haven College
Seniors at Harmony Haven	Seniors majoring in science at Harmony Haven
All achievement test scores	Scores on the mathematics achievement test

In perusing these examples note these characteristics of populations and samples: The sample is always smaller than the population, often representing only a fraction of it; the sample in one example may be the population in another; the population in one example may be the sample in another; and some populations (all college students, all elementary children) are too large to study in their entirety. In almost all educational research we study samples and not populations.

Random sampling This method of drawing a sample of a population guarantees that each population member has an equal chance of being selected. Kerlinger (1964, p. 52) states that in random sampling we have a "democracy of selection in which all members are equal before the bar of selection." He uses this example (p. 53):

Suppose we have a population of one hundred children. The children differ in intelligence. We want to know the mean IQ of the population, but for some reason we can only sample thirty of the one hundred children. If we sample

STEP 3

randomly, there are a large number of possible samples of thirty each. These samples have an equal and known probability of being selected. It can be shown that the means of most of these samples of thirty will be relatively close to the mean of the population. A few will not be close. The probability of selecting a sample with a mean close to the population mean, then, is greater than the probability of selecting a sample with mean not close to the population mean—if the sampling has not been random. If we do not draw our sample at random, however, some factor or factors unknown to us may predispose us to select a biased sample, in this case perhaps one of the samples with a mean not close to the population mean. If the one hundred children were known to us, we might unconsciously tend to select the more intelligent children. It should be emphasized that it is not so much that we would do so; it is that our method *allows* us to do so. Random methods of selection do not allow our biases or any other systematic selection factors to operate.

Several methods select and assign subjects at random. The best procedure is to use a table of random numbers often found in the appendix of statistics textbooks. These numbers have been machine-generated and have no discernible order. A number is assigned to each subject, and the subject in turn is selected and assigned on the basis of his number alone. A common randomizing procedure, somewhat less reliable than the use of a table of random numbers, involves placing the subjects' names on slips of paper which are tossed into a box and drawn by chance. You can also select and assign subjects by using the roll of dice.

Sources of sampling bias If the investigator uses random sampling, he is likely to avoid sampling bias. If he does not, you, in reading the report, must look for various sources of sampling bias. You can ask the following questions about the soundness of the sampling. First, did the investigator use volunteers? For example, if Hughes in Study VI had used only volunteers for answering the questionnaire on his program and on the amount of class time, he might have obtained many more favorable replies than he did because many disgruntled subjects might have chosen to express no opinion rather than to voice their complaints. Second, have subjects been lost? More technically, the loss of subjects, especially in studies conducted over periods of months and years, is called *subject mortality*. Unfortunately, subjects are not lost on a random basis, and they generally vary from those who remain. In Study IV, for example, if McNeil had lost many of his female and male subjects in the second phase of the experiment, it would be difficult to make his comparison of the effects of programed and live instruction. If, for example, some of the boys who were lost were the poorer readers, then he would find an even greater difference between the effects of the two types of reading instruction. Third, are common sources of school bias avoided? Campbell and Stanley (1963, p. 184) suggest these sources: time of day, day of the week, portion of the semester, nearness to examinations, and choice of investigators. For example, college students who register for an afternoon section of a required course may differ from those who register for a morning section. Also the performance of a student early in the semester may differ remarkably from his performance later on. Fourth, is the sample representative of the population to which the experimental results are applied? If a study of present-day sexual morality of American males and females uses a sample of college men and women, we would indeed question its validity for all American men and women. Fifth, have the subjects been assigned on a random basis? If the investigator wants to discover the effectiveness of programed instruction and assigns to the classes using programed instruction only the brightest students who have already learned well what the program will teach them and assigns to the control classes only the dolts who never seem to learn anything under any conditions, we may suspect a grievous case of sampling bias. The experimenter should not only randomly assign students to experimental and control groups but also randomly assign treatments to these groups. Which groups receive programed instruction should be determined by chance after the groups have been formed. Finally, has the investigator used a large enough sample? A common research rule is to use samples as large as possible. Some sample bias arises from sampling error, which is described next. Within limits, the larger the sample size, the smaller the sampling error. As you will see, the amount of sampling error can be estimated.

Sampling error Sampling error is the variability among the means of many samples drawn from the population. Consider this situation. You want to determine the level of achievement in physics of all graduating high school seniors. Since you do not have the time, resources, or authority to administer the test to the entire population of graduating seniors, you randomly select 1,000 samples of fifty students each from high schools throughout the nation. After determining the mean scores for each sample of fifty students, you discover that the means and the standard deviations vary. You must decide which mean and standard deviation are the most accurate for the graduating senior population. Unfortunately you have no direct way of finding the population mean and standard deviation, short of administering the test to all graduating seniors, an alternative we need only mention in order to discard. There is a method, however, of estimating the population mean and standard deviation. First you assume that the mean of the sample means is also the population mean. Then you assume that the standard deviation of the sample means is the standard deviation of the population. The resulting statistic is called the *standard error of the mean*. Table 17-5 shows you how this statistic is computed. Later you will see how the standard error of the mean is used in computing the t ratio, a method for determining the statistical significance of experimental differences.

CHECK THE VALIDITY AND RELIABILITY OF THE PROCEDURES   STEP 4

The investigator must use those procedures and instruments which yield valid and reliable data. Valid procedures and instruments provide the tests of hypotheses implied in the statement of the problem and of the description of the hypotheses. Using conventional televised and nontelevised lectures as the procedure in determining the effectiveness of programed instruction in mathematics achievement is an example of an invalid procedure. Using per-

TABLE 17-5   HOW TO COMPUTE THE STANDARD ERROR OF THE MEAN

Formula: $SE_M = \dfrac{s}{\sqrt{n}}$

SE_M = standard error of the mean
s = standard deviation of the sample means
n = the number of subjects in the sample

Problem: An investigator draws a sample of 400 IQ scores to estimate the intelligence of children in an American city. He obtains these values: mean = 100, standard deviation = 16. Find the standard error of the mean of the sample.

Step 1: Compute the square root of the same size
Step 2: Substitute the numbers in the formula as follows:

$$SE_M = \frac{s}{\sqrt{n}} = \frac{16}{20} = 0.80$$

sonality tests to determine IQ is an inappropriate and invalid use of these instruments. To a large extent the reader can judge the validity of the research procedures in much the same way he judges the validity of classroom tests. If the investigator has developed new instruments and tests, such as interview schedules, questionnaires, and tests of creativity, he must demonstrate their validity independently of the study in which he uses them.

It is also important to collect reliable evidence. This requires the correct application of the procedures and instruments. If, for example, the experimenter does not provide training and care in the use of programed materials and test administration, very good instruments may provide unreliable information. Carelessness in the use of well-designed questionnaires and interview schedules, lack of training in using observation schedules, carelessness in the recording of data, and modifications of procedures after the experiment is underway all result in untrustworthy data. The study should establish and report the reliability of its evidence.

STEP 5

CHECK THE ANALYSIS OF DATA

The report should outline and defend the methods of data analysis. As seen in the previous summaries, it is generally enough to mention the test of statistical significance used if it is a common test. If it is uncommon, the investigator must describe the method in sufficient detail for the competent critic to judge its appropriate and correct application. In the chapter section which follows we will consider several tests of statistical significance.

STEP 6

EVALUATE THE CONCLUSIONS OF THE REPORT

In his conclusions, the investigator must answer the question of whether the data confirm or do not confirm the hypothesis. He should present his results in statements, tables, and graphs that convey them clearly. He should then provide clear statements of the conclusions, substantiated by the evidence he has collected. He should consider alternative explanations which seem to fit his data. If you, as the reader of the report, can think of suitable alternative conclusions, the investigator has most certainly failed to support his hypothesis. The tone of this section should be scientific and objective rather than partisan and polemic. Most findings of sound research are not shocking violations of common sense. If the report arrives at conclusions which defy ordinary human experience, good judgment, and the findings of earlier related studies, you may suspect and discover serious shortcomings in the design and execution of the investigation.

Summary

We have described six steps in the evaluation of research reports. In the order in which they should be taken these are: (1) Read the entire report and identify the four major parts; (2) inspect the report for adequate descriptions of hypotheses, previous research, methods of data collection, and procedures and instruments; (3) evaluate the sampling procedure; (4) check the validity and reliability of the procedures; (5) check the analysis of data; and (6) evaluate the conclusions of the report.

QUESTION 17-2

A research educational psychologist was conducting a study on curiosity. His hypothesis was that school children subjected for one hour to low-stimulation environments would become more curious than children subjected for one hour to high-stimulation environments. A valid and reliable test of curiosity was his measure of the dependent variable. The children in the school volunteered for the experiment. As they lined up outside and entered his laboratory door he assigned each a number from the table of random numbers and then assigned each to one of three chambers: the high-stimulation chamber, the low-stimulation chamber, or a normal classroom. When the first child entered, for example, he was given a random number and was assigned to chamber 1. When the second child entered, he was also given a random number and was assigned to the second chamber. In this manner and order the other children were assigned to the different experimental conditions.

Which of the following statements is the best evaluation of the sampling procedure used?

(a) It is random in both assignment and selection of subjects.

(b) It is random in assignment but not in selection of subjects.

(c) It is random in selection but not in assignment of subjects.

(d) It is random neither in assignment nor in selection of subjects.

After selecting your answer, give the reasons for your choice.

Upon reading this section of the chapter, you should be able to meet these objectives:

17-16 Define and illustrate the null hypothesis and distinguish it from the research hypothesis.

17-17   Define statistical significance and explain $p = 0.01$, $p = 0.05$, and $p = 0.001$.

17-18   Define and illustrate the appropriate use of the t ratio and compute the t ratio of two sample means.

17-19   Define and illustrate the appropriate use of the F ratio and compute the F ratio when given the mean square between groups and the mean square within groups.

17-20   Define and illustrate the appropriate use of the Chi square test and compute Chi square for three classes of observed frequencies.

17-21   Distinguish and illustrate the differences between parametric and nonparametric tests.

17-22   Define and illustrate the use of factor analysis as a means of finding common variables.

ANALYSIS OF DATA

This chapter section should help you evaluate the statistical analyses of data which usually appear in the result section of the report. We will consider the testing of the null hypothesis and levels and tests of statistical significance. The significance tests discussed are the t ratio, based on the standard error of the differences between means; the F ratio, based on the analysis of variance; and the Chi square test. This section concludes with a brief consideration of nonparametric tests and factor analysis.

The Null Hypothesis

The null hypothesis states that there is no difference between two populations or samples. Here are some examples of null hypotheses:

1   There will be no significant difference in how quickly children read pseudowords constructed on the basis of grapheme-phoneme correspondence and how quickly they read those not constructed on this basis.

2   Boys will read as well under live female instruction as under programed instruction.

3   Students with the set for PA learning will learn the serial list in the same number of trials as will students without this set.

Although the forms of these statements vary somewhat, each statement asserts that the investigator will find no significant differences between experimental and control groups.

The research hypothesis, unlike the null hypothesis, usually has these characteristics: It asserts that there will be a difference between experimental and control groups, and it is expressed in verbal terms. The null hypothesis, on the other hand, is a statistical hypothesis either stating or clearly implying quantitative measure. Kerlinger (1964, p. 174) writes, "The *null hypothesis* is a statistical proposition which states essentially that there is no relation between the variables (of the problem). The null hypothesis says, 'You're wrong, there is no relation; disprove me if you can.' " In this sense, no matter what the research hypothesis asserts, the experiment must disprove the null hypothesis.

The test of the null hypothesis relates clearly to sampling error and the standard error of the mean. When you test this hypothesis, you try to determine if the difference between the means of the two samples (for example, the experimental group and the control group) is larger than can be expected from sampling error. This is why we say that the difference between the groups must be statistically significant—a small amount of difference may not be enough. If the difference between two samples is larger than that which the investigator can expect from sampling error, he can reject the null hypothesis and assert, with reasonable pride and confidence, that there is a significant difference.

Statistical Significance

For a difference to be statistically significant it must depart from chance expectation. In the previous summaries, note the appearance of these expressions: $p = 0.01$; $p = 0.05$; or $p = 0.10$. The p is the abbreviation for probability. The expression $p = 0.01$ means that the probability of the obtained difference occurring by chance is only one out of one hundred trials. The expression $p = 0.001$ means that the probability of the obtained difference occurring by chance is only one out of 1,000 trials. Although the practice of reporting the value of all p's is becoming widespread in behavioral science research, convention views all p's below 0.05 as not statistically significant—an insufficient basis, that is, for rejecting the null hypothesis. This convention has been frequently challenged because it may result in the rejection of potentially useful hypotheses (Rozeboom, 1960).

How large a difference is significant? Three general guidelines to follow are these: (1) the 0.05 level is about $2s$ from the mean; (2) the 0.01 level is about $2.5s$ from the mean; and (3) the 0.001 level is about $3s$ from the mean. The farther the level is from the hypothetical mean, the less chance there is that the differences are due to chance.

The *t* Ratio

The t ratio is the test of statistical significance used when the investigator is dealing with two sample means. In Study II, for example, Jensen used the t ratio to determine the possible significant difference in mean learning trials between the odd group (with the PA set) and the even group (without the PA set). McNeil in Study IV used the t ratio to determine the possible significant difference between the reading means of the boys and girls following programed instruction. Table 17-6 shows you how to compute the t ratio. You see that you must first compute the standard error of the mean and then use a t-ratio table to find out whether the t ratio is significant.

TABLE 17-6   HOW TO COMPUTE THE *t* RATIO

Formula: $t = \dfrac{M_a - M_b}{\sqrt{SE_{Ma}{}^2 + SE_{Mb}{}^2}}$

$t = t$ ratio (also called t test or critical ratio)

M_a = mean of sample a

M_b = mean of sample b

$SE_{Ma}{}^2$ = square of standard error of the mean for sample a

$SE_{Mb}{}^2$ = square of standard error of the mean for sample b

Problem: Mr. Patrick wanted to find out whether students learned programed mathematics better with overt (written) or covert (mentally rehearsed) responses. He selected two samples of one hundred each from the tenth grade population and assigned one group the overt and the other group the covert treatment. Both groups were given a test of mathematics achievement after completing their programs. Mr. Patrick found that the mean score of the overt group was 60, of the covert group 50. The standard deviations of both groups were 10. Using the t ratio, determine whether this difference is significant.

Step 1: Determine the means of samples a (overt) and b (covert).
         $(M_a = 60;\ M_b = 50)$

Step 2: Compute SE_{Ma} and SE_{Mb} by using Table 17-5.
         $(SE_{Ma} = 1;\ SE_{Mb} = 1)$

Step 3: Square the results of step 2.
         $(SE_{Ma}{}^2 = 1;\ SE_{Mb}{}^2 = 1)$

Step 4: Substitute the numbers in the formula and perform the indicated operations:

$$t = \frac{60 - 50}{\sqrt{1 + 1}} = \frac{10}{1.4142} = 7.07$$

Using a statistical table, we find $p < 0.01$ (significant).

The *F* Ratio

When the investigator compares more than two means, he often uses the *F* ratio to determine the possible statistical significance of his results. In Table 17-7 for example, Kerlinger uses the *F* ratio to compare two basic attitudes toward education—progressivism and traditionalism—of three groups of individuals. Kerlinger hypothesized that those individuals outside the university had the highest mean and that the graduate students of education had the lowest mean (i.e., were the least traditional). The independent variable was group membership; the dependent variable was the members' attitudes. The use of the *F* ratio enabled him to reject clearly the null hypothesis since the difference between the means is highly significant. His research hypothesis, therefore, found considerable support.

To compute the *F* ratio, one uses a method of data analysis known as the *analysis of variance*. This method uses variance (squared standard deviation) entirely instead of the standard error of the mean. In essence the investigator compares the variance between groups and the variance within groups. In experimental studies the between-group variance is the measure

Formula: $F = \dfrac{m.s._{bet.}}{m.s._{with.}}$

F = F ratio (or F test)

*$m.s._{bet.}$ = mean square between groups

*$m.s._{with.}$ = mean square within groups

	GRADUATE STUDENTS	UNDERGRADUATES	PERSONS OUTSIDE
n:	157	136	305
M:	3.84	4.43	5.19
S.D.:	0.93	0.84	0.86

SOURCE OF VARIANCE	DEGREES OF FREEDOM	*s.s.*	*m.s.*	*F*
Between groups	2	197.20	98.60	128.05 (0.001)
Within groups	595	457.85	0.77	
Total	597	655.05		

Data from study of attitudes toward education, based on the Traditionalism attitude scores (Kerlinger, 1964, p. 200).

In computing the *F* ratio, take these steps:

Step 1: Compute the mean square between groups.
($m.s._{bet.}$ = 98.60)

Step 2: Compute the mean square within groups.
($m.s._{with.}$ = 0.77)

Step 3: Substitute the numbers in the formula and divide.

$F = \dfrac{98.60}{0.77} = 128.05$

Consulting an *F* ratio table at the indicated degrees of freedom (explained below), you find that this ratio is highly significant ($p = 0.001$).

* For the computation of these statistics, see one of the standard statistics texts listed at end of this chapter.

of the dependent variable, the effect produced by the independent variable. The within-group variance is the measure of chance error. For the *F* ratio to reach the level of statistical significance the between-group variance must sufficiently exceed the within-group variance—that is, the groups must be more different from each other than the individuals are different within the groups. This relationship is shown in Figure 17-3, which is explained later. In Table 17-7 you can see that the between-group variance is far greater than the within-group variance, as indicated by the mean square for each one. Jimmy Amos and his associates (1965, p. 87), with the use of the curves in Figure 17-3, show how three groups of scores compare in two dif-

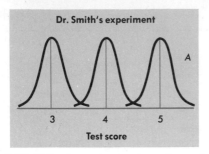

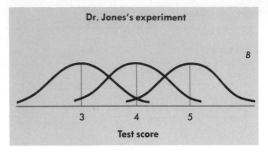

FIG. 17-3 Curves showing the variance of the groups in two experiments. Dr. Smith's groups show greater between-group variance, Dr. Jones's greater within-group variance (after Amos et al., 1965, p. 87). A: Means significantly different; B: Means not significantly different.

ferent experiments. In their respective experiments, Drs. Smith and Jones compared three methods of instruction. The curves show the distribution of scores for each method and both experiments. You can see that Dr. Smith's experiment will have a significant F ratio because the variance between groups is greater than the variance within groups (the scores are less spread out). Dr. Jones's experiment will not have a significant F ratio because there is much more overlap of scores and the variance within the three groups is considerably larger than the variance between the groups (the scores are spread out too much).

When $F = 1.00$ or less, the difference is always nonsignificant. The size of F in Table 17-7 indicates the high level of significance of this result.

The Chi-square Test

A third test of the null hypothesis is the Chi-square test. Whereas the t ratio and the F ratio deal with the means and the variances of groups, the Chi-square test deals with expected frequencies. Table 17-8 shows the computation of Chi-square as a test of the hypothesis stated there. The particular frequencies are those on an opinion survey of prospective teachers. The observed frequencies are those yielded by the actual survey. The expected frequencies are those hypothesized by the null (no-difference) hypothesis. After obtaining Chi-square (in this case 12.5), you obtain an entry from a Chi-square table according to what are called *degrees of freedom (df)*. Degrees of freedom are computed with this formula: $df = (r - 1)(c - 1)$, or $(2 - 1)(3 - 1)$, or 2, where r = row and c = column. Unlike the previous significance tests we have considered, the Chi-square test applies to scores which are and are not normally distributed.

Nonparametric Statistical Tests

The investigator uses nonparametric tests when he does not know or ignores the distribution shape and variance of the population scores. Ordi-

Formula $\chi^2 = \Sigma \left[\dfrac{(O - E)^2}{E} \right]$

χ^2 = Chi-square
Σ = sum of
O = observed frequencies
E = expected frequencies

Problem and
hypothesis (null):   There will be no difference in the number of responses for each of three kinds of responses. Thirty prospective teachers were asked their opinion about the desirability of introducing technological innovations into the classroom. The survey results are below.

Step 1:   Record expected and observed frequencies are follows:

		YES	NO	UNDECIDED
	O	20	5	5
	E	10	10	10

Step 2:	$O - E$	10	−5	−5
Step 3:	$(O - E)^2$	100	25	25
Step 4:	$\dfrac{(O - E)^2}{E}$	10	2.5	2.5

Step 5:   Substitute the numbers in the formula and perform the indicated operations.

$$\chi^2 = 10 + 2.5 + 2.5 = 15$$

Consult Chi-square table, with two degrees of freedom. $p = 0.01$.

---

narily (but not always), in using the parametric tests, the t ratio, and the F ratio, we assume that the scores are normally distributed and that variances within the groups are statistically the same. You should recall that in the F test, if the variances within the groups vary widely, the likelihood of finding significant differences between groups is greatly reduced. The F ratio, therefore, may not be significant when there is a significant difference between groups. The use of the t ratio and F ratio also assumes that the measuring instruments are continuous measures with equal intervals. We make this assumption, for example, in using intelligence and achievement tests. When, however, you are merely classifying data, as in the Chi-square test, or ranking scores, as in the rank-order correlation (*rho*), you cannot assume that your measures have equal intervals. In fact, Chi-square and *rho* (Chapter 16) are the two nonparametric tests you have already learned about.

In evaluating research reports, you may well follow Kerlinger's (1964, p. 260) advice: The investigator should be expected to "use parametric statistics, as well as the analysis of variance, routinely, but [to] keep a sharp eye on data for gross departures from normality, homogeneity of variance, and equality of intervals." Since nonparametric tests are often quick and easy to use, Kerlinger also suggests their use as preliminary but not definitive tests. Among the widely used nonparametric tests you will find in research reports are the following ones: the binominal test, the sign test, the median test, the sum of ranks test, the Kruskal-Wallis test, and the Friedman test.*

Factor Analysis

Factor analysis is a method of determining the number of basic variables underlying a large number of measures (Kerlinger, 1964, p. 650). These underlying variables are called *factors*. Kerlinger uses this example to illustrate factor analysis. We administer six tests to a large sample of seventh graders and hypothesize that the six tests are not measuring six different variables but a smaller number of variables. These are the names of the six tests and their labels: vocabulary *(V)*, reading *(R)*, synonyms *(S)*, numbers *(N)*, arithmetic *(AS)*, and a teacher-made arithmetic test *(AT)*. We score the tests and compute the coefficients of correlation between each test and every other test. We then make a matrix, or table, of coefficients. Table 17-9 shows the matrix for these six tests. Kerlinger (p. 651) states that we can now ask two questions: (1) How many underlying factors are there? and (2) what are these factors? To answer the first question note the circled coefficients in Table 17-9, cluster I and cluster II. The coefficients for tests *V, R,* and *S* in cluster I range between 0.57 and 0.72. Similarly, the coefficients for tests *N, AS,* and *AT* in cluster II range between 0.57 and 0.72. Finally, the tests in cluster I are relatively uncorrelated with those in cluster II, the correlations ranging from 0.00 to 0.16. The two clusters appear to be two underlying factors.

To answer the second question about what the factors are, you must

TABLE 17-9   A MATRIX OF CORRELATIONS SHOWING A VERBAL FACTOR (CLUSTER I) AND A NUMERICAL FACTOR (CLUSTER II) (after Kerlinger, 1964, p. 651)

		V	R	S	N	AS	AT
	V		0.72	0.63	0.09	0.09	0.00
CLUSTER I	R	0.72		0.57	0.15	0.16	0.09
	S	0.63	0.57		0.14	0.15	0.09
	N	0.09	0.15	0.14		0.57	0.63
	AS	0.09	0.16	0.15	0.57		0.72
	AT	0.00	0.09	0.09	0.63	0.72	

CLUSTER II

* For a discussion of these and other nonparametric tests see S. Siegel, *Nonparametric Statistics for the Behavioral Sciences.* New York: McGraw-Hill Book Company, 1956.

think of names which explain them. It appears that a factor called *verbal ability* is common to cluster I and that a factor called *numerical ability* is common to cluster II. Kerlinger stresses that the name of the factor should describe the common operations in the tests within the cluster. It would be inappropriate, for example, to call the factor in cluster II *arithmetic* since this would omit the operations in test *N*. You should also remember that these names are tentative or hypothetical. If you were to add a seventh test to this six-test battery, you might discover quite different clusters and you would then have to assign new and appropriate names to them.

The mathematical operations involved in factor analysis are beyond the scope of this book. Our illustration uses the cluster method, which depends on inspection and subjective judgment. Centroid methods use more objective factor analyses (see Thurstone, 1947). However, even this brief description of factor analysis should indicate its relationship to multifactor theories of intelligence (see Chapter 14) and to coefficients of correlation (see Chapter 16).

Summary

The evaluation of a research report requires knowledge of the statistical analysis of data. First, you must distinguish between the null hypothesis, which asserts no differences among groups, and the research or nonstatistical hypothesis, which usually asserts that there will be a difference. Second, a statistically significant difference must depart from chance expectation beyond the $p = 0.05$ level. We discussed several tests of statistical significance. In determining the difference between only two means, use the t ratio. When testing the difference between two or more means, use the F ratio, based on the analysis of variance. In determining the differences between frequencies, use the chi-square test. Use nonparametric tests, such as chi square and rho, when scores do not form a normal distribution, when variances are not homogeneous, and when measures do not have equal intervals. Finally, use factor analysis to determine underlying variables among a large number of factors.

QUESTION 17-3

The investigator administered a questionnaire to prospective teachers, asking their degree of agreement or disagreement with the use of team teaching in elementary schools. For each question the respondent could check one of these choices: strongly agree, agree, undecided, disagree, strongly disagree. The investigator wanted to test this hypothesis: There will be no difference among these response choices. Answer these questions:

(a) Which type of hypothesis is he testing?

(b) Which significance test should he use? (1) *t* ratio, (2) *F* ratio, (3) Chi square, (4) rho. Defend your choice.

SUMMARY

This chapter has dealt with the nature, use, and evaluation of research in educational psychology. It has stressed the importance of the relationship of applied and basic research and illustrated points along the research continuum with descriptions of various investigations. The chapter identified many characteristics of formal studies: independent and dependent variables, hypotheses, experimental and control groups, and experimental and correlational studies.

We examined six steps you can take in evaluating research reports: identifying the major parts—the problem and hypothesis, the procedures, the results, and the conclusions; distinguishing between adequate and inadequate descriptions of each part; evaluating the sampling procedures, especially for uncontrolled sources of sampling bias; evaluating the validity and reliability of the procedures and instruments; checking the analysis of data for adequate and clear reporting of results and the correct choice of significance tests; and, finally, evaluating the conclusions by testing alternative explanations.

The most technical aspect of your evaluation is the critique of the statistical analysis of data. To make this part of your evaluation, you must distinguish between the research and the null hypotheses and have familiarity with levels of statistical significance: t ratios, F ratios, Chi square, nonparametric tests, and factor analysis.

SUGGESTED READINGS

The following excellent texts and handbooks discuss the nature of psychological inquiry and research in education and educational psychology:

BACHRACH, ARTHUR J., *Psychological Research: An Introduction*. New York: Random House, 1962. (paperback)

GAGE, N. L., ed., *Handbook of Research on Teaching*. Chicago: Rand McNally & Co., 1963.

HYMAN, RAY, *The Nature of Psychological Inquiry*. Englewood Cliffs, N.J.: Prentice-Hall, Inc., 1964. (paperback)

KERLINGER, FRED N., *Foundations of Behavioral Research: Educational and Psychological Inquiry*. New York: Holt, Rinehart & Winston, Inc., 1964.

TRAVERS, R. M. W., *Second Handbook of Research on Teaching*. Chicago: Rand McNally, 1973.

TRAVERS, ROBERT M. W., *An Introduction to Educational Research*, 3rd ed. New York: The Macmillan Company, 1973.

The following guides and checklists are useful in the evaluation of research in educational psychology:

BORG, WALTER R., "Critical Evaluation of Research," in *Educational Research: An Introduction*, pp. 326–45. New York: David McKay Co., Inc., 1963.

RUMMEL, J. FRANCIS, "Criteria for Judging Research Reports," in *An Introduction to Research Procedures in Education*, 2nd ed., pp. 267–69. New York. Harper & Row, Publishers, Inc., 1964.

VAN DALEN, DEOBOLD B. and MEYER, WILLIAM J., "Evaluation," in *Understanding Educational Research: An Introduction*, pp. 442–54. New York: McGraw-Hill Book Company, 1966.

WANDT, EDWIN, *A Cross-Section of Educational Research*. New York: David McKay Co., Inc., 1965, pp. 7–13. (paperback)

The following useful texts deal with statistics in education and psychology:

AMORE, SIDNEY J., *Introduction to Statistical Analysis and Inference for Psychology and Education*. New York: John Wiley & Sons, Inc., 1966.

BLOMMERS, PAUL and LINDQUIST, E. F., *Elementary Statistical Methods*. Boston: Houghton Mifflin Company, 1960.

GLASS, GENE V. and STANLEY, JULIAN C., *Statistical Methods in Education and Psychology*. Englewood Cliffs, N.J.: Prentice-Hall, Inc., 1970.

POPHAM, W. JAMES, *Educational Statistics: Use and Interpretation*. New York: Harper & Row, Publishers, 1967.

TATE, MERLE W., *Statistics in Education and Psychology*. New York: The Macmillan Company, 1965.

The following authoritative texts are for students who want to explore advanced statistical procedures and research design:

McNEMAR, QUINN, *Psychological Statistics*, 3rd ed. New York: John Wiley & Sons, Inc., 1962.

WINER, J., *Statistical Principles in Experimental Design*. New York: McGraw-Hill Book Company, 1962.

ANSWERS TO QUESTIONS

QUESTION 1-1 The quotation describes mainly a philosophy of education. It refers to the goals and values which, according to the speaker, an educational system should embrace, such as the development of free minds. The passage is not a theory of teaching, despite the reference to classroom decisions, materials, and procedures. It does not answer the questions which tell how teachers should behave, for what reasons, and with what consequences. The passage is not a theory of learning because it does not describe and explain the conditions under which learning occurs. At best it describes conditions under which learning does not occur. It is not a theory of development because it does not describe changes occurring over time.

QUESTION 1-2 The first step of Herbart's method best fits the computer-based model and that part of the model described as the pretutorial phase. The interaction model is not a good choice because nothing in it is exactly equivalent to the apperceptive mass. Also, while Flanders assumes that learning and teaching should be the emergent

558

products of student and teacher interaction, Herbart assumes that what is to be taught is largely predetermined by the teacher. The purpose of his preparation is to find a common ground between preselected topics and students.

The lecture-recitation model is least similar to Smith's. The formalism of the Jesuit school made the flexible interaction implied in Smith's model difficult even though no teaching method entirely rules out the interaction Smith describes. The human relations model is not a good choice since its basic implication is the accommodation of the needs and interests of the students. The teacher can perceive those needs and interests only through an interaction such as described by Smith. In Smith's model, however, the teacher is probably more of a controlling stimulus than Combs and Snygg would like him to be. The Montessori model is most similar to Smith's model because it comes closest to the balance between student and teacher perceptions which Smith's model describes.

QUESTION 1-3

The best answer is (c). The second objective, you will see, however, fills only one of the requirements of adequate statements of instructional objectives. The two remaining objectives suggest but do not specifically describe observable performance.

QUESTION 2-1

The best answer is (a). The terminal performance is the selection of striated muscles, the standard of performance is 100 percent mastery, and the condition of performance is the list given to the student. Answer (b) is not acceptable because it does not clearly indicate the acceptable level of performance. Answer (c) lacks a clear description of the conditions under which the student should do the listing. For example, does he have access to charts, reference books? Is he selecting his list from a longer list?

QUESTION 2-2

The best choice is (b). To make the correct identification of fossils the student has to learn the abstract properties of fossils, those properties which characterize all fossils. Such learning involves more than correctly naming a fossil (verbal association) and involves less than the discovery of a higher-order principle (problem solving)—for example, the relationship of fossils to various geological ages.

QUESTION 2-3

The answer is (c). Selecting the proper vowel depends at least on distinguishing between vowels and nonvowels (consonants) and also on the specific recognition of vowels in the trigram context. She did not describe these entering behaviors. Answer (a) is not a good choice because Miss Pegg is not likely to succeed unless through happy coincidence or divine intervention the students know more than she is assuming they know. In the case of (b), terminal performance is adequately defined, but entering behavior is not.

QUESTION 3-1

The answer is (c). By working backward from the instructional objective to discover prerequisite learning, Mr. Chips was using Gagné's method of determining learning sets. The question of ordering examples for the purpose of acquiring concepts (in this case, figures of speech) pertains to selection strategies.

QUESTION 3-2

The correct answer is (a). Mr. Wright never prepared a test of entering behavior in the first place. He prepared a pretest or a posttest based on what the students were about to learn (terminal performance) not on what they had already learned (entering behavior). Neither alternative (b) nor (c) is acceptable because Mr. Wright

QUESTION 3-3

cannot make these decisions until he prepares the proper test and uses it to assess the entering behavior of his students.

QUESTION 4-1 The correct answer is (b). Maria seems to be moving from one period to another period of intellectual development so that her ability to coordinate two characteristics in her groupings (color and shape) does not appear stabilized. Disequilibrium is characteristic of transitional development and of intellectual development before the period of formal operations.

QUESTION 4-2 The correct answer is (c), the period of concrete operations. Arranging objects in parallel serial order is a capability of this period. The ability to reverse this order is also characteristic of this period. But reversibility seems to be the only other possibility Jacqueline considered. The color arrangement was completely ignored, although it is an obvious third alternative. But many other arrangements are possible (for example, shortest cane with tallest doll, the coordination of color with height and length).

QUESTION 4-3 The answer is (c). Such a statement indicates that the child is thinking at the level of concrete operations, which would be typical of a child in the third grade (age 8). Alternatives (a) and (b) are both adequate (if somewhat unsophisticated) statements of the law. They require the child to see a relationship between the plunger's angle of inclination and the ball's angle of reflection after it hits the wall. A child who understands this relationship is thinking at the level of formal operations—a feat we would not expect in the third grade. Answer (c) simply reports an observation which the child can use as an explanation.

QUESTION 5-1 The best answer is (c). Alternatives (a) and (b) both refer to surface structure which is more the concern of structural linguistics than transformational grammar. Alternative (d) does not refer specifically to language structure but to the ability and behavior of people using language.

QUESTION 5-2 The correct answer is (c) (*S-V-R* learning). Percival has reached the level at which he can make an internal verbal response (*V*) to an external stimulus (*S*, or the dog) and follow the verbal response with a physical movement (*R*, or touching the dog). Answers (a) and (b) refer to lower levels of verbal development in which the child's responses are still tied to the physical environment rather than to internal verbal responses and stimuli of his own. Answer (d) (*S-V-V-R* learning) is a more advanced level than that which Percival has attained—one in which he will be able to chain one verbal response to another.

QUESTION 5-3 The best answer is (c) since *little* is the pivot word and truck the open class word. This is evidence that Little Larry has reached at least the early part of the two-word-sentence stage of language development. Alternative (a) is wrong because echolalia is a preverbal stage, and (b) is wrong because it refers to a more advanced stage. Alternative (d) is misleading because two words cannot make a one-word sentence.

QUESTION 5-4 The correct answer is (a). Since disadvantaged children are often deficient in labeling behavior, their repetition of the label with each presentation of an example of the concept *sailor* should strengthen the use of that label. Answer (b) is less desirable because a yes response is not so effective as a label response in developing labeling behavior. Answer (c) encourages the use of labels with the nonexamples of *sailor* but not with *sailor,* which is the concept Mr. Peabody is teaching. Answer (d), again, may help the children learn the concept but not necessarily the label for the concept.

The best answer is (b). Only this alternative denotes a possible increase in the vigor of the individual's (Horatio's) effort. The alternatives can all be explained in terms of learning or innate ability, and so on. In (a), Hortense's steady progress is simply a measure of her increased learning. In (c), no evidence shows any increase in vigor, and it is suggested that Havelock possesses innate swimming ability. In (d), the reference to Henrietta's habit is also a reference to learning rather than to motivation.

QUESTION 6-1

The best answer is (a), although you may argue. By matching problem difficulty and student ability, Mr. Seiting is dealing with arousal and potential anxiety and frustration. High-anxiety students of superior ability find anxiety facilitating, where-as students of average ability ordinarily find it debilitating—which is why he gives the latter students easier problems. Also by allowing the students to make discoveries, he is heightening interest and arousal. Expectancy (b) may be the next best re-sponse in that by providing challenge he is kindling the motive to achieve—but this applies to only some of the students. Expectancies may also be involved in that the students are given problems which they expect to solve. As for incentives (c), no specific incentives are mentioned, unless you consider the successful solution of the problem the incentive—although no success is guaranteed.

QUESTION 6-2

The best answer is (b). The analogies Miss Litefull drew are incongruous and per-haps even ludicrous (depending on your political and social convictions). There is evidence in her analogies of almost deliberate mismatching. The item contains no reference to levels of student alertness (arousal), learned anticipations (incentives), and rewards and discipline. Mismatching expectancies, you learned, is a way of generating humor and increasing student motivation.

QUESTION 6-3

The brief description illustrates the elements in our definition of learning, answer (a). The change is relatively permanent (it has now lasted one month), practice has been obvious (over a period of two months), and reinforcement has been provided by the successful execution of the skill and by the approval of peers. We must, of course, infer the tendency. As for answer (b), undoubtedly some muscular and neural development is necessary for Leroy to learn this skill, but this develop-ment can well occur without the acquisition of this skill. As for answer (c), tricycle riding is not an instinct; many foreign children never exhibit this behavior. As for answer (d), habituation refers to reduced responsiveness, and, although Leroy has developed considerable poise he is not less alert to the situation and responses he has mastered.

QUESTION 7-1

The best answer is (b). The children are being taught to discriminate between examples and nonexamples of dogs. They must, in fact, make different responses to two stimuli. To the extent that they pick dogs and ignore the other animals, it may be said that they have learned to discriminate. As for (a), although reinforce-ment of their responses to the pictures is an important condition of learning, the

QUESTION 7-2

562

item made no reference to how the teacher may have provided (if he did so) for this condition. As for (c), in concept learning, practice must occur *after* the concept is learned and the indications in this situation are that the children are still engaged in learning the concept. As for (d), generalization is also important in concept learning, but the emphasis in this teaching situation is not on the similarities of the various examples of dogs (making the same response to different stimuli) but on the differences between dogs and other animals.

QUESTION 8-1   The correct answer is (a). The flashing light is the conditioned stimulus, the electric shock the unconditioned stimulus, and the reaction to the shock (and presumably later to the light) the unconditioned and conditioned response. As for (b), in this procedure Mr. Sternski could either reinforce desirable responses, those that conformed to classroom rules, or he could terminate the shock only when the deviant student complied with the rules (negative reinforcement). Since the answer is (a) and not (b), it cannot be (c) or (d).

QUESTION 8-2   The best answer is (b) (verbal mediation). Each of these words (*finger, button,* and *pfug*) is mediating the association between the drawing of the land mass and the name or label attached to it. Answer (a) (meaningfulness) is not so good a choice because pfug is not very meaningful to most students. Answer (c) (instructions to learn) refers to a prior statement of instructional objectives, something Mr. Werdee may or may not have provided. Answer (d) (reinforcement) is not an acceptable choice because we do not know which confirmation procedure Mr. Werdee is using. Since he is not providing the right answers, he is not using a prompting procedure.

QUESTION 8-3   The best answer is (d) (reducing interference). By providing practice on the individual associations, with the possibility of overlearning, she is taking precautions against interference which could arise because of the similarity of the learning materials. Answer (a) does not apply since she does not announce what the students are expected to do (although this is fairly clear because of the nature of the task). Answer (b) does not apply because she does not check these words against word-frequency lists. Answer (c) does not apply because we do not know how confirmation is provided.

QUESTION 9-1   The best answer is (b). Relationship among movements refers to coordination of the sequences in which the movements occur. The learning of these movements requires contiguity. As for (a) and (d), although the student will require the different modes and types of feedback for the proper execution of the skill, in this early stage of skill instruction, feedback does not appear to be Mr. Kinetic's major concern. As for (c), practice is a later step in skill instruction, following demonstration. As for (e), if Mr. Kinetic directed the students' attention to particular movement cues or to differences in movements he would be providing discrimination training. Instead, he seems to be providing generalization training.

QUESTION 9-2   The best answer is (d). It is less suitable than the individual tests because these latter tests could better assess the various psychomotor abilities required in different stages of skill learning. As for (a), the test may measure the abilities needed in the initial but not in the later stages of learning tennis. As for (c), the test is related to some but not to all relevant aspects of the entering behavior. As for (b), since the students may perform skills which employ quite different psychomotor abilities than does tennis, even a careful observation would be unrelated.

The correct answer is (e). He did not provide for one basic learning condition—feedback, or reinforcement. Although practice will provide some of its own feedback (knocking over or not knocking over the bowling balls), students need other forms of feedback in the early stages of learning this skill.

1. (c) (conjunctive concept); 2. (e) (relational concept); 3. (d) (disjunctive concept); 4. (a) (attributes); 5. (b) (attribute values); 6. (f) (principle). Your reasons ought to be a correct definition of each term.

The answer is (c). By leaving each card in view after presenting it, Miss D. Voted was performing step 5, which requires the teacher to present positive and negative examples of the concept either in close succession or simultaneously. Either procedure provides contiguity. As for (a), the student should be told the expected performance before instruction is underway. As for (b), the examples themselves are not verbal mediators, although mediators can be used by the student to sort out the examples. As for (d), the verification of concept learning (step 7) occurs after the original examples have been presented and requires the presentation of new examples.

The answer is (e). By asking the students to form the singular by removing the s of the plural form, Mr. Punctilious is performing step 5, which requires the student to demonstrate the principle fully. This demonstration, according to Gagné, should take varied forms, and Mr. Punctilious' procedure is one such variation. There appears to be no statement of objective (a), the decision about component concepts must precede instruction (b), he is providing no help in recalling these component concepts (c), and he is not, at least in the question, helping the students to order the components (d). All the alternatives refer to earlier steps in the instruction.

The correct answer is psychologist A. Problem solving is treated as a form of learning, and, since what is learned is higher-order principles, the learning necessarily must have wide application to the solution of many problems within a class of problems. The view of psychologist B is not acceptable because we took the position that present evidence does not warrant the assumption that such general techniques, if they exist, are teachable or learnable. Psychologist C refers to types of learning of a lower order than problem solving. The view of psychologist D is unacceptable because he makes no reference to transfer to out-of-school problems and it is unlikely that complex personal and social problems can be tackled in the same way that we tackle academic problems.

The correct order is as follows: 1. (e) (instructional objective); 2. (a) (assessment of entering behavior); 3. (c) invoking relevant principles); 4. (b) (verbal direction of thinking); and 5. (d) (demonstrating ability to solve new problems of the same class).

QUESTION 11-3   The correct matches are as follows: (a) Psychologist *A;* (b) psychologist *C;* and (c) psychologist *B.* As for (a), consistent patterns and types refer to personality traits and abilities. As for (b), psychologist *C* is expressing the view that this form of instruction can result in learning. As for (c), sensing gaps and missing elements describes problem solving (in part).

QUESTION 11-4   The best answer is (c). Wittrock arrived at this conclusion about the type of objectives for which discovery learning may be appropriate. Also adequate provision is made for entering behavior. As for (a), no evidence indicates that discovery learning is useful for these less complex learning types. As for (b), this may be an appropriate objective (according to Wittrock), but expository teaching can prove unsuccessful for several reasons; by providing improved learning conditions, one may eventually make it work. As for (d), this may be an appropriate objective (according to Wittrock), but creativity or creative problem solving is hardly a product of ignorance; intuitive leaps must bridge acquired knowledge. As for (e), an instructional situation without an objective is basically untenable, and there is little or no evidence that students develop this type of motivation in the pursuit of mysterious and unknown goals.

QUESTION 12-1   An *X* should follow (a), (b), and (d). The explanation for (a) is obvious since you are told at the start that there are frames. Active student response (b) is indicated by the blanks which the student must fill in. The frames use both formal and thematic prompts (d). Answer (c) is excluded because the correct response is not indicated. Answer (e) is excluded because the frames appear to be quite independent and because it is poor practice to use formal prompts after using thematic prompts for the same item of information. By doing this you fail to fade or vanish the prompting already introduced.

QUESTION 12-2   The best answer is (b) (systems analysis and design) since the major purposes are the selection of procedures and materials among alternatives and their comparison on the basis of effectiveness and efficiency. Answers (a), (c), and (d) could all be very costly without being comparably more effective and efficient. Although (e) (instructional kits and low-cost items) appear to be more efficient in terms of money, they are less efficient in terms of time and less effective in terms of achievement.

QUESTION 13-1   The answers are as follows: (1) *T;* (2) *F;* (3) *T;* (4) *T.* The first statement is true because the items have obvious validity—they can be directly validated. The second statement is false because the instructional objective states an absolute standard, and the item validly assesses achievement of this standard. It is true, however, that such an item can appear on a test using a relative standard of achievement. The third statement is true because the item, as far as we know, is clear and not necessarily too easy or too difficult. The fourth statement is true because it would be fairly easy to arrive at a consensus on the correct answers.

QUESTION 13-2   The difficulty index is 39 percent or $\dfrac{35 + 42}{200} \times 100$

The discrimination index is -0.07 or $(35 - 42)/100$. (2) Since an item of average difficulty has an index of 50 percent, this item is difficult. (3) The item is a poor discriminator. It discriminates negatively, against the high-scoring students. (4) A simple way of making the item easier is to increase the number of pounds in C and D until they are closer to 1,000 or above.

The answer is (a), by elimination. Most of the other things have been done. By observing score consistency they have checked (and presumably reported) test reliability. They have tested their scoring procedures (which also affect reliability). They have tested and presumably perfected the procedures for administering the test. And they are under no obligation to praise their rival test makers.

QUESTION 14-1

The answer is (c), special aptitude. This is a test of creativity, and we discussed creativity tests as special aptitude tests. In the number of problem solutions produced, the test is measuring fluency. In the quality of the solutions, it may be measuring originality.

QUESTION 14-2

Reading test: $M = 52.35$; Mdn. $= 51.5$. Science test: national $M = 50$. Reading test: national $M = 45$. Your class is below average in science, above average in reading. You must remember to use the means for the eighth grade in Table 15-10.

QUESTION 15-1

Science test: $s = 12.73$. If you use the second method for estimating s, $s = 14.5$ for the science test and $s = 17$ for the reading test. The national s for the eighth grade is 10 for the science test and 8 for the reading test. Your class is more variable on both tests than the national sample is.

QUESTION 15-2

The percentile scores are as follows: Science test: William, 16; Howard, 50; Elizabeth, 98; and Maynard, 8. Reading test: Dub, 80; Fred, 16; Julia, 50; and Kenneth, 98.

QUESTION 15-3

The grade-level scores are as follows: Science test: William, 6; Howard, 8; Elizabeth, off the scale; and Maynard, 5. Reading test: Dub, 9.5; Fred, 5.7; Julia, 8; and Kenneth, 11.2.

QUESTION 15-4

The percentile scores convey more valid information than the grade-level scores do because they compare the students with their own groups.

QUESTION 15-5

With the sixth-grade mean, six on the science test and four on the reading test. With the tenth-grade mean, eight on the science test and eight on the reading test.

QUESTION 15-6

(a) $r = 0.70$; (b) $rho = 0.70$; (c) Maynard in science; Maynard and Dub in reading; (d) Ronald and Russell in science; Hazen in reading.

QUESTION 15-7

Using Chart 1, (a) he will exceed less than 2 percent of the freshmen at Rolling Hills, about 12 percent at Pacifica State; (b) he should attend Pacifica State, where the competition should be less stiff.

QUESTION 15-8

The answer is (d) since it appears that he has not considered the effective range of scores on the tests, which may be greater or less than the effective range of scores on the activities. By utilizing the full range of scores for the activities, he has considered effective range for these scores. Although it is hard to reliably measure classroom discussion, this can be done if one can quantify the measure.

QUESTION 16-1

QUESTION 16-2 Dr. *A* is the most logical choice. All the information we have indicates that he is the best surgeon, particularly because he would have been graded on his surgical performance during his medical training. We can grant that Dr. *B* is better than Dr. *C,* but what information do we have that he is better than Dr. *A?* Sometimes students choose Drs. *B* and *C* because they believe that these men may combine surgical competence with a warm bedside manner. But to assume that Dr. *A* does not have a warm bedside manner is to be guilty of the stereotyping described previously.

QUESTION 17-1 (a) The intended study in the public schools occurs at step 5, in which previously tested materials (the film) are now tested under typical classroom conditions. The previous study under laboratory conditions illustrates step 4. (b) The independent variable in the intended (as well as in the previous) study is the film. (c) The dependent variables in the laboratory (as well as in the classroom) study are student scores on the achievement test. (d) Possible statement of hypothesis: If the students see the film on drug usage, then they will significantly improve their scores on the drug achievement test.

QUESTION 17-2 The best answer is (d). It is not random in selection because the children were volunteers and may have differed especially in degree of curiosity, from children who did not volunteer. It is not random in assignment because he assigned the children to the various experimental conditions in the order in which they entered his laboratory. It is not unlikely that some more curious children may have hurried to the laboratory before the others, and others may have been distracted en route. Although he assigned the children random numbers, he did not use these numbers for assigning them to groups.

QUESTION 17-3 He is testing the null hypothesis. He should use Chi-square because he is dealing with frequencies rather than means and variances. Furthermore, we do not know whether the questionnaire scores form a normal distribution, and the five response choices do not form an equal-interval scale.

BIBLIOGRAPHY

ADAMS, THURSTON (1939). *Motion Pictures in Physical Education*. New York: Teachers College Press, Columbia University.

ADKIN, DOROTHY C. (1958). "Measurement in Relation to the Educational Process." *Educational and Psychological Measurement,* 18: 221–40.

ALLEN, DWIGHT (1963). Demonstration of the Use of the Videotape Recorder in Teacher Training. Stanford, Calif.: Stanford University.

ALLPORT, GORDON W.; VERNON, PHILIP E.; and LINDZEY, GARDNER (1960). *Study of Values Test Booklet.* 3rd ed. Boston: Houghton Mifflin Company.

ALPERT, R., and HABER, RALPH N. (1960). "Anxiety in Academic Achievement Situations." *Journal of Abnormal and Social Psychology,* 61: 207–15.

ALSCHULER, ALFRED. *Human Relations Education: A Guidebook to Learning Activities.* Albany: Curriculum Development Center, State Education Department.

AMIDON, EDMUND J., and FLANDERS, NED A. (1963). *The Role of the Teacher in the Classroom: A Manual for Understanding and Improving Teachers' Classroom Behavior.* Minneapolis: Amidon & Associates.

AMMONS, ROBERT B. (1954). "Knowledge of Performance: Survey of Literature, Some Possible Applications, and Suggested Experimentation." *USAF WADC Technical Report No. 54–114.* Wright-Patterson Air Force Base, Ohio.

AMOS, JIMMY R.; BROWN, FOSTER L.; and MINK, OSCAR G. (1965). *Statistical Concepts: A Basic Program.* New York: Harper & Row, Publishers.

ANASTASI, ANNE (1958). *Differential Psychology.* 3rd ed. New York: The Macmillan Company.

———— (1961). *Psychological Testing.* 2nd ed. New York: The Macmillan Company.

———— (1968). *Psychological Testing.* 3rd ed. New York: The Macmillan Company.

ANDERSON, RICHARD C. (1967). "Educational Psychology." *Annual Review of Psychology,* 18: 129–64.

ANNET, JOHN (1964). *The Role of Knowledge of Results in Learning: A Survey.* Port Washington, N.Y.: U.S. Naval Training Device Center.

ARCHER, JAMES E. (1962). "Concept Identification as a Function of Obviousness of Relevant and Irrelevant Information." *Journal of Experimental Psychology,* 63: 616–20.

———— (1966). "The Psychological Nature of Concepts," in *Analyses of Concept Learning,* eds. H. J. Klausmeier and C. W. Harris, pp. 37–49. New York: Academic Press Inc.

ATKINSON, JOHN W., ed. (1958). *Motives in Fantasy, Action, and Society.* Princeton, N.J.: D. Van Nostrand Co., Inc.

AUSUBEL, DAVID P. (1959). "Viewpoints From Related Disciplines: Human Growth and Development." *Teachers College Record,* 60: 245–54.

———— (1960). "Use of Advance Organizers in the Learning and Retention of Meaningful Verbal Material." *Journal of Educational Psychology,* 51: 267–72.

———— (1963a). *The Psychology of Meaningful Verbal Learning: An Introduction to School Learning.* New York: Grune & Stratton, Inc.

———— (1963b). "A Teaching Strategy for Culturally Deprived Pupils: Cognitive and Motivational Considerations." *The School Review* (Winter), pp. 454–63.

———— (1965a). "A Cognitive Structure View of Word and Concept Meaning," in *Readings in the Psychology of Cognition,* eds. R. C. Anderson and D. P. Ausubel, pp. 58–75. New York: Holt, Rinehart & Winston, Inc.

———— (1965b). "The Effects of Cultural Deprivation on Learning Patterns." *Audiovisual Instruction,* 10: 10–12.

———— (1968). *Educational Psychology: A Cognitive View.* New York: Holt, Rinehart & Winston, Inc.

———— (1971). Paper read at Symposium on Teaching Psychology to Teachers. Annual meeting of American Research Association, New York.

AUSUBEL, DAVID P., and FITZGERALD, DONALD (1961). "The Role of Discriminability in Meaningful Verbal Learning and Retention." *Journal of Educational Psychology,* 52: 266–74.

AUSUBEL, DAVID P.; SCHPOONT, S. H.; and CUKIER, L. (1957). "The Influence of Intention on the Retention of School Materials." *Journal of Educational Psychology,* 48: 334–43.

AUSUBEL, DAVID P., and YOUSEFF, MOHAMED (1963). "The Role of Discriminability in Meaningful Parallel Learning." *Journal of Educational Psychology,* 54: 331–36.

BACHMAN, JERALD G. (1964). "Motivation in a Task Situation as a Function of Ability and Control Over Task." *Journal of Abnormal and Social Psychology,* 69: 272–81.

BAIR, MEDILL, and WOODWARD, RICHARD G. (1964). *Team Teaching in Action.* Boston: Houghton Mifflin Company.

BALDWIN, ALFRED L. (1967). *Theories of Child Development.* New York: John Wiley & Sons, Inc.

BANDURA, ALBERT (1962). "The Influence of Rewarding and Punishing Models on the Acquisition and Performance of Imitative Responses." An unpublished manuscript. Stanford University.

BANDURA, ALBERT, and WALTERS, RICHARD H. (1963). *Social Learning and Personality Development.* New York: Holt, Rinehart & Winston, Inc.

BARATZ, JOAN C. (1969). "Teaching Black Children to Read," in *Teaching Black Children to Read,* eds. J. Baratz and R. Shuy, pp. 92–116. Washington, D.C.: Center for Applied Linguistics.

BARSON, JOHN (1965). *A Procedural and Cost Analysis Study of Media in Instructional Systems Development.* Final Report, Grant No. OE-3-16-030.

BAYLEY, NANCY (1966). "Learning in Adulthood: The Role of Intelligence," in *Analyses of Concept Learning,* eds. H. J. Klausmeier and C. W. Chester, pp. 117–38. New York: Academic Press Inc.

BEACH, FRANK A.; CONOWITZ, M. W.; STEINBERG, F.; and GOLDSTEIN, A. C. (1956). "Experimental Inhibition and Restoration of Mating Behavior in Male Rats." *Journal of Genetic Psychology,* 89: 165–81.

BEBERMAN, MAX (1964). "An Emerging Program of Secondary School Mathematics," in *New Curricula,* ed. R. W. Heath, pp. 9–34. New York: Harper & Row, Publishers.

BECKER, HOWARD S. (1952). "Social Class Variations in the Teacher-Pupil Relationship." *Journal of Educational Sociology,* 25: 451–65.

BEHRINGER, MARJORIE P. (1966). "The Development of Differentiated Curricula for Ability Grouped Biology Classes, Including Teacher Training and Program Evaluation." *BSCS Newsletter, No. 30,* p. 23.

BERG, HARRY D. (1965). "The Objective Test Item," in *Evaluation in Social Studies,* ed. H. D. Berg, 35th Yrbk. of the National Council for the Social Studies, pp. 47–76. Washington, D.C.: National Education Association.

BERKO, JEAN (1958). "The Child's Learning of English Morphology." *Word,* 14: 150–77.

BERLYNE, DAVID E. (1957a). "Conflict and Information-Theory Variables as Determinants of Human Perceptual Curiosity." *Journal of Experimental Psychology,* 53: 399–404.

——— (1957b). "Recent Developments in Piaget's Work." *British Journal of Educational Psychology,* 27: 1–12.

BERN, HENRY A. (1967). "Wanted: Educational Engineers." *Phi Delta Kappan,* 48: 230–36.

BERNSTEIN, BASIL (1961). "Social Structure, Language and Learning." *Educational Research,* 3: 163–76.

BERNSTEIN, BASIL (1969). "Sociolinguistic Approach to Socialization, in *Direction in Sociolinguistics,* eds. H. Gumperz and D. Hymes. New York: Holt, Rinehart & Winston, Inc.

BEXTON, WILLIAM H.; HERON, WOODBURN; and SCOTT, T. H. (1954). "Effects of Decreased Variation in the Sensory Environment." *Canadian Journal of Psychology,* 8: 70–76.

BILODEAU, EDWARD A., and BILODEAU, INA M. (1961). "Motor-Skills Learning." *Annual Review of Psychology,* 12: 243–80.

BIRCH, HERBERT G., and RABINOWITZ, HERBERT S. (1951). "The Negative Effects of

Previous Experience on Productive Thinking." *Journal of Experimental Psychology,* 41: 121–25.

BLACKMAN, LEONARD S., and HEINTZ, PAUL (1966). "The Mentally Retarded." *Review of Educational Research,* 36: 5–36.

BLOOM, BENJAMIN S. (1964). *Stability and Change in Human Characteristics.* New York: John Wiley & Sons, Inc.

BLOOM, BENJAMIN S. *et al.,* eds. (1956). *Taxonomy of Educational Objectives: Handbook I: Cognitive Domain.* New York: David McKay Co., Inc.

BLOOMFIELD, L. (1933). *Language.* New York: Holt, Rinehart & Winston, Inc.

BOOK, WILLIAM F. (1908). *The Psychology of Skill.* University of Montana Publications in Psychology, No. 53.

BORG, WALTER R. (1963). *Educational Research: An Introduction.* New York: David McKay Co., Inc.

BRACKBILL, YVONNE; WAGNER, JOHN E.; and WILSON, DOROTHY (1964). "Feedback Delay and the Teaching Machine." *Psychology in the Schools,* 1: 148–56.

BRALEY, LOY (1963). "Strategy Selection and Negative Instances in Concept Learning." *Journal of Educational Psychology,* 54: 154–59.

BRIM, ORVILLE G. (1965). "American Attitudes Toward Intelligence Tests." *American Psychologist,* 20: 125–30.

BROUDY, HARRY S. (1963). "Historic Exemplars of Teaching Method," in *Handbook of Research on Teaching,* ed. N. L. Gage, pp. 1–43. Chicago: Rand McNally & Co.

BROWN, FRANK B. (1963). "The Non-Graded High School." *Phi Delta Kappan,* 44: 206–9.

BROWN, R. (1957). "Linguistic Determinism and the Part of Speech." *Journal of Abnormal and Social Psychology,* 55: 1–5.

BROWN, R., and BELLUGI, U. (1964). "Three Processes in the Child's Acquisition of Syntax." *Harvard Educational Review,* 34: 133–51.

BROWN, R.; CAZDEN, C.; and BELLUGI, U. (1968). *The Child's Grammar from I to III.* In J. P. Hill, ed., Minnesota Symposium on Child Psychology. Minneapolis: University of Minnesota Press.

BRUNER, JEROME S. (1960). *The Process of Education.* Cambridge, Mass.: Harvard University Press.

——— (1961a). "The Act of Discovery." *Harvard Educational Review,* 31: 21–32.

——— (1961b). "The Cognitive Consequences of Early Sensory Deprivation," in *Sensory Deprivation,* ed. Philip Solomon. Cambridge, Mass.: Harvard University Press.

BRUNER, JEROME S.; GOODNOW, JACQUELINE J.; and AUSTIN, GEORGE A. (1956). *A Study of Thinking.* New York: John Wiley & Sons, Inc.

BRYAN, W. L., and HARTER, N. (1897). "Studies in the Physiology and Psychology of the Telegraphic Language." *Psychological Review,* 4: 27–53.

——— (1899). "Studies on the Telegraphic Language: The Acquisition of a Hierarchy of Habits." *Psychological Review,* 6: 345–75.

BUROS, O. (1972). *The Seventh Mental Measurements Yearbook.* Highland Park, N.J.: Gryphon Press.

BUSS, ARNOLD H. (1950). "A Study of Concept Formation as a Function of Reinforcement and Stimulus Generalization." *Journal of Experimental Psychology,* 40: 494–503.

CAMPBELL, DONALD T., and STANLEY, JULIAN C. (1963). "Experimental and Quasi-Experimental Designs for Research on Teaching," in *Handbook of Research on Teaching,* ed. N. L. Gage, pp. 171–246. Chicago: Rand McNally & Co.

CARPENTER, CLARENCE R., and GREENHILL, LESLIE P. (1955). *Instructional Television Research Project No. One: An Investigation of Closed-Circuit Television for Teaching University Courses.* University Park, Pa.: The Pennsylvania State University.

———— (1968). *Instructional Television Research Project No. Two: An Investigation of Closed-Circuit Television for Teaching University Courses.* University Park, Pa.: The Pennsylvania State University.

CARPENTER, F. (1954). "Conceptualization as a Function of Differential Reinforcement." *Science Education,* 38: 284–94.

CARROLL, JOHN B. (1960). "Wanted: A Research Basis for Educational Policy on Foreign Language Teaching." *Harvard Educational Review,* 30: 128–40.

———— (1962). "The Prediction of Success in Intensive Foreign Language Training," in *Training Research and Education,* ed. R. Glaser, pp. 87–136.

———— (1963). "A Model of School Learning." *Teachers College Record,* 64: 723–33.

———— (1964a). "Words, Meanings, and Concepts." *Harvard Educational Review,* 34: 178–202.

———— (1964b). *Language and Thought.* Englewood Cliffs, N.J.: Prentice-Hall, Inc.

———— (1965). "School Learning Over the Long Haul," in *Learning and the Educational Process,* ed. J. D. Krumboltz, pp. 249–69. Chicago: Rand McNally & Co.

CARSON, ARNOLD S., and RABIN, A. I. (1960). "Verbal Comprehension and Communication in Negro and White Children." *Journal of Educational Psychology,* 51: 47–51.

CHAPANIS, ALPHONSE (1964). "Knowledge of Performance as an Incentive in Repetitive and Monotonous Tasks." *Journal of Applied Psychology,* 48: 263–67.

CHARTERS, W. W. (1963). "The Social Background of Teaching," in *Handbook of Research on Teaching,* ed. N. L. Gage, pp. 715–813. Chicago: Rand McNally & Co.

CHOMSKY, NOAM (1957). *Syntactic Structures.* The Hague: Mouton & Co.

———— (1965). *Aspects of a Theory of Language.* Cambridge, Mass.: M.I.T. Press.

———— (1968). *The Acquisition of Syntax in Children from 5 to 10.* Unpublished doctoral dissertation, Department of Linguistics, Harvard University.

CLARK, L. VERDELLE (1960). "Effect of Mental Practice on the Development of a Certain Motor Skill." *Research Quarterly,* 31: 560–69.

CLOWARD, RICHARD A., and JONES, JAMES A. (1963). "Social Class: Educational Attitudes and Participation," in *Education in Depressed Areas,* ed. Harry Passow, pp. 19–126. New York: Teachers College Press, Columbia University.

COFER, CHARLES N., and APPLEY, MORTIMER H. (1964). *Motivation: Theory and Research.* New York: John Wiley & Sons, Inc.

COLEMAN, JAMES S. (1961). *The Adolescent Subculture.* New York: Free Press of Glencoe, Inc.

———— (1971). "Education in the Age of Computers and Mass Communication," in *Computers, Communication and the Public Interest,* ed. M. Greenberger. Baltimore: The Johns Hopkins Press.

COMBS, ARTHUR W., and SNYGG, DONALD (1959). *Individual Behavior: A Perceptual Approach to Behavior.* New York: Harper & Row, Publishers.

Committee for the White House Conference on Education (1956). *A Report to the President.* Washington, D.C.: Government Printing Office.

CONNERS, KEITH C. (1964). "Visual and Verbal Approach Motives as a Function of Discrepancy from Expectancy Level." *Perceptual and Motor Skills,* 18: 457–64.

COOK, JOHN O. (1958). "Supplementary Report: Processes Underlying Learning a Single Paired-Associate Item." *Journal of Experimental Psychology,* 56: 455.

——— (1963). "Superstition in the Skinnerian." *American Psychologist,* 18: 516–18.

COOK, JOHN O., and KENDLER, TRACY S. (1956). "A Theoretical Model to Explain Some Paired-Associate Learning Data," in *Symposium on Air Force Human Engineering, Personnel and Training Research,* Publication No. 455, eds. G. Finch and F. Cameron, pp. 90–98. Washington, D.C.: National Academy of Sciences—National Research Council.

COOK, JOHN O., and SPITZER, M. E. (1960). "Supplementary Report: Prompting Versus Confirmation in Pair-Associate Learning." *Journal of Experimental Psychology,* 59: 275–76.

COOK, WALTER W.; LEEDS, CARROLL H.; and CALLIS, ROBERT (1951). *Minnesota Teacher Attitude Inventory Manual.* New York: Psychological Corp.

CORMAN, BERNARD R. (1957). "The Effect of Varying Amounts and Kinds of Information as Guidance in Problem Solving." *Psychology Monographs,* 71, No. 2 (Whole No. 431).

COVINGTON, MARTIN V. (1967). "Fostering Originality in Visual Problem Solving of Programmed Instructional Techniques." Paper read at the Western Psychological Association Meeting, San Francisco.

COX, JOHN A., and BOREN, LYNN M. (1965). "A Study of Backward Chaining." *Journal of Educational Psychology,* 56: 270–74.

CREMIN, LAWRENCE A. (1964). *The Transformation of the School: Progressivism in American Education.* New York: Vintage Books.

——— (1965). *The Genius of American Education.* New York: Vintage Books.

CROMWELL, RUE L. (1956). "Factors in the Serial Recall of Names of Acquaintances." *Journal of Abnormal and Social Psychology,* 53: 63–67.

CRONBACH, LEE J. (1960). *Essentials of Psychological Testing* (2nd ed.). New York: Harper & Row, Publishers.

——— (1963). *Educational Psychology* (2nd ed.). New York: Harcourt, Brace & World, Inc.

——— (1966a). "The Logic of Experiments on Discovery," in *Learning by Discovery,* eds. L. S. Shulman and E. R. Keislar, pp. 77–92. Chicago: Rand McNally & Co.

——— (1966b). "The Role of the University in Improving Education." *Phi Delta Kappan,* 47: 539–45.

CROSSMAN, E. R. F. W. (1959). "A Theory of the Acquisition of Speed-Skill." *Ergonomics,* 2: 153–66.

CROWDER, NORMAN A. (1960). "Intrinsically Programmed Teaching Devices," in *Invitational Conference on Testing Problems: 1959 Proceedings.* Princeton, N.J.: Educational Testing Service.

——— (1963a). "On the Differences Between Linear and Intrinsic Programming." *Phi Delta Kappan,* 44: 250–54.

——— (1963b). "The Rationale of Intrinsic Programming," in *Human Learning in the School,* ed. J. P. De Cecco, pp. 183–89. New York: Holt, Rinehart & Winston, Inc.

CUMMINGS, ALLANA, and GOLDSTEIN, LEO S. (1962). "The Effect of Overt and Covert Responding on Two Kinds of Learning Tasks," in *Technical Report 620919.* New York: Center for Programmed Instruction.

CURTIS, H. A., and KROPP, R. P. (1965). *Experimental Analyses of the Effects of Various Modes of Item Presentation on the Scores and Factorial Content of Tests Administered by Visual and Audio-Visual Means: A Program of Studies Basic to Television Testing.* Title VII, Project Number 385, National Defense Education Act of 1958, Grant Number 7–08–075, Office of Education, Dept. of

Health, Education, and Welfare. Dept. of Educational Research and Testing, Florida State University, Tallahassee.

DAVE, R. H. (1963). "The Identification and Measurement of Environmental Process Variables That Are Related to Educational Achievement." Doctoral dissertation, University of Chicago.

DAVIES, DOROTHY R. (1945). "The Effect of Tuition upon the Process of Learning a Complex Motor Skill." *Journal of Educational Psychology*, 36: 352–65.

DAVIS, ALLISON, and EELLS, KENNETH (1953). *Davis-Eells Games*. New York: Harcourt, Brace & World, Inc.

DE CECCO, JOHN P., and RICHARDS, ARLENE K. (1974). *Growing Pains: Uses of School Conflict*. New York: Holt, Rinehart & Winston, Inc.

DEESE, JAMES (1958). *The Psychology of Learning*. 2nd ed. New York: McGraw-Hill Book Company.

DEESE, JAMES, and HULSE, STEWART H. (1967). *The Psychology of Learning*. 3rd ed. New York: McGraw-Hill Book Company.

DEUTSCH, MORTON (1960). "The Effects of Cooperation and Competition on Group Process," in *Group Dynamics: Research and Theory*, eds. D. Cartwright and A. Zander, pp. 414–48. Evanston, Ill.: Row and Peterson.

DILLARD, J. L. (1972). *Black English: Its History and Usage in the United States*. New York: Random House.

DOLLARD, J.; DOOB, L. W.; MILLER, N. E.; MOWRER, O. H.; SEARS, R. R.; FORD, C. S.; HOVLAND, C. I.; and SOLLENBERGER, R. T. (1939). *Frustration and Aggression*. New Haven, Conn.: Yale University Press.

DOLLARD, JOHN, and MILLER, NEALE (1950). *Personality and Psychotherapy*. New York: The Macmillan Company.

DOMINOWSKI, R. L. (1965). "Role of Memory in Concept Learning." *Psychological Bulletin*, 63: 271–80.

DORÉ, L. R., and HILGARD, ERNEST R. (1938). "Spaced Practice as a Test of Snoddy's Two Processes in Mental Growth." *Journal of Experimental Psychology*, 23: 359–74.

DREHER, ROBERT E., and BEATTY, WALCOTT H. (1958). *Instructional Television Research Project Number One: An Experimental Study of College Instruction Using Broadcast Television*. San Francisco: San Francisco State College.

DUNCAN, CARL P. (1951). "The Effect of Unequal Amounts of Practice on Motor Learning Before and After Practice." *Journal of Experimental Psychology*, 42: 257–64.

———— (1959). "Recent Research on Human Problem Solving." *Psychological Bulletin*, 56: 397–429.

DWYER, FRANCIS M., JR. (1967). "Adapting Visual Illustrations for Effective Learning." *Harvard Educational Review*, 37: 250–63.

EBBINGHAUS, HERMANN (1885). *Ueber das Gedächtnis*. Translated by Henry A. Ruger and Clara Bussenius as *Memory*, Educational Reprint No. 3. New York: Teachers College Press, Columbia University, 1913.

EBEL, ROBERT L. (1963). "The Relation of Testing Programs to Educational Goals," in *The Impact and Improvement of School Testing Programs*, Part 2 of the 62nd Yrbk. of the National Society for the Study of Education, pp. 28–44. Chicago: University of Chicago Press.

———— (1965). *Measuring Educational Achievement*. Englewood Cliffs, N.J.: Prentice-Hall, Inc.

———— (1967). "Some Limitations of Basic Research in Education." *Phi Delta Kappan*, 49: 81–84.

574

—— (1972). *Essentials of Educational Measurement.* Englewood Cliffs, N.J.: Prentice-Hall, Inc.

Educational Policies Commission (1961). *The Central Purposes of American Education.* Washington, D.C.: Educational Policies Commission of the National Education Association.

EIGEN, LEWIS D., and FELDHUSEN, JOHN (1964). "Interrelationships Among Attitude, Achievement, Reading, Intelligence, and Transfer Variables in Programmed Instruction," in *Educational Technology,* ed. J. P. De Cecco, pp. 376–86. New York: Holt, Rinehart & Winston, Inc.

EIGEN, LEWIS D., and MARGULIES, STUART (1963). "Response Characteristics as a Function of Information Level." *Journal of Programed Instruction,* 2: 45–54.

EISENSON, J.; AUER, J. J.; and IRWIN, J. V. (1963). *The Psychology of Communication.* New York: Appleton-Century-Crofts, Inc.

EISNER, ELLIOTT W. (1967). "Educational Objectives: Help or Hindrance?" *School Review,* 75: 250–60.

ELLIS, HENRY (1965). *The Transfer of Learning.* New York: The Macmillan Company.

ELWELL, J. L., and GRINDLEY, G. C. (1938). "The Effect of Knowledge of Results on Learning and Performance. I: A Coordinated Movement of the Two Hands." *British Journal of Psychology,* 29: 39–53.

ELZEY, FREEMAN F. (1965). *A Programed Introduction to Statistics.* Belmont, Calif.: Wadsworth Publishing Co., Inc.

ENTWISLE, DORIS R., and HUGGINS, W. H. (1964). "Interference in Meaningful Learning." *Journal of Educational Psychology,* 55: 75–78.

ERICKSON, CARLTON W. (1965). *Fundamentals of Teaching with Audiovisual Technology.* New York: The Macmillan Company.

ERVIN-TRIPP, SUSAN (1961). "Changes with Age on the Verbal Determinants of Word Association." *American Journal of Psychology,* 74: 361–72.

—— (1964). "Language and Thought," in *Horizons of Anthropology,* ed. Sol Tax. Chicago: Aldine Publishing Co.

FEATHERSTONE, JOSEPH (1971). *Schools Where Children Learn.* New York: Laveright.

FERSTER, CHARLES B., and SKINNER, B. F. (1957). *Schedules of Reinforcement.* New York: Appleton-Century-Crofts.

FILEP, ROBERT T. (1961). "Programming for Your Classroom." *Programed Instruction,* 1, No. 1, 3–4.

FINLAY, GILBERT C. (1962). "The Physical Science Study Committee." *The School Review,* 7: 70.

—— (1964). "The Physical Science Study Committee." *ESI Quarterly Report* (Winter–Spring), pp. 5–16.

FITTS, PAUL (1951). "Engineering Psychology and Equipment Design," in *Handbook of Experimental Psychology,* ed. S. S. Stevens, pp. 1237–40. New York: John Wiley & Sons, Inc.

—— (1962). "Factors in Complex Skill Training," in *Training Research and Education,* ed. R. Glaser, pp. 177–97. Pittsburgh: University of Pittsburgh Press.

—— (1964). "Perceptual-Motor Skill Learning," in *Categories of Human Learning,* ed. A. W. Melton, pp. 243–85. New York: Academic Press, Inc.

FITZPATRICK, E. A. (1933). *Ignatius and the Ratio Studiorum.* New York: McGraw-Hill Book Company.

FLANAGAN, JOHN C. (1957). *Flanagan Aptitude Classification Tests.* Chicago: Science Research Associates, Inc.

FLANAGAN, JOHN C. *et al.* (1964). *Project Talent: The Identification, Development, and Utilization of Human Talents Final Report.* Pittsburgh: Project Talent Office, University of Pittsburgh.

FLANDERS, NED A. (1951). "Personal-Social Anxiety as a Factor in Experimental Learning Situations." *Journal of Educational Research,* 45: 100–110.

——— (1960). *Teacher Influence, Pupil Attitudes, and Achievement.* Minneapolis: University of Minnesota.

——— (1964). "Some Relationships Among Teacher Influence, Pupil Attitudes, and Achievement," in *Contemporary Research on Teacher Effectiveness,* eds. B. J. Biddle and W. J. Ellena, pp. 196–231. New York: Holt, Rinehart & Winston, Inc.

FLAVELL, JOHN H. (1963). *The Development Psychology of Jean Piaget.* Princeton, N.J.: D. Van Nostrand Co., Inc.

FLEISHMAN, EDWIN A. (1962). "The Description and Prediction of Perceptual-Motor Skill Learning," in *Training Research Education,* ed. R. Glaser, pp. 137–75. Pittsburgh: University of Pittsburgh Press.

——— (1964). *The Structure and Measurement of Physical Fitness.* Englewood Cliffs, N.J.: Prentice-Hall, Inc.

FLEISHMAN, EDWIN A., and HEMPEL, WALTER E., JR. (1954). "Changes in Factor Structure of a Complex Psychomotor Test as a Function of Practice." *Psychometrika,* 19: 239–52.

——— (1955). "The Relation Between Abilities and Improvement with Practice in a Visual Discrimination Reaction Task." *Journal of Experimental Psychology,* 49: 301–10.

FLEXMAN, RALPH E.; MATHENY, WILLIAM G.; and BROWN, E. L. (1950). "Evaluation of the School Link and Special Methods of Instruction." *University of Illinois Bulletin,* 47, No. 80.

FOWLER, HARRY (1965). *Curiosity and Exploratory Behavior.* New York: The Macmillan Company.

FOWLER, WILLIAM (1962). "Cognitive Learning in Infancy and Early Childhood." *Psychological Bulletin,* 59: 116–52.

FREEMAN, FRANK S. (1962). *Theory and Practice of Psychological Testing.* New York: Holt, Rinehart & Winston, Inc.

FRENCH, JOSEPH L. (1964). *Pictorial Test of Intelligence Manual.* Boston: Houghton Mifflin Company.

FRENCH, WILL *et al.* (1957). *Behavioral Goals of General Education in the High School.* New York: Russell Sage Foundation.

FRIEDLANDER, BERNARD Z. (1965). "A Psychologist's Second Thoughts on Concepts, Curiosity, and Discovery in Teaching and Learning." *Harvard Educational Review,* 35: 18–38.

FRIES, CHARLES C. (1963). *Linguistics and Reading.* New York: Holt, Rinehart & Winston, Inc.

GAGE, NATHANIEL L. (1963). "Paradigms for Research on Teaching," in *Handbook of Research on Teaching,* ed. N. L. Gage, pp. 94–141. Chicago: Rand McNally & Co.

——— (1964). "The Theories of Teaching," in *Handbook of Research on Teaching,* ed. N. L. Gage, pp. 268–85. Chicago: Rand McNally & Co.

GAGNÉ, ROBERT M. (1962a). "The Acquisition of Knowledge." *Psychological Review,* 69: 355–65.

——— (1962b). "Military Training and Principles of Learning." *American Psychologist,* 17: 83–91.

———— (1964). "Problem Solving," in *Categories of Human Learning*, ed. A. W. Melton, pp. 294–317. New York: Academic Press Inc.

———— (1965a). "Educational Objectives and Human Performance," in *Learning and the Educational Process*, ed. J. D. Krumboltz, pp. 1–24. Chicago: Rand McNally & Co.

———— (1965b). "The Analysis of Instructional Objectives for the Design of Instruction," in *Teaching Machines and Programmed Learning II: Data and Directions*, ed. R. Glaser, pp. 21–65. Washington, D.C.: Department of Audio-visual Instruction, National Education Association.

———— (1965c). *Conditions of Learning*. New York: Holt, Rinehart & Winston, Inc.

———— (1966). "The Learning of Principles," in *Analyses of Concept Learning*, eds. H. J. Klausmeier and C. W. Harris, pp. 81–96. New York: Academic Press Inc.

GAGNÉ, ROBERT M., and BASSLER, OTTO C. (1963). "Study of Retention of Some Topics of Elementary Nonmetric Geometry." *Journal of Educational Psychology*, 54: 123–31.

GAGNÉ, ROBERT M., and BROWN, LARRY T. (1961). "Some Factors in the Programming of Conceptual Learning." *Journal of Experimental Psychology*, 62: 313–21.

GAGNÉ, ROBERT M., and FLEISHMAN, EDWIN A. (1959). *Psychology and Human Performance*. New York: Holt, Rinehart & Winston, Inc.

GAGNÉ, ROBERT M.; MAYOR, J. R.; GARSTENS, H. L.; and PARADISE, N. E. (1962). "Factors in Acquiring Knowledge of a Mathematical Task." *Psychological Monographs*, 76, No. 7 (Whole No. 526).

GAGNÉ, ROBERT M., and PARADISE, N. E. (1961). "Abilities and Learning Sets in Knowledge Acquisition." *Psychological Monographs*, 75, No. 14 (Whole No. 518).

GALLAGHER, JAMES J. (1964). *Teaching the Gifted Child*. Boston: Allyn and Bacon, Inc.

GARRETT, HENRY E. (1958). *Statistics in Psychology and Education*. New York: David McKay Co., Inc.

"Gates-MacGintie Reading Tests" (1965). *Teacher's Manual Survey E*. New York: Teachers College Press, Columbia University.

GEIS, GEORGE L.; STEBBINS, WILLIAM C.; and LUNDIN, ROBERT W. (1965). *Reflex and Operant Conditioning*. New York: Basic Systems, Inc.

GENTILE, J. ROBERT (1967). "The First Generation of Computer-Assisted Instructional Systems: An Evaluative Review." *AV Communication Review*, 15: 23–53.

GETZELS, JACOB W. (1964). "Creative Thinking, Problem Solving, and Instruction," in *Theories of Learning and Instruction*, ed. E. R. Hilgard, Part 1 of the 63rd Yrbk. of the National Society for the Study of Education, pp. 240–67. Chicago: University of Chicago Press.

GETZELS, JACOB W., and JACKSON, PHILIP W. (1962). *Creativity and Intelligence: Explorations with Gifted Students*. New York: John Wiley & Sons, Inc.

GEWIRTZ, HAVA B. (1959). "Generalization of Children's Preferences as a Function of Reinforcement and Task Similarity." *Journal of Abnormal and Social Psychology*, 58: 111–18.

GHISELIN, BREWSTER, ed. (1952). *The Creative Process*. Berkeley, Calif.: University of California Press.

GIBSON, ELEANOR J.; PICK, ANNE; OSSER, HARRY; and HAMMOND, MARCIA (1962). "The Role of Grapheme-Phoneme Correspondence in the Perception of Words." *American Journal of Psychology*, 75: 554–70.

GIBSON, O. O. (1941). "A Critical Review of the Concept of Set in Contemporary Experimental Psychology." *Psychological Bulletin*, 38: 781–817.

GILBERT, THOMAS F. (1960). "On the Relevance of Laboratory Investigation of Learning to Self-Instructional Programs," in *Teaching Machines and Programmed Learning: A Source Book*, eds. A. Lumsdaine and R. Glaser, pp. 475–85. Washington, D.C.: Department of Audiovisual Instruction, National Education Association.

———— (1962a). "Mathetics: The Technology of Education." *Journal of Mathetics*, 1: 7–73.

———— (1962b). "A Structure for a Coordinated Research and Development Laboratory," in *Training Research and Education*, ed. R. Glaser, pp. 559–78. Pittsburgh: University of Pittsburgh Press.

GLASER, ROBERT (1962). "Psychology and Instructional Technology," in *Training Research and Education*, ed. R. Glaser, pp. 1–30. Pittsburgh: University of Pittsburgh Press.

———— (1965). "Toward a Behavioral Science Base for Instructional Design," in *Teaching Machines and Programmed Learning II: Data and Directions*, ed. R. Glaser, pp. 771–809. Washington, D.C.: Department of Audiovisual Instruction, National Education Association.

———— (1966). "Variables in Discovery Learning," in *Learning by Discovery*, eds. L. S. Shulman and E. R. Keislar, pp. 13–26. Chicago: Rand McNally & Co.

GLASER, ROBERT, and REYNOLDS, JAMES H. (1964). "Instructional Objectives and Programmed Instruction: A Case Study," in *Defining Educational Objectives*, ed. C. M. Lindvall. Pittsburgh: University of Pittsburgh Press.

GLAZE, J. A. (1928). "The Association Value of Nonsense Syllables." *Journal of Genetic Psychology*, 35: 255–67.

GLEASON, H. A., JR. (1965). *Linguistics and English Grammar*. New York: Holt, Rinehart & Winston, Inc.

GNAGEY, WILLIAM J. (1965). *Controlling Classroom Misbehavior*. Washington, D.C.: Department of Classroom Teachers, American Educational Research Association, National Education Association.

GOLDBERG, LEWIS (1965). "Grades as Motivants." *Psychology in the Schools*, 2: 17–23.

GOODLAD, JOHN I. (1964). *School Curriculum Reform in the United States*. New York: The Fund for the Advancement of Education.

GOODLAD, JOHN I., and ANDERSON, ROBERT H. (1963). *The Nongraded Elementary School*. New York: Harcourt, Brace & World, Inc.

GOROW, FRANK F. (1966). *Better Classroom Testing*. San Francisco: Chandler Publishing Co.

GOTKIN, LASSAR G., and GOLDSTEIN, LEO S. (1964). *Descriptive Statistics*, Vol. 1. New York: John Wiley & Sons, Inc.

GOTTLIEB, DAVID (1964). "Teaching and Students: The Views of Negro and White Teachers." *Sociology of Education*, 37: 345–53.

GOUGH, HARRISON G. (1957). *California Psychological Inventory Manual*. Palo Alto, Calif.: Consulting Psychologists Press.

GREENE, H. A. (1939). *The Iowa Every-Pupil Tests in Basic Skills*. Iowa City, Iowa: Extension Division, State University of Iowa.

GREENE, H. A., and KELLEY, V. H. (1943). *Iowa Silent Reading Tests*. (Elementary Tests: Manual of Directions for Forms Am (revised) and Bm (revised), Cm and Dm.) Chicago: World Book Encyclopedia, Inc.

GREENHILL, LESLIE P. (1964). "A Review of Some Trends in Research on Instructional Films and Instructional Television," in *Abstracts of Research on Instructional Television and Film: An Annotated Bibliography,* eds. D. W. MacLennand and J. C. Reid, pp. 1–32. Stanford, Calif.: Institute for Communication Research, Stanford University.

GREENSPOON, JOEL, and FOREMAN, SALLY (1956). "Effect of Delay of Knowledge of Results on Learning a Motor Task." *Journal of Experimental Psychology,* 51: 226–28.

GRONLUND, NORMAN E. (1965). *Measurement and Evaluation in Teaching.* New York: The Macmillan Company.

GROPPER, GEORGE L., and LUMSDAINE, ARTHUR A. (1961). "An Experimental Comparison of a Conventional TV Lesson with a Programmed TV Lesson Requiring Active Student Response. Studies in Televised Instruction, Reports No. 2, 3, USOE Project No. 336." *AV Communication Review,* 9: A-50–51.

GROSS, M. M. (1946). "The Effect of Certain Types of Motivation on the Honesty of Children." *Journal of Educational Research,* 40: 133–40.

GROSS, N. (1953). "Social Class Identification in the Urban Community." *American Sociological Review,* 18: 398–403.

GUILFORD, JOY P. (1950). "Creativity." *American Psychologist,* 5: 444–54.

———— (1959). "Three Faces of Intellect." *American Psychologist,* 14: 469–79.

———— (1962). "Factors That Aid and Hinder Creativity." *Teachers College Record,* 63: 380–92.

GUILFORD, JOY P., and LACEY, J. I. (1947). *Printed Classification Tests.* Washington, D.C.: Government Printing Office.

GUTHRIE, EDWIN R. (1952). *The Psychology of Learning.* New York: Harper & Row, Publishers.

GUTTMAN, NORMAN, and KALISH, HARRY I. (1963). "A Generalization Gradient Obtained from Pigeons," in *Principles of Psychology.* 2nd ed. Eds. G. A. Kimble and N. Garmezy, p. 145. New York: The Ronald Press Company.

HAMP, ERIC P. (1967). "Language in a Few Words: With Notes on a Rereading, 1966," in *Language, Thought, and Instruction,* ed. J. P. De Cecco, pp. 5–23. New York: Holt, Rinehart & Winston, Inc.

HARLOW, HARRY F. (1949). "The Formation of Learning Sets." *The Psychological Review,* 56: 51–65.

HARLOW, HARRY F.; HARLOW, MARGARET K.; and MEYER, DONALD R. (1950). "Learning Motivated by a Manipulation Drive." *Journal of Experimental Psychology,* 40: 228–34.

HARRISON, MAURICE (1964). *Instant Reading. The Story of the Initial Teaching Alphabet.* London: Sir Isaac Pitman & Sons, Ltd.

HAWKER, JAMES R. (1964). "The Influence of Training Procedure and Other Task Variables in Paired-Associate Learning." *Journal of Verbal Learning and Verbal Behavior,* 3: 70–76.

HEBB, DONALD O. (1949). *Organization of Behavior.* New York: John Wiley & Sons, Inc.

———— (1955). "Drives and C.N.S. (Conceptual Nervous System)." *Psychological Review,* 62: 243–54.

———— (1966). *A Textbook of Psychology.* Philadelphia: W. B. Saunders Co.

HEENAN, DAVID K. (1961). "Evaluation in the Humanities," in *Evaluation in Higher Education,* eds. Paul L. Dressel *et al.,* pp. 157–91. Boston: Houghton Mifflin Company.

HEMPEL, WALTER E., JR., and FLEISHMAN, EDWIN A. (1955). "A Factor Analysis of

Physical Proficiency and Manipulative Skill." *Journal of Applied Psychology,* 39: 12–16.

HERBART, JOHANN F. (1883). *The Science of Education.* Translated by H. M. Felkin and Emmie Felkin. Boston: D. C. Heath & Company.

HILGARD, ERNEST R. (1964). "A Perspective on the Relationship Between Learning Theory and Educational Practices," in *Theories of Learning and Instruction,* ed. E. R. Hilgard, Part 1 of the 63rd Yrbk. of the National Society for the Study of Education, pp. 402–15. Chicago: University of Chicago Press.

HILGARD, ERNEST, R., and BOWER, GORDON H. (1966). *Theories of Learning.* 3rd ed. New York: Appleton-Century-Crofts.

HILGARD, ERNEST R.; IRVINE, R. P.; and WHIPPLE, J. E. (1953). "Rote Memorization, Understanding and Transfer: An Extension of Katona's Card-Trick Experiments." *Journal of Experimental Psychology,* 46: 288–92.

HILL, WINFRED F. (1963). *Learning: A Survey of Psychological Interpretations.* San Francisco: Chandler Publishing Co.

HOBAN, C. F., and VANORMER, E. B. (1950). "Instructional Film Research, 1918–1950." *Technical Report No. SDC 269-7-19.* Port Washington, N.Y.: U.S. Naval Training Devices Center.

HOLLAND, JAMES G. (1960). "Design and Use of a Teaching-Machine Program." Paper read at the American Psychological Association Convention, Chicago.

——— (1964). "J. O. Cook's Tour de Farce." *American Psychologist,* 19: 683–84.

——— (1965a). "Research on Programming Variables," in *Teaching Machines and Programmed Learning II: Data and Directions,* ed. R. Glaser, pp. 66–117. Washington, D.C.: National Education Association.

——— (1965b). "Response Contingencies in Teaching Machine Programs." *The Journal of Programmed Instruction,* 3: 1–8.

HOLLAND, JAMES G., and SKINNER, B. F. (1961). *The Analysis of Behavior.* New York: McGraw-Hill Book Company.

HORN, ROBERT E. (1963). "The Rhetoric of Programming." *Programed Instruction,* 2, No. 6, 4–5.

HOVLAND, CARL I. (1938). "Experimental Studies in Rote-Learning Theory: II. Reminiscence with Varying Speeds of Syllable Presentation." *Journal of Experimental Psychology,* 27: 271–84.

HOVLAND, CARL I., and WEISS, WALTER (1953). "Transmission Information Concerning Concepts Through Positive and Negative Instances." *Journal of Experimental Psychology,* 45: 175–82.

HUGHES, JOHN L. (1962). "Effect of Changes in Programed Text Format and Reduction in Classroom Time on the Achievement and Attitude of Industrial Trainees." *Journal of Programed Instruction,* 1: 43–54.

HULL, CLARK L. (1952). *A Behavior System: An Introduction to Behavior Theory Concerning the Individual Organism.* New Haven, Conn.: Yale University Press.

HUNSICKER, PAUL (1963). *What Research Says to the Teacher: Physical Fitness.* Washington, D.C.: American Educational Research Association, National Education Association.

HUNT, EARL B. (1962). *Concept Learning: An Information Processing Problem.* New York: John Wiley & Sons, Inc.

HUNT, J. McVICKER (1964). "The Psychological Basis for Using Pre-School Enrichment as an Antidote for Cultural Deprivation." *Merrill-Palmer Quarterly,* 10: 209–48.

HURLOCK, ELIZABETH B. (1924). "The Value of Praise and Reproof as Incentives for Children," in *Arch. Psychology,* 11, No. 71.

580 ——— (1925). "An Evaluation of Incentives Used in School Work." *Journal of Educational Psychology,* 16: 145–59.

HUSÉN, TORSTEN, ed. (1967). *International Study of Achievement in Mathematics: A Comparison of Twelve Countries.* New York: John Wiley & Sons, Inc. In two volumes.

HUTTENLOCHER, JANELLEN (1962). "Some Effects of Negative Instances on the Formation of Simple Concepts." *Psychological Reports,* 11: 35–42.

HYMES, DELL H. (1967). "Linguistic Aspects of Cross-Cultural Personality Study," in *Studying Personality Cross-Culturally,* ed. B. Kaplan. New York: Harper & Row, Publishers, pp. 337–44.

INHELDER, BÄRBEL, and PIAGET, JEAN (1958). *The Growth of Logical Thinking from Childhood to Adolescence.* New York: Basic Books, Inc.

——— (1969). *The Early Growth of Logic in the Child: Classification and Seriation.* New York: The Norton Library, Humanities Press, Inc.

INSEL, SHEPARD A.; SCHLESINGER, KURT; and DESROSIERS, WINIFRED (1963). "Dependency Responses to Televised Instruction." *Journal of Applied Psychology,* 47: 328–31.

IRION, ARTHUR L. (1966). "A Brief History of Research on the Acquisition of Skill," in *Acquisition of Skill,* ed. E. A. Bidoleau, pp. 1–46. New York: Academic Press Inc.

ITARD, J. M. G. (1932). *The Wild Boy of Aveyron.* Translated by G. Humphrey and M. Humphrey. New York: Appleton-Century-Crofts.

JACOBS, PAUL I.; MAIER, MILTON H.; and STOLUROW, LAWRENCE M. (1966). *A Guide to Evaluating Self-Instructional Programs.* New York: Holt, Rinehart & Winston, Inc.

JAMES, WILLIAM (1892). *Talks to Teachers on Psychology and to Students on Some of Life's Ideals.* New York: W. W. Norton & Company, Inc., 1958.

JENKINS, J. G., and DALLENBACK, KARL M. (1924). "Oblivescence During Sleep and Waking." *American Journal of Psychology,* 35: 605–12.

JENSEN, ARTHUR R. (1960). "Programmed Instruction and Individual Differences." *Automated Teaching Bulletin,* 1: 12–17.

——— (1962a). "Spelling Errors and Serial-Position Effect." *Journal of Educational Psychology,* 53: 105–9.

——— (1962b). "Transfer Between Paired-Associate and Serial Learning." *Journal of Verbal Learning and Verbal Behavior,* 1: 269–80.

——— (1963). "Learning Ability in Retarded, Average, and Gifted Children." *Merrill-Palmer Quarterly,* 9: 124–40.

——— (1965). "Individual Differences in Learning: Interference Factor." *U.S. Office of Education Cooperative Research Project No. 1867.* Berkeley, Calif.: University of California.

——— (1966a). "Individual Differences in Concept Learning," in *Analyses of Concept Learning,* eds. H. J. Klausmeier and W. Harris, pp. 139–54. New York: Academic Press Inc.

——— (1966b). "Verbal Mediation and Educational Potential." *Psychology in the Schools,* 3: 99–109.

——— (1968). "Social Class and Verbal Learning," in *Social Class, Race, and Psychological Development,* eds. M. Deutsch, A. R. Jensen, and Irwin Katz. New York: Holt, Rinehart & Winston, Inc.

JOHN, VERA P., and GOLDSTEIN, LEO S. (1964). "The Social Context of Language Acquisition." *Merrill-Palmer Quarterly,* 10: 265–75.

JOHNSON, DONALD M., and O'REILLY, CHARLENE A. (1964). "Concept Attainment in

Children: Classifying and Defining." *Journal of Educational Psychology*, 55: 71–74.

JOHNSON, DONALD M., and STRATTON, R. PAUL (1966). "Evaluation of Five Methods of Teaching Concepts." *Journal of Educational Psychology*, 57: 48–53.

JOHNSTON, RAYMOND; DAVIS, ROBERT; FIEL, NICHOLAS; and HARTSELL, HORACE (1966). *Preparatory Laboratory for Physiology 501*. Laboratory 3, East Lansing, Mich.: Michigan State University.

JOKL, ERNEST (1966). "The Acquisition of Skills." *Quest*, Monograph VI, pp. 11–28.

JONES, JOHN GERALD (1965). "Motor Learning Without Demonstration under Two Conditions of Mental Practice." *Research Quarterly*, 36: 270–81.

JUDSON, ABE; COFER, CHARLES; and GELFAND, SIDNEY (1956). "Reasoning as an Associative Process: II. Direction in Problem Solving as a Function of Prior Reinforcement." *Psychological Reports*, 2: 501–7.

KAGAN, JEROME (1965). "Impulsive and Reflective Children: Significance of Conceptual Tempo," in *Learning and the Educational Process*, ed. J. D. Krumboltz, pp. 133–61. Chicago: Rand McNally & Co.

KAGAN, JEROME; PEARSON, LESLIE; and WELCH, LOIS (1966). "Modifiability of an Impulsive Tempo." *Journal of Educational Psychology*, 359–65.

KAGAN, JEROME; ROSMAN, BERNICE L.; DAY, DEBORAH; ALBERT, J.; and PHILLIPS, W. (1964). "Information Processing in the Child: Significance of Analytic and Reflective Attitudes." *Psychological Monographs*, 78, No. 1 (Whole No. 578).

KATES, SOLIS L., and YUDIN, LEE (1964). "Concept Attainment and Memory." *Journal of Educational Psychology*, 55: 103–9.

KATONA, GEORGE (1940). *Organizing and Memorizing: Studies in the Psychology of Learning and Teaching*. New York: Columbia University Press.

KAUSLER, DONALD H., ed. (1966). *Readings in Verbal Learning*. New York: John Wiley & Sons, Inc.

KEARNEY, NOLAN C., ed. (1953). *Elementary School Objectives*. New York: Russell Sage Foundation.

KELLER, FRED S. (1954). *Learning: Reinforcement Theory*. New York: Random House.

KELLEY, TRUMAN L.; MADDEN, RICHARD; GARDNER, ERIC F.; and RUDMAN, HERBERT C. (1964). *Stanford Achievement Test Directions for Administering. Intermediate I Battery*. New York: Harcourt, Brace & World, Inc.

KENDLER, HOWARD H. (1964). "The Concept of the Concept," in *Categories of Human Learning*, ed. A. W. Melton, pp. 211–36. New York: Academic Press Inc.

KENDLER, HOWARD H., and VINEBERG, ROBERT (1954). "The Acquisition of Compound Concepts as a Function of Previous Training." *Journal of Experimental Psychology*, 48: 252–58.

KENDLER, TRACY S., and KENDLER, HOWARD H. (1959). "Reversal and Nonreversal Shifts in Kindergarten Children." *Journal of Experimental Psychology*, 58: 56–60.

——— (1961). "Inferential Behavior in Children: II. The Influence of Order of Presentation." *Journal of Experimental Psychology*, 61: 442–48.

KENDLER, TRACY S.; KENDLER, HOWARD H.; and LEARNARD, B. (1962). "Mediated Responses to Size and Brightness as a Function of Age." *American Journal of Psychology*, 75: 571–86.

KENDLER, TRACY S.; KENDLER, HOWARD H.; and WELLS, D. (1960). "Reversal and Nonreversal Shifts in Nursery School Children." *Journal of Comparative and Physiological Psychology*, 53: 80–87.

KENNEDY, WALLACE A., and WILLCUTT, HERMAN C. (1964). "Praise and Blame as Incentives." *Psychological Bulletin*, 62: 323–53.

KEPPEL, FRANCIS (1967). "The Business Interest in Education." *Phi Delta Kappan,* 48: 186–90.

KEPPEL, GEOFFREY, and POSTMAN, LEO (1966). "Studies of Learning to Learn: III. Conditions of Improvement in Successive Transfer Tasks." *Journal of Verbal Learning and Verbal Behavior,* 5: 260–67.

KERLINGER, FRED N. (1964). *Foundations of Behavioral Research.* New York: Holt, Rinehart & Winston, Inc.

KERSH, BERT Y. (1963). "The Motivating Effect of Learning by Discovery." *Journal of Educational Psychology,* 53: 65–71.

———— (1964). *Directed Discovery Versus Programmed Instruction: A Test of a Theoretical Position Involving Educational Technology.* Monmouth, Oregon: Oregon State System of Higher Education.

———— (1965). "Programming Classroom Instruction," in *Teaching Machines and Programmed Learning. II: Data and Directions,* ed. R. Glaser, pp. 321–68. Washington, D.C.: Department of Audiovisual Instruction, National Education Association.

KERSH, BERT Y., and WITTROCK, MERLIN C. (1962). "Learning by Discovery: An Interpretation of Recent Research." *Journal of Teacher Education,* 13: 461–68.

KIENTZLE, MARY J. (1946). "Properties of Learning Curves Under Varied Distribution of Practice." *Journal of Experimental Psychology,* 36: 187–211.

KIMBLE, GREGORY A. (1964). "Categories of Learning and the Problem of Definition," in *Categories of Human Learning,* ed. Arthur W. Melton, pp. 32–45. New York: Academic Press Inc.

KIMBLE, GREGORY A., and BILODEAU, EDWARD A. (1949). "Work and Rest as Variables in Cyclical Motor Learning." *Journal of Experimental Psychology,* 39: 150–57.

KIMBLE, GREGORY A., and GARMEZY, NORMAN (1963). *Principles of General Psychology.* 2nd ed. New York: The Ronald Press Company.

KING, F. J.; KROPP, R. P.; CRAWFORD, W. R.; and MOYEL, I. S. (1961). "Changes in Delinquency-Proneness Scores Associated with Paced-Projected and Normal Modes of Test Administration." *Psychological Reports,* 9: 55–58.

KLAUS, DAVID J. (1961). "The Art of Auto-Instructional Programming." *Audiovisual Communication Review,* 9: 130–42.

KLAUSMEIER, HERBERT J., and GOODWIN, WILLIAM (1966). *Learning and Human Abilities: Educational Psychology.* 2nd ed. New York: Harper & Row, Publishers.

KNAPP, CLYDE G., and DIXON, W. ROBERT (1952). "Learning to Juggle: II. A Study of Whole and Part Methods." *Research Quarterly,* 23: 398–401.

KOHLER, W. (1925). *The Mentality of Apes.* New York: Harcourt Brace.

KORONAKOS, CHRIS, and ARNOLD, J. WILLIAM (1957). "The Formation of Learning Sets in Rats." *Journal of Comparative and Physiological Psychology,* 50: 11–14.

KOUNIN, JACOB S., and GUMP, PAUL V. (1958). "The Ripple Effect in Discipline." *Elementary School Journal,* 59: 158–62.

KOUNIN, JACOB S., and RYAN, JAMES (1961). "Explorations in Classroom Management." *Journal of Teacher Education,* 12: 235–46.

KRATHWOHL, DAVID R. *et al.,* eds. (1964). *Taxonomy of Educational Objectives: Handbook II: Affective Domain.* New York: David McKay Co., Inc.

KRECH, DAVID; ROSENZWEIG, MARK R.; and BENNETT, EDWARD L. (1962). "Relations Between Brain Chemistry and Problem Solving Among Rats Raised in Enriched and Impoverished Environments." *Journal of Comparative and Physiological Psychology,* 55: 801–7.

KREUGER, W. C. F. (1929). "The Effect of Over-Learning on Retention." *Journal of Experimental Psychology,* 12: 71–78.

KRUMBOLTZ, JOHN D., and KIESLER, CHARLES A. (1965). "The Partial Reinforcement Paradigm and Programed Instruction." *Journal of Programed Instruction,* 3: 9–14.

KRUMBOLTZ, JOHN D., and WEISMAN, RONALD G. (1962). "The Effect of Intermittent Confirmation in Programmed Instruction." *Journal of Educational Psychology,* 53: 250–53.

KUDER, FREDERIC G. (1953). *Kuder Preference Record. Examiner Manual for Vocational Form—C.* Chicago: Science Research Associates, Inc.

LABOV, WILLIAM. (1970). *The Logic of Non-Standard English.* Georgetown University Monograph Series on Language and Linguistics, Monograph No. 22. Washington, D.C.: Georgetown University Press.

LAVIN, DAVID E. (1965). *The Prediction of Academic Performance.* New York: Russell Sage Foundation.

LAWSON, REED (1965). *Frustration: The Development of a Scientific Concept.* New York: The Macmillan Company.

LAWTHER, JOHN D. (1966). "Directing Motor Skill Learning." *Quest,* Monograph VI, pp. 68–76.

LAZARUS, RICHARD S. (1963). *Personality and Adjustment.* Englewood Cliffs, N.J.: Prentice-Hall, Inc.

LINDAHL, LAWRENCE G. (1945). "Movement Analysis as an Industrial Training Method." *Journal of Applied Psychology,* 29: 420–36.

LINDEMAN, RICHARD (1967). *Educational Measurement.* Chicago: Scott, Foresman & Company.

LIPSIT, LEWIS (1961). "Simultaneous and Successive Discrimination Learning in Children." *Child Development,* 32: 337–47.

LOCKHART, AILEENE (1966). "Communicating with the Learner." *Quest,* Monograph VI, pp. 57–67.

LORENZ, K. (1937). "The Companion in the Bird's World," in *Auk,* 54: 245–73.

LORGE, IRVING (1930). *Influence of Regularly Interpolated Time Intervals upon Subsequent Learning,* Teachers College Contributions to Education, No. 438. New York: Teachers College Press, Columbia University.

LORGE, IRVING, and THORNDIKE, EDWARD L. (1935). "The Influence of Delay in the After-Effect of a Connection." *Journal of Experimental Psychology,* 18: 186–94.

LOVELL, K. (1959). "A Follow-Up Study of Some Aspects of the Work of Piaget and Inhelder on the Child's Conception of Space." *British Journal of Educational Psychology,* 29: 104–17.

LUH, C. (1922). "The Conditions of Retention." *Psychological Monographs,* 31, No. 142.

LUMSDAINE, ARTHUR A. (1964). "Educational Technology, Programed Learning, and Instructional Science," in *Theories of Learning and Instruction,* ed. E. R. Hilgard, Part 1 of the 63rd Yrbk. of the National Society for the Study of Education, pp. 371–401. Chicago: University of Chicago Press.

LYMAN, HOWARD (1963). *Test Scores and What They Mean.* Englewood Cliffs, N.J.: Prentice-Hall, Inc.

LYSAUGHT, JEROME P., and WILLIAMS, CLARENCE M. (1963). *A Guide to Programmed Instruction.* New York: John Wiley & Sons, Inc.

MCCLELLAND, DAVID O., ed. (1955). *Studies in Motivation.* New York: Appleton-Century-Crofts.

584   McCLELLAND, DAVID O.; ATKINSON, JOHN W.; CLARK, RUSSELL A.; and LOWELL, EDGAR L. (1953). *The Achievement Motive.* New York: Appleton-Century-Crofts.

MACCOBY, NATHAN, and SHEFFIELD, FRED D. (1961). "Combining Practice with Demonstration in Teaching Complex Sequences: Summary and Interpretation," in *Student Response in Programmed Instruction,* ed. A. R. Lumsdaine, pp. 77–85. Washington, D.C.: National Academy of Sciences—National Research Council.

McDONALD, FREDERICK J. (1965). *Educational Psychology.* 2nd ed. Belmont, Calif.: Wadsworth Publishing Co., Inc.

McDONALD, JAMES B. (1966). "Moral Concerns in Assessing Pupil Growth." *The National Elementary School Principal,* 45: 29–33.

MACE, LAWRENCE L. (1966). "Sequence of Vocal Response-Differentiation Training and Auditory Stimulus-Discrimination Training in Beginning French." *Journal of Educational Psychology,* 57: 102–8.

MACE, LAWRENCE L., and KEISLAR, EVAN R. (1965). "Reversibility of Stimulus and Response Terms Following Discrimination Learning of French Phonemes." *Journal of Educational Psychology,* 56: 46–49.

McGEOCH, JOHN A. (1942). *The Psychology of Human Learning.* New York: David McKay Co., Inc.

McGRAW, MYRTLE B. (1940). "Neural Maturation As Exemplified in Achievement of Bladder Control." *Journal of Pediatrics,* 16: 580–90.

McGUIGAN, F. J., and MacCASLIN, EUGENE F. (1955). "Whole and Part Methods in Learning a Perceptual Motor Skill." *American Journal of Psychology,* 68: 658–61.

McLAUGHLIN, BARRY (1965). "Intention and Incidental Learning in Human Subjects: The Role of Instructions to Learn and Motivation." *Psychological Bulletin,* 63: 359–76.

MacLENNAN, DONALD W., and REID, J. CHRISTOPHER, eds. (1964). *Abstracts of Research on Instructional Television and Film: An Annotated Bibliography.* Stanford, Calif.: Institute for Communication Research, Stanford University.

McNEIL, JOHN D. (1964). "Programed Instruction Versus Usual Classroom Procedures in Teaching Boys to Read." *American Educational Research Journal,* 1: 113–19.

McNEILL, DAVID (1970). "The Development of Language," in *Carmichael's Manual of Child Psychology,* ed. P. H. Mussen, vol. I, pp. 1061–1161. New York: John Wiley & Sons, Inc.

McNEMAR, QUINN (1964). "Lost: Our Intelligence? Why?" *The American Psychologist,* 19: 874–79.

MACOMBER, GLENN F., and SIGEL, LAURENCE (1960). *Final Report of the Experimental Study in Instructional Procedures.* Oxford, Ohio: Miami University.

McPHEE, JOHN (1965). *The New Yorker* (January 23), p. 42.

McV. HUNT, ed. (1964). *The Montessori Method.* New York: Schocken Books.

MAGER, ROBERT F. (1962). *Preparing Objectives for Programmed Instruction.* Palo Alto, Calif.: Fearon Publishers, Inc.

MAGER, ROBERT F., and McCANN, J. (1961). *Learner-Controlled Instruction.* Palo Alto, Calif.: Varian Associates.

MAIER, NORMAN R. F. (1930). "Reasoning in Humans. I. On Direction." *Journal of Comparative Psychology,* 10: 115–43.

MALTZMAN, IRVING (1955). "Thinking: From a Behaviorist Point of View." *Psychological Review,* 62: 275–86.

MALTZMAN, IRVING; BOGARTZ, W.; and BREGER, L. (1958). "A Procedure for Increasing Word Association Originality and Its Transfer Effects." *Journal of Experimental Psychology,* 56: 392–98.

MALTZMAN, IRVING; BROOKS, L. O.; and SUMMERS, S. S. (1958). "The Facilitation of Problem Solving by the Prior Exposure to Uncommon Responses." *Journal of Experimental Psychology,* 56: 399–406.

MALTZMAN, IRVING; SIMON, SEYMORE; RASKIN, DAVID; and LICHT, LENARD (1960). "Experimental Studies in the Training of Originality." *Psychological Monographs,* No. 493, pp. 1–23.

MANDLER, GEORGE (1967). "Verbal Learning," in *New Directions in Psychology,* Vol. III, pp. 1–50. New York: Holt, Rinehart & Winston, Inc.

MARGULIES, STUART (1964). "Some General Rules of Frame Construction." *Programed Instruction,* 4, No. 1, 6–8.

MARKLE, SUSAN MEYER (1961). *A Programed Primer on Programing,* Vols. 1 and 2. New York: Center for Programed Instruction.

——— (1964). *Good Frames and Bad: A Grammar of Frame Writing.* New York: John Wiley & Sons, Inc.

MARKS, MELVIN R., and RAMOND, CHARLES K. (1951). "A New Technique for Observing Concept Evocation." *Journal of Experimental Psychology,* 42: 424–29.

MARQUART, DOROTHY I. (1955). "Group Problem Solving." *Journal of Social Psychology,* 41: 103–13.

MARTIN, BARCLAY (1963). "Reward and Punishment Associated with the Same Goal Response: A Factor in the Learning of Motives." *Psychological Bulletin,* 60: 441–51.

MARTIN, WILLIAM E., and STENDLER, CELIA B. (1959). *Child Behavior and Development.* New York: Harcourt, Brace & World, Inc.

MASLOW, ALBERT H. (1954). *Motivation and Personality.* New York: Harper & Row, Publishers.

MASSERMAN, JULES M. (1943). *Behavior and Neurosis.* Chicago: University of Chicago Press.

MAUCH, JAMES (1962). "A Systems Analysis Approach to Education." *Phi Delta Kappan,* 43: 158–62.

MAY, MARK A. (1946). "The Psychology of Learning from Demonstration Films." *Journal of Educational Psychology,* 37: 1–12.

MEALS, DONALD W. (1967). "Heuristic Models for Systems Planning." *Phi Delta Kappan,* 48: 199–203.

MECHNER, FRANCIS (1961). *Programming for Automated Instruction,* Vol. 3. New York: Basic Systems, Inc.

——— (1965). "Science Education and Behavioral Technology," in *Teaching Machines and Programed Learning. II: Data and Directions,* pp. 441–507. Washington, D.C.: National Education Association.

MEHLER, JACQUES (1963). "Some Effects of Grammatical Transformations on the Recall of English Sentences." *Journal of Verbal Learning and Verbal Behavior,* 2: 346–51.

MELTON, ARTHUR W. (1959). "The Science of Learning and the Technology of Educational Methods." *Harvard Educational Review,* 29: 96–106.

MERRILL, MAUD A. (1938). "The Significance of IQ's on the Revised Stanford-Binet Scales." *Journal of Educational Psychology,* 19: 641–51.

MILLER, GEORGE A. (1956). "The Magical Number Seven, Plus or Minus Two: Some Limits on Our Capacity for Processing Information." *Psychological Review,* 53: 81–97.

———— (1962). "Some Psychological Studies of Grammar." *American Psychologist,* 17: 748–62.

———— (1965). "Some Preliminaries to Psycholinguistics." *American Psychologist,* 20: 15–20.

MILLER, GEORGE A.; GALANTER, EUGENE; and PRIBRAM, KARL H. (1960). *Plans and the Structure of Behavior.* New York: Holt, Rinehart & Winston, Inc.

MILLER, N. E. (1935). "The Influence of Past Experience upon the Transfer of Subsequent Training." Doctoral dissertation, Yale University.

MILLER, ROBERT B. (1962a). "Task Description and Analysis," in *Psychological Principles in System Development,* ed. R. M. Gagné, pp. 187–230. New York: Holt, Rinehart & Winston, Inc.

MONTESSORI, MARIA (1964). *The Montessori Method.* New York: Schocken Books, Inc.

MONTGOMERY, K. C. (1954). "The Role of Exploratory Drive in Learning." *Journal of Comparative and Physiological Psychology,* 47: 60–64.

MURRAY, EDWARD J. (1964). *Motivation and Emotion.* Englewood Cliffs, N.J.: Prentice-Hall, Inc.

NAYLOR, JAMES C. (1962). "Parameters Affecting the Efficiency of Part and Whole Training Methods: A Review of the Literature," in *NAVTRADEVCEN Technical Report,* N. 950-1. Port Washington, N.Y.: United States Training Devices Center.

NEDELSKY, LEO (1954). "Absolute Grading Standards for Objective Tests." *Educational and Psychological Measurement,* 14: 3–19.

NELSON, CLARENCE H. (1961). "Evaluation in the Natural Sciences," in *Evaluation in Higher Education,* eds. Paul L. Dressel *et al.,* pp. 113–56. Boston: Houghton Mifflin Company.

NELSON, DALE O. (1957). "Effects of Slow Motion Loop Films on the Learning of Golf." *Research Quarterly,* 27: 364–73.

NISSEN, H. W. (1953). "Instinct As Seen by a Psychologist." *Psychological Review,* 60: 291–94.

NOBLE, CLYDE E. (1952). "An Analysis of Meaning." *Psychological Review,* 59: 421–30.

NOLL, VICTOR H. (1965). *Introduction to Educational Measurement.* 2nd ed. Boston: Houghton Mifflin Company.

OLSON, LEROY A. (1963). "Concept Attainment of High School Sophomores." *Journal of Educational Psychology,* 54: 213–16.

OSBORNE, ALEX (1957). *Applied Imagination.* New York: Charles Scribner's Sons.

OSSER, HARRY (1971). "Language Development," in *Psychology and the Educational Process,* ed. G. S. Lesser. Chicago: Scott, Foresman & Co.

OZOLIN, N. G. (1958). "Motor Concepts in Teaching Sports Technique." *Theory and Practice of Physical Culture,* 21: 6. Translated from the Russian by Michael Yessis.

PACKARD, VANCE (1957). *The Hidden Persuaders.* New York: David McKay Co., Inc.

PAGE, ELLIS B. (1958). "Teacher Comments and Student Performance." *Journal of Educational Psychology,* 49: 173–81.

PARNES, SIDNEY J. (1961). "Effects of Extended Effort in Creative Problem Solving." *Journal of Educational Psychology,* 52: 148–52.

PARNES, SIDNEY J., and HARING, HAROLD F., eds. (1962). *Source Book for Creative Thinking.* New York: Charles Scribner's Sons.

PARNES, SIDNEY J., and MEADOW, ARNOLD (1959). "Effects of Brainstorming Instructions on Creative Problem-Solving by Trained and Untrained Subjects." *Journal of Educational Psychology,* 50: 171–76.

——— (1960). "Evaluation of Persistence of Effects Produced by a Creative Problem-Solving Course." *Journal of Educational Psychology,* 7: 357–61.

PARRY, SCOTT B. (1963). "Faulty Frames: Some Problems of Internal and External Evaluation of Programmes." *Programed Instruction,* 3, No. 2, 4–5, 7.

PAVLOV, I. P. (1927). *Conditioned Reflexes: An Investigation of the Physiological Activity of the Cerebral Cortex.* Translated and edited by G. V. Anrep. London: Oxford University Press, 1927.

PEEL, E. A. (1959). "Experimental Examination of Some of Piaget's Schemata Concerning Children's Perception and Thinking, and a Discussion of Their Educational Significance." *British Journal of Educational Psychology,* 29: 89–103.

PIAGET, JEAN (1932). *The Moral Judgment of the Child.* London: Routledge & Kegan Paul, Ltd.

——— (1952). *The Origins of Intelligence in Children.* New York: International Universities Press, Inc.

——— (1962). *Play, Dreams, and Imitation in Childhood.* New York: W. W. Norton & Co.

——— (1968). *On the Development of Memory and Identity.* Worcester, Mass.: Clark University Press.

——— (1970). "Piaget's Theory," in *Carmichael's Manual of Child Psychology,* ed. P. H. Mussen, Part I, pp. 703–32. New York: John Wiley & Sons.

——— (1970). *Psychology and Epistemology.* New York: The Viking Press.

PIAGET, JEAN, and INHELDER, BARBEL (1969). *The Psychology of the Child.* New York: Basic Books.

PIPE, PETER (1966). *Practical Programming.* New York: Holt, Rinehart & Winston, Inc.

POPHAM, W. JAMES (1967). *Educational Statistics: Use and Interpretation.* New York: Harper & Row, Publishers.

POSTMAN, LEO (1947). "The History and Present Status of the Law of Effect." *Psychological Bulletin,* 44: 489–563.

——— (1964). "Short-Term Memory and Incidental Learning," in *Categories of Human Learning,* ed. Arthur W. Melton, pp. 146–201. New York: Academic Press Inc.

POSTMAN, LEO, and SENDERS, VIRGINIA L. (1946). "Incidental Learning and Generality of Set." *Journal of Experimental Psychology,* 36: 153–65.

PRESSEY, SIDNEY L. (1963). "Teaching Machine and Learning Theory Crisis." *Journal of Applied Psychology,* 47: 1–6.

——— (1964). "Autoinstruction: Perspectives, Problems, Potentials," in *Theories of Learning and Instruction,* ed. E. R. Hilgard, Part 1 of the 63rd Yrbk. of the National Society for the Study of Education, pp. 354–70. Chicago: University of Chicago Press.

PRIEBE, ROY E., and BURTON, WILLIAM H. (1939). "The Slow Motion Picture as a Coaching Device." *School Review,* 47: 192–98.

PULASKI, MARY ANN SPENCER (1971). *Understanding Piaget: An Introduction to Children's Cognitive Development.* New York: Harper & Row, Publishers.

RAGSDALE, C. E. (1950). "How Children Learn the Motor Type of Activity," in *Learning and Instruction,* Part 1 of the 49th Yrbk. of the National Society for the Study of Education, pp. 69–91. Chicago: University of Chicago Press.

RAMSAY, OGDEN, and HESS, ECKHARD H. (1954). "A Laboratory Approach to the Study of Imprinting." *Wilson Bulletin,* 66: 196–206.

RHINE, R. J., and SILUN, B. A. (1958). "Acquisition and Change of a Concept Attitude as a Function of Consistency of Reinforcement." *Journal of Experimental Psychology,* 55: 524–29.

RIESSMAN, FRANK (1962). *The Culturally Deprived Child.* New York: Harper & Row, Publishers, Inc.

ROBB, MARGARET (1966). "Feedback." *Quest,* Monograph VI, pp. 38–43.

ROTHKOPF, ERNEST Z. (1966). "The Instructional Process." Paper presented at a symposium entitled Research Approaches to the Learning of School Subjects. Berkeley, Calif., 1966.

ROZEBOOM, WILLIAM W. (1960). "The Fallacy of the Null-Hypothesis Significance Test." *Psychological Bulletin,* 57: 416–28.

RUFFA, EDWARD J. (1936). "An Experimental Study of Motion Pictures as Used in the Teaching of Certain Athletic Skills." Master's thesis, Stanford University.

RUMMEL, FRANCIS J. (1964). *An Introduction to Research Procedures in Education.* New York: Harper & Row, Publishers.

RUSSELL, WALLACE A., and STORMS, LOWELL H. (1955). "Implicit Verbal Chaining in Paired-Associate Learning." *Journal of Experimental Psychology,* 49: 287–93.

SARASON, SEYMOUR B., and MANDLER, GEORGE (1952). "Some Correlates of Test Anxiety." *Journal of Abnormal and Social Psychology,* 47: 810–17.

SAUGSTAD, PER (1957). "An Analysis of Maier's Pendulum Problem." *Journal of Experimental Psychology,* 54: 168–79.

SAX, G. (1960). "Concept Acquisition as a Function of Differing Schedules and Delays of Reinforcement." *Journal of Educational Psychology,* 51: 32–36.

SAX, G., and CROMACK, THEODORE R. (1966). "The Effects of Various Forms of Item Arrangements on Test Performance." *Journal of Educational Measurement,* 3: 309–11.

SCHERER, GEORGE A. C., and WERTHEIMER, MICHAEL (1964). *A Psycholinguistic Experiment in Foreign Language Teaching.* New York: McGraw-Hill Book Company.

SCHILLER, BELLE (1934). "Verbal, Numerical, and Spatial Abilities in Young Children." *Archives of Psychology,* No. 161.

SCHULZ, RUDOLPH W. (1960). "Problem Solving Behavior and Transfer." *Harvard Educational Review,* 30: 61–77.

SCHUTZ, ROBERT E.; BAKER, ROBERT L.; and GERLACH, VERNON S. (1962). "Teaching Capitalization with a Programmed Text." *AV Communication Review,* 10: 359–62.

Science Research Associates (SRA, 1962). *ITED: The Iowa Tests of Educational Development. Examiner's Manual.* Chicago: Science Research Associates, Inc.

——— (1963). *ITED: The Iowa Tests of Educational Development. How to Use the Test Results: A Manual for Teachers and Counselors.* Chicago: Science Research Associates, Inc.

SEARS, PAULINE S. (1940). "Levels of Aspiration in Academically Successful and Unsuccessful Children." *Journal of Abnormal and Social Psychology,* 35: 498–536.

SEARS, PAULINE S., and HILGARD, ERNEST R. (1964). "The Teacher's Role in the Motivation of the Learner," in *Theories of Learning and Instruction,* ed. E. R. Hilgard, Part 1 of the 63rd Yrbk. of the National Society for the Study of Education, pp. 182–209. Chicago: University of Chicago Press.

SECHREST, LEE, and KAAS, JUDITH SCHMERLING (1965). "Concept Difficulty as a Function of Stimulus Similarity." *Journal of Educational Psychology,* 56: 327–33.

SECHREST, LEE, and WALLACE, JOHN (1962). "Assimilation and Utilization of Information in Concept Attainment Under Varying Conditions of Information Presentation." *Journal of Educational Psychology,* 53: 157–64.

SIEGEL, S. (1956). *Nonparametric Statistics for the Behavioral Sciences.* New York: McGraw-Hill Book Company.

SILBERMAN, HARRY R.; MELARAGNO, RALPH J.; COULSON, JOHN E.; and ESTAVAN, DONALD (1961). "Fixed Sequence Versus Branching Autoinstructional Methods." *Journal of Educational Psychology,* 52: 166–72.

SKINNER, B. F. (1938). *Behavior of Organisms.* New York: Appleton-Century-Crofts.

—— (1948). *Walden Two.* New York: The Macmillan Company.

—— (1953). *Science and Human Behavior.* New York: The Macmillan Company.

—— (1957). *Verbal Behavior.* New York: Appleton-Century-Crofts.

—— (1958). "Teaching Machines." *Science,* 128: 969–77.

—— (1961). "Why We Need Teaching Machines." *Harvard Educational Review,* 31: 377–98.

—— (1971). *Beyond Freedom and Dignity.* New York: Alfred A. Knopf.

SMEDSLUND, JAN (1961a). "The Acquisition of Conservation of Substance and Weight in Children. I. Introduction." *Scandanavian Journal of Psychology,* 2: 11–20.

—— (1961b). "The Acquisition of Conservation of Substance and Weight in Children. II. External Reinforcement of Conservation of Weight and of the Operations of Addition and Subtraction." *Scandanavian Journal of Psychology,* 2: 71–84.

SMITH, B. Othanel (1960). "A Concept of Teaching." *Teachers College Record,* 61: 229–41.

SMODE, A., and FITTS, PAUL (1957). Unpublished study made at Ohio State University on physical education instructors' opinions on training (see Fitts, 1962, p. 185).

SMOKE, KENNETH L. (1933). "Negative Instances in Concept Learning." *Journal of Experimental Psychology,* 16: 583–88.

SOLES, STANLEY (1963). "Educational Quackery External to Our Schools: What Is a Professional Response?" *Phi Delta Kappan,* 44: 299–302.

SOLLEY, WILLIAM H. (1952). "The Effects of Verbal Instructions of Speed and Accuracy upon the Learning of a Motor Skill." *Research Quarterly,* 23: 231–40.

SOLOMON, RICHARD L. (1964). "Punishment." *American Psychologist,* 19: 239–53.

SPEARMAN, CHARLES (1927). *The Abilities of Man.* New York: The Macmillan Company.

SPENCE, KENNETH W. (1956). *Behavior Theory and Conditioning.* New Haven, Conn.: Yale University Press.

SPIELBERGER, CHARLES D. (1966a). "Theory and Research on Anxiety," in *Anxiety and Behavior,* ed. C. D. Spielberger, pp. 3–20. New York: Academic Press Inc.

—— (1966b). "The Effects of Anxiety on Complex Learning and Academic Achievement," in *Anxiety and Behavior,* ed. C. D. Spielberger, pp. 361–98. New York: Academic Press Inc.

SPIKER, CHARLES C. (1963). "Verbal Factors in the Discrimination Learning of Children." *Monograph of the Society for Research in Child Development,* 28 (Whole No. 86), 53–69.

STAATS, ARTHUR W. (1957). "Verbal and Instrumental Response-Hierarchies and Their Relationship to Problem-Solving." *American Journal of Psychology,* 70: 442–46.

STAATS, ARTHUR W., and STAATS, CAROLYN K. (1963). *Complex Human Behavior.* New York: Holt, Rinehart & Winston, Inc.

590   STANLEY, JULIAN C. (1964). *Measurement in Today's Schools.* 4th ed. Englewood Cliffs, N.J.: Prentice-Hall, Inc.

STANLEY, JULIAN C., and HOPKINS, KENNETH D. (1972). *Educational and Psychological Measurement and Evaluation.* Englewood Cliffs, N.J.: Prentice-Hall, Inc.

STERN, CAROLYN (1965). "Labeling and Variety in Concept Identification with Young Children." *Journal of Educational Psychology,* 56: 235–40.

STEWART, NAOMI (1947). "A.G.C.T. Scores of Army Personnel Grouped by Occupation." *Occupations,* 26: 5–41.

STOLUROW, LAWRENCE M. (1964). "Social Impact of Programmed Instruction: Aptitudes and Abilities Revisited." *Educational Technology,* ed. J. P. De Cecco, pp. 348–55. New York: Holt, Rinehart & Winston, Inc.

STOLUROW, LAWRENCE M., and DAVIS, DANIEL (1965). *Teaching Machines and Computed-Based Systems. Teaching Machines and Programed Learning II: Data and Directions,* ed. R. Glaser, pp. 162–212. Washington, D.C.: Department of Audiovisual Education, National Education Association.

STRONG, EDWARD K. (1951). *Strong Vocational Interest Blank for Women.* Palo Alto, Calif.: Consulting Psychologists Press.

SUPPES, PATRICK (1964). "Modern Learning Theory and the Elementary-School Curriculum." *American Educational Research Journal,* 1: 79–93.

TABA, HILDA, and ELZEY, FREEMAN F. (1964). "Teaching Strategies and Thought Processes." *Teachers College Record,* 65: 524–34.

TABER, JULIAN I.; GLASER, ROBERT; and SCHAEFFER, HALMUTH H. (1965). *Learning and Programmed Instruction.* Reading, Mass.: Addison-Wesley Publishing Co., Inc.

TATE, MERLE W. (1965). *Statistics in Education and Psychology.* New York: The Macmillan Company.

TAYLOR, CALVIN, and BARRON, FRANK (1963). *Scientific Creativity: Its Recognition and Development.* New York: John Wiley & Sons, Inc.

TAYLOR, D. W.; BERRY, P. C.; and BLOCK, C. H. (1958). "Does Group Participation When Using Brainstorming Facilitate or Inhibit Creative Thinking?" *Administrative Scence Quarterly,* 3: 23–47.

TERMAN, LEWIS M., and MERRILL, MAUD A. (1937). *Measuring Intelligence.* Boston: Houghton Mifflin Company.

—— (1960). *Stanford-Binet Intelligence Scale: Manual for the Third Revision.* Boston: Houghton Mifflin Company.

TERMAN, LEWIS M., and OGDEN, MELITA H. (1950). *The Gifted Child Grows Up.* Stanford, Calif.: Stanford University Press.

THORNDIKE, EDWARD L. (1913). *The Psychology of Learning.* New York: Teachers College Press, Columbia University.

THORNDIKE, EDWARD L., and LORGE, IRVING (1944). *The Teacher's Work Book of 30,000 Words.* New York: Teachers College Press, Columbia University.

THORNDIKE, ROBERT L. (1963). "The Measurement of Creativity." *Teachers College Record,* 64: 422–24.

THORNDIKE, ROBERT L., and HAGEN, ELIZABETH (1969). *Measurement and Evaluation in Psychology and Education.* 3rd ed. New York: John Wiley & Sons, Inc.

THURSTONE, L. L. (1938). "Primary Mental Abilities," in *Psychometric Monograph No. 1.* Chicago: University of Chicago Press.

—— (1941). "Factorial Studies of Intelligence," in *Psychometric Monograph No. 2.* Chicago: University of Chicago Press.

—— (1947). *Multiple Factor Analysis.* Chicago: University of Chicago Press.

TORRANCE, E. PAUL (1960). "Creative Thinking Through the Language Arts." *Educational Leadership,* 18: 13–18.

———— (1961). "Priming Creative Thinking in the Primary Grades." *Elementary School Journal*, 42: 34–41.

———— (1962). *Guiding Creative Talent*. Englewood Cliffs, N.J.: Prentice-Hall, Inc.

———— (1963a). *Creativity: What Research Says to the Teacher*. Washington, D.C.: Department of Classroom Teachers and American Educational Research Association, National Education Association.

———— (1963b). *Education and the Creative Potential*. Minneapolis: University of Minnesota Press.

———— (1965). *Gifted Children in the Classroom*. New York: The Macmillan Company.

———— (1966). *Torrance Tests of Creative Thinking. Norms Technical Manual*. Princeton, N.J.: Personnel Press.

TORRANCE, E. PAUL, and HARMON, J. A. (1961). "Effects of Memory, Evaluative, and Creative Reading Sets on Test Performance." *Journal of Educational Psychology*, 52: 207–14.

TORRANCE, E. PAUL, and MYERS, R. E. (1963). "Teaching Gifted Elementary Pupils Research Concepts and Skills." *Gifted Child Quarterly*, 6: 1–6.

TRAVERS, ROBERT M. W. (1963). *Essentials of Learning*. New York: The Macmillan Company.

TRAVERS, ROBERT M. W.; McCORMICK, MARY C.; MONDFRANS, A. P.; and WILLIAMS, F. E. (1964). *Research and Theory Related to Audiovisual Information Transmission*. U.S. Office of Education Cooperative Research Project N. 3-20-003. Salt Lake City: Bureau of Educational Research, University of Utah.

TRAVERS, ROBERT M. W.; VAN WAGENEN, R. KEITH; HAYGOOD, DANIELLE H.; and McCORMICK, MARY (1964). "Learning as a Consequence of the Learner's Task Involvement Under Different Conditions of Feedback." *Journal of Educational Psychology*, 55: 167–73.

TWINING, WILBUR E. (1949). "Mental Practice and Physical Practice in Learning a Motor Skill." *Research Quarterly*, 20: 432–35.

TYLER, FRED T. (1964). "Issues Related to Readiness to Learn," in *Theories of Learning and Instruction*, ed. E. R. Hilgard, Part 1 of the 63rd Yrbk. of the National Society for the Study of Education, pp. 210–39. Chicago: University of Chicago Press.

TYLER, LEONA E. (1963). *Tests and Measurements*. Englewood Cliffs, N.J.: Prentice-Hall, Inc.

TYLER, RALPH W. (1934). "Some Findings From Studies in the Field of College Biology." *Science*, 18: 133–42.

———— (1949). "Achievement Testing and Curriculum Construction," in *Trends in Student Personnel Work*, ed. G. Williamson. Minneapolis: University of Minnesota Press.

———— (1950). "The Functions of Measurement in Improving Instruction," in *Educational Measurement*, ed. E. F. Lindquist. Washington, D.C.: American Council on Education.

———— (1964). "Some Persistent Questions on the Defining of Objectives," in *Defining Educational Objectives*, ed. C. M. Lindvall. Pittsburgh: University of Pittsburgh Press.

UNDERWOOD, BENTON J. (1949). *Experimental Psychology: An Introduction*. New York: Appleton-Century-Crofts.

———— (1957). "Interference and Forgetting." *Psychological Review*, 64: 49–60.

———— (1959). "Verbal Learning in the Educative Process." *Harvard Educational Review*, 29: 107–17.

———— (1961). "Ten Years of Massed Practice on Distributed Practice." *Psychological Review*, 68: 229–47.

———— (1964a). "The Representativeness of Rote Verbal Learning," in *Categories of Human Learning*, ed. Arthur W. Melton, pp. 48–78. New York: Academic Press Inc.

———— (1964b). "Laboratory Studies of Verbal Learning," in *Theories of Learning and Instruction*, ed. E. R. Hilgard, Part 1 of the 63rd Yrbk. of the National Society for the Study of Education, pp. 133–52. Chicago: University of Chicago Press.

———— (1966). "Some Relationships Between Concept Learning and Verbal Learning," in *Analyses of Concept Learning*, eds. H. J. Klausmeier and C. W. Harris. New York: Academic Press Inc.

UNDERWOOD, BENTON J., and RICHARDSON, JACK (1957). "Studies of Distributed Practice: XVII. Interlist Interference and the Retention of Paired Consonant Syllables." *Journal of Experimental Psychology*, 54: 274–79.

UNDERWOOD, BENTON J., and SCHULTZ, RUDOLPH W. (1960). *Meaningfulness and Verbal Learning*. Philadelphia: J. B. Lippincott Co.

VAN DER RIET, HANI (1963). "The Effects of Praise and Reproof on Paired-Associate Learning in Educationally Retarded Children." *Dissertation Abstracts*, 24: 1250.

VAN WAGENEN, R. KEITH, and TRAVERS, ROBERT M. W. (1963). "Learning Under Conditions of Direct and Vicarious Reinforcement." *Journal of Educational Psychology*, 54: 356–62.

VERDUCCI, FRANK (1967). Personal communication, April 6.

VERNON, PHILIP E. (1958). "Education and the Psychology of Individual Differences." *Harvard Educational Review*, 28: 91–104.

VERPLANCK, WILLIAM S. (1955). "The Control of the Content of Conversation: Reinforcement of Statements of Opinion." *Journal of Abnormal and Social Psychology*, 51: 668–76.

VETTER, HAROLD J., and HOWELL, RICHARD W. (n.d.). "Theories of Language Acquisition." Florida State University, in mimeo.

VINCE, M. A. (1953). "The Part Played by Intellectual Processes in a Sensory-Motor Performance." *Quarterly Journal of Experimental Psychology*, 5: 75–86.

VROOM, VICTOR H. (1964). *Work and Motivation*. New York: John Wiley & Sons, Inc.

WAGNER, JOHN (1960). "The Objectives and Activities of the School Mathematics Study Group." *The Mathematics Teacher*, 53: 454–59.

WALLACE, JOHN (1964). "Concept Dominance, Type of Feedback, and Intensity of Feedback as Related to Concept Attainment." *Journal of Educational Psychology*, 55: 159–66.

WALLEN, NORMAN E., and TRAVERS, ROBERT M. W. (1963). "Analysis and Investigation of Teaching Methods," in *Handbook of Research on Teaching*, ed. N. L. Gage, pp. 448–505. Chicago: Rand McNally & Co.

WANDT, EDWIN (1965). *A Cross-Section of Educational Research*. David McKay Co., Inc.

WARD, J. N. (1956). "Group Versus Lecture-Demonstration Method in Physical Science Instruction for General Education College Students." *Journal of Experimental Education*, 24: 197–210.

WARD, LEWIS B. (1937). "Reminiscence and Rote Learning." *Psychological Monographs*, 49, No. 4 (Whole No. 220).

WATERHOUSE, IAN K., and CHILD, IRVIN (1953). "Frustration and the Quality of Performance." *Journal of Personality*, 21: 298–311.

WAUGH, NANCY C. (1961). "Free Recall Versus Serial Recall." *Journal of Experimental Psychology,* 62: 496–502.

WEAVER, H. E., and MADDEN, E. H. (1949). "Direction in Problem Solving." *The Journal of Psychology,* 27: 331–45.

WEBER, MAX (1904). *The Protestant Ethic and the Spirit of Capitalism.* Translated by T. Parsons. New York: Charles Scribner's Sons, 1930.

WECHSLER, DAVID (1949). *Wechsler Intelligence Scale for Children: Manual.* New York: Psychological Corp.

——— (1955). *Wechsler Adult Intelligence Scale Manual.* New York: Psychological Corp.

WEIDEMANN, C. C. (1933). "Written Examination Procedures." *Phi Delta Kappan,* 16: 78–83.

——— (1941). "Review of Essay Test Studies." *Journal of Higher Education,* 12: 41–44.

WEITMAN, MORRIS (1965). "Item Characteristics and Long-Term Retention." *Journal of Educational Measurement,* 2: 37–47.

WERTHEIMER, MAX (1959). *Productive Thinking.* New York: Harper & Row, Publishers.

WHITE, ROBERT W. (1959). "Motivation Reconsidered: The Concept of Competence." *Psychological Review,* 66: 297–333.

WHITING, J. W. M., and MOWRER, O. H. (1943). "Habit Progression and Regression—a Laboratory Study of Some Factors Relevant to Human Socialization." *Journal of Comparative Psychology,* 36: 229–53.

WILDER, NANCY, and GREEN, DONALD ROSS (1963). "Expressions of Concepts Through Writing and Drawing and Effects of Shifting Medium." *Journal of Experimental Psychology,* 54: 202–7.

WILLIAMS, A. C., and FLEXMAN, RALPH E. (1949). "Evaluation of the School Link as an Aid in Primary Flight Instruction." *University of Illinois Bulletin,* 46, No. 71.

WITKIN, H. A. *et al.* (1954). *Personality Through Perception.* New York: Harper & Row, Publishers.

WITTROCK, MERLIN C. (1962). "Set Applied to Student Teaching." *Journal of Educational Psychology,* 53: 175–80.

——— (1963). "Verbal Stimuli in Concept Formation: Learning by Discovery." *Journal of Educational Psychology,* 64: 183–90.

——— (1966). "The Learning by Discovery Hypothesis," in *Learning by Discovery,* eds. L. S. Shulman and E. R. Keislar, pp. 33–76. Chicago: Rand McNally & Co.

——— (1967). "Focus on Educational Psychology." *Educational Psychologist,* 4, No. 2, 17, 20.

WITTROCK, MERLIN C., and KEISLAR, EVAN (1965). "Verbal Cues in the Transfer of Concepts." *Journal of Educational Psychology,* 56: 16–21.

WITTROCK, MERLIN C.; KEISLAR, EVAN; and STERN, CAROLYN (1964). "Verbal Cues in Concept Identification." *Journal of Educational Psychology,* 55: 195–200.

WOLFE, J. B., and KAPLON, M. D. (1941). "Effect of Amount of Reward and Consummative Activity on Learning in Chickens." *Journal of Comparative Psychology,* 31: 353–61.

WOMER, FRANK B. (1970). *What Is National Assessment?* Ann Arbor, Mich.: National Assessment of Educational Progress.

YAMAMOTO, K. (1964). "Role of Creative Thinking and Intelligence in High School Achievement." *Psychological Record,* 14: 783–89.

YUDIN, LEE, and KATES, SOLIS L. (1963). "Concept Attainment and Adolescent Development." *Journal of Educational Psychology,* 54: 177–82.

AUTHOR INDEX

SUBJECT INDEX